Essentials of

HUMAN RESOURCE MANAGEMENT

Essentials of
HUMAN RESOURCE MANAGEMENT

Indranil Mutsuddi
Senior Faculty
Department of Management Studies
Acharya Institute of Management and Sciences
(Bangalore University)
Bangalore, Karnataka

An Imprint of

NEW AGE INTERNATIONAL (P) LIMITED, PUBLISHERS
New Delhi • Bangalore • Chennai • Cochin • Guwahati
Hyderabad • Kolkata • Lucknow • Mumbai
Visit us at **www.newagepublishers.com**

Published by New Age International (P) Ltd., Publishers
First Edition: 2010
Reprint: 2014

BRANCHES

- **Bangalore** 37/10, 8th Cross (Near Hanuman Temple), Azad Nagar, Chamarajpet, Bangalore-560 018 Tel.: (080) 26756823, Telefax: 26756820, **E-mail: bangalore@newagepublishers.com**
- **Chennai** 26, Damodaran Street, T. Nagar, Chennai-600 017, Tel.: (044) 24353401 Telefax: 24351463, **E-mail: chennai@newagepublishers.com**
- **Cochin** CC-39/1016, Carrier Station Road, Ernakulam South, Cochin-682 016 Tel.: (0484) 2377303, Telefax: 4051303, **E-mail: cochin@newagepublishers.com**
- **Guwahati** Hemsen Complex, Mohd. Shah Road, Paltan Bazar, Near Starline Hotel, Guwahati-781 008 Tel.: (0361) 2513881, Telefax: 2543669, **E-mail: guwahati@newagepublishers.com**
- **Hyderabad** 105, 1st Floor, Madhiray Kaveri Tower, 3-2-19, Azam Jahi Road, Near Kumar Theater Nimboliadda, Kachiguda, Hyderabad-500 027, Tel.: (040) 24652456, Telefax: 24652457 **E-mail: hyderabad@newagepublishers.com**
- **Kolkata** RDB Chambers (Formerly Lotus Cinema) 106A, 1st Floor, S.N. Banerjee Road, Kolkata-700 014 Tel.: (033) 22273773, Telefax: 22275247, **E-mail: kolkata@newagepublishers.com**
- **Lucknow** 16-A, Jopling Road, Lucknow-226 001, Tel.: (0522) 2209578, 4045297, Telefax: 2204098 **E-mail:lucknow@newagepublishers.com**
- **Mumbai** 142C, Victor House, Ground Floor, N.M. Joshi Marg, Lower Parel, Mumbai-400 013 Tel.: (022) 24927869, Telefax: 24915415, **E-mail: mumbai@newagepublishers.com**
- **New Delhi** 22, Golden House, Daryaganj, New Delhi-110 002, Tel.: (011) 23262368, 23262370 Telefax: 43551305, **E-mail: sales@newagepublishers.com**

ISBN: 978-81-224-2815-5

₹ 399.00

C-14-03-7487

Printed in India at Saras Graphics, Rai, Haryana.
Typeset at In-house, Delhi.

PUBLISHING GLOBALLY
NEW AGE INTERNATIONAL (P) LIMITED, PUBLISHERS
7/30 A, Daryaganj, New Delhi-110002
Visit us at **www.newagepublishers.com**

Dedicated to

My beloved parents and grand parents for their uncompromising principles, constant encouragement and support

Riju & Rimi for being with me

and

Most importantly to my students for motivating me to author the book

PREFACE

Essentials of Human Resource Management had been a long cherished dream. The book has aimed to provide a practical and realistic perspective to HR practices in the corporate world, depicting their various challenges and recent trends. Keeping in mind of the new learners the book has also aimed to empower their subjective knowledge with fundamental concepts of human resource management. The supporting cases, theme readings, industry quotes and articles would enrich their perspective regarding what is really happening in the organizations. Each chapter is also supported by question banks, exercise cases for class discussion. Further the book also stimulates the readers in order to concentrate on learning the concepts, applying them in class presentations and encouraging the faculties to involve them in experiential exercises like games, research work and secondary information searching through internet sessions. The chapters and their supporting exercises would help the students to carry their studies out of their reading rooms into computer labs, libraries and even to their institute's amphitheatres to run around play HR related games and sharpen their presentation skills in class presentations and seminars organized by their respective institutes.

The purpose of the book would perhaps be not fulfilled without the inputs and suggestions of students, working professionals, industry experts and faculties for whom the book is meant.

Indranil Mutsuddi

ACKNOWLEDGEMENTS

I would like to express my sincere gratitude and thanks to Sri. V.R. Damodaran, Chief Editor, New Age International and his entire team for supporting me day and night in the publication of the book. The creative inputs of Sri Damodaran had been helpful in terms of making the book concise and improving its overall presentability.

I would like to express my deepest thanks to Prof. Kiran Reddy, CEO & Principal, Acharya Institute of Management & Sciences, Bangalore for her constant support, Dr. K. Aswathappa, Dean, Acharya Institute of Management & Sciences, Bangalore for his constant motivation and inputs and the entire AIMS management studies department faculty team for their unflinching support in bringing out this book. Last and not least it's the students who had always encouraged me in this pursuit.

I am immensely grateful to Mr. John Ditchburn for donating his cartoon on time management for the book. It was really a nice gesture on his part.

I am thankful to Mr. Anshuman Kumar, Program Design Content Manager, Infosys Technologies, Bangalore and the HR team for his contribution and inputs in the Infosys case, and Mr. Atul Rajbhushan, Hindustan Coca Cola Beverages Pvt. Ltd., Bidadi, Bangalore for his kind help.

I would like to thank my parents and grand parents for their uncompromising encouragement and support. Although Mom had been thoroughly optimistic & unflinchingly encouraging, Papa had been patient all through and constantly provided me all the necessary inputs in terms of looking ahead for further improvement. It would be selfish not to acknowledge the contribution of my son Riju who had particularly tolerated my presence in front of my laptop during the making of the book. My wife Rimi had been critical, yet been supportive in terms of her views in making the book presentable and more reader friendly.

Last and not least, I sincerely thank all those whose references have been quoted in for making the content more presentable for the readers.

CONTENTS

CHAPTER—2

CHAPTER—3

CHAPTER—4

CHAPTER 1

OVERVIEW AND INTRODUCTION TO HUMAN RESOURCE MANAGEMENT

THEME READING: HRM IN INFOSYS

Infosys has been a pioneer in innovative workforce practices and HR initiatives—be it in creating wealth for employees through wide distribution of stock option plans or in creating a enjoyable workplace with various amenities. Nandan Nilekani, President and Managing Director of Infosys, commented, "Attracting the best and the brightest and creating a milieu where they operate at their highest potential are very important for Infosys. Our campus and technology infrastructure is world-class, we pay a lot of attention to training and competency building, we try to have sophisticated appraisal systems, and we try to reward performance through variable pay".[8]

Recruitment: While recruiting new hires, Infosys takes into consideration so as to identify the right talents for the right jobs. And in this drive the company strictly focuses on hiring those individuals (talents) who have the capability of high degree of 'learnability'. The qualities mostly sought by the company involve high levels of analytical ability, teamwork and leadership, communication and creative skills, along with a practical and structured orientation to problem solving.

People Development and Training: Employee development and training at Infosys is a continuous process. When hired employees immediately go through induction and training programme. These programme mainly aim to emphasize on training these new recruits on new processes and technologies and orient them with the organization's culture and ethical practices. As they reach higher efficiency and performance levels, they are further trained on project management training sessions so that they could develop competencies for independently handling projects and assignments for the organization's clients. Infosys also emphasizes upon management and leadership development programme as and when required and caters to the requirements of management development for its senior employees and managers. The new recruits are trained at the Global Education Centre (GEC) in Mysore, which has world-class training facilities and the capacity to train more than 4,500 employees at a time. The company has a competency mapping system in place which takes into account individual performance, organizational priorities, and feedback from the clients so as to give comprehensive inputs for developing these training programme.

Infosys Leadership Institute (ILI): ILI set up in 2001 had an immense impact on the effectiveness of the HRD function at Infosys. The institute was primarily developed so as to develop and groom future talents in the company[12].

Fig. 1.1: The workplace at Infosys Technologies Limited[15]

Performance Appraisal System: The performance appraisal process at Infosys begins not only with performance evaluation but also encompasses the evaluation of individual skills for the tasks assigned to an employee during the assigned period of performance evaluation. In this regard, performance appraisal takes into consideration various performance criteria like timeliness, quality of work, customer orientation, peer satisfaction and performance improvement potential. The company has also launched an internal job posting mechanism and the concept of personal development plans, on the basis of 360 degree feedback[12].

Compensation and Rewards: The entire organization has restructured its compensations and reward system in order to match the performance of its employees, business needs and the growing scale of operations. The company started following a variable pay structure[10]. At the lowest level, 10 per cent of the salary is variable; it is 30 per cent at the middle level and 50 per cent at very senior levels. Salary at Infosys is linked to the topline, performance of the team and performance of the individual. The company also intends to compensate star performers more aggressively than average or poor performers in a move that has more similarities with American culture which promotes and rewards individual merit[11]. Another remarkable hallmark of Infosys had been its employee stock options plan (ESOP) framework for which the company has made a mark of its own in the industry. Many organizations had decided to adopt the Infosys ESOP system as an effective way to retain their employees.

Worklife Balance Programme: As part of its holistic HR policy, Infosys had opened a satellite centre in the heart of the city to enable its employees (particularly new and to be mothers) to cut down on travel time to work. The company has also initiated a pilot project for employees giving them an opportunity to opt for a one-year sabbatical at any point in their careers. This could be used for childcare, eldercare, higher studies or for health reasons[9]. Many working mothers and to be mothers have also been encouraged to work on their projects from their homes. Flexi timing of the working mothers also help these techniques to have enough time with their kids and family. Apart from these the company also emphasizes on organizing counseling programme for their employees so as to provide solutions for better worklife balance.

Infosys had always considered its people as its most valuable assets and had seeked opportunities for further improvement in performance, business development by fostering innovation and creativity in the workplace. In the coming years, how the company's HR philosophy would help the organization to steer into the new decade would well be worth watching and a learning experience for HR specialists.

(*Courtesy: Infosys Website, 2008*)

HUMAN RESOURCE MANAGEMENT

Prologue

In today's knowledge economy, business experts claim that the organizations who can constantly change and realign themselves with the fast changing business environment would survive for the long run. Fostering and building knowledge, developing and retaining talents and promoting creativity and innovation would thereby become the strategic needs for future organizations. For, only their abilities to learn, create, and innovatively utilize knowledge faster than those of the competitors – and quicker than the environmental changes – would provide them competitive advantage in the fast changing business environment. Hence the core competence of any organization would be their human capital, the collective learning of the people – and the value chain they would create by nurturing and developing new knowledge. Thus for ensuring organizational success CEOs and business captains would principally depend on how their people are being procured, developed, retained and nurtured into knowledge workers. Every organization believing in this philosophy would thereby be emphasizing on composing their people with such innovative capabilities and utilizing their services, developing their skills, motivating them to enhance their levels of performance and ensuring that they remain committed to the organization. This probably would be true for all types of organizations — government, business, education, health, recreation or social service organizations like NGOs irrespective of the type of business or service they are involved with. Organizations that can achieve these people capabilities have been suggested to be both effective as well as efficient. Inefficient or ineffective organizations without such people capabilities would face the threat of stagnating or being driven out of business by their rival organizations.

Hence from the above discussion it is evident that, the emphasis to acquire people capabilities would only be feasible if proper and effective human resource management principles and practices are fine tuned with the strategic needs of the business and the needs of the customers. HRM would thereby emerge as one of the most important strategic factor in contributing to the success of an organization. With the growing importance of knowledge workers to organizations and the rising expectations of employees, it is essential to have a good human resource management system in place. It is also important that all the different processes in an organization, like finance, HRM, marketing and operations align their objectives and strategies to those of the organization and work in harmony with each other.

Human Resource Management (HRM) can be primarily described to consist of four essential functions namely— acquiring, developing, motivating and retaining human resources. The acquisition of human resources is a crucial function that starts with planning for the number and categories of employees required (with the right capabilities and expertises) and ends with staffing. The development function has four dimensions namely— employee training, management development, and career development followed by succession planning. The motivation function is perhaps the most important for the retention of people in today's organizations. It involves identifying the individual motivational needs of employees and finding ways to motivate them. The retention function is perhaps the most complex function amongst all challenges in today's competitive business environment. It varies from industry to industry, business to business, capabilities of people and most importantly their changing needs and expectations. In a simpler way, it aims to provide a conducive work environment to the employees and nurturing them to make them feel committed and psychologically attached to the organization. The following caselet depicts how a reputed publishing house in India maintains excellent employee relations to retain their employees.

What is Human Resource Management?

Definition: According to Invancevich (2008)[1], Human Resource Management (HRM) is concerned with the most effective use of people to achieve organizational and individual goals. It is the strategic and coherent approach to the management of an organization's most valued assets—the people working there who individually and collectively contribute to the achievement of its goals.

HRM can also be described as a set of interrelated policies with an ideological and philosophical underpinning, concerned with the employment, development and reward of people in organizations and the conduct of relationships between the management and the employees. HRM is a strategic approach to the acquisition, motivation, development and management of the organization's human resources (Sharma, A.M.)[2]. It can be said that although all the line managers and team leaders play a pivotal role in managing an organization, the HR specialists play a vital role in shaping the overall strategy of an organization as well as acting as "Internal Consultants" for the organization. Today's HR professionals constantly need to nurture an empowering culture so as ensure effective retention of human resources in their organizations. This philosophy is nurtured well in an organization like ICICI Prudential India, as revealed by the following exhibit.

On the other hand for an organization like TCS, the company's success depends to a great extent on its ability to recruit, train and retain high quality IT professionals. TCS places emphasis on the human resources function in the organization, investing a substantial percentage of its annual revenues in training.

THEME CASE: THE 3Cs IN RAJSHRI PRODUCTIONS

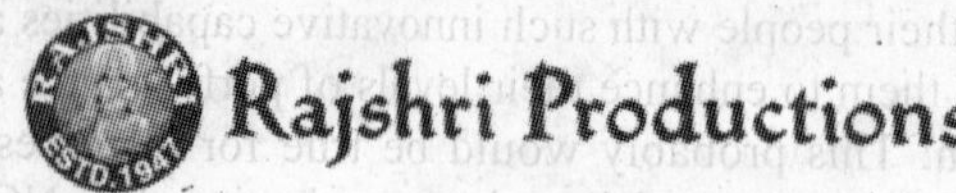

Excellence in HR practices is no longer the standalone buzzword in the corporates. The Indian film industry which is gradually shaping up into a growing corporate entity is no where behind any of these big giants in implementing innovative HR practices, like fostering confidence and empowerment in people and creating a culture where employees are allowed to participate and share their views on the final product or service offered by the organization. Rajshri Production is a bright illustration of the same.

(*Courtesy: Kunal M Shah, 2008: "A Marriage of Minds", Bangalore Mirror, 24th June, 2008, p. 36*)

HR Philosophy in Rajshri Productions: The organization over the years had focused on its people centric HR practices and the evidence of this can be had from one of the comments made by Mr. Sooraj Barjatya[14], Producer and the Chief of Rajshri Productions during an interview with a reputed daily. He said, "At Rajshri we believe that it is vital to take everyone's opinion, be it an assistant or a technician. As a producer, I should know if the film has touched people's soul or not".

By employing this practice, not only Rajshri Productions been able to inculcate a culture (The Ist C) of participation and employee empowerment, it had also ensured that the capabilities or competencies (2nd C) of its technicians, editors, crews and employees are wholeheartedly utilized, which also results in strong employee commitment (3rd C) and intrinsic motivation. These 3Cs have been instrumental in shaping Rajshri's success as a successful production house giving quality entertainment to the Indian film lovers. On the other hand, by instigating and successfully administering the 3Cs Rajshri had been able to enhance the quality of its production process, where the team members themselves have contributed to identify various technical as well as editorial flaws in the final print of the film, the company produced. In the post production works of Rajshri's latest movie "Ek Vivaah Aisa Bhi" a similar approach was used to rectify one such editing error. The company also encourages the family members of its employees to actively participate in the promotional activities of the production house, interact with the film stars; that have instilled a sense of belongingness and close association with the employees and the management of the organization.

The brains of the organization are widely distributed one per person. And ultimately it goes to the credit of that organization's HR practices so successfully utilize these untapped resources. Creative ideas are like insects, many which are born and few live up to their maturity (Gifford Pinchot, http://www.pinchot.com/). The chain of command in organizations which had been the order of many Indian film production houses are perhaps no more appropriate in the information age whether it be for a high profile ITES company like TCS or a film production house like that of Rajshri Productions. Could the 3Cs of Rajshri inspire Indian corporate giants would be worth watching.

Three Cs of HRM

The above case has brought about the importance of 3Cs which has been successfully used and implemented in a reputed Indian film production company. For any organization, irrespective of the industry type, in order to achieve organizational effectiveness, it is essential for HR managers to strictly emphasize upon these three Cs, namely:

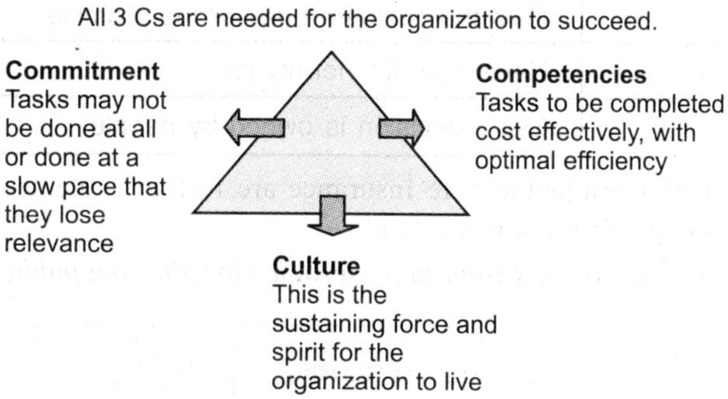

All 3 Cs are needed for the organization to succeed.

Commitment
Tasks may not be done at all or done at a slow pace that they lose relevance

Competencies
Tasks to be completed cost effectively, with optimal efficiency

Culture
This is the sustaining force and spirit for the organization to live

Fig. 1.2: The three important Cs of HRM

- **Commitment:** It is the psychological contract and the sense of belongingness of the human resources to the organization and its management.
- **Culture:** The second and one of the most important components of organizational success and development is the culture of the organization. Culture has been recognized as the vital sustaining force and background contributing to organizational growth and development.
- **Competencies:** Organizations need to depend strictly upon the competencies of their human capital rather than depending on individual knowledge, skills and abilities.

HR Practice: Thus carrying on with the above discussions, it can be said that HR practices can be described as:

- Any practice that deals with enhancing competencies, commitment and culture building can be considered as a HR practice.
- The practice could be a rule, a system, a process, and an activity, an accepted or expected way of doing things.
- For an organization like Arvind Mills, the HR practice acts as the foundation that integrates organizational culture, vision and values, fosters an environment that facilitates the maximization of human potential.

THEME READING: ICICI PRUDENTIAL'S EMPOWERING CULTURE

The culture at ICICI Prudential Life Insurance India stems from its core values, which comes from the following components

(Based on introductory presentation made by ICICI prudential representatives in their B School campus recruitment program Udaan)

Values @ ICICI Prudential Life Insurance	Hallmarks
Integrity	Be honest and fair in what you say
Passion	If it is to be, it is up to ones' commitment to what people do or say, boundaryless energy and enthusiasm
Customers first	Own the customer, deliver the promise
Boundaryless	Never say "It's not my job"
Ownership	Every decision is owned by people

These values at ICICI Prudential Life Insurance are further cemented by the following "People Cornerstones" that is unique in the organization:

(*Details can be had from http://www.iciciprulife.com/public/Others/Udaan-Home.htm*):

Learning and Growth	Supportive Environment
Meritocracy	Fairness

Fig. 1.3: People cornerstones at ICICI prudential life insurance

Assumptions of HRM

The fundamental assumptions of HRM are as follows:

- The members of an organization can be conceptualized as "Reservoirs" of untapped resources and people capabilities. Experts are of the opinion that organizations championing the cause of realizing such untapped potentials can create competitive advantage as compared to their business rivals.
- There is scope for unlimited development of knowledge and human resource capabilities in an organization.
- HRM is more involved with the development of individual potential and capabilities rather than emphasizing on the development thrust from outside (that is provided by conventional routine training programme).
- The organization also undergoes development with the overall benefits along with the development of its members.
- The organization should develop and nurture a culture in which prime importance is given on the harmonious boss-subordinate relations, teamwork, and collaboration among different groups of individuals including the customers of the organization. Managers should also emphasize on open communication and integration of goals of the organization with the needs and aspirations of the employees.
- The top management along with the team of employees should participatively take the initiative for HRM, formulate necessary plans and strategies and create an empowering climate in the organization and support for its implementation.

Concerns of HRM

Any HRM activity in an organization emphasizes on the following three important aspects, namely:

(a) ***Concern for the People***: It involves principles concerned with

- Respect and concerns for the individual
- Treat individual employees and team of people as internal customers of the organization.
- Ensuring an environment facilitating trust and interdependence at the workplace
- Ensuring administrative and procedural fairness and ethics involving all aspects of the ways in which decisions are taken with respect to the people in the organization.
- Ensuring transparency in the organizational decision making process with respect to policies and HR strategy implementation.

(b) ***Concern for Managing Organizational Performance***: One of the major concerns of HRM is to ensure that individuals as well as teams are constantly contributing to improve the overall organizational performance. Today's HRM therefore involves a holistic approach towards developing the right skills and competency frameworks and utilizing them for achieving the organizational goals and objectives. It is worth mentioning that managers should come out from traditional performance appraisal ratings and look into the broader perspectives of managing and developing organizational performance by instrumenting balance scorecards.

(c) ***Concern for Innovation***: The success of any organization in today's competitive perspectives should stem out from the capability of the people to constantly contribute to the organization's success through innovation. Hence it has become strategically important for today's HR professionals to create an environment in their corporations to foster knowledge building, sharing and utilizing the same for innovation.

HRM: Achieving Competitive Advantage through People

In the context of the challenging business environment, an organization's human resources have taken a critical role in terms of contributing to establishing an organizations' competitive advantage by contributing through constant innovation and creativity. In case of the knowledge-based organizations such as the IT and ITES corporations, organizational success increasingly had depended on innovative knowledge creation by their intellectual capital. These people-embodied know-hows include knowledge, skills and abilities (KSAs) of the employees and their ability to visualize the future needs of the organization. Industry experts have asserted that the key to an organization's success would be based on establishing a set of **Core Competencies** — integrated knowledge sets within an organization that distinguish it from its competitors and deliver value to customers. As for example, at Wal-Mart, its major competitive core competence is its superior logistics system. For its Indian counter part, Reliance Fresh the core competence had well been its ability to understand the needs of the middle class Indian customers and their unflinching service orientation. Just like, for a busy IT professional in Bangalore, Reliance Fresh is not only a one destination retail solution, it has further diversified its services into additional value-added services like two-wheeler insurance, payment of electric (BESCOM) bills, mobile phone bills and so on. Within IT organizations, skills, capabilities and functions are only core competencies if they directly support a business process that is itself a core competence. McDonalds has developed core competencies in management efficiency and training. In Bangalore McDonalds is more popular than any other Pizza outlet for its uncompromising service orientation. For any young couple, college students to a family, the employees working at the Brigrade Road or Forum Mall (Bangalore) McDonalds outlet are perhaps the most cool and smart people to interact with.

PARADIGM SHIFT IN HR PERSPECTIVES

The paradigm shift in considering people as the most valued assets of the organization had been the success mantra for any organization like McDonalds India, Reliance Fresh. On the other hand, for an organization like Big Bazaar any employee working at an outlet is empowered to contribute to innovatively promote the sales of a particular item. And the management makes it sure to reward such contributions by public announcements and incentive schemes. The core of this successful strategy had been the interest of the management to have confidence on the capabilities of their people. This has ensured that HR professionals and HR managers have emerged as the strategic business partners of the organizations to take decisions on people and guiding the top management to achieve the organization's strategic goals. This concept is illustrated by the following figure:

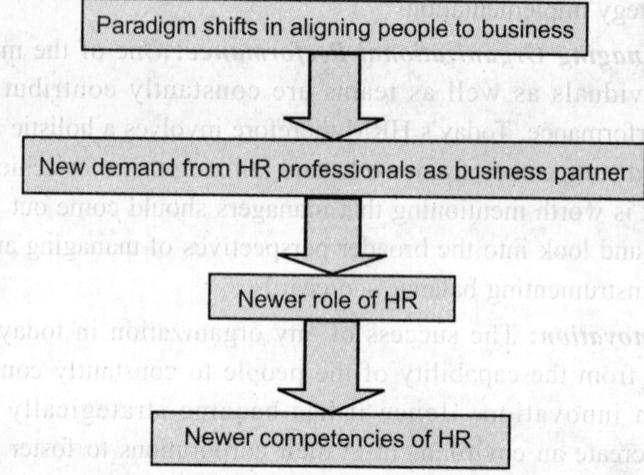

Fig. 1.4: Consequences of changing context – The newer role of HR

Taking the above factors into considerations, organizations and industry captains thereby need to emphasize on a paradigm shift in aligning people to the core of their business strategies. In order to achieve this, the HR function of an organization should emphasize upon five key elements (as illustrated by the following figure) like talent management, creating an open organization, developing leadership capabilities in people, encouraging creativity and innovation and most importantly developing a culture that promotes development of individual capabilities, participation and teamwork.

- **Talent Management:** It is holistic approach through which the keepers and superkeepers are identified, keepers are nurtured and developed into superkeepers and superkeepers are further engaged in the pursuit of higher knowledge and creatively challenging tasks in the organization. A talent management perspective also ensures a framework for retention and growth of the talents in an organization by fostering a comprehensive performance management and reward system in the organization. Professor Anil Sachdeva and his consulting firm (Grow Talent Organization) had been pioneers in promoting the concept of talent management. They had helped several client firms and business houses to institutionalize comprehensive talent management programme suiting their business profiles and needs.

- **Developing Leadership Capabilities:** One of the most successful strategies to foster organizational change and development had been to trap and realize the leadership capabilities of people. Organizations that endevaour on developing such leadership capabilities in their people had been instrumental to achieve customer satisfaction and attain competitive advantage in their business domains.

- **Creativity:** Fostering and encouraging creativity had been the long cherished success mantra for organizations having a vision to make their mark in the future.
- **Open Organizational Set up:** The HR professionals have to play an instrumental role in creating an open organizational set up from traditional bureaucratic structures. This would facilitate empowerment, teamwork and promote creativity of people and help them to attain higher pursuits in their careers in organizations.
- **Organizational Culture:** This is perhaps the most valuable component for organization's success. Customer centricity, business acumen and employee orientedness all stems out of a culture that values people and understands their needs and aspirations. Organizations must emphasize on nurturing a culture that promotes development of individual capabilities, participation and teamwork.

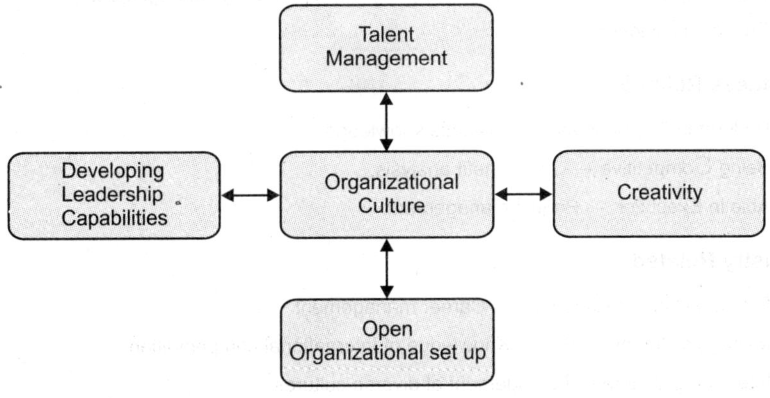

Fig. 1.5: HR must build 5 key elements of the enterprise

Proactive management of human capital and particularly the identification, selection, development and retention of the "superkeepers" or so called "talents" of an organization had become a daunting task for the HR professionals. The HR departments of most organizations seem to have been plagued by the "POGOSTICK" — the all illusive "Talent Volatility". In a cut throat competitive business environment, where rivals are bidding for one another's talent, luring away the "superkeepers" with sky-high compensation packages and benefits – savvy corporations need to understand the competitive value of their so called "superkeepers" and "keepers" and develop a strategic perspective to cater the challenges posed by the new business environment. Focus should be given in terms of identifying the human capital of the organization, which would involve.

— Defining required competencies
— Find the talent
— Growing the talent
— Retaining the talent

Another important aspect contributing to organizational success could well reside on their capability with respect to promptness and speed of service to their customers and even to their employees (internal customers). This would involve the level of adaptability of the organization through its innovative HR practices and would provide them competitive edge by ensuring "the first mover advantage" particularly when there are competitors from abroad.

According to Cambridge Solutions Ltd., a well known HR consultant the newer HR competencies for the future would involve the following:

CAMBRIDGE SOLUTIONS LTD.

Newer HR Competencies for future

Role Related

- Managing Change — Large group facilitation
- Responding Faster — e-HR application
- Managing Stake Holder Conflict — Building teams in the top management
- Coaching Leaders

Business Related

- Understanding Business — Business knowledge
- Being Competitive — Cost benefit analysis
- Able in Execution — Project management

Industry Related

- Providing Career Guidance — Career management
- Managing Compensation — Knowledge of international compensation
- Integrating Culture — Management of diverse cultures

Fig. 1.6: Newer HR competencies for future

(*Courtesy: Presentation by Cambridge Solutions Ltd. in an induction program for MBA students in Bangalore, Further reference can be had from http://www.cambridgesolutionsltd.com/*)

In this context role of senior HR professional must be seen as a(n):

- HR Expert
- Management Theory Expert
- Mentor and Counsellor
- Platform Speaker
- Influential Leader
- Objective and Ethical Leader
- Technologically Savvy Leader
- OD Expert
- Strategic Planning Expert
- Strategic Thinker
- Business Partner
- Morale Compass

Theme Reading: People Development Strategies at HCL Technologies

"Employees are the assets at HCL and there is a constant quest to promote an entrepreneurial culture that fosters creativity and innovation, encourages proactive and collaborative behaviour that ultimately increases the level of engagement of our employees", says Anand Pillai, Vice President and Global Head—talent Transformation and Entrepreneurship Development, HCL Technologies.

It is worth mentioning that the training wing at HCL has initiated a number of organizationally strategic programme that would help their employees at every level to get opportunities to discover and explore the entrepreneur within them. Two such initiatives are as follows:

- **Igen and Value Creation Portal:** Employees at HCL are encouraged to come forward with implementable ideas that would add value to the engagements that they are working for.
- **The Eagles Program:** Aimed at grooming high performance managers, who would be the torchbearers of entrcpreneurship in the organization.

(Courtesy: Bajpai, V., (2008): "Where the mind is without fear", Dare, Vol. 2, Issue: 4, January, 2008, p. 85.)

Characteristics of Core Competencies Achieved through People

Organizations can attain competitive advantage by having core competencies through people in the following ways:

- A core competency in people should make a significant contribution to the create value in the organization.
- People core competencies should be difficult for competitors to imitate. In many industries, such people competencies are likely to be unique. Such uniqueness in an organization's human resources should be rare.
- The capability of an organization in its human resources must be organized in such a way that the employee talents can be combined and deployed to work on new assignments.

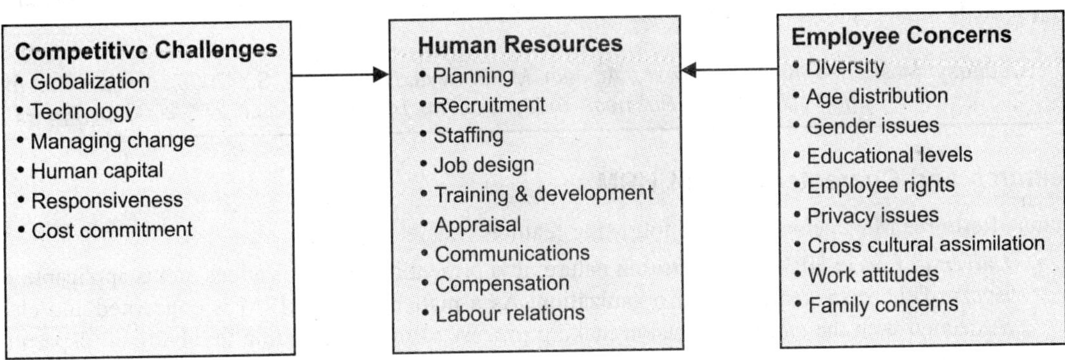

Fig. 1.7: Overall framework of HRM

Theme Reading: Managing Assets that go Home Every Evening

HRM is one of India's biggest challenges. In the new business environment, the quality of a organization's workforce has emerged as all that differentiating force that distinguishes corporations from one another. On the other hand, as new technologies continue to change the face of today's business, the last vestige of opportunity for a company in a competitive environment is its people. Globally, companies that manage their people the best have undergone radical transformation over the last decade. The changes that they made have been focussed in five key areas:

- Implementation of core values and leadership competencies
- Redefining the organization's philosophy
- Investment in the key HR productivity levers

- Realignment of the HR organization with the needs of the business
- The development of a clear and consistent leadership and succession planning model.

India Inc. is likely to find that the joy of exponential growth is accompanied by the frustration of talent scarcity. Leadership and succession planning are a key HR issue, not restricted to the top management, but a four step process spanning an organization's hierarchy.

Identifying talent through a robust performance appraisal system: India Inc. has traditionally relied on confidentiality reports (CR) based performance appraisals. Organizations across the world are moving towards Key Result Area (KRA) based performance management systems. KRAs drive a positive culture of result orientation. Further, being more objective in nature, they facilitate the process of identifying talents.

Identifying successors by matching available skills with job performance: This involves matching skill sets to job requirements. The key lies not just in individualized documentation of skill sets, but more in really knowing the potential successors.

Developing talent through adequate employee development and training processes: Typically there exists a gap between a role oriented skill set and that available in a candidate. For the candidate to play the desired role successfully, the gap should be bridged through training. Globally, best managed companies bridge such gaps by making training mandatory or by making subordinate development the supervisor's key performance criteria. Top corporations have also been found to use "study and learn as you go" approaches to encourage their employees being involved in continuous learning.

Retaining talent: In addition to providing exciting work, best managed companies also emphasize on creating qualitatively superior support mechanisms for their employees so as to encourage talent retention and growth.

(Courtesy: Mukherjee, K., Maheshwary, A., Jain, M., Bhavya, N.K., Lahiri, S., (2005): "India's best managed companies", Business Today, Volume 14, No. 6, March 27th, 2005, p. 106 –108.)

Features and Characteristics of HRM

Human Resource Management has the following features:

- ***Universal Force***: HRM is universal in nature; it is present in all organizations and is applicable at all levels of the management in an organization. As a matter of fact, HRM is concerned and closely associated with the strategic decision making process of the organization involving all departments and functions in the organization. Thus even for a budding SME entrepreneur knowledge of HRM would be instrumental for successfully managing his people without having any formal HR systems in his organization.
- ***Decision Oriented***: HRM emphasizes on decisions, rather than on record keeping, written procedures or rules, which had long been the responsibilities of traditional personnel management practices. These decisions might involve those with respect to performance improvement through further training, or a promotion decision based on satisfactory performance by an employee.
- ***Focus on Individual Needs and Aspirations***: HRM emphasizes on identifying the individual needs and aspirations of an individual employee on the basis of through analysis of their capabilities and future potential. Thus it makes an attempt to help these individuals to further develop their potential and encourage them to give their best to the organization. Thus for a B School faculty, his/her promotions to higher designations might well be related to contributions in research and development or management consultancy and such decisions would be at the discretion of the management of these institutes depending on the nature and framework used to assess the performance of the faculties.

- ***Employee Oriented*:** HRM is concerned about people. Conventionally HRM authors have denied concern for people with employees at work, both as individuals, as well as in groups and teams. But in today's highly competitive business perspective, concern for people has a wider domain conceptually. It mainly deals and revolves around the capabilities of the people rather than the individual. Thus the paradigm shift had been from assigning people on allotted tasks to utilize knowledge and human capabilities for higher performance outcomes.
- ***Development and Growth Oriented*:** Development had been long conceptualized as an initiative taken by an organization to acquire better work related skills and behaviours. In the context where organizations are emphasizing more upon sharing and developing knowledge, the concept of development attains a wider or broader meaning in terms of realizing the capabilities of people/rather knowledge workers. Behavioural scientists have argued that holistic development of people can be made instrumental if the former is coupled with reinforcement strategies ensuring the acquisition of the desired behaviour and capabilities among people. The reward and incentive structures of organizations are needed to be fine tuned along with the development oriented initiatives taken by the organization.
- ***Binding Force of an Organization*:** HRM has the additional responsibility of treating their employees as the "internal customers" of the organization. In this perspective HR professionals need to assume the role of experts (internal business consultants) in other functional domains of their organization like logistics, finance, supply chain management, total quality management, marketing and corporate relations so as to facilitate organizational effectiveness.
- ***Strategic Implication*:** In the perspective of today's highly competitive business environment, HRM should assume the role of the strategic decision making process in the organization. HR professionals in this regard need to assume the responsibility of being the strategic partners of the business and helping the organization to successfully achieve their business objectives by aligning people to the strategic goals of the organization.
- ***Support Functions*:** The HR function of an organization is service oriented. HR executives provide support services to the line managers working in other departments not only just accomplish their administrative or HR-related work more effectively, they so provide consultation as internal consultants and extend "subject-matter-expert (SME)" help and assistances whenever required. HR activities like talent tracking, reward management are examples of the service function.
- ***Multi-disciplinary Nature*:** HRM is a multi-disciplinary practice drawing the knowledge and inputs drawn from various disciplines and studies like those of psychology, sociology, anthropology, political science, economics, quantitative techniques and statistical applications, econometrics, ergonomics (Quality of life and work environment designing), financial concepts (Human resource accounting and HR-audit) etc. The multi-disciplinary aspect of HR function, helps HR professionals assume the role of strategic partners as well as internal consultants of the organization.
- ***Ongoing and Forward Looking Nature*:** HRM is an ongoing process that starts at the strategic level in the organization and pervades into each and every functional domain of the organization. Today's HR practices are mostly forward looking and they constantly take into consideration the future needs and requirements of the business.

Scope of HRM

The scope of HRM is immense for any organization plying in today's dynamic business environment. The entire process starts right from the manpower planning process and revolves around an organization's hiring practices, employee and executive motivation, maintenance, performance evaluation and compensation management, industrial relations and the employee retention plans and strategies. In case of a successful and fast growing company like ICICI Prudential Life Insurance, the scope of its HR function is clearly revealed from its HR philosophy. This is illustrated by the following exhibit.

Exhibit: HR Philosophy in ICICI Prudential Life Insurance

The core HR philosophy at ICICI Prudential Life Insurance revolves around the mantra, "People who achieve, grow and breathe success". This mantra at ICICI Prudential Life Insurance had helped the organization to increase and retain its manpower strength from 7700 in March 2006 to 16000 in March 2007 and 25000 in August 2007. The company relies on infusing young talents and that's why the average age of the professionals working in the organization is only 28 years. The company has an "Internal Job Posting (IJP) System" known as "**Career Scope**" through which about 30% of the vacancies in the organization are filled through internal growth. The company provides huge learning opportunities to its young professionals where freedom is given to each individual to cultivate new ideas and create a win-win culture at the workplace through wholehearted employee participation and commitment. The HR department continuously ensures long term grooming for its leaders. The company feels proud to admit that 80% of its top management team has an experience of more than 5 years stay in the organization; which also indicates the effectiveness of the retention plan in the organization.

(Courtesy: Presentation by representatives of ICICI Prudential Life Insurance in their B school campus recruitment program "Udaan" (http://www.iciciprulife.com/public/Others/Udaan-Home.htm)

Nature of HRM: The pervasive feature of human resource management makes its scope and applicability wider. Further the strategic role of HRM function and HR professionals now assuming the roles of strategic partners in the organization had further enhanced the scope of the HR function in the organization.

Employee hiring: Having the right employee at the right place is a challenge to any organization. Particularly when the rival organizations are attempting to poach away the best employees of one organization, it has become strategically crucial for today's HR managers to hire and retain their intellectual capital. This is facilitated by a comprehensive HR planning and a watch dog policy on rival organization's HR strategies.

Compensation management: Compensation management is one of the most important factors contributing to employee retention in today's organizations. When most of the firms are depending on their respective variable pay packages to attract talents and lure others from rival organizations, it is imperative that HR managers need to emphasize on a comprehensive compensation strategy.

Employee motivation: Retaining employees in the era of cut throat competition is hugely contributed by the extent through which employees are being motivated at their workplace. HR professionals have to play an instrumental role in creating a conducive environment at the workplace so as to facilitate constant learning, growth and employee development. At the same time there has to be an equal emphasis on enhancing the Quality of Work Life (QWL) and the overall ambience in the organization so as to enhance the psychological well being of employees in their workplace.

Employee maintenance: Today's HR managers go beyond the traditional "maintenance oriented" approaches towards a more holistic and developmental approach for nurturing their human capital. Organizations in this pursuit have emphasized on developing "assessment centres" and "growth laboratories/employee incubators" so facilitate holistic learning and development in the workplace.

Industrial relations: Today's HR functions had gone well beyond the traditional union-management conflict resolution platform to a more holistic and wide scenario. With majority of the organizations going global, the challenges of IR had been further complicated in terms of dealing with the labour laws and regulations of multiple countries where they operate. Further with employee empowerment creeping into the blood of most organizations and growing importance being laid upon self managed teams and quality circles, the relevance of unionism seemed to have been faded.

Fig. 1.8: A winning culture facilitates the growth of human resources

Prospects of HRM: This mainly includes emphasis on a broader outlook towards the people working in the organization. Issues include those of:

- HR functions assuming the role of strategic partners in the organization
- HR managers assuming the roles of "change agents" and "internal organizational development (OD) consultants"
- More involvement in to the personal lives of employees
- Focus on employee diversity management
- Emphasis on cross-cultural assimilation and training
- Emphasis on constant employee development and learning
- Emphasis and strategic focus on employee career planning and development
- Developing the next line of competent managers as a part of the organization's succession plan
- Performance management systems of organizations being linked with the strategic objectives of the organization
- Focus on developing employee capabilities rather than developing skills through conventional training activities.

Objectives and Functions of HRM

Human Resource Management has the following objectives and functions, namely:

- To ensure that it acts as the "Strategic fit (integration)" so as to effectively integrate the business and HR strategies in the organization.

- To ensure that the organization adopts a coherent approach to the provision of mutually supporting and integrated HR practices so as to enable the organization successfully accomplish its goals and objectives.
- To ensure the importance of achieving a holistic commitment of the people to the culture, values, mission and vision of the organization.
- To ensure the employees are treated as assets or "human capital" in the organization.
- To employ the skills and abilities of the workforce efficiently.
- To provide the organization with well-trained and well-motivated employees.
- To increase to the fullest, the employee's Job Satisfaction and Self-actualization.
- To develop and maintain a Quality of Work Life (QWL).
- To communicate HR policies to all employees effectively.
- To help maintain ethical policies and behaviour at the work place.
- To maintain discipline and address employee grievance and dissatisfaction more promptly and effectively.
- To maintain a cordial relationship in between the employees at various levels with the management of the organization.

Managing people: A step by step roadmap

- Start with recruitment. Don't recruit those people who will be the most difficult to retain.
- Adapt to attrition. It is the order of the day. Market forces are too strong.
- Focus on what you can change. Don't focus on what you can't change and lose sleep.
- Sometimes you don't have to recruit all high powered staff.
- Simplify and standardize jobs and use multi-skilling to meet any contingencies.
- Focus on retaining intellectual capital even when employees leave. Think of appropriate mechanisms and build organizational memories and knowledge systems to retain talent and intellectual capital.
- Electronic records of employee knowledge helps in many cases.
- Cooperate with competitors. Form clubs and associations.
- Work with local institutes and communities and develop a large source of skill base by giving projects and grants to local colleges.

Fig. 1.9: Managing people: a step by step roadmap
(Courtesy: Rao, T.V., 2006: "Old pillars of people management", Indian Management, Vol. 45, Issue: 6, p. 76).

Line and Staff Aspects of HRM

In any organization, as all managers get involved in activities like recruiting, interviewing, selecting and training; they take the role of HR managers. As for example, for most pharmaceutical companies the marketing managers or senior medical representatives take care of recruiting fresher professionals. In spite of this the HR function strictly resides to those of the HR professionals who come under the purview of the HR department of the organization. Taking this into consideration, the issue of concern is how the roles could and responsibilities of the HR managers and their staff relate to those of the "line managers" HR related duties. This would be clearly understood by clarifying the definitions of the line and staff authorities in an organization.

Table 1.1: HRM Objectives and Supporting Functions (William B Werther, Keith Davis et al.)[16]

HRM Objectives	***Supporting Functions***
1. Extra-organizational Commitments: The HR function of any organization should be concerned to foster commitment and service towards the society and environment in which the organization's operations is related or linked.	1. Legal Compliance/Statutory Compliance with Govt. bodies, International organizations and industry associations 2. Social welfare programme 3. Environment improvement initiatives 4. Supporting industrial associations for promoting social development programme (as done by Peenya Industrial Association in Bangalore) 5. Ensuring healthy union-management relations for promoting organizational and social obligations
2. Business Perspectives: The HR function of any organization should assume a strategic and consultative role in order to help the management of an organization achieve its business objectives. The HR function should also act as a change agent to foster growth and development and inculcate innovation in the organization.	1. Liaisoning with the top management for taking strategic decisions 2. Liaisoning with Govt. bodies, industry associations and international organizations for statutory compliance and quality management 3. Strategic Human Resource Planning (SHRP) and implementing the same for achieving business objectives 4. Employee development through competency mapping, performance evaluation and training 5. Employee career and succession planning 6. Employee motivation and welfare 7. Compensation and reward management 8. Acting as an "internal (OD) consultant" 9. Talent management and development 10. Involvement in developing knowledge systems and developing the same in liaison with technical experts in the organization
3. Functional Perspectives: The aim of this objective is to enhance the scope of the HR function of the organization beyond its conventional people management perspectives to a more proactive, development oriented approach.	1. Strategic HR planning 2. HR research 3. Consultative and OD activities 4. Liaison with statutory compliance authorities 5. Facilitating HR audit, and due diligence reviews to review organizational performance in terms of effectiveness of HR functions
4. Individual Perspectives: To assume the role of a mentor, coach, trainer and counselor so as to cater and meet the needs of individual employees.	1. Performance and potential appraisals 2. Performance evaluation, planning and development 3. Ongoing emphasis of training and management development activities 4. Career and succession planning 5. Reward and compensation management 6. Role as an internal counselor and consultant 7. Talent tracking and development

Line versus Staff Authority: Authority is the right to make decisions, to direct the work of others, and to give orders. It can be defined as the right to order or command and is delegated from the superior to the subordinate to discharge his responsibilities. Authority of a position could be in terms of the authority with respect to the position or designation held by an individual in the organization, it could also be the "Legal Authority" and also the "Authority of Knowledge/Expertise". The sources of authority in an organization could be illustrated by the following figure:

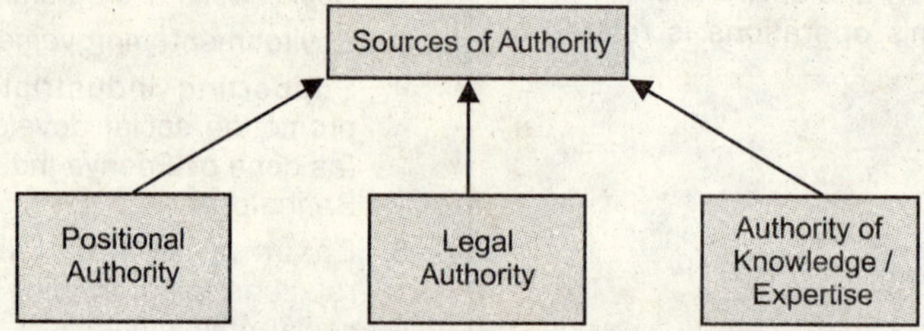

Fig. 1.10: Sources of authority in organizations

Line Authority

Line authority refers to those positions and elements of the organization which have the responsibility and authority and are accountable for the accomplishment of primary objectives of their jobs or duties. Line managers are authorized to direct the work of the subordinates and juniors. Line managers are in charge of accomplishing the organization's basic goals. Line authority acts as a chain of command from the CEO to the lower level subordinates. It provides the basic directions required for operating the enterprise for a systematic way. Line managers use this authority as a means of control by setting limits to the scope of their managerial actions.

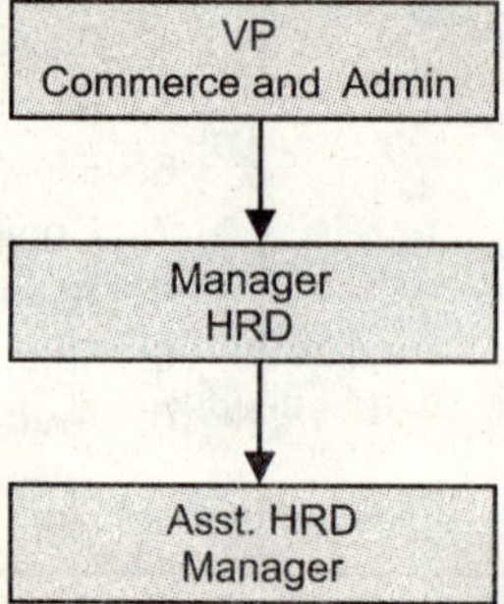

Fig. 1.11: Line structure in a HR department

Staff Authority

Staff authority refers to those elements which have the responsibility and authority for providing advice and services to the line positions in terms of assisting them for the attainment of their objectives and goals. Staff managers are authorized to assist and advise line managers in accomplishing their fundamental organizational goals. The roles of most HR managers are generally like staff managers. They are responsible for assisting and advising, consulting the line managers in areas like recruiting, hiring, and compensation related decisions and even helping them to find solutions to business related problems.

HR Roles and Responsibilities of Line Managers

The direct handling of people is, always has been, an integral part of every line manager's responsibility from that of the top management position to the lowest operation level of the organization. This is true for a CEO to a marketing manager or even a production manager. This could be illustrated by the following HR-related responsibilities of the line managers of an organization:

HR Roles of a Marketing Manager

- Hiring and placing the right person on the right job
- Orienting and training new hires and keep a team of supporting executives ready in case of immediate requirement and deployment.
- Catering to the development needs of the marketing executives as an when required to enhance their selling skills and capabilities.
- Improving the job performance of these employees by involving them in management development programme
- Gaining creative cooperation and developing smooth working relationships with the departments of the organization like the production department and the stores section.
- Taking responsibility in implementing the organization's policies and procedures in terms of incentive programme and reward strategies
- Ensuring controlling of labour costs by proper HR planning, preventing manpower wastage and loss.
- Motivating employees working in the marketing department to enhance their capabilities and contribute effectively into the business of the organization.
- Ensuring discipline and good employee relations at the workplace by facilitating communication at every level of the organization.
- Facilitating protection of employee rights, health and good working conditions and environment.

In SMEs, line managers like that of the administrative head may also carry out all these HR functions, where there could be even no formal HR department or HR manager to take care of these activities. Generally as an organization grows considerably the formal HR function under the leadership of a HR manager becomes a necessity for these organizations. In this aspect the HR department provides specialized assistance in terms of:

Functions of HR managers	Features/Hallmarks
1. Line function	Here the HR manager directs the activities (exerts line authority) of the people in his/her department and in related service areas. Outside their departments they generally exert implied authority.
2. Coordinative function	HR managers also coordinate personnel activities, a duty often referred to as functional control. They act as the "the right arm of the top management" so as to ensure that the line managers are implementing the organization's HR objectives, policies and procedures.
3. Staff (service) functions	Assisting and advising line managers is an integral part of the HR manager's responsibility. The HR manager helps in hiring, training, evaluating, rewarding, counselling, promoting and developing employees and also catering to various employee welfare and benefit programmes in the organization. They help line managers comply with statutory norms (legal norms, statutory compliances laid by the pollution control board, state establishment acts etc.), handle and manage employee grievances, safety and health practices, labour relations etc. They also take up the role of innovators by providing up-to-date information on the latest trends and new methods of solving problems, maintaining quality etc. They also act as change agents and internal consultants in terms of catering to the issues related to organizational change and development and most importantly play a strategic role by helping the top management and the CEO implement the firms' corporate strategy.

Approaches to HRM

The approaches to HRM can be broadly classified into three wings namely:

- Reactive and Supportive HRM
- Integrative HRM
- Independent HRM

Reactive and Supportive HRM: The key responsibilities and functions of the reactive and supportive approach to HRM are as follows:

- Management of employee contributions, administration of performance appraisals, performance development plans, career development plans etc.
- Listening and responding to employees
- Recruitment, compensation management, training/re-training, sustaining and facilitating growth and development of human capital.
- Union/association negotiations
- HR record maintenance and emphasis on HR research and statutory compliance management

Integrative Function of HRM: The role of HRM as an integrative function is more of being a strategic partner to the organization as a whole. This philosophy is guided mainly by the principles that:

- What was affine solution yesterday may not be valid tomorrow.
- Emphasizing on the 7Ss *i.e.*, Strategy, systems, staffs, skills, styles, structures and shared values.
- Generating a learning organization with knowledge workers

Independent Function/Role of HRM: Here the role of HRM is more of a change agent or internal consultant to the organization. This is facilitated by observing the organization's movement over time at a certain level of abstraction and provides inputs for organizational change and ensuring the right competence/skill/experience distribution of manpower in the organization so as to respond to changes more effectively.

HUMAN RESOURCE DEVELOPMENT (HRD)

HRD means developing or trapping hidden qualities in people in order to make them accomplish new functions leading to organizational and individual goals. Human resource development is concerned with the development and implementation of people strategies, which are integrated with corporate strategies, and ensures that the culture, values and structure of the organization, and the quality, motivation and commitment of its members contribute fully to the achievement of its goals. HRD is a set of systematic and planned activities designed by an organization to provide its members with the necessary skills to meet current and future job demands.

HRD is the process of increasing knowledge, skills, capabilities and positive work attitude and value of all people working at all levels in an organization. It constitutes the logical outcome of the argument than an organization's employees are its most valuable resource.

"The essence of Human Resource Management is that employees are valued assets and that their value should be increased by a systematic and coherent approach to investing in their training and development. Resourcing is about providing the skills base needed by the organization. Human Resource Development is about enhancing and widening these skills by training, by helping people to grow within the organization, and by enabling them to make better use of their skills and abilities" (Armstrong, 1992).

The Benefits of Human Resource Development

Armstrong (1992) claimed that investment in Human Resource Development could bring the following benefits to an organization:

- A signal to the employees that management believes they are important.
- Motivation to acquire new skills and consequent rewards.
- Commitment through the communication of values.
- Identification with company goals through better employee understanding.
- Two-way communication between management and employees.
- Needs satisfaction through achievement and recognition.
- Job enrichment through training and the acquisition of new skills.
- Increased awareness of the importance of change management.

The above list corresponds to the principles and findings of the Human Relations School of Management which stresses the importance of Human Resource Management to organizations.

HRD programme undertaken by RIL

- MPRE (Management Programme for Reliance Engineering), at IIM Bangalore.
- RCE (Reliance Certified Engineering), with IIT Mumbai.
- Leadership Programme, with HEWIIT Associates.
- In-house training programme (accounts and finance).
- System of assessment, aptitude tests, career mapping and other training programme.

Fig. 1.12: HRD programmes undertaken by Reliance India Limited

(*Courtesy: http://www.citehr.com/blogs/rohit_sachdeva/6613-hrd.html*)

Why is Human Resource Development So Important Now?

Tom Senge (1997) claimed there were three major driving forces to which organizations now had to respond:

- Technology.
- Globalization of business.
- Systems breakdown and control.

In order for organizations to cope with the above challenges and ensure reliable organizational outcomes, their managers will have to invest in Human Resource Development. Senge was one of the main originators of the learning organization and continues to stress the need for organizations to share knowledge: "Sharing knowledge occurs when people are genuinely interested in helping one another develop new capacities for action: it is about creating learning processes" (Senge P, 1997).

Objectives of HRD

- To acquire or sharpen capabilities of the human resources in order to facilitate them to perform functions associated with the organization's present as well as ***expected future challenges and roles***.
- To develop general capabilities of individuals and exploit their inner potential and capabilities for their own and/or organizational development purposes.
- To develop an organizational culture where team work and collaboration could contribute to the professional well being and motivation of the employees.

Hallmarks of HRD

HRD can be characterized under the following headings namely:

- **HRD as a system:** HRD as a system operates at the micro level to the macro level of the organization, facilitating the development of human capabilities for the present as well as for the futuristic needs of the business. HRD as a system makes an organization capable to proactively respond to organizational change by enhancing the potential and competence of the people.
- **HRD as a planned process:** HRD is a planned process as it strategically visualizes the future competence of the people and develops an action plan to achieve the same in an effective way. It emphasizes the participation of HR professionals in the strategic planning process of the organizations and linking individual employee's goals and objectives along with the strategic objectives and goals of the organization.
- **HRD Involves the development competencies:** One of the most striking features of HRD had been its capability to constantly contribute for the development of the capabilities and potential of the human resources. Emphasis is given on competency analysis and developing performance improvement plans based on the competency inventories of the people in the organization.
- **HRD is an interdisciplinary concept:** HRD like HRM is interdisciplinary in nature and its pervasiveness is strategically essential for an organization's sustainability and development.

HRM versus HRD: If we view the field carefully, we can easily differentiate the two field in the following manner:

HRD	HRM/Personnel Management
It is a continuous process.	It is a routine and administrative function.
It deals with the development and upgradation of the human capital in an organization.	It deals with the optimum utilization of the human capitals in the organization.
It is independent in nature.	It is integrative and supportive in nature.
HRD tries to bring about qualitative changes in the stock of human capital in an organization in accordance with the corporate objectives and needs.	HRM takes the stock of human capital as given and tries to optimally allocate it among different processes/activities in such a way that its effectiveness is maximized.
It is a sub-system of a large system, and more organizational oriented in nature.	It is a function of more independent activities with separate roles to play.
It is more proactive; it copes with the changing needs of the people as well as anticipate these needs.	It is mainly a reactive function responding to the demands which may arise.
It contributes to developing the whole organization, e.g., Organizational Development.	It is concerned with people only.
It is concerned with the involvement of the entire work force from top to bottom is more and a must in most of the cases.	It is basically the responsibilities of the HR department.

The **HRM (Function)** and **HRD (Profession)** have undergone tremendous change over the last two or three decades. Many years ago, large organizations looked to the "Personnel Department", mostly manage the paperwork around hiring and paying people. More recently, organizations consider the "HR Department." As playing a major role in staffing, training and helping to manage people so that people and the organization are performing at maximum capability in a highly fulfilling manner.

In recent years there has been a sudden spurt in the no. of organizations deciding to appoint HRD managers. However, many people are not clear as to what is the difference between personnel and HRD functions. As a result we find instances of personnel managers being redesignated HRD Manages or Human Resource Managers. Basically, HR consists of the value of productive capacity of a firm's human organization. HRD efforts aim at providing conditions in which the employees can improve their skill, knowledge, energy and talent, which in turn may lead to improved productivity. Basically, the main areas which have to be managed by HRD people are:

- Managing succession politics,
- Managing appraisal politics,
- Managing the reward system,
- Distribution of power across groups,
- Balancing power across groups,
- Influencing the key people.

It will be primary responsibility of the HRD people to develop the right kind of culture, values and norms to be followed by an organization.

HRD in India

Growth of HRD in India could be accounted to as early as that in the year 1970. The organizations which firstly introduced HRD in India are as follows:

- State Bank of India
- Bank of Baroda
- Larsen and Toubro (L&T)
- Voltas
- Crompton and Greaves
- Indian Oil Corporation
- Steel Authority of India Ltd. (SAIL)

But unfortunately in most cases the old personnel departments were just renamed as HRD departments.

Problems faced by most organizations in terms of HRD: The problems faced by most organizations with HRD were as follows:

- Lack of knowledge about HRD and dissemination of the same amongst people.
- The role of HRD in the corporate mission was most often confused. Business captains initially refused to accept the strategic role of the HRD.
- Lack of identification of elements of training programmes that could facilitate organizational development (OD) and learning.
- Conventional lecture methods were continued to be used for developing and training people that hardly brought about any changes in the capabilities of people.
- Language and cultural differences of people were hardly taken into consideration for holistic HRD.
- Unconducive environment for HRD caused by labour unrest and industrial disputes. Lack of interest from the side of the management to link HRD with the employee and industrial relations activities.
- Emphasis on job training only and failure of supervisors to ensure applicability of the learned skills in real life job situations.
- Lack of professional institutes, training organizations and experts.
- Lack of interest shown by HRD staff and senior management reluctance.
- HRD was not perceived as a lucrative profession as compared to the marketing, finance and production professionals.
- Pitfalls in the educational system, lack of focus on management education.

How a HRD system works can be illustrated by the following figure:

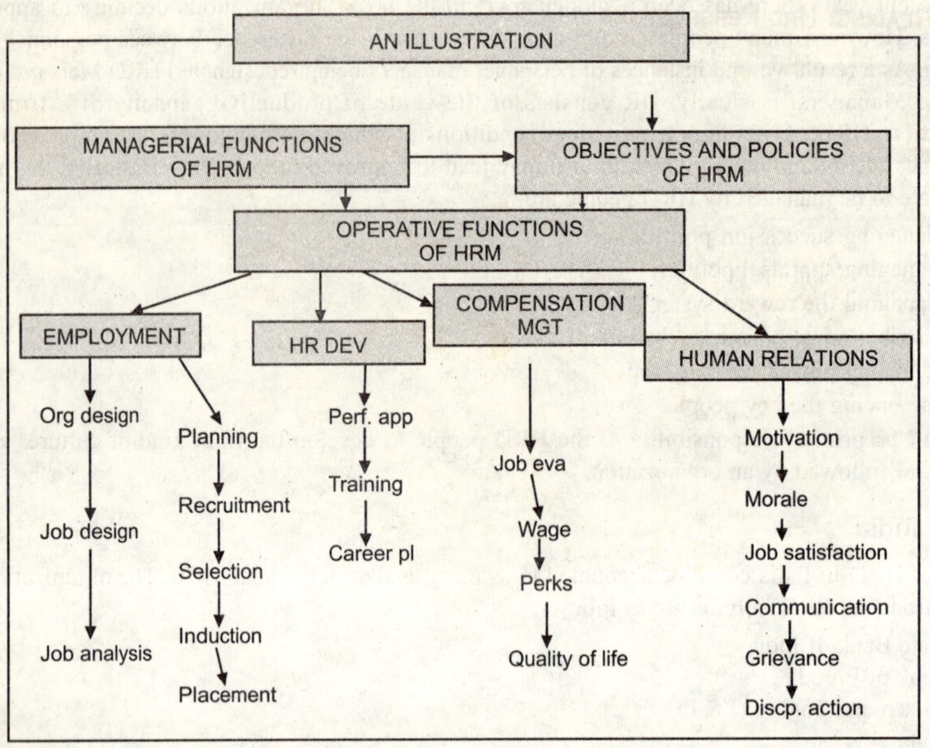

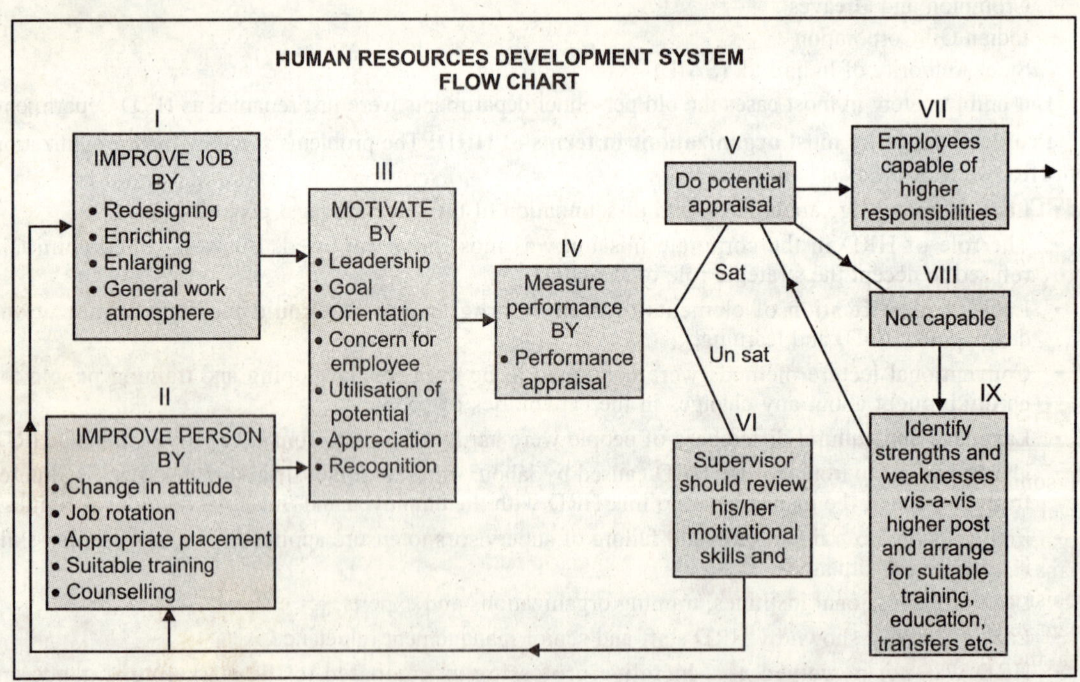

Fig. 1.13: HRD system

THEME READING: HRD PERSPECTIVES IN C-DAC

In C-DAC, the HRD managers act as co-coordinators to provide uniform inputs to all employees, irrespective of their level and function. HRD plans are evolved by staff participation and involvement. Developmental inputs contribute to learning, where learning builds professional competence and excellence.

Principal HRD Objectives in C-DAC

- To improve individual effectiveness.
- To inculcate pride, trust and satisfaction.
- To promote all-round growth and development.
- To initiate drive, innovation and creativity.
- To enhance the quality of work life (QWL).
- To prepare people for change and futuristic challenges.

HRD Activities in C-DAC

HRD objectives are achieved by the following:

- Identifying skills required in C-DAC.
- Recruitment and selection.
- Employee training and development.
- Compensation management.
- Rewards and recognition.
- Evolving employee centric policies.
- Conducting HR surveys.

HRD Functioning in C-DAC

Corporate HRD at C-DAC (HQ) in Pune functions in close collaboration with the HR incumbents at C-DAC's other centres to smoothly and correctly discharge HR duties and responsibilities across C-DAC.

(*Courtesy: http://www.cdac.in/*)

PERSONNEL MANAGEMENT

Personnel Management can be described as an administrative record-keeping function, at the operational level of the organization related to the maintenance and management of personnel related information in the organization. It attempts to maintain fair terms and conditions of employment, while at the same time, efficiently managing personnel activities for individual departments, managing personnel records for administrative decisions, catering to the welfare of employees and providing expert help and assistance to the higher management in terms of maintaining cordial industrial relations. The theory of personnel management assumes that the outcomes from providing justice and achieving efficiency in the management of personnel activities would ultimately contribute in terms of achieving organizational success. Personnel management can be defined as a set of programmes, functions and activities taken by an organization designed so as to maximize both personal and organizational goals and objectives.

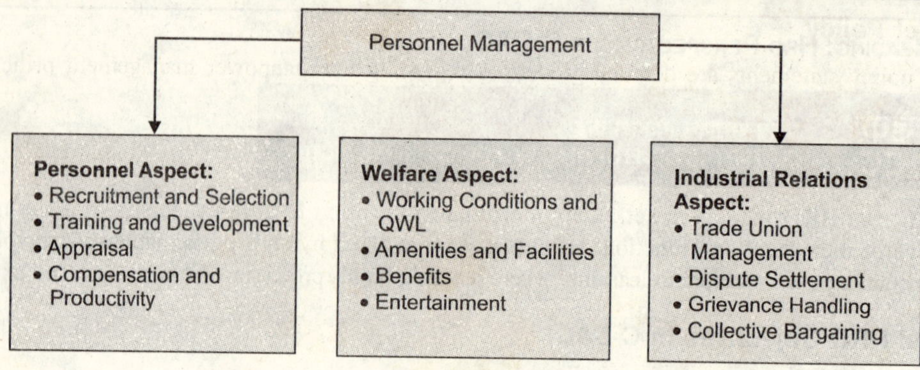

Fig. 1.14: Components of personnel management

Features of Personnel Management

- It is concerned with employees both as individuals as well as a group in attaining their goals and objectives for an organization.
- It is responsible for the development and growth of human resources in an organization.
- It entails and involves all levels and categories of employees in an organization.
- It is a continuous and ongoing process.
- It aims to attain organizational, individual and societal goals in an integrated way providing benefits to the employees, the organization and the society as the whole.
- It is a responsibility of all line managers and function of Staff managers.
- It caters to the welfare aspects of employees in an organization by emphasizing on their individual as well as their social needs and requirements.
- It also facilitates to manage cordial employee and industrial relations leading to industrial harmony and peace making.
- It provides the management of an organization an effective helping hand in terms of dealing with trade union related problems and managing the same in effective ways.
- Personnel managers facilitate to resolve industrial disputes and problems and aim to have liaison with concerned legal and state authorities.

Functions of Personnel Management

A	**Managerial**	Planning, Organizing, Directing, Supervising and Controlling
B	**Operative**	**Employee deployment related**: (Job Analysis, HRP, Recruitment, Selection, Placement, Induction and Orientation) **HRD**: (Performance Appraisal, Training and Development, Career and Succession Planning, Organization Development)
C	**Compensation**	Job Evaluation Wage and salary administration, Incentive, Bonus, Fringe Benefits Social security measures like provident funds, pension, life insurance benefits, gratuity etc.
D	**Human Relations**	Employee Relations
E	**Managing effectiveness of HRM**	Organization Health, Quality of worklife (QWL) Documentation and management of HR related records Organization Culture and Climate HR Accounting, Audit and Research

Personnel Policy

Personnel policy statements are detailed guidelines regarding the manpower management principles and practices pertaining to an organization. The personnel policies of an organization tend to vary from industry to industry and the nature of the business. They provide the fundamental guidelines regarding the procurement, management, retention, development of manpower in the organization and facilitate the organization to maintain cordial employee relationships, welfare activities of the employees and effective trade union management relationships at the workplace. The hallmarks of a personnel policy can be illustrated as that of a real life organization, as depicted below:

Exhibit: Hallmarks of Personnel Policy in Bata India Ltd. (Retail Section)

The personnel policies of Bata India Ltd. cover emotional intelligence. The ability to handle people skillfully, the art to build successful relationships is what distinguishes Bata from other companies. It makes workers to lead the work, to adopt to change, to give feedback on performance and motivate them. Bata has maintained an organization structure that supports the workers in every critical aspect. It has laid down various personnel policies. The primary function of the trade union (Bata Mazdoor Union) in Bata India Ltd. is to promote and protect the interest of its workers and put before the management their demands and grievances.

Personnel Team Mission in Bata (Retail)

- Partnering with the management in the creation and implementation of the business strategy.
- Ensuring that we have the right people in the right jobs.
- Developing our people in a planned and structured way, to improve performance, morale, motivation, quality and teamwork.
- Coordinating the alignment of our people's efforts to realize the company's mission.
- Ensuring that our organization has the ability to change.
- Creating an environment which is productive and efficient all in the context of good employee relations.

Table 1.2: Manpower in Bata India Ltd.

Category	***Years***							
	2001	***2002***	***2003***	***2004***	***2005***	***2006***	***2007***	***2008***
Managers	104	98	93	67	60	58	53	52
Fixed staff	124	120	108	96	72	67	62	65
Hourly fixed staff	41	38	34	34	38	32	32	38
Essential services staff	36	34	32	29	24	20	20	25
Accord staff (piece rate system)	1008	964	891	765	728	677	664	662
Total Manpower	1313	1255	1158	1021	922	854	831	842

The personnel department in Bata India Ltd., Bataganj plant is a small department, which is being headed by the personnel manager, who has been empowered by the top management to execute personnel policies farmed by the management. The personnel manager has also to take care and tackle the local problems of the plant. He has been given the authority to make modifications in the policies so as to suit the local conditions.

Contd...

Main Personnel Functions in Bata India Ltd.

- To maintain good industrial relationship
- Recruitment of staff, their training, development, preparing job descriptions
- Performance evaluation
- Compensation policy
- To provide retirement and pension schemes
- Promulgate an employee centric welfare policy

(*Courtesy: Organization study done by Mr. Syed Ghulam Sarwar at Bata India Ltd.*)

Advantages of Personnel Policy: The common advantages of having a personnel policy involve the following benefits:

- **Delegation:** Personnel policies ensure a framework for delegation of authority in terms of responsibilities of employees working at various levels of the organization.
- **Uniformity:** Personnel policies also facilitate the uniformity of personnel related decisions in organizations and provide a guideline for line managers and supervisors for managing employees at the workplace. They also form the basis of discipline and grievance management and help the managers of an organization to take decisions with respect to dispute settlement and union related problems.
- **Better Control:** Personnel policies facilitate better control to managers in terms of solving work related problems, settling grievances, disputes and maintaining an uniform code of conduct and discipline in the workplace.
- **Standards of Efficiency:** Many personnel policies also determine the standards of employee performance and efficiency indicators in organizations.
- **Confidence:** Personnel policies can instill an element of confidence amongst the employees by indicating the guidelines for various reward, incentive schemes and promotional as well as career upliftment opportunities in the organization.
- **Speedy Decision Making:** Personnel policies also promote speedy decision making with respect to manpower related decisions like payment of increments, bonus, promotions, transfers etc.
- **Coordination:** Personnel policies facilitate interdepartmental coordination, delegation of authority. It also acts as a guideline for managing union relations.

Characteristics of an Effective Personnel Policy: The personnel policies of an organization have the following features, namely:

- **Relatedness to Objectives:** The personnel policies help organizational members and managers to have their focus on the organizational objectives and help them to achieve the organizational goals by having the right people with right form of skills and capabilities for the right positions in the organizations.
- **Preciseness:** Personnel policies like any other organizational policies and strictly precise, objective in nature. They aim to realize the best potential of human resources in the organization, by encouraging them to higher performance levels, fostering training and development. They also decide the framework for reward and incentive schemes for employees catering to their motivation and retention in the organization.
- **Factual:** The personnel policies are based on facts and figures that are relevant to the organization and the industry standards, norms, rules and regulations. Personnel policies also take into consideration the statutory compliance frameworks and develop comprehensive guidelines for the organizations to adhere to the same.

- **Easily Understandable:** Personnel polices are generally simple; easily understandable to employees at all levels in an organization.
- **Stable and Flexible:** Personnel policies are generally stable in nature; yet they are flexible to changes in cases of impending organizations changes and administrative requirements.
- **Appropriateness:** All personnel policies are appropriate and factual in nature. They form the basis of managerial decision making with respect to personnel decisions as well as disciplinary guidelines for the employees in the organization. The personnel manual as maintained by most organization is based on such appropriate and factual information regarding the company's personnel activities.
- **Just, Fair and Equitable:** Any personnel policy by their very nature attempt to be fair, justifiable, rational, equitable and transparent in their very design and applicability.
- **Reasonable:** Personnel policies are reasonable in terms of decisions taken by the management based on actions or fact and figures related to an organization.
- **Reviewable:** Personnel policies are reviewable and changeable as and when required by the organization.
- **Development Oriented:** Personnel policies should emphasize on the overall development of the employees, catering to their training as well as career related development needs.

Distinction between Personnel Management and HRM

- Personnel management is ***workforce centered***, directed mainly at the organization's employees; such as finding their performance deficits and training them, arranging for them to be well compensated, explaining the management's expectations, justifying management's actions etc. While on the other hand, HRM is ***resource–centered***, directed mainly at the management, in terms of devolving the responsibility of HRM to line management, management and organization development etc.
- Although indisputably a management function, personnel management has never totally identified with management interests, as it becomes ineffective when not able to understand and articulate the aspirations and views of the workforce, just as sales representatives have to understand and articulate the aspirations of the customers. HRM has a more of an integrative role in the organization by involving in the strategic decision making process of the organization.
- Personnel management is basically an **operational** function, concerned primarily with carrying out the day-to-day people management activities. While on the other hand, HRM is **strategic** in nature, that is, being concerned with directly assisting an organization to achieve **sustained competitive advantage** over its business rivals.
- HRM is more *proactive* than Personnel Management. Whereas personnel management is about **maintenance** oriented and administrative in nature. On the other hand, HRM is about the visualizing and **forecasting** of organizational needs, the continual monitoring and adjustment of the existing HR systems so as to meet the current and future requirements of the business and cater the challenges pertaining to the management of organizational change and development.

Table 1.3: Distinction between Personnel Management and HRD

Sl. No.	*Dimension/Hallmarks*	*Personnel Management*	*Human Resource Development*
Beliefs and Assumptions			
1.	Contract	Careful delineation of written contracts	Aim to go 'beyond contracts'
2.	Rules	Importance of devising clear rules/mutuality	'Can-do' outlook; impatience with 'rule'

Contd...

3.	Guide to management action	Procedures	'Business – need'
4.	Behaviour referent	Norms/custom and practice	Values/Mission
5.	Managerial task *vis-à-vis* labour	Monitoring	Nurturing
6.	Nature of relations	Pluralist	Unitarist
7.	Conflict	Institutionalized	De-emphasized
STRATEGIC ASPECTS			
8.	Key relations	Labour management	Customer
9.	Initiatives	Piecemeal	Integrated
10.	Corporate plan	Marginal to	Central to
11.	Speed of decision	Slow	Fast
LINE MANAGEMENT			
12.	Management role	Transactional	Transformational leadership
13.	Key managers	Personnel/IR specialists	General/business/line managers
14.	Communication	Indirect	Direct
15.	Standardization	High (e.g. 'parity' an issue)	Low (e.g. 'parity' not seen as relevant)
16.	Prized management skills	Negotiation	Facilitation
KEY LEVERS			
17.	Selection	Separate, marginal task	Integrated, key task
18.	Pay	Job Evaluation (fixed grades)	Performance–related
19.	Conditions	Separately negotiated	Harmonization
20.	Labour management	Collective bargaining contracts	Towards individual contracts
21.	Thrust of relations	Regularized through facilities and training	Marginalized (with exception of some bargaining for change models)
22.	Job categories and grades	Many	Few
23.	Communication	Restricted flow	Increased flow
24.	Job design	Division of labour	Teamwork
25.	Conflict handling	Reach temporary truces	Manage climate and culture
26.	Training and development	Controlled access to courses	Learning companies
27.	Foci of attention of interventions	Personnel procedures	Wide ranging cultural, structural and personnel strategies
MANAGEMENT EFFECTIVENESS			
28.	Business impact	Short-term	Long-term

Contd...

29.	Decision making	Policy bound decision making	Strategic decision making
30.	Managing business challenges	Limited scope	Wider scope
31.	Managing diversity and cultural assimilation	Policy bound and limited scope	Greater flexibility is achieved by organizations having HRD capabilities
32.	Business expansion through JVs and M&A	Less helpful	Greater opportunities in terms of achieving success and effectiveness for the organization
33.	Mostly used by	Line managers hierarchical organizations	Leaders, teams and organizations believing in open and horizontal structural orientations
34.	Impact on organizational change and development	Limited applicability	Wider applicability and empowers organizations to manage change more effectively
35.	Organizational learning	Limited applicability	Facilitates learning organizations

Human Resource Management and Corporate Performance

Studies have revealed that progressive HRM practices can have a significant effect on corporate performance. Several authors in this regard have revealed the relationship between specific HR practices and critical outcome measures such as corporate financial performance, productivity, product and service quality, and cost control (as in case of linking the same through balance scorecard frameworks).

Many of the methods characterizing the so-called **"High-Performance Work Systems (HPWS)"** have been researched and developed by the HRM academic community. The characteristics of such HPWS are as follows:

Characteristics of High-Performance Work Systems (Becker, B., Huselid, M., Ulrich, D.: "The HR Scorecard", Boston: Harvard Business School Press, 2001)

- Large number of highly qualified applicants for each strategic position.
- The use of validated selection and promotion models/procedures.
- Extensive training and development of new employees.
- The use of formal performance appraisal and management.
- The use of multi-source (360 degree) performance appraisal and feedback.
- Linkage of merit increases to formal appraisal process.
- Above-market compensation for key positions.
- High percentage of entire workforce included into the incentive systems.
- High differential in pay between high and low performers.
- High percentage of HR activities spent on outsourced activities (e.g., recruiting, payroll etc.).
- High percentage of workforce working in self-managed, project-based work teams.
- Low percentage of employees covered by union contracts.
- Relatively low number of employees per HR professional.
- High percentage of jobs filled from within.

Human Resource Organization

Human Resource Organization is concerned with achieving organizational success by developing an effective organization design, catering the challenges related to organizational change and development, fostering employee motivation, facilitating application of effective leadership, and institutionalizing the process of getting across the message of promulgating team work and participative management at all levels of the organization. The fundamental objectives of the human resource organization are to ensure that every aspect of the organization, employment, motivation and management of people are strategically integrated with the objectives of the business and facilitate achievement of those objectives by the people in the organization. The human resource organization initiative also adheres various cultural and employee diversity related issues and attempts to seek and develop a conducive corporate culture that suits the customers and the needs of the business.

The two most important issues that are relevant for the organization of a HR department involve the following, namely:

- Place of the HR department in the overall organizational set up, preferably as the strategic partner in the organizational decision making; which eventually signifies the HR head being a member of the Board of Directors in the organization.
- Composition, design of the HR department itself and matching the same with the profile of employees and needs of the customers and other people in the value chain of the organization (like suppliers, distributors, retailers etc.).

Structural Considerations of a HR Department

The structures of the HR department of an organization could be as follows:

HRM in a small-scale unit: This structure is applicable to most SMEs, where the business is headed by an entrepreneur. The HR functions are either directly under the purview of the managing director/chairman of the company or it is managed by an administrative officer, who might be having a personnel assistant to help him out with the HR related activities and decisions.

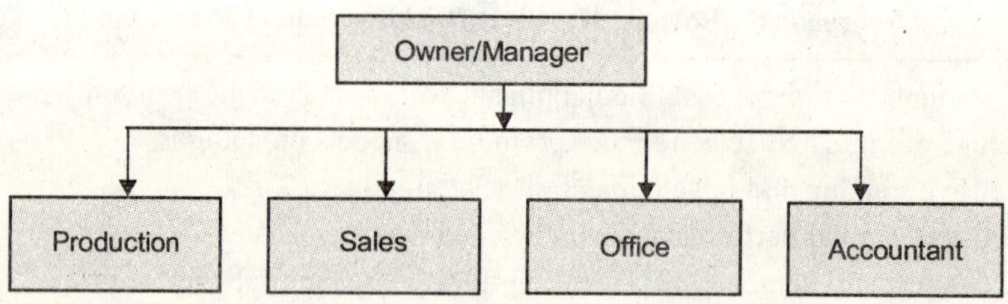

Fig. 1.15

HRM in a large scale unit: As an enterprise grows, every organization ensures that the HR functions and decisions are being taken by a person specialized in HR. The following figure illustrates one such organization, where the director HR heads the HR department in the organization and he reports directly to the chairman or the managing director of the company.

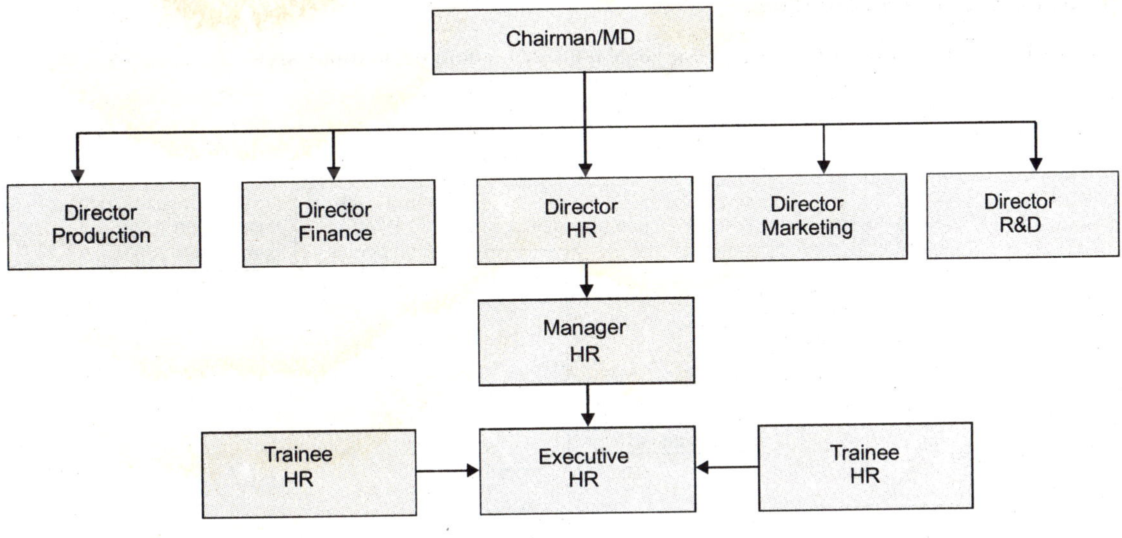

Fig. 1.16

Under the Director HR, the organization has a HR manager, who is again assisted by an HR executive. The HR executive on the other hand has one or two HR trainees working under him.

ONGC's HR/ER Department

The following figure depicts the organogram of ONGC's HR department:

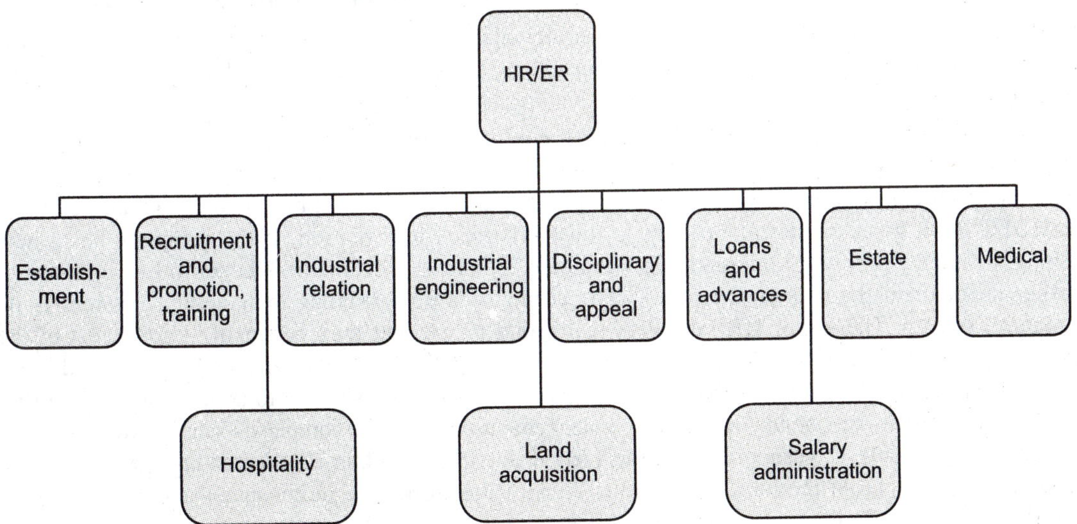

Fig. 1.17: ONGC's HR/ER department

(*Courtesy: Bodruzzaman Choudhury, "Organizational study report of ONGC"*)

HR Structure in a Retail Outlet

In case of a retail outlet the structure of the HR department could be as follows:

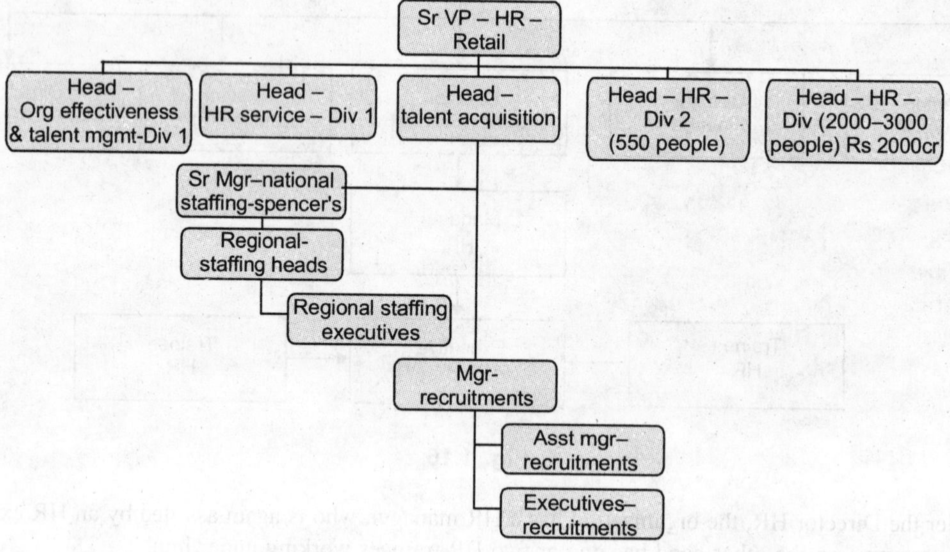

Fig. 1.18: Structure of the HR department in a retail store

Exhibit: HRM In HDFC Bank: "Achieving Success through People Centricity"

The HR department at HDFC Bank has 54 people, including the trainers. The HR department is present in Mumbai, Chennai, Delhi, Ahmedabad, Kolkata, Bangalore, Hyderabad, Chandigarh, Pune and Lucknow. All people here in HR are MBAs, except for those handling HR operations.

The most important thing in HR is to hold the confidence of people. Talent retention is a challenge today. Another challenge is managing expectations of youngsters, who are looking for fast tracking their career and want exposure quickly, they may not be lured by money alone, but the profile that they work for. HDFC Bank gives ample opportunity to those who seek job rotation. If the company has a new opening, it is being advertised internally. The company's philosophy is that it is better to lose a person to another department than to another bank. The company's performance management system is its 'signature' system. The senior HR managers feel proud to say that they personally know most of the people across various levels in the organization. They constantly help people move internally and assist them make a better career with the bank. In fact the HR department is proud to admit that the company has one of the lowest rates of attrition. Middle management onwards the company's salaries are good. The company is young only 12 years old where the average age in the bank is 27. Women have been rising up the ranks in the bank. At the junior level, over 33% of the workforce in consumer and retail banking comprises of women. In the senior levels, it is about 12% and in the top management, it is about 6 to 9%. Over the years HDFC was very cost conscious. Today the company has foreign tours, parties at national and regional levels, award nights and outings to motivate and encourage its employees. As an organization HDFC bank had constantly emphasized on celebrating its hard earned success.

(*Courtesy: Interview with Mandeep Maitra: "People Centric", Banking Frontiers, December 2006 issue, p. 4; www.bankingfrontierscom/coverstory0612_01.pdf*)

Human Resource Systems

Human Resource Systems are the essential programmes associated so as to effectively recruit, appraise, pay and look after the health, safety and well-being of the employees in an organization. The key elements of Human Resource Systems of an organization are as follows:

- ***Recruitment Management*:** It involves the process of obtaining (hiring/procuring) the required human resources for an organization.
- ***Information Management*:** It is the method of ensuring that all policies and practices are to be well articulated and effectively communicated to the workforce.
- ***Training Management*:** It is a system of identification of training needs, preparation of a training strategy and an appropriate training system.
- ***Performance Appraisal Systems*:** It is the objective and systematic technique of appraising performance of the organization against pre-defined criteria, reviewing performance progress to date and assessing the potential for further performance improvements. There are 3 main appraisal systems such as Performance Appraisal, Potential Appraisal and Performance Counselling.
- ***Reward Management*:** It is a method to ensure that people are rewarded in accordance with their contribution.
- ***Career Management*:** It is a system of charting special career paths for individual employees for advancement in the organization.
- ***Health and Safety Management*:** It is a system of maintaining a healthy and safe system of work in an organization.
- ***Discipline Management*:** It is a system of administering discipline so as to foster positive employee behaviour that will promote organizational objectives.
- ***Culture Management*:** It is a system of thinking and behaving shaped by the values, attitudes, rituals and sanctions in an organization.

Human Resource Relationships

Human Resource Relationships deal with the handling of employees individually and collectively as members of trade unions or staff associations. The main aim is to increase cooperation and trust and to involve employees actively in the organization's affairs. It also deals with problem-solving techniques, particularly to solve problems relating to disciplinary cases and grievances.

Human Resource Utilization: HR utilization mainly involves the following aspects namely:

- To conduct productivity drive in employees
- To improve manpower budgeting and control
- To introduce work measurement
- To use appropriate payment method by results, bonus and profit-sharing schemes
- To improve motivation
- To involve employees in improvement programmes
- To introduce new technology
- To negotiate appropriate productivity agreements
- To introduce training programmes based on an analysis of productivity needs.

Components of a HR Policy

Employment Policies: These are the policies that guide hiring practices, orientation of new employees, compliance with employment laws and confidentiality.

Employment status and records: These are the policies that define such issues as employment classifications access to personnel files and guidance on how background checks and performance reviews are to be performed.

Employee benefits: These are policies that explain employee benefits such as insurance, vacations, holidays, leave and employee reimbursements.

Payroll: These are policies that are related to salary and wage administration including deductions, pay advances and time keeping.

Workplace guidelines: These policies are quite varied and their purpose range from defining certain work arrangements such as flex time and telecommuting to offering guidelines on the use of company assets and record retention.

Employee conduct: These policies are guidelines that control employer behaviour and conduct on the job. The mainstay of this section is a code of conduct but also important are policies regarding substance abuse, smoking, harassment and workplace violence.

E-policies: These policies guide staff in the use of the organization's information technology. Policies defining acceptable and prohibited activities and use of e-mail and the Internet make up a majority of these policies.

Theme Reading: Highlights of the HR Policies in Syndicate Bank

The HR policies of Syndicate Bank are geared to meet the corporate objectives of accelerated and profitable growth. Taking into consideration the existing manpower, its age profile, likely attrition, the emerging scenario, need for additional manpower to support the growth and diversification of business, need for skilled staff to work in the networked banking environment and also the priorities attached to agricultural sector under the National policy, the bank has undertaken direct recruitment of General Banking Officers, Specialist Officers in the area of Agricultural Finance, Information Technology, Accounts and Financial Management, Security, Law etc. The bank has a well-planned succession arrangement by way of promotion, internal selection and direct recruitment to fill up the posts in key areas. The promotion policy has also been fine tuned to reward outstanding performers.

(*Courtesy: Syndicate Bank Annual Report, 2007–2008, p. 31*).

Assessing Effectiveness of the HR Function: HR Scorecard

In order to facilitate the assessment and communication of the effectiveness of an organization's HR and HRD efforts, HR scorecard is used by many HR professionals. A HR scorecard helps an organization on the following aspects, namely:

- It focuses on *leading* indicators defining the performance and the effectiveness of the HR function in the organization.
- It helps to identify the differences between HR *doables* and HR *deliverables.*
- It helps to demonstrate the HR's contributions to organizational strategy implementation and to the company's bottom lines.
- It helps HR managers to focus on and manage their strategic responsibilities.

- It encourages HR flexibility and change.
- It encourages "Customers" of an organization's HR function to become more self-sufficient.
- It provides focus for the HR and OD staff of an organization.

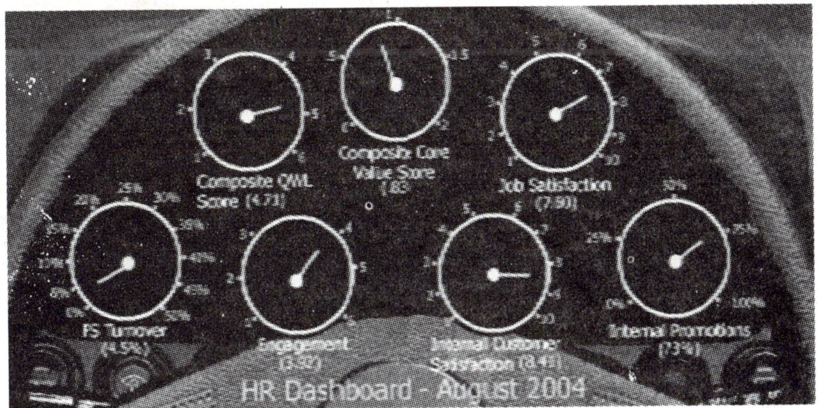

Fig. 1.19: The HR dashboard

(Courtesy:http://www.russellconsultinginc.com, 2005)

The HR Dashboard of an organization is a panel of dials that display HR effectiveness on the HR Deliverables like: Job Satisfaction (QWL, Values, 10 Values, 10–point), Organizational turnover, Engagement, Internal Customer Satisfaction and Internal Promotions etc.

Components of the HR scorecard: The HR Scorecard involves identifying both performance *drivers* and *enablers* to support to the company's strategic priorities. It helps in the process of balancing value creation of the HR activities and functions in an organization with emphasis on cost controls and efficiencies.

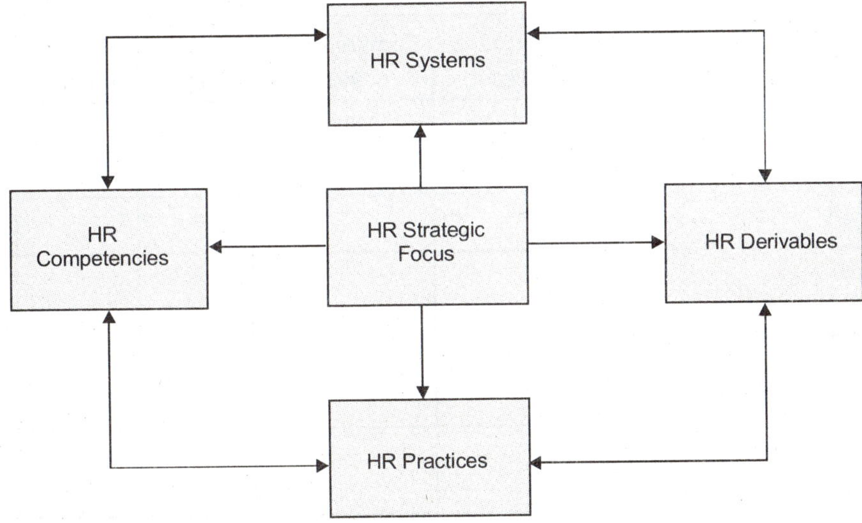

Fig. 1.20: Components of the HR scorecard

(Courtesy:http://www.russellconsultinginc.com, 2005)

HR Competencies: This component of HR scorecard includes those of:

- Role of HR as the change agent
- HR strategy execution
- Employee relations/advocacy
- Best practices in HR
- Operational efficiency

HR Systems: This component of the HR scorecard is characterized by:

- Differentiating HR services to match the different needs of different departments units
- Matching HR strategy to the organizational culture
- HR alignment with the organizational strategy
- Internal HR alignment

HR Practices: This includes various HR activities like those of:

- Succession planning
- Training and development
- Communication
- Internal customer satisfaction
- Effective work design
- Labour-management relations
- Performance measurement
- Compensation and benefits
- Employee orientation
- Recruitment and selection
- Staff competency models

HR Practices	Recruitment & selection	T&D	Performance Mgt	Compensation Mgt	Benefits & admn	HR Cost control	HR Value creation
Recruitment & selection							
T&D							
Performance Mgt							
Compensation Mgt							
Benefits & admn							

Fig. 1.21: Assessing the organization's internal fit

	High level of employee job satisfaction	High level of internal customer satisfaction	Low turnover in financial services specialist position	Highly competent financial services specialist staff	Staff engagement (with job and orgn. strategy)
Recruitment & selection					
T&D					
Performance Mgt					
Compensation Mgt					
Benefits & admn					

Fig. 1.22: Assessing HR systems support of the organization's HR deliverables

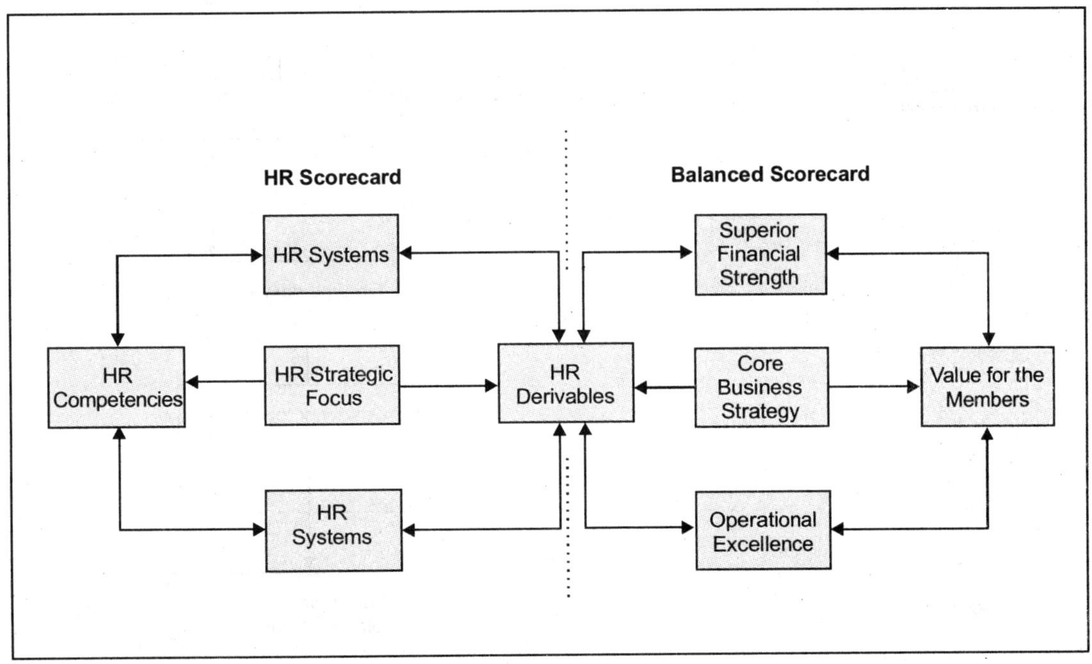

Fig. 1.23: Linking the HR scorecard with the balanced scorecard

(*Courtesy:http://www.russellconsultinginc.com, 2005*)

Linking the HR function with the organizational strategy: A strategy map (or a value chain) shows how the firm creates value in terms managers and employees can relate to. In other words, the strategy map details which organizational processes and capabilities drive firm performance. From an HR perspective, the strategy map is developed by seeking the answers to questions such as:

- "What strategic goals are critical to achieve rather than simply nice to have if possible?"
- "What are the performance drivers for each goal?"
- "How can progress towards each goal be measured?"
- "What are the barriers that can block the achievement of each goal?"
- "How do employees need to behave in order to ensure the firm achieves each of these goals?"
- "Is the HR architecture providing the firm with the employee competencies and behaviours needed to achieve those goals?"
- "If not, what needs to change within the HR architecture?"

Ideally, the strategy map will detail how HR and line management work together seamlessly as a partnership to create value within the firm. Specifically, the strategy map should outline how the six core HR competencies are integrated and measured. A strategy map details each link in that chain. For example, a simple strategy map would be:

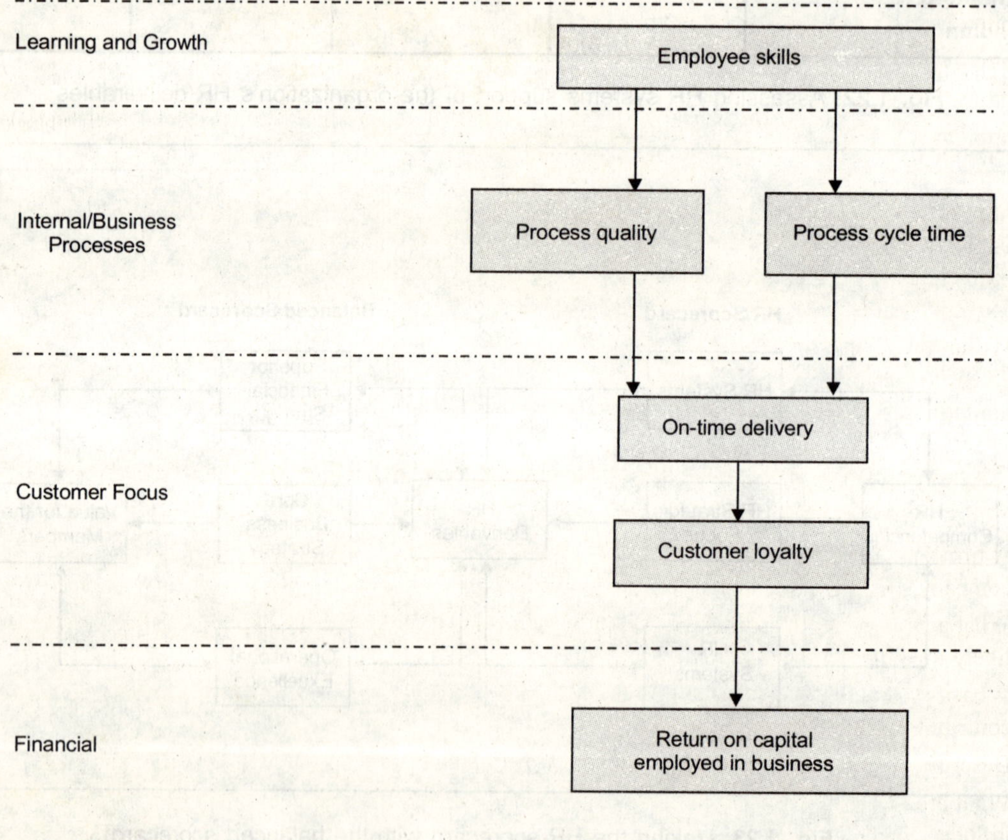

Fig. 1.24: A strategic map for effective utilization of human resources

REFERENCES

1. Ivancevich, J.M. (2008): "Human Resource Management", 10th Edition, McGraw-Hill, pp. 4–5.
2. Sharma, A.M. (2005): "Personnel and Human Resource Management", 5th Revised Edition, Himalaya Publishing House, p.16.
3. Page & Stephen, B. (2002): "Establishing a System of Policies and Procedures, Process Improvement Publishing", Westerville, Ohio: Process Improvement Publishing, p. 2.
4. McQuate, Craig, (2002): "Penning Effective Policies", Security Management, Dec. 2002.
5. Ramey, Ardella and Carl R.J. Sniffen (1999): "A Company Policy and Personnel Workbook", Central Point, OR: Oasis Press/PSI Research.
6. Armstrong (1992): "Handbook of Human Resource Management," Kogan page, London.
7. Senge, P. (1997): "The Fifth Discipline", Century Business.
8. http://www.icmrindia.org/casestudies/catalogue/Human% 20 Resource% 20 and % 20 Organization % 20 Behaviour/HROB090.htm
9. http://www.thehindubusinessline.com/2006/12/15/stories/2006121503380400.htm
10. http://www.financialexpress.com/old/fe_full_story.php?content_id=49326
11. http://www.ibef.org/artdisplay.aspx?cat_id=925&art_id=19040&arc=show
12. http://www.itpeopleindia.com/20020826/careers2.shtml
13. http://www.rediff.com/money/2006/jun/22infy.htm
14. http://www.rajshriproductions.com/aboutus.php
15. http://images.google.co.in/imgres?imgurl=http://www.transitionsabroad.com/publications/magazine/0409/india_workplace.jpg&imgrefurl=http://www.transitionsabroad.com/publications/magazine/0409/paid_software_internships_in_india.shtml&h=375&w=500&sz=43&hl=en&start=7&tbnid=TxBZs4WyHtCMwM:&tbnh=98&tbnw=130&prev=images%3Fq%3DInfosys%26gbv%3D2%26hl%3Den
16. William B. Werther, Jefferey M. Wachtel, David J. Veale (1995): "Global Deployment of Executive Talent", Human Resource Planning, Vol. 18, 1995.
17. http://www.hindu.com/2008/06/27/stories/2008062760640800.htm

QUESTION BANK

1. A firm's strategic HR choices cover the entire range of HR functions. Explain the strategic choices a company has regarding workflows, staffing, performance appraisal, training and development.
2. What according to you are the new challenges in the field of Human Resource Management that are likely to come up in future? How can these challenges be handled?
3. What is the purpose of human resource management? Identify and explain how its objectives contribute to that purpose.
4. Describe the relevance of HRM in the context of globalization and diversification of workforce.
5. What are the environmental factors influence the HRM function? Discuss with examples, how they influence the HR policies of an organization.
6. The context of the business environment has changes. How has this affected the HRM functions and what are the new roles, which the HR department is supposed to play?
7. What are the challenges for HR practitioners in the new millennium? What are your suggestions to successfully overcome these challenges?

8. Akbar has been an engineer for three years in Indian Engineering Company. It is a small firm employing only 50 workers and little over 5 officers. The firm manufactures ancillary products for TV sets. Because of the government reduction in excise duty the demand for TV has gone up. Indian Engineering Company has been able to get a large contract to manufacture ancillary components within a short time. Akbar has been given the target and the time. He is now wondering what he should do to his work force, so that they cooperate and help him fulfill the target in the given time. Help him to find a solution.
9. What are the factors influencing personnel environment in India and what are their implications?
10. Discuss the role of HRD in an organization in the changing environment.
11. Explain the environment of HRM. (BU July/August 2005, 2003).
12. Identify the major challenges of HRM and discuss how HR managers should face them? (BU July/August 2005).
13. "With overgrowing outsourcing of HR activities there is no place for HR department in the overall organization structure." Give reasons for your answer. (BU July/August 2005).
14. Can well-meaning HR programmes have negative effects on a firm? If so how? (BU 2004)
15. Sketch any model of HRM with which you are familiar. (BU 2002).
16. Identify five significant challenges confronted by an HR manager today. Elaborate each. (BU 2004).
17. What are the major functions of the HRM? Discuss in detail sub-functions of one major group. (BU 2003).

(Experiential exercises) Fun Games and Icebreakers

- Before starting the sessions, engage all the students into an icebreaker. Divide the entire group of students into small groups each consisting of at least six students. Give them 10 minutes time. Let them talk to each other and discuss the skills and strengths of each other. Now invite each participant and tell him/her to give a presentation on the skills and capabilities of the other person and so on.
- Involve two students into the shoot and win game. Let them stand infront of the entire class facing their backs to each other. Tell them to walk three steps away with the count of three and with the command "shoot" ask them to turn around and shout "bang" at each other. The participant shouting bang first wins. The game could be repeated by changing one participant taking the role of a beast (who is supposed to roar "HAAAAAA" and the other a hunter). The participant either roaring or shooting wins.
- **Prince Caspian:** Take the students to an open area. Arrange a chair in the middle of the ground or the open area and allow one student to adopt the role of Prince Caspian. Let your faculty take the role of prince Caspian's prime minister. Tell him to prepare a list of things (which may include anything like, pens, pencils, rubbers, I cards, shoe laces, ribbons, combs, exercise book etc. that fall under essential things used in the campus). Now divide the entire population of students into small groups of five students each. When your faculty would command "Prince Caspian wants you to find from the campus 4 shoe laces, seven I cards, ten pencils", the team members need to immediately leave and search the same and report back to the prince within 2 minutes. The team reporting first and with the correct items wins.

- **Char Minar game:** Divide the entire class into groups of students comprising of 5 students in each. Tell your faculty to assume the role of the game coordinator. Keep ready at least 30 old newspapers, five scissors, five cello tape rolls. Now the task ahead to each team would be to construct the "char minar" within 5 minutes time. The structure of the minar should be stable, erect and at least 4 feet tall. The team which is being able to make the same in the stipulated time and using the minimum numbers of newspapers would win. Tell your faculty to take record of the number of papers taken for constructing the minar and other observations during the game. Discuss the various skills important for the game and its outcomes after the game.

Internet Exercises

- Go to the internet and prepare a list of websites useful for HR professionals.
- Surf the websites of two public sector and private sector organizations and write a note on their respective vision and mission statements. Analyze with your friends the significance and importance of such mission and visions in the organizational strategy.
- Surf the following hyperlink http://careers.citigroup.com/careers/homepage/emea/gcib/humanres.htm and comment on the HR practices of the organization.
- Go to the following hyperlink related to Sony: http://www.sony.net/SonyInfo/Environment/ Analyze the CSR report 2007 and enumerate the contribution made by the organization towards CSR.

Games

- Form a group of three students with your faculty as the judge. Imagine that each of you are representing your company in a HR summit. Give a brief presentation of the highlights of your company's HR practices. Make sure that each of you speak for at least 3 to 4 minutes.
- 3 students are needed to participate in this game. Imagine that each you are the HR managers of Kingfisher Airlines, Go Air and Indian Airlines. Prepare a duty schedule for the flight attenders and air hostesses. The participant contributing the most attractive schedule wins the maximum points. Time limit 5 minutes.

STRATEGIC HUMAN RESOURCE MANAGEMENT

Theme Case: The Strategic Function of HRM Understood and Implemented in a Medium Sized Company

XYZ Ltd. is a medium sized engineering company with approximately 700 employees and an operating budget of approximately Rs. 90 million. Its head office and plant is located in an industrial estate in Bangalore, with other plants and offices being located in Pune, Baroda and Ghaziabad. In the company, the HR Manager reports to the Director Corporate and Administrative Services and the CEO of the organization. The company had decided to intervene significant changes in its overall corporate philosophy, legislation, technology and structure through its shift to the **funder**, purchaser, provider model and an output based management approach.

It was the HR Manager's intention to use a strategic analysis so as to have the basis for developing a comprehensive. The exercise was timely given the shift towards the funder, purchaser, provider model. As a result of this initiative, two of the executive positions have recently been filled, including the strategic planning director. The company further decided to hire a Delhi based reputed HR & OD consultant, who would work with the HR team to implement the necessary changes in the organization in its transformation interventions.

The Approach

Planning meeting: An initial meeting was held between the HR manager and the consultant firm. The meeting aimed to identify how the project would be approached and who should be taken or included into the intervention team. The organization has a medium sized HR structure with highly experienced staff, and it was deemed essential to gain their support and commitment from the beginning. They were subsequently briefed on the project, its rationale and the process that would occur.

Assessment: The consultant team conducted an individual interview with the Chief Executive Officer (CEO) of the company so as to ascertain the strategic and business issues facing the organization, the critical HR issues facing the organization and his assessment of the HR function. All of this was done using the **Strategic HR Framework**. The HR Manager was interviewed by the consulting team so as to obtain an assessment of the HR function. Key documents were reviewed and assessed including the company's Annual Report, recent HR audit reports, enterprise agreements, due diligence reports, details of the Structural Realignment of Service Delivery activities and Statutory Compliance reports.

Findings: Some of the major findings were as follows:

- There are no strategic or operational plans in place in the organization
- Performance and productivity indicators need to be more aligned throughout the company
- The organization needed a more diverse, outward looking approach to its recruitment
- There was an immediate need for competency assessment and modelling so as to ensure the necessary skills to meet the future needs of the business
- Performance management processes needed to instigate a balance scorecard approach for ensuring organizational effectiveness.
- There was a need to train and inform people more effectively on the statutory compliance requirements as the audit reports revealed that most of the times the HR people were either delayed or failed to meet the compliance requirements specified by the state authorities.

Action planning: A three hour workshop was held with a mix of directors, middle managers, HR staff and the consultant team. The aims of the workshop were to:

- agree on the critical business related issues facing the organization
- agree upon the critical HR priorities
- agree upon implementing a balance scorecard framework for evaluating organizational performance
- agree upon a comprehensive employee development program on compliance management for all the HR people and business managers to work together.

The CEO and the HR team did not waste any time and immediately organized several meetings with their staffs and employees at various levels of the organization followed by involving all into workshops and management development programmes on various functional disciplines to implement the above action plans.

Learning's from the case

The above intervention jointly coordinated by the OD consultant and the HR people in the organization ensured that it provided an edge to the prevalent HR practices and aligning the same for strategic perspectives of the organization. One of the important learnings that emerged out of this case was that the management realized the importance of linking their HR practices with the overall organizational strategy and information requirements. The organization also learned the importance of a comprehensive balance scorecard framework for its performance management and how to utilize the same for strategic purposes. The need for constantly upgrading the capabilities of people through competency assessment and management development programmes was a key learning in terms of performance improvement interventions.

What is Strategic Management?

Strategy: A strategy is a way of doing something. It usually includes the formulation of a goal and set of action plans for the accomplishment of that goal.

Strategic management is the process of formulating, implementing and evaluating business strategies to achieve organizational objectives.

Strategic management involves those sets of managerial decisions and actions which determine the long-term performance of a business organization. It includes environmental scanning, strategy formulation, strategy implementation, evaluation and control.

Steps Involved in Strategic Management

- To analyze the opportunities and threats or constraints that exist in the external environment of business.
- To formulate strategies that will match the organization's strengths and weaknesses with the environmental threats and opportunities.
- To implement the business strategies effectively.
- To evaluate and control activities so as to ensure that the organization's objectives are being achieved.

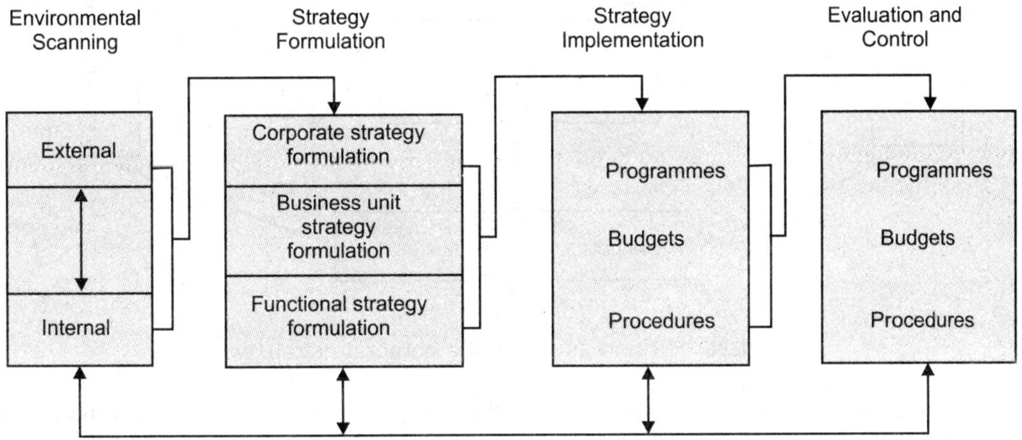

Fig. 1.25: Process of strategic management

What is Strategic Human Resource Management?

The beginning theme case has clearly revealed the importance of aligning the human resource function with the strategic objectives of the organization. Strategic HRM is a concept that integrates traditional human resource management principles and activities with the organization's overall strategic planning and their implementation. SHRM integrates human resource considerations with other physical, financial, and technological resources in the setting of organizational goals and solving complex organizational problems (Legnick-Hall & Legnick-Hall, 1988).[2] SHRM also emphasizes the implementation of a set of policies and practices that aims to develop pool of employee competencies and capabilities (Jackon and Schuler, 1995)[3] that are relevant to organizational goals and objectives.

Strategic HRM is an approach involving effective decision making with respect to successfully implement the strategic objectives of an organization concerning their employment relationship and HR processes and systems involving recruitment, training, development, performance management, reward and employee relations management. The key characteristic of strategic HRM is that it aligns and integrates the HRM strategies with those of the business strategy. The HRM strategies developed by a strategic HRM approach are thereby one of the most essential components of an organization's business strategy.

Boxall (2003)[4] has strongly supported that strategic HRM is concerned with explaining how HRM influences organizational performance. Strategic HRM is based on HRM principles incorporating the concept of strategy. So if HRM is a coherent approach to the management of people, strategic HRM implies that is done on a planned way that integrates organizational goals with policies and action sequences taken in the organization. This can be best understood by the following figure:

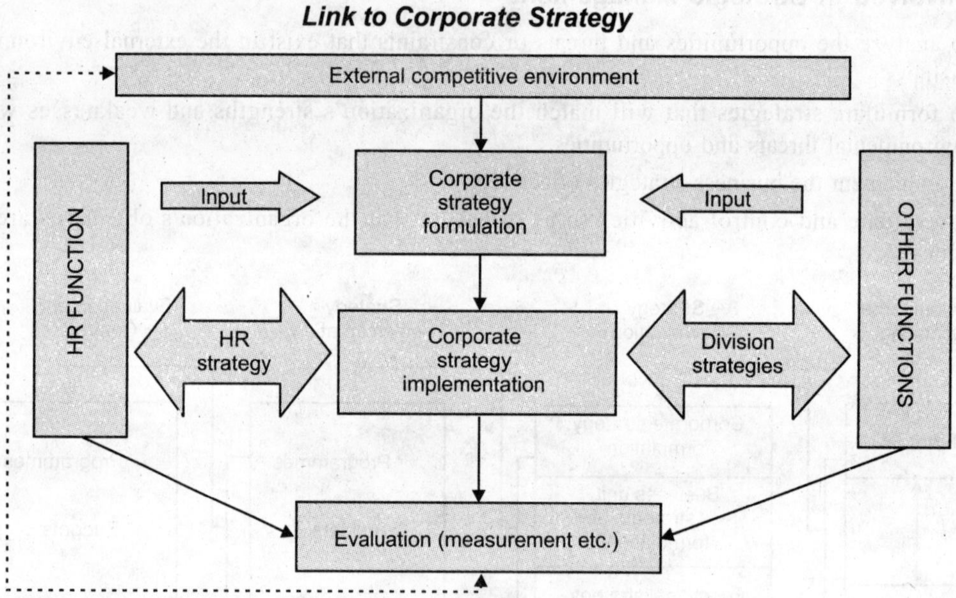

Link to Corporate Strategy

Fig. 1.26: HR and its link to the corporate strategy

HR's strategic architecture: The development of the strategic HR architecture requires special sets of skills from the HR executives and HR professionals in the organization. The HR professionals in this regard should make an effort so as to enhance their level of competency in terms of their knowledge regarding the strategic perspectives. To ensure this they need to develop the following set of competencies, namely:

- Knowledge of the business
- Strategic business acumen
- Mastery in HR practices, particularly in organizational development
- Capabilities as a change agent and an internal consultant
- Individual credibility and instrumentality
- Capability for managing strategic performance management

Exhibit: HR strategies of Corporation Bank

In an interview with Mr. B Sambamurthy, Chairman Corporation Bank, it was revealed that the bank had recruited around 1300 employees in the past 1.5 years. In spite of this the bank faced challenges of attrition.

To cope this, the bank had made plans for emphasizing recruiting more staffs at the clerical as well as in the specialist positions. After the back-office processes and the accounting work have been fully automated, the need had been for largely soft skills at the front end. Therefore the management of the bank had decided to emphasize on only recruiting HSC qualified personnel for clerical positions. For other executive positions the bank would emphasize on recruiting specialist officers. The organization also had plans for outsourcing some kind of contractual relationship apart from acquiring the skill mix.

(Courtesy: Mayur Shetty, The Economic Times, ET Finance, 14th January, 2008)

Meaning of Strategic HRM

Strategic HRM has the following four meanings:

- SHRM involves the use of planning in order to establish a strategic link between the HR systems and the goals and objectives of the organization.
- SHRM involves a coherent approach to ensure the design and management of the HR systems based on an employment policy and manpower strategy
- It involves the matching of HRM activities and policies to the business strategy
- SHRM aims to consider people of the organization as the 'strategic resource' for the achievement of 'competitive advantage' for the organization.

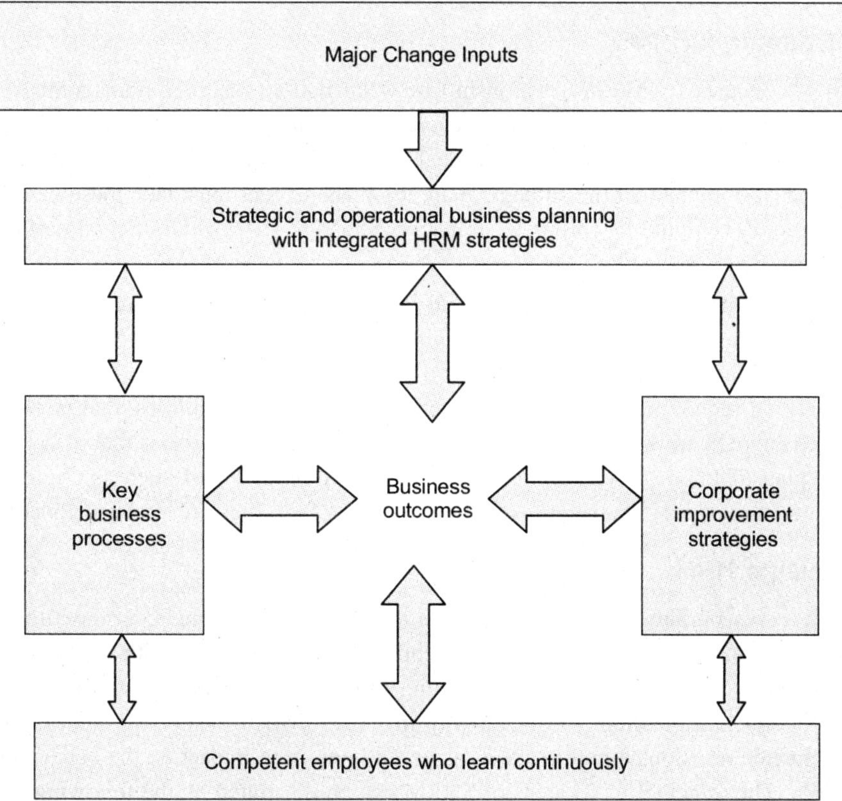

Fig. 1.27: Role of SHRM in achieving business objectives

Hence it is evident that SHRM is a process that involves:

- Integrating HR into the Strategic Planning Process of the organization.
- Aligning HR practices to business strategy and to one another.
- Developing a partnership between the strategic thinkers of the organization alongwith the line management so that the organizational HR programmes could meet real life business needs and challenges.
- Internally transforming of HR structure and staff according to the needs of the business.
- Enhancing the overall HR and administrative efficiency.
- Assessing the bottom-line impact of the HR activities in organizational performance improvement.

Hence an organization's HR policies and practices must fit with its business strategy so as to constantly meet the challenges of its competitive business environment. The concept of such integration has three aspects:

- The linking of the HR policies and practices with the strategic management process of the organization
- The internalization of the importance of HR on the part of line managers
- The integration of the workforce into the organization so as to foster whole hearted commitment or an 'identity of interest' for the strategic goals.

Concerns of Strategic HRM

Strategic HRM is concerned with the relationship between human resource management and strategic management in an organization. It caters to provide overall direction to the organization in order to achieve its goals through people. As people or the intellectual capital is a major source of competitive advantage, and it is the people who implement the strategic plan, top management must take these key considerations fully into account for developing its corporate strategies. Strategic HRM is an integral part of such people strategies.

Strategic HRM addresses broad organizational issues relating to organizational effectiveness and performance, changes in structure and culture, matching resources to future requirements, the development of distinctive capabilities, knowledge management and the management of change. It is concerned with both meeting human capital requirements and the development of process capabilities, that is, the ability to get things done effectively. On an overall, SHRM considers any major people issues that affect or are affected by the strategic plan of the organization. 'The critical concerns of HRM such as choice of executive leadership and formation of positive patterns of labour relations form the core strategic concern in any firm.

Focus of Strategic HRM

Strategic HRM focuses on actions that differentiate an organization from its competitors. It develops declarations of intent which define means to achieve ends, and it is concerned with the long-term allocation of significant company resources, and with matching those resources and capabilities to the external environment. Strategy is a perspective on the way in which critical issues or success factors can be addressed, and strategic decisions aim to make a major and long-term impact on the behaviour and success of the organization. The principal focus areas of SHRM can be illustrated by the following table:

Table 1.4: Focus areas of SHRM

Focus Areas of SHRM	***Hallmarks***
Universal approach	SHRM involves the transformation of traditional HR practices into a limited set of "correct" HR procedures and practices
Strategic fit	SHRM involves matching specific HR practices to the organization's overall strategy
HR service	SHRM emphasizes upon involving HR professionals taking up providing the right HR services to the employees (internal customers) of the organization which is in fact a part of the strategic objective of the organization
Configurational perspective	SHRM emphasizes on bundling or configurating HR practices so as to enhance the capability of the human resources of the organization and utilize the same for achieving the organizational goals and objectives
Resource based perspective	SHRM engenders organizational success by enhancing an organization's ability to acquire, develop, utilize, and retain employees with high competence levels relevant to firm activities.

THEME READING: ROLE OF HR IN THE RETAILING SECTOR

"With the dawn of the concept of an employee being seen as an asset, the gamut of focus, for HR, has enlarged from mere salary administration to more concrete activities like employee empowerment and change management. The paradigm shift of HR being perceived as a much as a line function, has brought a huge change in how HR professionals are remunerated," says Ms. Dipali Goenka, Director Welspun Retail. HR plays a critical role in the retail industry, particularly in areas of sourcing and deployment, experts say. Goenka emphasizes that the industry therefore is trying to adequately compensate HR, in comparison to other sunrise industries. She claims that HR salaries in the retail industry have gone up, considerably, in the last five years. "The skills required to perform a HR manager's role has changed and hence, what was applicable a few years ago, today, stands redundant. And these competencies today aren't easily available in the industry and hence, there is a huge supply demand pushback and this condition poses a great challenge for the recruiters seeking quality HR talent," says Goenka.

(Courtesy: "The Need of the Hour", Times Ascent, Wednesday, 20th August, 2008.)

Aim of Strategic HRM

The fundamental aim of strategic HRM is to generate strategic capability by ensuring that the organization has the skilled, committed and well motivated employees so as to achieve sustained competitive advantage. Its objective is to provide a sense of direction in the often turbulent business environment, so that the needs and goals of the organization, and the individual and collective needs of its employees, can be met by the development and implementation of coherent and practical HR policies and programmes. Strategic HRM should provide unifying frameworks which are at once broad, contingency based and integrative.

Strategic HRM and Human Capital Management

A number of authors have argued that strategic HRM and human capital management (HCM) are one and the same thing. The main features of strategic HRM, according to Dyer and Holder (1988),[5] depicts its similarity with the human capital management initiatives taken in organizations:

- **Applicability at the Organizational Level:** As organizational strategies involve decisions about key goals, major policies and the allocation of resources they tend to be formulated at the top. These people strategies should enable the organization to integrate operations at the bottom-line of the pyramid.
- **Focus:** HR strategies are typically business-driven and focus to achieve organizational effectiveness; thus in this perspective people are viewed primarily as resources to be managed towards the achievement of strategic business goals.
- **Framework:** HR strategies by their very nature provide unifying frameworks which are at once broad, contingency-based and integrative. They incorporate a full complement of HR goals and activities designed specifically to fit extant environments and to be mutually reinforcing or synergistic.

This argument has been based on the fact that both HRM in its proper sense and HCM rest on the assumption that people are treated as assets rather than costs and both focus on the importance of adopting an integrated and strategic approach to managing people which is the concern of all the stakeholders in an organization not just the people management function. However, the concept of human capital management complements and strengthens the concept of strategic HRM rather than replaces it[1]. It does this by:

- drawing attention to the significance of 'management through measurement', the aim being to establish a clear line of sight between HR interventions and organizational success
- providing guidance on what to measure, how to measure and how to report on the outcomes of measurement
- underlining the importance of using the measurements to prove that superior people management is delivering superior results and to indicate the direction in which HR strategy needs to go
- reinforcing attention on the need to base HRM strategies and processes on the requirement to create value through people and thus further the achievement of organizational goals
- defining the link between HRM and business strategy
- strengthening the HRM belief that people are assets rather than costs
- Emphasizing role of HR specialists as business partners.

Hence both HCM and HRM can be regarded as vital components in the process of people management and both form the basis for achieving human capital advantage through a resource-based strategy. Strategic HRM could therefore be viewed as the defining framework within which these evaluation, reporting and management process take place and ensure that they are iterative and mutually reinforcing.

Importance of HRM in Strategic Thinking

HR activities and practices typically focus on a small number of outcomes or criteria or outcome measures. These criteria include the following:

Major criteria of interest for evaluation in HRM for strategic perspectives:

- Performance (Individual, team, unit)
- Quantity, quality, timeliness, cost-effectiveness, effect on others
- Productivity
- Customer (Internal/External) satisfaction
- Absenteeism
- Turnover/Retention/Tenure/Intentions to stay/Leaves
- Employee theft
- Violence at the workplace
- Job Stress (Role Conflict, ambiguity)
- Job satisfaction/Motivation/Attitudes/Commitment
- Creativity and Innovation
- Perceived fairness (Procedural, Interactional)
- Error rates
- Accidents, health-related variables (work stress, injuries)
- Organizational citizenship behaviour

Model of SHRM

One of the most commonly used models in SHRM is the 'matching' model. This model was evident in Devanna et al.'s (1984)[6] research: 'HR systems and organizational structure should be managed in a way that is congruent with organizational strategy'. In this model, HR–strategy–structure follows and feed upon one another and is influenced by environmental forces (as shown in the following figure). Similarly, the notion of 'fit' between an external competitive strategy and the internal HR strategy is a central tenet of thc HRM model advanced later on by Beer et al. (1984)[7]. The authors have emphasized the analysis of the linkages between the two strategies and how each strategy provides goals and constraints for the other. This means that there must be a 'fit between competitive strategy and internal HRM strategy and a fit among the elements of the HRM strategy contributes to organizational effectiveness. The relationship between business strategy and HR strategy is said to be 'reactive' in the sense that HR strategy is subservient to 'product market logic' and the corporate strategy.

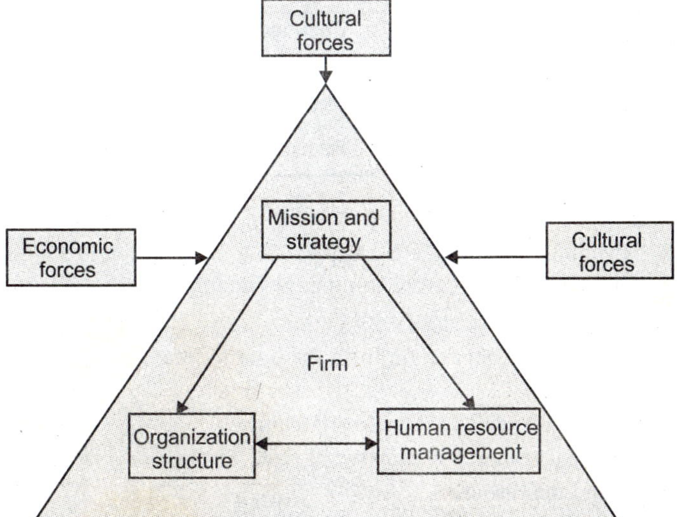

Fig. 1.28: Devanna et al.'s strategic human resource management 'matching' model

Benefits of SHRM

SHRM has the following advantages, namely:

- Identifying and analyzing external opportunities and threats that may be crucial to the company's success.
- Provides a clear business strategy and vision for the future.
- To supply competitive intelligence that may be useful in the strategic planning process.
- To recruit, retain and motivate people.
- To develop and retain of highly competent people.
- To ensure that people development issues are addressed systematically.
- To supply information regarding the company's internal strengths and weaknesses.
- To meet the expectations of the customers effectively.
- To ensure high productivity.
- To ensure business surplus thorough competency

The above benefits could be further understood by studying the differences between the conventional and strategic HR capabilities.

Traditional HRM capabilities	Strategic HRM capabilities
Specialist approach	Generalist approach
Focus on HR policy and procedures	Emphasis on being effective communicators
Focus on the present perspective (reactive approach)	Focus on both the present as well as the future perspective (proactive approach)
Monolingual approach (emphasis on only HR related discussions)	Emphasis on the language of the business
Management hierarchy focused	Customer focused
Few financial or marketing skills	Championing business acumen (emphasis on holistic/multi skills)
Stays "within the box"	Thinks "outside the box"
Focused on the internal organization	Focused on the internal organization as well as on the broader aspect of the business
Factual communicator	Persuader
Nationalist in approach	Internationalist in approach

Barriers of SHRM

Barriers to successful SHRM implementation are complex. The main reason is a lack of growth strategy or failure to implement one. Other major barriers are summarized as follows:

- Inducing the vision and mission of the change effort.
- High resistance due to lack of cooperation from the bottom line.
- Interdepartmental conflict.
- The commitment of the entire senior management team.
- Plans that integrate internal resource with external requirements.
- Limited time, money and the resources.
- The status-quo approach of employees.

- Fear of incompetence of senior level managers to take up strategic steps.
- Diverse work-force with competitive skill sets.
- Fear towards victimization in the wake of failures.
- Improper strategic assignments and leadership conflict over authority.
- Ramifications for power relations.
- Vulnerability to legislative changes.
- Resistance that comes through the legitimate labour institutions.
- Presence of an active labour union.
- Rapid structural changes.
- Economic and market pressures influenced the adoption of strategic HRM.
- More diverse, outward looking approach.

Factors Influencing HR Strategies

The organization's HR strategies depend mainly on the overall business strategy and the culture of the organization, which contributes to shape and determine the need for human resources, both in terms of quantity and quality and also helps to identify the requisite skill levels to achieve the same. On the other hand, the competitive business environment, particularly the economic scenario and the position of the organization in the context of the said scenario, determines the extent to which financial resources could be budgeted for the development of HR strategies and action plans in the organization.

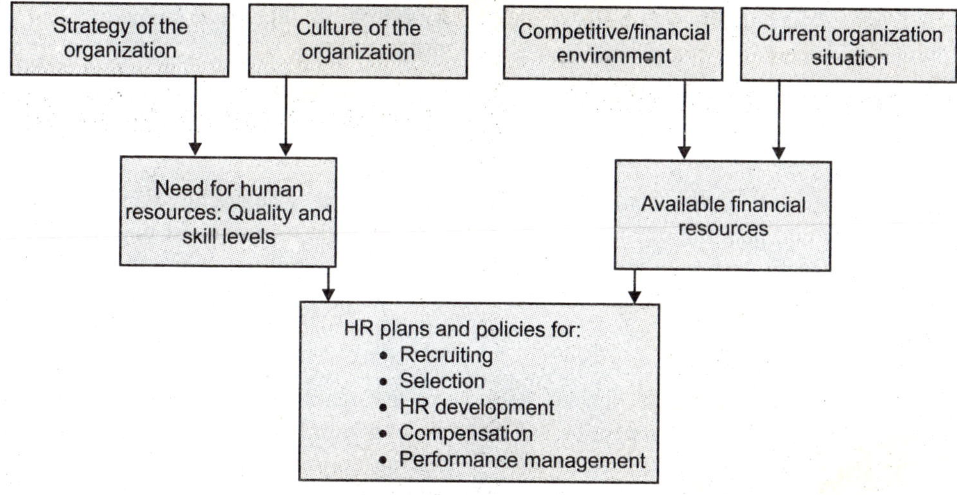

Fig. 1.29: Factors determining HR plans and strategies

The combination of these ensures the organization to go for strategic human resource planning that forms a comprehensive action plan or map in terms of identifying the future organizational strategies in terms of its recruitment, selection, HR development, compensation and performance management strategies. The entire process is typically cyclical and ongoing in nature. The cycle thereby starts with laying down the organizational strategic plan, linking HR functions in it, and then providing the same as the basis for Manpower planning and employee development initiatives.

Linkage of Organizational and HR Strategies			
Organizational Strategy	**Strategic Focus**	**HR Strategy**	**HR Activities**
1. Cost Leadership	• Cost control	• Alignment of right people for right jobs	• Continuous development
	• Zero waste		• Participative and team management
	• Lean production	• Emphasis on strategic HR planning	• Employee communication programmes
		• Employee retention	• Employee reward and incentive schemes
2. Differentiation	• Innovation	• Competency assessment and development	• Performance evaluation
	• Focus on R&D	• Performance management linked strategic objectives of the organization	• Employee reward and incentive schemes
	• Quality improvement		• Total quality HRM practices

The next stage would involve sustaining and retaining individuals who are hired and making sure that they work efficiently and help the organization move in the selected direction. At this juncture strategic focus should be given to ensure rating of employee performance and comparison of the same with established standards or benchmarks. On the basis of such analysis performance deviations should be identified and precautionary measures as well as corrective measures should be taken so as to improve future performance.

The table given above takes into consideration two of the generic strategies and the strategic focus required to generate each of these competitive advantages along with HR strategy and activities needed to be done by HR Department to help the organization in generating these strategic advantages and to move successfully towards desired goals and objectives. The selected strategic focus should be very clear and well integrated into organizational policy and clearly communicated to HR Department to help in drafting suitable HR strategy and last in carrying out all activities.

Strategic HRM Concepts

Strategic human resource management (SHRM) is concerned with the contributions human resource strategies make to organizational effectiveness, and the ways in which these contributions are achieved. There are three SHRM concepts: high performance management (high performance working), high commitment management and high involvement management.

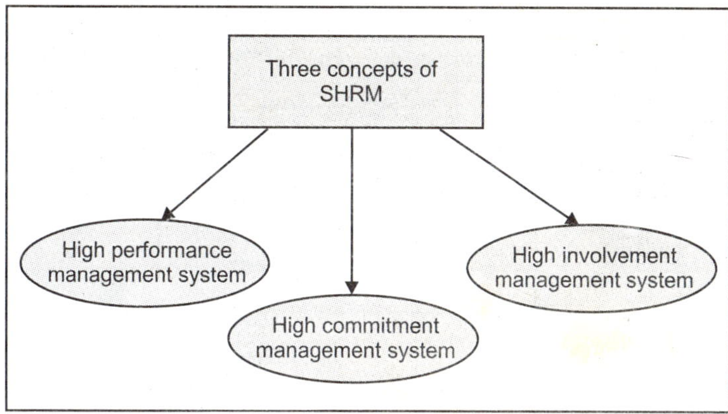

Fig. 1.30: Concepts of SHRM

Within the framework of the concept of strategic HRM, these describe various approaches to its development and implementation.

SHRM scholars like Dyer & Shafer, 1999[8] had adopted a contingency perspective emphasizing on institutionalizing of the concept of domain of fit or alignment of the HR strategies with the business strategy of the organization. Here such fit is being achieved in two ways. One is vertical, or the degree of alignment between (a) components of a firm's human resource strategy and (b) core features of its business strategy. The other is horizontal fit, or the degree of alignment among components of a firm's business strategy (typically activities or programmes such as selection, training and compensation). Conceptually, the two notions of fit have been used to derive normative models to show how intuitively derived typologies of human resource strategy should be paired with similarly derived typologies of business strategy to maximize firm performance (Dyer & Holder, 1988)[5]. Empirically, the contingency (or configurational) perspective has informed a series of empirical studies designed to determine whether business units that had achieved vertical and horizontal fit performed better than those that had not (Arthur, 1994[9]; Delery & Doty, 1996[10]; Ichniowski, Shaw & Prennushi, 1997[13]; MacDuffie, 1995[11]; Youndt, Snell, Dean & Lepak, 1996[12]). In general, these studies have produced, at best, mixed opinions (Wright & Sherman, 1999[14]). As a result some SHRM scholars have come to advocate a universalistic or "best practice" approach to human resource strategy; that is, to argue that a single high performance human resource strategy (HPHRS) enhances organizational effectiveness regardless of organizational goals, work systems, or context in which they are being implemented (Becker & Huselid, 1999[15]; Pfeffer, 1998[16]).

High Performance Management Systems/High Performance Work Systems (HPWS)

High performance working systems involve the development of a number of interrelated processes that together make an impact on the performance of the organization through its people in such areas as productivity, quality, and levels of customer service, growth, profits, and ultimately ensuring the delivery of increased shareholder value. This is achieved by 'enhancing the skills and engaging the enthusiasm of employees' the starting point of which is leadership, vision and benchmarking so as to create a sense of momentum and direction amongst employees at various levels in the organization. HPWS also emphasize on the concept of continuous performance assessment and evaluation for future performance improvement and development.

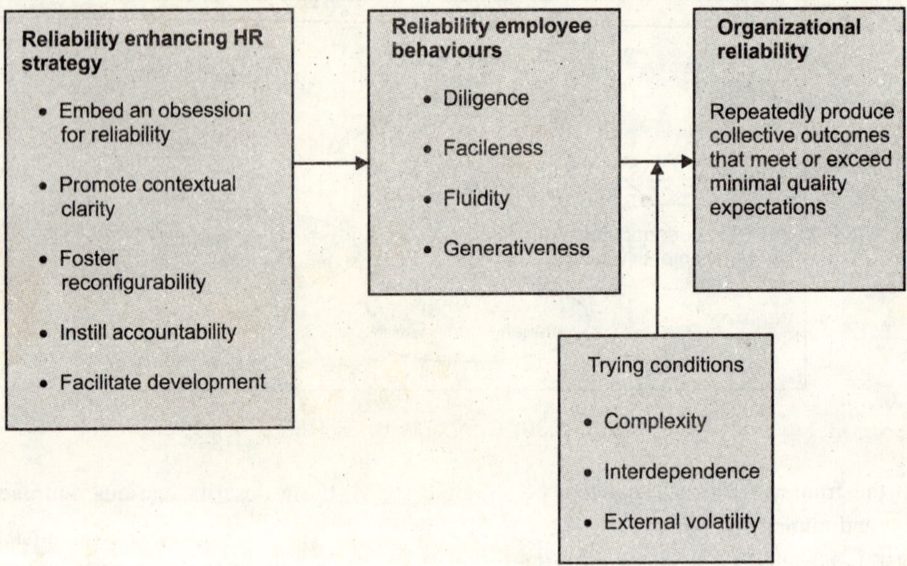

Fig. 1.31: Towards a SHRM model of high performance organization

Characteristics of High Performance Work Systems: The features of high performance work systems (HPWS) are as follows:

- These organizations and their HR set ups evaluate large numbers of highly qualified applicants for each strategic position
- HPWSs use validated selection and promotion models/procedures
- They implement extensive cross training and development of new employees
- HPWS use formal performance appraisal and management
- HPWSs use multi-source (360 degree) performance appraisal and feedback
- They link merit increases to formal appraisal processes
- HPWSs consider above-market compensation for key positions
- They high percentage of entire workforce included in incentive system
- They take into consideration high difference in pay between high and low performers
- They involve high percentage of workforce working in self-managed, project-based work teams
- In HPWSs low percentage of employees are covered by union contract
- In HPWSs high percentage of jobs are filled from within

Key strategies for enabling a HPWS: High performance work systems (HPWS) ensure that business and HR issues are strategically linked with each other. Such linkages facilitate catalyzing organizational changes in terms of structures, procedures and systems and adjust the overall HR strategy and processes to cope with the same. This radical transformation is achieved by developing competencies and skills of people, instigating a holistic performance management system and motivating employees by a comprehensive compensation and reward management system.

Key Strategies for Building a Performing Organization Illustration

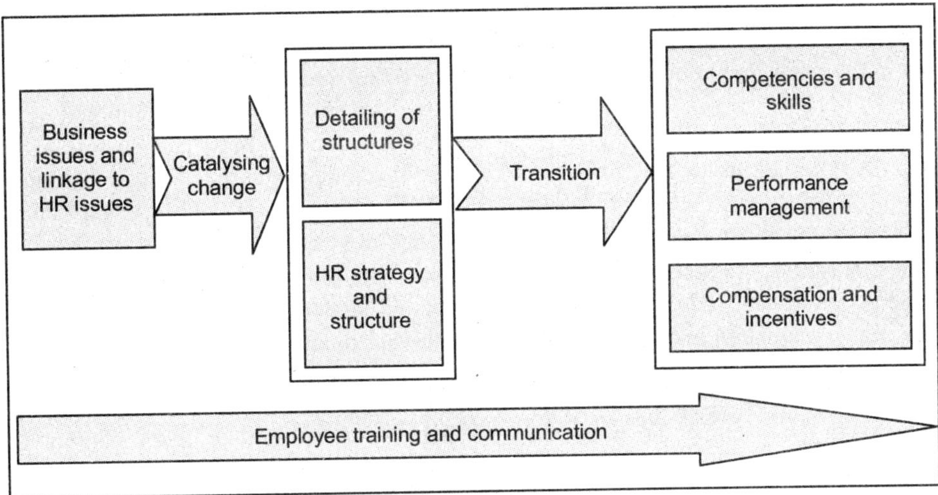

The various strategies involving such organizational development may be summarized by the following table:

Table 1.5: High Performance Human Resource Strategy

Criteria	***High performance work systems (HPWS)***	***High performance human resource systems (HPHRS)***	***Reliability enhancing human resource strategy (REHRS)***
Focus	Organizing system	HR management	Organizing system
Emphasis	HR principles	HR activities	HR principles
Specificity	High	Low	High

The HPWS stream, at its name implies, focuses on organizing systems: in particular, the organization's operations or the production systems (Appelbaum, Bailey, Berg & Kalleberg, 2000[17]). Rooted in socio-technical systems theory, HPWS research digs deeply into interrelationships among people, process and technology. MacDuffie, 1995[18] had emphasized the "organizational logic" in favour of matching HPWSs to flexible production systems and control-oriented human resource strategies to classic mass production approaches. Since the focus is on the organizing system, the HPWS stream also tends to emphasize human resource strategy principles — general themes that theoretically guide the selection and grouping of human resource activities — rather than just the human resource activities themselves.

HPWSs ensure to enhance workforce skill levels, providing employees discretion and opportunity to use their skills in collaboration with other workers, and offering an incentive structure that enhances employee motivation and commitment (Batt, 2002[19]). HPWS are typically characterized as focusing on the work system performance, emphasizing human resource management principles, and greatly specifying human resource activities.

A Six Principle of Reliability-Enhancing HR Strategy (REHRS) for Organizational Effectiveness:

Principle 1: Creating obsession for reliability: Human resource work systems must inculcate a sense of reliability in the organization by enabling people to track down past mistakes in decisions and enhance the effectiveness in strategic decision making. To embed such an obsession for reliability HR systems must entrench reliability objectives into their organizational missions, values, and performance metrics (Weick et al., 1999)[20]. They ensure that virtually every piece of formal organizational communication going to employees reinforces some aspect of reliability (Roberts & Bea, 2001a[28]). They reward and celebrate reliability way over and above productivity or efficiency issues (Roberts & Bea, 2001b[22]).

Principle 2: Promote contextual clarity: This involves understanding that reliability is the uncontested organizational priority is not enough. According to Weick and Sutcliffe (2001)[21], another "key to effective performance lies in maintaining situational awareness, the big picture of current situations. HR systems should thereby seek to promote such contextual clarity. This means that HR systems should work hard to ensure that employees can effectively integrate their local knowledge with the overall situational and operational status of the system and then extend their analysis forward in time to envision potential future implications.

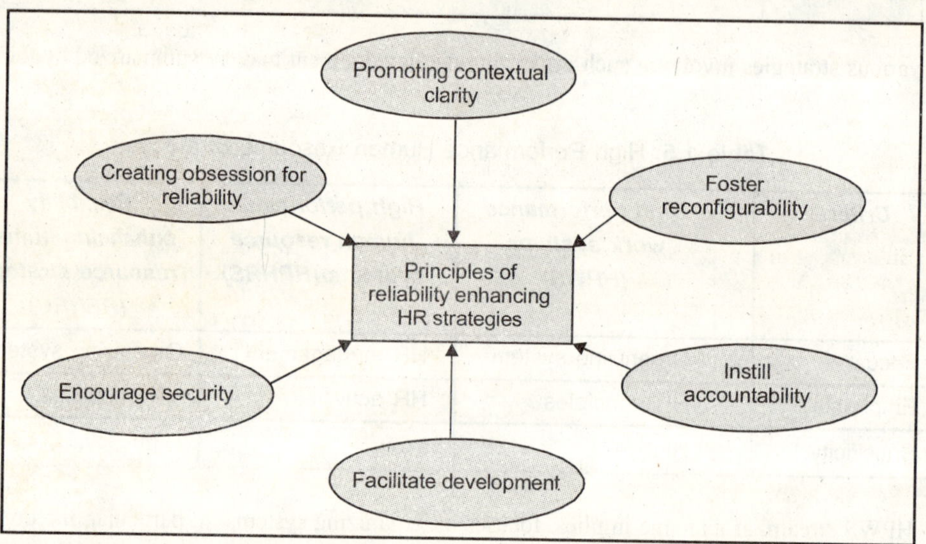

Fig. 1.32: Principles of reliability enhancing HR strategies for organizational effectiveness

Principle 3: Foster reconfigurability: HR system in order to achieve resiliency in the face of challenging business demands, should emphasize on fostering reconfigurability. They should strive to develop people and infrastructures flexible enough not only to routinely handle a wide-range of unexpected events but also to effectively manage all contingencies through successful ad hoc actions.

Principle 4: Instill accountability: HR systems should also work hard to ensure that irrespective of whether employees are executing routine tasks or responding to an emergency, they are always operating within the boundaries (and the best interests) of the system (Vaughan, 1999[23]). HR systems should thereby instill accountability in organizational practices by regularly asking employees to explain their conduct both formally and informally.

Principle 5: Facilitate development: HR systems should strive to facilitate the continual development of their systems and people. The objective of such initiatives should be to ensure that the organization is constantly forcing, and then helping, people to know what they don't know (Roberts & Bea, 2001a[32]).

To facilitate development, HR systems should regularly assess core processes and procedures and develop competencies of the people.

Principle 6: Encourage security: HR systems tend to employ people with highly specialized skills and then ask them to be diligent, facile, fluid, and generative under challenging and stressful circumstances. On the other hand, employee turnover and hiring mistakes can lead to serious system disruption and even instability of such systems and processes. Thus, for achieving organizational effectiveness HR systems should work hard to encourage employment and psychological security at the workplace. To encourage security, HR systems should formally and informally encourage rewarding people for raising concerns and pointing out errors (Weick et al., 1999[24]).

High Commitment Management

One of the defining characteristics of HRM is its emphasis on the importance of enhancing mutual commitment. High commitment management has been described as a form of management which is aimed at eliciting a commitment so that employee behaviour is primarily self-regulated rather than controlled by sanctions and pressures external to the individual, and relations within the organization are based on high levels of trust.

High Involvement Management

This approach involves treating employees as partners in the enterprise whose interests are respected and who have a voice on matters that concern them. It is concerned with communication and involvement. The aim of this approach is to create a climate in which there is a continuing dialogue between managers and the members of their teams in order to define expectations and share information on the organization's mission, values and objectives. This establishes mutual understanding of what is to be achieved and a framework for managing and developing people to ensure that it will be achieved.

Emerging Roles of HR Professionals in the Perspective of SHRM

The HR managers need to be instrumental in taking the responsibility of the effective planning and implementation of the policies and decisions in tune with the business changes. They should act as strategic partners and be proactive in their role than mere reactive, passive spectators. The HR managers should understand how far their decisions contribute to business surplus incorporating human competency and performance to the organization. Strategic HR managers need a change in their outlook from seeing themselves as relationship managers to strategic resource managers. Kossek (1987[26], 1989[27]) argues that major HRM innovations occur when senior management takes the lead and adoption of innovative SHRM practices is dependent on the nature of relationship of the HR department with the CEO and the line managers. HR department and HR managers in these innovative organizations play a strategic role (Ulrich, 1997[28]) linking the HR strategy with the business strategy of the organization. A crucial aspect concerning SHRM is the concepts of fit and flexibility. The degree of fit determines the human resource system's integration with organization strategy. It is the role of HR managers to ensure this fit in between Human Resource System with the Organization Strategy.

Ideally HR and the top management of an organization should work together so as to formulate the company's overall business strategy; that strategy then provides the framework within which HR activities such as recruiting and appraising must be crafted. If it is done successfully, it should result out in the employee competencies and behaviour that in turn should help the business implement its strategies and realize its goals.

THEME READING: SENIOR HR EXECUTIVES OF DERCY LACK OF STRATEGIC INPUTS

Though many HR management gurus have championed the evolving and expanding strategic role of HR professionals, a recent report from the Conference Board of Canada seems to indicate that most HR executives feel they aren't very involved with their companies' strategic plans. The recent survey of 155 senior-level HR executives found that 63 per cent of the respondents felt that 'HR is never, rarely or only sometimes' a major part of their companies' overall strategy. The remaining 37 per cent did feel that HR plays a significant role in their companies' strategic planning. According to researchers with the Conference Board, employees at companies that encourage HR participation in strategic planning have a stronger understanding of their functions within the organization. 'There is a strong correlation between those companies that say HR is always linked to the strategic process, and how well the companies' employees understand where the company wants to go', says Brian Hackett, a senior HR specialist with the board.

(*Ref: HR Magazine, 1999, January, pp. 21–2*)

International and Comparative Strategic Human Resource Management

The assumption that SHRM is a strategically driven management process points to its international potentialities. The employment relationship is shaped by national systems of employment legislation and the cultural contexts in which it operates. Thus, as the world of business is becoming more globalised, variations in national regulatory systems, labour markets and institutional and cultural contexts are likely to constrain or shape any tendency towards 'convergence' or a 'universal' model of best HRM practice (Clark & Pugh, 2000; Kidd et al., 2001). This section addresses aspects of the international scene to help us place the discourse on the SHRM model into a wider global context. In doing so, we make a distinction between international HRM and comparative HRM. The subject matter of the former revolves around the issues and problems associated with the globalization of capitalism. Comparative HRM, on the other hand, focuses on providing insights into the nature of, and reasons for, differences in HR practices across national boundaries.

Trends Enhancing the Importance of SHRM

- Trend 1: The increased globalization of the economy
- Trend 2: Technological changes, challenges and opportunities
- Trend 3: The need to be flexible in response to changing business environments
- Trend 4: Increase in litigation related to HRM (proliferation of regulations and compliance checks related to HR decisions)
- Trend 5: Changing characteristics of the workforce (workforce diversity)
- Trend 6: Intellectual capital-knowledge has become a direct competitive advantage for organizations selling ideas and relationships. The challenge to organizations is to ensure that they have the capability to find, assimilate, compensate and retain talents.

The Role of the Strategic HR Practitioner

What is Expected from HR Professionals?

- HR professionals should be proficient in business management and deliver effective people strategies so that they could effectively contribute to achieve organizational objectives.
- Maintaining and managing ethical standards at the workplace and ensuring a strategic framework so as to continuously support its corporate social responsibility related obligations/perspectives.
- Adapting and managing techniques for people management and development so as to effectively fit the future needs of the organization and the employees.
- Effectively managing and implementing change and acting as "internal consultants" for the organization.

- Being committed and encouraging other people (employees) to learning and inculcating the spirit of professional development.
- Act as auditors/inspectors so as to ensure compliance checks and record maintenance.
- To lead and effectively involve people into public relations activities
- To be the spearheads of the internal marketing initiatives of the organizations by emphasizing "people" of the organizations as "internal customers".
- Promulgating the best in class workplace facilities and environment and lead the organization towards "organizational excellence" model.

Qualities of a Strategic HR Manager

- People mindedness
- Strategic planner
- Thorough business knowledge
- Fairness and firmness
- Tact and resourcefulness
- Sympathy and consideration
- Knowledge of manpower management and their holistic development
- Broad social outlook
- Change agent capabilities (internal consultant)
- Competence to perform activities relating to personnel better than his/her subordinates.
- Academic qualifications and quest for research work

Role of a HR/Personnel Manager

- ***The Reactive/Proactive Role***: Today's HR managers need to have reactive as well as proactive roles in the organization. They should not only provide regular day-to-day administrative systems and support to the management, but at the strategic level their role should be more as a visionary, business partner, or more as a change agent or "internal consultant" so as to effectively develop integrated HR strategies, innovations and interventions.
- ***Strategist Role***: As strategists, HR professionals have the major responsibility of addressing long-term issues concerning the management and developing a strong and healthy employment relationship at the workplace as well as building an effective HR (Employability) Brand for the organization. They should also be considered as business partners involving sharing responsibilities with their line managers for the successful attainment of organizational goals and objectives.
- ***Advisory Role***: Advising, suggesting, counselling and helping people in discharging their responsibilities relating to grievance redressal, conflict resolution, employee selection, training etc.
- ***The Conscience Role***: To inform the management about the humanitarian approach-towards moral and ethical obligations to its employees.
- ***Counsellor Role***: To discuss various problems of employees relating to career, supervisors, colleagues, health, family, financial, social etc. and suggest means to minimize and overcome work stress.
- ***Mediator's Role***: Resolving conflicts so as to effectively maintain industrial harmony.
- ***Representative Role***: To act as a representative of the organization so as to give an overall picture of the organizational operations to the employees particularly in case of industrial disputes or grievance redressal.

- ***Innovator Role*:** HR professionals should have a strong acumen for creativity and innovation, so as to effectively introduce new processes and procedures which would contribute to enhance organizational effectiveness.
- ***Fire-fighting/Legal Role*:** Grievance handling, settlement of disputes, handling disciplinary cases, collective bargaining, joint consultation, interpretation and implementation of various labour laws, contacting lawyers, handling industrial tribunals etc.
- ***Welfare Role*:** To provide and maintain canteens, hospitals, educational institutes, office, clubs, libraries, conveyance facilities, cooperative credit societies, consumer stores etc.
- ***Problem-solver Role*:** To effectively handle this role regarding various short range and long range problems of the company involving the interests of human resources.
- ***Role of Change Agent*:** To convince workers and the management and take the lead in implementing changes in technology, organization, production and installing the organization development techniques etc.
- ***Decision-making Role*:** To play a dominant role in the decision-making process, regarding both major and minor issues of the organization involving human resources.
- ***Executive Role*:** Once decisions are taken HR manager plays a dominant role in executing those decisions and programmes.
- ***Internal Consultant Role*:** HR professionals should actively take part in analyzing problems, diagnosing issues and proposing solutions for ensuring organizational effectiveness.

Exhibit: HRM in ONGC

HR Vision

"To attain organizational excellence by developing and inspiring the true potential of company's human capital and providing opportunities for growth, well being and enrichment".

HR Mission

"To create a value and knowledge based organization, by inculcating a culture of learning, innovation and team working and aligning business priorities with aspiration of employees, leading to development of an empowered, responsive and competent human capital".

Factors Affecting the HR Image in ONGC: In ONGC, the effectiveness of its HR image depends on its various HR services (like establishment matters, IT Based systems, estate, hospitality, medical facilities, healthy working conditions etc.), HR policies and procedures, staffing practices, training activities, rewards and benefits, performance management, career and succession planning, information sharing and OD initiatives.

Fig. 1.33: Factors affecting the HR image in ONGC

HR policies at ONGC revolve around the basic tenet of creating a highly motivated, vibrant and self-driven team. The company cares for each and every employee and has in-built systems to recognize and reward them periodically. Motivation plays an important role in HR development. In order to keep its employees motivated the company has incorporated schemes such as **Reward and Recognition Scheme, Grievance Handling Scheme** and **Suggestion Scheme**.

Initiatives Taken to Improve the Organizational HR Image

Aligning Organizational HR Practices with Customer Needs and Aspirations

One of the factors influencing successful HR practices in ONGC had been its endeavour in aligning its organizational HR practices along with the customer needs and aspirations. The core HR mantra supports the organizations concern in this regard.

The core HR mantras: The core HR mantras at ONGC instills all around its customers and how the organization needs to gear up the effectiveness of its HR services so as to achieve the same.

"Think like a business with a product to be developed, marketed and reliably delivered to customers who need our services".

- **WHAT DO THE CUSTOMERS WANT FROM HR?**
- **HOW WELL DO WE DELIVER?**
- **HOW TO IMPROVE OVERALL HR IMAGE?**

Changes in the Overall HR Perspective in the Organization

The organization's past HR practices could be typically attributed as a reactive, tactical, conservative, cost centred approach that was described to contribute hardly anything productive to the organization in terms of aligning its human resources to its business needs.

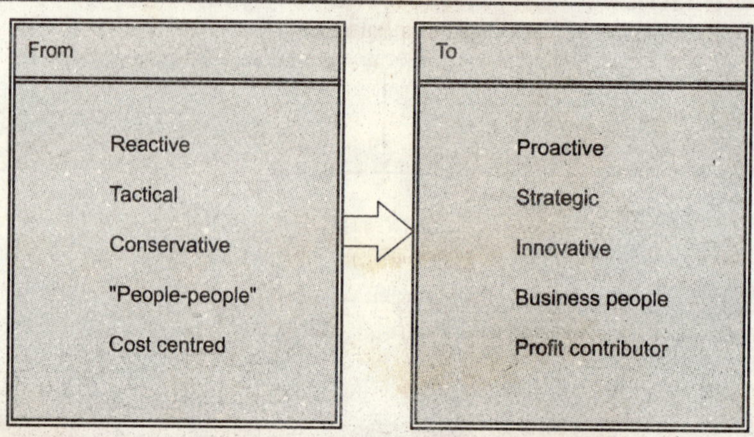

ONGC has undertaken an organization transformation exercise in which HR has taken a lead role as a change agent by evolving a communication strategy to ensure involvement and participation among employees in various work centres. Exclusive workshops and interactions/brainstorming sessions are organized to facilitate involvement of employees in this project. The new HR practices at ONGC could be described as a more proactive, strategic, innovation oriented, profit contributing that contributed not only to its organizational transformation process but also improving the overall effectiveness of the organization. Some of the transformational HR initiatives included the introduction of the "Project SHRAMIK" and instigating a participative culture at the workplace.

(a) **Project "Shramik":** To move towards worldclass systems, processes and practices, a project for integrated System of Human Resource Automated Management Information for KAIZEN (SHRAMIK) based on software platform SAP R/3 has been launched which is an attempt to address key issues in HRM through comprehensive process reengineering and remodelling of HR functions.

(b) **Participative Culture:** Policies and policy makers at ONGC have always had the interests of the large and multidisciplined workforce at heart and have been aware of the nuances and significance of cordial Industrial Relations. By enabling workers to participate in management, they are provided with an informative, consultative, associative and administrative forum for interactive participation and for fostering an innovative culture.

In fact, ONGC has been one of the few organizations where this method has been implemented. It has had a positive impact on the overall operations since it has led to enhanced efficiency and productivity and reduced wastages and costs.

HR Philosophy at ONGC

"HRM must demonstrate competency in areas such as strategic thinking, diagnostic ability, critical evaluation, financial analysis, business analysis, marketing and communicating with influence".

Roadmap to Achieve the Change in Traditional HR

(a) **Delivering Promises**

- Be more responsive.
- Ensure that HR personnel, practices and systems work to support the goal.
- Identify the HR personnel who are willing to go the extra mile.

(b) Updating the HR Image

- Presenting the HR Dept. as a Business Partner.
- Identifying and removing the 'Road Blocks' in the change process.
- Providing value added services.

(c) Spreading the Word

- Talk about the success stories.
- Quantify the impact of HR services.
- Communicate in Board Meetings, Bilateral Meetings and through the Intranet.

(d) Enhance Visibility and Transparency

- Publish success stories in HR Journals.
- Present case studies in HR Conferences.
- Compete for HR Awards.

(e) Kaizen

- Continuously review and update the HR services.

(f) Emphasis on customer perceived thrust areas

- **Policy Related Issues**

  Recruitment
  - Periodical recruitment at staff levels
  - Monitoring of manpower by HR Department
  - Right Man for the Right Job

  Promotion
  - Transparent policy
  - University and consistency

  Training
  - Retraining
  - Training on behavioural aspects

  Performance Evaluation
  - Through assessment development centre
- **Clarity in Roles and Responsibilities**
- **Planned and Transparent Job Rotation**
- **Job Enrichment**

(g) Feedback Mechanism

- HR/Finance Team to visit Drill Sites/Installation/Field Party.
- Telephonic or email interaction with every employee.

(h) Value Added Services

- Liaisoning of HR department with RTO/police for NOC and registration of vehicles.

HR Issues in Mergers and Acquisitions

There has been an unprecedented growth in the numbers of mergers and acquisitions that took place (or were announced) in last calendar year. The total number of M&A deals announced during the year 2007 rose up to 661 with a total announced value of $51.17 billion as compared to 2006 in which only 480 such deals took place. Sectors like steel, telecom and aviation witnessed amalgamation of big brands and thus, were clear leaders in sectoral values. With such a whooping number of M&As taking place every year, some concerns of employees also rise apparently. This is because HR issues are the most neglected issues as financial considerations are given more importance.

Fig. 1.34: The most waited M&A of the year: Kingfisher and the Air Deccan merger

When a merger is announced, employees of the company become worried about issues like job security, role conflicts, interpersonal conflicts, cultural adaptations, etc. Such factors hold the power to make or break the deal. It is believed that most of the overseas mergers fail because of people centric issues as the management fails to deal with them aptly. It becomes the responsibility of HR personnel of the organization to take care of such issues before and after the amalgamations takes place.

Prevalent HR Concerns

The success of M&A always depends on the how well the HR issues are managed after the merger takes place. There are also some major human resource concerns that need to be dealt with before the merger actually takes place. HR issues that form greatest challenge to the success of a M&A deal include the following:

- **Consolidating and Integrating:** The uncertainties of M&As shift the focus of employees from productive work to issues related to interpersonal conflicts, layoffs, career growth with the acquirer company, compensation, etc. Moreover, employees are concerned with how well they will go with new colleagues. The mergers involve downsizing, hence the first thing that comes to the minds of employees is related to their job security. Mergers also lead to changes in the well-defined career paths of employees, as defined by the acquired company. Due to these reasons, employees find themselves in a completely different situation with changes in job profiles and work teams. This may have a negative impact on the performance of the employees.
- **Cultural Integration:** An organization's culture defines its managerial style, structure and organizational practices. Each company has its own set of values which may conflict with those of the acquired company. The employees may not be able to accommodate themselves in a new culture and thus may lead to cultural shock. Inability to adapt to a new culture increases stress levels among employees and results in low job performance. The need therefore is to follow a structured approach in dealing with cultural differences. As in the case of Kingfisher and Air Deccan M&A this was perhaps one of the greatest challenges ahead Mr. Malya, but he handled the challenge in smart way and the outcome was a smarter gate up and look of the new Air Deccan.

Fig. 1.35: The new smart Air Deccan

- **Employee Communication:** Whenever there is news of any merger in an organization, anxiety prevails among the employees. This atmosphere of apprehensions leads to company wide rumours. The employees lose faith in their organization and tend to become demotivated. To free employees from such fears, proper communication has to take place between the management and the employees. The management should instill a sense of security among them. Attrition: Most mergers bring with them downsizing, reallocation of work, change in work profiles, changes in career paths, etc. Moreover apprehensions about the new company also create anxiety among employees. If they fail to adopt to the new culture they face high levels of stress and thus end up leaving the organization.
- **Differences in Organizational Structures:** Another problem is the difference between the organizational structures of the companies. Since the organizational structures are different, differences in compensation packages and designations can take place. The company has to maintain employees at equal levels. Unable to do so, employees can feel dissatisfied.

Cross Cultural Integration and HR Issues

In the first phase of mergers and acquisitions there are various aspects of business that is affected which needs to be streamlined. These processes have a direct relation with the success of the integration. This process such ideally called synergy but it is called integration as not all mergers and acquisitions synergies the processes of both the parties. Closer look at the different aspects that can be affected by a crosscultural integration.

The flow of an M&A proces is as follow:

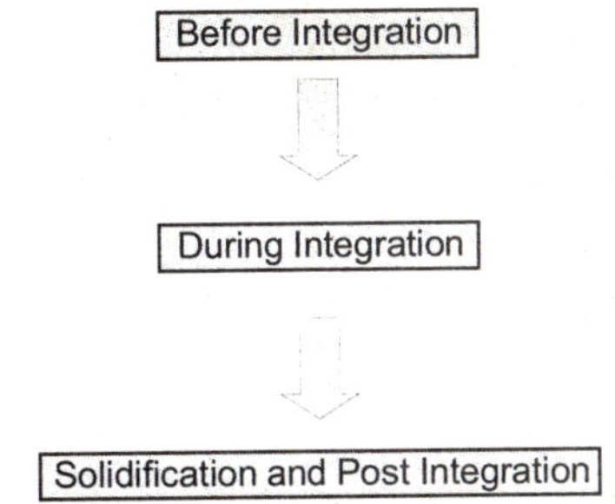

Fig. 1.36: Flow of an M&A process

HR issues: People issues in case of M&A are the most sensitive and critical aspect to handle. Effective communication is the key to keeping the rumours of an effective M&A. In today's world there is always a continuous struggle to get the right talent for your job. Imagine loosing your war just because your warriors have lost path to your goal.

Very little importance is given to human capital concerns at the time of M&A. Following can be the reasons:

- People issues are not viewed as priority since there are other process driven challenges to be addressed.

- Top management views people issues too sensitive to address so try not to discuss the same.
- Lack of information with the top management.
- In case of lay-offs don't know how to deal or communicate with the employees.
- The value for human capita is marginal for some managers.
- There are concerns of having their ground stable first then people issues would be addressed.

Step 1: HR issues during integration

- Identifying a pilot who can spread the information. This person should be a very good communicator, have good analytical abilities, have the good connect with the staff and should be unbiased.
- Keep infusing accurate information with the help of that pilot. Constant communication to be in touch with your employees.
- Cultural assessment.
- Creating practices for learning and knowledge transfer.

Step 2: HR issues during combination

During integration of the company there needs to be an extra care to be taken care of

- Deciding on who will be retained and who will be not communication here is the most critical. Communication should be handled in the most sensitive manner
- Establishing a HR culture, policies and practices is essential
- Systematic approach towards the selection of the team

Integration can be poorly implemented leading to specific implications:

- The attrition rate will shoot up
- The leadership rate will also go down, as he will have lesser information the current scenario
- Employee satisfaction will drop down
- Integration efforts differ from company to company so the processes to be put in place should be in alignment with the new vision and mission
- Most of the employees think that the employees care more about financials than about their human resources

There needs to be a selection of a integration manager who with the help of the inputs from communication manager should implement the integration. The integration manager should be:

- The integration manager should have good HR sense, good analytical skills, good leadership skills
- Achieved good business sense
- Retained a high credibility in the system before

Also the HR is responsible for setting up a Steering committee that will be responsible for

- Selection of a leader
- Selection of goals and objectives
- Role definition, processes and procedures
- Redefine or reinforce the company values
- Redefine or reinforce the R&D processes

Step 3: Solidification and post integration

Clearly there is a new entity that has been created at the outset of the two companies. There are various HR issues that can be addressed at this stage. A new joint will bring in issues of solidifying, fine tuning, readjusting. The other HR related issues:

- Creating and evaluating a new structure
- Meddling two cultures need assessment and fine tuning and change
- Help manage the change as a facilitator
- Revising the new model
- Selection of the new entrants
- Deciding the leaders who are going to chalk out the culture of the new entity

Role of HR in Making M&A Successful

The success of a merger and acquisition depends on how well an organization deals with issues related to its people and cultural integration. The HR departments of an organization act as a strategic partner. The role of HR becomes strategic when it takes decisions about what kind of people, capability and commitment the company would want after the deal. The HR can help the employee in the following ways:

- HR helps in managing interpersonal conflicts and makes employees better team players. It also helps them in dealing with cultural differences. Clear communication content and channels are customized to address cultural differences.
- HR also deals effectively with the integration issue. Effective employee communication acts as a key here. Questions about job security, relocation, changes in benefit programmes and new reporting relationships are answered by the HR only. Keeping a check on rumours, anxiety, resentment and the loss of top talent, has also to be dealt with.
- The M&A phase is very sensitive for employees as they feel insecure about their future in the transitional times. HR in such a situation makes people retain their faith in the organization. The HR has to retain the confidence of employees and assure them job security.

Develop the 'HR' Project Plan

A project plan is a critical document that directs and supports the whole process of integration and should be continuously updated to include the latest developments. The project plan should define the tasks to be performed in order of their priority. The owner for each task has to be identified and the responsibilities assigned. But, how many HR departments take the pains of designing a project plan exclusively for the HR activities planning.

Conduct the 'HR' Due Diligence Review

A due diligence review helps the merging companies identify the presence of any hidden liabilities for the integrated business. This review would help the companies have a relook at their decision and recheck its feasibility. It would also help the companies identify those critical areas which need immediate attention if the deal is to be carried out successfully. The common belief is that HR does not have any role to play during the due diligence review. Some organizations are even looking at specific issues like "culture due diligence review". Some of the components for the HR due diligence review are: (a) Organizational culture and structure (b) Employee compensation and benefits (c) Industrial relations (d) Pending employee litigations (e) HR policies and procedures and (f) Key talent analysis.

Managing M&A the HR Way

Clearly defined communication strategy during M&A plays an important role in removing the employee fears and kill rumours floating around in the organization. Studies show that communication strategy that involves senior managers of the acquired organizations work well. Involving other employees who are trusted by the employees for instance trade union leaders are also helpful. The employees meeting in small groups so as to discuss their concerns, fears and positive feelings also helps to lessen the stress on employees of acquired firm. The group meetings seem to help because many-a-times employees are reluctant to come out and speak their concerns, whereas in groups where everyone shares same set of feelings to an extent, it becomes easier to come out with the common set of concerns and fears. This also provides confidence to employees that the new management is willing to listen to their concerns and feelings, building an atmosphere of mutual trust.

HR Takes Control

- Train managers on the nature of change
- Technical retraining
- Family assistance programmes
- Stress reduction programme
- Meeting between the counter parts
- Orientation programmes
- Explaining new roles
- Helping people who lost jobs
- Post merger team building
- Anonymous feedback helpline for employees

Case: Acquisition Strategy of GE Capital

GE Capital uses a successful model called "Pathfinder" for acquiring firms. The model disintegrates the process of M&A into four categories which are further divided into subcategories. The four stages incorporate some of the best practices for optimum results. The pre-acquisition phase of the model involves due diligence, negotiations and closing of deals. This involves the cultural assessments, devising communication strategies and evaluation of strengths and weaknesses of the business leaders. An integration manager is also chosen at this stage. The second phase is the foundation building. At this phase the integration plan is prepared. A team of executives from the GE Capital and the acquiring company is formed. Also a 100 days communication strategy is evolved and the senior management involvement and support is made clear. The needed resources are pooled and accountability is ensured. The third is the integration phase. Here the actual implementation and correction measures are taken. The processes like assessing the work flow, assignment of roles etc. are done at this stage. This stage also involves continuous feedbacks and making necessary corrections in the implementation. The last phase involves assimilation process where integration efforts are reassessed. This stage involves long-term adjustment and looking for avenues for improving the integration. This is also the period when the organization actual starts reaping the benefits of the acquisition. The model is dynamic in the sense that company constantly improves it through internal discussions between the teams that share their experiences, effective tools and refine best practices.

TOTAL QUALITY IN MANAGING HUMAN RESOURCES

The TQM approach is changing the role of HR professionals by changing the expectations of the stockholders, within and outside the profession, with regard to the HRM responsibilities of these individuals in the organization. Thus while, HR executives and managers reflect the organizational culture within which they are expected to influence and shape it. The difference in the traditional HR approach and the total quality HRM approach is depicted in the following table:

Table 1.6: Comparison of Traditional and Total Quality HRM Approaches

Hallmarks	***Traditional HRM Approach***	***Total Quality HRM Approach***
Philosophy	A fair day's work for a fair day's pay	Shared responsibility, commitments, rewards
Business objectives	Increased productivity, profitability; quality is secondary; focus on labour	Increased quality, productivity, customer satisfaction, employee satisfaction and loyalty
Quality objectives	Adequate quality to remain in business; self driven approaches to quality improvement	TQM and continuous improvement at and across every level
Business information sharing	Limited to information on as needed basis for job performance	Open books, share broad information on profits, productivity, quality, costs, capital spending plans etc
Major constituencies	Managers, stockholders, customers and employees	Customers, all employees, stockholders
Employee involvement	Programmes: suggestions, plans, individual employee awards; usually no formal system	Extensive within and between levels and functions
Education and training	On the job training, feedback on job performance	Quality and economic education, multi-skill training, problem solving and group process
Reward structure	Management designed and administered	Designed and adjusted by management-employee committees; formal, early union involvement
Job security	Labour as a variable cost; layoffs common during business downturns	Formal commitment a key consideration in all decisions

Another way to perceive the total quality difference in HRM is to examine the relevant HRM areas identified by the Baldrige Award criteria to determine similarities and differences between traditional and total quality HRM approaches is exhibited by the following table:

Table 1.7: Comparison of Traditional and Total Quality HRM Approaches using the Baldrige Award Criteria

HRM-related Baldrige Award Criteria	***Traditional HRM Approach***	***Total Quality HRM Approach***
1. HRP	• Alignment with organizational strategy • Employee selection for job fit • Hiring for individual knowledge, skills and/or abilities match	• Alignment with organizational strategy • Employee selection for organization and job fit • Hiring for "whole person" match

Contd...

2. Employee participation	• Involvement and empowerment within a contingency framework	• Involvement and empowerment as a universalistic prescription
3. Employee development	• Endorsement of systematic, ongoing education and training • Horizontal career development as an expedient response to vertical blockage	• Endorsement of systematic, ongoing education and training • Horizontal career development as desirable for acquiring a total system orientation
4. Employee performance and recognition	• Assumes that person factors are primary the influence on performance • Assessment of individual differences in performance is always meaningful • Limited attention to recognition rewards • Reliance on individual based incentive pay systems that reinforce short-term, quantity oriented achievement of personal objectives	• Assumes that system factors are the primary influence on performance • Assessment of individual differences in performance is rarely meaningful • Heavy emphasis on recognition rewards • Reliance on team and individual pay systems that reinforce long-term, quantity oriented achievement of organization objectives
5. Employee fulfillment	• Focus on employee work performance, rather than satisfaction, as contributing to organizational effectiveness • Assume, at best, a modest relationship between job satisfaction and work performance	• Emphasize on employee satisfaction as necessary to support continuous improvement and organizational effectiveness • Assume strong correlations among job performance and organizational citizenship behaviour

(***Source***: Adapted from Dean, James W. Jr. and Bowen, David E. (1994): "Management Theory and Total Quality: improving research and practice through theory development." Academy of Management Review, Vol. 19, No.3, pp. 399–403.)

Barriers of Total Quality HRM Practices

The common barriers of total quality HR practices are as follows:

- **Management System Response:** Differences over strategic priorities is often a major corporate barrier that might restrict the HR function in the organization adopt a total quality perspective.
- **Limitations Caused by Inflexibility in the Organizational Structures and Systems:** Resistance to the HRM/senior management strategic perspective from either side can become a barrier to effective implementation of total quality HR practices. Further intensive divisionalization encourages identification with groups, departments or subdivisions rather than the total organization.

- **Cultural Barriers:** An underdeveloped organizational ethical work culture could be also a potent barrier for adopting total quality HR practices. Unrealistic social expectations and organizational norms could also resist people from adopting a total quality HR perspective.
- **Specialization Barrier:** HR specialists who focus on staffing, compensation and benefits, training and development, or other specialities may resist the expansion of role responsibilities beyond the narrow technical areas in terms of adopting a total quality HR approach.
- **Operational Barriers:** HR managers can claim that there is insufficient time to do their jobs and work on job improvement, but that is the total quality operational challenge — to simultaneously do the job and improve the way HR is handled and managed in the organization.
- **Attitudinal Barriers:** Employees may regard total quality as a passing fad which would not work and which focuses attention on internal processes rather than the external results.

Exercise Case Study: China's Lenovo Takes Over IBM PCs

Lenovo, the reputed Chinese computer company now in charge of IBM's legendary PC business said it will waste no time in proving itself in the global market place. In a statement released recently, Lenovo Group said it has completed its $1.25 billion acquisition of IBM's (Quote) "Think" brand, including its ThinkPad laptops, ThinkCentre desktop PCs, ThinkVantage software tools and ThinkVision monitors.

Lenovo's strengths: "Lenovo is well-positioned, with competitive strengths in branding, world-class scale and industry-leading efficiency," Ward said in a statement. "Lenovo's leading R&D and product differentiation capabilities, experienced management team and global distribution network—through our unique alliance with IBM—give us a powerful competitive position in global markets."

Highlights of the M&A: As part of the deal, Lenovo now has its executive headquarters in the city of Purchase, New York, in Westchester County. The company's principal operations would remain in Beijing, China and Raleigh, North Carolina, with R&D facilities in Beijing, Shenzhen, Xiamen, Chengdu, and Shanghai, China; Tokyo, Japan; and Raleigh. Lenovo's primary PC manufacturing and assembly facilities will remain in Shenzhen, Huiyang, Beijing, and Shanghai, China. Lenovo's

Lenovo employee insights: The new Lenovo would be expecting a worldwide workforce of more than 19,000 people who seem to be elated with the deal.

"The closing of this transaction is an historic event for Lenovo and marks a new era for the global PC industry," Yuanqing Yang, Lenovo chairman of the board, said in a statement. "The new Lenovo's strategy is based on what our customers want: high-quality products and world-class service."

Lenovo executives further believed that due to this M&A, the quickest path to transitioning IBM's Think brand lines to Lenovo would come through their procurement and marketing expenses as well as expanding to new markets. The new Lenovo would have combined annual PC revenue of approximately $13 billion and volume of approximately 14 million units.

"We expect to capture synergies starting today through leveraging the complementary nature of Lenovo and PCD's customer bases, product offerings and geographic coverage while utilizing Lenovo's highly sophisticated operating platforms," Ward said in a statement.

The restructuring: As part of the acquisition announcement, Lenovo firmed up its executive management team. As expected, Yang has become chairman of Lenovo succeeding Liu Chuanzhi, Lenovo's founder, who has been named a non-executive director of the board. Ward, previously IBM senior vice president and general manager of IBM's Personal Systems Group, will serve as CEO and as a board member. IBM said it has nominated Bob Moffat and Henry Chow to sit on the Lenovo board as non-voting observers. Moffat is a senior vice president with IBM's Integrated Supply Chain division and also serves as member of the Board of Trustees for The Manufacturing Institute, an educational and research affiliate of the National Association of Manufacturers. Chow is general manager and CEO of IBM in Greater China.

Which Employees of IBM Would be Affected?

- There are approximately 10,000 IBM regular and supplemental employees globally whose employment would transfer to the new Lenovo. Excluded from this transfer would be those who are approved for and receiving benefits under the Medical Disability Income Plan (MDIP) and the Long Term Disability (LTD.) Plan at closing. Those employees currently on pre-retirement bridge leaves of absence would also excluded.
- All employees who are part of IBM's Personal Computing Division (PCD) and whose primary work responsibility is in support of the PCD mission/business.
- Employees in other IBM business units whose primary work responsibility is in support of the PCD mission/business.
- Additional employees deemed necessary to meet the new Lenovo requirements may be selected based upon business need and an assessment of their current job responsibilities.
- Employees defined above who are receiving benefits under the IBM Sickness and Accident Income Plan as well as those on leave of absence will also become employees of the new Lenovo.

New Employment Terms and Conditions

Accordingly, Lenovo will maintain compensation and benefits that are comparable in value in the aggregate to those currently offered by IBM. This guarantee will be extended at least through the end of 2007 and perhaps beyond. This commitment to maintain comparable compensation and benefit value is intended to reassure employees making the transition to the new Lenovo about the level of the company's investment in its human resources and in the future strength of the business.

In the U.S., this means that at the time employees join the new Lenovo, their base salaries will remain the same, and performance bonus opportunity and sales commission plans will provide a substantially similar opportunity. The new Lenovo will also offer comprehensive retirement and health benefits that are comparable to current IBM programme. Generally, IBM employees who join the new Lenovo will receive service credit for benefit purposes. The new Lenovo employees can expect continued professional growth and challenge, along with the opportunity to participate in a new and expanding business venture. Lenovo and IBM are committed to making this a smooth transition that minimizes personal disruptions and loss of work productivity.

Issues Related to Downsizing

As the two company structures are highly complementary, industry experts have commented that there could be the need for rebalancing the new organization and its structure would be minimal. If resource reductions are foreseen, Lenovo had agreed to provide affected employees with severance benefits equal to those provided by IBM, with service credit for employment with both IBM and the new Lenovo.

Compensation and Benefits

Lenovo has agreed that at the time an employee joins the new Lenovo, base salary would remain the same, and current performance bonus targets would be initially maintained for the first year, with new targets established for the new Lenovo thereafter. Incentive and sales commission plans would provide a substantially similar opportunity, with targets based on the objectives of the new Lenovo. Lenovo has also agreed to maintain the same compensation concepts that IBM has used, with key measurements tied to the new Lenovo's business performance and success.

Lenovo had also agreed to offer an overall package of benefits that is comparable in value in the aggregate to the current IBM program. Special provisions and a five-year guarantee apply to pension and savings benefits, as follows:

- **Prior Retirement Formula** under the IBM Personal Pension Plan (Prior Plan)**:** The new Lenovo would deliver comparable pension benefits to Prior Plan participants through a new pension plan (the new Lenovo Pension Plan) that would be established by the new Lenovo.
- **Personal Pension Account (cash balance) formula** under IBM Personal Pension Plan**:** The new Lenovo would deliver comparable benefits to Personal Pension Account participants through a defined contribution plan (the new Lenovo Defined Contribution Plan).
- **Match with IBM Savings Plan:** Lenovo had indicated an intent to continue the current IBM Savings Plan.
- **Health Benefits:** Regarding this aspect, the new Lenovo employees would have immediate access to a comprehensive program of health benefits coverage, with no exclusions or pre-existing condition limitations other than those currently found in IBM's plans. Participants will receive credit for amounts applied to 2005 deductibles, if any.

Issues Related to International Assignments

The new Lenovo had indicated that international assignees would continue in their current assignments until they are completed, and that the terms and conditions currently in place would continue for the assigned duration of the international assignment.

Conclusion: The new Lenovo and its HR policies is expected to reap rich dividends for the organization in its future performance. But to what extent it would be effective would well be worth watching for most academicians and management experts.

Exhibit: The Lenovo SWOT Analysis

Strengths

- National image (China)
- Knowledge about the local market
- Strong R&D
- Mass manufacturing capability
- Quick responsiveness
- Government policies in favour of Industry includes infrastructure development, reduction in excise duty
- Capability of integrating the overseas operations

Weaknesses

- Little knowledge about Indian market
- Poor brand perception (global)
- No pure electronics sales
- Low inventory turnover
- After sales services are not adequate
- Limited knowledge of global market

Opportunities

- Import barrier
- Increasing global demand

- Internet boom
- Growing wireless PC/Notepad/Thinkpad/Laptop market
- Government association

Threats

- Heavy competition from global counterparts
- Industry reaching maturity
- Software piracy and clone market in China
- Little firm's growth

(*Courtesy: http://www.bracuniversity.net/nbc/06/findu.pdf*)

Mutsuddi, I., Mutsuddi, R., (2008): "Has the growth of Indian conglomerates been a threat to foreign multinationals", ICFAI Journal of marketing management, Vol. VII, No. 3, August 2008, pp. 52–53.

Questions for analysis

1. Discuss the HR challenges associated with this take over.
2. What factors do you think had ensured effective amalgamation of these two organizations?
3. What future challenges could lay ahead this new amalgamation?

REFERENCES

1. http://www.allianceibm.org/hr_us_qa.pdf
2. Legnick-Hall, C.A, Legnick-Hall, M.L. (1988), "Strategic Human Resources Management: A Review of the Literature and a Proposed Typology", *Academy of Management Review*, Vol. 13 No.3, pp.454–70.
3. Jackson, S.E. and Schuler, R.S. (1995): "Understanding Human Resource Management in the Context of Organizations and their Environments". *Annual Review of Psychology*, 46, 237–264.
4. Boxall, P., (2003): "HR Strategy and Competitive Advantage in the Service Sector", Human Resource Management Journal, Vol. 13, No. 3, pp. 5–20.
5. Dyer, L., & Holder, J. (1988): "A Strategic Perspective of Human Resource Management"; In L. Dyer (Ed.) *Human Resource Management: Evolving Roles and Responsibilities:* 1–35. Washington, DC: American Society for Personnel Administration/Bureau of National Affairs.
6. Devanna, M., Fombrun, C. and Tichy, C. (1984): "A Framework for Strategic Human Resource Management". In Fombrun, C., Tichy, C. and Devanna, M. (Eds) *Strategic Human Resource Management*. New York: Wiley, pp. 33–51.
7. Beer, M., B. Spector, P.R. Lawrence, D. Quinn Mills and R.E. Walton (1984): "*Managing Human Assets*", N.Y., The Free Press.
8. Dyer, L., Shafer, R. (1999): "Creating Organizational Agility: Implications for Strategic Human Resource Management", in Wright, P., Dyer, L., Boudreau, J., Milkovich, G. (Eds), *Research in Personnel and Human Resource Management*, JAI Press, Stamford, CT and London, (Supplement 4: Strategic Human Resource Management in the Twenty First Century).
9. Arthur, J.B. (1994): "Effects of Human Resource Systems on Manufacturing Performance and Turnover"; *Academy of Management Journal,* 37, 670–687.

10. Delery, J., & Doty, D.H. (1996): "Modes of Theorizing in Strategic Human Resource Management: Tests of Universalistic, Contingency and Configurational Performance Predictions", *Academy of Management Journal,* 39 (4), 802–35.

11. MacDuffie, J.P. (1995): "Human Resource Bundles and Manufacturing Performance: Flexible Production Systems in the World Auto Industry". *Industrial Relations and Labour Review,* 48, 197–221.

12. Youndt, M., Snell, D.A., Dean, J.W. and Lepak, D.P. (1996): "Human Resource Management, Manufacturing Strategy, and Firm Performance". *Academy of Management Journal,* 39(4), 836–66.

13. Ichniowski, Casey, Kathryn Shaw and Giovanna Prennushi (1997): "The Effects of Human Resource Management Practices on Productivity: A Study of Steel Finishing Lines," American Economic Review, Vol. 87, pp. 291–313.

14. Wright, G., & Sherman, R. (1999): "Let's Create a Comic Strip" *Reading Improvement*, 36(2), 66–72.

15. Becker, B. E. & Huselid, M. A. (1999): "Overview: Strategic Human Resource Management in Five Leading Firms"; Human Resource Management Journal, 38, (4), Winter, 287–301.

16. Pfeffer, J., (1998): "The Human Equation: Building Profits by Putting People First", Harvard Business School Press (Boston), p. 345.

17. Appelbaum, E., Bailey, T., Berg, P. and Kalleberg, A. (2000): "*Manufacturing Advantage: Why High Performance Work Systems Pay Off*" , ILR Press, Ithaca, New York, 2000.

18. MacDuffe, J.P. (1995): "Human Resource Bundles and Manufacturing Performance: Organizational Logic and Flexible Production Systems in the World Auto Industry", Industrial and Labour Relations Review, 48(2): 197–221.

19. Batt, R. (2002): "Managing Customer Services: Human Resource Practices, Quit Rates, and Sales Growth". *Academy of Management Journal,* 45: 587–597.

20. Weick, K.E., Sutcliffe, K.M., and Obstfeld, D. (1999): "Organizing for High Reliability: Processes of Collective Mindfulness"; In B.M. Staw & R. Sutton (Eds.), *Research in Organizational Behaviour,* Vol. 23: 81–123. Greenwich, CT: JAI Press.

21. Weick, K.E. and Sutcliffe, K.M. (2001): "*Managing the Unexpected*". San Francisco: Jossey-Bass.

22. Roberts, K.H. & Bea, R. (2001b): "When Systems fail"; *Organizational Dynamics*, 29: 179–191.

23. Vaughan, D. (1999): "The Dark Side of Organizations: Mistake, Misconduct, and Disaster"; *Annual Review of Sociology*, 25: 271–305.

24. Roberts, K.H. Stout, S.K. and Halpern, J.J. (1994): "Decision Dynamics in Two High Reliability Military Organizations"; *Management Science*, 40: 614–624.

25. Roberts, K.H. and Bea, R. (2001a): "Must Accidents Happen? Lessons from High Reliability Organizations". *Academy of Management Executive*, 16: 70–78.

26. Kossek, E. E., 1987. Human Resource Management Innovation. *Human Resource Management Journal*, 26(1): 71–92.

27. Kossek, E. E., 1989. The Acceptance of Human Resources Innovation by Multiple Constituencies. *Personnel Psychology*, 42: 263–281.

28. Ulrich, D., (1997): "Human Resource Champions: The Next Agenda for Adding Value and Delivering Results"; Harvard Business School Press (Boston), p. 281.

29. Mutsuddi, I., Mutsuddi, R., (2008): "Has the Growth of Indian Conglomerates been a Threat to Foreign Multinationals", ICFAI Journal of Marketing Management, Vol. 7, No. 3, August 2008, pp. 52–53.

QUESTION BANK

1. A firm's strategic HR choices cover the entire range of HR functions. Explain the strategic choices a company has regarding workflows, staffing, performance appraisal, training and development.
2. What is strategic management? Describe the steps involved in the process of strategic management.
3. What is strategic HRM? What are its components? What are the concerns and focus areas of SHRM?
4. Define SHRM. What are the aims of SHRM?
5. What is the role of SHRM in ensuring effective human capital management?
6. What is the importance of HR in an organization's strategic planning?
7. Describe a model of SHRM.
8. What is the contribution of SHRM in business performance?
9. Distinguish between traditional HR practices and SHRM.
10. What are the barriers of SHRM? How can they be removed?
11. Categorize HR strategies and mention what are the factors which influence such HR strategies?
12. What do you mean by high performance work systems? Describe their characteristics. What is the role of an organization's HR function in developing a high performance work system?
13. What is the role of HR professionals in SHRM?
14. What are the roles HR professionals in the changing business environment?
15. What are the HR issues influencing mergers and acquisitions?
16. What is the role of total quality in HR practices?
17. What are the barriers of Total Quality in HR practices?
18. What is the benefit of having a strategic HR approach in today's organizations? How does it provide competitive advantage to organizations?

Internet Exercises

- Visit the website www.shrm.org and share your learnings with your friends.
- Collect the highlights of the HR policy of an organization of your choice from the internet and make a presentation to your class. Add your own comments and analysis.
- Collect the pictures of eminent CEOs/HR leaders in reputed organizations, study their profiles and present to your class their contributions in their respective organizations.
- Use internet resources (specially surfing job portals and newspapers like Times Ascent) to prepare a presentation on various job openings/career options available as HR professionals in reputed organizations. List what are the desired qualities and experience levels required for such positions.

Games

- Two students are required in this game. Imagine that both of you are the VP-HR of your respective organizations. Recently your companies have decided to go for a 50-50 joint venture. Now in this role play session you are supposed to hold a meeting to discuss the terms and conditions of the joint venture in terms of managing your human resources. Time limit: 6 mins
- Suppose you are the HR manager of your company. Your organization had promised to give bonus to all the employees during the coming festivals. Your CEO due to some unavoidable circumstances had withheld this decision. Prepare an action plan in 5 mins and present to the class.

INTERNATIONAL HUMAN RESOURCE MANAGEMENT

THEME CASE: CRISIS IN THE CITIGROUP

Joseph Bipin* was reading the economic times and was shocked to find, "Citigroup had planned to cut thousands of trading and investment banking jobs this week, part of previously reported plans to slash about 10% of its investment bank division". Joseph, who had been working for one of the investment banking divisions in India as a senior regional manager, sales and promotions was about to fly next Friday to the States for a six month project assignment was obvious to be shaken by the news. This was not only the case of Joseph, it meant a lot for employees working in the various international divisions of the respective organization.

The crisis ahead: According to confirmed sources, the Citigroup had planned to slash thousands of jobs, which would mean that 10% of its 65,000 investment bank staff would be facing loss of jobs. Inspite of still being the largest US bank, with a US $ 5.1 first-quarter loss in April, Citibank has been reported not to increase the number of job cuts from about 6,500. The entire group, which has more than 3,50,000 employees globally, had reduced its workforce by about 9,000 employees through the end of March. And now the situation seems to be so grave that it could also involve the departures of several senior managing directors.

HR@Citigroup

Citigroup's Human Resource Division is the leader in its field and has experts in all areas of the Human Resource function. Citigroup's HR function works as a partner with all its businesses to recruit, manage and develop the company's most important asset: its people. The company had emphasized upon putting tremendous efforts to develop and manage its policies so as to ensure that it is in line with its core values and also comply with regulatory demands. Thus over the years Citigroup had been able to offer its employees a harmonious and dynamic environment to work in. Citigroup employees are aligned by function covering the broad spectrum of human resource management including the following:

Compensation and benefits: The company's compensation and benefit package comprises of compensation, benefits, relocation, tax, deferred compensation and pensions. HR specialists develop and implement compensation strategies to ensure that the organization is being able to offer and execute some of the most effective compensation plans in the industry. The HR professionals at Citigroup work with all its businesses to provide strategies that are seamless and fully integrated solutions. They also deliver high quality and easy to use benefit, pensions and relocation services to all the employees in the organization.

Resourcing function: Citigroup's "Professional Resourcing team" provides key recruitment strategies for implementation at all levels across the company. They have a strong graduate recruitment team who work in partnership with the businesses to recruit the most talented graduates in the market. The company's "Permanent Resourcing team" supports all its businesses with their lateral hiring needs and lastly the "Senior hiring specialists" work with managers in hiring the future business heads and leaders of the company. The company's "Temporary Resourcing" function provides temporary workers and contractors to all Citigroup businesses and divisions.

Training and development function: The company's Training and Development specialists develop and execute leading edge programme across the banking industry. They are specialists in the development of people and work with the organization's key businesses to ensure continuous training and development of talents at all levels across the company.

Generalist functions: The HR Generalists support specific businesses and act as partners in the decision-making and planning processes of the organization. They support the line managers on a range of issues and processes, essential in the successful management of all people in the organization.

Diversity management: The Diversity team is pre-eminent in developing diversity strategies within the banking industry. They direct and inspire a vision of openness and participative work culture in the organization.

Employment relations and policy: HR department at Citigroup also works diligently so as to develop and implement policies and procedures in line with best practice and current legislative frameworks in order to maintain healthy employee relations at the workplace[11].

Challenges ahead: Inspite of having a very effective HR practice and a diligent management to lead the organization, it is worth watching how the HR function of the Citigroup would manage this organizational restructuring.

*(Courtesy: Economic Times, Bangalore, 24th June, 2008; *Joseph Bipin is an imaginery character having no resemblance to any person living or dead working in the company. The character has been created to do justice with the case.)*

Introduction to Multinational Organizations

Multinational organizations are primarily located and managed from the country of origin, but diffuse the production of goods and services throughout the world to serve local markets with subsidiaries that operate relatively autonomously (Barlett & Ghoshal, 1989)[14]. Multinational organizations are typically characterized by their cultural, social and political diversity (Harzing and Ruysseveldt, 1995)[15]. They seldom see themselves as being in competition with other countries, but rather as serving a profitable market wherever they exist. Industries producing branded packaged goods (such as food, softdrinks, clothing, electronic appliances and even services like retailing, banking etc.) are good examples of multinational organizations (Beamish et al., 1991)[16].

Table 1.8: Strategy, Structure, Knowledge and Skills in MNCs in Comparison to Global, International and Transnational Organizations (Adapted from Barlett & Ghoshal, 1989)

Hallmarks	***MNC***	***Global corporation***	***International organization***	***Transnational organization***
1. Strategic focus	National responsiveness To meet local needs products and services are differentiated	High efficiency Identification of low cost production locations and high skill—R&D locations	Transfer of new technology from home country to foreign countries Prime importance on the development and diffusion of innovations	Locally responsive Globally efficient Emphasis on continuous innovation
2. Organizational structure	Decentralized	Managed from home country	Flexible decentralization	Coordination of interdependent units both nationally and worldwide High flexibility Diversity Complexity
3. Knowledge and skills	Country specific skills and knowledge	Global standardization Centralized knowledge of R&D, production, purchasing and marketing	Leverage central core competencies into national markets	Develop, transfer and diffuse knowledge and skills from wherever found

What is International Human Resource Management?

Broadly defined, international human resource management (IHRM) is the process of procuring, allocating, and effectively utilizing human resources in a multinational corporation. If the MNC is simply exporting its products, with only a few small offices in foreign locations, then the task of the international HR manager is relatively simple. However, in global firms human resource managers must achieve two somewhat conflicting strategic objectives. First, they must integrate human resource policies and practices across a number of subsidiaries in different countries so that overall corporate objectives can be achieved. At the same time, the approach to HRM must be sufficiently flexible to allow for significant differences in the type of HR policies and practices that are most effective in different business and cultural settings.

Organizations like Procter & Gamble, IBM, Pepsi and Coca Cola have had extensive International experience and their success can only be attributed to their capability of constantly deploying the right people at the right place, facilitating knowledge and innovation dissemination and constantly identifying and developing talents on a global basis. Thus for Ford which has a global HR perspective "The company requires understanding different cultures, what motivates people from different societies, and how they are reflected in the structure of international assignments".

Morgan's Model of IHRM

Morgan (1986) had developed an unique model to depict how IHRM works. He asserted that IHRM basically is comprised of three components, namely,

- The wide spectrum of HR activities particularly with reference to the added responsibilities of the international HR managers in terms of managing cultural diversity and developing international executives.
- The National/Country specific people and cultural categories involved in IHR activities and lastly
- Types of international employees deployed in various international organizations (Dowling & Welch, 2007).

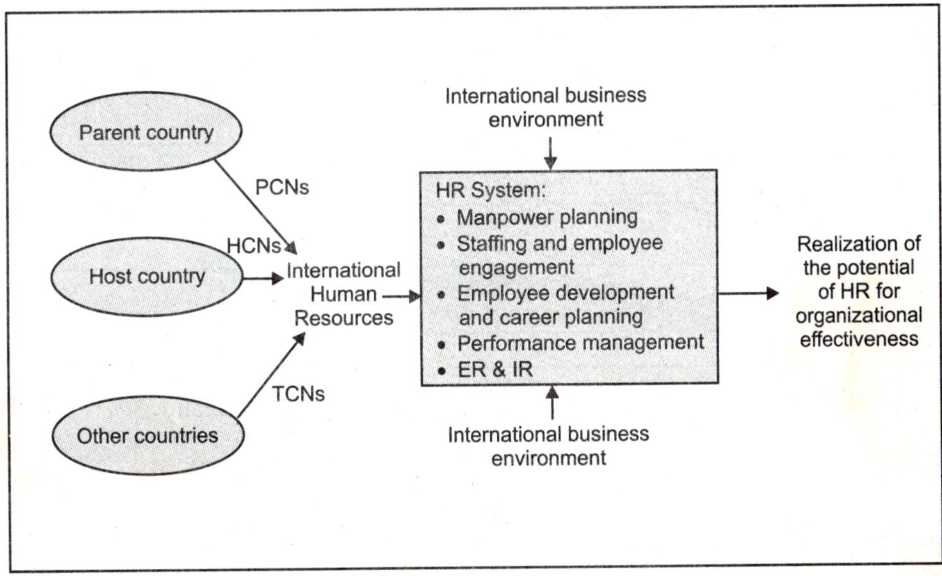

Fig. 1.37: A model of IHRM

(Inspired from P.V. Morgan, International Human Resource Management, Fact or Fiction. Personnel Administrator, Vol. 31, No. 1986, p. 44)

HR activities: The HR activities on an International perspective can be broadly depicted as those of procurement, allocation and utilization of human resources in the organization. These activities include international human resource planning, staffing (recruitment, selection, induction and placement), performance management, training and development, compensation and reward management and managing international employee relations and industrial relations. These HR activities with respect to an international scenario have a broad spectrum mainly in terms of the complexity created by country differences, level of control, cultural differences and so many factors influencing the international business environment.

Industry Opinion

"Moving a manager from New York to California could be tougher than moving someone Delhi to Chennai." … Ayoyendra Mukherjee, Global Head-HR, TCS.

(*Courtesy: Indian management, July 2008, Vol. 47, Issue: 7, p. 20.*)

Country categories involved in IHRM: The model further depicts that in an international perspective three types of country categories may be involved, namely:

- The host country where the subsidiary could be located or be operating.
- The home country where the MNC/International firm could be headquartered.
- The "third-country" from where employees, capital and other resources like technology or logistics could be availed or procured by the organization.

Employee categories involved in IHRM: Depending on the above country categories, the employees in an international perspective could be broadly classified as under:

- Host Country Nationals (HCNs) representing the employees hired from the host country.
- Parent Country Nationals (PCNs) representing the employees expatriated to the foreign subsidiary from the home country of the MNC.
- Third Country Nationals (TCNs) representing the employees deployed from third/other countries other than that of the home country of the MNC.

Table 1.9: Comparison of Advantages in Sources Overseas Managers

HCNs	*PCNs*	*TCNs*
Less cost	Talent available within the company	Broad experience
Preference of host country governments	Greater control	International outlook
Intimate knowledge of environment and culture	Company experience Mobility	Multilingualism
Language facility	Experience provided to corporate executives	

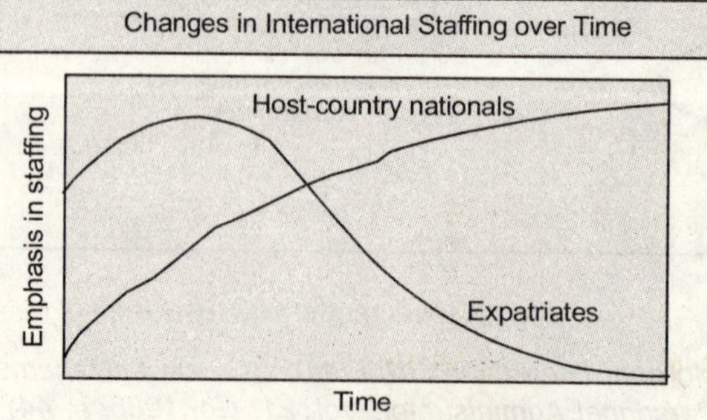

Fig. 1.38: Changes in international staffing over time

The above figure shows that, at early stages of international expansion organizations tend to have a high need for expatriates as most international business ventures might not have the right human resources at the right time. Lack of presence in a particular region or country might also influence dependency on PCNs. With the establishment of the business and subsequent proliferation and expansion of international subsidiaries, most multinationals tend to depend on local talents (HCNs) or even depute specialists from other countries (TCNs) for a project or assignment. This is why the above figure depicts a slowdown in the inflow of expatriates and rise in HCNs in international ventures.

IHRM Practices Compared with Domestic HR Practices

A multinational corporation's HR practices vary from firm to firm and the nature of business it does in the context of the international scenario. It also depends on whether the manager is located in a global corporation's headquarters or onsite in a foreign subsidiary. This problem of balancing integration (control and coordination from HQ) and differentiation (flexibility in policies and practices at the local subsidiary level) have long been acknowledged as common dilemmas facing HR and other functional managers in global corporations. Although some argue that IHRM is not unlike HRM in a domestic setting, others point out that there are significant differences. Specifically compared with domestic HRM, IHRM has the following features, namely:

- IHRM encompasses more HR functions (like more involvement in employee's personal lives, focus on diversity training, cross cultural assimilation etc.)
- IHRM involves more heterogeneous functions
- It involves constantly changing perspectives
- It requires more involvement in employees' personal lives
- IHRM is influenced by more external sources
- It involves a greater level of risk than typical domestic HRM.
- Emphasis put on HR activities changed when workforce mix varies

Wider Spectrum of HR Functions

When compared with domestic human resource management, IHRM requires a much wider spectrum on even the most common HR activities. This is particularly so for HR managers operating from a MNC's headquarters. The number and variety of IHRM activities are daunting. International HR managers must deal with issues as varied as international taxation; international relocation and orientation; various other administrative services for expatriates; selecting, training and appraising local and international employees; and managing relations with host governments in a number of countries around the world. Other relevant issues might involve those of (a) international taxation and legal obligations, (b) International relocation and orientation, (c) providing special or additional administrative services for the expatriates, (d) managing host government relations and (e) statutory/legal compliance management etc. A final aspect of the broader scope of IHRM is that the organization needs to deal with people with different cultural backgrounds. The HR manager must coordinate policies and procedures to manage expatriates from the firm's home country parent country nationals, (PCNs), host-country nationals (HCNs), as well as third country nationals (TCNs, e.g., a French manager working for an American MNC in the firm's Nigerian subsidiary) in subsidiaries around the world. The HR manager must develop HR systems

Fig. 1.39: Managing a multi-cultural workforce is one of the greatest challenges of IHRM

that are not only acceptable to the host country but also compatible with company-wide systems being developed by the HQ-based officer. These policies and practices must effectively balance the needs and desires of local employees, PCNs and TCNs.

More heterogeneous HR activities: Even when dealing with one particular HR function area such as compensation, the international HR manager is faced with a great variety of national and international pay issues. For example, while dealing with pay issues, the HQ-based HR manager must coordinate pay systems in different countries with different currencies that may change in relative value to one another over time. An American expatriate in Tokyo who receives a salary of $100,000 may suddenly find the buying power of that salary dramatically diminished if the Japanese yen strengthens in value relative to the US dollar. A US dollar purchased 248 yen in 1985, but less than 110 yen in 2000. In the case of fringe benefits provided to host company employees, some interesting complications might arise. For instance, it is common in the United States to provide health insurance benefits to employees and the employee's family, which usually means spouse and children. In some countries however, the term "family" may include a more extended group of relatives—multiple spouses, aunts, uncles, grandparents, nephews and nieces. One important decision which most HR managers need to take at the International level is to determine the right mix of their employees deployed for an international assignment.

Fig. 1.40: Dr. Santrupt Misra, Group HR Head, Aditya Birla (Picture (*Courtesy: http:/ www.adityabirla.com/ the_group/images/Dr-Santrupt_misra_new01.jpg*)

Exhibit: Aditya Birla Group's Global Talent Management Model

In an interview with a reputed business journal, Dr. Santrupt Misra, Group HR Head, Aditya Birla Group, commented, "Our way is a combination of geocentric and polycentric. There is an Aditya Birla way that we implement but we adapt to it to local conditions where necessary. In HR terms, a very simple example is that the performance appraisal method will be common everywhere. But compensations will be different, in line with the company's social security and taxation laws. Likewise, the reporting structure may be tuned to a geography where there is a sharp perceived differentiation between management and non-management cadres, for example in India and Europe. And there are regions like the US and South East Asian countries where the differentiation is not as sharp. So we will adapt to that.

(*Courtesy: Indian Management, Vol. 47, Issue: 7, July 2008, p. 22.*)

Advantages	Disadvantages
• Lower labour costs • Demonstrates trust in local citizenry • Increases acceptance of the company by the local community • Maximizes the number of options available in the local environment • Leads to recognition of the company as a legitimate participant in the local economy • Effectively represents local considerations and constraints in the decision-making process	• Makes it difficult to balance local demands and global priorities • Leads to postponement of difficult local decisions until they are unavoidable, when they are more difficult, costly, and painful than they would have been if implemented earlier • May make it difficult to recruit qualified personnel • May reduce the amount of control exercised by headquarters

Fig. 1.41: Advantages and disadvantages of using local employees to staff international subsidiaries (Gomez-Mejia, Balkin, Cardy, 1995: "Managing Human Resources", PHI)

Advantages	Disadvantages
• Cultural similarity with parent company ensures transfer of business/management practices • Permits closer control and coordination of international subsidiaries • Gives employees a multinational orientation through experience at parent company • Establishes a pool of internationally experienced executives	• Creates problems of adaptability to foreign environment and culture • Increases the »foreigness« of the subsidiary • May involve high transfer and salary costs • May result in personal and family problems • Leads to high failure rate • Has disincentive effect on local-management morale and motivation • May be subject to local government restrictions

Fig. 1.42: Advantages and disadvantages of using expatriate employees to staff international subsidiaries (Gomez-Mejia, Balkin, Cardy, 1995: "Managing Human Resources", PHI)

More Involvement into Employee's Personal Lives

It is at the subsidiary level that the increased involvement of IHRM in the personal lives of employees becomes particularly apparent. It is not unusual for subsidiary HR managers to be involved in arranging housing, healthcare, transportation, education, and recreation activities for expatriate and local staff.

IHRM activities are also influenced by a greater number of external forces than are domestic HR activities. The HQ-based manager may have to set equal employment opportunity (EEO) policies that meet the legal requirements of both the home country and a number of host countries. Because of the visibility that foreign firms tend to have in host countries (especially in developing countries), subsidiary HR managers may have to deal with ministers, other political figures, and a great variety of social and economic interest groups than would normally be encountered in a purely domestic HRM.

Such involvement into employee's personal lives may arise from the necessity of (a) selecting, training and effective management of expatriates on foreign assignments, (b) providing accommodation, health care and compensation package, Banking investments and home rental services etc.

Various factors which moderate the differences between domestic and international HRM are as follows:

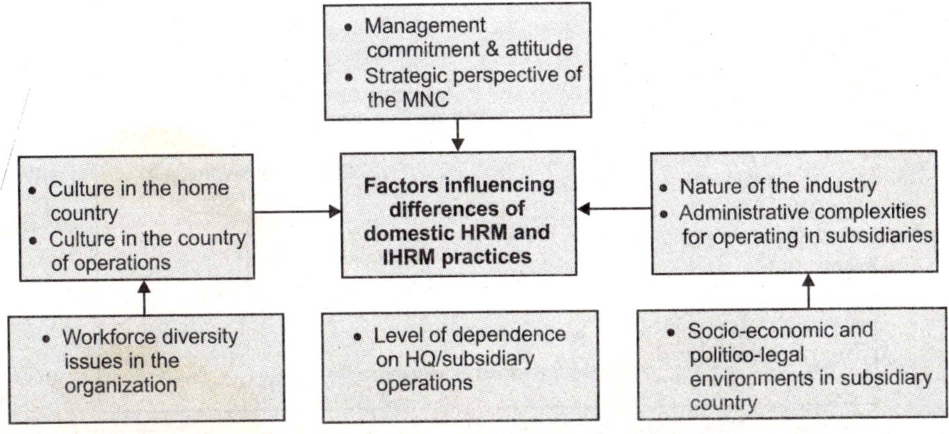

Fig. 1.43: Factors moderating the differences between domestic and international HRM

What is Expatriation?

Expatriation can be described as a foreign assignment given to an employee of a MNC or international organization where the individual has to operate in a foreign country/subsidiary away from the home country. In this regard these employees are described as "**expatriates**". Thus expatriates are employees who are working and temporarily residing in a foreign country for the purpose of an international assignment or project. For this reason many authors have also described expatriates as '**international assignees**'. Thus expatriates could be in the form of PCNs i.e. from the parent country operations, TCNs transferred to either HQ or another subsidiary, and HCNs transferred into the parent country.

The international assignment can be principally described as a cyclical process as depicted by the following figure. It starts with the recruitment and selection of the expatriate followed by hiring, and thorough training and development for the international assignment. This preparation stage leads to expatriation. The subsequent stages follow a typical cyclical pattern leading to either completion of the foreign assignment and repatriation.

Theme Reading: Expatriation the Bengaluru Experience

Expatriates experience a very different work environment in the city as compared to the culture back at home. There are hundreds of expatriates working across the various offices Bengaluru. A major chunk of them work in the MNCs which have become important hubs for outsourcing in the country today. But, is the work environment in the city similar to that of their native countries had been a daunting question for corporates. The US based MNCs in the city follow traditional American work culture, which make some expatriates feel at home with their work. According to Monika Nikore, an American employee with AOL, "I don't find a huge difference working with Indians as the work environment is very similar to that of the US. This is because American work conditions are followed here. One of the differences I can point out is that most Indians are not as outspoken as their American counterparts. But there are a few differences which can be attributed to the geographical and cultural factors. The office jokes back at home speak a lot of politics, life and culture there whereas here in India they are more Indian context based. Also, here in Bengaluru everything runs on schedule and people are really hard working, which is amazing." Carryme M. an Iranian expatriate, who worked with the Cloth Fashion Management, feels the difference in the work environment of the city based companies. He says, "It's initially difficult to adjust to the Indian work system which is very different from that of theMiddle East. There are more rules and regulations at office here than back in Iran. One has to get used to this to survive here. You basically have to work hard to counter the cut throat competition.

Contd...

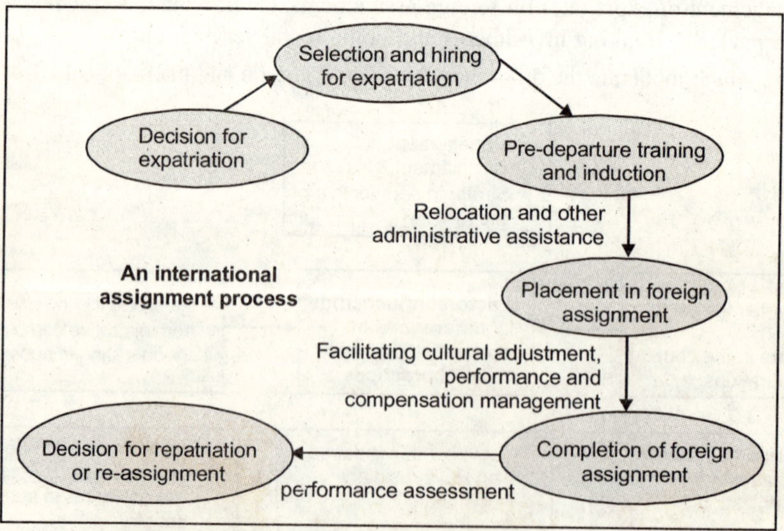

Fig. 1.44: International assignment process

Though language and communication is not a major problem with so many cultural differences it's very tough for a foreigner to adjust". Laura Navarro who taught Spanish language at "The Language Centre" says, I noticed that Indians are more open to learning a new language than others".

On an overall working in a cosmopolitan city as that of Bengaluru is an experience by itself.

(Courtesy: Kundu, R., (2008): "The Office Blues", Deccan Chronicle, Expats, Sunday, 31st August, 2008, p. 35)

Once the international assignment is over the employee may be repatriated (relocated or redeployed in the home country) back to his home country. In this context each step during the expatriation process, before and after can have considerable impacts on the behaviour and orientation in an expatriate. As revealed in the following figure the stay of an expatriate in an international assignment can be categorized before, during and after the international assignment. The problems that might be associated during an international assignment could be due to language problems, lack of cultural adjustments, and lack of support from the management as well as incapability of the family members of the expatriate to get adjusted with the new socio-cultural environment in the organization.

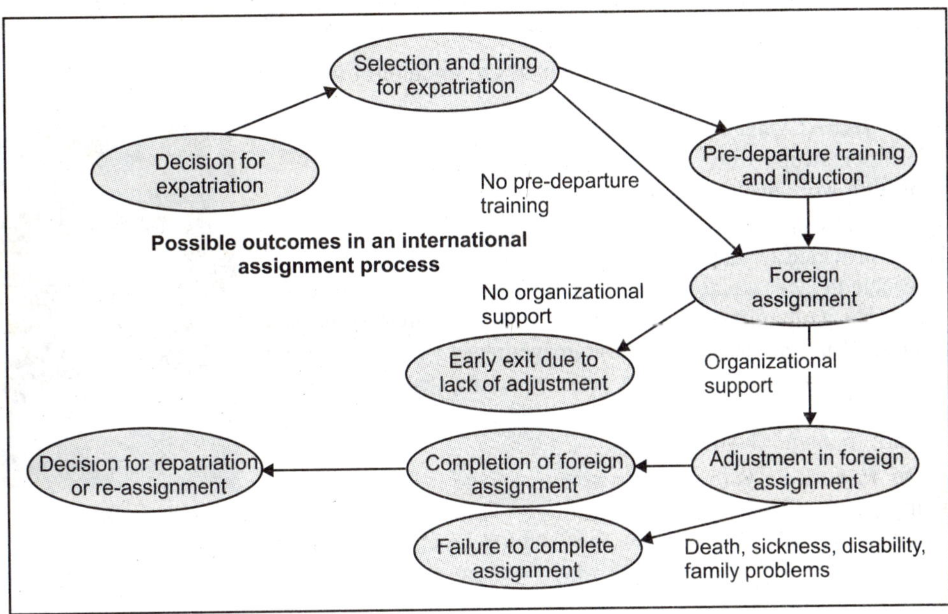

Fig. 1.45: Possible outcomes of an international assignments

Cross cultural adjustment and diversity management: Hence, it is evident that for the success of any international assignment, cross cultural adjustment is crucial for the success if any expatriate. Lack of cultural adjustment leads to apathy, depression, frustration and may influence the expatriate to either resign or demand for an early repatriation. **Repatriation** involves the reentry of the expatriate into the home country from his/her foreign assignment which is mainly associated with what is known as "reentry shock" or reverse cultural shock, that happens when an individual starts his international assignment. The phases of cultural adjustment can be described as a four stage process, namely:

***Cultural sensitivity*:** In every organization it is important that a certain internal sensitivity or awareness develops with respect to the various cultural differences (cultural diversity) within the global concern which is often known as cultural sensitivity. In other words, it can be said that cultural sensitivity is an awareness of cultural differences that is essential for the HR manager at the corporate headquarters as well as in the host location (Tung, 1993)[13]. So as to decide upon activities such as hiring, promoting, rewarding etc. which could be determined by the practices of the host country and based on the value system peculiar to that country's culture. It has been claimed by Tung (1993) that cultural sensitivity could not only be essential and crucial internally but externally to the organization located internationally.

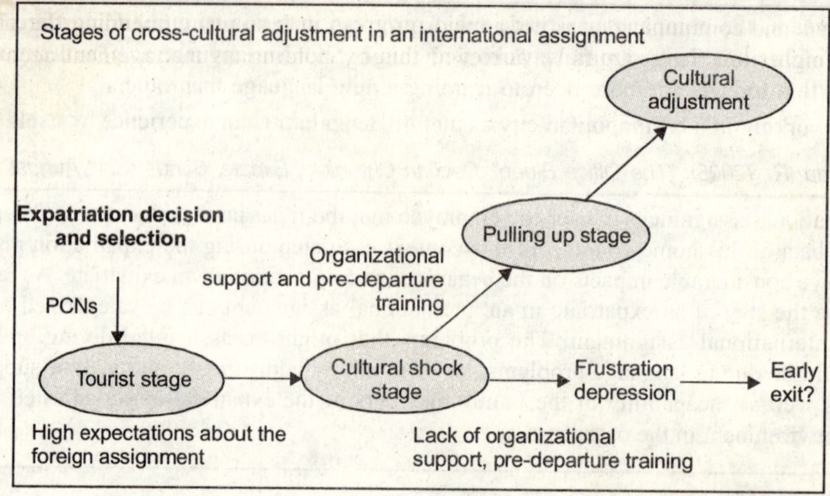

Fig. 1.46: Stages of cross-cultural adjustment

***Stage 1 or Tourist Stage*:** This stage is characterized by expatriates having high expectations from their international assignments or the probability of high work status and enrichment of life style.

***Stage 2 or Cultural Shock Stage*:** This stage is characterized by the "reality-shock" provided by the workplace in a foreign country which is caused mainly due to lack of adjustment with the local culture, habits and language which has its impact on the performance of the individual in the foreign location. If not supported by the management or by the family members, the individual can go into a stage of acute depression and stress which might lead him/her to either quit the job or demand for a premature return to his/her home country.

Fig. 1.47: Expatriate jraining

***Stage 3 or Pulling up Stage*:** If the previous stage is supported by proper training, support from the management and family members, the individual may considerably recover from the "cultural shock/stress". This ultimately leads to the "Pulling up" stage where the candidate makes an effort to recover from the cultural shock and stress. This phase could be slow or incremental depending on the nature of social and organizational support received by the expatriate.

***Stage 4 or Adjustment Stage*:** This stage involves the recovery stage when the candidate gets habituated/adjusted with the local culture and work environment. This stage is characterized by steady performance and development of individual capabilities.

Fig. 1.48: International assignments provide a wider career opportunity

Exhibit: Diversity Management in Citigroup

One of the most important elements of Citigroup's leadership has been its longstanding commitment to diversity. For Citigroup employees, it is a culture where the best people want to work, where people are promoted on their merits, where the organization treats each other with dignity and respect, and where opportunities to develop are widely available to all—regardless of all sorts of cultural differences in people.

Over the years, the company has made great progress in terms of embedding the principles of diversity and inclusion. Citigroup have achieved this by holding its management accountable, by strengthening its efforts to attract and develop talent, and by creating innovative programme for the employees to share an even greater sense of pride and fulfillment in their individual or team-based endeavours. Some of these initiatives involve those of:

- The senior managers are committed to develop diversity plans and review their progress on an on going basis with the organization's Board of Directors.
- Citigroup ensured that the organization continued to attract top diverse talent through core partnerships.
- The company launched a global initiative on flexible work systems by developing a common set of guidelines, tools, and resources through which employees and managers can consider and strengthen their flexible work strategies.
- The company also took initiatives so as to reinforce its diversity efforts with its business partners by creating opportunities among affinity markets.

Role of Citigroup's diversity councils: Citigroup's 24 diversity councils are fundamental to the successful implementation of the organization's overall diversity strategy. The Citigroup diversity operating council is made up of senior diversity and HR leaders from core businesses and regions. It meets biweekly so as to review the progress of their strategy, share best practices, align policies globally, develop and execute initiatives. These councils focus on gender issues along with other dimensions of diversity, such as disability, ethnicity, race, or sexual orientation. The Global Consumer Group and Corporate and Investment Banking diversity councils in India were among the new councils launched recently.

(*Courtesy: Citigroup website*[12])

THEME READING: THE TEN COMMITMENTS OF CULTURAL DIVERSITY

- ***Clarify the motivation***: There must be a strong business case for diversity issues.
- ***Clarify the vision***: The aim of diversity programme should be to tap the full potential of every person in the workforce.
- ***Expand the focus***: Diversity should go beyond race, gender, creed and ethnicity to include background, education, function and personality differences.
- ***Audit the corporate culture***: Culture building is a key part of any diversity initiative.
- ***Modify the assumptions***: Every time changes are made, the culture may resist them.
- ***Modify systems***: The systems should not just be optimal but also work for all employees.
- ***Modify models***: Mental models should not stand in the way.
- ***Tell people they are pioneers***: Implementing diversity initiatives involves change management. People should be judged as pioneers, not as seasoned practitioners.
- ***Ask some key questions***: Does this program, policy or principle give special consideration to one group? Will it only produce benefits for a disadvantaged group? If the answer is yes, many more challenges remain to be addressed.
- ***Continue affirmative action***: The ultimate goal is to manage the company without any unnatural advantage or disadvantage for a member of the workplace. But affirmative action may be needed initially to have a truly diverse workforce.

(Courtesy: R Roosevelt Thomas Jr., (1998): "Making Diversity pay off", leader to leader, Winter.)

THEME READING: MCDONALD'S COMMITMENT TO WORKFORCE DIVERSITY

McDonald's commitment to diversity is well established on the foundational belief that diversity is not just a moral and ethical issue, but also a business issue (McDonald's, 2005)[18]. Due to the global expanse of McDonald's business, diversity has become an integral part of the internal company culture. McDonald's has over 30,000 restaurants around the world, which means franchise owner/operators, employees, and customers represent just about every culture, religion or ethnicity on earth. In addition, McDonald's promotes the use of local suppliers and based on their policies of diversity, expects and retains suppliers that have a similar diversity culture. Knowing and understanding the local customs and traditions of the communities where McDonald's has established businesses, integrating people from these communities into the company, and adapting locally to the tastes and cuisines of the community, has made McDonald's the leader in their industry.

In the United States alone, McDonald's has won numerous awards and received national recognition for diversity. According to McDonald's website, www.mcdonalds.com, awards include; PUSH-Excel Corporate Partner Award, Corporate Achievement and Image Award, Nullities Corporate Award, Corporate Vision Award, and the Circle of Inclusion Award. These awards and recognitions are not the result of a surface attempt to appease the critics. They are the result of McDonald's embracing and integrating diversity into their company ethos as an asset and an ally.

McDonald's realizes that having diversity as an asset greatly enhances the profitability of the company. Diversity is a direct reflection of a company's interpersonal relationships. These relationships, if positive, result in a rewarding venture. Conversely, if the relationships are negative, the company's morale declines and if not addressed, leads to the deterioration of the company. This deterioration directly impacts the company's income and the community's acceptance of the business. However, McDonald's leadership encourages diversity through their policies and programme. McDonald's proven success with leveraging the advantages of diversity can be attributed to their core value of ethics. McDonald's success is built on the foundation of personal and professional integrity (www.mcdonalds.com). From the beginning, McDonald's has based its reputation on trust and dependability, and their commitment to the community made them a household name. Founder Ray Kroc, believed in giving something back to the community in order to make the world a better place. Throughout the 1970's, McDonald's became involved with a lot of charity work. In 1974 established a charity called Ronald McDonald House. The purpose of this program was to provide temporary housing for the families of seriously ill children receiving treatment at nearby hospitals. Since the 70s, more than 10 million families around the world benefited from the comfort provided by Ronald McDonald Houses (www.rhmc).

(*Courtesy: http://www.freeonlineresearchpapers.com/external-internal-factors-affecting-mcdonalds*)

Cultural Sensitivity: Its Acquisition and Development

Cultural sensitivity has emerged as one of the most essential competence on the part of most expatriates in their foreign assignments. It can be mentioned that learning a foreign language could be best done in conjunction with getting to know the culture, customs and taboos of the country where the language is to be spoken. This makes the language learning much less tedious and mechanical and adds the essential dimension of cultural awareness to the knowledge of the language. It may also be necessary for other members of the organization who are not going to learn the language — but still to have sensitivity to the culture of a country they are going to visit or whose nationals are visiting them.

One method of developing "cultural sensitivity" is to read about the culture of the people with whom an expatriate or a HR manager has to deal or watching films made with the specific purpose of explaining cultural variations. A refinement is needed from the repatriates in order to prepare case studies on their experiences abroad regarding the host country cultures, beliefs or practices that should be diligently shared with the trainee expatriates.

Expatriate failure: Expatriate failure is a term encompassing a broad range of themes such as premature return, low performance, adjustment problems etc. It has been shown by many authors that under-performance during an international assignment, and retention upon completion, could also be included as major factors influencing expatriate failure in MNCs. The factors influencing expatriate failure are as follows:

- Inability to adjust to the foreign culture
- Length of assignment could be too long to cope with
- Willingness to move
- Work-related factors
- Psychological contract to the home country work environment

Strategic Planning in the International HRM Perspective

Strategic planning in the international context seeks to match markets with products and other corporate resources in order to strengthen an organization's competitive position with respect to its global business rivals. It attempts to engage all the functional and corporate levels of the MNC. In order to be able to perform the matching process with that of the global market, a corporation must execute both an external and internal analysis so as to result in a product/market combination also known as "strategic business units (SBUs)". In case of a MNC firm the strategic planning process must define its market entry participation strategy and its competitive strategy for a particular SBU. The principal elements of this are as follows:

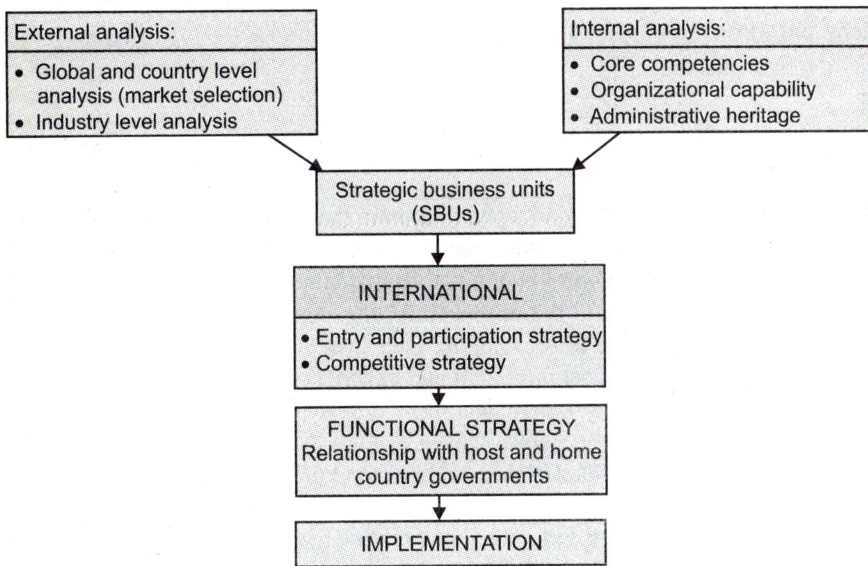

Fig: 1.49 Strategic planning process in a multinational corporation

The management literature devoted to strategic planning presents many very different models. The fundamental differences between the strategic planning process in a domestic and MNC firm could be represented as follows:

Classical Planning Model	Strategic Planning in a domestic perspective	Strategic Planning in a MNC
1. Proposing a change and collecting relevant information for the same	• Defining goals • Competitive analysis • Analysis of internal arrangements	• Global and country level analysis for market selection • Industry level analysis

Contd...

2. Analyzing the information and projecting past and present conditions into the future	• Analysis of competitive advantage	• Development of core competencies • Organizational capability • Administrative heritage
3. Designing a set of alternative plans for making the change and selecting the best plan	• Design of competitive strategy	• SBUs • Design of international: entry and participation strategy; competitive strategy
4. Implementing the selected plan and monitoring and reviewing the implementation	• Implementing the appropriate competitive strategy	• Developing the functional strategy: relationship with host and home country
5. Making necessary modifications based on implementation and business outcomes		

THEME CASE: CONTROLLING UNILEVER

Unilever is a large multinational corporation, operating more than 500 companies in about 80 countries. Most of the corporation's business is in consumer goods, such as food, personal products and detergents. The Anglo-Dutch parent companies are in London and Rotterdam.

In order to control and coordinate the corporation, top management sets the major goals. The decentralized divisions are responsible for developing their own strategic plans. To maintain control in this decentralized structure, only the most proficient and experienced managers are given profit and loss responsibility; these managers also have a great deal of flexibility in decision-making.

However, decentralization has not always worked. One of Unilever's U.S. subsidiaries, Lever Brothers, once responsible for all household, personal, and food products, had a great deal of freedom to make decisions. The hands-off approach by headquarters, less than sufficient investments, and a too careful approach to marketing may have contributed to a relatively poor performance in the United States. In the late 1980s, however, things began to change. For one, Lever now handles only laundry and soap products, marketed under names such as Wisk, Surf, Snuggle, Dove and Lifebuoy. Snuggle, for example, had over 20 per cent of the U.S. market in 1989.

The U.S. operations include Lever Brothers, Chesebrough-Pond's, Elizabeth Arden, Calvin Klein Cosmetics, Thomas J.Lipton (teas, dried foods, and other foods) Van Den Bergh Foods, and Ragu Foods. To control and integrate the U.S. operations and the other operations around the world demands coordination.

Committees play an important part in the coordination of the enterprise. To become a member of the top management team, one has to prove himself or herself by performing well in special committee assignments, which serve as a kind of apprenticeship program for future managers. Committees, in general, are notorious for delaying decisions. Not so at Unilever. These committees are driven by a sense of urgency for action.

[*Courtesy: AIMA, (2008)*]

Training and Development in the International Perspective

Primarily driven by an upsurge in international joint ventures and strategic alliances as well as the emergence of small to medium-sized organizations as key players in the global marketplace, an increased importance has been placed on the ability of today's organizations to develop managers for international work assignments. The complex and ever-changing world of international management requires not only cultural awareness and sensitivity, but also the ability to change, develop, and improve on the job performance. In response to this challenge, most multinational corporations have pursued cross-cultural training programme for their expatriate managers in order to make them more culturally aware and effective in their international assignments (Harris and Kumra, 2000). In fact, one recent survey indicated that almost two-thirds of MNCs offer some type of cultural development programme for their expatriates (Fitzgerald-Turner, 1997).

Although expatriate cultural training is now widely accepted and used, there has been to date very little attention devoted to evaluating this training's effectiveness and better fitting expatriate managers to the local culture to make them more effective once on the job.

Importance of developing expatriates for overseas assignments: One of the main reasons for effective cultural training is to help control the failure rate of expatriate managers. Defined as the premature return by an expatriate from an overseas assignment, failure rates are between 25 and 40 per cent when the expatriate is assigned to a developed country and a whopping 70 per cent when the expatriate is assigned to a still-developing country (Shay and Tracey, 1997). An overwhelming majority of these failures is attributed to the expatriate's and/or spouse's inability to adapt to the new culture (Thomas, 1998; Tung, 1988).

The importance of developing expatriate managers for their overseas assignment through the utilization of cross-cultural training seems apparent. Caudron (1991) highlights some specific dimensions which cultural training can help in reducing costly expatriate failure and increase the effectiveness of their assignment:

Negotiation styles: Expatriates should be made aware that negotiation styles vary widely from country to country. For example, in Russia negotiations are conflict oriented. However, in Asian cultures, more of a consensus-oriented negotiating style is more appropriate.

Communication: In the USA, business associates have a tendency to address each other by first names right after being introduced. However, in France it may take three to six months before business associates feel comfortable addressing each other without a formal title. Non-verbal cues can also be barriers to effective communication. For example, standing too far from a Middle Easterner or standing too close to a Spaniard can be interpreted by both as a lack of interest.

Social relations: Americans tend to place a high value on informality as a way of creating a comfortable environment. Conversely, Europeans tend to be more formal, both in dress and demeanor, while conducting business or entertaining guests. As a result, Europeans may interpret the informal environment as a sign of disrespect. On the other hand, Americans may interpret European formality as stiff and unfriendly.

Family lifestyle adjustment: Concerns associated with everyday lifestyle adjustment in another country, such as where to shop, how to get the kids to school, and how to decode the public transportation system can be quite stressful for expatriates and their families.

How to Improve Expatriate Training

The expatriate cultural training for the above types of dimensions must be tailored to each country and even subcultures (e.g., social vs business) to be effective. In other words, a contingency or "if-then" approach should be utilized when designing and delivering cultural training programme (Luthans *et al.*, 1997). This training should not only include the above four dimensions but also help the expatriate develop their management and interpersonal skills and a sense of efficacy (confidence) and leadership effectiveness.

There is no question that comprehensive cultural training can have many benefits for MNCs. For starters, it can help orient and develop expatriates to better communicate, understand, and work effectively with people from different cultural, religious and ethnic backgrounds. Comprehending and valuing cultural differences can also help expatriates in the effective management of multicultural teams. Understanding global markets, customers, suppliers, and competitors is another indirect benefit. Pragmatically, cultural training can have a positive impact on combating very expensive expatriate failure.

Besides these obvious benefits that mainly result from simple cultural awareness and sensitivity gained from the training received, the more important and sustainable interpersonal skills (e.g., listening, providing feedback and recognition, and a caring, empathetic concern for associates) and management skills (e.g., planning, coordinating and controlling the work and coming up with and implementing innovative ideas to improve the work) in other cultures are not found in most training programme for expatriates. The more subtle, but potentially even more important, efficacy (confidence) building and leadership effectiveness in other cultures are badly neglected or ignored in expatriate training programme and may be the reason for performance problems.

Cross-cultural Training

To cope with the mix of nationalities now common at most MNCs, top managements are emphasizing training particularly with a 'cross-cultural" dimension. The fundamental aim of such training is to secure a successful adjustment to a new position and to ease the pain of repatriation when their foreign assignments are completed. MNCs use a number of various types of training and development programme which can be grouped into two general categories, namely:

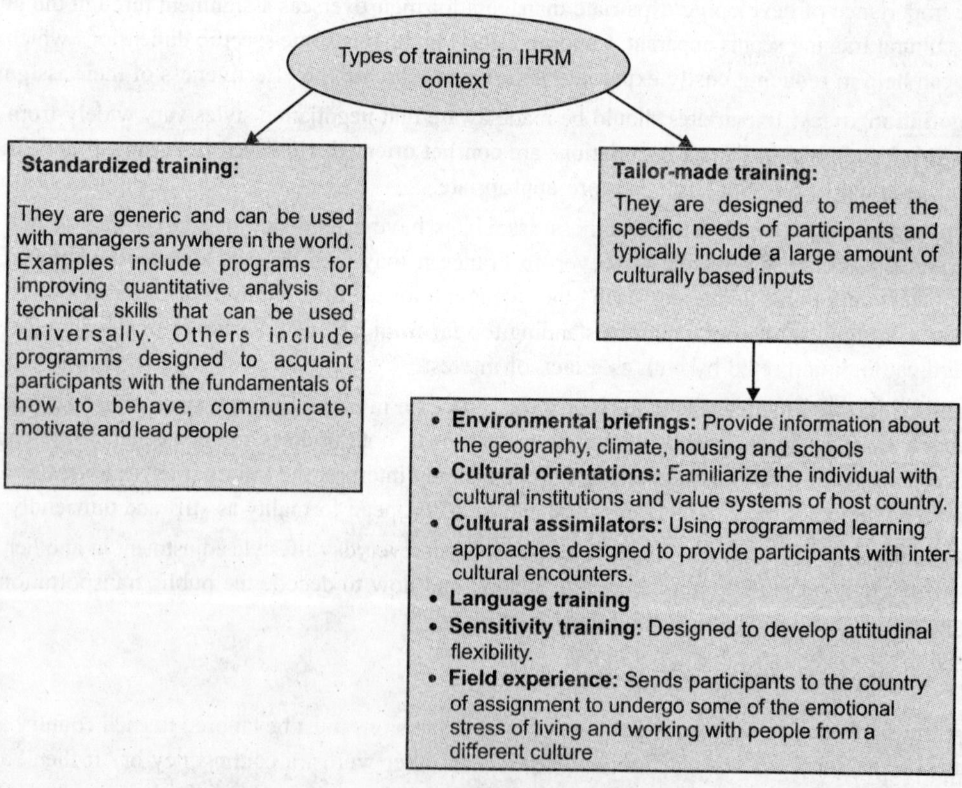

Fig. 1.50: Training in the international context

Exhibit: Methods of Cross-cultural Training

Cross-cultural Training	Hallmarks
1. Role playing	Participants are asked to imagine themselves in situations presented by the trainer related to an international assignment given by the organization in a foreign country. The memebers are then asked to subsequently enact and simulate the given roles. Feedback follows immediately after each role play.
2. Case studies	Case studies developed by repatriates and international managers are given to participants who are asked to analyze and present the cases to the trainer with requisite solutions and suggestions to the problems identified.
3. Instructional games	Essential features of these games include the competition factor and a simplified representation of a real life problem during a foreign assignment. Problems are mutually discussed and solved by participants.
4. Cultural assimilators	These are computerized programmes (or written materials) which aim to increase the participant's abilities to see situations from the perspective of the members representing other cultures. The underlying idea is that individuals can learn to make attributions that are appropriate to different cultural environments.
5. Lectures	These include oral presentations from the trainer which may be supported by audio-visual aids.
6. Reading assignments	Suggested reading materials or relevant topics that may be studied by the trainee expatriates by means of self learning are also encouraged.
7. T Group sessions	Here participants are expected to unfreeze from their habitual roles and thereby adopt a novel situation developed by the trainer. This helps them to develop new and often unexpected roles. The behavioural changes of the participants are subsequently studied by other participants of the group.
8. Drill and practice	This is a method in which practice and feedback are alternated frequently in such a way that undesired behaviour has little chance of establishing itself. It is frequently used in the context of language training.
9. Modelling	The basic assumption of this method is that learners, by observing models perform the desired behaviours and being reinforced doing so can adopt the same behaviours on repeated practice.
10. Field trips	A pre-visit to the country of assignment helps the trainee expatriates to have a real-life experience of the country of their assignment.
11. Assignment to micro-cultures	Here the trainees are placed in situations for a limited period of time in which they are forced to interact with people whose way of life and values are different from their own.
12. Interaction with International manager	The informal interaction with experienced international managers helps the trainees to exchange much valuable information that are required for their cultural adjustments in the foreign assignments.

Performance Management in the International Perspective

Performance management and particularly performance appraisal is a part of the strategic human resource management (HRM) process. These mechanisms enable the MNC to continuously evaluate and improve individual, subsidiary unit and corporate performance against clearly defined, preset objectives that are directly linked to company strategy (Dowling, Welch & Schuler, 1999). Thus, an effective performance appraisal creates a mechanism that can ensure the HCM and their overseas subsidiaries are acting in accordance with the parent MNC's interests. While there is wide recognition of the importance of performance appraisals, most MNCs have not effectively managed their international appraisals. It has been argued that mismanagement of international performance appraisals is primarily due to information asymmetry and goal incongruence between the parent company and its subsidiaries (Shen, 2005).

Performance appraisal is considered as one of several key elements of performance management (Suutari & Tahvanainen, 2002), the others being the communication of company strategy through individual objective setting, development and compensation. Taking the international perspective into consideration, three aspects of performance appraisal are important, namely:

Performance criteria: Goals tend to be translated into performance appraisal criteria. Performance cues are important aspects, and International HR managers need to recognize that hard, soft, and contextual goals as the basis for defining the performance criteria for their employees.

Hard goals are objective, quantifiable, and can be directly measured such as return-on-investment (ROI), market share, and so on.

Soft goals tend to be relationship or trait-based, such as leadership style or interpersonal skills.

Contextual goals attempt to take into consideration factors that result from the situation in which performance occurs. For example, multinationals commonly use arbitrary transfer pricing and other financial tools for transactions between subsidiaries in order to minimize foreign exchange risk exposure and tax expenditures. Another consideration is that all financial figures are generally subject to the problem of current conversion, including sales and cash positions. Further complications arise because host governments can place restrictions on repatriation of profits and currency conversion. The nature of the international monetary system and local accounting differences may preclude an accurate measurement of performance results.

Who Conducts the Performance Appraisal?

Another issue concerning appraisals in the international context is who conducts the performance appraisal. Typically, employees are appraised by their immediate superiors, and this can pose problems for subsidiary managers. They work in countries geographically distant, yet are evaluated by superiors back at headquarters who are not in the position to see on a day-to-day basis how to expatriate performs in a particular situation. Consequently, subsidiary managers tend to be assessed according to subsidiary performance, with a reliance on hard criteria similar to that applied to heads of domestic units or divisions. Of course, there is a danger that a PCN or TCN subsidiary managers will make decisions and implement local strategies that favour short-term performance to the detriment of long-term organizational goals — her or his subsidiary performance will not be affected if the expatriate assignment has been completed before the consequences of those decisions and strategies begin to take effect.

Appraisal of other expatriate employees is likely to be conducted by the subsidiary's chief executive officer, the immediate host country supervisor, or the individual's home country manager, depending on the nature and level of the position concerned. Host country managers may have a clearer picture of expatriate performance and can take into consideration contextual criteria, but they may have culturally bound basis (e.g., about role behaviour) and lack an appreciation of the impact of the expatriate's performance in the broader organizational context. Some expatriates may prefer to have parent company evaluators given that their future career progression may depend on how the evaluation data is utilized back at headquarters; this may be especially so in cases where foreign operations are relatively less important than domestic U.S. operations. Others, may prefer hostcountry evaluation if they perceive it as a more accurate reflection of their performance. Multiple raters are sometimes used in the domestic context—such as the "**360-degree feedback**". It has been argued that, given the cross-cultural complexity of the foreign assignment, a team of evaluators should be used for expatriate performance evaluation.

Standardized or Customized Performance Appraisal Forms

Domestic companies commonly design performance appraisal forms for each category, particularly those using a traditional performance appraisal approach rather than performance management. Such standardization assists in the collection of accurate performance data on which personal decisions can be made and allows for cross-employees comparisons. The question often posed is, should these standardized forms be adapted when used for evaluating international managers?

One of the problems with annual appraisal is that employees do not receive the consistent frequent feedback considered critical in order to maintain or improve their performance. It is also suggested in the performance literature that regular feedback is an important aspect in terms of meeting targets and revising goals, as well as assisting in motivation of work effort. The difficulty for the expatriate who is being evaluated by a geographically distant manager is that timely, appropriate feedback is only viable against hard criteria.

Compensation Management in the International Context

Compensation in international organizations and MNCs are more challenging than that being managed in the domestic HRM perspective. International HR managers have to constantly fine tune their compensation package according to the country of operations, workforce combination and in doing so they require a thorough knowledge of employment and taxation rules, customs and legislations in various countries, currency fluctuations and the effect of inflation on compensation and also understanding of various special allowances for expatriates working in different foreign subsidiaries. All these factors make international compensation management a complex and more challenging in its basic nature. The fundamental objectives of international compensation management are as follows:

- The compensation policy should be consistent with the overall organizational HR strategy, structure, business needs of the MNC.
- The policy must work to attract and retain talents on the global perspective.
- The compensation policy should facilitate transfer of international employees in the most cost effective way.
- The policy should facilitate the organization and the HR professionals in order to cater the issues caused by difference in taxation laws, employment legislations in different countries of operations.
- The international compensation policy should also address the issue of equity both in terms of external and internal equity.

Components of International Compensation: The components of international compensation are as follows:

Components of International Compensation	Features/Hallmarks
Base Salary	• For expatriates base salary is the primary component or the foundation block of a package of allowances (e.g., Foreign service inducement or hardship premium, cost of living allowance, housing allowance etc.) which are/could be related to the base salary itself.
Foreign Service Premium	• PCNs or even TCNs may receive a salary premium as an inducement to accept a foreign assignment or as a compensation for any hardship caused by the transfer or relocation to a foreign subsidiary.
Allowances	**Cost of Living Allowance (COLA):** • Cost of living allowance involves a payment to compensate for differences in expenditures between the home country and the foreign subsidiary where the expatriate has been deputed/posted.

Contd...

	Housing Allowance: • It is the allowance provided to expatriates so as to maintain their home country living standards or receive accommodation in the country where the foreign subsidiary is located. **Home-leave Allowance:** • These allowances are given to the expatriates for enabling them to bear the costs of returning to their home country once a year. **Education Allowances:** • These are meant for bearing the cost of education for the expatriate's children in the subsidiary country. **Relocation Allowances:** • These allowances are meant to facilitate the moving, shipping and storage charges, temporary living expenses, subsidies for the expatriates working in foreign subsidiary. **Spouse Assistance Allowances:** • These are the allowances given to the expatriates for compensating the loss of job of the expatriate's spouse due to their relocation or transfer to a foreign subsidiary. Many MNCs may provide "Dual Career" options for working couples to facilitate their employment in the same organization or different organizations in the subsidiary country.
Benefits	These could include pension plans, medical coverage, insurance benefits, social security benefits, support in terms of legal help and help in terms of coping with taxation norms in the host country.

Approaches to International Compensation: There are mainly two approaches to international compensation, namely: (a) The Going Rate (Market rate) approach, (b) The Balance Sheet (Build-up) approach. The various features of these approaches are depicted by the following table:

Approaches of International Compensation	Features/Hallmarks
Going Rate/Market	• Based on the rates of the subsidiary country • Compensation based on selected survey comparisons • Base pay and benefits may be supplemented by additional payments for low-pay subsidiary countries • It relies comparisons amongst (a) HCNs (b) PCNs and (c) TCNs and (d) Expatriates of all nationalities
Balance Sheet/Build-up Approach	• It helps to maintain home country living standards in the foreign subsidiary and also provides financial inducements caused by the differences in the cost of living between the host and the home countries • Home-country pay and benefits act as the foundations of this approach • Financial incentives (e.g., Foreign Service inducement or hardship premium) are provided to make the compensation package attractive.

International Labour Relations

MNCs and international organizations opening subsidiaries in foreign countries need to find substantial differences in labour relations practices among the world's countries and regions. MNC headquarters involvement in industrial relations is influenced by several factors such as:

- The degree of inter-subsidiary production integration
- Nationality of ownership of the subsidiary

- International HRM approach of the organization
- MNC prior experience in International IR
- Nature and characteristics of the subsidiaries
- Characteristics and features of the home product market
- Management attitude towards the unions

Impact of trade unions in IHRM: Trade unions may limit the strategic choices of MNCs by three ways, namely:

- By influencing the wage levels to the extent that cost structures may become uncompetitive
- By constraining the ability of the MNC to vary employment levels at will in terms of investing or divesting in a particular subsidiary
- By hindering or preventing global integration of the operations of the MNCs.

Response of trade unions to MNCs: Trade unions have long seen MNCs as a potential threat to the bargaining power of labour because of the considerable wealth, autonomy and power and influence exerted by the MNCs in host country (subsidiary) operations. The following factors or issues can be depicted as the reasons contributing to the growing concerns of the trade unions caused by the MNC operations. These are:

- MNCs have formidable financial resources which may even include the ability to manage and withstand losses in a particular subsidiary that might be in dispute or conflict with the local trade unions.
- MNCs are strong in terms of their alternative sources of supply of manpower and other resources.
- MNCs are highly capable in terms of shifting their operations facilities to other countries having favourable climate for IR.
- Most MNCs have remote locus of control and authority that might not be influenced by the industrial disputes occurring in a particular foreign subsidiary unit.
- MNCs are strong in terms of their operations facilities in many industries and other product lines.
- MNCs are good at superior knowledge and expertises in industrial relations
- MNCs have the capacity to stage an "investment strike" in a particular country where IR environment is unfavourable for business.

Considering the above issues posed by the superior strengths and capabilities of most MNCs, the response of trade unions to MNCs can be categorized into a three fold entity, namely:

- Forming International Trade Secretariats (ITSs) which can function as loose confederations so as to provide worldwide support for trade unions from various countries
- Lobbying to the national governments in respective subsidiaries for restrictive national legislations
- Regulation of MNCs by International Organizations like those of the European Trade Union Confederation (ETUC) and the International Confederation of Free Trade Unions (ICFTU) etc.

Career Management in the International Perspective

One of the greatest challenges faced by HR professionals in the international context is to manage the career paths of their expatriates sent for international assignments. Generally most executives sent for international assignments assume that a foreign assignment would bring about an increase in the status of their position in the organization both in terms of monetary as well as indirect benefits. It is the role of HR professionals to not only to ensure attractive career paths for these executives but also provide an opportunity for their growth and development. Further the challenge becomes more complex when the issue gets mingled with the career development of HCNs and TCNs. The firm at this juncture needs to develop a clear cut strategy to decide the career options for each of these PCNs, HCNs and TCNs.

Theme Reading: Capabilities of Indian Managers for Better Career Opportunities

A recent study conducted by Korn/Ferry International along with International Management Association (IMA) have revealed that there was a significant difference between the leadership styles of C-level Indian executives and their North American counterparts. Indian executives were found to be more task focused, complex and creative, which means they make decisions considering many options with a focus on high quality. In other words, they are strategic — in fact, they are as strategic as western best-in-class executives. These capabilities of Indian executives provided better career opportunities as compared to their global counterparts. The study also indicated that Indian executives were found to have high intellectual and social capabilities that made them successful even in International assignments. These capabilities facilitated best-in-class leadership progression and career growth for most of the Indian professionals and executives. The following figure illustrates the above mentioned capabilities facilitating career growth in Indian executives and professionals with respect to various positions like supervisory positions to that to the level of CEO.

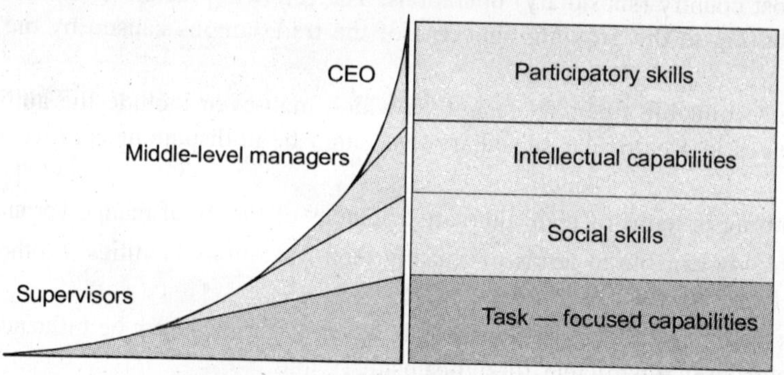

Fig. 1.51: Best-in-class leadership progression

(*Courtesy: "How Indian Managers Compare with the Rest", Indian Management, Vol. 47, Issue: 1, January, 2008, p. 14.*)

Dual career challenges: International organizations over the years have witnessed the spurt in the increasing number of working husbands and their spouses. Many had accepted offering dual career options for both the husband and the working wives when one is being sent for an international assignment. Bangalore being the hub of MNCs, have witnessed many such corporations adopting dual career options for their expatriates. The following case highlights the various problems and issues related to career options for expatriates working in India. The case also highlights the increasing trend of husbands taking the role of house-husbands and wives taking the responsibility of being the bread earners for the family. HR managers of most international organizations now need to consider these issues for effective people management strategies in their organizations.

Theme Case: Career Issues for Expatriates Working in Bangalore

Bangalore city is today buzzing with an ever-growing expatriate population. With growing number of expert housewive, there is now a chunk of house-husbands who, having followed their wives' professional commitments, have taken up the responsibility of handling household duties. While their wives focus on climbing the corporate ladder, these men are content with being stay-at-home dads or house-husbands.

"The trend is definitely not popular in the West. Rather the number of dual income families is more in the West as compared to those in India. And one generally sees the mothers opting to stay at home," says Alex Heihn, software engineer, father of a six-year old son and a three-year-old daughter, who is two months into his role as a stay at home dad and loves it already. A part of the growing tribe of house-husbands in Bangalore, Alex along with Tom Murphy and Shawn Webb, feels that the opportunity to visit India, a better position offered to the wives and a chance to spend quality time with their kids made them opt to be stay-at-home dads. Tom Murphy owned a small business in the USA but when his wife was offered a high paying position in Bangalore, he decided to get someone else to manage his business and decided to be with his kids. "If we were back in the US, we would require a double income to maintain our living standards so the pressure for me to work would be high there," commented Alex, though all of them admit that the fact they are away from home does make things easy for them. The Webbs family took a practical decision when they decided that Shawn who was earning less than his wife would stop working to take care of their two adopted kids.

Alex feels the new role comes easier. "In the US, ambitious women are under more pressure to perform than men. It's easier for us to take a career break here in India".

(Courtesy: Mehta, D., (2008): "Bangalored dads love it", Bangalore Mirror, Sunday, July 6th, 2008, p. 11)

Role of HR in Compliance Management

With more and more organizations going global, it has become strategically important for most MNCs to ensure that their HR functions take care of handling the problems related to statutory compliance management. One example could be cited here. William J. Teuber, CFO of EMC has emphasized on the importance of such compliance management for the sustainability of International organizations like EMC. In an interview with a reputed business magazine he commented, "If you watch TV, you'll see a rash of top executives on trail who say they did not know about the financial irregularities that were taking place in their own companies". He further commented, "Compliance is a theme sweeping across the world". Compliance regulations like Sarbanes-Oxley (SOX) that US corporations as well as Indian companies doing business with US corporations will have to adhere have become the concerns for most organizations. In Europe there is Basel-II, there are new rules for banks in the US as well the new "Hippa" rules for US medical institutions. These International compliance regulations would enhance the responsibility of the HR function to ensure transparency in the organization's functioning and business.

Employee Retention in the International Context

Employee retention and engagement is also another important aspect of international HR practices. MNCs inspite of their thriving profitabilities had encountered the challenge of retaining their employees in their international operations. Indian companies as compared to their foreign counterparts over the few years have been reported to have adopted a more proactive approach towards employee retention keeping in mind their global operations. Let us discuss this issue with respect to a fast growing Indian MNC which had excelled in its IHR practices.

Essar Group (Sanjai, P.R. Kalesh, B., 2008)[17], the Mumbai Based Conglomerate with interests in steel, oil, power and shipping has set up an inhouse "Global Talent Acquisition Cell", borrowing the concepts from MNCs like GE and Coca Cola. The group controlled by the Ruia family, has already recruited 28 executives for the cell and plans to raise the count for 50 this year. "Engaging a search firm for talent acquisition is **acostlier** alternative as you will end up paying huge fees", said Mr. Adil Malia, group President — HR, Essar Group. In the last few years, Essar has expanded its overseas presence to the US, Canada, Africa, West Asia, the Carribean and South East Asia and added new lines of business including outsourcing and telecommunications. Mr. Malia said that his groups' employee turnover rate is nearly 9% much below the industry's 13–15%. But how far this HR initiative would help Essar Group in its international venture could well be worth watching.

HR Challenges in International Joint Ventures (IJVs)

Apart from the above situations MNCs and even domestic giants are frequently entering into International Joint ventures (IJVs), Mergers and Acquisitions (M&A). In these cases the most frequent and obvious HR challenges faced by these organizations can be summarized as follows:

Table 1.10: HR Challenges Associated with International Joint Ventures (IJVs)

Focus areas of HRM	*HR Challenges*
Staffing	Management of the host country partner may perceive providing jobs for their citizens (HCNs) as a more important objective than increasing profits
Promotion	Blocked promotion of HCNs in the IJV may result from revising top positions for expatriates (PCNs) deputed in the foreign assignments.
Loyalty	Because of the multiplicity of entities involved in the IJV, loyalty and cultural conflicts may occur
Delegation	Partner companies limit the delegation of authority and/or disagree on the desired extent of autonomy
Decision making	Decision making is a particularly complicated process because of the conflicting expectations of the entities involved
Unfamiliarity	Each employee group may experience feelings of strangeness and lack of familiarity with the employees of the other entities
	Expatriates (PCNs) may be unfamiliar with the environment and culture of the host country
Communication	Communication blockages can result because of the interpersonal problems and cross-cultural differences between geographically dispersed managers and executives
Information sharing	Information flow from the host or foreign partner in the IJV may be restricted because of suspicion regarding the intentions of the other partner.
Compensation	Dissatisfaction with compensation gaps between HCNs and PCNs can develop.
	Difficulties in assessing the performance of IJV staff stem from the different procedures and performance standards of the parent companies.

(*Source:* Adapted from Oded Shenkar and Yoram Zeira, "Human Resources Management in International Joint Ventures: Directions for Research," Academy of Management Review, Fall 1987, pp. 546–557)

Exhibit: Internet Laboratory: List of useful IHRM Websites

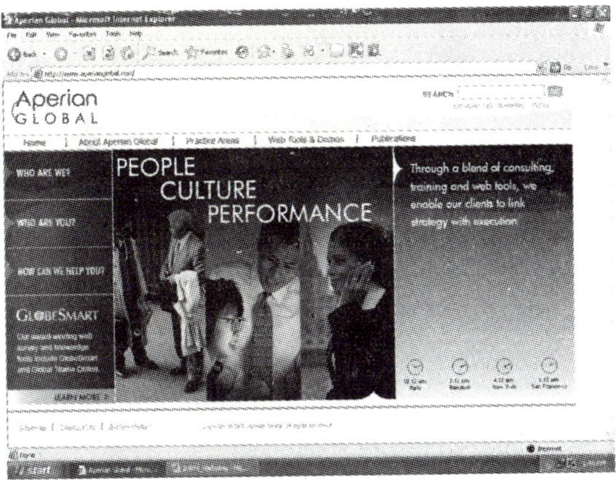

http://www.aperianglobal.com/ (A website useful for tracking organizational culture and performance at the International level)

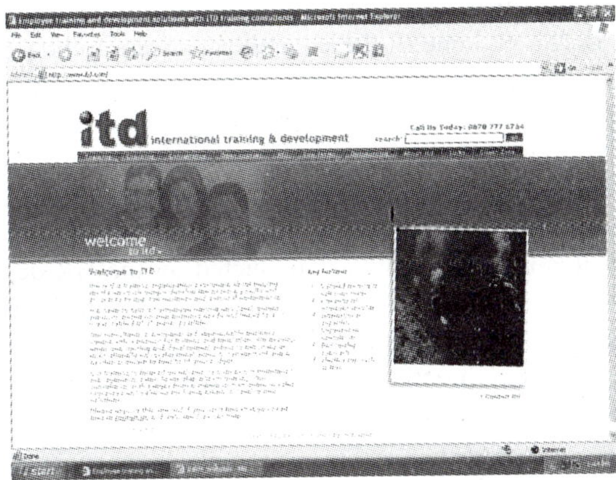

http://www.itd.com/ (A website useful for international training and development)

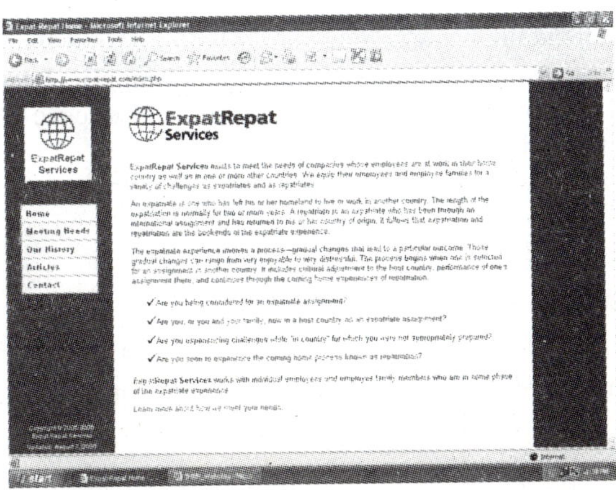

http://www.expat-repat.com/ (A website providing coaching for expatriate performance in international assignments)

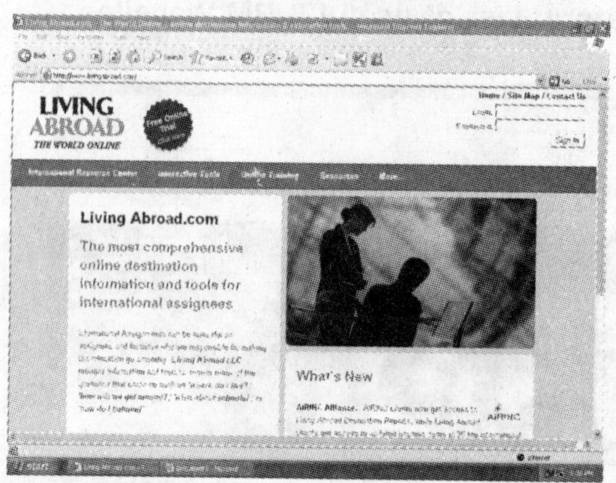

http://www.livingabroad.com (An e-magazine for expatriates)

Exercise Case Study 1: Mr. Sam's Woes

XYZ International a reputed US based MNC is well known for its people centric policies. The company was spending enormously on three of its employees. Mr. Wang, Ms. Suzan and Mr. Sam. The company was opening a new office in Berlin and one of these candidates were to be posted as the Regional Head. The three employees were then subsequently subjected to a rigorous orientation followed by training for the aforesaid assignment. The candidates were informed that only one of them would be selected for the post and all of them in spite of having an excellent track record were giving their all during their training. The Group HR Head also promised them great rewards and benefits in their foreign assignment and also an equal benefits and positions on their return home after the foreign assignment. After comprehensive training and orientation an evaluation program was conducted by the HR department and Mr. Sam was identified as the best performer. Mr. Sam was congratulated by all his colleagues and was in high spirits. Later on he requested the HR department to sanction a leave of 7 days to be with his family as his mother was not keeping well for the last three months. He said that he would compensate his leave of absence during the next week after coming back from his leave.

The HR Department first was astonished at his request as career meant everything to Mr. Sam and that had shown in his performance. Mr. Sam was refused permission to go on leave. There was a lot at stake. Instead he was ordered to go to Germany and take charge of the operations over there. The HR Department promised that they would help him to relocate his family at Berlin and would bear all the expenses in the same. Mr. Sam did not know how to react. The next day without a word of explanation he gave in his resignation. The very next day he got a better offer from ABC International a reputed FMCG company with better parks and compensation. They also granted a leave of 10 days to Mr. Sam on permission from the MD of the company.

QUESTIONS

1. What do you think went wrong in XYZ International?
2. How could these types of incidents be avoided, if you were the HR head of XYZ International?
3. What would have been your reactions as the HR head of XYZ International after hearing the news of Mr. Sam being hired by ABC International?

REFERENCES

1. Dowling P.J., Welch, D.E. (2007): "International Human Resource Management: Managing People in the Multinational Context," 4th edition, Thomson-South Western.
2. Christensen, C., Harzing, A.W. (2004): "Expatriate Failure: Time to Abandon the Concept", Career Development International.
3. Harris, H. and Kumra, S. (2000), "International Manager Development: Cross-cultural Training in Highly Diverse Environments", *The Journal of Management Development*, Vol. 19, No. 7, pp. 602–14.
4. Fitzgerald-Turner, B. (1997), "Myths of Expatriate Life", *HR Magazine*, Vol. 6, pp. 64–74.
5. Shay, J. and Tracey, J. (1997), "Expatriate Managers", *Cornell Hotel and Restaurant Administration Quarterly*, Vol. 38, No. 1, pp. 30–6.
6. Thomas, D.C. (1998), "The Expatriate Experience: A Critical Review and Synthesis", in Cheng, J.L. and Peterson, R.B. (Eds), *Advances in International Comparative Management*, JAI Press, Vol. 12, Greenwhich, CT, pp. 237–73.
7. Tung, R. (1988), *The New Expatriates: Managing Human Resources Abroad*, Ballinger, Cambridge, MA.
8. Caudron, S. (1991), "Training Ensures Success Overseas", *Personnel Journal*, Vol. 70, No. 12, pp. 27–30.
9. Luthans, F., Marsnik, P. and Luthans, K. (1997), "A Contingency Matrix Approach to IHRM", *Human Resource Management Journal*, Vol. 36, No. 2, pp. 183–99.
10. http://www.citigroup.com/citigroup/corporate/history/index.htm
11. http://careers.citigroup.com/careers/homepage/emea/gcib/humanres.htm
12. http://www.citigroup.com/citigroup/citizcn/divcrsity/index.htm
13. Tung, R.L., (1993): "Managing Cross-cultural and International Diversity," Human Resource Management, 32, No. 4, pp. 461–477.
14. Barlett, C.A., and Ghoshal, S., (1989): "Managing Across Borders: The Transnational Solutions", Boston, MA: Harvard Business School Press.
15. Harzing, A.W., J.V. Ruysseveldt, (1995): "International Human Resource Management", London: Sage Publications.
16. Beamish, P.W., J.P. Killing, D.J. Le Craw and H. Crookell (1991): "International Management: Text and Cases", Homewood Ill: Irwin.
17. Sanjai, P.R., Kalesh, B., (2008): "Essar Gets Scouting Cell to Hunt for Better Talent and Cut Costs", Mint, Vol. 2, No. 168, July 15th 2008, p. 5.
18. McDonald's, (2005). Retrieved October 9, 2005, from McDonald's website: http://www.mcdonlads.com/corp/values/diversity/supplierdiversity/commitment.html

QUESTION BANK

1. Why has the study of international HRM gained so much importance today? What are the differences between issues bothering domestic and international HRM?
2. What are the factors of an effective Human Resource function in a multinational corporation? Discuss the HRM policies of any multinational corporation operating in India.
3. Highlight the specific International HRM activities of a multinational firm. Explain the inter-relationship between HR functions and a firm's expansion in International business.

4. What performance criteria are used in evaluating expatriate performance and what precautions have to be taken while using them?
5. Outline the factors associated with the appraisal of expatriate managerial performance. What is the relevance of hard, soft and contextual goals in the assessment of expatriate managerial performance?
6. Can standardized domestic appraisal forms be used for international managers or should they be customized?
7. How frequently should the performance be evaluated?
8. What are the factors that affect selection decision of expatriates? Analyze the consequences of ignoring these factors.
9. Imagine that you are a training manager in a large multinational organization. What training strategy would you adopt for training your expatriate employees? Justify your answer.
10. Discuss the importance of expatriate pre-departure training. What should be essential components of this training and how can this training be made relevant and effective?
11. What are the factors that affect selection decision of expatriates? Analyze the consequences of ignoring these factors.
12. Discuss the main differences in salary compensation for PCNs and TCNs. How critical are these differences in so far as individual performance is concerned?

Internet Exercises

- Visit the following website and give a presentation on your learning from the same: http://www.humanresourcesmagazine.com.au/
- You are the HR manager of an Indian multinational company which has its branch at New York. Very soon two of your officers from the Bangalore HQ would be expatriated to the New York office. Now one of these employees would be taking his 10 year old boy and wife to the states along with him. Now your job is to surf the net (google search) and find out websites that could provide valuable information regarding the schooling to your employees' kid, information regarding retail shops in New York and Bank facilities for the employee. Collect the relevant information and present to your class.
- You are the HR trainee of a reputed FMCG company. Your company is supposed to participate in an International symposium in Paris the next month. Collect information from the net regarding the arrangements for flight booking from Bangalore, hotel booking and other amenities in Paris for the said symposium. Regarding the hotel arrangements prepare a comparative study of the tariff of at least three 5 star hotels in Paris.

Games

- Suppose you are the training officer in a reputed Japanese car manufacturing company having their regional office in Delhi. Now your company had sent 4 technicians from Japan to your Delhi office for the production of a new car and helping the Indian technicians for the said project. Now these technicians would join by the next one month. You being the training officer at the India office have been invited to go to Tokyo and conduct an orientation session on India, its habits and habitats. Prepare a presentation and present to your class assuming that the audience comprises of these Japanese technicians.
- You are the public relations officer of a reputed International travel maker. Very recently the students of a reputed Indian B School would be going for an International study trip in Singapore. Prepare a presentation for the same and deliver it to your class with illustrations assuming that your friends are those Indian students who would be visiting Singapore very shortly.

CHAPTER 2

HUMAN RESOURCE PLANNING

(*Courtesy: www.perssyst.com/consulting_hrp.htm*)

THEME CASE: MANPOWER NEEDS IN THE INDIAN CEMENT INDUSTRY

Fast rising Government Expenditure on Infrastructure sector[1] in India had resulted a higher demand of cement in the country. In the same direction, participation of larger companies in the sector has increased. Presently the Indian cement industry comprises of 125 large cement plants with an installed capacity of 148.28 million tonnes and more than 300 mini cement plants with an estimated capacity of 11.10 million tonnes per annum.[2] Domestic cement demand growth has surpassed the economic growth rate of the country for the past couple of years. The growth rate of cement demand over the past five years at 8.37% was higher than the rate of growth of supply at 4.84% as also the rate of growth of capacity addition during the same period. Demand for cement in the country is expected to continue its buoyant ride on the back of robust economic growth and infrastructure development in the country. The key drivers for cement demand are real estate sector, infrastructure projects and industrial expansion projects. Among these, real estate sector is the key driver and accounted for almost 55% in FY 07.

(*Courtesy: "Cement cos too face hiring retention woes", The Economic Times, 24th June, 2008, p: 7*)

HR Challenges in the Indian Cement Industry

In the wake of a huge boom in the real estate and construction sector, thanks to growing metros like Bangalore and Hyderabad, the cement industry is going through significant changes especially related to the management of human capital. There is concerted effort among leading cement organizations to manage people linked with this huge growth. In fact with the boom of the Indian economy and fast growing metro cities in India, the cement industry has shifted its focus on two vital HR related issues namely, talent acquisition and retention of talents. In order to cope with the growing demand of cement, most of these organizations are focussing on enhancing their production capacities for which they also need to consider increasing supply of manpower.

Industry figures reveal that the Indian cement industry has an installed capacity of 196 million tonnes and the industry has declared a 30 million tonnes addition in the last financial year. There are news that the industry had made proposals to install another 90 million tonnes so as to reach an operational capacity of 275 million tonnes by 2011. This expected growth would no doubt result in a shortage of manpower. Over the next 4–5 years, the cement sector would need around 20,000 more people, which would account to a 50% growth over the headcount of the cement industry in India.

Industry experts have further revealed that technical profiles in the domains of project management and operations management would be most demanded profiles, which would mean that technical institutes need to supply quality engineers so as to successfully meet this huge demand of manpower. Further as the cement industry is also expected to undergo a paradigm shift from being labelled as accommodity industry to a brand conscious one, the sector would also require a huge number of marketing and brand development professionals so as to successfully meet these needs and challenges.

As most of the HR departments in this challenging scenario would need to hire large number of well trained, capable professionals and technicians, without having an effective HR planning process supported by a talent management framework in their organizations might lead them to face shortage of manpower, leading to their inability to manage future projects and balance effectively with their "go-to-market strategy". Hence manpower planning is expected to be a key strategic lever for these organizations so as to cater to the future challenges in the cement industry as well as manage the competition of the industry itself with other sectors in terms of competitive compensation and retention practices.

HR figureheads, like that of Mr. Amandeep, Executive Director HR, Dalmia Cements, believe that the industry has taken note of the talent situation and is preparing to adopt strategies so as to successfully retain and engage employees with their companies. Thus many of the HR practices that were critically the hallmarks of IT, Service sector organizations and FMCG companies are now being implemented in the organizations belonging to the cement industry.

Industry captains had also opined that their organization's manpower planning systems would also need to tackle the challenges of keeping the compensation packages high as compared to similar positions in other industries with an equal emphasis on the market trends, cost reduction and putting into action comprehensive employee benefit programs like those of employee stock option plans (ESOPs) so as to effectively attract capable professionals and technicians from other industries. How the cement industry would be able to manage this upcoming challenge in terms of attracting and retaining their human capital would be worth watching.

PREFACE: THE NEED OF MANPOWER PLANNING

The penalties for not being correctly staffed are costly to any organization in today's business context. On the other hand understaffing loses the business economies of scale and specialization, orders, profits and most importantly the customers. Overstaffing is wasteful and expensive, if sustained, and it is costly to eliminate because of modern legislation in respect of redundancy payments, consultation, minimum periods of notice, etc. Hence in order to ensure the competitive efficiency of the business, any organization requires meticulous planning of its staffing activity. This involves the assessment of present and future needs of the organization to be compared with the present resources and future predicted resources along with the involvement of appropriate steps so as to effectively plan and balance the demand and supply of manpower in the organization. This is known as human resource planning (HRP) or manpower planning.

What is Human Resource Planning (HRP)/Manpower Planning?

Definition: HRP is an ongoing function involving the acquisition, utilization, improvement and preservation of Human Resources in an organization aimed so as to assess the manpower requirements in advance keeping the production schedules, market fluctuations, demand forecasts etc in the background.

E.W. Vetter[4], has described "Human resource planning is the process by which the management determines how an organization should move from its current manpower position to its desired manpower position to its desired manpower position. Through planning the management strives to have the right number and the right kinds of people at the right places, at the right time, to do things which result in both the organization and the individual receiving the maximum long-range benefit".

E. Geisler[5], has described "Manpower planning is the process including forecasting, developing and controlling by which a firm ensures that it has the right number of people and the right kind of people at the right places, at the right time doing work for which they are economically most useful".

Leon Megginson[4], has described "Human resource planning is an integrated approach to performing the planning aspects of the personnel function in order to have a sufficient supply of adequately developed and motivated people to perform the duties and tasks required to meet organizational objectives and satisfy the individual needs and goals of organizational members".

Coleman[6], has described "Human resource planning is the process of determining manpower requirements and the means for meeting those requirements in order to carry out the integrated plan of the organization".

Workforce planning is the strategic alignment of an organization's human capital with its business direction. It is a methodical process of analyzing the current workforce, determining future workforce needs, identifying the gap between the present and future, and implementing solutions so the organization can accomplish its mission, goals, and objectives.

As a process, workforce planning includes elements such as strategic planning (by both the organization and its partners), workload projections, legislative forecasts, turnover analyses, and budget projections. Workforce planning forecasts the numbers of people and types of skills needed to achieve success by comparing the available workforce with future needs to determine needs that may be unmet (gaps). Workforce planning is a management tool that affects the full life cycle and range of human resources activities including recruitment/selection, classification and compensation, training and development, performance management, and retention.

THEME READING: "INCREASING DEMAND OF MANPOWER IN INDIAN IT COMPANIES IN THE NEXT 3 YEARS"

Indian IT and ITES giants have been reported to feel the challenge of scaling up their human resource needs in the coming next 3 years. Over the years Indian IT companies have shown their great ability to enhance their capabilities by the competencies of their efficient intellectual capital strengths and particularly by adopting a business model known by industry experts as "the body shopping one" which is best suited to them. This was the opinion given by Mr. Francois Enaud, CEO, Steria, in a recent interview with a leading Indian business daily.

(Courtesy: Singh, H., 2008: "India headcount to double in next 3 years", The Economic Times, June 25th, 2008, p. 5.)

Who is Responsible for Workforce Planning?

It requires involvement of the entire organization in identifying its vision, goals and core business functions. The HR professional's role is to examine how work and the workforce of the organization are fast changing. By analyzing information from multiple sources to define current and future workforce needs, HR professionals need to develop and implement strategies so as to fill in any gaps to be better positioned in order to meet stakeholders' increased service expectations. This dynamic, data-driven process is the core of workforce planning. Work planning is one aspect of overall strategic planning processes.

Basic aspects of HR planning: HR planning involves "Planning for Future Needs" by deciding how many people with what skill the organization will need in the organization. In other words this approach can be termed as "finding the right person at the right number and right capabilities for the right positions in the organization". Hence the basic aspects of HR planning would involve the following:

- Planning for future balance of workforce by comparing the number of needed employees to the number of present employees who can be expected to stay with the organization, which leads to
- Planning for recruiting or laying off employees
- Planning for the development of the employees to be sure the organization has a steady supply of experienced and capable personnel.

Four essential things should be added to HR planning to make it more strategic and useful for the organization. These are:

- Facilitate organization's strategic goals and ensure that the HR system functions as a strategic partner to the top management.
- Assess the readiness of the workforce in order to implement the overall HR strategy and also identifying knowledge gaps, study the organizational structural change needs etc.
- Involved in the communication of the HR strategy at all levels in the organization.
- Measure the result and implications of the HR functions in terms of contributing to the organization's performance.

Planning staff levels requires that an assessment of present and future needs of the organization be compared with present resources and future predicted resources. Appropriate steps then be planned to bring demand and supply into balance.

Thus the first step is to take a 'satellite picture' of the existing workforce profile (numbers, skills, ages, flexibility, gender, experience, forecast capabilities, character, potential, etc. of existing employees) and then to adjust this for 1, 3 and 10 years ahead by amendments for normal turnover, planned staff movements, retirements, etc, in line with the business plan for the corresponding time frames. Hence it is evident that the HRP should need to integrate the bottom line of the organization with that of the top level of the organization (as shown below).

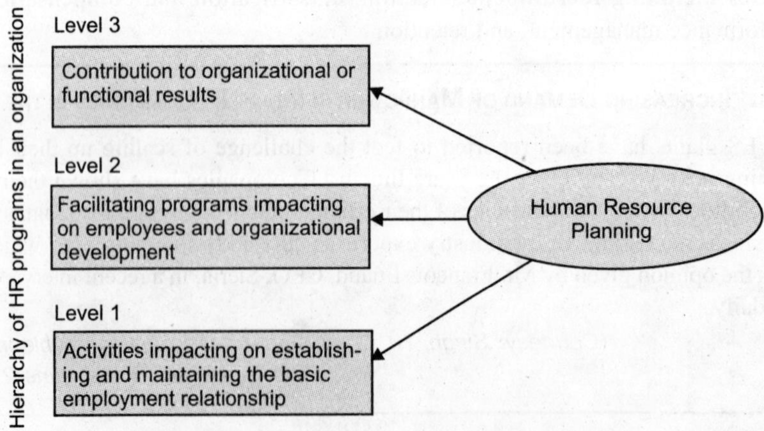

Fig. 2.1: Link of HRP with the hierarchy of HR programs in an organization

Linking the Processes of HRP and Strategic Planning

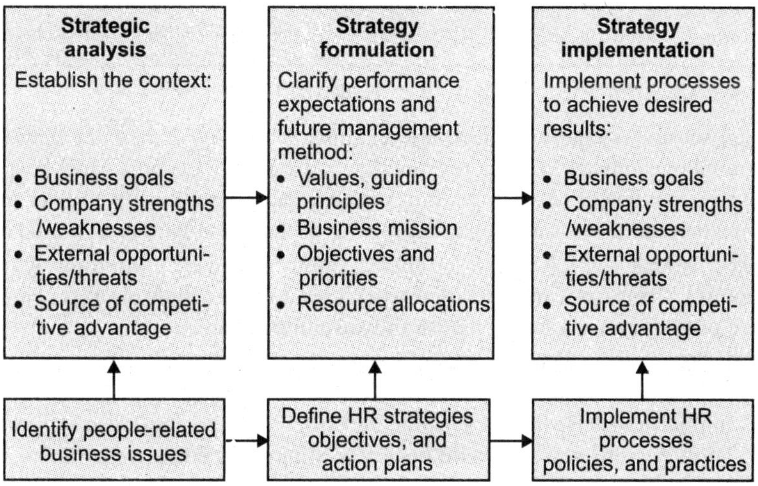

Strategic analysis	Strategy formulation	Strategy implementation
Establish the context: • Business goals • Company strengths /weaknesses • External opportunities/threats • Source of competitive advantage	Clarify performance expectations and future management method: • Values, guiding principles • Business mission • Objectives and priorities • Resource allocations	Implement processes to achieve desired results: • Business goals • Company strengths /weaknesses • External opportunities/threats • Source of competitive advantage
Identify people-related business issues	Define HR strategies objectives, and action plans	Implement HR processes policies, and practices

Fig. 2.2: HRP linked with the strategic planning process in the organization

The above figure clearly depicts the importance of aligning the HRP process with the strategic planning process in the organization. This could be achieved by effectively mapping the organization's human capital architecture and recognizing the same as a part of the strategic objectives of the organization. This mainly involves:

- Identifying the "Core knowledge workers" in the organization ("**Super-keepers**")
  - These are the employees who have firm-specific skills that are directly linked to the company's strategy (Example: Senior software programmer).
- Identifying the "Traditional job-based employees" or the so called "**Keepers**"
  - These include those employees with skills to perform a predefined job that are quite valuable to a company, but not unique. (Example: Security guard).
  - Contract labour.
- Identifying the employees whose skills are of less strategic value and generally available to all firms (Example: General electrician).
- **Identifying the Alliance/partners:** These involve those individuals and groups with unique skills which may not even be directly related to a company's core strategy (Example: Independent product label designer).

Role of HRP in Ensuring the Fit between HR and Organizational Strategy

HRP contributes to facilitate the right fit between an organization's human capital with that of the organization's strategy. This is achieved by ensuring (a) an external fit as well as an (b) internal fit.

External fit (or External alignment): It focuses on the connection between the business objectives and the major initiatives in HR. These may involve initiatives pertaining to the organization's growth strategy in the form of mergers and acquisitions and joint ventures. On the other hand when an organization might need to benchmark or develop a particular competency that may pose to be strategically important for the organization's long-term sustainability, HRP would facilitate the organization in terms of achieving a competitive edge over its business rivals in terms of adjusting its HR with the external needs of the business.

Internal fit (or internal alignment): It involves aligning the organization's HR practices with one another to establish a configuration that is mutually reinforcing. This could involve strategic requirements like that of organizational restructuring, retrenchment requirements, organizational stability and so on. HRP would empower organizations to ensure a strategic fit with these internal requirements of its business objectives.

Illustration of Manpower Planning in the Hospital Industry

In a typical hospital set up, expenditure on salary amounts to roughly 25–30 per cent of total income or 30–35 per cent of total expenditure. This is not healthy statistics, say experts. Most hospitals are believed to operate with excess manpower. As competition increases and margins come under pressure, hospitals tomorrow will have no option but to rationalize manpower, which, in other words, would mean downsizing.

Most times, downsizing has led to further chaos, mainly because of improper manpower planning. Health-care consultants stress on a multi-skilled workforce to carry multiple tasks in order to maintain optimum employee per bed ratio, a key to boost and sustain profits.

To achieve this, manpower planning becomes crucial. But, such tasks are rarely undertaken in hospitals, say experts. Most hospitals operate on excess man power, says Dr. K. C. Ojha, managing director, Hospic, Mumbai-based Hospital Consultancy Firm. "Ideally, employee to bed ratio should be 3 per bed," he says. Three persons per bed could be a little stingy, say some, who find 4–5 persons per bed more acceptable.

Factors affecting manpower in hospitals: The type of hospital, the set-up and even the structure of the building counts when it comes to manpower allocation.

Specialty: The number of employees depends not on the size of hospital but more on its specialty, say experts. "Ideally for multi-specialty and super specialty hospitals the ratio of bed to employee should be around 1:6. This is an ideal situation and is practiced in developed countries as mandatory requisition," says Dr. C. P. Kamle, international associate of American Institute of Medicine and Hans Finne International.

Setup: More classes of wards means more staff. For instance, a deluxe room may have one staff for just 2 beds since the patients are charged higher and consequently demand better care. In median class, one employee can look after 6 patients.

Structure: Hinduja Hospital has more staff than other hospitals in Mumbai because the building is designed to have four separate wings. A ward boy in one wing may not be able to give his best to all the wings on the same floor. So the staff increases. Says Col Rampal, director, HR, Hinduja Hospital, "The solution is to economize without effecting patient care. For example, non-core sector like support staff, house keeping can be outsourced. We have outsourced security and are thinking of outsourcing food service too."

Measures to be taken: Audit: Manpower audit, which must be carried out regularly is seldom done. According to Dr. Vivek Desai, MD of Hosmac Consultancy, Mumbai, knowledge among healthcare professionals on manpower audits is not satisfactory.

Multi-skilling and multi-tasking: Employee per bed ratio can be kept optimum, provided effective utilization of manpower is done by creating multi-skilled and multi-tasked personnel. Explains Dr. Ojha, "In any hospital, an ECG technician does the job of just taking the ECG. And if it is a male technician, he can see only male patients. Most of the times therefore he is left without work." The right way he says is to employ female employees or train nurses to carry out the same for full utilization of man power.

Giving an example of multi-skilled employee, Dr. Ojha says that a peon must have knowledge of computers, lift operation, vehicle driving and handling patients. He emphasizes that even class IV staff be given training and apprenticeship. Full orientation for computer application must be given. This will reduced manpower requirement, say experts.

Outsource: Consultants advice that hospitals must explore services which can be outsourced. Dr. Desai says that contracting some services can bring down manpower to 4 persons per bed.

(*Courtesy: http://www.citehr.com/28045-manpower-planning-industry.html*)

Objectives of manpower planning: Manpower planning has the following principal objectives. These objectives not only help the organization to facilitate proper functioning of the organization, but also act like a bridge so as to ensure that the HR practices are linked with the strategic goals and objectives of the organization:

- To ensure having an estimate of employee requirement along with matching skill or competency so as to efficiently meet organizational needs and objectives.
- To provide information about how existing manpower are to be employed and what types of skills and or competencies are to be developed for achieving the desired levels of performance.
- To indicate the requirement of additional manpower when and wherever required by the organization.
- To cope immediate changes or fluctuations regarding the requirement of a particular skill and or competency in the workforce.
- To ensure productive and efficient utilization of human resources and reduce manpower wastage.
- To assess and forecast future skills requirements of the employees in the organization.
- To provide control measures so as to ensure that necessary resources are being made available as and when required.
- To provide guidelines so as to enable employees to train and develop themselves for higher pursuits and effective performances.
- To form the basis of career planning and succession planning in the organization.

Importance: The importance of manpower planning is as follows:

- To determine recruitment levels.
- Understaffing loses the business economies of scale and specialization, orders, customers and profits.
- Overstaffing is wasteful and expensive, if sustained, and it is costly to eliminate because of modern legislation in respect of redundancy payments, consultation, minimum periods of notice, etc. Very importantly, overstaffing reduces the competitive efficiency of the business.
- To anticipate redundancies and avoid unnecessary dismissals.
- To determine optimum training needs and levels.
- To provide a basis for management development programs.
- To deploy the manpower in new projects.
- To assist in productivity bargaining.
- To study the cost of overheads and value of service functions and effectively control costs.
- To decide whether certain activities need to be subcontracted.
- To form the basis for effective talent management.
- Enabling the organization to expand or contract its business activity.
- Providing a basis for career and succession planning.

Benefits: Manpower planning has several benefits. These are as follows:

- Reducing labor costs associated with attrition.
- Reducing recruiting and replacement costs.
- Focus training resources appropriately.
- Increase the ability to take advantage of new business opportunities.
- Improve employee morale and satisfaction.
- Control rapid expansion or reduction of the workforce.
- Monitor staffing and retention policies of the organization.

The Process of HRP: The steps in the HRP process are as follows:

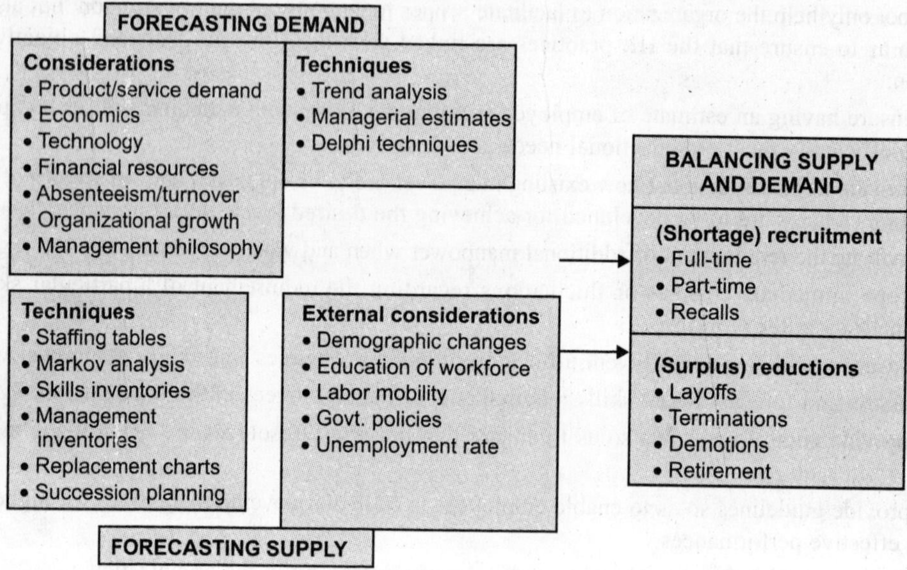

Fig. 2.3: Process of HRP

As discussed above HRP is all about balancing the demand and the supply of manpower requirements of an organization that ultimately gives to identification of the corresponding HR strategies. The process as illustrated above takes into consideration forecasting the demand and supply of manpower. The information regarding the same is collected both from external as well as internal (organizational) sources. The details of these are discussed below:

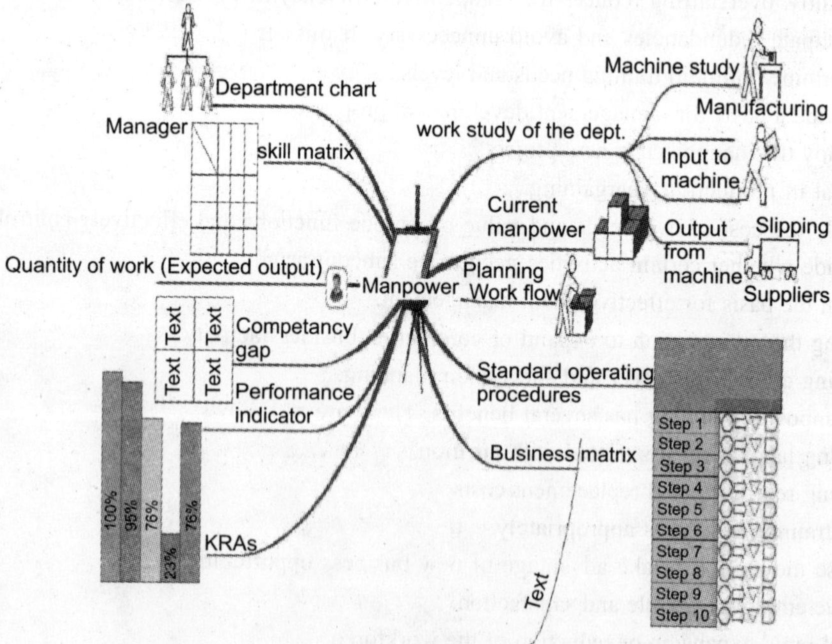

Fig. 2.4: A model of manpower planning

The above figure depicts a simple model of HRP. It depicts how HRP relates the employee capabilities with the job related requirements of the organization. These include the relation of the HRP process in terms of determining performance indicators, developing skill matrix, identifying KRAs, competency gaps, managing work flows, determining operating procedures, ensuring the right skill-job requirement fits, assessing the present manpower strengths in the organization and so on.

Information regarding employee capabilities is drawn from departmental charts, skill matrix charts, performance standard records, competency gap analysis records, performance indicators and KRAs. These are then matched with the positional requirements related to the job based on work study of the department, current manpower review records, work flow records, standard operating procedures and so on. One of the most valuable outcomes of HRP had been in its capability of linking the HR functions with the strategic planning framework of the organization.

It is by strategic HR planning through which HR and line managers can focus on linking all HR activities with the organization's strategic objectives, whether be it in the terms of linking employee allocations with the organizational structure or ensuring the right match between people capabilities and their contributions towards the productivity of the organization.

Exhibit: HR Plans in Cognizant Technologies

Cognizant technology solutions is devising new plans to attract talents from campuses such as offering internships to MBA students, tapping alumni network and even publishing exclusive newsletter to B schools. But some of them – such as conducting business plan contests, and helping B schools with case study presentations – are designed specifically to tap MBAs. Mr. T. Sridhar, Chief People Officer, Cognizant Technologies have commented, "MBAs join the company to work in areas of consulting, analytics, business development, opportunity assessment, relationship management, corporate development, and domain excellence. We do not redirect B School graduates to technical roles." Reports indicate that today, Cognizant has at least one MBA holder/domain expert for every 30 software professionals. Four years back the ratio was one for every 40–45 software professionals. In 2007 alone the company had hired more than 700 MBAs both from premier campuses as well as from the lateral market.

(Courtesy: "Cognizant technology hunts for MBAs to drive growth"; The Economic Times, 10th January, 2008, p: 6)

COMPONENTS OF THE HRP PROCESS

Future manpower planning is directly linked to the strategic business plans of an organisation. The estimation on manpower and budgets are governed by customers' demands. Ashwin Thacker[7], Managing Director, Flamingo Pharma, states, "Business needs are achieved from effective management of materials, machines, money and manpower. Manpower needs, if planned properly, in terms of profile required, numbers, time and place, will give the company mileage over competitors in terms of consistency in output. Effective human resources planning give optimal productivity in terms of timelines and quality of deliverables."

HRP is the process of anticipating and carrying out the movement of people into, within, and out of the organization. It is done in order to achieve the optimum utilization of human resources and to have the right number and types of employees needed so as to meet the organizational goals and objectives.

As discussed above, the components of HRP can be broadly classified into two categories, namely: (a) Forecasting the demand of human resources and secondly (b) Analyzing the supply of manpower. This is illustrated by the following figure:

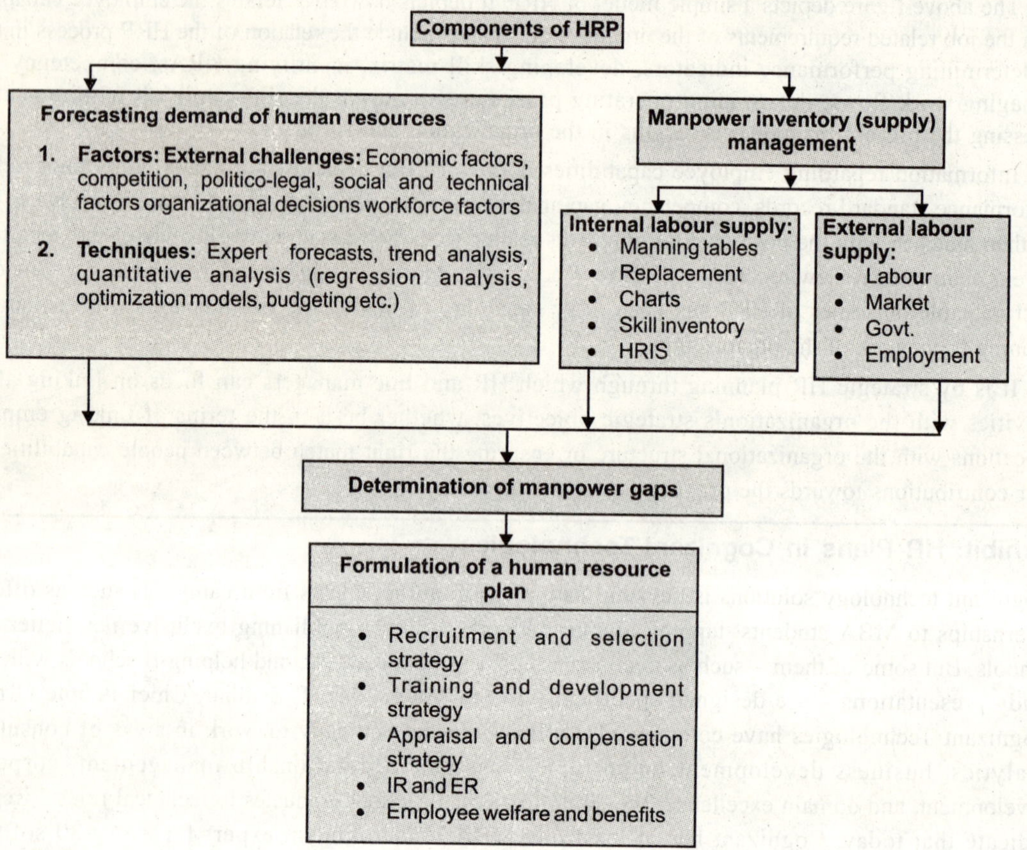

Bramham (1994)[8] had argued that there is a wide spectrum difference in the **concepts** of manpower planning and human resource planning. He described "Manpower Planning" as a purely QUANTITATIVE approach which is concerned with the forecasting demand and supply of labour. Whereas, "Human Resource Planning" is a far wider concept encompassing a whole range of activities including those of the motivation of employees, employee attitudes, and organisational culture. According to Taylor (2002)[9], MP and HRP are concerned with 'looking ahead', using systematic techniques, i.e. auditing skills to be able to meet org. requirements of the future and having 'the right people, with the right skills, in the right places at the right time. Taylor (2002)[9] had further emphasized on a HR planning cycle which comprises of stages like those of (a) Forecasting future demand of HR, (b) Forecasting future internal supply of HR, (c) Forecasting future external supply of HR and (d) Formulating responses to the forecasts.

Forecasting the Demand for Human Resources

This is one of the most important aspects of human resource planning activity. This is particularly important for organizations like that in the IT/ITES sector where the attrition rate is considerably higher and organizations have little or no control on the same. Analysis of manpower demand would not only help managers focus on the present requirements of manpower in their companies but it also help them to have an insight of the future manpower needs in the organization and even in the industry. Many HR outsourcing firms conduct these types of research activities for their clients and the industry. This entire process primarily depends on three factors, namely:

(a) **External Challenges:** The external challenges are purely external to the organization and beyond the control of the organization or the industry as a whole. These depend on variables like the economic scenario of the region, politico-legal system, socio-technical system and nature of competition in the market.

- **Economic Developments:** Liberalization, opening up of the banking sector, capital market reforms, on-line trading systems etc. has created a huge demand for finance professionals. Inflation and economic recessions also have tremendous impacts on manpower demand. As in the later case most organizations prefer to go for manpower crunch and downsizing as a strategic choice to cater survival and adjust to recession trends. In recent years India's growing service sector has facilitated a tremendous boost to the hiring of more trained professionals in this sector. Retailing, financial services, Insurance etc. all these booming sectors have ensured the increase in manpower demand in these fast growing sectors.
- **Political, Legal, Social and Technical Changes:** The politico-legal system also plays a vital role in terms of shaping the economic policy of a country and the future of business development in a region. These policies tend to vary from government to government, which again are being influenced by their respective political ideology and beliefs. Trade and fiscal policies of various governments in India had changed by frequent changes in a ruling party which may also have a destabilizing impact on the business scenario in the country. The socio-technical changes in terms of people's capabilities and skills, behaviour and attitudes have a very important influence in the business development and growth in a nation. The most prominent change so far, influencing the Indian economy had been the profuse growth in the IT/ITES sector. Over the last few years young graduates had been found to be most interested in terms of having their careers in this sector. Nowadays preference for the service sectors like retailing had also been found to be growing.
- **Competition in the Market:** Competition in the market also plays a vital role for shaping the demand of manpower in the industry. This has become more strategically important in terms of growing needs of talent retention in the industry and incidents of talent poaching by business rivals becoming more and more frequent.

(b) **Organizational Decisions:** The organizational decisions are mainly influenced by the company's strategic plans, sales and production forecasts and new ventures are taken into account for employment planning.

(c) **Workforce Factors:** Manpower demand is also modified by factors like those of retirements, termination of services, resignations, deaths and leaves of absence, attrition rates, absenteeism rates and most importantly their capabilities in terms of the future requirements of the business. With the business environment becoming more and more complex, organizations have been reported to engage themselves more proactively on these variables.

Manpower Demand Forecasting Techniques: The manpower forecasting techniques commonly employed by modern organizations are as follows:

- ***Expert (Management) Forecasts***: Here, managers or HR professionals or consultants engage themselves in estimating the future human resource requirements, where their experiences and judgements on such issues are taken into good effect. Apart from this, the opinions of supervisors, department managers, customers (customer feedbacks, opinion of retailers, suppliers etc.), experts (Subject Matter Experts/SMEs), or others knowledgeable about the organization's future employment needs are also taken into consideration. Many HR Consultants use their SMEs/consultants to conduct rigorous research and provide their industrial clients valuable suggestions in terms of identifying their manpower needs for their organizations. This method is effective to use when the experts are unbiased, large changes are unlikely to occur in the organization/industry, relationships and market dynamics are well understood by experts (e.g., demand goes up when prices go down), experts possess privileged information, and experts receive accurate and well-summarized feedback about their forecasts.

- ***Demand Forecast***: The ability to predict manpower needs is crucial[10] for an industry. On the demand side, companies formulate manpower planning strategies based on these forecasts, while, on the supply side, they provide job seekers with a basis to assess the attractiveness of a given sector. Manpower forecasts are also important for assisting the government in the policy-making process by serving as pointers to help avoid redundant investments and achieve efficient and balanced growth for an industry. Meanwhile, forecasts based on an inaccurate market analysis can cause imbalances such as undersupply or oversupply of manpower. Demand forecast is the process of estimating the future quantity and quality of manpower required. Since it's an open system that we exist in, a variety of organizational factors, including competitive strategy, technology, structure, and productivity can influence the demand for labor. For example, utilization of advanced technology is generally accompanied by less demand for low-skilled workers and more demand for knowledge workers. The basis of this forecast primarily depends on the annual budget and long-term corporate plan, which are then translated into activity levels for each function and department of the organization. It also takes into consideration both internal as well as external factors. The external factors include economic climate, competition, laws and regulatory bodies, changes in technology, social factors and demographic factors. The internal factors include budget constraints, production levels, new products and services, organizational structure and employee separations.
- ***Market Prediction Method***: This method also known as betting markets, information markets, and futures markets have a long history in predicting manpower requirements in an organization/industry. Some commercial organisations provide internet markets and softwares that to allow participants to predict manpower needs. Consultants can also setup betting markets within firms to bet on such things as the sales growth of a new product. These predictions can produce accurate sales forecasts when used within companies. However, there are no empirical studies that compare forecasts from prediction markets and with those from traditional groups or from other methods.
- ***Supply Forecast***: HR demand analysis provides the management with the means of estimating the number and kind of employees that would be required in an organization. The next logical step is to determine whether it will be able to procure the required number of personnel and the sources of such procurement are also to be considered. Supply forecasting provides this information. It measures the number of people that are likely to be available from within and outside the organization, after making allowance for absenteeism, employee turnover, internal movements and promotions, and changes in hours and other conditions of the work.
- ***Ratio-trend Analysis***: This is one of the quickest forecasting techniques. It involves studying past ratios, say, between the number of workers and sales in an organization and forecasting future ratios, making some allowance for changes in the organization or its methods. Ratio analysis means making forecasts based on the ratio between (1) some causal factor like sales volume and (2) the number of employees required (for instance number of sales people). For example, suppose as salesperson traditionally generates $500,000 in sales. If the sales revenue to salespeople ratio remains the same, you would require six new salespeople next year (each of whom produces an extra $500,000) to produce an expected extra $3 million in sales. Like trend analysis ratio analysis assumes that productivity remains about the same – for instance, that each salesperson can't be motivated to produce much more than $500,000 in sales. If sales productivity were to increase or decrease, the ratio of sales to salespeople would change. A forecast based on historical ratios would then no longer be accurate.

- ***Work Standards Data*:** Many organizations have established comprehensive sets of data for man-hours or unit times to perform a great many production tasks. For each department the projected units of output are converted into man-hours, man-days and number of employees by applying the established time standards.
- ***Key Predictive Factors*:** The essence of key predictive technique is to locate key indicators with which total manpower correlates highly. To identify such a factor, the HRP department must examine several business factors such as sales volume units produced, clients served, and so on.
- ***Delphi Technique*:** It is a qualitative method of forecasting HR needs. It solicits estimates of personnel needs from a group of experts, usually managers. It is an attempt to decrease the subjectivity of forecasts by soliciting and summarizing the judgements of a pre-selected group of individuals. The Delphi technique helps managers to capture the knowledge of diverse experts while avoiding the disadvantages of traditional group meetings. The latter include bullying and time-wasting. To forecast with Delphi the administrator should recruit between five and twenty suitable experts and poll them for their forecasts and reasons. The administrator then provides the experts with anonymous summary statistics on the forecasts, and experts' reasons for their forecasts. The process is repeated until there is little change in forecasts between rounds – two or three rounds are usually sufficient. The final forecast represents a composite group judgement. The HR experts act as intermediaries, summarizes the various responses and report the findings back to the experts. The experts survey again after they get this feedback. Summaries and surveys are repeated until the experts' opinion begins to agree. The Delphi forecast is the median or mode of the experts' final forecasts.

The forecasts from Delphi groups are substantially more accurate than forecasts from unaided judgement and traditional groups, and are somewhat more accurate than combined forecasts from unaided judgement.

- ***Trend Analysis*:** HR needs can be forecast through projecting past trends. Past rates of change can be projected into the future or employment growth can be estimated by its relationship with a particular index. Trend analysis means studying variation in your firm's employment levels over the last few years. One might compute the number of employees in an organization at the end of each of the last five years, or perhaps the number in each subgroup (like sales, production, secretarial, and administrative) at the end of each of those years. The purpose is to identify trends that might continue into the future. Trend analysis can provide an initial estimate, but employment levels rarely depend just on the passage of time. Other factors like changes in sales volume and productivity also affect staffing needs.
- ***Structured Analogies Method*:** The outcomes of similar situations from the past (analogies) may help a manager to forecast the outcome of a new (target) situation in terms of manpower and their relevant skill requirements. For example, the introduction of new products in the markets can provide analogies for the outcomes of the subsequent release of similar products in other countries. People often use analogies to make forecasts, but they do not do so in a structured manner. For example, they might search for an analogy that suits their prior beliefs or they might stop searching when they identify one analogy. The structured-analogies method uses a formal process to overcome biased and inefficient use of information from analogous situations. To use the structured analogies method, an administrator prepares a description of the target situation and selects experts who have knowledge of analogous situations; preferably direct experience. The experts identify and describe analogous situations, rate their similarity to the target situation, and match the outcomes of their analogies with potential outcomes in the target situation. The administrator then derives forecasts from the information the experts provided on their most similar analogies. Structured analogies are more accurate than unaided judgement in forecasting decisions.

Forecasting as a Part of Human Resource Planning

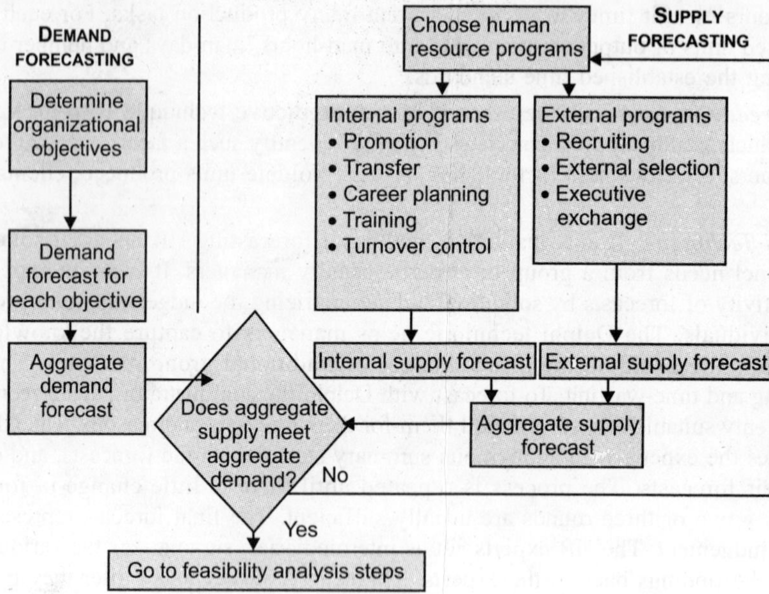

Fig. 2.5: Forecasting as a part of effective HRP

(*Courtesy: www.bus.ucf.edu/jones/SHRM/Chp5.HRP.ppt*)

Trend Analysis in HRP: This involves forecasting of manpower demand based on an organizational index such as sales:

- Selecting a business factor that best predicts human resources needs.
- Plotting the business factor in relation to the number of employees to determine the labor productivity ratio.
- Computing the productivity ratio for the past five years.
- Calculating human resources demand by multiplying the business factor by the productivity ratio.
- Projecting human resources demand out to the target year(s).

2006–07	Production of Units	:	4,000
2006–07	No. of workers	:	100
	Ratio	:	100:4000
2007–2008	Estimated Production	:	5,000
No. of workers required		:	5,000 × 100/4,000 = 125

If supervisors have a span of 10 workers, 12 supervisors would be required in 2007–2008.

Year	Business factor (sales in thousands)	÷	Employee productivity (sales/employee)	=	Demand of HR (number of employees)
1999	Rs. 3412		8.1		421
2000	Rs. 3892		10.4		374
2001	Rs. 4230		13.1		322

Contd...

2002	Rs. 4500	15	300
2003	Rs. 4900	17.5	280
2004	Rs. 5000	16.7	299
2005	Rs. 5345	16.8	318
2006	Rs. 5767	17.3	333
2007	Rs. 5986	17.6	340

Fig. 2.6: Examples of trend analysis

- ***Other Methods*:** Several mathematical models, with the aid of computers are also used to forecast HR needs in an organization. These include: Regression Analysis, Optimization models, Budget and planning analysis.

(e) **Workforce Analysis:** The average loss of manpower due to leaves, retirement, death, transfer, discharge etc during the last 5 years are taken into account. The rate of absenteeism and labor turnover are also taken into account.

(f) **Work-load Analysis:** The need for manpower is also determined on the basis of work-load analysis, wherein the organization tries to calculate the number of persons required for various jobs with reference to a planned output- after giving weightage to factors such as absenteeism, idle time spent etc.

(g) **Job Analysis:** Job analysis helps in finding out the abilities or skills required to do the jobs efficiently. A detailed study of jobs is usually made so as to identify the qualifications and experience required for them.

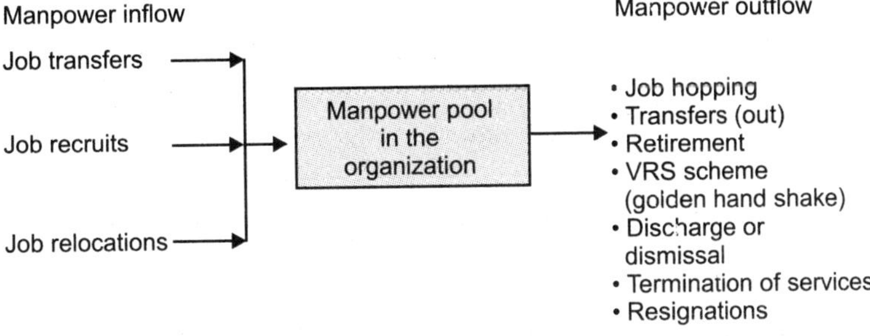

Fig. 2.7: Manpower flow in an organization

Planned output for the year	15,000 units
Standard hours per piece	5 Hours
Planned Hours required	75,000 Hours
Productive hours per person per year (allowing for absenteeism, turnover, idle time etc.)	1,000 Hours
Number of workers required	75
If span of control in the unit is 15/team leader, then 5 team leaders would be needed for the production	

Fig. 2.8: Illustration of Work-load analysis

Preparing Manpower Inventory (Supply Forecasting):

The basic purpose of preparing manpower inventory is to find out the size and quality of personnel available within the organization to man various positions. Any organization has 2 major sources of supply of manpower, namely: Internal and External Sources.

Internal sources: A profile of employees in terms of age, sex, education, training, experience, job levels, past performances and future potential are kept ready for this purpose. Requirements in terms of growth, internal movement of employees (transfer, promotions, retirement etc) must also be assessed in advance. Replacement charts and/ Succession plans are also utilized for this purpose. Frequent Manpower Audits are carried out so as to find out the available talent in terms of skills, performance levels and potentials. Forecasting internal labor supply involves the following methods, namely:

- **Skill Inventories:** These involve analysis of files of personnel education, experience, interests, skills, etc., that allow managers to quickly match job openings with employee backgrounds. They can help HR manager to:
  - identify qualified employees for different jobs.
  - determine which skills are present or lacking in the organization.
  - assess longer term recruitment, selection and training and development requirements.
- **Replacement Charts:** These are the listings of current jobholders and persons who are potential replacements if an opening occurs. They can help to summarize the skills information in visual form for key managers so they can easily identify:
  - The present incumbents
  - Potential replacements (or lack of) for given positions.

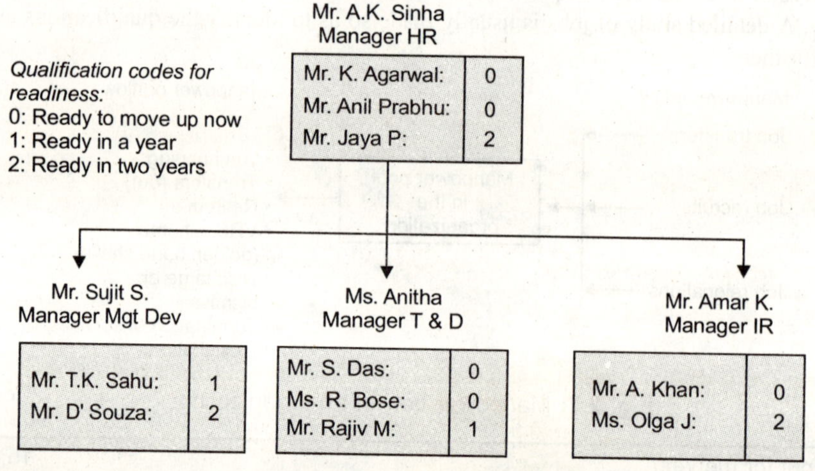

Fig. 2.9: An executive replacement chart in the HR department of an organization

- **Succession Planning:** This is the process of identifying, developing, and tracking key individuals for executive positions.
- **Analysis of Manning/Staffing Tables:** These are graphic representations of all organizational jobs, along with the numbers of employees currently occupying those jobs and future (monthly or yearly) employment requirements.
- **Turnover Analysis:** A detailed turnover analysis of **why** people leave is essential for meaningful information regarding loss of manpower in an organization. Assessment of **Exit interviews** and labour turnover rates from past years are the best source of this information. Turnover for each **job classification** and department should also be calculated.

- **Markov Analysis:** This is a method used for tracking the pattern of employee movements through various jobs in the organization. It is mathematical technique that helps to forecast the availability of **internal** job candidates in an organization. It assumes that the **movement** of personnel among various job classifications can be predicted from past movements. The limitation of this method is that it is used only in very large organisations. The basic assumption of this model is that an employee in a particular grade or a status group has a fixed chance of promotion in a given year, independent of vacancy.

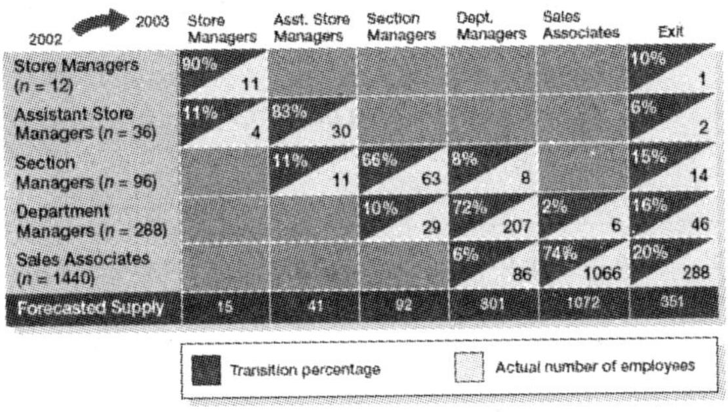

2002 → 2003	Store Managers	Asst. Store Managers	Section Managers	Dept. Managers	Sales Associates	Exit
Store Managers (n = 12)	90% 11					10% 1
Assistant Store Managers (n = 36)	11% 4	83% 30				6% 2
Section Managers (n = 96)		11% 11	66% 63	8% 8		15% 14
Department Managers (n = 288)			10% 29	72% 207	2% 6	16% 46
Sales Associates (n = 1440)				6% 86	74% 1066	20% 288
Forecasted Supply	15	41	92	301	1072	351

Fig. 2.10: Hypothetical Markov analysis for retail company

(Courtesy: Bohlander, Snell, (2004): "Managing Human Resources", Thomson-South Western, Indian edition)

Thus number receiving promotions depends on the number of eligible staffs in the grade below, subject to fulfillment of eligibility criteria, which may be age, seniority, qualifications or experience. The central equation for this model is:

$$N(t + 1) = n(t)P + R(t + 1)r$$

where, **n(t)** is the vector of stocks at a given time **t**, i.e. number of employees in each status group.

P is the matrix of transition probabilities between each of status groups.

r is the vector of probabilities of a recruit starting in particular status groups

R(t) is the number of new recruits at the time **t**.

If the number of employees n(t) in each status group at a particular time is known, the equation may be used to predict the value of n(t), i.e. the number of employees in each status group at a later time t. This is however, subject to the conditions that recruitment levels, i.e., R(t) during the period, i.e. t = 0 to t = T, are already known. Alternatively, the total number of the staff in the organization, which is N(t) may be specified. The prediction equation, therefore, may be written as:

$$N (t + 1) = n(t)q + m(t + 1)r$$

Here, M(t + 1) = N(t + 1) and includes not only transition within the organization but also the effects of wastage and recruitment to maintain the balance in the organization.

- **Wastage Analysis:** Manpower wastage is an element of labour turnover. Wastage is severance from the organization, which includes voluntary retirement, normal retirement, resignations, deaths and dismissals. Marginal recruitment decisions without wastage analysis may lead to inaccuracies in manpower planning. The various methods of wastage analysis are as follows:

Method of wastage analysis	Features
Labour Turnover Index	It indicates the number of employees leaving an organization as a percentage to average number of employees. It is given by the formula: Labour Turnover = Number of employees leaving × 100/Average number of employees employed
Stability Index	This index indicates stable workforce percentage for a given period and can be given as: Stability Index = Number with more than 1 year service now × 100/Total employed one year ago
Cohort Analysis	It takes into account the length of service, which is an important variable of labour wastage analysis. It eliminates the defect of labour turnover index and is more accurate for a small homogeneous group of employees. It is calculated by the formula: Number remaining at a given time × 100/Number engaged at the start

Analysis of External Sources: When an organization grows rapidly, diversifies into newer areas of operations, it needs to fill its vacancies or meet its manpower requirement through outside sources like manpower supply through consultant firms or by outsourcing.

Table 2.1: Factors influencing Internal and External Manpower Supply Forecast

Internal Supply Forecast	*External Supply Forecast*
• **Manning Tables:** It shows the number of employees in each job and tries to classify employee on the basis of age, sex, position, category, experience, qualifications, skill etc. The study of this table indicates whether current employees are properly utilized or not. • **Replacement Charts:** It shows the profile of job-holders, department-wise and reveals those who could be used as replacements whenever the need arises. • **Skill Inventory:** It indicates the routine and strategic skills of an employee before or since joining the organization.	• **Labour Market Conditions:** Such as local employment trends of relevant categories of employees, competition for such skills, availability of parttime labour, migration trends of labour, housing facilities available, transport needs etc. • **Macro Level Factors:** Such as availability of a certain category of jobs to "outsiders", cultural factors, customs and social norms, training schemes of the Govt. etc.

Determining Manpower Gaps: The existing number of personnel and their skills (from manpower inventory) are compared with the forecasted manpower needs (demand forecasting) so as to determine the quantitative and qualitative gaps in the workforce. Reconciliation of demand and supply forecasts will give the number of people to be recruited or made redundant as the case might be. This forms the basis for preparing the manpower plan.

Appendix: Features of HRP in Mastek (Software Company).

- Strategic and operational business objectives and desired competencies are made available for developing manpower plans.
- Experienced/professionally trained individuals perform HRP activities.
- The strategic competency and workforce needs are documented on a regular basis.
- For each of the organization's/unit's required competencies, a competency development plan is produced.
- HRP is prepared for the organization and its units, tracked quarterly and revised, if needed.
- The organization develops succession plans for its key positions.
- Measurements are made and used to determine the status of strategic and near-term HRP activities across the organization and units.

Exhibit: Manpower Requirement Facts in the Airlines Sector in India

Employment: The Indian aviation sector is likely to generate nearly 2.5 lakh jobs by 2010 as fleet expansion is on the rise. As a consequence of Commonwealth games, approximately 10 million tourists will be visiting India by 2010. There is a growing demand for training 1,500 pilots every year due to the phenomenal growth in the civil aviation sector. With such a robust growth, the sector would be facing a dearth of qualified commercial pilots, expatriates and technicians. It is estimated that a requirement of 40,000 cabin crew members will arise in coming five years.

Attrition: Skilled employees are leaving their companies on a large scale thus, resulting in dearth of talented professionals in the companies. The attrition among pilots and cabin crew is as high as 46 per cent. Moreover, maximum attrition is observed in employees in age group of 26 to 30 years with experience of two to four years.

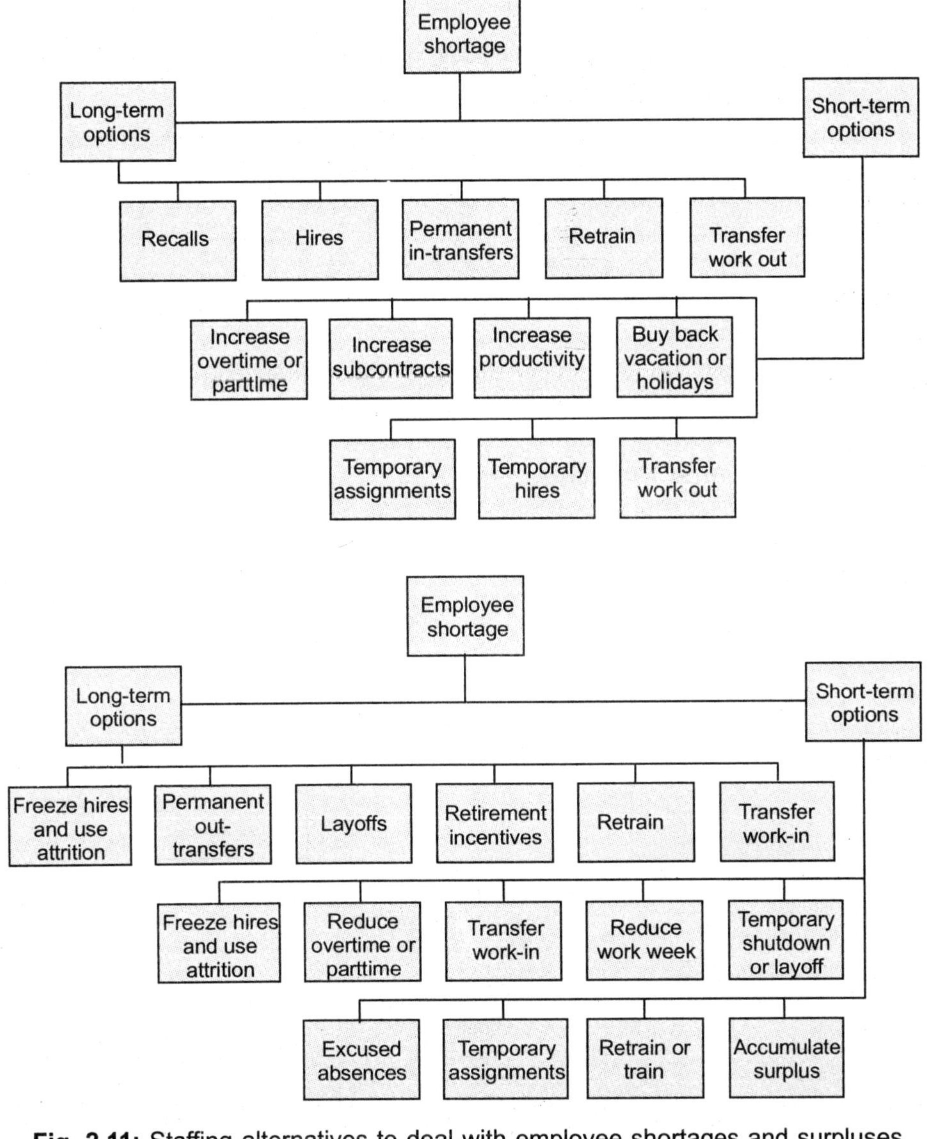

Fig. 2.11: Staffing alternatives to deal with employee shortages and surpluses

Exhibit: HR Planning Software

Information Technology has greatly facilitated the HR planning in organizations. One example of such software used by organizations for HR planning is known as Oriador staff scheduling software. Oriador staff scheduling software takes the pain out of HR scheduling, shift planning and staff rotations. With Oriador managers can prepare and distribute the staff schedule easier and faster, saving time and money for the business and reducing stress for analysis complex datas and information related to employees in the organization. Unlike traditional spreadsheet style staff scheduling softwares, Oriador has been developed from the ground up to provide an attractive, easy to use graphical interface for defining and maintaining schedules and work plans. Oriador staff scheduling software (Oriador Rota) takes care of an organization's staff schedules and rosters quickly and easily, enabling managers with more time and energy for other, more important tasks. The finished schedule can be exported to the web or a company intranet, while payroll or timesheet data can be exported to Microsoft Excel for further analysis. The following figure illustrates how Oriador is used for employee work scheduling in a particular organization.

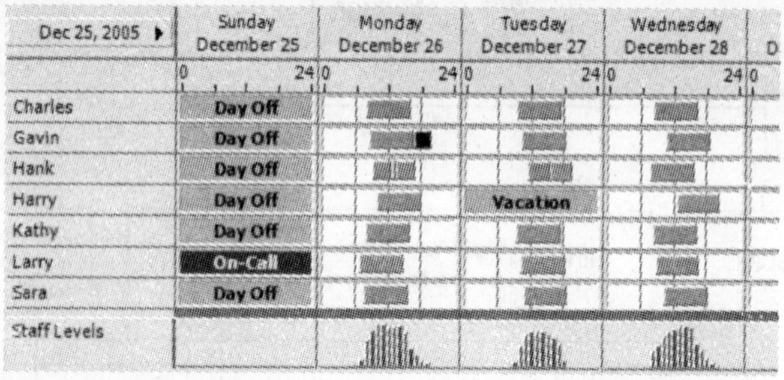

Fig. 2.12: Oriador: simple, graphical staff scheduling

(*Courtesy: http://oriador-staff-scheduling.com/hr-human-resource-planning.htm*)

Strategic Human Resource Planning

Strategic workforce planning is not limited to hiring and retaining talent, but anticipating future manpower needs of an organization. In a dynamic business scenario, manpower planning is critical to organizational

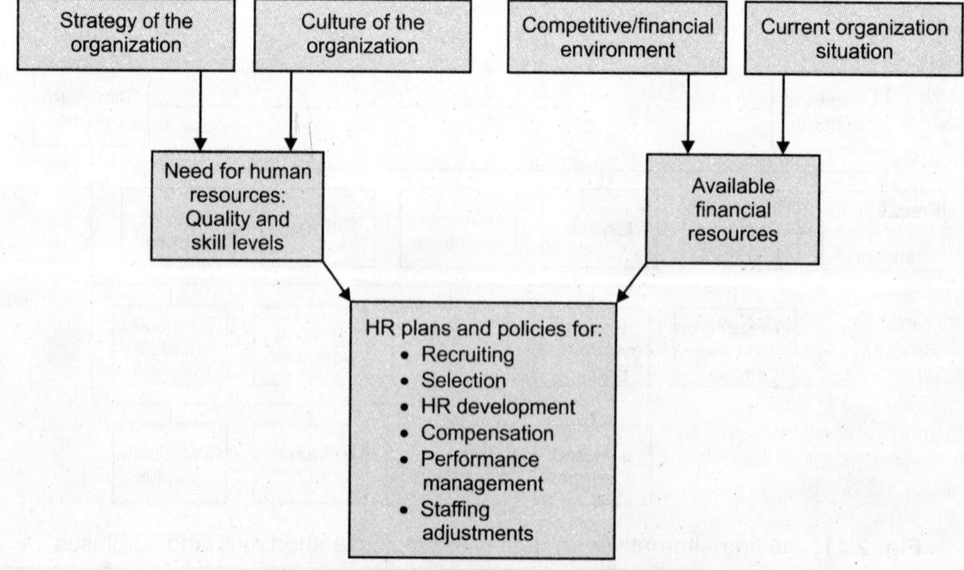

Fig. 2.13: Factors influencing HR plans

growth and stability. It is integral to recruiting, retaining, retraining and redeployment of talent. Linked to business needs of the organization, the process is much more complicated than it seems, primarily because it also involves developing skills and competencies of existing employees to meet market demands which can change with time. Having a contingent plan in place in case of any eventuality (talent shortage) is also critical to the process. The following figure shows the relationship among the variables that determine the HR plans an organization would adopt.

The inter-relationship of organizational strategy and corresponding strategic implications for the HR functions can be illustrated by the following figure.

Table 2.2: Linkage of Organizational and HR Strategies

Organizational Strategy	*Strategic Focus*	*HR Strategy*	*HR Activities*
Cost Leadership	• Efficiency • Stability • Cost-control	• Long HR planning horizon • Build skills in existing employees • Job and employee specialization efficiency	• Promote from within • Extensive training • Hire and train for specific capabilities
Differentiation	• Growth • Innovation • Decentralization	• Shorter HR planning horizon • Hire the HR capabilities needed • Broader, more flexible jobs and employees	• External staffing • Less training • Hire and train for broad competencies

It is necessary for organizations like those of pharmaceutical companies, particularly large and medium sized companies, to have a workforce plan in place. Kris Lakshmikanth, Founder and CEO, The Headhunters India, believes that while the industry will not face manpower crunch like the BPO sector, there will be a shortage of quality people. The obvious reasons are:

- Entry of new MNCs which require people for production, development, sales and product management. People working in existing medium and large pharmaceutical companies will be their targets.
- On the retail front, all big retail groups—Future Group, Reliance, RPG, etc. are setting up pharmacies across India. Subhiksha and Apollo already exist in the South and are set for expansion. These stores will require trained people and the best are obviously available in pharmaceutical companies.
- Clinical research, which requires specialists, is increasingly shifting to India. The salaries of such people have gone up significantly in the last two to three years. Most BSc graduates who were the prime source of supply will shift to clinical research/trials as it offers them better salaries and greater chances of career development. Quality young people will be lost to such companies.
- Finally, many of the pharmaceutical companies are expanding fast, both in India as well as abroad, further aggravating the war for talent.

Significance of strategic workforce plan

- What makes workforce plan very critical is the possible negative repercussions that excess and under recruitment can lead to. It is people who build the organization, consequently any mismatch in employee-related statistics, whether in terms of number, skill set or core competencies may upset the whole organization dynamics and its objectives.
- The employee head count has direct impact on cost but indirect impact is far more sensitive. Workforce planning has a direct link with employee development, multi-skilling and succession planning.
- An organization must forecast its business and expansion strategy correctly and also have its workforce planning in place. There are various management approaches in use for determining either shortage or surplus.

Contd...

- Apart from forecasting, an organization's capability to sustain the current business and to grab the new business makes a big difference.
- A pharmaceutical company should consider factors like current business needs, future plans, growth areas, addition/deletion of business, change in technology, attrition trends and talent availability in the market to ensure that they recruit the right amount of workforce.

Source: *Oasis executive search and management consultancy*[7]

The Time Span of HRP

The time span of human resource planning differs from organization to organization, and can range from the immediate quarter to five years. Both short-term and long-term planning is essential, varying as per the industry or organizational demands. This also differs as per the level of the manpower recruits, whether it is planning for entry level positions or that for senior positions. "Workforce planning is driven by the need at different management levels as the business evolves. At junior level/entry level it make sense to have a yearly plan broken into four quarters whereas at senior level the forecasting for professionals is over a period of two-three years," says Sampath Shetty, VP, Permanent Staffing Business Unit, TeamLease Services. HR planning in pharmaceutical companies requires to be designed on short-term (one-five years) and long-term (more than five years) basis, concede most industry captains from the pharma industry. Career progression and succession planning in this industry is drawn in such a manner that company needs and employee profile are synchronized. This way the industry ensures that employee enriches learning and grows with company. "Workforce planning is reviewed every month to check requirements, status on positions, separations, additional manpower requirements and surplus staff," adds most industry captains[7].

HR Planning for Contingencies

Organizations which have fairly evolved HR systems in place know the importance of a contingent plan for any unexpected situations in terms of aligning their people requirements in the organization. Planning for the future manpower requirements is not just an issue of ascertaining the right number of people requirement, but it also emphasizes how well an organization can deal and realize their skills and capabilities. Hence, the HR planning process should be effective enough so as to avoid talent surpluses or shortages.

A contingency HR plan is put to action when something outside the control of the organization happens. These situations should ideally be over and above those mentioned in the main HR plan of the organization. "The need for a contingency HR plan would come during market fluctuations, stringent deadline, natural calamity, change in technology and may be an unexpected opportunity," states Geeta A Sundrani, Director, Oasis executive search and management consultancy. Sundrani points out that while approved/standard workforce strength as decided for the organization is sufficient even during difficult times, existing employees should be given authority with responsibility to meet the business needs for the hour. Stretch, during crises, could lead to realizing of hidden potential and loyalty of an employee towards the organization.

A buffer/pipeline of suitable candidates is necessary to prevent any last minute surprises. "The recruitment team today works along with business line managers to plan ahead of their manpower needs. Organizations which have gone on rampant panic hiring spree to manage their short-term business needs without considering the flip side of layoffs has led to negativity of the market credibility. If a company is more efficient, it can avoid such unpleasantries and image tarnishing for themselves.

Industry Opinion: BP Chairman and CEO Robert Horton's Opinion on Strategic Human Resource Planning in his Organization

Human resource planning is by its very nature a future-oriented concern. What assumptions about BP's future guide HR practices and policies? These issues were discussed by Mr. Robert Horton in a recent interview with Alan White, in a reputed HR journal.

Horton: I agree that HR is an investment in the future. This long-term investment must sustain over the peaks and troughs of the business cycle. In order to justify this continuous investment, BP, like any other employer, must have a long-term view of the world and its competitive position. BP has such a view of the world and the industry in which we compete. This serves as the basis upon which our investment in HR is made and sustained.

Having said that, the days when we could put a long- or medium-term strategy in place are over. We must continue to develop flexible strategies, and more importantly, flexible processes for looking at strategic directions. HR strategy must be equally flexible, but must assist in pushing strategic options forward.

White: A common failing is for companies to chart strategic directions and to make business plans without effective consideration of HR needs. How will BP ensure the integration of corporate strategic business planning and HR planning?

Horton: HR Planning is used to determine what skills, abilities and knowledge will be needed to compete effectively. HR systems are then aligned with the needs analysis. Currently, we are experimenting with bringing the strategic planning function and the HR function closer together. Initially, we included HR elements is our strategic methodology. We asked questions regarding cultural fit and HR deliverability.

Now, through cooperation between the two staff functions, we are preparing systems and methods where the business strategy and the HR strategy can be aligned. Development of analytical tools as well as diagnostic and prescriptive tools is being tested. The next step will be to provide the businesses with the systems to do their own analysis.

White: BP has a good track record in responding successfully to major changes in its operating environment. What HR practices have contributed to BP's success?

Horton: BP has been able to respond successfully to the changes in the environment. We attribute that ability to the quality of our people. We have been able to recruit the very best people and because of our success, offer them a challenging career with plenty of opportunity for professional diversity among functions. Also, being a worldwide company, we have provided opportunities for international experience. In return, BP people have expressed their loyalty and dedication; they have a high regard for the organization and its goals. It is these qualities that give us the ability to meet the challenge of our changing world.

But we can't become complacent. Our continued ability to respond to change is being challenged, not because our people or our systems are lacking, but because the pace of change is accelerating. Competition is becoming more nimble and technological half-life is forever decreasing. BP, like all other global companies, must find new and better ways to respond to these challenges.

(Courtesy: White, Alan F., (1992): "Organizational transformation at BP: an interview with chairman and CEO Robert Horton", Human Resource Planning, Saturday, February, 1st, 1992. (www.allbusiness.com/business-planning/business-structures/328843-1.html)

Roles and Responsibilities of Human Resource Planning Teams

It is important to remember that when employees are involved in the HR planning process, they also accept the plan and promote it to other employees. A HR planning team should consist of dedicated and knowledgeable employees from different occupations, locations, and levels within an organization. The National Academy of Public Administration's *Building Successful Organizations: A Guide to Strategic Workforce Planning*[11] provides a specific list of team members. These include:

Top Leaders	Heads of agencies are responsible for recognizing the need for workforce planning, demonstrating commitment, and providing the resources to make it happen.
Line Managers	Line managers should serve on workforce planning teams. Managers are also responsible for using workforce planning as a process for aligning people actions, such as recruitment and training, with strategic goals and objectives.
HR Professionals	HR professionals should serve on workforce planning teams and provide support and workforce data. They should also work closely with line managers in developing and implementing workforce plans.

Contd...

IT (Information Technology) Professionals	IT professionals should serve on workforce planning teams, especially if the process is being automated.
Strategic Planners	Strategic planners should serve on workforce planning teams to ensure linkage between the strategic plan and the workforce plan.
Budget Analysts	Budget analysts should serve on workforce planning teams to ensure linkage between the budget and workforce planning.

(*Courtesy: http://www.hr.state.tx.us/workforce/guide.html*)

Exhibit: A Sample Replacement Chart

Emp code	Name	Designation	Date of joining	Key skills	Training/ certificates	Exp	Comments
ACM01	Sam	Mkt Mgr	13-04-2002	Presentation, negotiator won 12 million order from wal mart in last FY	MBA marketing	10	Ready for promotion
ACH07	Tom	HR executive	1/2/2004	Good in pay roll, sharp analytical skills valuable inputs in formulating incentive plans for sales force	MBA, pursuing HR certification	3	Ready for future promo-tion/training recommended in manage-rial, people handling skills. (Ref personal files-record ACH 07)
ACF109	Bob	Sr. accountant	1/7/1999	CA, experienced in accounting and finalizing	CA, pursuing MBA	15	Satisfactory, lacks depth in project financing fund analysis recommend certification in AMFI (Ref personal files-record ACH 109)

Exhibit: Manpower Requisition Procedure

MANPOWER REQUISITION FORM

Category	C-D4

Date:	**Department Name:**
Requisitioned raised by: **Name:** **Designation:**	
Justification/reason for new manpower (please tick the category and mention the reason)	
Recruitment 1 **Replacement 1**	**Position:** **Supervisor____/Sr. Asst____/** **Asst_____/Jr. Asst______/Helper or Peon_______**
Reason	**Qualification**
	• M. Com/B.com______Nos • H.S.C_________Nos • S.S.C_________Nos • Other _______Nos
Prepared by: **Manager/Dept. Head** Received by: **Manager, HRD**	Reviewed By: **Director** Approved By: **Chief Executive Officer**
Actions taken:	
1. Adverts published/circulated________ 2. CVs received__________ 3. Test (written) taken ___________ 4. Oral test taken _________	

Exhibit: Separation Clearance Sheet

<table>
<tr><td colspan="2">Employee Name</td><td colspan="2">Employee No.</td></tr>
<tr><td colspan="4">Department/Designation</td></tr>
<tr><td colspan="4">Last Day of Work</td></tr>
<tr><td colspan="4">Mode of Disassociation: Resignation/Retirement/Termination/Death
(Please cut the irrelevant)</td></tr>
<tr><td colspan="2">Have You reviewed and completed the Asset Tracking Form and returned to your Supervisor or Department Representative:</td><td>Employee Initials and Date</td><td>Supervisor's Initials and Date</td></tr>
<tr><td>All Keys?</td><td>☐Yes ☐ Not applicable</td><td></td><td></td></tr>
<tr><td>Data in Soft and/or Hard Files</td><td>☐Yes ☐ Not applicable</td><td></td><td></td></tr>
<tr><td>Account Codes and Passes?</td><td>☐Yes ☐ Not applicable</td><td></td><td></td></tr>
<tr><td>Computer/Info Tech Equipment?</td><td>☐Yes ☐ Not applicable</td><td></td><td></td></tr>
<tr><td>Telecommunications Equipment? Sins etc.</td><td>☐Yes ☐ Not applicable</td><td></td><td></td></tr>
<tr><td>Vehicles/Transport Equipment?</td><td>☐Yes ☐ Not applicable</td><td></td><td></td></tr>
<tr><td>Parking Pass? If any Issued</td><td>☐Yes ☐ Not applicable</td><td></td><td></td></tr>
<tr><td>Stationery Items?</td><td>☐Yes ☐ Not applicable</td><td></td><td></td></tr>
<tr><td>Other Equipment and Materials? Like Calculations</td><td>☐Yes ☐ Not applicable</td><td></td><td></td></tr>
<tr><td>Brief Case?</td><td>☐Yes ☐ Not applicable</td><td></td><td></td></tr>
<tr><td>Travel Expense Receipts and Reports?</td><td>☐Yes ☐ Not applicable</td><td></td><td></td></tr>
<tr><td>Sales Manual?</td><td>☐Yes ☐ Not applicable</td><td></td><td></td></tr>
<tr><td>HAVE YOU</td><td>also</td><td></td><td></td></tr>
<tr><td>Given your <u>Forwarding Address</u> to your HR/Payroll for further communication?</td><td>☐Yes ☐ Not applicable</td><td></td><td></td></tr>
<tr><td>If working in Sales Department, taken clearance from Distributors?</td><td>☐Yes ☐ Not applicable</td><td></td><td></td></tr>
<tr><td>Attended your <u>exit interview</u> – for info about benefits- continuation after separation (if applicable) and to offer confidential comments?</td><td>☐Yes ☐ Not applicable</td><td></td><td></td></tr>
</table>

NEXT PAGE completed by Supervisor, HR/Payroll Rep, and Dept Head →

SEPARATION CLEARANCE
SHEET, PAGE-2

Employee Name			**Employee No.**
Department/Designation			
Last Day of Work			
Mode of Disassociation: Resignation/Retirement/Termination/Death (*Please cut the irrelevant*)			
SUPERVISOR:			
HAVE YOU:			**Authorized rep initials and date**
Terminated the individual's access rights to official email?	☐ Yes	☐ Not applicable	
Terminated the individual's signature authority on bank accounts (such as foundation accounts)	☐ Yes	☐ Not applicable	
Collected from the individual all assets listed on Asset Tracking Form?	☐ Yes	☐ Not applicable	
Forwarded materials as appropriate to HR?	☐ Yes	☐ Not applicable	
Submitted appropriate separation actions(s) to HR department prior to the payroll cutoff deadline for the final pay date?	☐ Yes	☐ Not applicable	

DEPARTMENT HEAD:

My signature certifies that all separation requirements for the individual have been satisfied.

Dept head signature	**Dept head name**	**Date**

HR/PAYROLL DEPARTMENT			
HAVE YOU:	**Authorized Rep**		
Cancelled any training scheduled but not yet incurred?	☐ Yes	☐ Not applicable	
Cancelled any travel scheduled but not yet incurred?	☐ Yes	☐ Not applicable	
Receive all liabilities information from finance?	☐ Yes	☐ Not applicable	
Set up an exit interview?	☐ Yes	☐ Not applicable	

A copy of this completed form should be submitted for the individual's permanent personnel file

TO:	**HR Department**	
HR Use Only		

Exhibit: Work Analysis Report Required for HRP Generated by an ERP Package

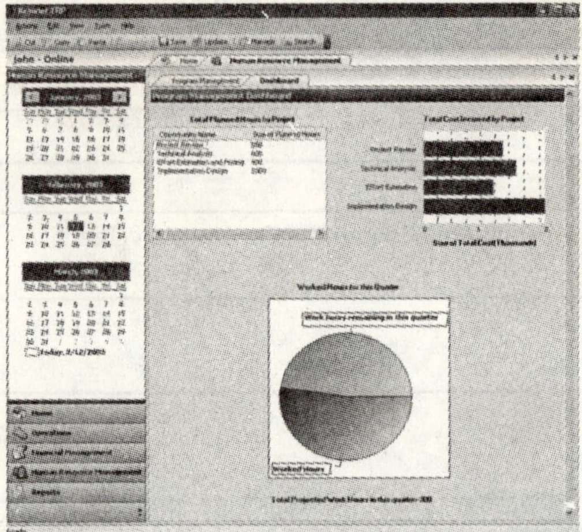

(*Courtesy: www.krawlernetworks.com/ea-hra-1b.jpg*)

Exercise Case Study: Metro Department Store

Metro departmental store is a multi-division, multi-locational largest departmental store based in New Delhi. Its growth in Delhi has been phenomenal. The store sells through its exclusive outlet to its growing number of customers—a variety of consumable goods and electronic items of household requirements.

The proprietors have decided to start in about a years period from now four more departmental stores in other metros' such as Mumbai, Kolkata, Chennai and Bangalore. The director in-charge of this expansion plan is not aware of the planning, recruitment and selection techniques in operation in the industry having grown through experience in family business. Prepare a manpower plan for this project. The requirements for experienced, fresh personnel in various activities of the departmental stores in the large metros stated above should be in keeping with consumer demand. The departments would include HR, Finance, Stores, Purchase, Marketing, Security, Cash counters, Godown keeper, warehousing, transport, housekeeping and customer guides. These departmental stores would be two storied buildings.

REVIEW QUESTIONS

1. Identify the basis on which the manpower plan for each store in each city would be made.
2. Suggest recruitment and selection methodology that you would consider.
3. Identify the kind of training requirements and the approach you would take to ensure effective deployment of staff.
4. What would be your approach to settling compensation to the staff?

REFERENCES

1. http://business.mapsofindia.com/cement/
2. http://www.economywatch.com/business-and-economy/cement-industry.html
3. http://www.pr-inside.com/in-india-s-cement-industry-the-real-r626781.htm
4. http://www.citehr.com/4272-human-resources-planning.html

5. Edwin B. Geisler (2006): "Organizational placement of manpower planning", Human Resource Management, Vol. 7, Issue: 1, pp. 29–35.
6. Bruce P. Coleman (1970): "An integrated system for manpower planning", *Business Horizons*, 1970, Vol. 13, Issue: 5 pp. 89–95.
7. http://www.expresspharmaonline.com/20070831/pharmalife01.shtml
8. Bramham, J. (1994) Human resource planning, 2nd edition, London, Institute of Personnel Development, 1994.
9. Taylor, S. (2002) People Resourcing, 3rd edition, London, Chartered Institute of Personnel and Development.
10. Sang-hyun Park, Seung-jun Yeon, Sang-wook Kim, "Building a Dynamic Manpower Planning Model: Focused on the Information Security Manpower Policy of Korea" http://www.systemdynamics.org/conferences/2006/proceed/papers/PARK415.pdf
11. http://www.hr.state.tx.us/workforce/guide.html

QUESTION BANK

1. Define human resource planning. State its importance in organizations.
2. Define manpower planning. State its objectives and importance. What are the benefits of manpower planning?
3. What is the need for human resource planning?
4. Describe the components of HRP.
5. How is HRP linked with the strategic planning process in the organization?
6. What is the role of HRP in human capital management?
7. What is the relation of HRP and setting organizational strategies?
8. Describe the process of HRP with relevant diagrams.
9. What are the techniques used for forecasting manpower demand in HRP?
10. How manpower supply is determined for HRP?
11. What is manpower gap analysis? How does it help in formulating a HR plan?
12. Describe what you mean by strategic HRP.
13. How does HRP help in effective staffing?

Internet Exercises

- Study the labour bureau website in details. Give a presentation to your class how this website related information could he helpful for human resource planning.
- Go to the business portal of India and CII websites and identify their importance in manpower planning.

Games

- Assume that you have been hired by Reliance Fresh as a Retail manager. Your job also includes some HR activities like recruiting. Now your boss has allocated a budget of 5 lakhs for the upcoming recruitment project. How would you go ahead?
- Assume that you are an entrepreneur of a SME selling pickles. How would you go ahead for managing your company? Give a presentation.

JOB ANALYSIS

Theme Case: Why Job Analysis Matters

Manjunath, a 34 year old, worked as an order-filler cum team leader in the shop floor section of an engineering firm located in the Peenya Industrial Estate, Bangalore. The job required him to lift as much as 80 kgs of load, until a back injury took him off work temporarily. His other responsibility was as a supervisor and team leader for a group of workers whom he used to supervise regularly. Covered by the workers' compensation policy of his company, he received physical therapy for several weeks from a private hospital in Bangalore and then returned to his job. After a short time, however, he again reinjured his back, and was off work again to receive physical therapy and treatment. Manjunath returned to work a second time, only to have the same injury flare up again.

A hard worker and a valued employee, Manjunath was frustrated by the back injury that kept him off the job. In addition, his employer was paying thousands of rupees in disability-related costs because of his injury, and the company lost the benefit of having him at work as more than a worker, he was an efficient team leader in the shop floor. It was perhaps the time for a new strategy.

The company turned Manjunath's case over to a disability-management department of a famous private hospital located in the Airport road, Bangalore which searched for the underlying reason for his injury. Each time he returned to work, his doctor had pronounced him fit for duty. Yet what then was the problem no one could understand. The company and HR department was in full support to what happened to Manjunath, yet everybody was confused what to do.

The answer was discovered in a complete job analysis conducted by an ergonomist from a consultant firm which was subsequently consulted on advice from the disability-rehabilitation department of the private hospital. The analysis broke down the tasks and components of Manjunath's job, as well as the aptitudes, skills, physical environment and work schedule. This revealed that the amount of weight that Manjunath had to lift was only part of the problem. The compounding factor was that his job required mandatory overtime, which proved to be too much, too soon, for him as he returned to work. Without a thorough job analysis, Manjunath could have continued the cycle of injuries, perhaps until he was no longer able to perform his job. In the end, it was the job analysis that uncovered the problem and provided the solution.

Job Analysis is Something More than a Checklist

More than just a checklist of requirements (such as the ability to type a certain number of words per minute) or physical demands (for example, lifting 50 pounds or standing for a certain number of hours), a true job analysis can breakdown and catalog the movements, motions, and aptitudes of the tasks that make up a job. Everything from the purpose of the job to the physical environment is noted. With complete information and understanding of what a job entails, employers like that of Manjunath's can have a powerful tool for assisting and placing their workers. At the shopfloor where Manjunath worked, employees were later videotaped as they performed their duties, which yielded a wealth of detail about the kinds of tasks, the physical postures, and other demands of their jobs. This case, in fact became the eye opener for the entire organization where a simple job analysis became the basis of a plan for Manjunath's return to work.

With input from his physician, transitional duties were assigned to Manjunath, who performed his regular job for the first few hours of the day and then worked as a stores data operator. The job analysis showed that the skills-set of the stores data operator matched many of the functions that Manjunath performed as a team leader while recording the activities and events done by his team. The stores data operator job, however, was far less physically demanding for Manjunath, which gave him sufficient time for recovery.

A Benchmarking Tool

Manjunath's case is a clear-cut example of the value of job analysis, particularly to determine if ill or injured employees can return to their jobs and to assign temporary, modified tasks to them. But that only scratches the surface of usage for in-depth job analyses. Job analyses are important documentation for interviewing, selecting, and training employees, as well as promoting them. In this instance, the job analysis serves as a kind of benchmark to measure and quantify employee performance, and to determine if an employee has the qualifications to move into a new position. Further they can be used for safety and prevention to identify and address potential hazards and stress factors before they become a problem. Later on in a Peenya Industrial Association meeting Mr. Suresh, the Managing Director of the company expressed the importance of job analysis in his organization and expressed his concern for other organizations having similar problems in the Peenya Industrial estate.

What is a Job?

A job may be defined as a "collection or aggregation of tasks, duties and responsibilities which as a whole, are regarded as a regular assignment to individual employees". Thus each job has a definite title based upon standardized trade specifications within a job; two or more grades may be identified, where the work assignments may be graded according to skill, the difficulty in doing them, or the quality of workmanship. Further, a job may include many positions, for a position is a job performed by, related to, a particular employee.

What is Job Analysis?

Definition: Job analysis can be described as the process involving formal and detailed examination of the jobs, which involves the identification of the required tasks, knowledge and the skills necessary for performing them and the conditions under which they should be performed.

Edwin Flippo has described "Job analysis is the process of studying and collecting information relating to the operations and responsibility of a specific job".

Harry Wylie has described "Job analysis deals with the anatomy of the job. This is the complete study of the job embodying every known and determinable factor, including the duties and responsibilities involved in its performance; the conditions under which performance is carried on; the nature of the task; the qualifications required in the worker; and the conditions of employment, such as pay hours, opportunities and privileges".

The 3 basic parts of Job analysis are (a) Identifying the job (b) obtaining information about the tasks, duties, responsibilities and working conditions of the job and (c) determining the worker characteristics needed for successful performance of the job.

Job analysis can be written as:

Job Analysis = Job Description + Job Specification + Job Performance Standards

Importance of Job Analysis

The general purpose of job analysis is to document the requirements of a job and the work performed. Job and task analysis is performed as a preliminary to successive actions, including to define a job domain, write a job description, create performance appraisals, selection and promotion, training needs assessment, compensation and organizational analysis/planning.

In the fields of Human Resources (HR) and Industrial Psychology, job analysis is defined as process involving gathering information for the use in personnel selection, training, classification, and/or compensation.

Job analysis is a systematic approach to defining the job role, description, requirements, responsibilities, evaluation, etc. It helps in finding out required level of education, skills, knowledge, training, etc. for the job position. It also depicts the job worth i.e. measurable effectiveness of the job and contribution of job to the organization. Thus, it effectively contributes to setting up the compensation package for the job position.

Job analysis helps in analyzing the resources and establishing the strategies to accomplish the business goals and strategic objectives. It forms the basis for demand-supply analysis, recruitments, compensation management, and training need assessment and performance appraisal.

What Aspects of a Job are analyzed: Job Analysis should collect information on the following areas:

- **Duties and Tasks:** The basic unit of a job is the performance of specific tasks and duties. Information to be collected about these items may include: frequency, duration, effort, skill, complexity, equipment, standards, etc.
- **Environment:** This may have a significant impact on the physical requirements to be able to perform a job. The work environment may include unpleasant conditions such as offensive odors and temperature extremes. There may also be definite risks to the incumbent such as noxious fumes, radioactive substances, hostile and aggressive people, and dangerous explosives.
- **Tools and Equipment:** Some duties and tasks are performed using specific equipment and tools. Equipment may include protective clothing. These items need to be specified in a Job Analysis.
- **Relationships:** Supervision given and received. Relationships with internal or external people.
- **Requirements:** These include the knowledge, skills, and abilities (KSA's) required performing the job. While an incumbent may have higher KSA's than those required for the job, a Job Analysis typically only states the minimum requirements to perform the job.

Job analysis is a systematic procedure to analyze the requirements for the job role and job profile. Job analysis can be further categorized into following sub components.

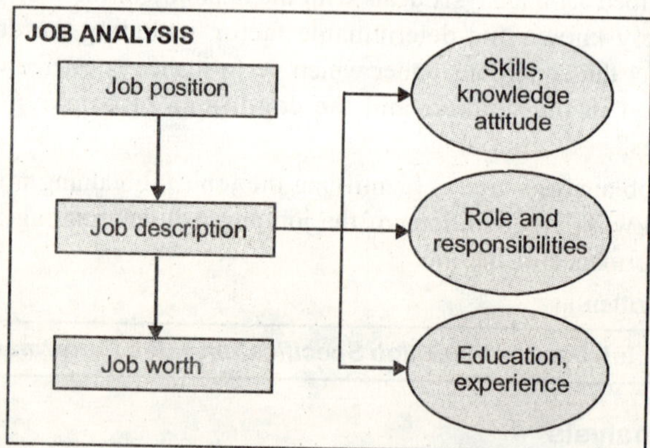

Fig. 2.14: Components of job analysis

Job Position

Job position refers to the designation of the job and employee in the organization. Job position forms an important part of the compensation strategy as it determines the level of the job in the organization. For example, management level employees receive greater pay scale than non-managerial employees. The non-monetary benefits offered to two different levels in the organization also vary.

Job Description

Job description refers the requirements an organization looks for a particular job position. It states the key skill requirements, the level of experience needed, level of education required, etc. It also describes the roles and responsibilities attached with the job position. The roles and responsibilities are key determinant factor in estimating the level of experience, education, skill, etc. required for the job. It also helps in benchmarking the performance standards.

Job Worth

Job worth refers to estimating the job worthiness i.e. how much the job contributes to the organization. It is also known as job evaluation. Job description is used to analyze the job worthiness. It is also known as job evaluation. Roles and responsibilities helps in determining the outcome from the job profile. Once it is determined that how much the job is worth, it becomes easy to define the compensation strategy for the position.

Therefore, job analysis forms an integral part in the formulation of compensation strategy of an organization. Organizations should conduct the job analysis in a systematic at regular intervals. Job analysis can be used for setting up the compensation packages, for reviewing employees' performance with the standard level of performance, determining the training needs for employees who are lacking certain skills.

Purposes of Job Analysis

The purpose of job analysis is to establish and document the '*job relatedness*' of employment procedures such as training, selection, compensation and performance appraisal.

Determining Training Needs

Job analysis can be used in training/"needs assessment" to identify or develop:

- training content
- assessment tests to measure effectiveness of training
- equipment to be used in delivering the training
- methods of training (i.e., small group, computer-based, video, classroom...)

Compensation

Job analysis can be used in compensation to identify or determine:

- skill levels
- compensable job factors
- work environment (e.g., hazards, attention, physical effort)
- responsibilities (e.g., fiscal, supervisory)
- required level of education (indirectly related to salary level)

Selection Procedures

Job analysis can be used in selection procedures to identify or develop:

- job duties that should be included in advertisements of vacant positions;
- appropriate salary level for the position to help determine what salary should be offered to a candidate;
- minimum requirements (education and/or experience) for screening applicants;
- interview questions;

- selection tests/instruments (e.g., written tests, oral tests, job simulations);
- applicant appraisal/evaluation forms;
- orientation materials for applicants/new hires.

Performance Review

Job analysis can be used in performance review to identify or develop:

- goals and objectives
- performance standards
- evaluation criteria
- length of probationary periods
- duties to be evaluated

Job Analysis Information: The job analysis provides the following information:

- ***Job Identification***: Job title, job code number
- ***Characteristics of the Job***: Job location, Physical setting, supervision levels required, union jurisdiction, hazards associated etc.
- ***Job Duties (Principal activities)***: A detailed list of the duties along with the probable frequency of occurrence of each duty.
- ***Equipments and materials used:***
- ***How a Job is done***: Focus lies mainly on the nature of operations associated with the job.
- ***Required Personnel Attributes***: Experience levels, trainings undertaken, apprenticeships, physical strength, coordination levels, mental capabilities, social skills, communication skills etc.
- ***Job Relationships***: Opportunities for advancement, working conditions, essential cooperation etc.

Uses of Job Analysis: Job analysis has the following uses and implications in an organization:

- ***Human Resource Planning (HRP)***: Job analysis helps in forecasting HR requirements in terms of knowledge and skills. By showing lateral and vertical relationships between jobs, it facilitates the formulation of a systematic promotion and transfer policy.
- ***Recruitment***: It is used to find out how and when to hire people for future job openings. An understanding of the skills needed and the positions that are vacant in the future helps managers to plan and hire people in a systematic way.
- ***Selection***: Without a proper understanding of what is to be done on a job, it is not possible to select a right person for the right job.
- ***Placement and Orientation***: After selecting people, the newly recruited employees have to be placed for the jobs best suited to their interests, activities and aptitude. Job analysis helps to determine to effectively identify the right person for the right job. Similarly, it also helps in the implementation of effective job orientation by enabling a proper understanding of the needs of each concerned job.
- ***Training***: If there is any confusion about what the job is and what is supposed to be done, proper training efforts cant be initiated.
- ***Counseling***: Managers can properly counsel employees about their careers when they understand the different jobs in the organization.
- ***Employee Safety***: A thorough job analysis reveals unsafe conditions associated with a job and thereby helps to reduce risks and associated with jobs at the workplace.
- ***Performance Appraisal***: By comparing what an employee is supposed to be doing (based on Job analysis) to what the individual has actually done, the worth of that person can be assessed.

- ***Job Design and Redesign***: Once the jobs are understood properly, it is easy to locate weak spots and undertake remedial steps.
- ***Job Evaluation***: Job analysis helps in finding the relative worth of a job, based on criteria such as degree of difficulty, type of work done, skills and knowledge needed etc.

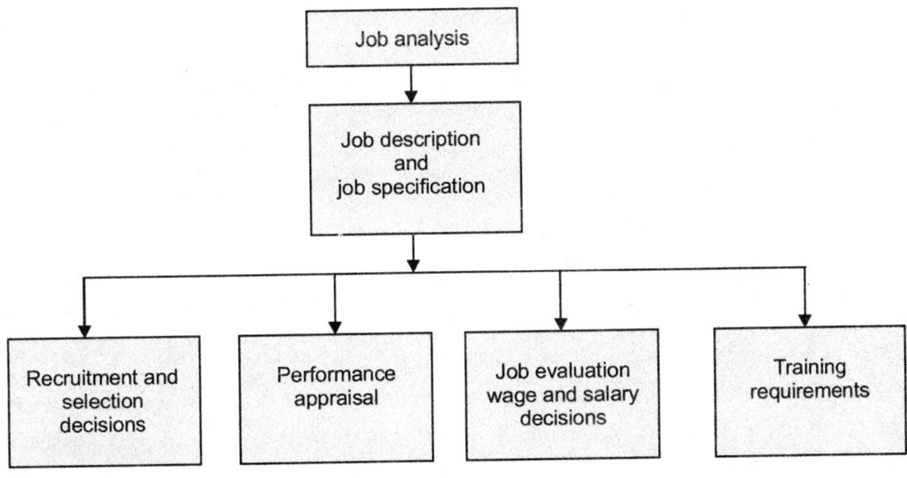

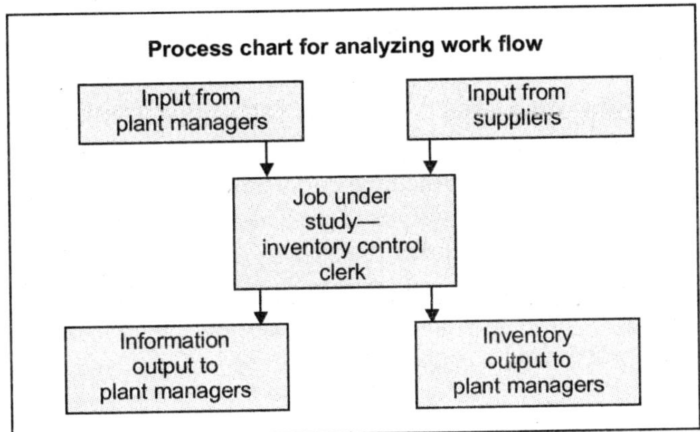

Fig. 2.15: Process chart for analyzing work flow

Benefits of Job Analysis

Job analysis has the following advantages:

- It serves as a basis for clarifying job expectations with workers.
- It facilitates worker performance since there is specific information about job tasks and competencies necessary for assessing the outcomes.
- It serves as an information base for assessing the staffing process.
- It serves as a tool for monitoring the relationship between the work performed by staff and the goals and objectives of organization.
- Job analysis could be effectively used so as to identify the training needs of workers.

Methods of Job Analysis: The various methods of job analysis are as follows:

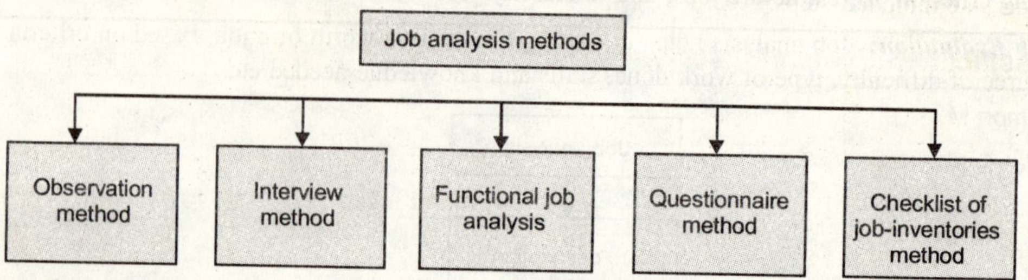

***Observation Method*:** Three methods of Job Analysis are based on observation. These are: Direct Observation; Work Method Analysis, including time and motion studies and micro-motion analysis; and critical incident method.

***Interview Method*:** It involves discussions between job analysis and job occupants or experts. Job analysis data from individual and group interviews with employees are often supplemented by information from supervisors of employees whose jobs are to be analyzed.

***Daily Method*:** It requires the job holders to record in details their activities on a daily basis.

***Technical Conference Method*:** In this method, services of the supervisors who possess extensive knowledge about a job are used with the help of a conference of the supervisors. The analyst initiates discussion which provides details about the job.

***Functional Job Analysis (FJA)*:** It is a method that uses precise terminology and a structured job analysis "schedule" to record information regarding the job content. It is especially useful to the recruiting and selection functions.

***Questionnaire Method*:** These can be filled out by the employees on an individual basis or by job analysts for a group of employees.

***Job Inventories or Checklists*:** These are structured questionnaires that require a respondent to check or rate behaviour and/or worker character necessary to a particular job or occupation. Job inventories can either be Task/Job Oriented or Qualifications/Worker oriented.

***Job Performance Method*:** In this method the job analyst actually performs the job in question and thus receives 1st hand experiences of contextual factors on the job including physical hazards, social demands, emotional pressures mental requirements.

Task Inventories

The task inventory emphasizes work activities. In this approach a list of tasks pertinent to a group of jobs is developed. Then the tasks involved in the job under study are rated on a number of scales by incumbents or supervisors. Finally the ratings are manipulated statistically, usually by computer, and a quantitative job analysis is developed. Actually any method of job analysis, even narrative job descriptions, could be termed a task inventory if an analysis of the data can provide quantitative information from appropriate scales. One example of this type of job analysis is the **Comprehensive Occupational Data Analysis Program (CODAP).** After the task list has been prepared by incumbents, supervisors, or experts, incumbents are asked to indicate whether they perform each of the tasks. They are then asked to indicate on a scale the relative amount of time spent in performing each particular task. Other ratings are also obtained, such as training time required and criticality of performance. The ratings are then summed across all tasks and an estimated percentage of time on each task is derived. The total percentages account for the total job. The relative times are then used to develop a group job description. Computer programs are used to analyze, organize, and report on data from the task inventory. The CODAP is most useful for large organizations and is relatively costly. The descriptor employed is *work activities*, and the output of the analysis is the *work performed*. *Worker requirements* must be inferred, as in conventional job analysis. Data developed by this method have been used in selection to identify training needs and design training programs, to validate training completion as a training criterion, to restructure jobs, and to classify jobs.

Classification Systems used as basis for or resulting from job analyses[1].	
Common Metric Questionnaire (CMQ)	The Common Metric Questionnaire (CMQ) is targeted toward both exempt and non-exempt jobs. It has five sections: (1) Background, (2) Contacts with People, (3) Decision Making, (4) Physical and Mechanical Activities, and (5) Work Setting. The CMQ is a relatively new instrument. It has been field tested on 4,552 positions representing over 900 occupations in the Dictionary of Occupational Titles (DOT), and yielded reasonably high reliabilities. (Harvey, 1993)[2]
Fleishman Job Analysis Survey	Another job analysis methodology—the Fleishman Job Analysis Survey (FJAS), formerly the Manual for Ability Requirements Scales—contains a taxonomy of abilities that is buttressed by decades of research (Fleishman and Mumford, 1991)[1]. FJAS uses level of ability rating scales that specify level of functioning requirements for jobs.
Functional Job Analysis Scales	Beginning in the 1940s, Functional Job Analysis (FJA) was used by U.S. Employment Service job analysts to classify jobs for the DOT (Fine and Wiley, 1971)[1]. The most recent version of FJA uses seven scales to describe what workers do in jobs: (1) Things, (2) Data, (3) People, (4) Worker Instructions, (5) Reasoning, (6) Math, and (7) Language. Each scale has several levels that are anchored with specific behavioural statements and illustrative tasks. Like other job analysis instruments, FJA is a methodology for collecting job information.
MOSAIC	The Office of Personnel Management (OPM) is in the process of developing a database of information on federal jobs using Multipurpose Occupational Systems Analysis Inventory-Closed Ended (MOSAIC). Toward that end, OPM has been conducting a series of occupational analysis projects, each project handling a different set of occupations (e.g., clerical, managerial, etc.). Each job analysis inventory used to collect data for OPM's system includes a variety of descriptors. The two primary types of descriptors in each questionnaire are tasks and competencies. Tasks are rated on importance and competencies are rated on several scales including importance and requirement for entry.
Occupational Analysis Inventory (OAI)	The Occupational Analysis Inventory (OAI) contains 617 "work elements." It was designed to yield more specific job information than other multi-job questionnaires such as the PAQ while still capturing work requirements for virtually all occupations. The major categories of items are five-fold: (1) Information Received, (2) Mental Activities, (3) Work Behaviour, (4) Work Goals, and (5) Work Context. OAI respondents rate each job element on one of four rating scales: part-of-job, extent, applicability, or a special scale designed for the element. Reliabilities obtained with the OAI have been moderate, somewhat lower than those achieved with the PAQ.

Contd...

Position Analysis Questionnaire (PAQ)	The Position Analysis Questionnaire (PAQ) developed by McCormick, Jeanneret and Mecham (1972)[3] is a structured job analysis instrument to measure job characteristics and relate them to human characteristics. It consists of 195 job elements that represent in a comprehensive manner the domain of human behaviour involved in work activities. The items that fall into five categories: Information input (where and how the worker gets information), Mental processes (reasoning and other processes that workers use), Work output (physical activities and tools used on the job), Relationships with other persons, and Job context (the physical and social contexts of work).

Exhibit: A Sample Page from the PAQ

1. Information input

1.1. Sources of job information

Rate each of the following items in terms of the extent to which it is used by the worker as a source of information in performing his job.

	Extent of Use (U)
NA	Does not apply
1	Nominal/very infrequent
2	Occasional
3	Moderate
4	Considerable
5	Very substantial

1.1.1 Visual sources of job information

01 U Written materials (books, reports, office notes, articles, job instructions, signs, etc.

02 U Quantitative materials (materials which deal with quantities or amounts, such as graphs, accounts, specifications, tables of numbers, etc.)

03 U Pictorial meterials (pictures or picturelike materials used as sources of information, for example, drawings, blueprints, diagrams, maps, tracings, photographic films, X-ray films, TV pictures, etc.)

04 U Patterns/related devices (templates, stencils, patterns, etc., used as sources of information when observed during use; do not include here materials described in item 3 above)

05 U Visual displays (dials, gauges, signal lights, radarscopes, speedometers, clocks, etc.)

06 U Measuring devices (rulers, calipers, tire pressure gauges, scales, thickness gauges, pipettes, thermometers, protractors, etc., used to obtain visual information about physical measurements; do not include here devices described in item 5 above)

Systems Exchange Model of Job Analysis

Since the job is the connection between the organization and the employee, it may be useful to develop a model based upon this common connection. We can say that both the organization and the employee contribute to the job and expect to receive something from it. In order for these results to come about, something has to happen inside the job. This dual systems exchange model is illustrated in the following figure. The vertical dimension of the model is the person-job relationship. The person brings his or her abilities and effort to the job (cell 1). These are used in activities, which are divided into physical, mental and interactional types (cell 3). The results, for the person, are the rewards and satisfaction received from working on the job (cell 5). These rewards can be both intrinsic and extrinsic.

The horizontal dimension of the model is the organization-job relationship. The organization brings to the job resources needed to perform the job and ways to do the job that coordinate with organizational needs; the latter are perceived as constraints (cell 2). These resources and constraints determine the way the job activities (cell 3) are carried out. The organizational results are some product created or service performed by the employee; these outcomes are in the form of a change in data, people, and/or objects (cell 4). These results can be defined in terms of quantity, quality and time. This model suggests that information (descriptors of jobs) can be collected on the purpose of the job (cell 4), the activities of the job (cell 3), the worker requirements of the job (cell 1), the organizational context of the job (cell 2), and the rewards of the job to the worker (cell 5).

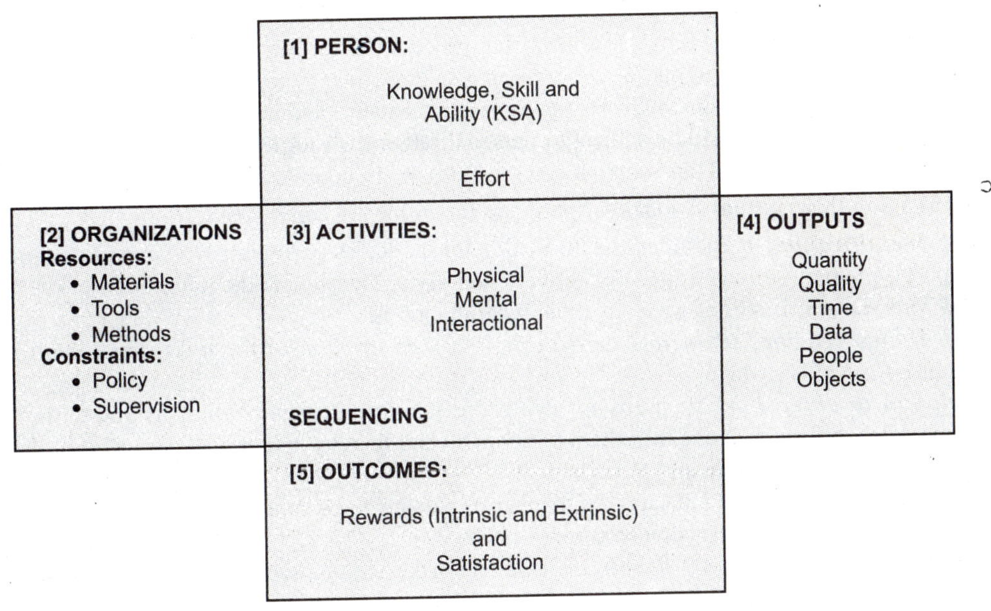

Fig. 2.16: Systems exchange model of job analysis

Role of Job Analysts

Employees, supervisors, and job analysts perform the tasks of collecting and analyzing job information. Job incumbents have the most complete and accurate information, but getting this information and making the results consistent requires attention to data-collection methods. Also, employee acceptance of the results is a priority, and employee involvement in data collection and analysis tends to promote this. Supervisors may or may not know the jobs of their subordinates well enough to be useful sources of job information. If they do know the jobs well enough, a great deal of time and money can be saved.

Job analysts have been trained to collect job information. They know what to look for and what questions to ask. They also know how to standardize the information and the language employed. People with various educational backgrounds have been trained as job analysts. Most organizations train their own job analysts by having them work with experienced analysts. Experience suggests that limited training suffices to provide these skills.

Exhibit: Job Analysis Software[6]

Occupational Assessor™ Professional Edition is a job analysis software which provides detailed job descriptions for more than 20,000 position titles. It also analyzes job for FLSA exempt/non-exempt determinations, transferable skills assessment, career counseling and vocational rehabilitation.

(Courtesy: http://www.paq.com/index.cfm?FuseAction=bulletins.job-analysis-questionnaire)

Components of Job Analysis

Job Description: A Job Description (JD) is a written statement of what the job holder does how it is done, under what conditions it is done and why it is done. It describes what the job is all about, throwing light on job content, environment and conditions of employment. It is descriptive in nature and defines the purpose and scope of a job. It is a statement of duties, tasks and activities of a position. It elucidates the primary and secondary activities of a position. It also presents the reporting relationship and also the conditions under which the position holder should work. (For example, desk job, lot of traveling involved, always on the field, etc.). The main purpose of writing a Job Description is to differentiate the job from other jobs and state its outer limits.

An accurate job description, composed with clarify and brevity and based on the careful analysis of the tasks performed, is essential not only for the staffing process but for job evaluation and the full range of Human Resources functions. Without job description as a guideline, interviewing job candidates would be difficult selecting the right person would be a gamble. Performance appraisals would be more guess work, evaluations for promotions would be subject to personal rather than professional considerations, selecting for training would be haphazard, and comparison structure might be invalid.

Contents of a Job Description: A job description has the following components.

- ***Job Identification***: It includes the Job title, Job code, Department, Division, Location, Plant, Reporting Supervisor and aims to effectively identify and designate the job properly.
- ***Job Summary***: It is a brief write-up about what the job is.
- ***Job Duties/Activities (Principal activities)***: It is a description of the tasks done, facilities used, extent of supervisory help etc.
- ***Relation to other Jobs***: It helps to locate the job in the organization by indicating the job immediately below or above it in the job hierarchy and thereby also provides an idea of the vertical relationships of work flow and procedure.
- ***Supervision Required***: It indicates the number of persons to be supervised along with their job titles and to the extent of supervision required.
- ***Machine/Tools/Equipments Required***: It indicates the various types of tools/equipments used by the job incumbent in his/her day to day job duties.
- ***Working Conditions Involved***: It indicates the physical environment of the job in terms of heat, noise and other hazards.
- ***Social Environment***: Size of the work Group and Interpersonal interactions required for the job.

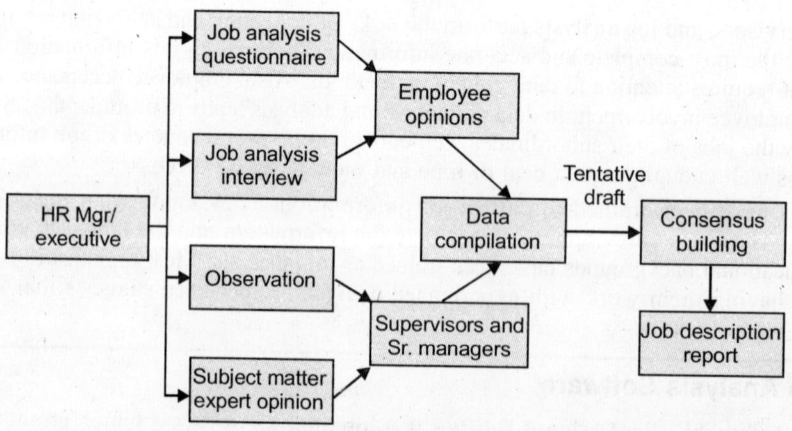

Fig. 2.17: Process of preparing job descriptions

Guidelines for Job Description: The following guidelines can be presented for developing an effective job description:

- The JD should indicate the nature and scope of the job, including all important relationships.
- It should be brief, factual and precise and provide a clear picture of the job.
- It should indicate (a) kind of the work (b) the degree of complexity associated with the job (c) the skills required for the job (d) the extent to which problems are standardized (e) the degree and type of accountability.
- The extent of supervision available.
- The reporting relationships should be clearly indicated.

Managerial Job Descriptions

Managerial job descriptions differ from non-managerial job descriptions in what are called *scope data*. For example, financial and organizational data are used to locate managerial jobs in the hierarchy. The identification section of managerial job descriptions is usually more elaborate and may include the reporting level and the functions of jobs supervised directly and indirectly. The number of people directly and indirectly supervised may be included, as well as department budgets and payrolls. The work-performed section of managerial job descriptions, like that of non-managerial job descriptions, includes the major tasks, but gives special attention to organization objectives. Writers of managerial job descriptions need to remember that "is responsible for….." does not tell the reader what the manager does.

Table 2.3: A Non-managerial Job Description

JOB TITLE: Sales Clerk

JOB SUMMARY: Serves customers, receives and straightens stock, and inspects dressing rooms.

PRINCIPAL ACTIVITIES

1. Serves customers to make sales and to provide advice: Observes customers entering store, approaches them and asks to help, locates desired articles of clothing, and guides customers to dressing rooms. Decides when to approach customers and which articles of clothing to suggest. Sometimes gets suggestions from other sales clerks or supervisor. Rings up purchases on cash register and takes cash or check or processes credit card. Decides whether check or credit card acceptance is within store policy (80%).
2. Receives and arranges stock to attractively exhibit merchandise: Unpacks boxes, counts items, and compares with purchase orders. Reports discrepancies to supervisor. Arranges and inspects new and old merchandise on racks and counters. Removes damaged goods and changes inventory figures. Decides where to place items in the store, within guidelines of supervisor. Twice a year helps with taking inventory by counting and recording merchandise (15%).
3. Inspects dressing rooms to keep them neat and discourage shoplifting: Walks through dressing area periodically, collecting clothing left or not desired. Remains alert to attempts to shoplift clothing from dressing area. Decides when security needs to be called in. Re-hangs merchandise on sales floor (5%).

Table 2.4: A Managerial Job Description

JOB TITLE: Branch Bank Manager

JOB SUMMARY: Promotes bank in community and supervises branch operations and lending activities

PRINCIPAL ACTIVITIES

1. Promotes bank services in the community to increase total assets of the bank: Engages in and keeps track of community activities, both commercial and social. Identifies potential customers in community. Analyzes potential customer needs and prospects, plans sales presentation, and meets with potential customers to persuade them to use bank services (40%).

Contd...

2. Supervises branch operation to minimize cost of operation while providing maximum service: Plans work activity of the branch. Communicates instructions to subordinate supervisors. Observes branch activity. Discusses problems with employees and decides or helps employees decide course of action. Coordinates branch activities with main office. Performs personnel activities of hiring, evaluating, rewarding, training, and disciplining employees and financial activities of budgeting and reviewing financial reports (35%).
3. Evaluates and processes loan requests to increase revenues of the bank: Reviews and analyzes loan requests for risk. Seeks further information as appropriate. Approves (or denies) requests that fall within branch lending limits. Prepares reports to accompany other loan requests to bank loan committee. Keeps up with changes in bank lending policy, financial conditions, and community needs (25%).

Types of Job Descriptions

McCormick[3] had classified job descriptors as follows:

- On the basis of work activities: (a) job-oriented activities (b) worker-oriented activities
- On the basis of machines, tools, equipment used
- On the basis of work performed
- On the basis of job context
- On the basis of personnel requirements

This classification suggests that job analysis can yield six kinds of useful job information. These descriptors presumably flow from McCormick's model[3] of the operational functions basic to all jobs, sensing (information receiving), information storage, information processing, and decision and action (physical control or communication). These functions vary in emphasis from job to job. It is not clear how the five descriptors flow from this model, however it can be suggested that the following job information is needed by organizations: (1) job content factors; (2) job context factors; (3) worker characteristics; (4) work characteristics; and (5) interpersonal relations (internal and external).

Table 2.5: Five Types of Job Descriptions

1. **Worker Functions:** The relationship of the worker to data, people and things.
2. **Work Fields:** The techniques used to complete the tasks of the job. Over 100 such fields have been identified. This descriptor also includes the machines, tools, equipment, and work aids that are used in the job.
3. **Materials, Products, Subject Matter, and/or Services:** The outcomes of the job or the purpose of performing the job.
4. **Worker Traits:** The aptitudes, educational and vocational training, and personal traits required of the worker.
5. **Physical Demands:** Job requirements such as strength, observation and talking. This descriptor also includes the physical environment of the work.

***Source*:** U.S. Department of Labour, Handbook for Analyzing Jobs (Washington, D.C.: U.S. Government Printing Office, 1972[4].

Job Specification

Job specification summarizes the human characteristics needed for satisfactory job completion. It translates the job description into terms of the human qualifications which are required for a successful performance of a job. It is a statement of the eligibility criteria. It describes the qualifications, skills required for the position. It spells out the important attributes of an individual in terms of education, experience, knowledge skills and abilities (KSAs) to perform a particular job.

The personal attributes that are described in a job specification are classified into 3 categories, namely:

- ***Essential Attributes*:** Knowledge, Skills and Abilities (KSAs) of an individual
- ***Desirable Attributes*:** Qualifications of an individual
- ***Contra-indicators*:** Attributes that act as barriers to effective performance of an individual.

It states about the minimum **acceptable** requirement of skill, qualification, knowledge, physical and mental characteristics than an incumbent must posses. Elaboration of these terms is as follows:

Physical Specification: It includes the vision, hearing, height, weight, age and ability to carry the weight etc. as most of the job require physical needs like operating heavy machinery and all.

Mental Specification: It shows the incumbent ability in respect to creativity, analytical ability, data interpretation ability and decision-making ability etc.

Emotional and Social Specification: It shows the ability of incumbent to work in a team, to lead a team and above all the ability to adjust etc.

Behavioural Specifications: The behavioural specifications play an important role in the section of the candidate for higher level jobs. These may include capabilities like those of ability to undertake responsibilities, creativity, emotional maturity etc.

SUCCESS PROFILING

The process for determining the essential requirements for an incumbent to perform effectively at a given level or in a business-critical role is called **Success Profiling**. As illustrated below, Success Profiling is a critical link between business strategy and the identification of development gaps. Success Profiling is similar to **Job Analysis** or **Competency Profiling** but the information that stems from Success Profiling is more detailed, comprehensive and focused on the future.

Success Profile Elements

A well-defined Success Profile should contain four types of information:

1. **Competencies** – clusters of behaviours that are related to success in a given role.
2. **Enablers and Derailers** – personal attributes that may facilitate or hinder success in a role even when everything else is effective. Cognitive ability is sometimes included here as it is, in the broadest sense, a personal attribute.
3. **Key Knowledge** – the degree of understanding that incumbents need to have about the organization and how it operates.
4. **Key Experiences** – the kinds of situations that someone entering a business critical role or progressing to a more challenging role should have experienced or at least have had some exposure to.

Fig. 2.18: A model of success profiling

Success Profiling Process

The core elements that underpin an effective Success Profiling process are as follows:

Background Review and Analysis: An effective Success Profile emerges from a clear understanding of an organization's vision, strategy, values and critical success factors. A review and analysis of documents that contain this type of information is the foundation of a successful Success Profiling process.

***Data Collection*:** The most effective data collection methods used in success profiling are:

***Incumbent Interviews or Focus Groups*:** The aim here is to determine what high performing incumbents actually do in their role.

***Critical Incident Meetings*:** The aim of a Critical Incident Meeting is to find out specific behavioural examples of specific incidents or events that define effective (and sometimes ineffective) performance in the role.

***Repertory Grid Analysis*:** This is a well established method used with managers who operate above the target level being analyzed, to map out their broader perspectives on job/role issues and demands. A structured interviewing process is used to compare and contrast different employees' performance with one another. The technique is used to capture systematically a top down management perspective on the behaviours which lead to superior and less effective performance.

***Visioning Discussions*:** Normally conducted with senior executives to gather information to help understand the broader organizational vision and strategy as well as the desired values and culture.

***Validation*:** This is a critical step that can make or break the utility of a Success Profile. This normally involves asking participants to review the Success Profile(s) and rate comprehensiveness. And, there is often a process for rating and ranking the competencies contained in the profile.

Success Profiling in a FMCG Company: A Case

The common approach adopted by most organizations for developing success profiling is by outsourcing the same from an external OD/HR consultant organization. One case can be cited here how a HR consultant firm helped its large FMCG client in developing the Success Profile for the organization. This FMCG business was under pressure to leverage top-line revenue performance. As part of an overall sales effectiveness strategy, they sought assistance in building the capability of people in business development roles across the organization.

Solution provided by the HR consultant: A HR consultant firm was engaged to help the FMCG client understand the success criteria for different business development roles. The resultant Success Profiles were to be utilized for feedback and development planning and to target and drive the highest pay-off organization development (OD) activities.

Fundamentally different roles were identified through consultation with ***client stakeholders***. These included roles such as sales managers, key account managers and sales representatives.

Through a highly consultative process focus groups were conducted with incumbents to gather data on the range of responsibilities, activities and time applications required in each role. Using the critical incident methodology, managers of incumbents were interviewed to share performance data: the situations or examples that best capture or define strong or poor performance in the roles. Data was also collected to understand the potential derailers in the roles: those personality attributes that may undermine performance even when incumbents are endowed with the ability to display required behaviours. These data enabled the drafting of competencies that captured the behaviours that were thought to underpin success in each role.

Additional data were collected from incumbents and their managers regarding knowledge requirements to perform effectively in the role as well as the key experiences incumbents had previously had that helped them to prepare for the challenges of their current role.

All the data were then analyzed by the consultant firm to draft a provisional Success Profile for each of the different business development roles in the enterprise. The provisional Success Profiles were formatted into a validation questionnaire that gave a wide variety of business development stakeholders the opportunity to comment with respect to the accuracy and comprehensiveness of the provisional data.

Outcome: Following some minor adjustments based on feedback from the validation questionnaire, the finalized Success Profiles were presented for each key business development role in the organization.

Due to the high levels of consultation, robustness of approach, and quality of analysis, the key stakeholders in the organization embraced the Success Profiles and they have been actively deployed through the business.

All people in business development roles have subsequently undertaken development centers to help focus them on leveraging their identified strengths and to close development gaps. The profiles are being used in this organization as the platform for ongoing feedback and performance management and as the basis for recruiting talent from the external labor market and for promoting within. Finally, the profiles are providing the management of this a valuable input into the construction of organization wide capability development programs, ensuring that the focus for development is aligned with the very elements that underpin strong performance.

WORKFLOW ANALYSIS

A **workflow** is a depiction of a sequence of operations, declared as work of a person, work of a simple or complex mechanism, work of a group of persons, work of an organization of staff, or machines. Workflow may be seen as any abstraction of real work, segregated in work share, work split or whatever types of ordering. For control purposes, workflow may be a view on real work under a chosen aspect, thus serving as a virtual representation of actual work. A workflow is a model to represent real work for further assessment, e.g., for describing a reliably repeatable sequence of operations. More abstract a workflow is a pattern of activity enabled by a systematic organization of resources, defined roles and mass, energy and information flows, into a *work process* that can be documented and learned. Workflows are designed to achieve processing intents of some sort, such as physical transformation, service provision, or information processing.

Why Should a Business Use Workflow?

The Evolution of Workflow Management consists of the automation of business procedures or "workflows" during which documents, information or tasks are passed from one participant to another in a way that is governed by rules or procedures. Work flow analysis is the process of examining how work creates or adds value to the ongoing processes in a business.

The Key Benefits of Workflow Analysis

- **Improved efficiency** – automation of many business processes results in the elimination of many unnecessary steps
- **Better process control** – improved management of business processes achieved through standardizing working methods and the availability of audit trails
- **Improved customer service** – consistency in the processes leads to greater predictability in levels of response to customers
- **Flexibility** – software control over processes enables their redesign in line with changing business needs
- **Business process improvement** – focus on business processes leads to their streamlining and simplification

Workflow Mapping: Workflow (process) mapping is one of the fastest ways to lower errors, increase productivity, and affect customer service. It generally follows these steps:

- **Choose a process:** You have to first decide what you want to improve. Some examples are the process of making reservations at a corporate travel center, handling a customer's repair order at a car dealership, or registering students at a college. The best bet is a process which is time-consuming, error-prone, or critical to success; starting where there is a strong potential for improvement will build morale and help launch later mapping projects.
- **Assemble a team:** Preferably, the team will include people from the lowest and highest levels directly involved in the operation, such as customer service agents, their supervisors and managers, and the head of operations. The team must be empowered (given the responsibility and sufficient authority or leeway) to make significant changes in the work flow.
- **Map out the way work is currently done:** Diagram each step, showing decision branches, time spent, any distances traveled or people contacted, and other important aspects of the work. It is often be easier to sketch out the individual tasks first, then go back and fill in the details.
- **Identify problem areas:** These are areas where people feel there are currently major issues to be resolved, such as poor customer satisfaction, "dropping the ball," large expenses, or significant delays. Where there are many areas to choose from, try to follow the 80/20 rule: work on the 20% of the areas that cause 80% of the problems.
- **Brainstorm solutions:** Identify all possible action steps for each problem area, without evaluating them.
- **Evaluate action steps:** Set up a set of "final" action steps by group consensus.
- **Assign responsibilities.** Ask people to volunteer to take responsibility for each action step judged to be worthwhile by the group, and to set deadlines.
- **Create a master plan:** Summarize who has responsibility for what actions and the deadlines. Distribute the plan and make sure everyone agrees with it and that it accurately reflects the decisions made during the sessions.
- **Follow through:** The meetings are useless without appropriate follow-through. Try meeting again every two weeks to see what went well and what did not. When the time is right, try having another brainstorming session. This is where having a detailed, clear, and well communicated master plan is invaluable.

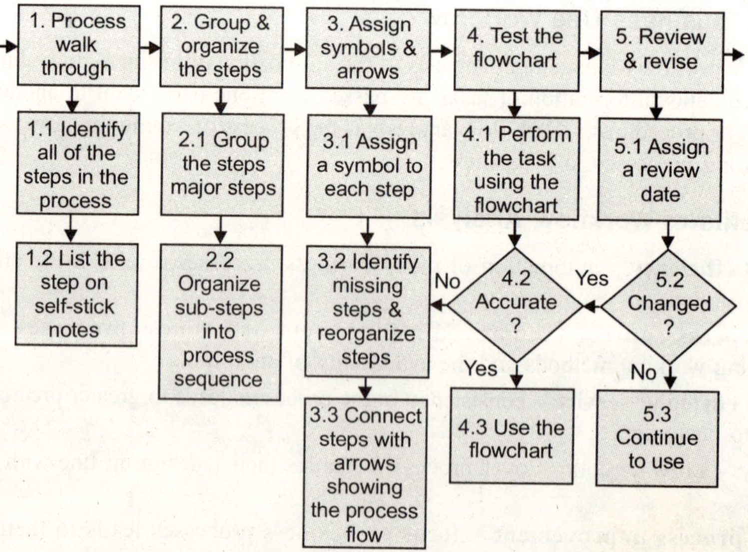

Fig. 2.19: A sample workflow chart

WorkFlow Analysis using softwares: Most organizations carry out their workflow analysis by applying software applications like that of "Ultimus Workflow". The following figure illustrates how this software works.

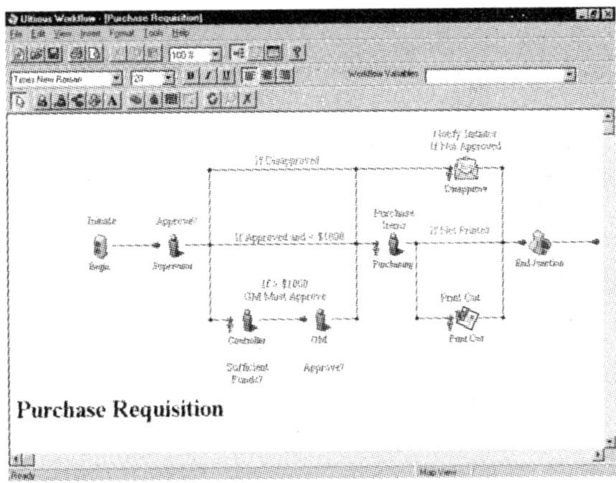

Fig. 2.20: ULTIMUS workflow on the web screen[5]

(*Courtesy: http://www.softscout.com/screenshot/ULTIMUS-WORKFLOW-ON-THE-WEB/91AB7502185DEC8885256F9900187696*)

Exhibit

JOB DESCRIPTION FORM	
Job Title:	Section:
Reports to:	Immediate Subordinate:
PURPOSE OF THE JOB: (What are the objectives or end results of this position?)	
JOB SPECIFICATIONS	
FACTORS	**REQUIREMENTS**
Min. Age Min. Formal Qualification/ Education Min. job related experience required Any specific job-related skills required (e.g., technical skills, communication skills, interrelationship skills, computer skills, etc.) Knowledge Tools	
FUNCTIONS and RESPONSIBILITIES (duties to be performed by this position)	
AUTHORITIES: (type of personnel supervised, level of authority to hire or fire or to make recommendations or to sanction leaves, etc.)	
ANY PHYSICAL DEMANDS OF THE JOB: (physique, eyesight, traveling, lifting operations, etc.)	
Prepared by: Reviewed by: Approved by:	Date: Date: Date:

Exhibit: Sample Job Description Form of a HR Executive

Title:	HR Executive
Department/Business Unit:	Human Resources
Reports to:	Manager (Human Resources)
Location:	
Basic Function	To Co-ordinate Planning, Implementation and Monitoring of all Human Resource Management Systems, Policies and Procedure and co-ordinate other Human Resources activities.
Principal Responsibilities:	– Liaise with other functional/departmental employees so as to understand all necessary aspects and needs of HR development, and to ensure they are fully informed of HR objectives, purposes and achievements. – Monitor the implementation of the ERP system. – Co-ordinate training and development activities. – Maintain the General Administrative matters on day to day basis in co-ordination with HR Manager. – Maintain the employee relation matters like employee discipline, grievance, counseling, motivation, culture and attitudinal change etc. – Co-ordinate with other departments regarding the effective implementation of HR policies and procedure. – Report the HR issues and development plans and achievements within agreed formats and timescales.
Key Performance Indicators	– Successful Implementation of HRMS – Effective Presentations and Communication – Effective Interpersonal Relationship – Time Management
Knowledge, Skills, Qualifications and Experience	– MBA or equilent. – Good knowledge of HR Policies and Procedure – Good command in English, both written and verbal – Proficiency in all computer applications and knowledge in ERP system.

What is a Role?

A role is a set of expectations people have about the behaviour of an individual in a position. A position holder may perform 3 types of roles, namely:

- ***Expected Role***: It is what other people expect from an individual
- ***Perceived Role***: It is how the individual thinks how he/she should behave so as to fulfill the expected role.
- ***Enacted or Actual Role***: It is the way the individual actually behaves in an organization.

Role Analysis

Role analysis is a process of analyzing the role of a manager in relation to the roles of other managers or members of the organization who get affected by his performance.

P. N. Singh, has described "Role analysis is a participatory process which aims at defining the work content of a role in relation to all those with whom the role occupant has significant interaction in the performance of his jobs".

Process of Role Analysis

The following figure illustrates the process of role analysis:

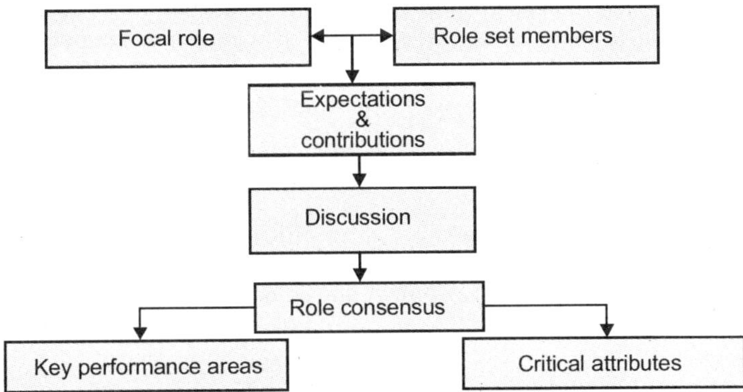

Fig. 2.21: Process of role analysis

Identifying the Focal Role: The first step is to identify the focal role. This involves identification of the key positions in the organization related to a particular task or a job. The focal role is the manager whose role is to be analyzed.

Identification of Role Set Members: The next step is to identify the role set members. The role set members are the various members in the department or organization with whom the focal role has to interact to accomplish goals.

Listing out Expectations and Contributions: The Focal Role (Role Holder) has to write down his expectations from and his contributions to the Role Set Members. The Role Set Members also have to write down their expectations from and contributions to the Focal Role.

Discussion Stage: The focal role and role set members hold discussion. In this discussion, they compare the two lists of expectations and contributions.

Role Consensus: The discussion leads to role consensus which the focal role needs to undertake. The role consensus is arrived only after a good discussion on the expectations and contributions are stated in the two lists.

Identification of Key Performance Areas (KPAs): The group i.e. focal role and the role set members identifies **'key performance areas'** in which the focal role needs to concentrate.

Identification of Critical Attributes: The role set members may be asked to indicate the critical attributes in the areas of knowledge, attitude, skills and behaviour required for the focal role. Such critical attributes enable the focal role to perform his role effectively.

Review of Performance: The performance of the focal role is reviewed either by the superior of the focal role or by the role set members or any other appraising authority. Necessary feedback is provided to the focal role so that he can correct his weaknesses and consolidate his strengths.

Applications and Advantages of Role Analysis

Role analysis is applicable in the following areas, namely:

- Providing role clarity to various job incumbents
- Identification of main functions related to a particular role
- Identifying critical attributes related to a role
- Setting individual goals
- Facilitating placements
- Facilitating performance appraisal
- Identifying training needs
- Preparing and developing second line executives
- Facilitating career planning

Difference between Job Analysis and Role Analysis

Hallmarks	Job Analysis	Role Analysis
Meaning	It is systematic collection and studying information relating to operations and responsibilities of a specific job.	It is participatory process, which aims at defining the role content in relation to all those roles of Role Set Members.
Suitability	Suitable for Operative jobs	Suitable for Managerial Jobs
Who conducts	Job Analyst who occupies advisory position	Interaction between the Focal Role and the Role Set Members
Frequency	Not very frequently done	More frequently done
Information	Information regarding the job is documented through job description and job specification	Information regarding the role is given by the Key Performance Areas of the **Focal Role** as well as by the critical attributes of the **Focal Role**
Type of concept	Old concept	New concept

Exhibit: Sample Job Analysis Checklists

ROUTINE CLERICAL RESPONSIBILITIES

Activity	Frequency			
	D	W	M	O
Types labels, letters, envelopes and invoices.				
Determine layout and format, and type in finished format.				
Proofread and correct errors.				
Set up an type financial and statistical reports.				
Take dictation and transcribe.				
Transcribe dictation from voice recordings.				
Record, type and distribute meeting minutes.				
Compose standard letters in response to routine correspondence				
Schedule appointments without prior clearance, schedule meetings and conferences, and make travel arrangements including reservations.				
Prepare meeting and conference rooms.				
Maintain, process, distribute and update records, files and documents.				
Maintain confidential records and files, and handle confidential correspondence and records.				
Open, sort and distribute mail.				
Answer telephones, screen and place calls, monitor and follow up on voice mail recordings, refer callers to appropriate parties.				
Prepare, process and verify invoices, bills, checks and receipts.				

Maintain and report expense account activity.				
Receive and welcome visitors, and refer to appropriate parties.				
Maintain and update mailing lists. Enter data electronically and verify.				
Process payroll records.				
Perform calculations, post and verify figures, trace and adjust errors.				
Maintain inventory of office supplies, requisition new supplies, and distribute supplies to authorized parties.				
Schedule and monitor equipment repairs and service contracts.				
Maintain locks and keys for storage cabinets and other facilities, and distribute to authorized parties.				
Orient and train new employees.				
Schedule work for coworkers as requested.				
Handle cash and negotiable instruments.				
Maintain cash box.				
Sign legal documents.				
Act as resource for others as to staff and locations.				
Maintain records of cash receipts and disbursements.				
Review job applicants/applications and conducts screening interviews.				
Collate and bind.				
Make copies.				
Date and stamp documents.				
Recommend improvements in operations and procedures. Modify operations and/or procedures.				
Maintain procedures and information manuals.				
Develop operating budget for approval.				
Research, tabulate, and summarize information of routine, periodic or special reports.				
Present findings in oral or written form.				
Record and verify entries or accounts, journals, logs and general ledgers.				
Balance accounts and reconcile statements.				

Indicate the equipment that is operated as a regular part of the responsibilities of the job:

- Calculator, Camera, Cash register/petty cash
- Computer, Dictation equipment, Facsimile machine
- Microfilm equipment, Photocopier, Postage machine
- Security equipment, Sorter switchboard
- Word processor
- Other equipment
- Other activities

What is TASK ANALYSIS?

Task analysis is the analysis of how a task is accomplished, including a detailed description of both manual and mental activities, task and element durations, task frequency, task allocation, task complexity, environmental conditions, necessary clothing and equipment, and any other unique factors involved in or required for one or more people to perform a given task. Task analysis emerged from research in applied behaviour analysis and still has considerable research in that area. Task analysis analyses what a user is required to do in terms of actions and/or cognitive processes to achieve a task. A detailed task analysis can be conducted to understand the current system and the information flows within it. These information flows are important to the maintenance of the existing system and must be incorporated or substituted in any new system. Task analysis makes it possible to design and allocate tasks appropriately within the new system. The functions to be included within the system and the user interface can then be accurately specified.

Information from a task analysis can then be used for many purposes, such as personnel selection and training, tool or equipment design, procedure design (e.g., design of checklists or decision support systems) and automation. The term "task" is often used interchangeably with activity or process. Task analysis often results in a hierarchical representation of what steps it takes to perform a task for which there is a goal and for which there is some lowest-level "action" that is performed. Task analysis is often performed by human factors professionals. Task analysis may be of manual tasks, such as bricklaying, and be analyzed as time and motion studies using concepts from industrial engineering. Cognitive task analysis is applied to modern work environments such as supervisory control where little physical works occurs, but the tasks are more related to situation assessment, decision-making, and response planning and execution. Task analysis is also used in education. It is a model that is applied to classroom tasks to discover which curriculum components are well matched to the capabilities of students with learning disabilities and which task modification might be necessary. It discovers which tasks a person hasn't mastered, and the information processing demands of tasks that are easy or problematic. In behaviour modification, it is a breakdown of a complex behavioural sequence into steps. This often serves as the basis for Chaining.

Task Analysis: Data collection

Task analysis analyses what a user is required to do in terms of actions and/or cognitive processes to achieve a task. A detailed task analysis can be conducted to understand the current system and the information flows within it. These information flows are important to the maintenance of the existing system and must be incorporated or substituted in any new system. Task analysis makes it possible to design and allocate tasks appropriately within the new system. The functions to be included within the system and the user interface can then be accurately specified.

Benefits

It provides knowledge of the tasks that the user wishes to perform. Thus it acts as a reference against which the value of the system functions and features can be tested.

Method

Task Decomposition: The aim of 'high level task decomposition' is to decompose the high level tasks and break them down into their constituent subtasks and operations. This will show an overall structure of the main user tasks. At a lower level it may be desirable to show the task flows, decision processes and even screen layouts (see task flow analysis, below).

The process of task decomposition is best represented as a structure chart (similar to that used in Hierarchical Task Analysis). This shows the sequencing of activities by ordering them from left to right. In order to break down a task, the question should be asked 'how is this task done?' If a subtask is identified at a lower level, it is possible to build up the structure by asking 'why is this done?'. The task decomposition can be carried out using the following stages:

1. Identify the task to be analyzed.
2. Break this down into between 4 and 8 subtasks. These subtasks should be specified in terms of objectives and, between them, should cover the whole area of interest.
3. Draw the subtasks as a layered diagram ensuring that it is complete.
4. Decide upon the level of detail into which to decompose. Making a conscious decision at this stage will ensure that all the subtask decompositions are treated consistently. It may be decided that the decomposition should continue until flows are more easily represented as a task flow diagram.
5. Continue the decomposition process, ensuring that the decompositions and numbering are consistent. It is usually helpful to produce a written account as well as the decomposition diagram.
6. Present the analysis to someone else who has not been involved in the decomposition but who knows the tasks well enough to check for consistency.

Developing Task Flow Diagrams

Task flow analysis will document the details of specific tasks. It can include details of interactions between the user and the current system, or other individuals, and any problems related to them. Copies of screens from the current system may also be taken to provide details of interactive tasks. Task flows will not only show the specific details of current work processes but may also highlight areas where task processes are poorly understood, are carried out differently by different staff, or are inconsistent with the higher level task structure.

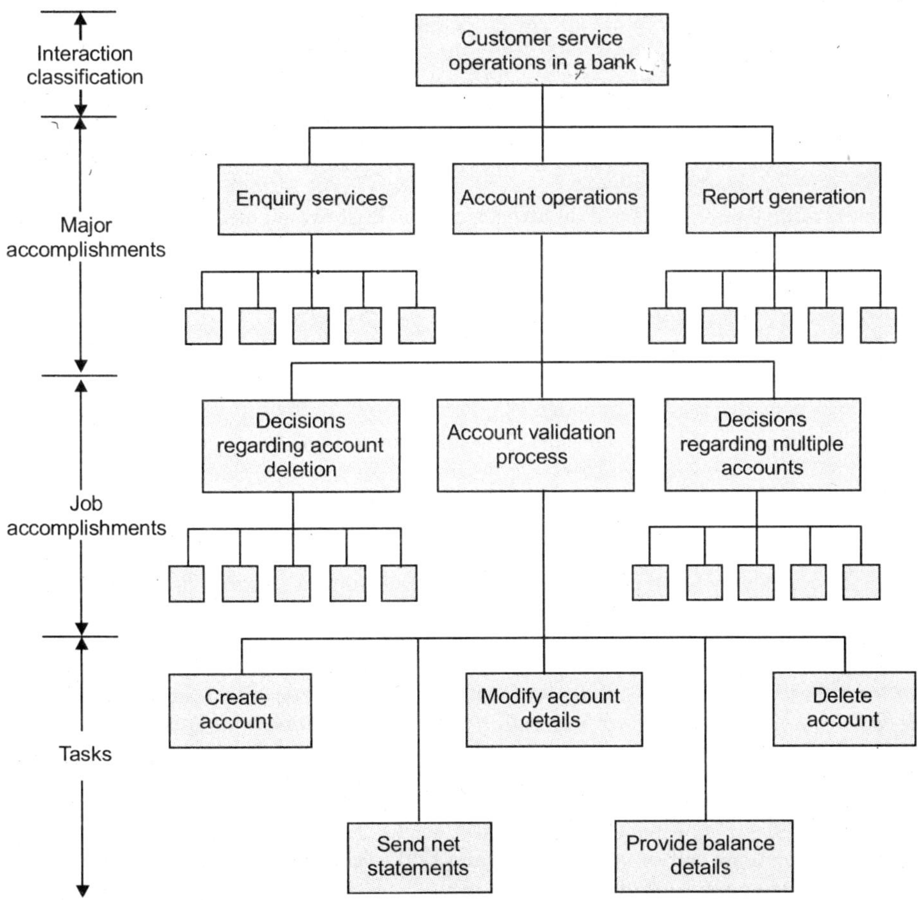

Fig. 2.22: Task analysis in a bank

REFERENCES

1. http://www.hr-guide.com/data/G012.htm
2. Harvey (1993): "*Research Monograph: The Development of the CMQ*". Monograph Describing the Development and Field-testing of the Common Metric Questionnaire (CMQ). (Word for Windows 6 format; 113K)
3. McCormick, E.J., Jeanneret, P.R., and Mecham, R.C. (1972): "A Study of Job Characteristics and Job Dimensions as Based on the Position Analysis Questionnaire (PAQ)". Journal of Applied Psychology Monograph, 56, 347–368
4. U.S. Department of Labour, Handbook for Analyzing Jobs (Washington, D.C.: U.S. Government Printing Office, 1972.
5. http://www.softscout.com/screenshot/ULTIMUS-WORKFLOW-ON-THE-WEB/91AB7502185DEC8885256F9900187696)
6. *http://www.paq.com/index.cfm?FuseAction=bulletins.job-analysis-questionnaire*

QUESTION BANK

1. Define job analysis. State its importance in organizations.
2. What is the difference between job analysis and task analysis?
3. What are the components of job analysis?
4. What do you mean by role? What are the essentials of role analysis? How can role analysis help in improving employee performance?
5. What are the various methods of job analysis? Give suitable illustrations.
6. What is workflow analysis? Why is it important in organizations?
7. What is the role of a job analyst? What strategies are taken by this individual to ensure effective job analysis?
8. Describe the relative advantages and disadvantages of at least two methods of job analysis known to you.
9. What do you mean by job description? Describe the steps in preparing a job description with a neat diagram.
10. What do you mean by job specification? How is it different from job description?
11. How can be job specification be useful in recruitment?
12. How can job description help in effective performance management?
13. What do you mean by job performance standards? Why are they important?
14. How would you plan a job analysis survey in an organization?
15. How job analysis information could be useful for human resource planning in organizations?

Internet Exercises

- Go to naukri.com website and collect the job specification for marketing managers representing various sectors. Comment on the common skills and attributes required in these profiles.
- Go to the internet and collect at least three management cartoons on the themes related to job analysis and give a presentation explaining what had been your comments on or your learning from the same.
- Download the demo version of the Job Analysis software in the following hyperlink (*http://www.paq.com/index.cfm?FuseAction=bulletins.job-analysis-questionnaire*) and study the various features of the software and share your learnings with your friends.

Games

- Collect Times Ascent Newspapers for at least 3 weeks. Assume that you are heading the placement and corporate relations cell of your institute and find relevant job openings related to the MBA and BBM students. Give a presentation on the same.
- Using the above newspapers and the information given in the job specification advertisements organize a Job Description writing contest in your class.

JOB DESIGN

WILDLIFE MANAGEMENT

Theme Case: Crisis in Sharma Motors Pvt. Ltd.

Sharma Motors had been a well-known company in the Peenya Industrial Estate, Bangalore. The company was dealing with manufacturing automotive parts and its clients were Maruti India, Hero Honda, Hindustan Motors, Bajaj, TVS Motors and to name a few.

The company's track records over the years had been excellent keeping its growing profit into consideration. But for the last six months or so, the senior management had been quite worried about the increasing lack of interest among the workers in the shop floor level with respect to their jobs which were complained to be monotonous, repetitive and boring. But this issue was also crucial for Sharma Motors in terms of stringent regulations in terms of maintaining quality of its products with whom the company would never compromise.

One case reported by Manjunath, a senior shop floor supervisor came as shocking news to Mr. Nagraj, the production manager of the company. Due to the negligence of one worker, one batch of the switch gears had defective quality according to the standards maintained by the company. The management later on decided to abandon this batch of product. Mr. Manjunath was instructed to conduct a full fledged enquiry on the issue and report the same within 24 hrs. to Mr. Nagraj. The management called a meeting that evening with all the senior officers of the company.

Mr. Nagraj, the production manager complained that the problem was entirely a technical one and due to lack proper job design employees made mistakes or were careless in their duties. He blamed that the problem was entirely due to the lack of consideration and regular inspection by the engineering department. The chief engineer, Mr. Ramesh, was furious with this comment and passed the buck on the HR manager and blamed that it was lack of training and application of job analysis studies that made the employees more incompetent. He further showed the evidence that his section regularly inspected the performance of the machines, raw materials and conducted product quality tests to ensure quality. And the report of the same was being regularly submitted to the executive working in the production department.

Mr. Reddy, the HR manager agreed that there were some problems in the system but it was not alone the sole responsibility of the HR department to make the jobs interesting for the employees. The company conducted regular training assessment programs to evaluate the skill levels of the employees and frequently trained the shop floor workers on the job training. But perhaps attention and care from the part of the supervisors were not sufficient enough to make things easy for the workers at the shop floor. He also complained that the environment at the shop floor was not conducive for work in terms of illumination and ventilation which might also could have contributed to the disliking of the employees.

The meeting was characterized by blames and counter blames, the management could not yet decide what could be the solution for the problem. The managing director Mr. Sudheer Sharma who had been to Japan since the last two weeks for a business deal was disappointed to know about the latest turnaround in his company. He instructed the HR manager to wind up the issue and identify a solution on a priority basis.

What is Job Design?

Job design is the logical sequence of the process of job analysis and involves conscious efforts to organize tasks, duties and responsibilities into a unit of work so as to business objectives.

"Job design is the process of deciding on the contents of a job in terms of its duties and responsibilities, on the methods to be used in carrying out the job, in term of techniques, systems and procedures and on the relationships that should exist between the jobholder and his superiors, subordinates and colleagues" Ibid.

Job design is the logical sequence to job analysis. It involves conscious efforts to organize tasks, duties and responsibilities into a unit of work so as to achieve organizational objectives. It deals with the allocation and arrangement or organizational work activities and tasks into sets where a singular set of activities constitutes a "job" and which is subsequently performed by a job incumbent. Technically speaking job design attempts to integrate work content like those of tasks, functions, relationships with that of the skill requirements applicable for each job that meets the needs of the employees and also the organization as a whole.

Job design is about the way that tasks are combined to form complete jobs in the workplace, whilst job redesign has its focus on how existing jobs are changed: for example, by redesigning jobs management may able to increase motivation around, say, the introduction of self managed work teams. Job design therefore encompasses a specification of tasks that are to be performed by employees in the organization and it includes any anticipated interpersonal and task relationships. This occurs all the time in the workplace as people communicate and is increasingly so in the flat, lean organization structures. The following figure represents a framework for job design.

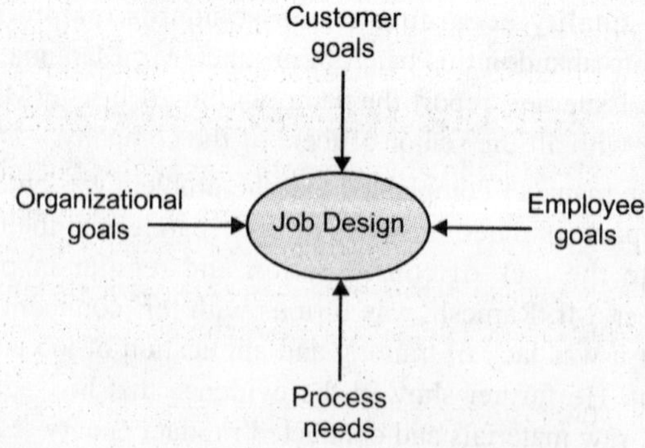

Fig. 2.23: Framework of job design

Two important goals of job design

- To meet the organizational requirements such as higher productivity, operational efficiency, quality of product/service etc. and
- To satisfy the needs of the individual employees like interests, challenges, achievement or accomplishment, etc.

Poorly designed jobs often result in

- Boredom
- Increased turnover
- Reduced motivation
- Low levels of job satisfaction
- Less than optimal productivity
- Increase in organizational costs

Steps of job design: Job design involves the following three steps:

- The specification of individual tasks
- The specification of the method (s) of performing each task
- The combination of tasks into specific jobs to be assigned to individuals.

Factors affecting job design

The various factors influencing job design are depicted by the following figure:

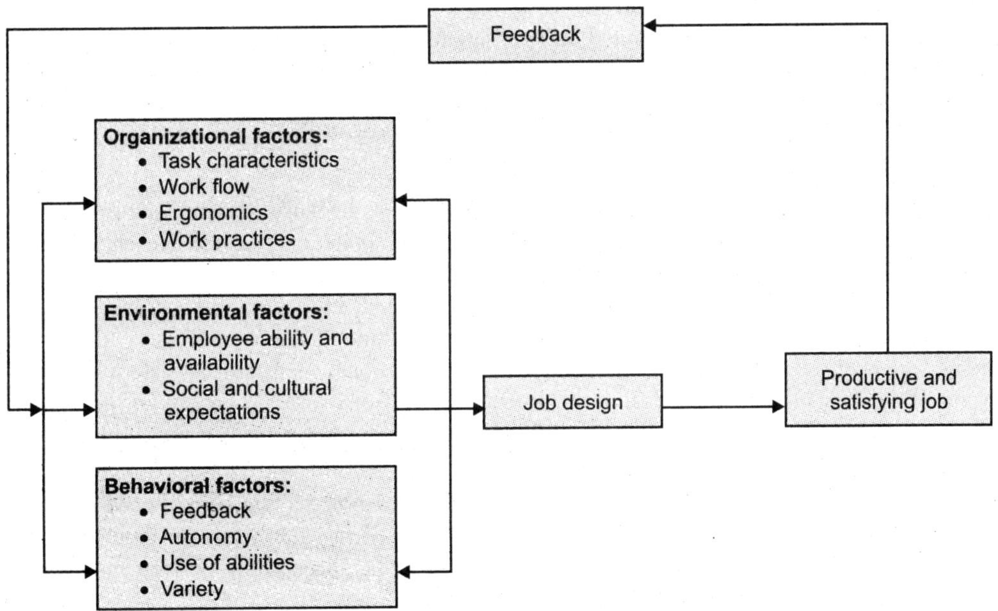

Fig. 2.24: Factors influencing job design

Impact of Organizational Factors

Organizational factors are of great importance for deciding the job design in an organization. The nature of business has a significant influence in terms of task characteristic of a particular job. Task characteristics would again demand different levels of skill and knowledge sets from the job incumbents. Other issues/

factors like those of workflow schedules, ergonomical factors and work practices or norms also decide the nature of job design in an organization.

Environmental Factors

These mainly involve the availability of the right manpower for the right job. This means not only there should be adequate manpower requirement for a particular job, the job incumbents should also have the right KSAs (Knowledge, Skills, Abilities) for the relevant jobs. The environmental factors also take into due consideration of the social and cultural expectations of the job incumbents as well as that of the entire organization.

Behavioural Factors

Behaviour factors or elements mainly relate to the behavioural traits or characteristics of the employees. These involve the level of empowerment given by the higher management to take decisions (autonomy), opportunity to use or apply different skills and the extent to which the job incumbents receive feedback from their superiors, peers, customers to improve their performance and other aspects related to the job. The behavioural factors also define or decide what elements or characteristics of the job could contribute to the motivation level of the job incumbents (as explained in the Job Characteristic Model).

Fig. 2.25: Job Design: A challenging task

Approaches to Job Design

Approaches to job design have concentrated on two variables in achieving the balance between meeting needs and goals:

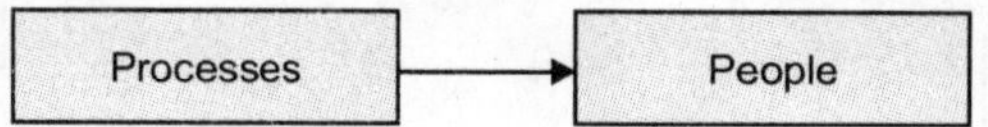

There is an interaction between job design/redesign and process because accomplishing anything in an organization more often than not requires knowledge of whom to see and how to present an idea to that person. Process refers to how tasks are carried out, and regardless of how the job is designed or redesigned, all workers participate in such processes as decision-making, leadership, communication, motivation, and conflict-resolution, and process is closely related to decision-making. It may be necessary to make changes in job design and process in order to meet individual and organizational needs process determination depends on the ways of working and the individual personalities and teams involved. There are key groups who may need to be consulted, e.g., team leaders, and customers; not to do so is likely to minimize or nullify an effective process.

In order to achieve organizational effectiveness, collectively process and people need to be balanced and the search for this stabilization leads to the consideration of the alternative methods of job design. Gaining such a balance is often related to the areas of job satisfaction and job performance. This can be illustrated by the following figure:

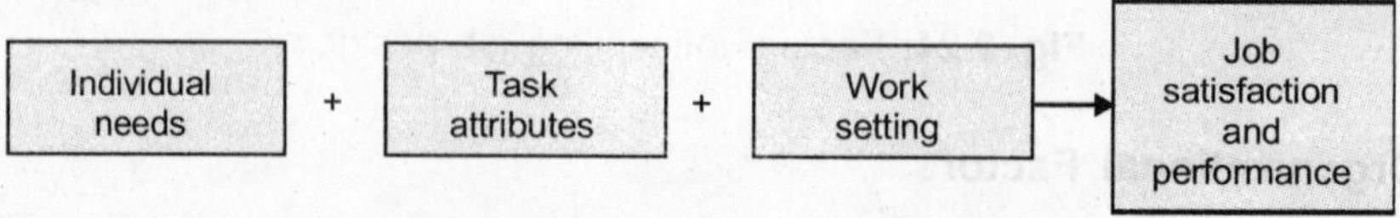

Fig. 2.26: Job design and motivation

Job Characteristic Model (Hackman and Oldham, 1976[1]) of effective Job Design and Job Satisfaction

The Job Characteristics Model (JCM) (e.g., Hackman and Oldham, 1976[1]) is a widely studied model of motivational job design that has explained important work outcomes (e.g., satisfaction, tenure) for workers in a wide variety of blue and white-collar jobs. Hackman and Oldham sought to "measure" the motivating potential of jobs. In other words, to measure the extent that a job exhibits the five characteristics listed above. Their research found that jobs scoring high in terms of a combination of these five characteristics resulted in higher job satisfaction and productivity than jobs scoring low. For a job to be intrinsically motivating, all five characteristics must be simultaneously present, to some extent. According to the JCM, certain core features of jobs *as seen by the worker*, impact psychological reactions to the job and the outcomes that follow from those reactions. In other words, as shown in the following figure, the JCM posits that Perceived Core Job Characteristics impact work outcomes through their effects on psychological reactions to the job (i.e., Critical Psychological States).

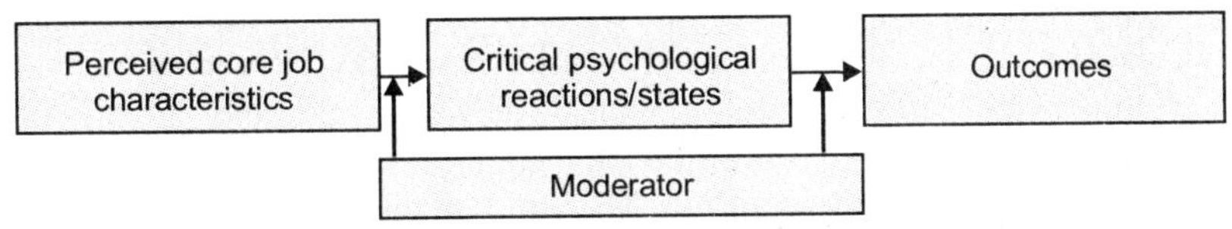

Fig. 2.27: Key components of the job characteristics model

The five core job characteristics are: "skill variety" (i.e., the perceived variety and complexity of skills and talents required to perform the job); "task identity" (i.e., the extent the job is seen as involving a whole, identifiable task); "task significance" (i.e., the extent that the job affects the well being of others); "autonomy" (i.e., the extent the job is seen as allowing for personal initiative in performing the work); and "feedback from the job" (i.e., the extent that the job, itself, provides information about job performance).

(i) Skill Variety	:	Degree to which the worker uses a multiplicity of skills and talents
(ii) Task Identity	:	Degree to which tasks require completion with an identifiable outcome
(iii) Task Significance	:	Degree to which the task is significant to the worker
(iv) Autonomy	:	Degree to which the job provides ultimate freedom
(v) Feedback	:	Degree to which the worker receives feedback on the process and results of the task.

The JCM posits that the way jobs are perceived in terms of these five core job characteristics impact three particular psychological reactions to the job. These reactions, referred to as "critical psychological states", include "experienced meaningfulness of work" (i.e., the extent that the work is seen as making a difference to others), "felt responsibility" (i.e., the extent that the worker assumes responsibility for his/her work), and "knowledge of results" (i.e., the extent to which the worker is aware of the quality of his/her work). Jobs seen as high in the five core job features (e.g., high in autonomy) are expected to be seen as more meaningful by workers, are expected to engender greater feelings of responsibility on the part of workers, and are expected to provide clear cues to workers about the quality of work. Finally, critical psychological states are expected to explain variability in five specific work outcomes which include: general job satisfaction, perceived job performance, internal work motivation (i.e., the extent that the worker is motivated by doing good work), satisfaction with growth (i.e., the extent that the worker is satisfied with the opportunity to learn new things on the job); and thoughts of quitting. In addition, the linkages shown in the model (above Figure) are expected to be moderated by "growth need strength". In other words, the linkages are expected to be significantly stronger for those individuals who are highly motivated to learn and grow on the job.

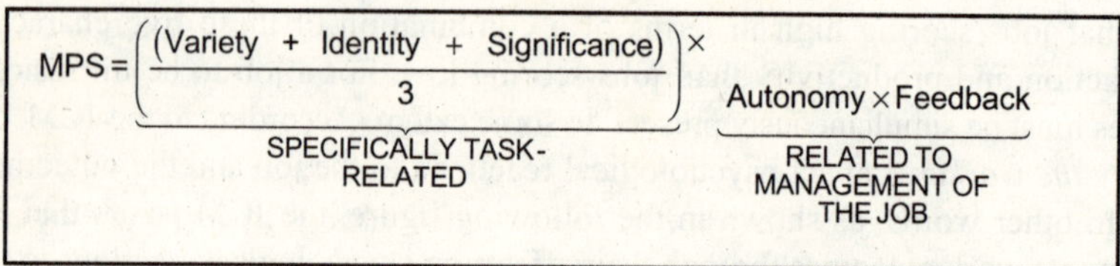

Fig. 2.28: Motivation potential score

The score calculated using this equation is only a crude indication of a job's motivational potential. First, it is important to remember that different individuals may respond to the variables differently — the values assigned to the 5 variables are a matter of the job incumbent's perception. Thus, two different people may produce a different MP Score for the same job. The utility in this equation lies in its ability to pinpoint particular problems for a specific job. Then, having pinpointed the problem, the job can be "redesigned" to correct the shortcomings in one or more of the five critical components.

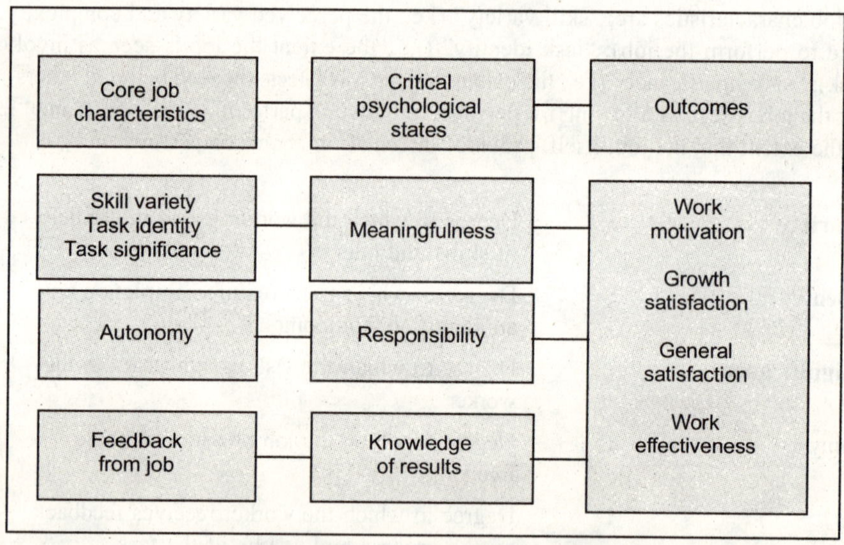

Fig. 2.29: Job characteristic model

As revealed in the above discussion, it is clear that the Job Characteristic Model (JCM) includes the two factors of growth and strength (the desire to self-actualize) which act as a moderator. People with a high growth need strength usually respond more positively to tasks with high motivating potential score (MPS), whilst workers with a low growth need strength tend to respond less favourably to such jobs. The job characteristic model tends to suggest that core job dimensions could stimulate three critical psychological states according to the relationships specified in the model. These are as follows:

- **Experienced meaningfulness of the job:** The degree to which the job incumbent feels the job has meaning and is valuable and worthwhile.
- **Experienced responsibility for work outcomes:** The degree to which the job incumbent is personally accountable for the results of his or her work.
- **Knowledge of results:** The results to which the employee receives feedback on the performance and effectiveness of his or her work.

Table 2.6: Examples of High and Low Job Characteristics

Job Characteristics	***Examples***
	Skil! Variety
• **High variety**	The owner-operator of a garage who does electrical repair, rebuilds engines, does body work, and interacts with customers
• **Low variety**	A body-shop worker who sprays paint eight hours a day
	Task Identity
• **High identity**	A cabinetmaker who designs a pieces of furniture, selects the wood, builds the object, and finishes it to perfection
• **Low variety**	A worker in a furniture factory who operates a lathe to make table legs
	Task Significance
• **High significance**	Nursing the sick in a hospital intensive care unit
• **Low significance**	Sweeping hospital floors
	Autonomy
• **High autonomy**	A telephone installer who schedules his or her own work for the day, and decides on the best techniques for a particular installation
• **Low autonomy**	A telephone operator who must handle calls as they come according to a routine, highly specified procedure
	Feedback
• **High feedback**	An electronics factory worker who assembles a radio and then tests it to determine if it operates properly
• **Low feedback**	An electronics factory worker who assembles a radio and then routes it to a quality control inspector who tests and adjusts it

Implications of the JCM

The JCM could be helpful for effective job design and motivation of employees. This could be helpful in the following ways, namely:

1. Forming Natural Work Units:
    - First, identify the basic work items
    - Second, group the items in natural categories
2. Combining Tasks:
    - To form new and larger modules of work
    - Remember: Scientific Management had fractionalized jobs

3. Establishing Client Relationships:
   - To establish direct relationships with the "customers" of their work
4. Vertical Loading of Jobs and Activities:
   - *doing* vs *planning and controlling*
   - Responsibilities and controls that used to belong to higher levels of management are added to the job
5. Opening Feedback Channels:
   - To help individuals learn whether their performance is improving, deteriorating or remaining at constant level
   - Direct feedback

Limitations of the Job Characteristics Model (Parker and Wall, 1998[2]): The JCM has been criticized by several authors (Parker and Wall, 1998[2]) in the following ways:

- Regarding the distinctiveness of the 5 Job Characteristics stated in the JCM, it is doubtful whether they are separable aspects of the job. Further another issue could be whether they could be perceived individually.
- Role of Critical Psychological States is not clear from the JCM particularly in terms of:
  (*i*) Whether Job Characteristics relate to other psychological states
  (*ii*) Whether a model without the Psychological States could work just as well (Job characteristics effect on outcomes)
- Effect of moderators is not clearly understood from the JCM:
  - Research has focused on testing moderating effect between job characteristics and psychological states but not the moderator effect between psychological states and outcomes.
  - The moderating effect of growth need has been shown in research, unlike the other moderators proposed.
- Little support for the efficacy of the motivating potential score proposed.
- The JCM fails to identify the relationship among outcome variables and the implications of these are at odds with known evidence.

Limitations of the Job Characteristics Model (Kelly, 1992[3]): The Twin-Track Model of Job Design

Kelly (1992[3]) has taken the JCM forward by stating that the model does not give consideration to developments in motivation, job satisfaction and performance. He criticized the underlying research methodology stating that this might account for the JCM being limited in its application.

Kelly found that there were rises in job performance after there had been a pay rise and/or losses in the jobs which had occurred simultaneously with job design/redesign. Kelly subsequently propounded his own twin-track model of job design as depicted above.

Kelly proposed that there are two key pathways related to job design/redesign: satisfaction/motivation, and job performance. This model depicts that any change in work methods, pay rates, job security, and individual rewards can come about because of job design/redesign as well as or instead of changes in job characteristics. Any change in job characteristics would affect job satisfaction and motivation. However, the other changes have a more direct impact on job performance.

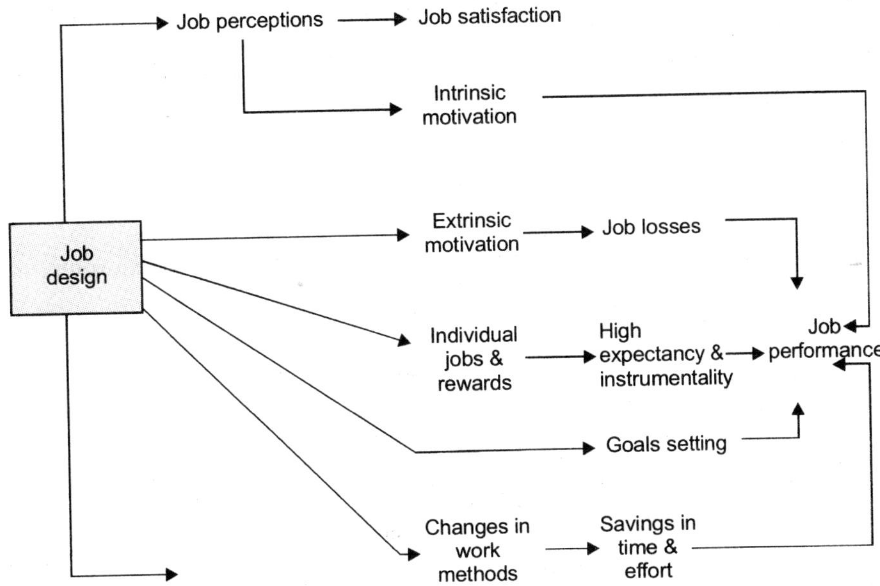

Fig. 2.30: Twin-track model of job design (Kelly, 1993)

Redesigning Works/Jobs to enhance levels of Motivation: It is possible to contrast approaches to job redesigning in terms of impact and complexity. Impact is the extent to which a particular approach is likely to be linked to factors unrelated to the job in hand, for example, performance, reward systems, appraisal methods (top down, bottom up or 360 degree), organizational structure, leadership and participation styles, empowerment, working conditions, team composition and organizational norms; in addition, the effects these are likely to have on both productivity and quality. Complexity means the extent to which the job design approach is likely to require:

- Changes in multiple factors.
- Involvement of individuals with diverse skills at various organizational levels.
- High levels of decision-making skills for successful implementation.

The relationship between impact and complexity can be seen in the following figure:

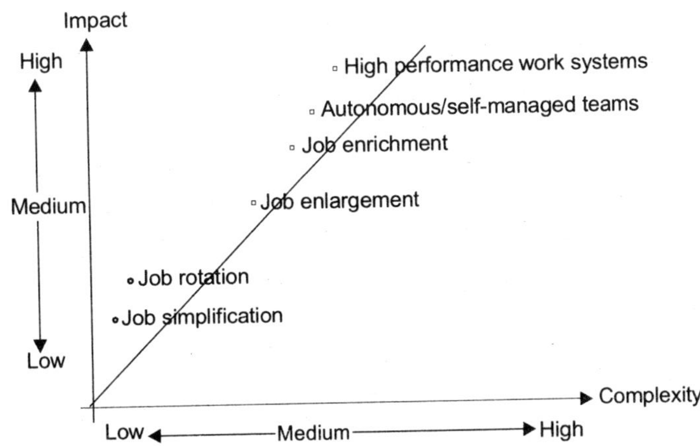

Fig. 2.31: The common approaches to job design contrasted in terms of impact and complexity

Job Specialization: In many organizations, one finds that job specialization is the rule. There are clearly many advantages to creating specialized jobs:

- job are mastered quickly
- jobs can be changed quickly and easily
- training costs are minimized

However, there are also negative consequences to specialized jobs:

- monotony of tasks causes worker alienation
- employees may have to be paid extra because of the alienation created by monotonous jobs
- monotony and boredom may result in poor quality workmanship
- worker motivation is reduced

Table 2.7: Approaches to Job Satisfaction and Job Designing

Job-design Approaches	*Positive Outcomes*	*Negative Outcomes*
1. **Work Simplification:** Here a job is broken into small sub-units and each sub-units are assigned to an individual	Job is highly specialized, so that less trained and less paid employees can effectively perform.	Over simplification results in boredom with attendant risks of errors and resignations
2. **Job Rotation:** It implies the movement of employees from alienated. job to job, although the job remains unchanged, but the incumbents shift.	Job's intrinsic reward potential is likely to increase. Organization too stands to gain because of the versatility of its employees. Worker's self image grows. There is enhanced interdepartmental cooperation.	Jobs do not improve. Workers may feel rootless and
3. **Job Enlargement:** It involves expanding the number of tasks or duties assigned to a given job	Claims to have motivational impact	Could have resistance from employees until the quality of the job is enhanced.
4. **Job Enrichment:** It seeks to improve both the task efficiency and human satisfaction by building into people's jobs, quite specifically, greater scope for personal achievement and recognition, more challenging and responsible work, and more opportunity for individual advancement and growth.	Increased motivation, reduced absenteeism, psychological needs of employees is met. Brings about empowered teams.	People may not like to accept new responsibilities.Union resistance.
5. **Autonomous Work Teams:** It is an intact group of employees who are responsible for a "whole" work process or segment that delivers a product or service to an internal or external customer.	There is greater involvement of employees in the decision-making.	Resistance from employees, unions, managers and supervisors.

Contd...

6. **High Performance Work Systems (HPWS):** It is a means of improving performance in an environment where positive and demanding goals are set. It starts from the principle of Self-managed teams and develops an approach which enables them to work effectively together in situations where the rate of innovation is high.	Works in an environment of high rate of innovation operational freedom.	May not work in large bureaucratic organizations.

Importance of the Human Factor (Ergonomics)

The approaches to job design has become more sophisticated as organizations endeavoured to strive for quality and excellence in a globalized market with an ever increasing diversity of workers. There developed a perspective known as the human factor approach which focuses on minimizing the physical demands and the biological risks in the workplace. This approach is sometimes referred to as **ergonomics** and is particularly related to equipment design, being: '*the analysis and design of work equipment and environments to fit human physical and cognitive capabilities*'.

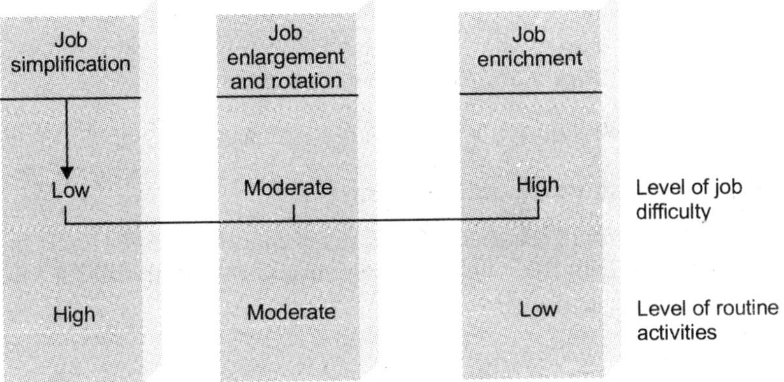

Fig. 2.32: A continuum of job design strategies[4]

(*Source: Schermerhorn, R.C., Nosborn, J.G.H.R., (2001): "Organizational Behaviour" (7th Edition) John Wiley & Sons, Inc., New York, p: 155*)

Ergonomics is usually associated with job design and new technology. Social scientists and psychologists have researched into a variety of concerns related to new technology. Particularly, ergonomics have worked to improve the compatibility of new technology with the information-processing capabilities of human beings. The positive outcomes of ergonomics and its application in job designing had been encouraging in the form of ensuring:

- less physical effort
- less physical fatigue
- fewer health complications and medical concerns
- lower absenteeism
- higher job satisfaction.

However, there are negative outcomes in the form of higher financial costs because of changes in equipment or in the job environment.

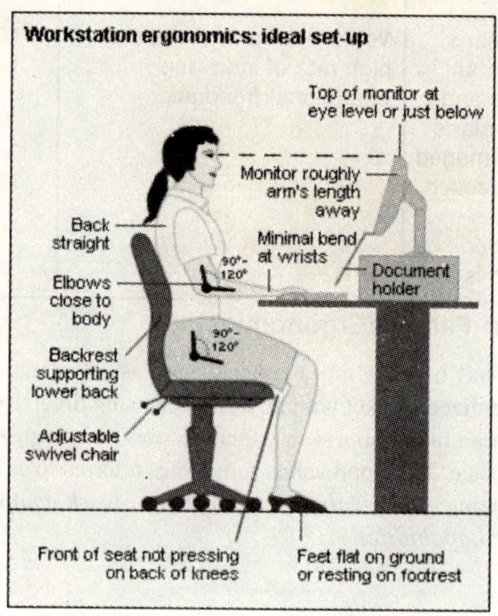

Fig. 2.33: Application of ergonomics

(*Courtesy: http://www.mydr.com.au/content/images/categories/worksafety/desk_ergonomics.gif*)

Recent Models for Understanding Job Design

To understand more recent theories of job design, there is a need to look more closely at the nature of the work and the way it has changed, together with the requirement for the analysis of the nature of the work. The model considers three concepts namely:

- Workflow Uncertainty
- Task Uncertainty
- Task Interdependence

- **Workflow Uncertainty:** It is the amount of knowledge that a worker has concerning when the inputs are due to be received and when they will require processing. If there is little work flow uncertainty, the employee will as a consequence have little autonomy to decide which, when or where tasks will be performed – there is minimum discretion available for the job incumbent.
- **Task Uncertainty:** It relates to the amount of knowledge that a job incumbent has about how to perform the task when the time comes for it to be carried out. If there is little task uncertainty, the employee has a considerable amount of knowledge about how to produce the required results. However, high task uncertainty is accompanied by very few pre-specified ways for dealing with some or all of the tasks related to the job. As a result, in order to complete the task to a required level, the employee must have experience, accurate judgement, intuition and problem solving skills of the highest standard.
- **Task Interdependence:** It is the degree to which decision-making and cooperation between two or more workers are needed for them to perform their jobs effectively. There are three basic types of interdependent task relations, namely:
  - Pooled task interdependence
  - Sequential task interdependence
  - Reciprocal task interdependence

Pooled task interdependence: It occurs when employees can carry out their jobs without communicating much with others in the organization.

Sequential task interdependence: It is the result of when one worker has to complete certain tasks before another worker can perform his or her specific tasks. That means that the output of one employee is the input for another employee or other employees.

Reciprocal task interdependence: It occurs when outputs from one individual (or team) become the inputs for others and vice versa. Such interdependence is a common factor in everyday life and particularly relates to team working. Reciprocal interdependence requires sophisticated interpersonal skills such as collaboration, communication and team decision-making.

REFERENCES

1. Hackman, J.R. and Oldham, G.R., (1976): "Motivation Through the Design of Work: Test of a Theory", Organizational Behaviour and Human Performance, 16, pp. 250–279.
2. Parker, S.K. and Wall, T.D. (1998): "Job and Work Design", Sage, London.
3. Kelly, J. (1992): "Does Job Redesign Theory Explain Job Redesign Outcomes?" *Human Relations,* 45(8), 753–774.
4. Schermerhorn, R.C., Nosborn, J.G.H.R., (2001): "Organizational Behaviour" (7th Edition) John Wiley & Sons, Inc., New York, p. 155.

QUESTION BANK

1. How can be jobs made interesting for the employees?
2. Define job design. What are the principles of job design?
3. What are the various approaches of job design?
4. How can organizations ensure effective job design?
5. Describe the job characteristic model of job design. How can job design contribute to employee motivation?
6. Crtically analyze the job characteristic model of job design? What other view points have been supported by other authors while criticizing this model?
7. What is job enrichment? How is it different from job enlargement?
8. What is job simplification? How is it different from job rotation?
9. What are socio-technical systems? How do they work towards employee motivation and performance?
10. How do organizations go ahead for job redesigning? Is redesigning strategically important for organizations? Give suitable illustrations.
11. How can you reduce boredom in the job settings of a call centre office?

Games

- Divide your class into small teams. Preparing card castles is always a trouble some job when one is all alone. Give the task of preparing card castles to each team and ensure the team with the tallest and most attractive design wins. Discuss the various strategies adopted by each team and how they negated their job difficulties.

- Divide the class into small teams. Take a bundle of waste papers, cello tapes and prepare a paper basket with the same. Hung this basket with a thread on a hook or rope and throw an egg inside each basket. The basket which is being able to hold the egg wins. Discuss the strategies adopted by each team to make the task possible.

Experiential Exercises

- Maintaining student records by your institute's administration department is a burden some task? Prepare a strategy how this task could be made simple and less complex.
- Develop a strategy for maintaining the notice board of your department and ensuring that the old notices are preserved well for reference.
- In what way job enlargement could be used in your institute's campus for better performance. Talk to various staffs in your college and prepare a strategy and present the same in your class.

HRIS

THEME CASE: THE NEW HR MANAGEMENT SYSTEM AT ABC ENGINEERING LTD.

Introduction

Multinational employees find a home at ABC Engineering Ltd. Previously the company used to have hrSQL, through which it hired and retained the people to help them compete and grow as a world class manufacturing organization. With increasing business challenges and particularly for effectively managing the organization's most valuable assets the Human capital, the management replaced hrSQL with a new HR management system known as **Perfect HR.**

For over the years, the company's systems have been the products of choice in steam cycle and geothermal power plants throughout the world. The organization is an international company which manufactures large industrial pumps. The primary application of these pumps is in the pulp and paper industry.

Problems before Implementation

Prior to selecting hrSQL, the HR Department relied on their mainframe human resource system. This system used **"green screen"** terminal technology and required the custom programming of a number of internal employees in order to create new screens or reports. Reporting and analysis took days, not minutes. The MIS and HR staff needed to have extensive knowledge in the proprietary system, but were keenly aware of the Y2K and other growth issues associated with staying on their current platform. The major contact from the organization to the vendor came at an International trade show. Here, representatives from the vendor company were able to demonstrate to the ABC staff the benefits of moving out from the age old hrSQL system with its custom reporting, standard platforms, scalability and more. The company's IT staff, in conjunction with their HR team, did an exhaustive evaluation of the needs and capabilities required by all participants in the venture. Included in the special considerations were interoperability between the hrSQL system and particularly the company's payroll system (provided by ADP). Also, the ability to take data from the hrSQL system into the BAAN system which was currently being implemented at Nash sites across the globe. There was no shortage of email, paper and phone lines being burned up in the process of this evaluation.

The management after meetings with the technical departments took the decision to go for the deal with Perfect Software. In this perspective a review committee was developed along with the team from

Perfect Software to study the context of how HR functions were carried on in the organization and identify the areas where Perfect HR could do justice for the organization and its HR department. Subsequently a thorough need analysis study was organized, followed by the trail and implementation of the new HR application.

Perfect HR: Perfect Software's HRIS

The Perfect Software Human Resource software module known as **Perfect HR** is designed to help companies in any industry, or any size, bring the challenging task of HR record keeping and government reporting under control. The software can truly aid the HR professional by combining bits of information to produce studies and analyses that help businesses define their future. Perfect HR is a browser-based software solution, providing capabilities for a human resources department to manage thousands of employee records in a clear easy to use format. Extensive information can be available at a HR manager's fingertips through this HR software aiding in protecting an organization's most valuable asset, the Human Capital.

Perfect HR makes viewing employee data simple and easy. There are custom search capabilities to aid in finding employee information and working on employee records. A HR manager can tailor the HR software by changing field names and search options. This can make the system easier to navigate and to use, maximizing the effectiveness of time and other resources. Further, integrated e-mail capabilities in this software make communication with individual employees and employee groups quick and easy. With the software's human resource management system, an HR executive can send e-mails directly to employees from their demographic records. Part of Perfect HR also provides interoperability with Perfect Payroll or any other payroll outsource providers. This ensures organizations real-time updating between HR and Payroll systems ensuring that the HR and Payroll departments are working with the most current and up to date employee data. Apart from these, with the system's **Reports and Tools** managers can think, analyze and provide top management with significant facts and figures that would aid in running the business in an optimal and effective manner.

Results: Perfect Software satisfied the needs of ABC engineering Ltd. in one comprehensive package that was perhaps not provided by the previous hrSQL system. As a result of this, not only the organization was being able to effectively track its employees more accurately than before, but they became more effective by using the package to disseminate Employee Benefit Statements in record time. A project that used to take 3 months was now being generated on demand at any time. Customized work was done to track retiree benefits, pension plans and foreign employees.

The company also choose PerfectSoftware for its ease of use, and the ability to customize many of the user fields. Some of the many reports the managers in the organization can now generate include EEO Analysis, Headcount processing, Audit logs and Benefits Analysis. In addition, the company now dealt and managed their employees "directly within the factory" instead of using separate sales, training and support facilities.

(Courtesy: www.perfectsoftware.com & http://www.poweronline.com/storefronts/nasheng.html)

Human Resource Information Systems

Human Resource Management Systems (HRMS), Human Resource Information Systems (HRIS), HR Technology or also called **HR modules**, shape an intersection in between human resource management (HRM) and information technology. It merges HRM as a discipline and in particular its basic HR activities and processes with the information technology field, whereas the programming of data processing systems evolved into standardized routines and packages of enterprise resource planning (ERP) software. On the whole, these ERP systems have their origin on software that integrates information from different applications into one universal database. The linkage of its financial and human resource modules through one database is the most important distinction to the individually and proprietary developed predecessors, which makes this software application both rigid and flexible.

Definition

A human resource information system (HRIS) can be defined as an integrated approach to effectively acquiring, storing analyzing and controlling the flow of information related to the human resources throughout an organization.

A HRIS can also be defined as interrelated components working together to collect, process, store and disseminate information to support decision-making, coordination, control, analysis and visualization of an organization's HRM activities.

Human Resources Information Systems (HRIS) is an integration of HRM and Information Systems (IS). HRIS or Human Resource Information System helps HR managers perform HR functions in a more effective and systematic way using technology. It is the system used to acquire, store, manipulate, analyze, retrieve and distribute pertinent information regarding an organization's human resources. A human resource information system (HRIS) is a system used to acquire, store, manipulate, analyze, retrieve and distribute pertinent information about an organization's human resources (Tannenbaum, 1990). The HRIS system is usually a part of the organization's larger management information system (MIS) which would include accounting, production and marketing functions, to name just a few. Human resource and line managers require good human resource information to facilitate decision-making.

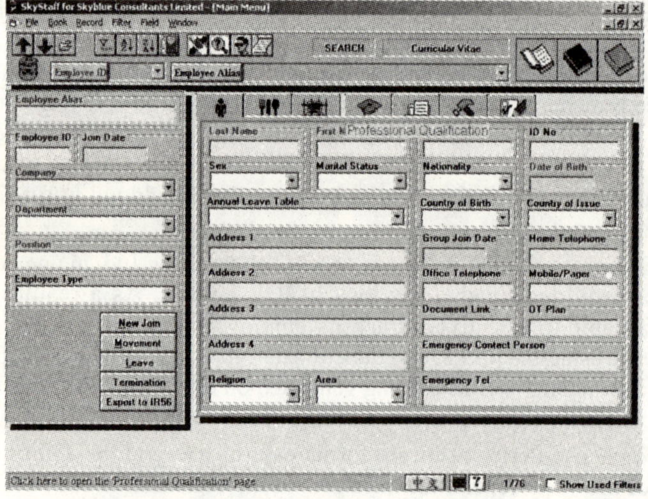

Fig. 2.34: Sample HRIS

(*Courtesy: www.skyblue.com.hk/skyblue_family.htm*)

Purpose

The function of Human Resources departments is generally administrative and common to all organizations. Organizations may have formalized selection, evaluation and payroll processes. Efficient and effective management of "Human Capital" has progressed to an increasingly imperative and complex process. The HR function consists of tracking existing employee data which traditionally includes personal histories, skills, capabilities, accomplishments and salary. To reduce the manual workload of these administrative activities, organizations began to electronically automate many of these processes by introducing specialized Human Resource Management Systems. Due HR executives rely on internal or external IT professionals to develop and maintain an integrated HRMS. Before the "client-server" architecture evolved in the late 1980s, many HR automation processes were relegated to mainframe computers that could handle large amounts of data transactions. In consequence of the high capital investment necessary to purchase or program proprietary software, these internally developed HRMS were limited to organizations that possessed a large amount of capital. The advent of client-server, Application Service Provider, and **Software as a Service** or **SaaS** Human Resource Management Systems enabled take increasingly higher administrative control of such systems. Currently Human Resource Management Systems encompass:

1. Payroll
2. Work time
3. Benefits administration
4. HR management information system
5. Appraisal module
6. Recruiting

Payroll module: The Payroll module automates the pay process by gathering data on employee time and attendance, calculating various deductions and taxes, and generating periodic pay cheques and employee tax reports. Data is generally fed from the human resources and time keeping modules to calculate automatic deposit and manual cheque writing capabilities. This module can encompass all employee related transactions as well as integrate with existing financial management systems.

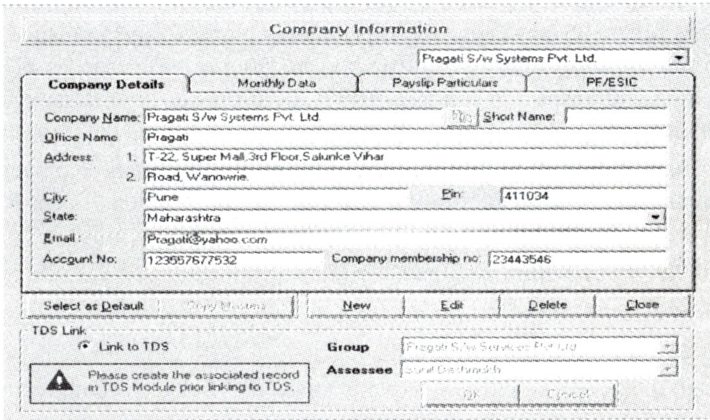

Fig. 2.35: Illustration of payroll software

Pragti S/w Systems Pvt. Ltd. — For the month : April, 2007

T-22, Super Mall, 3rd Floor, Salunke Vihar Road, Wanowrie.
Pune - 411034

Payslip

Employee No.	Name	Grade	Designation	Department	Date of Joining
[illegible]	Dipti	A	Web Designer	Software Development	March 19, 2007

Attendance		Earnings			Deductions		
		Particulars	For the Month (Rs.)	Year to Date (Rs.)	Particulars	For the Month (Rs.)	Year to Date (Rs.)
Earned days	30	Basic	10,000	10,000	PT	175	175
		DA	5,000	5,000	PF	1,800	1,800
		HRA	3,000	3,000			
		Conveyance	1,000	1,000			
		Medical	1,000	1,000			
Total Days	30	Total Earnings	20,000	20,000	Total Deductions	1,975	1,975

Net Salary : Rs. 18025/- (Rupees Eighteen Thousand Twenty Five only)

Net Salary Credited to Your Icici Bank Account Number 123344556[illegible]

Fig. 2.36: Illustration of an e-pay slip

Work Timegathers Module: The Work Timegathers module standardized time and work related efforts. The most advanced modules provide broad flexibility in data collection methods, labour distribution capabilities and data analysis features. Cost analysis and efficiency metrics are the primary functions.

Benefits Administration Module: The Benefits Administration module of a HRIS provides a system for organizations to administer and track employee participation in benefits programs. These can typically encompass, insurance, compensation, profit sharing and retirement information of an organization.

HR Management Module: The HR management module is a component covering many other HR aspects from application to retirement. The system records basic demographic and address data, selection, training and development, capabilities and skills management, compensation planning records and other related activities. Leading edge systems provide the ability to "read" applications and enter relevant data to applicable database fields, notify employers and provide position management and position control. Human resource management function involves the recruitment, placement, evaluation, compensation and development of the employees of an organization. Initially, businesses used computer based information system to:

- produce pay checks and payroll reports;
- maintain personnel records;
- pursue talent management.

Appraisal Module: This is characterized by high profile human resource capital management applications like those of Peoplesoft, Adrenalin etc. These HCMSs not only manage e-performance appraisals, they also ensure a holistic approach towards managing team and organizational performances. Generally the appraisal module stores information with respect to appraisal scores, performance criteria/standards, KPIs/KRAs and other information related to performance improvement pertaining to the needs of the employees.

Recruiting Module: Online recruiting has become one of the primary methods employed by HR departments to garner potential candidates for available positions within an organization. Talent Management systems typically encompass:

- analyzing personnel usage within an organization;
- identifying potential applicants;
- recruiting through company facing listings;
- recruiting through online recruiting sites or publications that market to both recruiters and applicants.

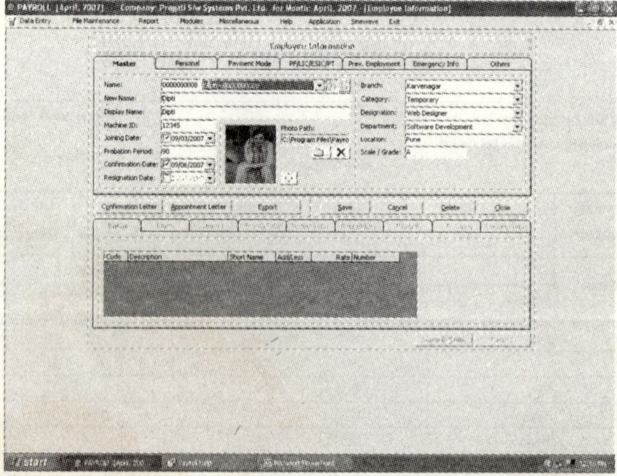

Fig. 2.37: Illustration of a HRIS (General Employee Information and Payroll)

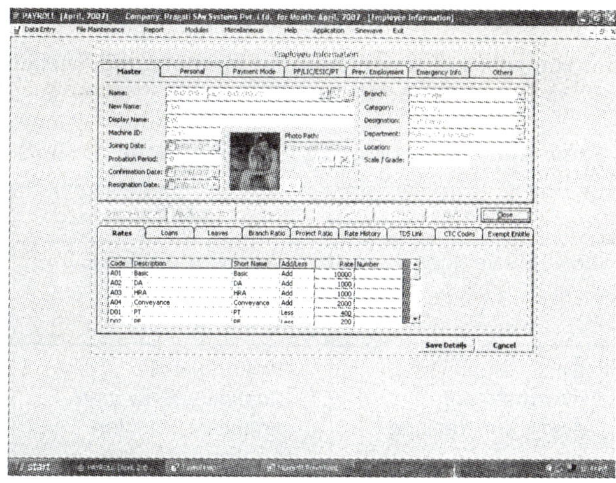

Fig. 2.38: Illustration of a HRIS (General Employee Information and Payroll)

Levels of using HRIS

Kavanagh et al. (1990)[1] stated that HRIS functions interactively with human resources management systems such as human resource planning, staffing, training and career development, performance management and compensation management. They further explained HRIS in a three level continuum, namely electronic data processing (EDP), management information system (MIS), and decision support system (DSS). For easy reference, a comparison of these three levels of HRIS is presented in the following Table. Combinations of these systems can occur within a single firm Kavanagh et al. (1990)[1].

Table 2.8: Comparisons of the Three Levels of HRIS

Dimension	*EDP*	*MIS*	*DSS*
Target users	Basic level operators	Middle managers	Top managers and executives
Focus	Data, files, storage, transaction processing and reports	Information retrieval, Plan and analyze data against expected values, integration	"What if" analysis through use of models, generation of decision alternatives
Characteristics	Basic personnel information	Inquiry capability, report-generation capability	Interactive for users
Examples	Payroll	Turnover reports, age and gender distribution, EEO compliance report	Human resource planning, compensation simulation

(*Courtesy:* Lin, C. Y. Y., (1997)[2]. Human Resource Information Systems: Implementation in Taiwan, *Research and Practice in Human Resource Management,* 5(1), 57–72).

Modules of a HRIS

As discussed earlier HRIS is comprised of several modular functions, the functions and hallmarks of which are as follows:

Table 2.9: Various Modules and Functions of HRIS

Dimension	*EDP*	*MIS*	*DSS*
Human resource planning	Skills inventory	Turnover analysis, Organizational charting	Succession planning, Work force dynamics analysis
Staffing	Basic employee information, Applicant tracking	Recruitment analysis, Selection analysis, Position analysis, Manpower structure analysis	Staffing simulation
Training and career development	Employee training data, Training courses Career profile	Training needs analysis, Training cost-benefit analysis, Promotion analysis	Career management simulation, Training evaluation and decisions
Performance management	Performance data	Performance appraisal analysis, Attitude survey, Attendance management analysis, Productivity analysis	Performance management simulation
Compensation management	Payroll, Health insurance Routine reports (e.g., income tax)	Manpower cost analysis, Compensation structure analysis	Compensation management simulation

(*Courtesy: Lin, C. Y. Y., (1997)*[2]. *Human Resource Information Systems: Implementation in Taiwan,* Research and Practice in Human Resource Management, *5(1), 57–72*).

Maintaining and Managing HRIS

One of the most important factors influencing the proper maintenance of HRIS is the support of the information system (IS) department of the organization. Apart from playing a major role in facilitating the computerization of human resource information, the IS department plays a crucial role in terms of making the HRIS trouble free, upgradation and constant vigil in terms of maintenance and development according to the needs of the organization. They also need to be in constant touch of the vendors and other competitive application packages in the market and make the HR department be aware of the advancements in HRIS application modules available. They along with the HR people are also being held responsible for constantly training the personnel in handling and using the HRIS for day to day administrative activities and thereby facilitating managerial decision making related to the human resources of the organization.

Another important factor identified for effective management of the HRIS is obviously the cost factor. The HR department needs to constantly identify areas where the HRIS could be effectively utilized in order to make the HR functions more cost effective. As for example, it is a well known fact that most organizations encounter a significant cost in terms of maintaining their recruitment efforts, cross-posting within and across general or industry-specific job boards and maintaining a competitive exposure of manpower availabilities. In fact this day to day HR challenge can be negated by the development and implementation of a dedicated Applicant Tracking System, or 'ATS' module in the organization's HRIS that would significantly contribute to control recruitment costs. Many organizations have gone beyond the traditional functions and developed human resource management information systems, which support recruitment, selection, hiring, job placement, performance appraisals, employee benefit analysis, training development, health, safety and security, while others integrate an outsourced Applicant Tracking System (ATS) that encompasses a subset of the above functions.

Functions of HRIS

Typically, the Human Resource Information Systems (HRIS) provide the following functions, namely:

- Management of all employee information.
- Reporting and analysis of employee information.
- Company related documents such as employee handbooks, emergency evacuation procedures and safety guidelines.
- Benefits administration including enrollment, status changes and personal information updating.
- Complete integration with payroll and other company financial software and accounting systems.
- Applicant and resume management.

HRIS can help HR professionals of various organizations effectively monitor:

- attendance and PTO use,
- pay raises and history,
- pay grades and positions held,
- performance development plans,
- training received,
- disciplinary action received,
- personal employee information, and occasionally,
- management and key employee succession plans,
- high potential employee identification, and
- applicant tracking, interviewing and selection.

Human Resource Management Information System Objectives

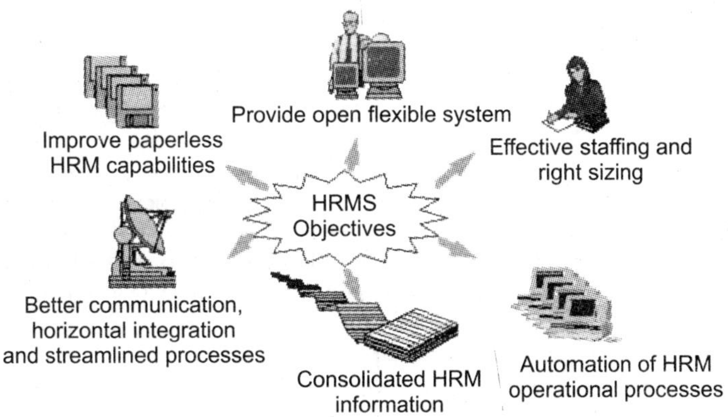

Fig. 2.39: Objectives of HRIS

An effective HRIS provides information on just about anything the company needs to track and analyze about employees, former employees and applicants. Any organization which needs to implement a suitable HRIS would essentially need to customize it to meet the needs of effectively managing its human resources.

With an appropriate HRIS, Human Resources staff enables employees to do their own benefits updates and address changes, thus freeing HR staff for more strategic functions. Additionally, data necessary for employee management, knowledge development, career growth and development, and equal treatment is facilitated. Finally, managers can access the information they need to legally, ethically, and effectively support the success of their reporting employees.

Components of HRIS

A human resource information system for a larger organization is comprised of the following components and capabilities:

- Computerized Database Management System
- Screens for cross-checking
- Modules for performing specific functions
- Query programs for requesting special information

Components of HRIS	Features
Databases	• State of the art Relational Database Management Systems (RDBMS) can reduce the need to keep and maintain duplicate data. • With the use of database systems, information appears only once, in an appropriate table; for e.g., a table on employment information, a table on benefits or on employee skills.
Screens	• Each module in the HRIS will have its own screens for data entry and retrieval • Screen for basic personnel data can be effectively organized employee-wise.
Modules	• Most systems in the HRIS would have a number of modules that perform specific functions and produce regular reports. • The most basic module, which virtually all systems have, contain employee information such as age, sex, date of appointment·
	• And the like which can be accessed by other modules as needed.
Query programs	• More sophisticated HRISs do not just produce regular reports; they also can produce special reports, answer queries and play an important role in support of the decision-making process.
Reports	• It involves the extent to which HRIS caters to the task of manipulating the human resources data to appear in the appropriate format and then delivering the data to the appropriate destination or individual for important HR decisions.

Benefits of HRIS

HRIS would be very critical for organizations in the near future. HRIS has showed many benefits to the HR operations. A few of them can be detailed as:

- Large amount of data and information to be processed.
- Project based work environment.
- Faster information process
- Increase of knowledge workers and associated information.
- Employee empowerment.
- Greater information accuracy
- Improved planning and program development and
- Enhanced employee communications.

Significant Accomplishments of HRIS

The accomplishments of a HRIS in an organization can be understood in terms of their contribution to effectively identify the inputs, maintenance and outputs (as revealed by the following table).

Accomplishments of HRIS	Features
Inputs	This involves the extent to which adding data to the system is made easy by a HRIS
Maintenance	It is the extent to which a HRIS caters to the tasks of updating, integrating and organizing of the data
Outputs	It involves the extent to which HRIS caters to the task of manipulating the human resources data to appear in the appropriate format and then delivering the data to the appropriate destination or individual for important HR decisions.

Barriers to the success of an HRIS: The primary reason for delay in HRIS implementation in organizations is because of the fear psychosis created by "technology" and "IT" in the minds of senior management. They may not be very tech savvy and fear being left out.

- Lack of management commitment
- Satisfaction with the status quo
- No or poorly done needs analysis
- Failure to include key people
- Failure to keep project team intact
- Politics/hidden agendas
- Inter and intra departmental conflicts
- Failure to involve/consult significant groups
- Lack of communication
- Lack of union support and recognition
  Bad timing (time of year and duration of implementation)

Factors Contributing to the Effectiveness of HRIS

The effectiveness of HRIS in an organization depends on several factors, namely:

- **Adequacy of Information:** This mainly caters to the HR information available in the organization. Any organization in order to successfully implement a HRIS should emphasize on the adequacy of the relevant HR information, that should be fed into the databases for future decision-making. The HR managers and executives should take outmost care so as to choose the right information for feeding into the organization's HRIS.

- **Specificity:** The success of a HRIS would also depend on the specific functions in terms of outputs to be derived from the system. The HR managers associated with the use of the HRIS application must be sure what type of HR functions they need to automate by the use of the HRIS.
- **Relevance:** The HRIS and its features should be strictly customized according to the needs of the organization. Hence the software provider should emphasize on a needs assessment survey before installing the application in their client's office.
- **Flexibility:** The HRIS should be flexible enough to instigate any form of change or modifications as and when needed by the organization with respect to its HR practices and organizational change and development related decisions.
- **Comprehensiveness:** the HRIS should be comprehensive in terms of covering all aspects of the HR functions and procedures in the organization.
- **Reliability:** One of the most important criteria of a HRIS is its reliability. The information collected from a HRIS and the outputs generated should facilitate the management to take vital decisions with respect to the management of the organization's human resources.
- **Delivery:** The HRIS should be result oriented in its delivery and should help the HR managers to take HR decisions both in terms of qualitative as well as in terms of quantitative parameters.
- **Promptness:** The HRIS should be able to provide the management prompt responses in terms of queries made by the users. The system should provide easy and fast data retrieval as when required.
- **User Interface:** The HRIS should provide a very simple and effective user interface for its users for their ease. Each modules and functions should have special online help and guideline manuals so as to facilitate users.
- **Training and Software Maintenance Support:** The application/software company installing the HRIS in an organization should ensure that they provide adequate training and orientation to the employees associated with the use of the HRIS. Training should focus on the overall use of the HRIS and also on system maintenance and administration.

Recent Trends in the use of HRIS

Recent trends have indicated that organizations are changing for the better as more and more of business heads and HR professionals are realizing the importance of IT and technology. Major HRIS providers are concentrating on the small and middle range organizations as well as large organizations for their products. They are also coming up with very specific software modules, which would cater to any of their HR needs. SAP and Peoplesoft provide HR modules within their business intelligence software. Hence HRIS would soon be an integral part of HR activities in all organization.

Application Softwares used for HRIS

HRIS Software	Features
Abra Suite	Used for human resources and payroll management
ABS (Atlas Business Solutions)	General information, Wages information, Emergency information, Reminders, Evaluators, Notes customer information, Documents and photos, Separation information.
CORT: HRMS	Used for applicant tracking, Attendance tracking and calendars, Wage information, Skills tracking, Reports-to information, Status tracking, Job history tracking, Cost center tracking, Reviews and tracking, Mass update and change tools etc.

Contd...

HRSOFT	Identify and track senior managers, Assess management skills and talents, Generate a wide range of reports, resumes, employee profiles, replacement tables and succession analysis reports, Identify individuals for promotion, skills shortages, unexpected vacancy, Discover talent deep, Competency Management, career development, align succession plans etc.
Human Resource Microsystems	Used for sophisticated data collection and reporting, flexible spending accounts, compensation, employment history, time off, EEO, qualifications, Applicant/Requisition Tracking, Position Control/Succession Planning, Training Administration, Organization Charts, HRIS-Pro Net (employee/managerial self-service), HR Automation (eNotification and eScheduler) and Performance Pro (performance management)
ORACLE-HRMS	Oracle iRecruitment, Oracle Self-Service Human Resources, Payroll, HR Intelligence, Oracle Learning Management, Oracle Time and Labour
PEOPLESOFT	Enterprise eRecruit, Enterprise Resume Processing, Enterprise Services Procurement, Workforce Planning, Warehouse
SAP HR	Human Capital Management (HCM) for Business, All-in-One: Rapid HR, SPECTRUM HR: iVantage® and HRVantage®. iVantage is a Web-based HRIS product designed for organizations with up to 10,000 employees.
VANTAGE: HRA	'Point-and-Click' report writing, internal Messaging System for leaving reminders to yourself, to someone else or to everyone using HRA - very useful for Benefit Applications, Disciplinary Actions, Special Events, Employee Summary Screen for Basic, Leave (Absenteeism) and Salary/Position History, skills and training module, Leave Tracking Module

REFERENCES

1. Kavanagh, M.J., Gueutal, H.G. and Tannenbaum, S.1. (1990), Human Resource Information Systems: Development and Application, PWS-Kent Publishing Co., Boston.
2. Lin, C. Y. Y., (1997). Human Resource Information Systems: Implementation in Taiwan, *Research and Practice in Human Resource Management*, 5(1), 57–72.
3. http://www. rphrm.curtin.edu.au/1997/issue1/taiwan.html
4. www.perfectsoftware.com
5. http://www.poweronline.com/storefronts/nasheng.html

QUESTION BANK

1. Define Human Resource Information System. What are its objectives? How can an organization be benefitted by a HRIS?
2. What are the functions of HRIS?
3. How can a HRIS enhance the effectiveness of the HR function in an organization?
4. "HRIS facilitates effective human capital management in organizations". Comment on the statement.
5. What are the various features of an effective HRIS?
6. Write a note on latest HRIS packages available in the market. How do various organizations have been benefitted by the use of these applications?
7. HRIS helps in effective human resource planning. Explain the statement.
8. What are the emerging trends in the use of HRIS in today's organizations?
9. What are the barriers of implementing HRIS in organizations? How can these barriers be removed?
10. Do HR professionals need to be tech savvy for managing HRIS effectively? Comment, giving suitable explanations.
11. What are the factors or attributes that contribute to the effectiveness of HRIS?

Internet Exercises

- Go to the internet and collect information on the various latest HRIS software available in the market. If possible make a cost benefit analysis of the same.
- Surf the internet. Prepare a list of organizations where HRIS have been successfully implemented and comment on how they have been benefitted.

Project

- Use MS Excel spreadsheet and try to prepare a database of the student profile of your class. How would you prepare a concise report out of this database? You may organize this project into a team of five members and consult you IT faculty for the same

JOB EVALUATION

(*Courtesy: www.ahajokes.com*)

THEME CASE: RAMESH'S WOES

Ramesh had started looking after his family garments factory in Bangalore after the accident of his uncle. Ramesh had done his BE from a reputed institute in Karnataka and was a tech savvy, enthusiastic, enterprising young man. Prior to this assignment he was working with a reputed management consultant as a trainee for the last 2 years before he had to take charge of his family business. Ramesh's garments factory employed almost 400 employees working in different shifts. There was a manager to look after the work shifts and the productivity. Whereas the accounts officer took care of the compensation, which was a very complex activity. Being in an industry which had high attrition rates, particularly with respect to others in and around Bangalore Ramesh had no idea what to do. Jobs were not properly aligned, designations were all done without any job analysis. Further there was no system to record employee performance and track their achievements. As a result in spite of good contribution from the employees, rewards could not be allocated at the right time for the deserving candidates which led to growing dissatisfaction among the employees. Ramesh did his best to ensure that the factory had proper layout, design and he even took the help of his institute's senior professor to streamline the production process. But linking employee performance to their compensation was still at bay. The supervisors didn't know how to convince their employees. The administrative department were of the opinion that this was a passing phase and the company would adjust things with time.

Last week Ramesh was travelling to Chennai for a business deal with one of his clients when he met Raj his class friend in Shatabdi express. Raj had completed his MBA degree after finishing his BE and joined a MNC as a training coordinator. He suggested, "when you need to have a job evaluation to fix things, go to a consultant! I have some good contacts in Bangalore". Ramesh started to give it a serious thought, even though he was aware of the opinion of his staffs.

Problems faced by that of Mr. Ramesh was not unknown in most small scale industrial units in Bangalore. In fact, it was a syndrome affecting most of the companies.

What is Job Evaluation?

Job evaluation is the systematic way of determining the value/worth of a job in relation to other jobs in an organization. The aim of job evaluation is to provide a systematic and consistent approach to defining the relative worth of jobs within a workplace, single plant or multiple site organization. It is a process whereby jobs are placed in a rank order according to overall demands placed upon the job holder. It therefore provides a basis for a fair and orderly grading structure.

Job evaluation does not determine actual pay. That is a separate operation, normally the subject of negotiation between management and employees or their trade union representatives. Only the job is evaluated, not the person doing it. It is a technique of job analysis, assessment and comparison and it is concerned with the demands of the job, such as the experience and the responsibility required carrying out the job. It is not concerned with the total volume of work, the number of people required to do it, the scheduling of work, or the ability of the job holder.

Features of Job Evaluation

The purpose of job evaluation is to produce a defensible defensive ranking of jobs on which a rational and accepted pay structure can be established.

- It tries to assess jobs, not people.
- The standards of Job Evaluation are relative, not absolute.
- The basic information on which Job Evaluations are made is obtained from Job Analysis.
- Job evaluations are carried out by groups, not by individuals.
- Job evaluation is not fix pay scales, but merely provides a basis for evaluating a rational wage structure.

Process of Job Evaluation

The process of job evaluation can be described under the following stages, namely:

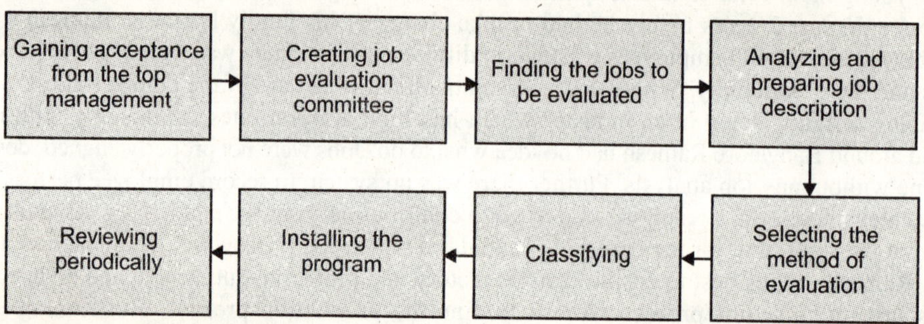

Model of Job Evaluation

The following figure indicates the Hay method of Job Evaluation. The model depicts that the job evaluation process starts with job evaluation meetings, which aims to develop knowhow scores with respect to each job in the organization. The knowhow scores mainly emphasize upon depth and range of technical and management knowhows. The participants or the experts subsequently contribute to construct problem solving scores on the basis of their creative opinions. In the next level focus is given on assessing the financial impact of job, which ultimately is used to develop the accountability score. The accountability score along with the knowhow and problem solving scores help to establish the final evaluation of the job complexity.

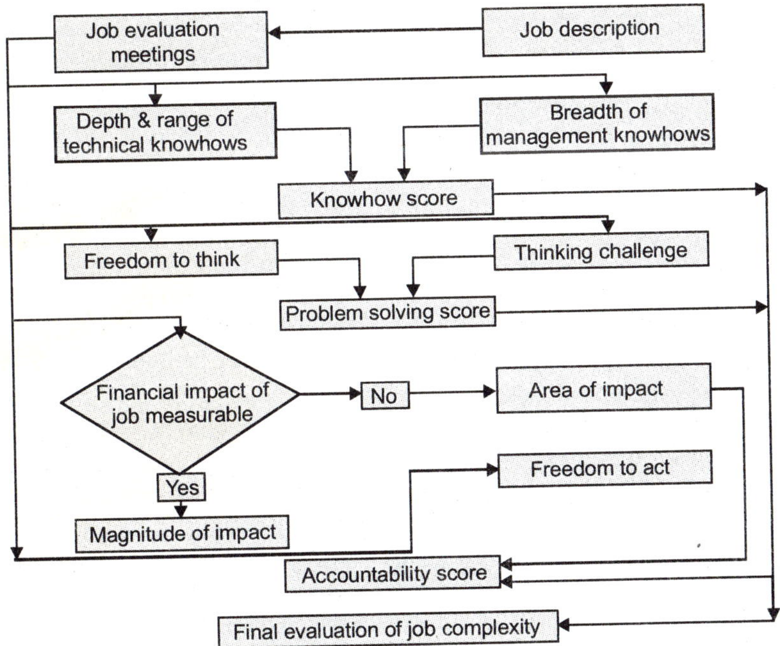

Fig. 2.40: Hay method of job evaluation

(Courtesy: Business Today, Jan 7–21, 1996, p. 119)

Industry Opinion

"If you want to understand which job stands where in a hierarchy, Job Evaluation is the only objective way of doing so". Debashish Mitra, Group Vice President (HR), Ballarpur Industries.

(Courtesy: Business Today, January 7–21, 1996, p. 119)

Methods of Job Evaluation

A. Ranking Method: In this method, jobs are arranged from highest to the lowest, in order of their value or merit of the organization. Jobs can also be arranged according to their relative difficulty in performing them. The jobs are then examined as a whole rather than on the basis of important factors in the job; and the job at the top of the list has the highest value and the job at the bottom will have the lowest value. The variation of the payment of salaries depends on the variation of the nature of the job performed by the employees. The ranking method is one of the simplest to administer. Jobs are compared to each other based on the overall worth of the job to the organization. The 'worth' of a job is usually based on judgements of skill, effort (physical and mental), responsibility (supervisory and fiscal) and working conditions.

Advantages	Disadvantages
• Simple. • Very effective when there are relatively few jobs to be evaluated (less than 30).	• Difficult to administer as the number of jobs increases. • Rank judgements are subjective. • Since there is no standard used for comparison, new jobs would have to be compared with the existing jobs to determine its appropriate rank. In essence, the ranking process would have to be repeated each time a new job is added to the organization.

B. Classification Method: Here, a predetermined number of job groups or job classes are established and jobs are assigned to these classifications. The method places groups of jobs into classes or job grades. Separate classes may include office, clerical, managerial, personnel etc. Jobs are classified into an existing grade/category structure or hierarchy. Each level in the grade/category structure has a description and associated job titles. Each job is assigned to the grade/category providing the closest match to the job. The classification of a position is decided by comparing the whole job with the appropriate job grading standard. To ensure equity in job grading and wage rates, a common set of job grading standards and instructions are used. Because of differences in duties, skills and knowledge, and other aspects of trades and labour jobs, job grading standards are developed mainly along occupational lines. The various job classes could be in the form of:

- ***Class I — Executives***: Further classification under this category may be Officer, Manager, Deputy office manager, Office superintendent, Departmental supervisor etc.
- ***Class II — Skilled Workers***: Purchasing assistant, Cashier, Receipts clerk etc.
- ***Class III — Semiskilled Workers***: Stenotypists, Machine operators, switchboard operators etc.
- ***Class IV — Semiskilled Workers***: File clerks, Office boys, sweepers, cleaners etc.

Advantages	Disadvantages
• Simple. • The grade/category structure exists independent of the jobs. Therefore, new jobs can be classified more easily than the Ranking Method.	• Classification judgements are subjective. • The standard used for comparison (the grade/category structure) may have built in biases that would affect certain groups of employees (females or minorities). • Some jobs may appear to fit within more than one grade/category.

C. Factor Comparison Method: In this method, instead of ranking complete jobs, each job is ranked according to a series of factors. These factors include mental effort, physical effort, skill needed, supervisory responsibility, working conditions and other relevant factors like knowhow, problem solving abilities, accountability etc. Pay is assigned in this method by comparing the weights of the factors required for each job. A set of *compensable* factors are identified as determining the worth of jobs. Typically the number of compensable factors is small (4 or 5). Examples of compensable factors are:

- Skill
- Responsibilities
- Effort
- Working Conditions

Next, benchmark jobs are identified. Benchmark jobs should be selected as having certain characteristics.

- equitable pay (not overpaid or underpaid)
- range of the factors (for each factor, some jobs would be at the low end of the factor while others would be at the high end of the factor).

The jobs are then priced and the total pay for each job is divided into *pay* for each factor. The following job comparison matrix illustrates this:

	Cost clerk	File clerk	Adresso-graph op.	Ledger clerk	Junior typist	Order clerk	Mes-senger	Total
Cost clerk								
File clerk								
Addresso-graph op.								
Ledger clerk								
Junior typist								
Order clerk								
Messenger								

Fig. 2.41: A job comparison matrix

This process establishes the rate of pay for each factor for each benchmark job. Slight adjustments may need to be made to the matrix to ensure equitable dollar weighting of the factors. The other jobs in the organization are then compared with the benchmark jobs and rates of pay for each factor are summed to determine the rates of pay for each of the other jobs.

Table 2.10: Job Evaluation: Factor Comparison

Job	***Hourly Rate***	***The hourly rate is divided into pay for each of the following factors:***			
		Pay for Skill	***Pay for Effort***	***Pay for Responsibility***	***Pay for Working Conditions***
HR executive	Rs. 90	45	20	20	5
HR assistant	Rs. 55	30	10	10	5
Supervisor	Rs. 45	25	10	4	6

Contd...

Advantages	Disadvantages
• The value of the job is expressed in monetary terms. • Can be applied to a wide range of jobs. • Can be applied to newly created jobs.	• The pay for each factor is based on judgements that are subjective. • The standard used for determining the pay for each factor may have build in biases that would affect certain groups of employees (females or minorities).

D. Point Method: Here, jobs are expressed in terms of key factors. Points are assigned to each factor after positioning each factor in the order of importance. The points are summed up to determining the wage rate for the job. Jobs with similar point totals are placed in similar pay grades. A set of *compensable* factors are identified as determining the worth of jobs. Typically the compensable factors include the major categories of:

1. Skill
2. Responsibilities
3. Effort
4. Working conditions

These factors can then be further defined.

1. Skill
   (a) Experience
   (b) Education
   (c) Ability
2. Responsibilities
   (a) Fiscal
   (b) Supervisory
3. Effort
   (a) Mental
   (b) Physical
4. Working conditions
   (a) Location
   (b) Hazards
   (c) Extremes in environment

The point method is an extension of the factor comparison method. Each factor is then divided into levels or degrees which are then assigned points. Each job is rated using the job evaluation instrument. The points for each factor are summed to form a total point score for the job. Jobs are then grouped by total point scores and assigned to wage/salary grades so that similarly rated jobs would be placed in the same wage/salary grade.

Basis for Job Hierarchy	Non-quantitative comparison involving job as a whole	Quantitative comparison involving job comparisons
Jobs versus Job comparison	Job ranking	Factor comparison
Jobs versus Scale comparison	Job grading or classification	Point method Hay Plan

Fig. 2.42: Job evaluation procedures

(*Courtesy: Ivancevich, J.M., (1992): "Job Evaluation procedures," from Foundations of Personnel.*)

Advantages of Job Evaluation

- It is the logical and objective method of ranking jobs relating to one another.
- For newer jobs, this method often facilitates fitting them into the existing wage structure.
- It helps to replace the many accidental factors, occurring in less systematic procedures on the basis of comparative job requirements.
- Job Evaluation information also reveals that workers are engaged in jobs requiring less skill and other qualities than they possess, thereby pointing to the possibility of a making more efficient use of an organization's labour force.
- It provides a benchmark for comparing job complexities.
- It facilitates career planning in an organization.
- It streamlines responsibility levels.
- It can be used to equate pay with jobs for senior managers.

Sample Job Evaluation Questionnaire

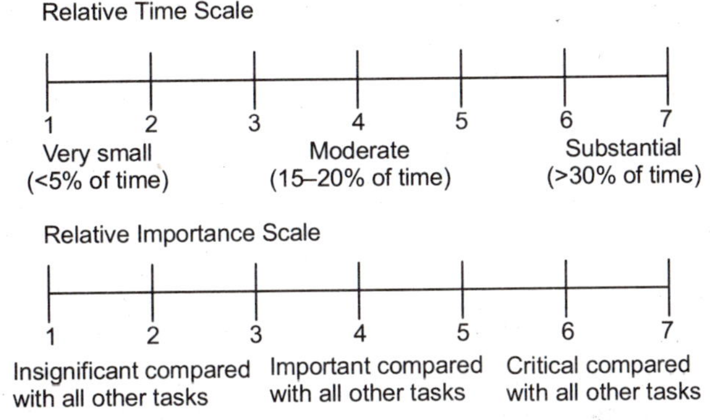

Statements	Relative Time Spent		Relative importance
	Performing	Supervising	
Allocates acquired work resources			
Interfaces with suppliers and vendors			
Coordinates work resources for maintenance and replacements			
Addresses usefulness and usage of work resources			
Arbitrates differences of opinions on work-related decisions			
Sets direction on work-related subjects and makes appropriate assignments			
Establishes appropriate work environment such as productive, creative or team oriented			
Determines desired work action after assessing alternatives			
Determines policy and procedural needs using company manual and other sources			

QUESTION BANK

1. What is job evaluation? State its importance.
2. How does job evaluation help in compensation management?
3. What are the various methods of job evaluation? State their respective merits and demerits.
4. Describe the steps in the process of job evaluation.
5. How can one ensure effective job evaluation in organizations?
6. What are the features of job evaluation?

Games

- Suppose you are the team leader of a team consisting of 10 members. Each of you had contributed Rs. 500 to start a business venture as a project. Describe the plan how would you all share the earnings or your return of investment.
- Can you apply the concept of job evaluation for a differential pay system/performance based pay system in the Indian Cricket (test, one day/20–20 cricket) team? Use a suitable presentation to support your research.

RECRUITMENT, SELECTION AND PLACEMENT

Theme Reading: Root Cause of Talent Poaching

Often, we come across hiring managers complaining about talent poaching by their competition. An easy hire would be to make a +10 per cent offer to the people and woo them to your side. The same holds good for your competition too. How do you eliminate/minimize talent/people poaching? What does it say about the position being filled? If anyone can fill the position, doesn't it call for elimination/automation of that position?

If value addition is not expected of a position but mere mundane execution of a procedure, then it is a candidate for automation (or elimination). Why do companies fight over filling such positions? If human deployment is cheaper than automation, then, get temp staff. Organizations that rely on temp staff for longer periods should consider redesigning their business processes.

The real value-adding positions are unique to each business and are tightly integrated with their business models. Poaching will seldom help fill such positions. A meaningful talent search is needed to ensure value generation by that position. It is difficult to find an exact or near exact match in the open market. The collection of such positions in organizations forms the competitive advantage platform. The selection process would be to seek out people with basic business acumen, maturity, near zero ego, and a willingness to learn and adapt. People engaged in such positions form the human capital for their organization.

Those seeking such positions would see their role to be meaningful and adequate on the economic front. They would not be available for a +10–30 per cent offer by the competition. The world is opening up with global opportunities. It is difficult to tie employees up for long in one place unless they see it as home.

The HR challenge should be to make the job/position meaningful rather than to entertain poaching. With rapid obsolescence of business models, the hiring manager's focus should be on role design and engaging the right people. Human capital is not built with deadwood. Poaching is a transitional phenomenon in static (high inertia) business models and soon becomes irrelevant in the information/knowledge society.

Then, why do hiring managers complain about talent poaching? Are high inertia, static business models the root cause? Why are organizations looking for answers somewhere else?

(Ref: K. V. Ramesh (2005): Business Line, Dec. 20, 2005)

What is Recruitment?

Recruitment is the process of finding and attracting capable applicants for employment. The process begins when new recruits are sought and ends when their applications are submitted. The result is a pool of applicants from which new employees are selected.

The recruitment and selection is the major function of the human resource department and recruitment process is the first step towards creating the competitive strength and the strategic advantage for the organizations. Recruitment process involves a systematic procedure from sourcing the candidates to arranging and conducting the interviews and requires many resources and time. A general recruitment process is as follows:

Definitions

According to Subbarao (2005) Human Resource Management: Recruitment is defined as a process to discover the source of manpower to meet the recruitment of starting schedule and to employee effective measure for attracting that work force in adequate numbers to facilitated effective selection of an effective work force.

According to Dr. C.B. Mamoria (2000): Recruitment is essential to every organization and it is the post stage of employee entering the organization Recruitment is an systematic process finding/attracting applicants skills knowledge for knowledge process of individual recruitment is recruit is employee carefully and right place and right job, it makes possible to acquire the number and types of people unnecessary to ensure the continued operation of this organization.

According to Misra (1990): Recruitment is the differences between job recruitment and individual performance recruiting is a process of recruiting to employee right place in right job, that is ensure the person industry to working and it is an identified eligible person on the time of recruiting, if person recruitment level of select to applicant an proper manner,

According to Edwin B. Flippo (1969): The process of searching for prospective employee and stimulating them to apply for jobs in organization,

According to Denerely and Plumblay (1969): Recruitment is concerned with both engaging the required number of people and measuring their quality. It is not only a matter of satisfying a company's needs, it is also an activity which influences the shape if the company's future.

Recruitment has been regarded as the most important function of manpower management and administration. Unless the right matches of people are not hired, even the best organizational plans and control systems will be of no effectiveness. A company cannot prosper, grow, or even survive without adequate human resource and particularly when the right people with the right skills are not available. Need for skilled manpower in recent years has created a pressure on the industry to establish an efficient recruitment function. Many organizations who are not good at this function have been found to outsource the recruitment activity from an outside HR consultant firm. Recruitment if not planned and executed wisely, lead to ineffective management. Manpower costs increases and bottlenecks worse. Training costs increase and customer service suffers.

Now a days the recruitment process is strategically meant to locate the source of work force so as to meet job related requirements and skills or experience related specification as well has or the first stage the process with continues with selection and carrier with the placement of candidate recruitment is the process of attracting the applicants with certain skills abilities and other personal character has to job vacancies on organization. A successful recruitment strategy should be well planned and practical to attract more and good talent to apply in the organization.

Identifying the Vacancy

The recruitment process begins with the HR department receiving requisitions for recruitment from any department of the company. These contain:

- Posts to be filled
- Number of persons
- Duties to be performed
- Qualifications required
- Preparing the job description and person specification.
- Locating and developing the sources of required number and type of employees (Advertising etc.).
- Short-listing and identifying the prospective employee with required characteristics.
- Arranging the interviews with the selected candidates.
- Conducting the interview and decision-making

As for example, a marketing manager of a FMCG company might have his own choice of manpower requirement as compared to that of an IT manager. This not only varies in terms of the number of manpower but also in terms of the different skills, experience and capabilities of the targeted employees. But in all the cases the basic purpose is to ensure the right people with right capabilities and skills for the right jobs.

Industry Opinion

"Restricting our hiring strategy to traditional methods or channels will not suffice. As Tata Motors works towards becoming an International player, we are using a multitude options". Mr. Sangram Tambe, VP, HR, Tata Motors

(Courtesy: Bajpai, V., 2008: "Innovative Hiring Strategies", Dare, Vol: 2, Issue: 10, July 2008, issue, p. 55).

Purpose and importance: Considering the above discussions related to employee retention and organizational success the purpose of the recruitment initiative taken by any organization could be immense. Some of the most important purposes could be as follows:

- To determine the present and future requirements of the organization in conjunction with the personnel planning and job analysis activities.
- To enhance the pool of potential job aspirants with minimal cost.
- To enhance the success rate of the selection process by reducing the number of, underqualified or overqualified job applicants.
- To effectively reduce the probability of job applicants, once recruited and selected, will leave the organization only after a short period of time.
- To meet the organization's legal and social obligations regarding the composition of its workforce.
- To start identifying and preparing potential job applicants who will be appropriate candidates.
- To increase organizational and individual effectiveness in the short- and long-term.
- To evaluate the effectiveness of various recruiting techniques and sources for all types of job applicants.
- To support and form the basis of the manpower retention plan of the organization.
- To form the basis of the manpower development process by hiring the future talents.

Factors Governing Recruitment Process

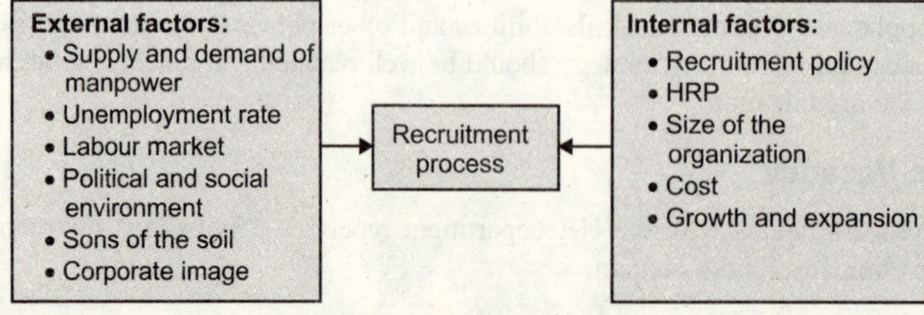

Characteristics of a Firm's Recruitment Policy

An organization's recruitment policy is the statement of guidelines describing the overall objectives of the recruitment process and action plans and thereby acts as a facilitator of effective decision-making so as to ensure the right people with right skills and capabilities for the right jobs in the organization. The recruitment policy of an organization may vary according to the nature of the business, or the type of industry where the organization is belonging. But in terms of the objectives and goals all recruitment policies bear a similar theme and approach:

An effective Recruitment Policy of an organization should contain the following elements:

- Organization's Objectives: Both short-term and long-term.
- Financial allocation and guidelines regarding the use of the same
- Identification of the recruitment needs
- Preferred sources of recruitment
- Criteria of selection and preferences
- The cost of recruitment and financial implications/outcomes of the same.

Exhibit: How Pepsi Recruits for ITS Fit

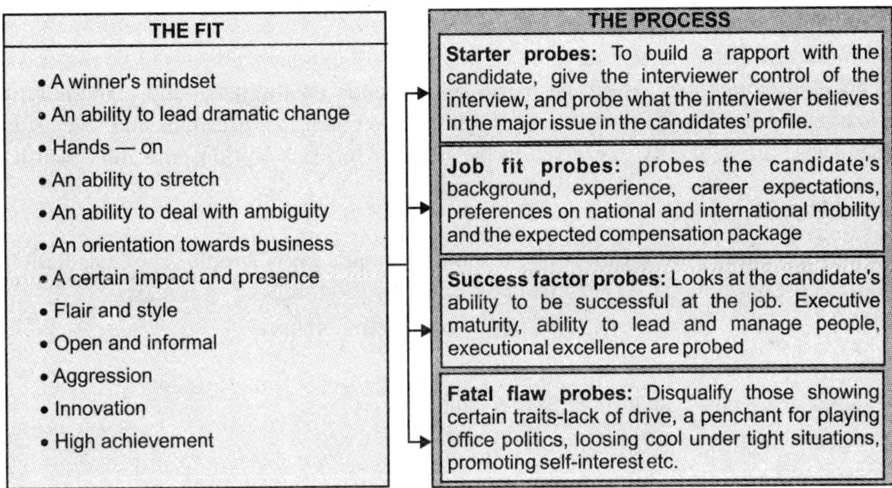

(*Courtesy: "Managing People", The Business Today, January 7–21, 1996, p. 73*)

The Recruitment Process

The various stages in the recruitment process can be illustrated by the following figure:

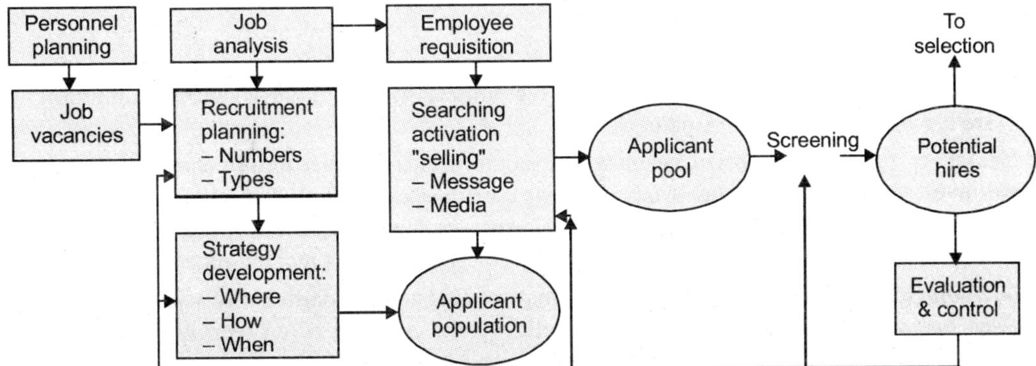

Fig. 2.43: Stages in the recruitment process

Recruitment Planning

Recruitment planning forms an essential component of the human resource planning activity in an organization. It is done in conjunction of job analysis and manpower audit study reports or on the basis of the information provided by the organization's human resource information system (HRIS). Recruitment Planning involves the translation of likely "Job Vacancies" and information about the nature of these jobs into a set of objectives or targets that specify the (a) number and (b) type of applicants to be contacted.

(a) ***Number of Contacts***: Organizations need to plan and attract more applicants than that what they actually need to hire. This is a safeguard to control the costs incurred in cases where candidates take decisions not to accept offers given by the company. In this process, generally computation of the **"Yield Ratios" (YRs)** which expresses the relationship of the applicant inputs to outputs at various decision points becomes strategically essential. A yield ratio is the percentage of applicants from a particular source that makes it to the next stage in the selection process. Thus;

Yield Ratio (YR) = Number of Applicant Inputs/Number of Applicant Outputs

This approach helps the HR department to have an eye on the targeted requirements of manpower hiring in the given/allotted time frame and deadlines keeping the financial constraints also into consideration.

(b) ***Type of Contacts***: This refers to the type of people (skill/experience level) to be informed about the job vacancies or openings. The type of people depends on the tasks and responsibilities of the labour markets comprising of the job seekers and also on their qualifications and level of experiences involved. These are generally expressed in the form of Job Descriptions and Job Specifications.

Cost of Recruitment

The cost of various recruiting procedures can be compared using a fairly simple set of calculations. Thus, if the average source cost per hire (SC/H) can be determined by the following formula:

$$SC/H = (AC + AF + RB + NC)/H$$

where,

AC = advertising costs, total monthly expenditure

AF = agency fees, total for the month

RB = referral bonuses

NC = no-cost hires, walk-ins, non-profit agencies etc

H = total hires

The above computations would help an organization to determine and evaluate the effectiveness of their hiring initiative in a given time.

Recruitment Strategy Development

In order to ensure that a recruitment plan is being effectively implemented, organizations need to employ recruitment strategies. For developing an effective recruitment strategy in an organization, the following elements are taken into consideration, namely:

- ***"Make" or "Buy" Decisions***: Organizations should decide whether to hire less skilled employees and invest on TandD programs (Make Strategy), or they can hire skilled labour and professionals (Buy Strategy). Make strategy seems to be effective for hiring freshers, whereas for the senior and middle level positions, but strategy is a better fit for getting things moving on an immediate basis.
- ***Technological Sophistication***: Use of Information Technology, particularly with the help of web based business solutions. Companies now a days have emphasized on recruiting people through

their own websites with lots of information regarding the candidate's future career and job related challenges. This helps to clarify doubts and filters candidates who are not sure which company to apply for.

- ***Where to Look***: In order to reduce costs, organizations look into labour markets most likely to offer the required job seekers. They generally look into the national market for managerial and professional employees, regional or local markets for technical employees and local markets for clerical and blue-collar employees. Now a days job portals have become an one-stop destination for most hirers for identifying and getting close to their future recruits.
- ***Knocking at the Right Door***: This refers to identify the right sources of recruitment, namely in terms of both (a) External Sources and (b) Internal Sources.
  - **(a) Internal Sources of Recruitment:** Present Employees: Promotions and transfers from amongst present employee lists; Employee referrals; Referrals of former employees; Previous applicant databases; company contacts etc.
  - **(b) External Sources of Recruitment:** Professional Trade Associations; Advertisements; Employment exchanges; Campus Recruitments, Walk-ins and Talk-ins; Unsolicited applications, Recruitment consultants; Contractors; Displaced persons; Job Portals etc.

THEME READING: RECRUITMENT PLANS IN J P MORGAN

Investment bank JP Morgan, which now employs 3200 people had planned to recruit atleast 700 staffs to its Asia Pacific HQs in Hong Kong over the next three years, and lease up to 11 floors in a new office block to accommodate the growth.

(Courtesy: "JP Morgan to add 700 staff in Hong Kong", The Economic Times, 8th January, 2008, p. 10)

THEME READING: RECRUITMENT IN HDFC BANK

HDFC's campus strategy is to look at tier one campuses like Bajaj, SP Jain, IMI, SCMHRD, etc and not only IIM's. HDFC visits to 70 business schools, covering far away places like Bhuvaneshwar, Ludhiana, Baroda, etc. Students from these institutes understand the psyche of the upcountry customers and are ambitious about working for private sector banks. It hires B.Com, M.Com, engineers and other graduates, as well as MBA's. Today the requirement is not just globalization, but localization. To achieve this, the company hires people from various towns and cities. The company also emphasizes on hiring managers from rural background. HDFC Bank has a need to locate people in 500+ branches across 300 cities. Ms. **Mandeep Maitra,** the Country Head HR at HDFC Bank, believes that the bank is being able to attract IIM graduates after they have worked for 3 to 5 years of work experience and have also experienced the real world and are likely to be less disillusioned. The company takes its screening process very seriously. HDFC also emphasizes on referring to current employers and ask questions about performance and integrity of newly joined employees.

(Courtesy Interview with Mandeep Maitra: "People Centric", Banking Frontiers, December 2006 issue, p. 4; www.bankingfrontierscom/coverstory0612_01.pdf)

Factors Influencing the Recruitment Process

Recruitment process is influenced by the following factors namely:

- **Organization Size and Dimension:** This is actually dictated by the nature of service required by the organization from their manpower. Bigger companies have demands of higher volumes of skilled manpower. Now a days service sectors have attracted the largest inflow of expert manpower and the trend seems to be climbing with days to come.

- **Employment Conditions:** This refers to the terms and conditions of employment in the given organization and this depends on the HR policies of the organization.
- **Past Recruitment Efforts or Initiatives:** The performance of the organization in its past recruitment efforts in terms of employee retention or attrition or availability of skilled manpower also influences the budgetary allocation in the present recruitment initiative.
- **Working Conditions, Compensation and Benefits, Career Growth Opportunities:** These variables depend mainly on the policy of the organization and the concerned HR approaches, whichever applicable.
- **Organizational Growth:** The performance and the growth rate of an organization also have an immense role in terms of shaping its manpower hiring initiative. This could be explained by the fact that the recruitment drive of a company in a small industrial area of Bangalore would not be the same as that of Infosys or TCS.
- **Organizational Climate and Culture and Corporate Image:** The employability brand and the culture of an organization have an immense impact on its recruitment plan.

Methods of Recruitment

The various recruitment methods can be classified as follows:

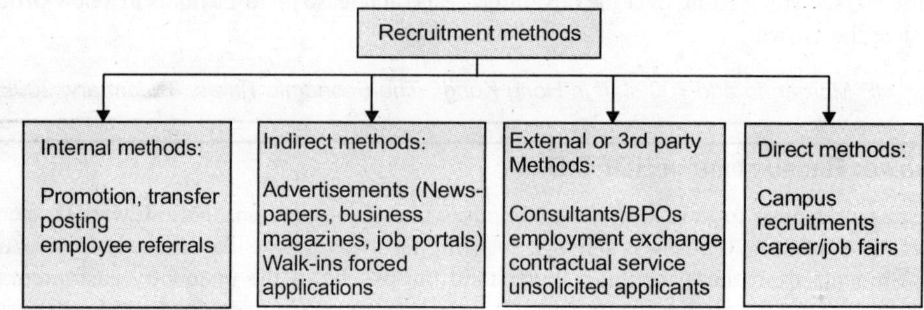

Fig. 2.44: Recruitment methods

- **Internal Recruitment:** This refers to the hiring of employees from within the organization in case of a vacancy in a given position. This depends on whether the candidate has requisite experience and skill levels to meet the needs of the same.
- **Indirect Methods:** This involves hiring candidates from outside or extra-organizational sources. They involve sources like advertisements in newspapers, business magazines, job portals, forced applications and walk-ins.
- **External or 3rd Party Hiring:** This method emphasizes on hiring through an agent or consultant. The advantage is obviously time saving. But sometimes it could be very costly.
- **Direct Recruitment:** It involves the hiring candidates through campus recruitments and career/job fairs.

Fig. 2.45: A recruitment advertisement from perotsystems

Merits and Demerits of External and Internal Recruitment:

Type of Recruitment	Merits	Demerits
1. **Internal recruitment**	• Less costly • Job candidates are already oriented for the organization • Managements have better knowledge for the candidates. • Enhanced employee morale and motivation	• It perpetuates the old concept of doing things. • It abets raiding • Candidates' current work may be affected • Politics play greater roles • Morale problems for those not promoted.
2. **External recruitment**	• Benefits of new skills-competencies, new talents and experiences. • Compliance with reservation policy becomes easy. • Scope for resentment, jealousies and heartburn are avoided.	• Better morale and motivation associated with internal recruiting is denied to the organization. • It is costly. • Chances of creeping in false positive and false negative errors.

Recent Trends in Recruitment

The following trends are being seen in recruitment:

HR Poaching/Raiding

"Buying talent" (rather than developing it) is the latest mantra being followed by the organizations today. Poaching means employing a competent and experienced person already working with another reputed company in the same or different industry; the organization might be a competitor in the industry. A company can attract talent from another firm by offering attractive pay packages and other terms and conditions, better than the current employer of the candidate. But it is seen as an unethical practice and not openly talked about. Indian software and the retail sector are the sectors facing the most severe brunt of poaching today. It has become a challenge for human resource managers to face and tackle poaching, as it weakens the competitive strength of the firm.

The Recruitment Industry

The recruitment industry has four main types of agencies. Their recruiters aim to channel candidates into the hiring organization's application process. As a general rule, the agencies are paid by the companies, not the candidates.

Traditional Recruitment Agency

Also known as employment agencies, recruitment agencies have historically had a physical location. A candidate visits a local branch for a short interview and an assessment before being taken onto the agency's books. Recruitment Consultants then endeavour to match their pool of candidates to their clients' open positions. Suitable candidates are with potential employers.

Remuneration for the agency's services usually takes one of two forms:

- A contingency fee paid by the company when a recommended candidate accepts a job with the client company (typically 20%–30% of the candidate's starting salary), which usually has some form of guarantee, should the candidate fail to perform and is terminated within a set period of time.
- An advance payment that serves as a retainer, also paid by the company.
- In some states it may still be legal for an employment agency to charge the candidate instead of the company, but in most states that practice is now illegal, due to past unfair and deceptive practices.

Outsourcing

In India, the HR processes are being outsourced from more than a decade now. A company may draw required personnel from outsourcing firms. The outsourcing firms help the organization by the initial screening of the candidates according to the needs of the organization and creating a suitable pool of talent for the final selection by the organization.

Outsourcing firms develop their human resource pool by employing people for them and make available personnel to various companies as per their needs. In turn, the outsourcing firms or the intermediaries charge the organizations for their services. Advantages of outsourcing are:

- Company need not plan for human resources much in advance.
- Value creation, operational flexibility and competitive advantage.
- Turning the management's focus to strategic level processes of HRM.
- Company is free from salary negotiations, weeding the unsuitable resumes/candidates.
- Company can save a lot of its resources and time.

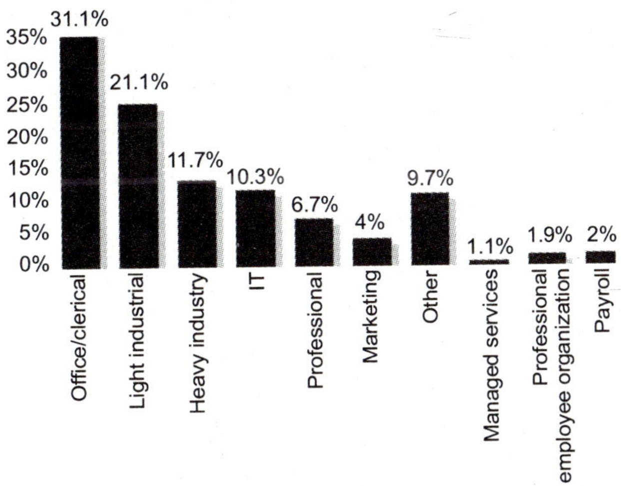

Fig. 2.46: Occupational breakdown of temporary help agency placements

(*Source*: Steve Jones, "You've Come a Long Way, Baby: What the Staffing Industry Offers Today," *Canadian HR Reporter* 14, no. 19, November 5, 2001; 15.)

Online Recruitment Websites

Such sites have two main features: job boards and a resume/Curriculum Vitae (CV) database. Job boards allow member companies to post job vacancies. Alternatively, candidates can upload a résumé to be included in searches by member companies. Fees are charged for job postings and access to search resumes. The details of e-recruitment are included in the e-HR chapter. The following two figures illustrate one job portal and e-recruitment through a company's website.

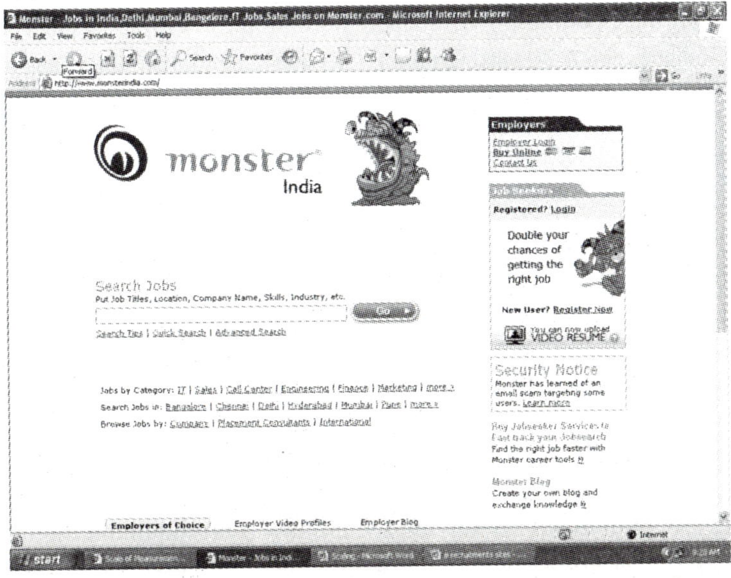

Fig. 2.47: Illustration of a job portal

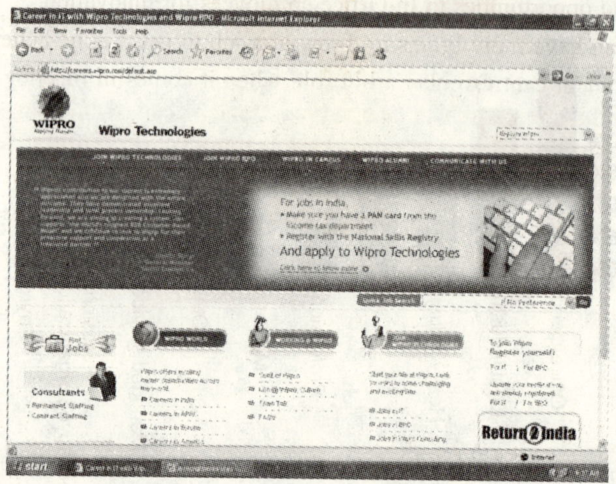

Fig. 2.48: Illustration of recruitment through a company's website

Employee Leasing

Employee leasing now a days have become one of the most convenient ways of hiring human resources in an organization. Outsourcing organizations, consultants etc. provide their client organizations the most dependable, sincere and creative employees. These employees work remotely from the consultant's offices. In this type of staffing or hiring, from a technical and productive standpoint, there is no difference between an engineer sitting 6000 miles away and the one sitting in the next cubicle in the office on a local area network. Employee leasing is similar to the process of hiring temporary workers, but the key difference is permanency. A company wishing to pursue employee leasing will first contact a **professional employment organization (PEO)** to discuss its particular employment needs. The PEO or other employment leasing company might set up an interview process for recruiting new staff, or might take responsibility for existing workers. The company can still participate in the hiring process, but any hired personnel will officially work for the employee leasing company.

Employers often pursue employee leasing options in order to eliminate the need for accountants and human resource managers. The employee leasing agency charges a fee in addition to the employees' wages, much like temporary employment agencies. This fee is often less than the cost of hiring human resource experts and payroll accountants. Because workers are not considered employees of the company in a legal sense, personal injuries and workers' compensation claims become the responsibility of the employee leasing agency.

Employee leasing is not a perfect solution for some companies, however, since workers are not completely under the control of management, communications may become strained. Conflicts may have to be arbitrated by representatives of the employee leasing agency. Termination of non-productive workers may not be as simple as handing out pink slips. Certain union contracts actually prohibit the use of employee leasing agencies or PEOs in order to prevent companies from outsourcing their human resource departments.

Applicability of Employee Leasing

The concept of employee leasing can be highly profitable for the company and the existing staff as:

- Better product and great customer service are the two most important factors for growth and prosperity of every company. Remote employees can help you develop efficient, bug less products and free In-Office or (say) In-House employees' time to communicate with customers to understand and design their requirements efficiently.

- Give more time and opportunities to In-Office employees for innovation.
- Client Company can have more brains to throw at a job to get it done better and faster.
- Stress-free environment can also play a big role when it comes in meeting tight deadlines. A fresh brain can work ideally smarter than a talented one. Infact if an offshore employee is also surrounded by an equally talented Project manager*, Results are golden.

Headhunters

Headhunters are third-party recruiters often retained when normal recruitment efforts have failed. Headhunters are generally more aggressive than in-house recruiters. They may use advanced sales techniques, such as initially posing as clients to gather employee contacts, as well as visiting candidate offices. They may also purchase expensive lists of names and job titles, but more often will generate their own lists. They may prepare a candidate for the interview, help negotiate the salary, and conduct closure to the search. They are frequently members in good standing of industry trade groups and associations. Headhunters will often attend trade shows and other meetings nationally or even internationally that may be attended by potential candidates and hiring managers.

In-house Recruitment

Larger employers tend to undertake their own in-house recruitment, using their Human Resources department. In addition to coordinating with the agencies mentioned above, in-house recruiters may advertise job vacancies on their own websites, coordinate employee referral schemes, and/or focus on campus graduate recruitment. Alternatively a large employer may choose to outsource all or some of their recruitment process (Recruitment process outsourcing).

Recruitment Management System

Recruitment management system is the comprehensive tool to manage the entire recruitment processes of an organization. It is one of the technological tools facilitated by the information management systems to the HR of organizations. Just like performance management, payroll and other systems, Recruitment management system helps to contour the recruitment processes and effectively managing the ROI on recruitment. The features, functions and major benefits of the recruitment management system are explained below:

- Structure and systematically organize the entire recruitment processes.
- Recruitment management system facilitates faster, unbiased, accurate and reliable processing of applications from various applications.
- Helps to reduce the time-per-hire and cost-per-hire.
- Recruitment management system helps to incorporate and integrate the various links like the application system on the official website of the company, the unsolicited applications, outsourcing recruitment, the final decision-making to the main recruitment process.
- Recruitment management system maintains an automated active database of the applicants facilitating the talent management and increasing the efficiency of the recruitment processes.
- Recruitment management system provides and a flexible, automated and interactive interface between the online application system, the recruitment department of the company and the job seeker.
- Offers tolls and support to enhance productivity, solutions and optimizing the recruitment processes to ensure improved ROI.
- Recruitment management system helps to communicate and create healthy relationships with the candidates through the entire recruitment process.

The Recruitment Management System (RMS) is an innovative information system tool which helps to sane the time and costs of the recruiters and improving the recruitment processes.

Profile Analysis: Evaluating Employees Against Job Requirements

Few aspects of management command more attention and are fraught with more difficulties than that of managing human resources. First line supervisors feel the pressure daily to find the right persons for each position and, when found, to keep the individual challenged against the requirements of the position.

Unfortunately, there are no scientific formulas for defining position requirements and evaluating job applicants. The position/person matching process seems more art than science. While it is performed daily by many, few feel comfortable at handling the required complexities. One reason is that they have no analytical framework for addressing this process of balancing with people.

Whether

- establishing a new position,
- seeking qualified applicants to hire,
- evaluating performance of existing personnel,
- or attempting to develop personnel **career advancement**.

To evaluate the performance of an existing employee, a supervisor compares the expectations for the position with the employee's actual performance. The requirements of the position must be determined, the performance or capabilities of individuals must be evaluated against these requirements. This process is carried out continually, often without the aid of any concrete discipline. Each case seems unique. The need is for an ordered methodology for doing this that accommodates the different environments and the non quantifiable elements that must be taken into account. Profile analysis is the tool of choice in these circumstances, namely:

Job position profiling: It consists of the following elements, namely:

- oral and written communication skills,
- knowledge of the industry,
- knowledge of accounting systems,
- knowledge of and experience using Cobol programming language,
- knowledge of the computers operating system, and
- skills in database management.

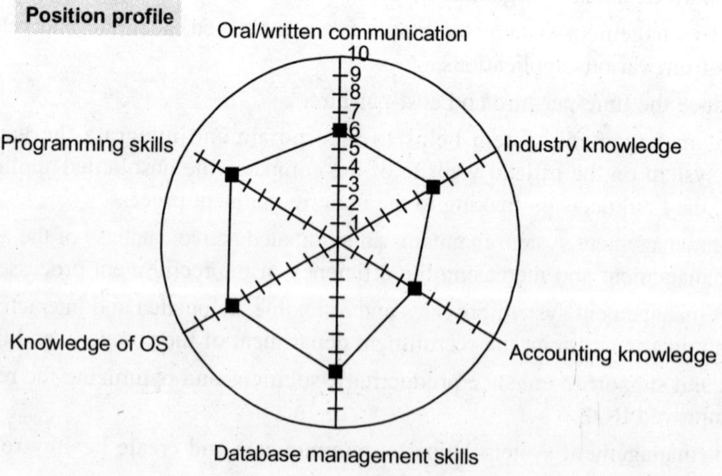

Fig. 2.49: Position profiling diagram

Personnel profile: Once the position requirements are established, attention can turn to evaluating the job applicant side of the equation. Input for this part of the evaluation will come from a variety of sources, including

- a job application
- resume/CV,
- a job interview,
- discussion with former employers,
- actual on the job observations and
- discussion with peers.

Using the information obtained, a personnel evaluation of each job candidate can be performed in which the individual qualifications are matched with the previously developed knowledge/skill factors required, factor by factor. Using a spider chart, the individual's level can then be annotated for each factor.

HR Challenges in Recruitment

Recruitment is a function that requires business perspective, expertise, ability to find and match the best potential candidate for the organization, diplomacy, marketing skills (as to sell the position to the candidate) and wisdom to align the recruitment processes for the benefit of the organization. The HR professionals-handling the recruitment function of the organization-are constantly facing new challenges. The biggest challenge for such professionals is to source or recruit the best people or potential candidate for the organization. The major challenges faced by the HR in recruitment are:

- **Adaptability to globalization** — The HR professionals are expected and required to keep in tune with the changing times, i.e., the changes taking place across the globe. HR should maintain the timeliness of the process.
- **Lack of motivation** — Recruitment is considered to be a thankless job. Even if the organization is achieving results, HR department or professionals are not thanked for recruiting the right employees and performers.
- **Process analysis** — The immediacy and speed of the recruitment process are the main concerns of the HR in recruitment. The process should be flexible, adaptive and responsive to the immediate requirements. The recruitment process should also be cost effective.
- **Strategic prioritization** — The emerging new systems are both an opportunity as well as a challenge for the HR professionals. Therefore, reviewing staffing needs and prioritizing the tasks to meet the changes in the market has become a challenge for the recruitment professionals.

Improving Effectiveness of External Recruitment

External recruitment can be improved by assessing the (a) Yield ratios (b) Realistic Job Previews and (c) Ensuring frequent training of the recruiters.

Yield Ratio Analysis

Yield ratio is the percentage of applicants from a recruitment source that make it to the next stage of the selection process. If in a recruitment process 100 resumes are received, and 50 are being found to be acceptable then we can say that there is 50% yield. On the other hand, the **Cost of Recruitment (per employee hired)** would be determined by the formula:

$$\frac{SC}{H} = \frac{AC + AF + RB + NC}{H}$$

where,

SC = source cost

AC = advertising costs, total monthly expenditure (example: $28,000)

AF = agency fees, total for the month (example: $19,000)

RB = referral bonuses, total paid (example: $2,300)

NC = no-cost hires, walk-ins, non-profit agencies, etc. (example: $0)

H = total hires (example: 119)

Cost to hire one employee = $414

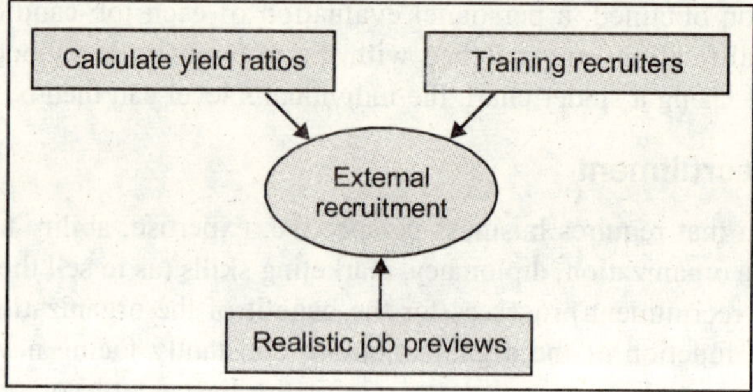

Fig. 2.50: Improving the effectiveness of external recruitment

Realistic Job Previews (RJP): These involve informing applicants about all aspects of the job, including both its desirable and undesirable facets. The positive benefits of RJPs involve those of:

- Improved employee job satisfaction
- Reduced voluntary turnover
- Enhanced communication through honesty and openness
- Realistic job expectations

Requirements for Effective Recruiters: These involve the following aspects related to:

- Knowledge of the recruited job's requirements and of the organization
- Training as an interviewer
- Personable and competent to represent the organization

Recruitment Strategies

Recruitment is of the most crucial roles of the human resource professionals. The level of performance of an organization depends on the effectiveness of its recruitment function. Organizations have developed and follow recruitment strategies to hire the best talent for their organization and to utilize their resources optimally. A successful recruitment strategy should be well planned and practical to attract more and good talent to apply in the organization. For formulating an effective and successful recruitment strategy, the strategy should cover the following elements:

1. **Identifying and prioritizing jobs:** Requirements keep arising at various levels in every organization; it is almost a never-ending process. It is impossible to fill all the positions immediately. Therefore, there is a need to identify the positions requiring immediate attention and action. To maintain the quality of the recruitment activities, it is useful to prioritize the vacancies whether to focus on all vacancies equally or focusing on key jobs first.

2. **Candidates to target:** The recruitment process can be effective only if the organization completely understands the requirements of the type of candidates that are required and will be beneficial for the organization. This covers the following parameters as well:
   - Performance level required: Different strategies are required for focusing on hiring high performers and average performers.
   - Experience level required: The strategy should be clear as to what is the experience level required by the organization. The candidate's experience can range from being a fresher to experienced senior professionals.
   - Category of the candidate: The strategy should clearly define the target candidate. He/she can be from the same industry, different industry, unemployed, top performers of the industry etc.
3. **Sources of recruitment:** The strategy should define various sources (external and internal) of recruitment. Which are the sources to be used and focused for the recruitment purposes for various positions? Employee referral is one of the most effective sources of recruitment.
4. **Trained recruiters:** The recruitment professionals conducting the interviews and the other recruitment activities should be well-trained and experienced to conduct the activities. They should also be aware of the major parameters and skills (e.g., behavioral, technical etc.) to focus while interviewing and selecting a candidate.
5. **How to evaluate the candidates:** The various parameters and the ways to judge them i.e. the entire recruitment process should be planned in advance. Like the rounds of technical interviews, HR interviews, written tests, psychometric tests etc.

Exhibit: Recruitment Waterfall at TCS

At TCS the recruitment process translates into a sound foundation for the organization. In the dynamic software industry, with the demand far outgrowing the supply, it is the quality of people and workforce practices that are the deciding factors for any organization's success. With process orientation so intricately woven into the HR practices, system thinking is the key for the design of all design of all workforce practices at TCS. TCS has a very sound recruitment process starting from accrediting institutes to training on interview techniques. The following figure illustrates the waterfall recruitment at TCS.

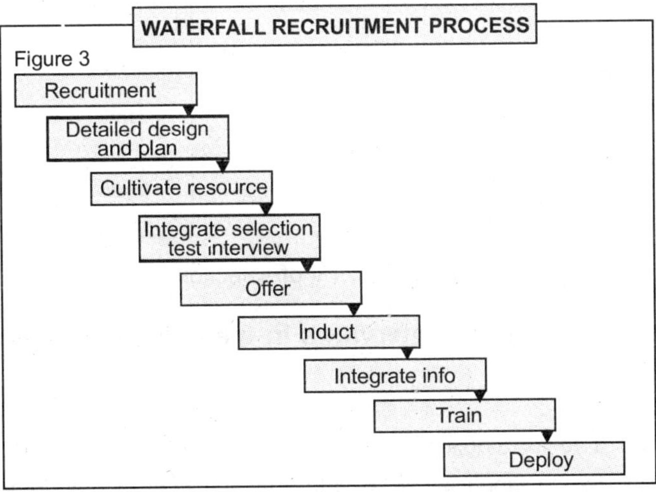

Fig. 2.51: Waterfall recruitment in TCS

SELECTION

What is Selection?

Selection is the process of differentiating between applicants in order to identify (and hire) those with a greater likelihood of success in a job. It is the process of picking individuals having relevant qualifications and experiences for filling job vacancies in an organization.

Selection Procedures

According to Roe and Greuter (1989), it is important that selection procedures in an organization fulfill four main functions:

- ***Information Gathering***: It involves generating information about the organization, the job, career paths and employment conditions on the one hand; and on the other, about the candidates, including their experience, qualifications and personal characteristics.
- ***Prediction***: Using information on past and present candidate characteristics as a basis for making predictions about candidates' future behavior.
- ***Decision-making***: Using the predictions about candidates' future behavior as a basis for making decisions about whom to accept or reject.
- ***Information Supply***: Providing information about the organization, the job and employment conditions to candidates etc.

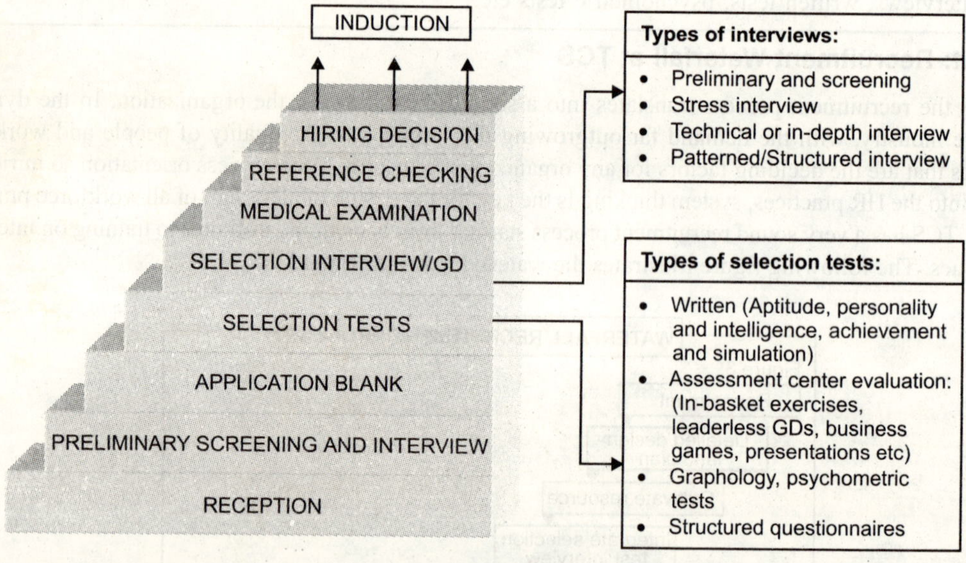

Fig. 2.52: Steps of selection

Importance of Selection Tests and Interviews in the Selection Process:

Selection Tests

The various selection tests used for the selection process are as follows:

(a) ***Performance Tests***: Here the applicant is asked to demonstrate his/her ability to do the job for which he/she is supposed to be recruited.

(b) ***Intelligence Tests***: These are mental ability tests and aim to evaluate the incumbent's learning ability and the ability to understand instructions and take decisions or make judgements.

(c) ***Aptitude Tests***: They measure an individual's potential to learn certain skills like clerical, mechanical, mathematical etc. They indicate whether or not an individual has the ability to learn a given job quickly and efficiently.

(d) ***Personality Tests***: These tests seek to assess an individual's motivation, adjustment to the stresses of everyday life, capacity for inter-personal relations and self-image. These are expressed in terms of relative significance of such traits within the person as self-confidence, ambition, decisiveness, optimism, patience, fear and distrust. Personality Tests are used to measure basic aspects of an individual's personality such as motivation, emotional balance, self-confidence, interpersonal behavior, introversion etc.

- **Projective Tests:** These tests expect the candidates to interpret problems or situations based on their own motives, attitudes, values etc.
- **Interest Tests:** These are meant to find how a person in tests compare with the interests of successful people in a specific job. These tests show the areas of work in which a person is most interested.
- **Preference Tests:** These tests try to compare employee preferences with the job and organizational requirements.

(e) ***Achievement Tests***: These are designed to measure what the applicant can do on the job currently that is, whether, the **testee** actually knows what he or she claims to know.

(f) ***Simulation/Situational Tests***: Simulation exercise is a test, which duplicates many of the activities, and problems of an employee faces while at work. These exercises are commonly used for hiring managers at various levels in an organization.

(g) ***Assessment Centres***: An assessment centre is an extended work sample. It uses procedures that incorporate group and individual exercises. These exercises are designed to stimulate the type of work which the candidate is expected to do. Examples of the real-life but simulated exercises included in a typical assessment centre are as follows: **In-Basket exercise; Leaderless group discussion; Business games; Individual presentations; Structured interviews.**

(h) ***Graphology Tests:*** It involves using a trained evaluator to examine the lines, hooks, strokes, curves and flourishes in an individual's handwriting so as to assess the individual's personality and emotional make up.

(i) ***Polygraph Tests***: The polygraph tests are designed to ensure accuracy of information given in the applications.

(j) ***Integrity Tests***: These are designed to measure an employee's honesty so as to predict those who are more likely to steal from an employer or otherwise act in a manner unacceptable to the organization.

(k) ***Medical Tests***: They reveal the physical fitness of a candidate.

How are they hiring: Tata Motors
Employee referrals: The automotive giant seeks involvement of its current workforce to attract key talent.
Online recruitment process: Tata Motors holds selection tests to recruit its graduate and postgraduate trainees. Applicants can take test from any location.
Internal job postings: The automotive arm is also part of the Tata Group's internal job postings service, and harps on employee movement across companies.
Employer branding: The Company sponsors scholarships at the prestigious Indian School of Business
Other sources: Jobsites, placement consultants, collabouration with industrial training institutes etc.

Hiring in Tata Motors

(Bajpai, V., 2008: "Innovative Hiring Strategies", Dare, Vol. 2, Issue: 10, July 2008, p. 55)

Selection Interviews

Interviews form an essential component of the selection process. It provides an opportunity to the recruiters to be in direct interaction with the screened candidates. The types of selection interviews are as follows:

Types of Employment Interviews	Features/Hallmarks
1. One-to-One Interview	• This interview involves two participants — the interviewer and the interviewee. • This interview can be considered as a preliminary or interactive interview
2. Sequential Interview	• It involves a series of interviews, usually utilizing the strength and knowledge-base of each interviewer, so that each interviewer can ask questions in relation to his/her subject area of each candidate, as the candidate moves from one room to another room.
3. Panel Interview	• It consists of two or more interviewers who might come from different subject specializations.

Objectives of Interviews

The overall purpose of selection interviews in an organization are as follows:

- Help to obtain additional information from the applicant
- Facilitate giving general information to the applicant such as company policies, job, products manufactured etc.
- Help to build the company's image among the applicants.

Types of Interviews

Types	Type of Questions	Usual Applications
1. Structured	A pre-determined checklist of questions, usually asked of all applicants	Useful for valid results, especially when dealing with large number of applicants.
2. Unstructured	Few planned questions, which are made during the time of the interview.	Useful when the interviewer tries to probe personal details of the candidate to analyze why they are not right for the job.
3. Mixed	A combination of structured and unstructured questions, which resembles what is usually done in practice.	A realistic approach that yields comparable answers plus in-depth insights.
4. Behavioral	Questions limited to hypothetical situations and where the process of evaluation is based on the solution and the approach of the candidate.	Useful to understand the applicant's reasoning and analytical abilities under modest levels of stress.
5. Stress Interviews	A series of harsh, rapid-fire questions intended to upset the applicant.	Useful for stressful jobs, such as handling customer complaints.

Job Interview Questioning Techniques

The way a HR manager approaches and opens the interview is important to its overall success. The types of questions he/she asks and the way the candidates are being asked are of prime importance. There are two types of questions.

- Directive
- Non directive

Both can be used effectively in the interview to gain the information the manager might require from the job applicant.

Directive Questions

A directive question leads the applicant onto making a specific response by limiting him to a choice of a yes or no answer.

- "Do you prefer early morning or late afternoon schedules?"
- "Did you hear about us through an employment agency?"

Directive questions can often be effective in gaining precise answers or exact information, but, because they limit the applicant to a choice or yes or no answer, they often discourage free response and result in very little information. Questions that provide for little information are generally those that can be answered in one or two words. A definite answer will be offered, but the applicant probably will volunteer any additional information.

Non-directive Questions

Non directional questions allow the applicant to respond freely without being forced to make a choice or respond with a yes or no answer.

- "What type of work schedule do you prefer?"
- "How did you happen to hear about our company?"

They may be used to direct the conversation to an area of the interviewer's interest, but do not control the applicants response. Thc applicant is free to express his thoughts without being forced to make a choice, or respond with a yes or no. Non directive questions are prefixed by the following: how, why, what, when and where.

Exhibit: An Outline Employee Evaluation Interview Guide

Here are seven top tips when conducting job interviews:

1. Put the employee at ease.
2. Explain how the interviewee and organization can benefit from an open interview.
3. Explain areas that will be covered during evaluation review.
4. Ask evaluation questions that elicit answers to the dimensions in each area.
5. Describe the job function and its contribution to departmental and organizational success.
6. Ask the interviewee if he or she has any questions.
7. Close the interview.

BEHAVIOURAL EVENT INTERVIEW

A common type of job interview in the modern workplace is the **behavioural interview** or **behavioural event interview**. In this sort of interview, the interviewers tend to ask questions about general situations, with the candidate asked to describe how they handled a specific problem. A bad hiring decision now a days can be immensely expensive for an organization — cost of the hire, training costs, severance pay, loss of productivity, impact on morale, cost of re-hiring, etc. Structured selection techniques have a better track record of identifying the soundest candidate than the old-style 'biographical' interview. Typical behavioural interview questions:

- "Describe a time you had to work with someone you didn't like".
- "Tell me about a time when you had to stick by a decision you had made, even though it made you very unpopular".
- "Give us an example of something particularly innovative that you have done that made a difference in the workplace".
- "What was the last time you were late with a project?"

THE BEHAVIOURAL DIMENSIONS

I. INITIATIVE

Q. Tell me about something you're glad you got a chance to do in your institute. How did it come about?

☐ Confident ☐ Possible ☐ Doubtful ☐ Didn't see

II. TAKING OWNERSHIP

Q. Tell me about a situation when you had to work in a group that wasn't functioning Well. What did you do?

☐ Confident ☐ Possible ☐ Doubtful ☐ Didn't see

III. SELF CONTROL

Q. Tell me about a situation in which you were frustrated with someone? What was it? What did you do?

☐ Confident ☐ Possible ☐ Doubtful ☐ Didn't see

IV. ADAPTABILITY

Q. Tell me about a time when the situation you were in changed suddenly? What did you do?

☐ Confident ☐ Possible ☐ Doubtful ☐ Didn't see

Fig. 2.53: Sample behavioural event interview questions

The goal of the interview is to assess the candidate's ability to respond to the sorts of situations that the job may present them with. The questions asked will therefore be based on the job description, the performance indicators, the skills/personal qualities required and the interviewer's knowledge of operating in the role. Questioning will either be hypothetical ('how would you deal with situation X?') or based on historical examples from your current or previous experience ('when situation X arose, how did you deal with it?'). Either way, the interviewer is interested (a) the thought process used and (b) the values of the candidate and the outcome of the situation.

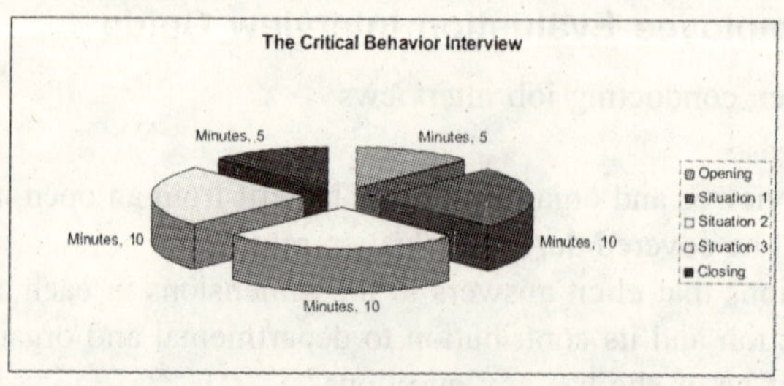

Fig. 2.54: Components of critical behaviour interview

(*Courtesy: Managing People, Business Today, January 7–21, 1996, p. 85*)

Using the STAR Technique: In a behavioural interview, the interviewer will ask questions about your past experiences. A useful way to prepare for this style of questioning is to use the STAR technique. The STAR technique is a way to frame the answers to each question in an organized manner that will give the interviewer the most information about your past experience. Questions might involve like those of:

What was the **S**ituation in which you were involved?

What was the **T**ask you needed to accomplish?

What **A**ction(s) did you take?

What **R**esults did you achieve?

Sample Behavioural Interview Questions

- Tell me about a time when you were on a team, and one of the members wasn't doing his or her share.
- Tell me about a time when you felt a need to update your skills or knowledge in order to keep up with the changes in technology. How did you approach that?
- Describe a time when a customer got angry with you. How did you react? How did you resolve the situation?
- Please give me an example of a time when you took the initiative to improve a specific work process.
- Give me an example of a time when you surpassed a customer's expectations.
- Tell me about a time when a customer requested special treatment that was out of the scope of normal procedures. What was the situation and how did you handle it?
- Describe a time when you had to use logic and good judgment to solve a problem.
- Tell me about a time when you had to cope with a stressful situation.
- Give me an example of a time when you had to make a split second decision.
- Give me an example of a time when you used your fact-finding skills to solve a problem.
- Describe a time when you put your needs aside to help a co-worker understand a task. How did you assist them? What was the result?

What is a Competency Based Interview?

Competency Based Interviewing is founded on the notion that the best predictor of a candidate's future performance is his or her past performance. Therefore, competency based interview questions are built around specific incidents that have happened rather than hypothetical situations. The questions ask candidates to describe things that they have actually done, as opposed to what they would do in a given situation. Therefore, this interview approach is most useful for higher level positions; however, modifications may be made to suit the needs of any position. You may also create an interview that includes different types of questions (i.e., situational, competency based, and job knowledge-based).

It is an interview in which each candidate is asked the same broad questions which are designed to obtain information about the match between the candidate's competencies and those required for the job. These questions concentrate on the most important parts of a candidate's past experience. This enables the interviewer to draw from each candidate his or her ability to demonstrate successful performance in the job.

The emphasis of a competency based interview is on the applicants' life learning; interviews of the past have focused on accomplishments and future plans; competency based interviewing assesses the individual as a whole.

Competency based interviewing emphasizes excellent communication throughout the interview; with the focus on learning, applicants with substantial learning generally interview better than those applicants with good interviewing skills, but who possess little self awareness. Competency based interviewing places the emphasis on the applicant's individual ability to relate learning from experience to the position in question.

Interview styles range from highly intuitive processes to those that are strictly fact-based. While no technique is perfect, Competency Based Interviewing can alleviate some of the common problems associated with other interview methods. Common errors include:

- Lack of a clear purpose;
- Inadequate preparation;
- Lack of structure;
- Failure to utilize job analysis;
- Personal bias; and
- Premature decisions.

Competency Based Interviewing increases the likelihood of receiving honest and revealing responses to, job-related questions. The information obtained may be used to gauge candidates' job-related competencies and assist employers in determining which candidate is most qualified for a position.

Answers to competency based interview questions should provide verifiable, concrete evidence as to how a candidate has dealt with issues in the past. This information often reveals a candidate's level of experience and his or her potential to handle similar situations in your organization. The information may also be highly useful in conducting final reference checks, as one may verify that the candidate actually did what he or she has claimed.

What Will the Interview be Like?

The Competency Based Interview, will in general, will be conducted as follows:

- Introductions
- Brief discussion of job
- Competency based interviewing
- Validation of technical/functional skills where necessary
- Interviewee's opportunity to ask questions
- Close out/next steps

For an interview to be most effective, it should:

- Be based on a recently updated description of the position resulting from a job analysis;
- Follow a pre-determined rating guide with which interview panel members are familiar; and
- Include sufficient, factual documentation regarding the candidates' responses.

This provides a more accurate basis for selection, as well as documentation of a logical objective and legally defensible selection procedure.

Exhibit: Examples of Competency Based Interview Questions

Competency: Creative and Innovative Thinking: Develop innovative ideas that provide solutions to all types of workplace challenges.

Question: Describe a situation in which you developed a brand new idea for a product or service that your organization offered to its clients. What was unusual or innovative about this idea? What resistance, if any, did you encounter as you attempted to "sell" your idea to your colleagues or customers, and how did you overcome it?

Describe a situation in your career in which you were asked to develop a product or service that no one had ever thought of before. This should be something that really had no previous "blueprint" from which you could build your idea. What was the product or service? Describe how you took things from the "concept phase" to the "reality phase".

Medical Examination: It provides the following information:

- Whether the candidate is medically suitable for the job
- Whether the candidate has health problems or psychological attitudes
- Whether the candidate suffers from bad health
- Whether the applicant's physical measurements are in accordance with the requirements of the job.

Reference Checks

Once the interview and medical examination of the candidate is over, the HR department will engage in checking the candidate's references. The procedure places reliance on the evaluation of former employers, friends and professional personnel.

Hiring Decision

The HR manager of the HR department has to make the final decision-whether to select or reject the candidate after soliciting the required information collected through the different stages of the selection process. The organization sends the appointment orders to the successful candidates either immediately or after sometime depending upon its time schedule..

Exhibit: Written Test/Oral Test Score Sheet

WRITTEN/ORAL TEST RESULT FOR THE POST OF (POST NAME)

(DATE OR EXAM (WRITTEN/ORAL):

Canditate and MRF particulars					Result		Decision	Appointment and joining data		
Sl. no.	Id No.	Name	Qual	Ref: MRF	Written	Oral	Selection	Appointed as	Joined on	Remarks
1.	3	Mr. XYZ	MBA	ACC-01/02/06	59	45	Yes or no			
2.	8	Ms. ZXY	M. Com	ACC-01/02/06	55	59	Yes or no			

Prepared by:

(Name)

Desig of HRD Personnel

Selected by:

Annexure 1

COMPANY NAME: Resources International, Inc. (RII)

Job Vacancy Form

Is this an established post:

Title of Post:

Department:

Date when post becomes vacant:

Who will this be replacing:

Is the post permanent/temporary/fixed-term/contractor

(Give details e.g. length of fixed-term contract)

Grade of Post (if applicable)

Salary range:

Full Time/Part Time (give number of hours).

Comments:

Signed (Appointing Manager)________________ Date:

Authorized by (Appropriate Director)________________

I confirm availability of funding

Director of Finance________________________

Annexure 2

COMPANY NAME: Resources International, Inc. (RII)

INTERVIEW RECORD FORM

Post Title:

Date of Interview:

Panel Members:

Summary of Panel's comments on interviewees (including recommendation(s) to appoint).

Name	Comments

Signed ....Appointing Manager/Panel Chairperson

PLACEMENT AND EMPLOYEE ENGAGEMENT

What is Placement?

Placement involves deciding, which jobs are to be assigned after the selected candidates have been hired for the job. It also indicates which job best matches the selected candidate's talents and abilities.

Placement requires a clear-cut match between employee's skills, knowledge, aptitude and value systems. Placements can be made more effective by measures such as Job Rotation, Team Work, Continuous Training and Development Programs, Job Enrichment and Empowerment.

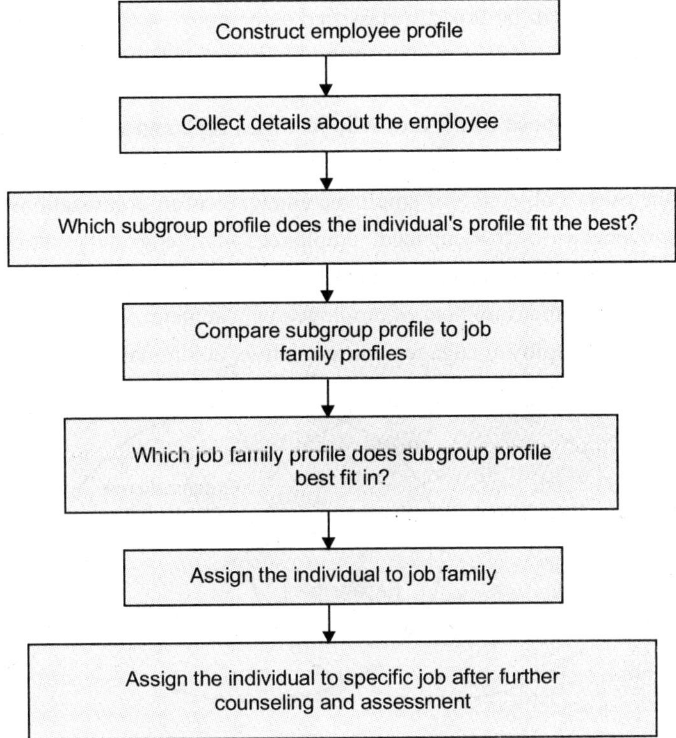

Fig. 2.55: Assessment-classification model of employee placement

What is Employee Engagement?

Employee engagement is the extent that an employee believes in the mission, purpose and values of an organization and demonstrates that commitment through their actions as an employee and their attitude towards the employer and customers. Employee engagement is high when the statements and conversations held reflect a natural enthusiasm for the company, its employees and the products or services provided.

Components of Employee Engagement

There are three components of employee engagement, namely:

Components of employee engagement	Features/Hallmarks
Cognitive	It is the belief that an employee has about his company and its values.
Emotional	It is the feeling an employee has about his colleagues, supervisors.
Behavioural	Is what the employees exhibits at work commitment.

On the basis of this employees can be broadly classified as being:

- **Engaged:** These are those employees who are highly motivated and can go an extra mile to achieve the organizational goals and objectives.
- **Not Engaged:** These are those employees who just pass time and wait to return to house
- **Disengaged:** These are those employees who complain about their work

So it can be said that the overall objective of employee engagement in organizations is:

- To ensure the conversion of "Not engaged" employees into "engaged" employees.
- To facilitate planning for employee engagement.
- To ensure evaluation and measurement of employee engagement.
- To touch all aspects of employee engagement (cognitive, emotional, behavioural)

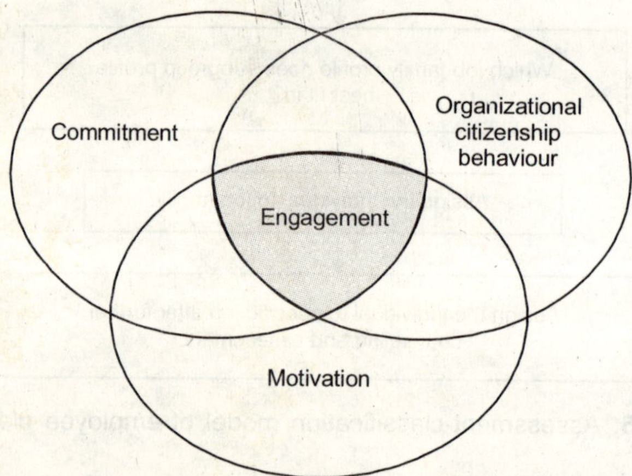

Fig. 2.56: Relation of employee engagement with motivation, commitment and organizational citizenship behaviour

Employee engagement depends upon three elements, namely: interpersonal support, individual values, and facilitating focused work in organizations. Interpersonal support could be build by teamwork and collabouration at the workplace. Whereas, individual values can be contributed by support and recognition from the superiors, peers and the top management of the organization as well as by the developmental plans initiated by the company's HR department also form integral elements of employee engagement. On the other hand, focused work environment could be ensured by employee empowerment and by aligning individual performance and efforts with the organizational strategy.

Types of Employee Engagement

The following are the various types of employee engagement, namely:

Types of employee engagement	Features/Hallmarks
Communication Activities	These help employees find out what is going on within the company outside of their immediate team. They also help to create an environment of trust and openness within the organization where they are able to talk openly. Employees who feel they are listened to are able to express dissatisfaction and work together to resolve their causes, without it affecting their performance.
Reward Schemes	Reward schemes are an important part of a company's overall employee engagement program. Studies have long shown that, while money in itself is not a motivating factor, the absence of financial reward can be a significant de-motivator. Thus the role of reward schemes in boosting employee engagement is to remove barriers to satisfaction in the organization: To provide a framework for rewarding everyone in the organization for their performance: To give those who are motivated by financial gain an opportunity to achieve this.
Organizational Culture	Giving employees a feeling of belonging is crucial in creating a thriving organization that people feel committed to and others want to join.
Team Building Activities	Culture-building activities are great for generating a feeling of belonging, but all organizations are build out of smaller teams who can get on and work together.
Leadership Development Activities	A great organization needs not just a great leader, but people with leadership skills. This stimulates good performance, boosts creativity and eases succession planning.

How Organizations Take Care of Employee Engagement?

Organizations take care of their employee engagement activities by using an instrument known as "**Employee Engagement Matrix**". It is a comprehensive analysis tool that helps HR managers to align employee engagement types with various engagement activities taken in the organization. The following figure provides an illustration of such an engagement matrix.

Theme Caselet: Employee Engagement in Practice *(Courtesy: Goyal, M., "Indians seek respect, clarity of role at work"; The Economic Times, 8th January, p: 6)*

Organizations, their track record, leadership and HR policies have a significant bearing on how engaged their employees are Watson and Wyatt's Study, one of the most comprehensive studies to understand workers' attitudes have revealed such findings.

***Realities of employee engagement*:** Watson and Wyatt's Study had revealed that regionally Europe workers lead with the highest levels of engagement followed by the Asia-Pacific. American workers are the least engaged. A combination of rapid growth in Eastern European countries, generous employee welfare activities and benefit programs and Government support in these countries have facilitated such high levels of employee engagement in these countries. According to Ms. Anita Belani, Country Head, Watson and Wyatt India operations, "Attitudinally, the centrality of work in an executive's life in Europe is not as

Engagement Type	Engagement Activities					
Initial recruit and induction	**Pitching of organization**	**Website**	**First day**	**Induction**	**Goal setting**	**KRA's**
Communications activities	Communication forums to provide regular feedback to all people, including team meetings, conference and "away days"	In-house e-magazines	Online communications, including discussion boards and blogs by company personnel including senior management	Monthly updates on corporate goals and directions	Regular employee opinion and satisfaction	Active soliciting of employee feedback including opinion
Reward schemes	Compensation and benefit program.	Stock and profit sharing	Recognition program.	Idea collection schemes linked to rewards for idea generation	Long service and good performance awards	
Organizational culture	Clear and humane HR policies	Pro-social corporate objectives and corporate social responsibility	Equal opportunities policies and practices	Initiatives to maintain the quality of work life and a balance between personal/professional lives.	Developing a safe, clean and inspiring work environment	Demonstrating commitment to employees' well being
Team building activities	Small team recreational activities, such as bowling, skating, trips to the cinema		Community outreach activities such as volunteering and fund-raising.		Social activities, such as family gatherings.	
Leadership development activities	Effective leadership	Fair evaluation of performance	Empowerment through effective delegation	Coaching and mentoring activities to give honest feedback by supervisors and peers	An open and transparent culture to empower people and develop entrepreneurs	

Fig: An Employee Engagement Matrix

high as in many other places. Yet people are well engaged because they are encouraged by shorter work weeks, work-life balance programs and vacation opportunities which keep the level of their engagements high." In case of Asia pacific, the sheer growth momentum had been identified as the most important factor contributing to high employee spirits in their workplace. Even though the work conditions in this region might be far below as compared to Western standards, the buoyancy in the economy and optimistic job outlook have kept the employees modestly engaged to their workplace.

***Employee Engagement in India*:** India, with a buoyant economy and particularly with the Diaspora of Indian corporate going stronger and stronger, employee engagement levels have been found to be fairly high at 78%. Most amazing finding was that China, in spite of its lead over the Indian economy, did not score that high on employee engagement figures. The study revealed that Indian employees were happiest about their role clarity and how they fit into the entire scheme of things in their respective organizations. The respect at their individual workplaces and outside the organizations played a vital role in their job satisfaction. In spite of this compensation, training and development were identified as major problem issues restricting effective employee engagement in India. Strategic leadership and direction were considered to be important for employee engagement in most Indian organizations.

Table 2.11: Employee Engagement Facts and Figures

Asia Pacific	%	***Regional***	%
India	78%	Asia Pacific	65%
Philippines	735	USA	63%
China	67%	Europe	73%
Japan	395		

Table 2.12: Top three drivers in employee engagement

Regions	***Engagement Drivers***
Asia Pacific	Customer focus, compensation and benefits, communication
USA	Customer focus, trust in leaders, compensation and benefits
Europe	Strategic direction and leadership, communication, customer focus

Exhibit: A Sample Offer Letter

Date: 24.05.2008

To,
Mrs. Suman Das
S/O. Mr. R.K. Das

Dear Mrs. Suman,

Ref: Offer Letter

With reference to your application and subsequent interview, we are pleased to offer you the job for the post of 'xxxxxxxx' in our company, at xxxxxx Branch.

The detailed appointment letter will be given to you at the time of joining. You have to join on or before 27-11-06 otherwise this offer will stand withdrawn automatically.

You will be paid salary as discussed with the undersigned.

You are requested to bring attested copies along with the original certificates/ testimonials at the time of joining the following:

- Educational certificates
- Experience certificates from previous employers
- Copy of resignation/acceptance letter and relieving letter
- Three passport size photographs
- Passport
- Medical fitness certificate

Please contact Ms.xxxxxx in case you require any accommodation or transport facilities so that arrangements will be made for you prior to your reaching to the place here. Please send us an e-mail/ telegram confirming the receipt of this offer letter as a token of acceptance of terms and conditions mentioned therein.

Thanking You,

FOR xxxxxxxxxxxxx

Exhibit: A Sample Appointment Order

Date: 24.05.2008

To,

Mrs. Suman Das

S/O. Mr. R.K. Das

Dear Mrs. Suman,

Sub: Appointment Order

We are happy to appoint you with us as "______________________________" w.e.f. __________ in our organization on the following terms and conditions.

EMOLUMENTS PER MONTH

1. You will be paid salary comprising of the following,

   BASIC : Rs.

   HRA : Rs.

   CONVEYANCE : Rs.

   EDUCATION ALLOWANCE : Rs.

   OTHER ALLOWANCE : Rs.

   Rs. per month

2. You will also be eligible for bonus and gratuity as per the rules and policies of the company.

NATURE OF WORK

3. You will be reporting to ______________________ .
4. The Company and the Management expects a performance from you of the highest order and would be pleased to accord to you due recognition based on the merits of your performances.
5. Your overall responsibility would cover output quality, discipline and other allied matters of work assigned to you by your superiors from time to time to the best of your ability and skills.
6. Your nature of work and designation are liable to be changed as and when required by the Management without necessarily assigning any reason and you shall on receipt of such orders act accordingly with immediate effect.

PROBATION

7. You will be on probation for a period of **6 months**. Your progress will be reviewed periodically and your absorption in our company on a regular basis will depend on the progress made by you. The management reserves the right of extending your probation in our company and the decision of the management in this regard will be final and binding on you.

PLACE OF WORK AND TRANSFER

8. Your present place of work is ______________________.
9. You are liable to be transferred to any other department or branch or sister concern of the company anywhere in India and outside India at the discretion of the Management.

CONFLICT OF INTEREST

10. You shall always devote the whole of your time and services to the duties allotted to you and you shall not without the consent in writing of the Management be interested, employed or otherwise engaged directly or indirectly in any other business or employment.
11. Non-adherence to this condition would amount to willful suppression of facts and breach of contract, and shall entail termination of your services.

TERMINATION OF SERVICES

12. Either party may terminate the service by giving **six-month** notice to the other or salary in lieu of such notice.
13. In case at any time the management finds that the information furnished by you in your application and related papers is false or you are found to have suppressed any material information, the appointment itself will be deemed to be void and your services will be liable to be terminated without notice or compensation in lieu thereof.
14. You will abide by the rules and regulations made by the Company as are in force or as may be introduced or amended or extended from time to time.
15. Your services can be terminated without noticc or salary in lieu of notice at the discretion of the management if it is found that you have violated the model standing laws in force or lost confidence of the management.

GENERAL

16. During the period of your employment or thereafter at any time, you shall not disclose, divulge or communicate to any person or persons whatsoever information or secret relating to any trade or business of the Company you may have acquired as an employee of the company.
17. Subject to the statutory provisions, the management may require you to work on holidays/off days as may be necessary and you shall promptly act in accordance with the instructions in this behalf.
18. You shall be responsible for safe keeping and returning the property of the company under your custody, If misused or lead to damage, the cost of the property may be recovered from your salary.
19. Any change in your residential address should be notified in writing to the company immediately. All communications will be addressed to you on the last address notified by you and it will be presumed that you have received such communications addressed to you within the normal time taken for this purpose. The management shall not be held responsible for non-receipt of such communication for whatever reasons.
20. If required you are liable for medical check-up at all times by a Registered Medical Practitioner of the Management's choice. The Management may terminate your employment if you are found to be unfit physically or otherwise.
21. All disputes will be subject to BANGALORE jurisdiction only.

If the above terms and conditions of employment are acceptable to you, kindly return the duplicate copy of this letter duly signed as a token of your acceptance.

We welcome you to our organization and look forward to a long and mutual beneficial association with us.

Best Wishes,

For ______________________________

AUTHORISED SIGNATORY

I hereby accept the above Terms and Conditions

Signature ______________________________ Date ______________

Exercise Case Study: Only Asians wanted here

It was a HR manager's nightmare. IBM Japan Ltd., IBM's Japanese subsidiary, seemed to have been recruiting through Japanese magazines in the US in a discriminatory fashion. Although IBM Japan insists they never instructed their employment agency to screen out white people and black people in favour of Asians, it does seem that some discriminatory actions might have taken place.

The problem revolved around the employment agencies owned by a Japanese firm called Recruit. According to allegations made by Recruit USA's former staffers. Recruit USA had set up a fairly formal system to see that only Asians were hired for the IBM Japan jobs. According to one memo submitted by a former staffer to the EEOC (Equal Employment Opportunity Commission), Recruit officials summarized the hiring policy as: "Foreigners, no good-IBM current rule…white people, black people, no, but second-generation Japanese or other Asian descent o.k." Another Recruit agency in US allegedly set up a system of code words to discriminate against people it didn't want to hire. For example, if the job order said, "see Adam," it meant the client only wanted a male employee. If the job order said "Talk to Haruo," it meant the client only wanted a Japanese worker.

The whole story first broke, when former Recruit employees took their allegation to the San Francisco Chronicle. Then the EEOC got involved and more allegations were unearthed. Japanese firms and other MNCs are therefore learning the truth of the old saying, "When in Rome, do as the Romans." But in this case it means that when you are doing business in a certain country, you would better know and follow the laws of the land.

QUESTIONS FOR REVIEW

1. Do you think a client (in this case IBM Japan) should be held responsible for the actions of an independent employment agency that it hires? Why or who not?
2. Do you think it would be right for a company to discriminate in hiring people in the US for work overseas, since it's not hiring them to work in the US? Why or Why not?
3. If you were the HR manager of a company using an employment agency, how would you avoid the sort of discrimination problem described in the case?

QUESTION BANK

1. Recruitment is considered to be the foundation stone on which the entire organizational edifice stands.
2. Differentiate between recruitment and selection.
3. Explain the purpose of reliability and validity in administration of selection test. Elucidate the various types of reliability and validity test.
4. A top ranking business school of India has invited you for campus recruitment. What preparations you would like to make before you visit the business school?
5. Should applicants be selected primarily on the basis of ability or on personality fit? How can fit be assessed?
6. What is placement? What are the steps involved in the placement process?
7. Describe the steps involved in a recruitment process. Identify the constraints which could limit the freedom of a manager to recruit at various stages and your suggestions to cope with the same.
8. What factors determine the recruitment policy of a company? How has Internet, affected recruiting? What have been its advantages and disadvantages in the selection process?
9. "Selection Process begins where the recruitment process ends". Discuss. (BU 2002).
10. Critically examine the selection methods employed for managerial personnel in Indian organizations. (BU 2001).
11. Discuss aptitude tests and achievement tests. What is the difference between the two? For admission in medical college which test would you use and why?
12. What is employee engagement? What are the strategies influencing employee engagement?

Internet Exercises

- You are the HR trainee of a reputed FMCG company. Your organization conducts campus recruitment for hiring employees for various entry level positions of your organization. Now you have to prepare a plan for your senior officers for visiting various campuses. Your job would be to surf the net and scrutinize the information that can be useful regarding the information on various B schools in India. Submit a report from your study to your faculty assuming that he is the HR manager of your organization.
- Visit at least four job portals and make a comparative study of their attributes and present to your class.

Experiential Learning

- If you or any of your friends in the class had ever faced an interview board share the experience of the same with all emphasizing on the learnings from the same.
- Suppose you are representing Johnson and Johnson for campus recruitment. Deliver a presentation to your class assuming yourself to be the senior marketing manager of the company.
- Organize an appointment letter writing competition amongst your friends and ask your faculties to judge. The position could be considered for a marketing trainee in a retail outlet.

EMPLOYEE ORIENTATION/INDUCTION

THEME CASE: AJAY'S FIRST DAY AT XYZ LTD.

Ajay had passed his MBA with distinction marks from a reputed B school in South Bangalore. This was his first day in office after he was selected in a campus recruitment program. His company was an associate of GE and was mainly involved in providing total lighting solutions to corporate clients. With his joining on the first day he was warmly welcomed by the managing director of the company Mr. Srinath, who personally introduced him to his to be colleagues. "Wow the starting was a grand feeling", thought Ajay.

Ajay was hired as a business development officer for this company XYZ Ltd. which was an associate of GE. Ajay's job was to frequently visit corporates and real estate offices in and around Bangalore for providing lighting solutions in their offices. In the context of several IT complexes and business centers growing in Bangalore his company had a huge business opportunity. Ajay also felt that this break would help him to have a learning experience and be a handful platform to shape his future career. Ajay was not worried about his compensation as his company was a medium sized one. Yet he had dreams to learn and grow and that was his greatest motivation.

After Mr. Srinath went back to his cabin, Ajay was taken to his department by the company secretary where he met Mr. Sanjay, Mr. Amit and Mr. Rakesh. Sanjay was working as a senior Business Development Manager for the last 3 years. Looking at Ajay, "Ah there's our new friend, we had been expecting you. I am Sanjay and he is Amit and Rakesh". Amit and Rakesh were working with the company for the last 1 and 2 years respectively. Ajay was quite surprised to find the "happy to go" attitude of his colleagues. He expected Mr. Sanjay to have a serious talk with him, but nothing happened.

To Ajay's great astonishment, Mr. Sanjay said, "My dear young friend today's the first day for you here. You relax and settle down, tomorrow I will take you with me to a meeting with one of our clients in Jayanagar and show how we work. Have some coffee. Now we are all moving out. May be I will talk with you in the evening, when I return". Ajay was left alone with his doubts, until he was called back by Mr. Srinath, who handed over Ajay a file of the company having information regarding its history and various products/services. Ajay went back to his desk disappointed and took the initiative to open the website of the company and at least have a self study.

The day ended quite uneventful and disappointing for Ajay, until the evening, when Mr. Sanjay took Ajay to a nearby cafeteria and had a long chat about how things were supposed to be at XYZ Ltd.

What is Orientation/Induction?

Orientation or induction is the process of introducing new employees to an organization, to their specific jobs and departments, and in some instances, to their community. It also marks the beginning of the process by which employees are integrated into the organization.

An orientation program principally conveys 3 types of information, namely:

(a) General information about the daily work routine to be followed

(b) A review of the organization's history, founders, objectives, operations and products or services, as well as how the employee's job contributes to the organization's needs.

(c) A detailed presentation of the organization's policies, work rules and employee benefits.

Items	Topics covered in employee orientation programs
1. Organizational Issues	• History of the employer • Organization of employer • Names and titles of key executives

Contd...

	• Employee's title and department • Layout of physical facilities • Probationary period • Product line or services provided • Overview of production process • Company policies and rules • Disciplinary regulations • Employee handbooks • Safety procedures and enforcement
2. Employee Benefits	• Pay scale and pay days • Vacations and leaves • Rest breaks • Training and development benefits • Counseling • Insurance benefits • Retirement program • Employer-provided services to employees • Rehabilitation programs
3. Introduction	• To supervisor • To trainers • To co-workers • To employee counselor
4. Job Duties	• Job location • Job tasks • Job safety requirements • Overview of jobs • Job objectives • Relationship with other jobs

Orientation Objectives

- To welcome the new employee, relieve anxieties and make him/her free comfortable.
- To develop a rapport between the company and the new employees and make them feel part of the organization as quickly as possible.
- To inspire the new employee with good attitude towards the organization and the job.
- To acquaint new employees with the organizational goals, history, management, traditions, policies, departments, divisions, products and physical layouts.
- To communicate to new employees what is expected out of them, their responsibilities and how they should handle themselves.
- To present the basic information the employee wants to know: rules and regulations, benefits, paydays, procedures and general practices followed in the organization.
- To encourage the new employee to have an inquiring mind and assist him/her towards a discipline effort in developing additional knowledge.
- To provide basic skills, terms and ideas of the business and help the new employee in building effective human relations.

Importance of Induction Programs

"Do not ask what will happen if we train people and they leave? Instead ask what will happen if we do not train people and they stay on". This is what the motivational speaker Zig Ziegler said to summarize the importance of induction programs. Induction is essential for any company because it helps an individual grow within a company and motivates him or her. It inculcates in the employee, more confidence to progress, which in turn helps the company. An effective induction helps a new employee feel assured and comfortable in the new environment, which is critical for early uptake in the new role. A new entrant should culturally fit in an organization and interaction at this stage shapes an individual's disposition and outlook for work and motivation levels.

It is during induction that a new employee gets to know about the organization's employment philosophy, culture and values along with key business processes and his responsibilities. The importance of induction cannot be underestimated, especially in the knowledge intensive pharmaceutical sector, where technical knowledge is critical to the survival of an employee. Such programs are all the more important for the pharmaceutical because employees have to get accustomed not just to the key processes but also to the quality philosophy in terms of compliance and quality management systems.

Fig. 2.57: Infosys lateral induction

Companies like Infosys uses the state of the art information technology to provide what is known as "lateral induction", where a new employee may be oriented simultaneously by several top executives of the organization through video conferencing and live interaction sessions, apart from being trained or oriented by their departmental heads.

> **Developing an ideal induction program**
>
> The first and foremost thing is integrating company's mission and vision with training curriculum, says Tiwari and adds that there should be a good balance between technical training and personality development. For long-term success, it is absolutely essential that training curriculum is continuous and progressive. This helps in creating the winning culture in the organization. "High time we realized that in today's competitive world, where creating product differentiation is getting difficult, the key success factor is people and one can never over invest in this," emphasizes Suresh Tiwari.

Does Good Induction Lead to Employee Retention?

Do induction programs help in reducing attrition rates? Apparently yes. The first impression is very important when a person comes into a new organization and how you interact with these new entrants plays an important role on how they discharge their duties later, according to P Dwarakanath, Director-HR (India and South Asia), Glaxo Smithkline consumer health care. However, he adds that this alone cannot give guarantee for retention because how you deal with that person later is also very important to motivate and retain them. In an HR exercise at Eli Lilly, it was found that employees who received an effective induction were more engaged, compared to those who rated the quality of induction as below average. The thought of leaving the organization creeps in at early stage in cases where the induction is not done with passion, informs Suresh Tiwari, Associate Director, HR, Eli Lilly. A good induction prepares an employee better to compete in fiercely competitive market place, which has a direct impact on the early success and hence motivation, he adds.

(1) Terms and conditions of employment:

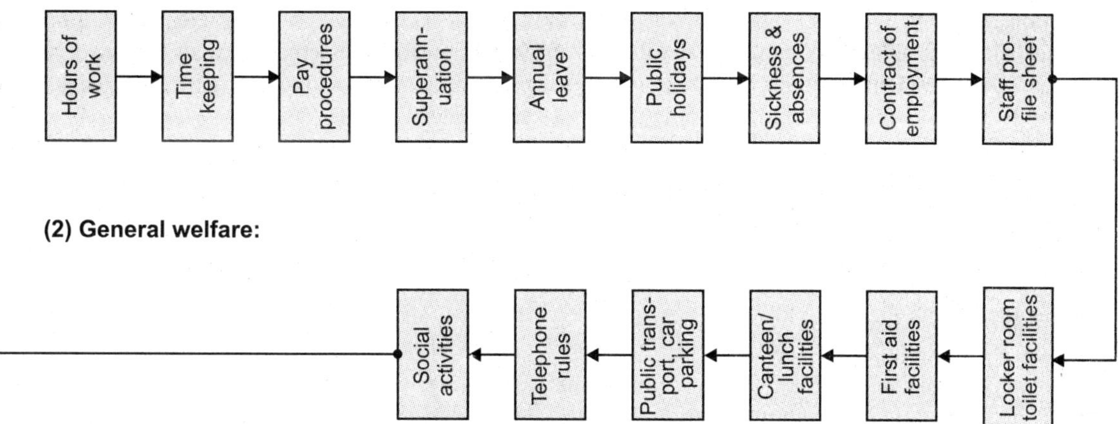

(3) Workplace health and safety:

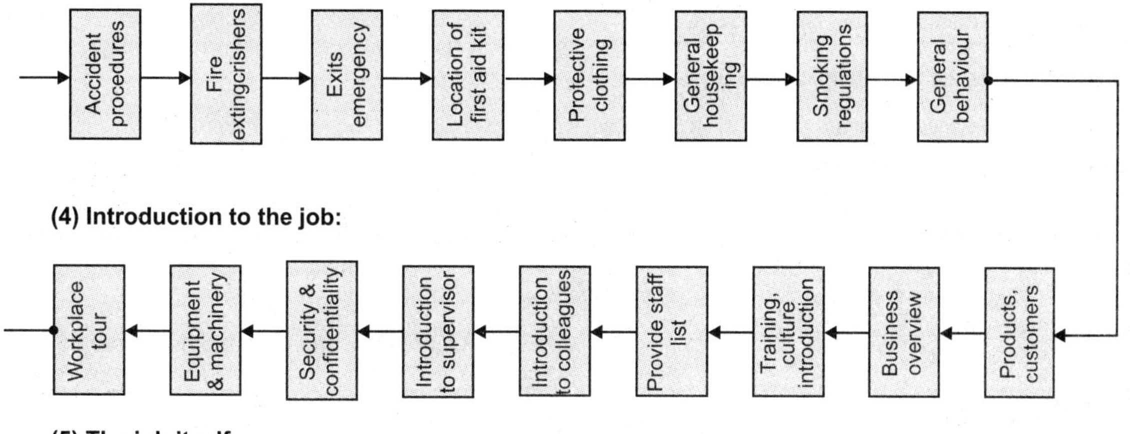

(5) The job itself

Fig. 2.58: Induction flow chart

When it comes to pharmaceutical sales and training, good induction programs certainly help in reducing attrition. For instance, a new medical representative (MR) who has just graduated from a college finds the first few days in the field quite trying, usually in a new place. In such a scenario, says K Gopal, a Chennai based pharmaceutical sales and training consultant, the area manager will act like a friend, philosopher and guide, who instills the necessary confidence that the new MR so badly needs during this critical period. If one looks around there are numerous incidences where new MRs have resigned on the very first day because there was no one to guide them, adds Gopal.

Theme Reading: Induction Programs in Pharmaceutical Companies

Typically, at the entry level, the new MR, who joins the field after the classroom training, is briefed by the frontline manager on various facets of the job like detailing, retail chemist call, prescription audit, personal order booking and stockiest handling. Later, he joins an MR during actual fieldwork and walks him through all the above activities. This critical on-the-job-training helps shape the new entrant for the future, avers Gopal. He adds that this induction period comprises of a lot of briefing, fieldwork, continuous mid-course corrections, guiding, counseling and a lot more. However, different companies have different set of training modules and approaches. For example at Eli Lilly, the induction for sales employees starts with a three weeks in-house residential training program, which is a blend of technical training, market knowledge and personality development. During the training, heavy focus is placed on values through presentations, case studies and role-plays, informs Tiwari. The first day is dedicated only to company values, where the CEO spends half day with the employees, taking them through company history, achievements and values.

On the other hand, at GSK, there are two types of induction training programs. One is designed for the management trainees (from management schools and technical schools) and the other type for people who come from outside companies. Dwarkanath informs training fresh talent from management schools requires more time than people with experience. For instance, a management trainee will undergo an induction-training program of two months; however, for an experienced person it is as low as three days.

There is a standard program called "neutral zone" for management trainees for helping them make a smooth transition from the campus to corporate culture at GSK, says Dwarkanath. Here, they are trained on managing the transition because campus life is different from the corporate life. This generic program has been developed for all the trainees, after taking inputs from the functional heads. For employees who come from other companies, depending on their background, the programs are devised with the help of the HR in association with the line managers for various processes like financing, accounts, supply chain management, manufacturing and marketing.

Components of Orientation Program

An organization needs to make four strategic choices before designing its Orientation Program. These include:

Type of Orientation Program	Features/Hallmarks
1. Formal or Informal	• In case of informal orientation, new recruits are directly put on to the job are expected to acclimatize themselves with the work environment and the organization • In case of Formal Orientation, the management provides a structured program.
2. Individual or Collective	• The individual approach aims to develop far less homogeneous views in individuals about their respective jobs and is also likely to preserve individual differences and perspectives. • Collective orientation aims to socialize individuals with themselves and with the organization as a whole.
3. Serial or Disjunctive	• A serial orientation is the one where an experienced employee inducts a new hire. • When new hires do not have any predecessors available to guide them or to model their behaviour in the organization, it is known as disjunctive orientation.
4. Investiture or Divestiture	• Investiture Orientation seeks to ratify the usefulness of the characteristics that the person brings to the new job. • Divestiture Orientation, seeks to make minor modifications in the characteristic of the new hire and this is done to so as to seek a better fit between a new member and the organization.

Components of a Formal Orientation Program

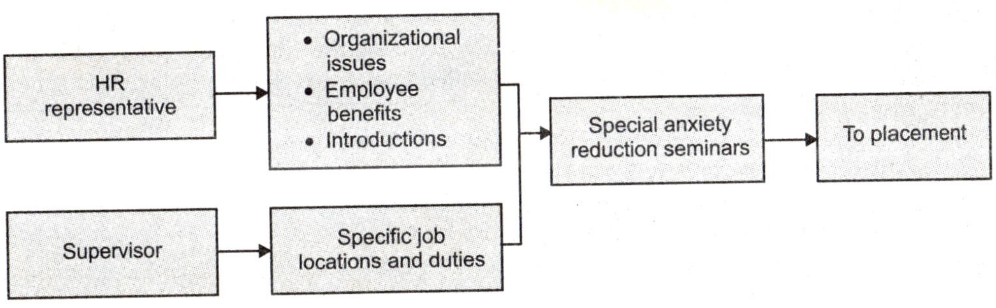

Requisites of An Effective Orientation Program

- To prepare new employees
- To determine information, which the new employees might want to know
- To determine how to present information
- Completion of paperwork.

Evaluation of Orientation Program

A systematic orientation program should have an evaluation and follow-up. Evaluating the costs and benefits of the orientation program can follow several approaches. Trainees can be asked to evaluate the benefits of orientation by administrating a questionnaire. To measure how well the orientation program has met its objectives, the HR manager may use:

- Testing or questionnaires to check if factual material was being learned.
- The checklist
- Evaluation forms or opinions
- Discussions with immediate supervisors of newly oriented employees
- Formal or informal interviews during probationary periods or at the end of a month's employment.
- Exit or terminal interviews

Exhibit: Infosys Conducts Induction Ceremony

(Courtesy: http://www.efytimes.com/efytimes/fullnews.asp?edid=19599)

Infosys has already recruited 90 students out of the 125 it targets this year for its internship program

Monday, June 11, 2007: Infosys' global internship programme, InStep, held its induction ceremony, for its eighth batch of interns. Present on the occasion were 50 interns who will intern in Bengaluru over the next few months. The company will recruit a total of 125 interns for financial year 2007–08.

Addressing the occasion was N.R. Narayana Murthy, chairman and chief mentor, Infosys Technologies. "We believe InStep is a crucial platform for tomorrow's global workforce to groom themselves. We initiated InStep to gain mindshare with students from top colleges as they could be clients, employees, competitors or even leaders of tomorrow. Today, we are confident of having shaped the careers of around 500 InStep alumni who are working across the world in different sectors." he said.

Sharing her experience with InStep, Brianna Dieter, BA, Smith College, currently employed with Infosys Technologies in Bengaluru as an executive Academic Relations, said, "After completing my internship with the Global Academic Relations team in 2005, I realised I wanted to gain more business experience in an emerging economy. With so much energy in the business climate and an exciting range of possibilities opening with the economy, I choose to return to Infosys India. The experience has been a synthesis of formative business learning in a flattening economic environment and fascinating cultural climate".

As of now, Infosys has already recruited 90 students out of the 125 it targets this year. So far, the program has a representation of students from 28 nationalities and 54 universities. This year, interns have been recruited from new geographies like Italy, Spain, Denmark, Israel, Chile and Norway. The interns are slated to work at various offices of Infosys including India, France and the US.

Exhibit: Induction Checklist

Personal Details

Name
Department/Base
Post
Date employment commenced
Date for start of checklist
Details of previous employment/experience:
....
....
....

This form must be completed within one month of commencement of employment and sent to the Personnel and Development Department for inclusion on the employee's personal file.

Exhibit: Process Flowchart for Systematic Induction

Timescale days	Action	Responsibility
	Selection process	MGR/PDS
-21-0	Background information documents sent and regular contact maintained. Co-worker identified	PDS
-21	Offer letter and 'contract' sent	MGR
-14	Induction course date notified to employee and manager	PDS
1	Employee welcomed and introduced to work environment Payroll documentation completed and dispatched. Staff handbook issued	MGR
1	Personal Development Portfolio (PDP) is issued to employee	MGR
1-7	Checklist commenced parts A, B, C	MGR/CO
2-28	Checklist continued part D, E, F, G, (H)	MGR/CO
By 28	Checklist completed	MGR/CO
By 42	Checklist sent to Personnel for filing	PDS
By 42	Induction course held (non-attendees names sent to manager for action)	MGR/EMP
By 49	Outcome of Induction course and checklist evaluated	MGR/PDS
-	Ongoing supervision sessions implemented	MGR
-	Objectives and development needs identified and fed into PDP	MGR/EMP

PDS – Personal Development Services
MGR – Manager
CO – Co-Worker
EMP – Employee
MEN – Mentor

INDUCTION TRAINING FOR NEW EMPLOYEES

(FOR STAFF ONLY)

Name:		**Designation**	
Deptt.		**Date of Joining**	

Date	**Time**	**Deptt.**	**Topics to be covered**	**Responsibility/**	**Signature**
20.07.07	9.00 AM	Director	* Introduction and Company Policy		
20.07.07	9.15 AM	ED	* Introduction and Company Policy		
20.07.07	9.30 AM	G.M.	* Introduction and Company Policy		
20.07.07	10.00 AM TO 11.00 AM	HR	* Organization Structure,Vision and Mission * Company's HR Policies * About Group Companies (for Sr.Engr.and above) * Organization Culture * Brief detail of Activities like Kaizen, 5-S etc.		
20.07.07	11.00AM TO 12.00PM	Despatch	* Departmental working system * About Products * About Customers		
20.07.07	12.00PM TO 1.00PM	Purchase Store	* Departmental working system * About Vendors * About Customers * About Kanban, FIFO, Bin System etc.		
20.07.07	2.00PM TO 3.30PM	QC MR	* ISO/TS 16949, ISO 14001 and OHSAS 18001 POLICY * Departmental working system * About Customers and Products * About Internal Audits and Systems Handling		
20.07.07	3.30PM TO 4.30PM	Accounts Excise	* Payment Procedure and Bill passing * Departmental working system * About Customers * About company's turnover and growth * About IT functions		
20.07.07	4.30PM TO 5.30PM	Design and Development	* Departmental working system * About Customers * Drawing issuance procedure		

Contd...

21.07.07	9.00AM TO 11.00AM	Press Shop Weld Shop	* About components running in Press/Weld Shop * About Press/Weld shop capacity * About Press/Weld shop operations * About Customers		
21.07.07	11.00AM TO 12.00PM	Injection Moulding	* Business Parameters/ Plan * About Department Functions * About Customers		
21.07.07	12.00PM TO 1.00PM	Machine Shop	* About components running in M/c shop * About M/c shop capacity * About M/c shop operations * About Customers		
21.07.07	2.00PM TO 3.00PM	PU / PIP	* Departmental working system * About Customers * Types of toolings/presses		
21.07.07	3.00PM TO 4.00PM	Assembly	* Departmental working system * About Customer and products * About M/c shop operations * About components running in M/c shop		
21.07.07	4.00PM TO 5.00PM	Maintenance	* Departmental working system * About Customers * TPM		
21.07.07	5.00PM TO 5.30PM	Tool Room	* Departmental working system * Safety Measures * TPM		

(EMPLOYEE)

Indranil M.
(Executive - HR)

Exhibit: Days' Learning Points from Training

Induction Program on Leadership for Management Trainees

Session	**What I have Learnt**
1. The Paradigms of Effective Leadership	1.
	2.
2. Managing Cultural Transformation at Work Place	1.
	2.

Contd...

3. Building Relationships and Teams at Work Place: Leadership Inputs	1.
	2.
4. Transcendence from a Manager to Leader: Transactional Perspectives	1.
	2.
5. Leadership and Power: Ethical Explorations	1.
	2.
6. Transformational Leadership (Part-I)	1.
	2.
7. Transformational Leadership (Part-II)	1.
	2.

What I propose to apply:

(Please be specific and list down only those proposed applications for which the progress can be monitored by you and others. The area of application could be related to work and/or improvement in self)

Sl. No.	What I propose to apply	Time frame

Name of Trainee	:______________	**Name of HOD**	:__________
Designation	:______________	**Designation of HOD**	:__________
Date	:______________	**Department and Plant**	:__________

QUESTION BANK

1. What is induction? What is its importance in organization?
2. What are the objectives of an induction program in an organization?
3. What are the components of an induction program?
4. What are the prerequisites of an effective induction program?
5. How is induction different from orientation training?
6. How is an induction program planned and executed?
7. What is the role of the HR manager in designing an induction program?

Induction

Internet Exercises

- Prepare notes on induction programs organized by various organizations after going through the net and submit a report to your faculty using your own words.
- Suppose you are in charge of conducting the induction program for a group of foreign students who have enrolled for an internship program in your organization, which is a reputed IT company based in Bangalore. Prepare an induction session based on life in Bangalore by taking help from the internet for the same.

Role Play

- Imagine that your faculty had asked you to introduce your college to the freshers, give a presentation assuming your friends to be the newcomers.
- Imagine that you are the manager of Planet M music and entertainment retail outlet. You have recently recruited 5 young graduates as Customer support staffs for your store. Involve yourself into a role play session assuming that you are conducting an induction program for them.

CHAPTER 3

TRAINING AND DEVELOPMENT

THEME CASE: TRAINING AND DEVELOPMENT AT BHEL

BHEL is the largest engineering and manufacturing enterprise in India in the energy-related/infrastructure sector. The company was established more than 40 years ago, ushering in the indigenous heavy electrical equipment industry in India — a dream that has been more than realized with a well-recognized track record of performance. BHEL conducts regular training programs for its employees in order to develop them into fulfilled individuals and effective managers. BHEL has been a pioneer in the area of Human Resource Development, being the first Public Sector Undertaking of its kind, in India, to have setup an extensive HRD infrastructure as way back as in the early sixties. Human Resource Development Centre (HRDC) of BHEL R.C. Puram, Hyderabad occupies a significant place not only among other HRDCs of BHEL but also as an important Training and Development Centre in the twin cities of Hyderabad [Andhra Pradesh]. In BHEL training and development is basically concerned with identifying, assessing and helping employees to attain their key competencies which would enable them to perform current or future jobs.

Role of HRDI: The campus of Human Resource Development Institute (HRDI), Bharat Heavy Electricals Limited (BHEL), is a virtual treat and ideal for the overall development of the individual. Far from the madding crowd, nestling next door to the film city in Noida, near Delhi, India, HRDI has sprawling lawns and a four-storey glass building. BHEL is the largest engineering and manufacturing enterprise in the country and ranks among the top 10 power equipment manufacturers in the world. Started in 1956 in Bhopal, India, today the company has 14 manufacturing plants and 150 sites in India and abroad. HRDI aims to secure all-round development of employees. This includes their technical skills and behaviour to improve their efficiency and integration of individual and organizational needs for growth in all areas— team spirit, relationships with superiors and subordinates.

Hallmarks of BHEL's training initiatives: Training programs conducted by BHEL include those on general management, behavioural science and functional management. For behavioural sciences, HRDI has specially trained some of its employees from the Institute of Human Behaviour and Allied Sciences, Delhi. According to senior managers, the company's aim has been to inculcate strong leadership qualities amongst its employees. The company strongly believes that successful team leaders would not only envision the organization's future goals and objectives, they would also facilitate and enlist the support of others in achieving them. This initiative taken by BHEL explains the prospects of future leaders, the difference between modern and traditional leaders, style of leadership, also persuasion and politeness. Other aims of this development program are imparting creativity, goal setting, assertiveness, listening and motivation. The company strongly believes in the philosophy "Only when an individual is fully developed himself can he transform the organization and make it successful." The entire program meant for this is a well-structured with a duration of five days consisting of lectures, case studies and sharing experiences of the executives and employees.

Training for senior managers: For Senior Managers and above BHEL conducts "General Management Programs" [GMP]. The objectives of GMP are as follows:

- Creating an awareness of the influence of Business Environment on Organization,
- Enhancing Inter-Functional awareness in critical functional areas of BHEL
- Conceptual and experiential understanding of behavioural process in an organization so as to enhance Personal, Inter-Personal and Organizational Effectiveness
- Reviewing the present status of the organization and challenges ahead through interactions amongst the group and with the Top-Management
- Facilitating "Self-Learning" and development

Behavioural training programs: Some of the "Behavioural Training Programs" which BHEL conducts emphasize on the development of the following skills, namely:

- Assertive Skills
- Presentation Skills
- Emotional Intelligence
- Neuro Linguistic Psychology
- Conflict Management
- Stress Management
- Achievement Motivation
- Negotiation Skill
- Creative Problem Solving Skills
- Leadership and Decision Making Skills

Special skill development workshops in BHEL: The key services associated with the skill development workshops in BHEL are as follows:

- One to one coaching for approximately 30 staff on the program
- Design and co-delivery of management development training course
- Creation of job descriptions for all sales staff from Sales Director down
- 'Perception is Reality' participative workshops to support culture and role changes
- Presentation-skills training
- Training needs analysis and individual training plans to support the integration of ongoing development into the organizational culture following the program
- Combination of detailed personal assessment on "Critical Thinking Skills" and "Innovation Potential Indicators" along with structured discussion to enable individuals to:
    - Explore and understand their development needs

- Take responsibility for creating their own development opportunities
- Create realistic development plans that supported genuine personal change
- Explore creative options for career planning and development

Module-wise development programs: For the specific group of executives, where there is a change in cadre/grade, BHEL conducts "Module oriented programs" for that particular group. These programs include those of:

- EDP[Executive Development Programs]
- SDP [Supervisor Development Programs]
- TDP [Technician Development Programs]
- ADP [Artisan Development Programs]

The key focus in all these modules is to bring role-clarity and role-effectiveness among the participants in their new assignments. The program duration varies from 4 to 6 days.

Computer training programs: Every year BHEL conducts a number of Computer Training Programs [like those of MS Office, MS Access, Autocad-Basic/Advanced, Solid Modeling, Oracle, VB, Networking and Windows NT Server] for the employees.

Customer training programs: As a Corporate Policy, the HR department at BHEL always gives top priority to "Customer Service and Satisfaction". And, of course, as a part of this policy, HRDC conducts regular Customer Training Programs for its employees and marketing executives.

Environment management system (EMS) training: BHEL Unit being now been certified for ISO-14001 ensures that all its employees must get acquainted with this standard and put their best efforts for the implementation of the same. The company also ensures that its employees also adhere with reference to the statutory compliances regarding environmental legislation/regulations, conservation of natural resources, reduction in waste, pollution prevention and control. The senior managers also take initiatives so as to create environmental awareness in the employees, customers and suppliers. Broadly, the EMS training is of two-types: Awareness Training and Competence Training. The key-focus in EMS-Training Program is to continually improve environmental performance in our activities, products and services emphasizing the element of "Clean and Green".

Quality, productivity training: Keeping pace with changing times, the training programs are organized in these areas highlighting the latest trends, advancement and applications.

Conclusion: The success of BHEL can be rightly asserted to the people centric and development oriented policies. The top management had been instrumental to inculcate the spirit of holistic development in each and every employee working in the organization, irrespective of their departments and level of the management to which they belonged. In the context of the new economy where changes of technology and development of new people competencies would be critical for the survival of any corporation, it would be well worth watching how BHEL would steer its people development perspective for its sustained growth and enhanced competitiveness.

(*Courtesy:* Organization study by Ms. Padmaja N., http://www.lifepositive.com/mind/work/corporate-management/Bhel.asp, www.productfinder.co.in/Nov2007/bharat.htm)

TRAINING, EDUCATION AND DEVELOPMENT

According to Flippo, training is the act of increasing the knowledge and skills of an employee for doing a particular job. Training can also be defined as any organizationally planned effort to change the behaviour or attitudes of employees so that they can perform jobs on acceptable standards.

Development, in contrast, is considered to be more general than training and more oriented to individual needs in addition to organizational needs and it is most often aimed towards management people. Usually the objective of development is to provide knowledge and understanding that will enable people to carry out non-technical organizational functions more effectively, such as problem solving, decision-making and relating to the people.

The term "education" is wider in scope and more general in purpose when compared to training. Education is the process of increasing the general knowledge and understanding of the employees in an organization. It is a person-oriented, theory-based knowledge whose main purpose is to improve the understanding of a particular subject or theme or conceptual learning. Education is imparted with the help of schools or colleges and the contents of such a program generally aim at improving the talents of an individual.

Exhibit: Distinction Between Training and Learning

Hallmarks	Training	Learning
Definition	A planned and systematic effort to modify or develop knowledge/skill, attitude through learning experience, so as to achieve effective performance in an activity or range of activities	The process whereby individuals acquire knowledge, skills and attitudes through experience, study or instruction
Purpose	To enable individuals to acquire abilities in order that he/she can perform adequately a given task or job	To enable an individual to acquire knowledge, skills and attitudes through experience, study so as to effectively perform an activity
Nature	More specific or related to the present or future job More predictable and generally uniform	More general in nature Less predictable and generally variable in nature
Process	Training tends to be more of a mechanistic process that emphasizes uniform and predictable responses to standard guidance and instructions reinforced by practice and **repeatation**	Learning is a more of organic process depending upon the person itself, his/her attitude, culture and the way he/she perceives and interprets a particular event
Duration	Training is a short term process generally destined to be finished within a particular time period	Learning is a life long process

Contd...

Content	Training aims to provide knowledge and skills and to inculcate the attitudes which are needed to satisfy specific tasks previously settled	Learning is acquired from various practical, real-life situations from which an individual picks up (what is known as experience) from his/her mistakes and/or steps taken in response to a particular unknown or often known situations.
	Training implies the learning of specific behaviours with a certain degree of uniformity within the limits set by individual differences	Learning attempts to increase the variability of individual differences and determines how each individual comes to behave in a way which is particular to him.
Implications	The changes brought about by a training are often more immediately observable.	Learning, education and development are more likely to show their influence in the long run and in a more profound way.
	Training has its limitations to deal with uncertainties.	An individual can better tackle an uncertainty from his/her experience and learning in comparison to a formal training
	The outcomes of training can be specified as behaviours or performances, typically expected from such training and instructional procedures	The end products of learning can be specified in terms of particular instances of performances
Factors influencing	Training depends on the nature of activities, practices and procedures in the organization, its values and perceptions and culture also play important roles in terms of developing the content of a training program	Learning depends fundamentally on the individual himself/herself-personality, culture, attitude and perception as well as the environment by which the person is being influenced. Learning is also influenced by the societal factors including values and practices.

Importance of Training

Benefits to the organization	Benefits to the employee/individual
• Trained workers can work more effectively and can contribute to achieve organizational goals and objectives on a regular basis.	• Training makes employees more useful to an organization. It upgrades one's knowledge and skills relevant for his/her job
• Employees can effectively use machines, tools, materials in a	• Training makes employees more efficient and effective in terms of

Contd...

proper way and thereby also helps to eliminate wastage. Quality consciousness increases and this leads to customer satisfaction	effectively utilizing their individual potential at their workplace.
• Training reduces accidents at the workplace. It enhances concern for occupational health and safety management.	• Individuals become more aware of their own safety, rather being dependent on others. • Training enables employees to secure promotions easily and realize their career goals more effectively
• Trained workers can show superior performance and can turn out better quality goods by putting the materials, tools and equipment to good use. • Trained employees become capable of accepting future job challenges when and wherever required by their organization.	• Training enhances employee confidence and awareness regarding their own developmental needs. • Training helps and facilitates effective career planning and growth.
• Training makes employees more loyal to an organization. • Training enhances the level of employee engagement.	• Training contributes to motivate individuals for higher pursuits and future job challenges.

Objectives of Training

Broadly speaking training and development has the following objectives, namely:

- To impart the basic knowledge, and job related skills to the new entrants and enable them to understand and perform their jobs well.
- To equip the employees to meet the challenges of the changing requirements of the job and the organization. This is mainly concerned with adopting and developing newer skills and competencies for futuristic jobs.
- To ensure that employees are being updated with new techniques and ways of performing the job or operations. This involves upgrading the technical expertise of the employees according to the needs of the business or changing business environment.
- To prepare employees for higher level tasks and build up a second line of competent managers. Keeping the high attrition rate in IT/ITES sectors this is a very important strategic aspect for any organization to breed a line of competent successors to fill in vacancies whenever they come.

The PDCA Model of Training

Training like any managerial activity is well planned and implemented. Hence the concept of "Plan-Do-Check-Act" (PDCA) fits well with the process of training followed in any organization. The importance of a systematic approach towards training can be well flavoured by the following theme reading related to Infosys.

Plan: This starts with the training needs assessment phase in a T&D cycle. The training plan on an overall emphasizes mainly on the "learning plan", which means what should be learned, who should learn and what to learn and how to learn. All these informations are processed from a comprehensive training needs assessment (TNA). The apparently simple activity may be internally arranged by the HR department or with the help of a HR consultant.

Do: This phase mainly is concerned with developing and designing the "learning program" based on the learning plan or the training needs of the employees in an organization. Subject Matter Experts (SMEs), supervisors, HR heads/consultants, trainers need to get well so as to develop a comprehensive training curriculum with the needs of the employees and the organization as a whole.

Check: This stage is mainly concerned with the implementation of the training curriculum followed by subsequent evaluation of the extent to which employees had been able to learn or accumulate the required knowledge and skills relevant to their works/jobs. On an overall this stage is known as "Training Evaluation phase". This phase is subsequently followed by the stage known as "Act".

Act: This stage is a continuation of the "Check" approach, where the organization makes an effort to take actions so as to counter training gaps or deploy individuals who had successfully accomplished the training program to jobs with higher levels of skills and capabilities.

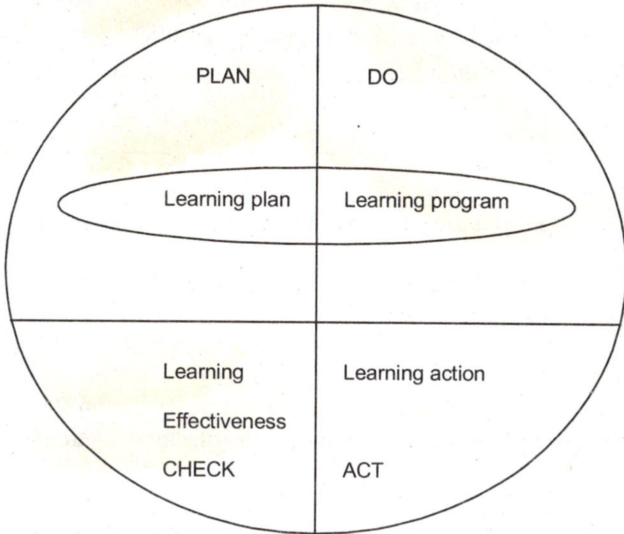

Fig. 3.1: The PDCA Cycle Model of Training

THEME READING: MATCHING TRAINING INTERVENTIONS WITH ORGANIZATIONAL NEEDS AT INFOSYS

Infosys is one of the fastest growing and most successful IT services companies in the world. Founded by seven professionals in 1981, it relocated to Bangalore the following year. It is a global player in the knowledge economy with headquarters in India. In the words of the Head of Education and Research at Infosys, Dr M.P. Ravindra; "Our aim is to become a provider of business solutions leveraging technology to compete with any consultancy in the world." This ambition is built on the vast pool of talent available in India, but demands a commitment to maintain, enhance and update skills at all levels.

Investment in knowledge and learning

Infosys corporate message is "powered by intellect, driven by values" and the company makes a considerable investment in knowledge and learning. The human resource concerns mirror those of any large knowledge intensive company. They have moved from 15 to 6 tiers of staff and they have introduced an Employee Stock Option Plan (the first in India). There is a competency system in place and every individual must have a training plan, based on these competencies, which takes account of individual performance, organizational priorities and, where appropriate, client feedback. Training interventions are organized in four key areas:

- Technical training (which accounts for 50% of training effort)
- Managerial and skills training (25%)
- Domain training (knowledge of specific industry 12.5%)
- Quality processes (12.5%)

The training department intervenes through just-in-time training courses, mainly delivered off the job and mainly project specific. There is an ambitious knowledge management program in place with rewards and reorganization for those staff who submit knowledge assets, which are highly rated by their peers. A new knowledge product, Kspeak, is under development — the idea is that someone telephones in with an enquiry, probably on a technical subject. The answer or solution will be generated through voice recognition and intelligent systems and mailed back to the person concerned. Despite this technical sophistication, to date Infosys has not committed heavily to e-learning. There is probably more reliance on the classroom than in a US or European firm. Dr Ravindra expresses his perspective in the following terms: "Learning should be supported not automated."

(Courtesy: "The Changing role of the trainer". www.learningarray.com/live index2. php?option = com_docmanandtask = doc_viewandgid=8anditemid=159).

Training: Core Concepts

From the above discussions we can understand that training involves the following core concepts, namely:

- Training should be a systematic process with some planning and control rather than random learning from experience
- It should be concerned with changing concepts, skills or attitudes of people treated both as individuals and as groups (Bramley, 1996)[1].
- It is intended to improve performance in both the present and the following job and through this should enhance the effectiveness of the part of the organization where the individual or group works (Hartle, 1995)[2]

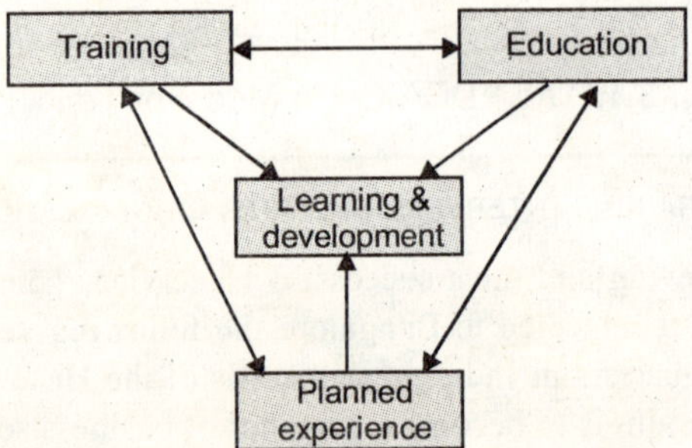

Fig. 3.2: Elements which contribute to learning and development

Essential Models of Training

Bramley's Model: Peter Bramley (1996) has considered training as an investment that produces returns that can be related to the business plans of the organization and had thereby proposed a model based upon improving organizational effectiveness. The model depicts to what extent investment in training contributes to enhance the levels of effectiveness or performance levels in the organization. It also makes an attempt to identify what behaviours of trainees are necessary so as to achieve the desired performance levels.

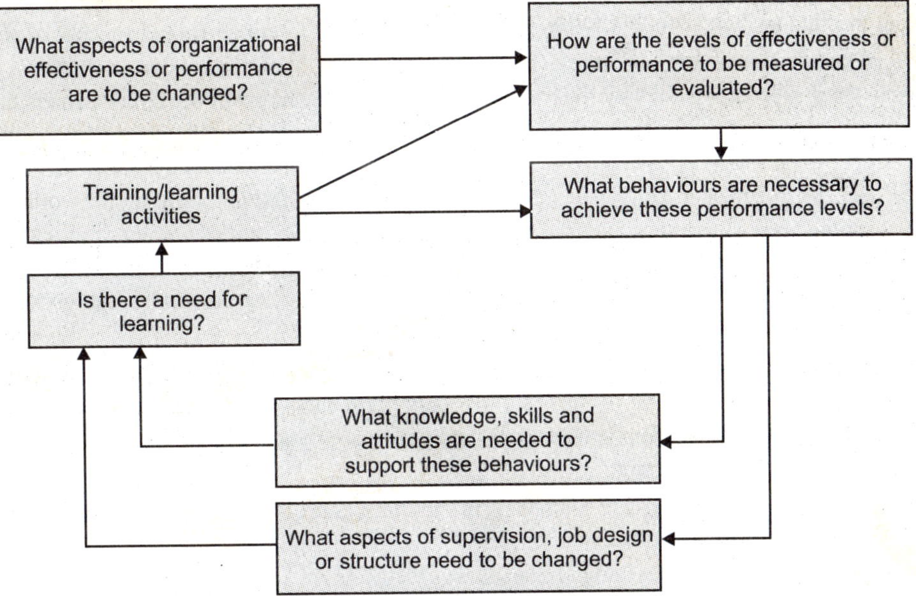

Fig. 3.3: Bramley's model of training based upon improving effectiveness

Traditional Training Model: A more traditional model of training process, based upon individual learning through technical education is depicted in the following figure. The problem is that, this model is a learning model rather than a training model and thus lends itself to evaluation at the learning rather than at the application level. Hence this model is suitable for training and testing off-the-job, but the application is usually left to the learner alone to accomplish.

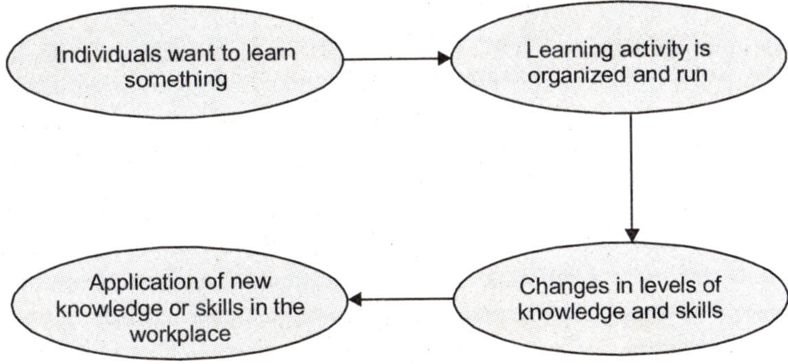

Fig. 3.4: A traditional model of training based upon individual education and learning

Factors to be Considered while Organizing a Training Program

Choice of the Trainer: Choice of the trainer is a vital factor for the effectiveness and success of any training program. Trainers who are involved in the delivery of training are likely to have to call upon a variety of skills which is not always appreciated by the training managers nor by many of the direct trainers themselves. In fact the training manager or the coordinator should ensure that the trainer appointed for the training program possesses the necessary general, technical and specialized knowledge of the subject (Subject Matter Experts or SMEs) and that his/her experience or skills are properly reflected in managing the working sessions, adapting the training style, using various training methods and creating interests in the trainees. The trainer should also have the essential attributes in terms of personality and attitudes such as openness to new ideas, observation, listening to others, a questioning mind and willingness to experiment and undergo research whenever needed.

Trainees or the Learners: The success of the training program also depends on the modalities of the subjects for whom the training is being developed. Thus their background, experience, intellectual and physical capacities, diagnostic and application skills and personality attributes as well as attitudes also form an integral part of the training program.

Training/Learning Conditions: The trainer or the training coordinators need to be aware of the ways in which people learn and how conditions of learning can be arranged so as to aid the learning process. The trainer must know how the training material would facilitate learning and what type of learning environment should facilitate the same. Conditions that hinder the learning process must be identified and taken care off with utmost care.

Individual Differences: Apart from some obvious differences in individuals like those of intelligence, aptitudes, age and previous learnings or experiences other differences have been seen to have an important bearing on the ease of learning. These include personality factors and individual learning styles.

Training Curriculum: The training curriculum should be designed for the optimal utilization of resources available towards the achievement of training objectives. The training department should ensure the relevance of their training curriculum to those of the trainees in terms of the degree of their complexity or suitability and matching the same with the level of maturity or capabilities of the learners.

Training Material: Closely linked with the training conditions and training curriculum is the influence that the material to be learned should have on the arrangement and organization of the learning conditions.

Training Methods and Techniques: The training methods and techniques should contribute to maintain the interest and high degree of participation among the participants so that they could be effective in the process of inducing fruitful transfer of knowledge and skills.

Sequencing Training Events and Materials: An obvious but most often neglected aspect influencing training programs is how the events or the materials used in the training process are being sequenced and presented to the trainees. The ordering of certain kind of training content has been reported to have critical difference on the level of retaining the learnings in a training session.

Timing of the Training Materials: Timing of the placing of the training materials is also another important aspect contributing to the success of raining. It has been suggested that ideally any training session should not extend beyond the duration of $1\frac{1}{2}$ hours and the optimal number of training sessions in a day should be around four, where only in cases of residential programs one could think about incorporating an additional session, particularly during evening or before the dinner.

Other Factors: Other factors like the venue of the training program, physical facilities and training equipments also play important roles in the success of any training program.

Process of Training: A Systematic Approach

The following steps outline the various events in a typical training process:

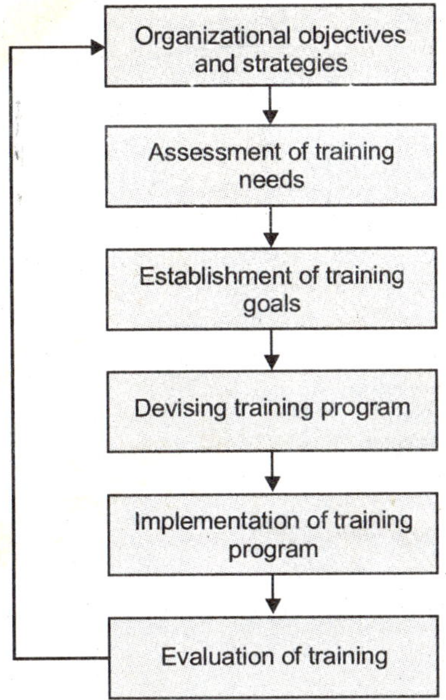

Fig. 3.5: A systematic approach to training

For ensuring a systematic approach to training and development organizations need to develop an **"Instructional Systems Design (ISD)"** model like that presented in the following table and figure. The ISD process consists of four principal phases, namely: (a) Needs assessment, (b) Design and development of training, (c) Delivery of training and (d) Evaluation of Training.

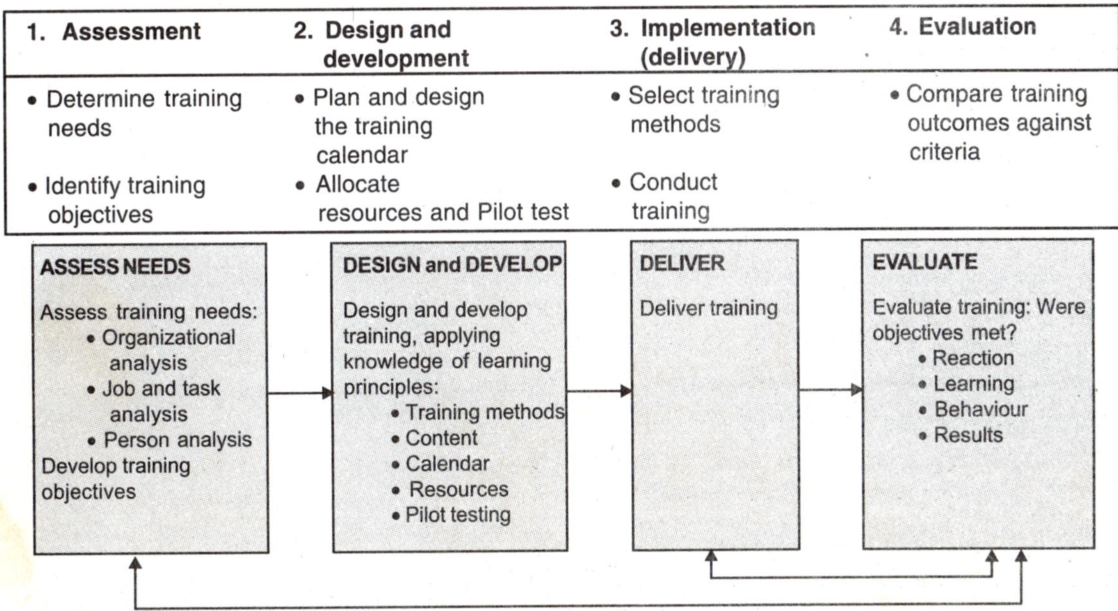

1. Assessment	2. Design and development	3. Implementation (delivery)	4. Evaluation
• Determine training needs • Identify training objectives	• Plan and design the training calendar • Allocate resources and Pilot test	• Select training methods • Conduct training	• Compare training outcomes against criteria

Fig. 3.6: A systematic approach to training

How the systematic approach to training works: The approach towards systematic training is not as simple as depicted in the above figures. The process in reality is more complex than what it appears. The following model illustrates the details of this process.

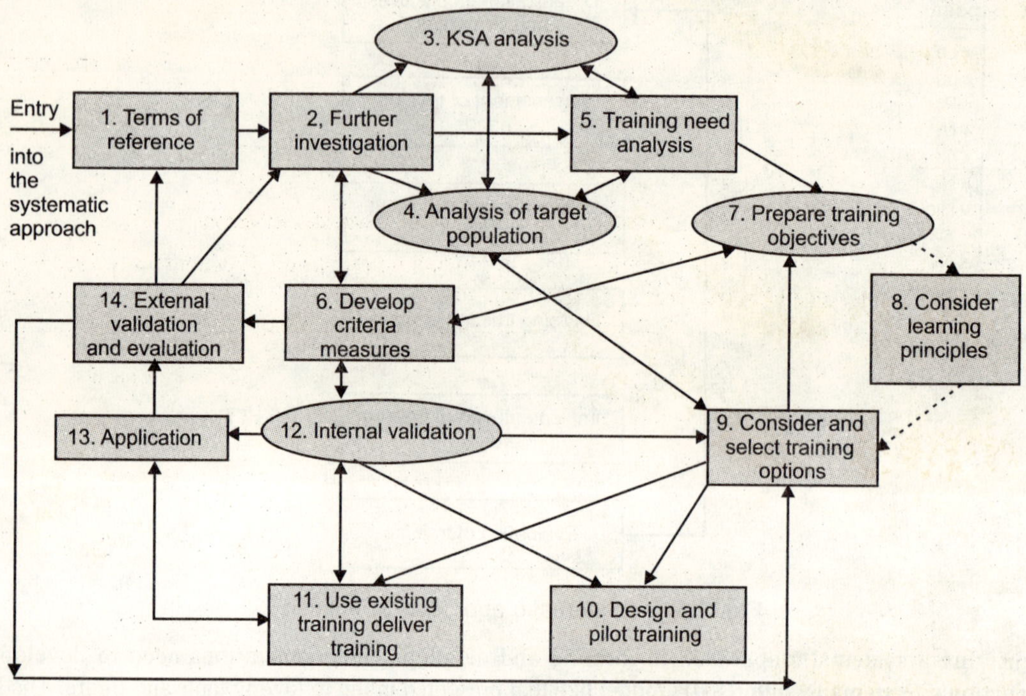

Fig. 3.7: A model depicting systematic approach to training

Training Needs Assessment

Training efforts must aim at meeting the requirements of the organization (long term) and the individual employees (short term). This involves the assessment of Training Needs Analysis (TNA). According to Thayer and McGhee et al., the components of TNA are as follows:

- Organizational Support and Organizational Analysis
- Requirement Analysis and Task, KSA and Role Analysis
- Person or Manpower Analysis

The following figure illustrates the various aspects of the TNA process:

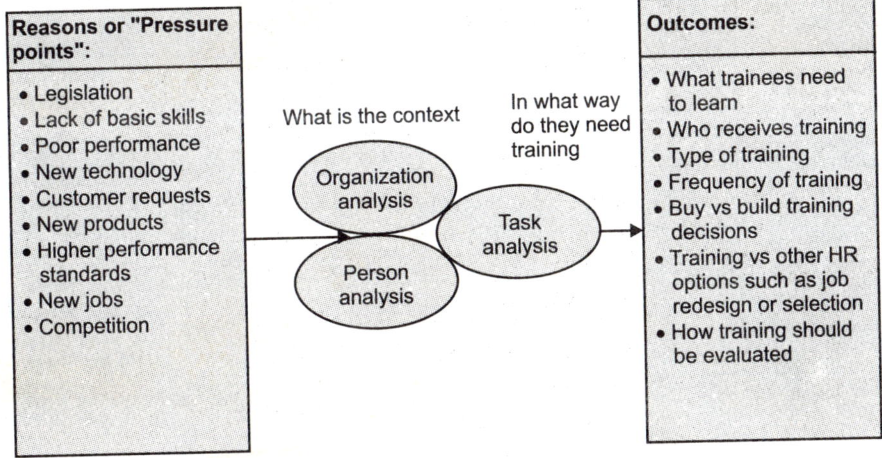

Fig. 3.8: Causes and outcomes of TNA

Organizational Support for the TNA Process

(a) Establishing relationship with the Top Management (French and Bell, 1999):

- Creating an open dialog with the top level management.
- Establish whether the organization is ready to lend support, time and effort towards the successful completion of the TNA.
- Exchange of information
- Resolving expectation dilemmas
- Issues concerning confidentiality of the results.

(b) Establishing relationship with organizational members (Bennis, 1969):

- To ensure that the various components of the organization are represented.
- To include members who are recognized leaders of their respective units
- To choose members who are generally in time with the idea of helping by being a problem solver for the organization.

Organizational Analysis: The process of Organizational Analysis consists of the following steps namely: (a) Specifying Goals, (b) Determining the Training Climate, (c) Identifying External and Legal Constraints, (d) Resource Analysis

Requirement Analysis: The phases involved in the requirement analysis are as follows:

- Understanding the job in the context of the organization.
- Defining the target job.
- Choosing the methods for conducting the needs assessment (like: Observation method, questionnaire method, key consultation method, interview method, GD method, Tests, records, Work Sample method)
- Determining the participants in the Needs assessment process.
- Determining points of contact in the organization.
- Anticipating problems to be resolved
- Developing a protocol.

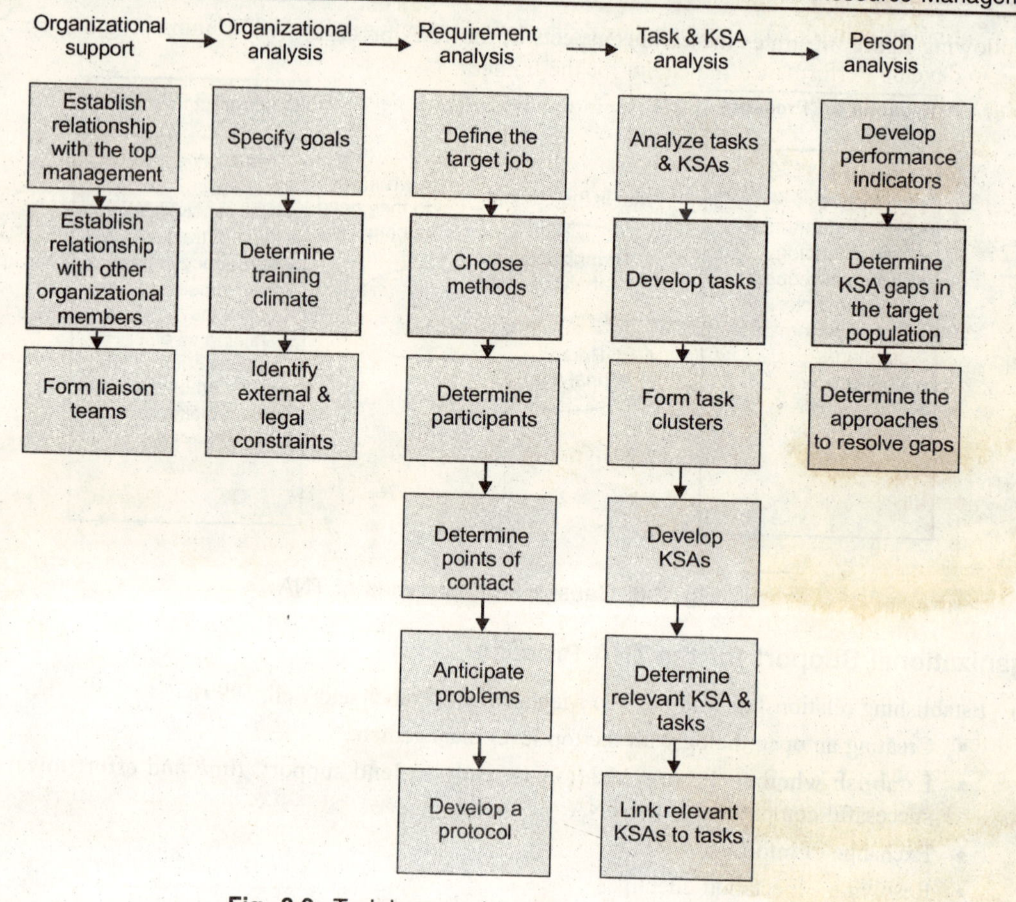

Fig. 3.9: Training needs assessment process

Task and KSA Analysis: Task Analysis results in a statement of the activities or work operations preferred on the job and the conditions under which the job is performed. This involves the following steps, namely:

- ***Developing Task Statements***
- ***Determining Task Clusters:*** Task Clustering is the collection of the complete task set from the Job Observations, panels and interviews.
- ***Developing the KSA Analysis***
- ***Determining Relevant Task and KSA Characteristics.***
- ***Linking the KSAs to the Tasks***
- ***Competency Modeling:*** It is the holistic approach utilized in organizations in order to successfully identify and map the KSAs consistently used by exemplary performers which is aimed to provide a detailed information about the KSA-Task Relationship that can be used for the design of Training programs targeted at specific audiences.

Person Analysis: Here the focus is on the individual in a given job position. The key issues that are involved with the process of person analysis are as follows:

- To identify who needs training
- To identify and assess whether the individual is capable of being trained and the specific areas in which the training is needed.

- To find out what kind of instructions do those individuals need for the training program.
- To develop Performance Indicators for the trainees.
- To determine KSA gaps and developing approaches so as to effectively resolve them.

Identifying the Training Objectives

Once training needs are being identified, training objectives should be set so as to meet these needs:

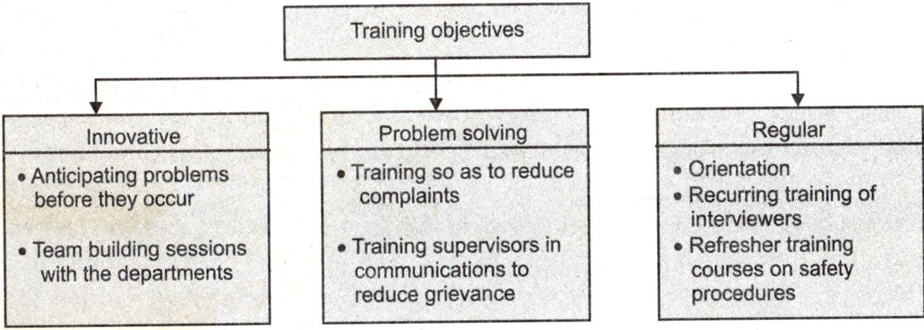

Exhibit: Training in Taj Group of Hotels

The employees of the Taj Group are trained in varied field like sales and marketing, finance, hospitality and service, front office management, food and beverages, projects, HR and more. They also have to take part in various leadership programs, so that they could develop in them a strong, warm and professional work culture. Through these programs, the Taj group ensures assessment of the future potential of their employees and training required to further develop their skills. The group offer excellent opportunities to employees both on personal as well as organizational front. In order to achieve the "Taj Standards", employees are made to undergo a rigorous training program. The Taj group strives hard to standardize all its processes and evolve a work culture, which appeals to all its employees universally.

The Taj Exotica, one of the Taj groups of hotels offers on-the-job training to its employees. It considers HRM and Training and Development as its key strength in the competitive hotel industry. It has a trainer for each department and division of the hotel. It also offers department-centric training programs based on the individual skills and training needs of each person.

(Courtesy: www.tajhotels.com/)

TRAINING METHODS

On-the-Job Training Methods

Job-Instruction Training (JIT)

These are provided to the employees when they are being taught relevant knowledge, skills and abilities at the actual workplace. This training occurs in the presence of an able supervisor and involves the following steps:

- The trainee receives an overview of the job, its purpose and its desired outcomes, with a clear focus on the relevance of the training.
- The trainer demonstrates the job to give the employee a model to copy. The trainer shows a right way to handle the job.

- In the next stage, the employee is permitted to copy the trainer's way. Demonstrations by the trainer and practice by the trainee are repeated until the trainee masters the right way to handle the job.
- Finally, the employee does the job independently without supervision.

Table 3.1: Merits and Demerits of JIT

Merits	***Demerits***
• Trainee learns fast through practice and observation.	• The trainee should be as good as the trainer. If the knowledge of the trainer is not good, transference of knowledge and skills would be poor.
• It is economical, as it does not require any special settings. Also, mistakes can be corrected immediately.	• Trainee while learning may damage equipments, waste materials, cause accidents frequently.
• The trainee gains confidence quickly as he does the work himself in actual settings with the help of the supervisor.	• Experienced workers cannot use the machinery while it is being used for training.
• It is most suitable for unskilled and semiskilled jobs where the job operations are simple.	

Coaching and Mentoring

Coaching is a one-to-one relationship between trainees and supervisors which offers workers continued guidance and feedback on how well they are handling their tasks. The coach assigns the task, monitors the trainee behaviour, and provides reinforcement and feedback. Coaching is commonly used for all kinds of trainees, from unskilled to managerial positions. This method is critically dependant on the quality of the coach.

Mentoring is a particular form of coaching used by experienced executives to groom junior employees. Normally, mentoring involves on-on-one coaching for a period of several years until the individual is eventually capable of replacing the mentor.

Exhibit: Coaching vs. Mentoring

Coaching	**Mentoring**
• A coach is someone available for the performer to learn with. Coaching is the process whereby one individual helps another to unlock their natural ability; to perform, learn and achieve.	• A mentor is someone available for the performer to learn from. Mentoring is the process whereby one senior individual is available for a junior for a period of several years until the individual is eventually capable of replacing the mentor.
• The roles overlap when a person performs successfully as a coach. He or she is likely to be adopted as a mentor of coaching skills.	• A mentor on the other hand can never be a coach unless he deliberately adopts the skills involved with successful coaching.
• A coach concentrates on helping the performer learn how to achieve more.	• The mentor's aim is to be available for the performer to use as a resource.

Apprenticeship Training

Apprentices are trainees who spend a prescribed amount of time working with an experiences guide or supervisor or trainer. Assistantships and internships are similar to apprenticeship programs, because they use high levels of participation by the trainee. An internship is a kind of on the job training that usually combines job training with classroom instruction in business schools, colleges or universities. One important disadvantage of the apprenticeship method is the uniform period of training offered to the trainees.

Committee assignments: In this method the trainees are asked to solve an actual organizational problem. The trainees have to work together and offer solution to the problem. This method of training helps them to develop team spirit and work **unitedly** towards common goals.

Job Rotation Training

This training involves the movement of the trainee from one job to another. This helps him to have a general understanding of how the organization functions. Apart from releasing boredom, Job rotation allows workers to build rapport with a wide range of individuals within the organization, facilitating future cooperation among various departments. Such cross-trained personnel offer a great deal of flexibility for organizations when transfers, promotions or replacements become inevitable.

Off-the-Job Training Methods

Vestibule Training

In this method, actual work conditions are simulated in a class room. Materials, files and equipments those are used in actual job performance are also used in the training process. This type of training is commonly used for training personnel for electrical and semi-skilled jobs. Although vestibule training uses learning principles, there may be some problem with the transfer of learning unless machinery and tools are identical to those on the job. Also, vestibule training cannot simulate the actual work environment conditions such as noise, disturbance, distraction of co-workers and job pressures. It allows the employees to develop the necessary skills in a pressure-free environment.

Role Playing

It is defined as a method of human interaction that involves realistic behaviour in imaginary situations. This method of training involves action, doing and practice. The participants play the role of certain characters, such as the production manager, mechanical engineer, supervisor etc. This method is mostly used for developing interpersonal interactions and relations.

Lecture Method

It is a traditional and direct method of instruction. The instructor organizes the material and gives it to a group of trainees in the form of a talk. To be effective, the lecture must motivate and create interest among the trainees. An advantage of this method is that it is direct and can be used for a large group of trainees. The major limitation of this method is that it does not provide for the transfer of training effectively.

Conference/Discussions Method

This method is a directed discussion on a specific topic conducted with a relatively small group of trainees. Trainees have a large degree of verbal interaction with the discussion leader and with one another. This method is useful for teaching and exploring difficult conceptual materials, and for changing attitudes and opinions. It provides opportunity for feedback, reinforcement practice, motivation, and transfer, largely due to the active interchange of ideas between the participants. This method as compared to the lecture method is expensive, but popularly used for managerial training purposes.

Programmed Instruction (PI)

Programmed Instruction (PI) presents information in small books, either in book form or through a teaching machine. After reading each book of material, the learner must answer a question about it. Feedback in the form of correct answers is provided after each response. PI involves: a) presenting questions, facts or problems to the learner; b) allowing the person to respond; c) providing feedback on the accuracy of answers of the learner; d) If the answers are correct, the learner can proceed to the next level or next block. A major advantage of PI is that it is self-paced; trainees can progress through the program at their own speed, In terms of learning principles, PI provides a high degree of reinforcement and knowledge of results and motivates most trainees in that they are actively engaged in the learning experience. One of the major drawbacks could be that the transfer of learning can be problematic since the learning situation is unlike the real-life job situations.

Films and Televisions

Films are pre-recorded and can be shown on either movie screen or television sets and/or well-suited to any number of trainees. An advantage of films and television over lectures is that the films can show objects and processes in detail and in motion. This facilitates the transfer of skill because visual images tend to be remembered longer than the verbal ones.

Computer-Assisted Instruction (CAI)

It is the method similar to programmed instruction which utilizes the computers' storage and memory capabilities to individualize instruction. The computer analyzes the learners' responses and determines what material is presented next. In terms of learning principles, CAI is very much like PI except that feedback from CAI can be as rich and colourful like modern electronic games.

Simulated Work Settings

Training simulators are those which replicate the essential characteristics of the real world that are necessary to produce learning and transfer of knowledge and skills. Simulation on the other hand can thereby be described as an attempt to create a realistic decision-making environment for the trainee by presenting likely problem situations and decision alternatives. The reasons for the applicability of this form of training is that they ensure controlled reproducibility, ensure safety considerations and cost effectiveness, involve learning considerations including those of providing feedback, arrangements for practice, designing/altering the environment and using part/whole and massed/spaced methods. In this exercise, the results of the decisions taken by the trainee are generally reported back in the form of feedbacks, which enables them to improve their working skills and facilitate their decision-making capabilities.

Theme Case: Training Employees of IBM Through E-Learning

Ever since its inception, IBM had been focusing on human resources development. The company concentrated on the education and training of its employees as an integral part of their development. During the mid 1990s, IBM reportedly spent about $1 billion for training its employees. However, in the late 1990s, IBM undertook a cost cutting drive, and started looking for ways to train its employees effectively at lower costs. After considerable research, in 1999, IBM decided to use e-learning to train its employees. Initially, e-learning was used to train IBM's newly recruited managers. IBM saved millions of dollars by training employees through e-learning. e-learning also created a better learning environment for the company's employees, compared to the traditional training methods. The company reportedly saved about $166 million within one year of implementing the e-learning program for training its employees all over the world. The figure rose to $350 million in 2001.

Andrew Sadler, director of IBM Mindspan Solutions, explained the benefits of e-learning to IBM, "All measures of effectiveness went up. It's saving money and delivering more effective training, while at the same time providing five times more content than before." By 2002, IBM had emerged as the company with the largest number of employees who have enrolled into e-learning courses. However, a section of analysts and some managers at IBM felt that e-learning would never be able to replace the traditional modes of training completely. Rick Horton, general manager of learning services at IBM, said, "The classroom is still the best in a high-technology environment, which requires hands-on laboratories and teaming, or a situation where it is important for the group to be together to take advantage of the equipment."

Hallmarks of e-Learning at IBM

The e-learning part included articles, simulations, job aids and short courses. The founding principle of Basic Blue was that 'learning is an extended process, not a one-time event.' Basic Blue was based on a '4-Tier blended learning model'. The first three tiers were delivered online and the fourth tier included one week long traditional classroom training. The program offered basic skills and knowledge to managers so that they can become effective leaders and people-oriented managers. The managers were divided into groups of 24 members each. Each group then entered the first tier of the Basic Blue program (without interaction with the other members of the group-learning from information).

BEHAVIOURALLY EXPERIENCED TRAINING METHODS

Behavioural modeling: Behaviour modeling is a newer method for teaching interpersonal skills and attitude change, is very specific in its training objectives. It teaches specific supervisory skills by: (a) Presenting a model or good example of the behaviour to be learned; (b) allowing the trainees to practice the modeled behaviour; and (c) Providing feedback and reinforcement on practice attempts. This method is flexible and is based on the idea that workers learn the best when they see a task being performed and then practice the task with feedback until they are competent.

Case study method: It presents the trainees with a written description of a business or organizational problem. The object of the case method is to teach the trainees how to analyze information, generate alternative decisions, and evaluate the alternatives. Cases can be analyzed by individuals or small groups. Feedback and reinforcement are provided through oral discussion or written comments from the instructor. Through this method the trainees can learn to transfer appropriate principles to the examples of "real" problems.

Business games: The business game technique requires trainees to make sequential decisions. Business games are more dynamic than those of case study analysis. This is because in this method the decisions made early in the game affect the alternatives available later in the game and its outcome. Trainees work by themselves in teams in which each team member takes the role of the manager of a functional area such as HR, marketing, finance etc. Trainees usually regard business games as highly involving andmotivating since, like any game, a score is maintained and the trainees compete with each other.

In-basket technique: This training method places the trainee in the role of a person who must suddenly replace a manager. In this role, the trainee receives background information about the organization and the person he or she is replacing, along with letters, memos and relevant files and information regarding the job. The trainee then must organize the information, make decisions, and prepare memos, letters and organize files so as to handle the problems or present themselves to the trainers. This exercise can be developed for almost any type of jobs, involving managerial or professional decision-making. The major value of in-basket exercise as a training technique depends upon the amount of feedback and reinforcement provided.

T-group technique: The T-group method uses a small group of trainees, who meet with a passive trainer and gain insight into their own and other's behaviour. Meetings have no agenda, and questions deal with the "hear and know" of the group process. The discussions focus mainly on "why participants behave as they do, how they perceive one another, and the feelings and the emotions generated in the interaction process." T-groups are highly involving and give participants some opportunity to practise new behaviours, but material to be learned is much unstructured.

Sensitivity training: Sensitivity training is a part of human relations training which aims to make act, feel differently. According to Argyris, Sensitivity training is a group experience designed to provide maximum possible opportunity for the individuals to expose their behaviour, give and receive feedback, experiment with new behaviour and develop awareness of the self and of others. It is based on the concept of empathy, which is to actually perceive a situation with another person's viewpoint and emotions. This method was introduced by Kurt Lewin and popularized by the National Training Laboratories, USA.

The objectives of this type of training are to provide the participants with increased awareness of their own behaviour and how others perceive them. Specific outcomes of this form of training involve increased ability to empathize with others, enhance listening skills, greater openness, increased tolerance of individual differences and increased conflict-resolution skills. The major demerit of this method is that once this training is over, the participants might resort to their own or previous day to day habits.

Neuro-Linguistic Programming (NLP): NLP is a set of techniques aimed to help trainees change from mediocre to excellent performers. It helps them to think differently and positively so that it affects their behaviour and also affects the behaviours of others. It teaches techniques for improved communication within the organization and helps to develop and improve interpersonal skills. It is a technique designed to bring together various aspects of trainees' thinking patterns, their spoken language and even their non-verbal languages. The concept relates neurology (the way people think and take actions) and both the inherited (inborn) as well as the learned patterns which produce or determine their language or communication skills. The model is described simply as the way people use their mental mechanisms in relation to their sensory perceptions.

NLP uses many different techniques some of which relates to self management. One example is "outcome thinking" which requires the subject to go through a number of stages, namely:

- Thinking of a positive outcome associated with a certain situation and continually rehearsing it by imagining it through as many senses as possible.
- Identifying the personal resources such as confidence required to bring about a positive outcome and to find those resources using stimulus-response techniques that require the individual to think of a time when he/she possessed that resource, to relieve the emotions he/she possessed.
- Rehearsing the use of these resources in the new situation to try to ensure a positive outcome.

Action learning: It is probably one of the most challenging ways to develop people within an organization. It is challenging both for the developer and those being developed. Action learning sets are similar to Quality Circles in that the solutions require changes to be made in the organization, which poses challenge to the senior management. An element of risk is therefore involved, but the benefits are immense as people can learn to take responsibility of their own problems and so also their solutions.

Synergogy: It refers to the learning design which provides an important strategy for dealing problems associated with the actual learning of an individual. It also provides a systematic framework for approaching the problems found in the process of education, training and development. Synergogic learning designs contribute a set of instructions and instruments which helps to direct what is known as "students'-colleague oriented training". Synergogy are introduced in comparison with more traditional approaches to three aspects of learning, namely:

- Comprehending knowledge such as facts, data, principles and generalizations
- Acquisition of conceptual and mechanical skills
- Development of attitudes, values and beliefs.

Building Training Design

Planning a training session involves the following aspects, namely:

- Establishing learning objectives based upon identified training needs
- Identifying the components to be covered in the training session
- Assembling specific methods and activities in a coherent design
- Implementing the training programs planned
- Evaluating the training program.

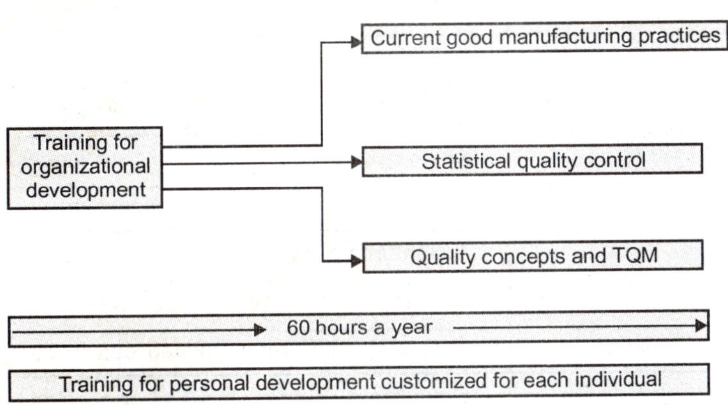

Fig. 3.10: Ranbaxy's quality training

(*Courtesy: Business Today, Jan 7–21, 1996, p. 205*)

Implementing the Training Program

Once a training program is being designed, the training and development professionals are being held responsible for their implementation. This responsibility includes the planning and execution of the training sessions and building a corpus of competent trainers, to be involved in the training process. Another important aspect that needs constant attention is the scheduling training around the present work. This also involves the problem of record keeping about the performance of the trainees during their training period. The process of Training implementation involves the following steps, namely:

- Deciding the location and organizing the training and other facilities required for the training
- Scheduling the training program
- Conducting the program
- Monitoring the progress of the trainees
- Taking feedback about the training from the participants.

Exhibit: Modern Training Techniques (Source: Business Today, Jan 7–21,'96)

Modern Training Techniques	Hallmarks
1. Ice Breakers	Games to get team members know each other
2. Leadership Games	Exercises to teach different styles of leadership
3. Skill Games	Tests to develop analytical skills
4. Communication Games	Exercises to build bias-free listening and talking skills
5. Strategic Planners	Games to test the ability to plan ahead
6. Team-building Games	Exercises requiring collaborative efforts
7. Role Reversal Games	Brings out ideas that are not often expressed.
8. Doubling	Brings out ideas that are not often expressed.
9. Tag Teams	One role played alternately by two participants
10. Mirroring	Training with an external perspective
11. Monodrama	Insight into a given situation
12. Shifting Physical Positions	Highlighting of communication problems
13. Structured Role Playing	Role play with predetermined objectives
14. Multiple Role Playing	Providing a common focus of discussion
15. Built-in-tension	Teaching the importance of resolving matters
16. Shadowing	Working under a senior to watch and learn
17. Outward-bound Training	Adventure sports for teams
18. 9+1+23	Self-assessment by a leader of leadership skills
19. Lateral Thinking	Thinking randomly to come up with new ideas.
20. Morphological Analysis	Listing of alternative solutions to problems
21. Gordon Technique	Steering a discussion to crystallize solutions
22. Attribute Listening	Isolation, selection and evaluation of a problem.
23 Cross-cultural Training	Programs to teach specifies of varied cultures.

THEME CASELET: TRAINING IN SYNDICATE BANK

Training is an integral part of any business to grow and sustain. The management of Syndicate bank realises this key factor and accounts significant importance to its training process. In order to achieve the objectives of the training, the bank emphasizes on designing suitable training programs in tune with the corporate strategic direction and goals. The knowledge levels and skills across all cadres — executives, officers and workmen – are upgraded on a continuous basis through appropriate need based training modules. Training programs on Risk management, Credit, Lending to SMEs, Agricultural lending, Recovery Management, Foreign Exchange Business and Information Technology and development of soft skills are the focus areas.

Syndicate Institute of Bank Management (SIBM), the apex training institute of the bank at Manipal, assumes the prime position in organizing customized special training programs for senior officials of the bank. The infrastructure of the institute is periodically upgraded on par with the institutes of similar standing in India.

The training centres at Bangalore, Delhi, Mumbai, Chennai, Ernakulam, Hyderabad, and Kolkata impart training to the junior level officers and workmen employees. All training centres are equipped with the state of the art computer labs for imparting training in CBS operations. During the year 2007 a full fledged Training Centre was opened at Chennai to cater to the training requirements of the employees in the state of Tamil Nadu. In order to meet the ever increasing need for technology based training, the capacity of the CBS Computer Labs at Bangalore and Kolkata were increased.

The Bank adopts scientific methods to identify the training requirement of its employees through "Training Need Analysis". Specific training programs, based on the jobs performed, are also imparted to the employees. The training requirements are identified to meet three objectives, namely: (a) reward those who perform exceedingly well, (b) impart the skills required in a new assignment and (c) upgrade the skills for doing a better job.

During the year 2007–08, 6823 officers and 6675 workmen employees were trained by the bank's Training System in different functional areas. In addition, 138 executives and 272 officers were deputed to external training programs conducted by reputed training institutes in India. 20 executives/officers were also deputed for overseas training programs. In addition, two in-company programs on executive development were conducted.

The first training program on "Credit management" through "Distance Learning Program" was completed. The program that was launched in January 2007, envisages learning through self-reading materials and contact classes through video conferences. 41 officers have been successful in the first batch of the said program.

During the year, the Bank recruited General Banking Officers, Specialist Officers and Clerks. Customized training programs were developed and imparted to meet the job requirement of these employees.

The investment made by the bank in the video-conference infrastructure is being productively used by the training system to organize special flexible training programs. These programs impart skills to the identified subjects to the participants with least disturbance to the functioning of the branches and at the minimal cost.

(Courtesy: Syndicate Bank Annual Report, 2007–2008, p: 32)

Importance of the Trainers in the Success of a Training Program

A trainer must possess sufficient knowledge, skill and practical experience in the training. A trainer, thus, can be described as someone who is competent in three fields, namely:

- Training know-hows
- Training approaches
- Training cooperation and coordination skills and abilities

One of the major tasks of the trainer is to provide leadership in establishing goals for the training and development activity.

Trainer Tasks

- To identify training needs, by facilitating the needs assessment process
- To identify all the tasks performed on-the-job in the organization
- To determine learning requirements for the said tasks

- To appraise trainees' capacities to learn the tasks
- To formulate a training approach that matches the learning requirements for those tasks
- To develop a training program that implements the approach
- To try out the training program with a sample of the intended audience
- To make revisions based on test results
- To establish reasonable measurable qualitative and quantitative standards and plan the total input of the training activities.
- To undertake a comprehensive training audit periodically

Trainer Roles: Desirable Qualities Needed for an Effective Trainer

Bennett (1988) had described five trainer roles depending on two dimensions namely, maintenance and change orientations. According to Bennett, a trainer is concerned only with the maintenance oriented functions providing the present job related skills for the employees. A trainer assumes the role of a provider when he/she focuses beyond the conventional maintenance oriented roles into more of a developer or change oriented role.

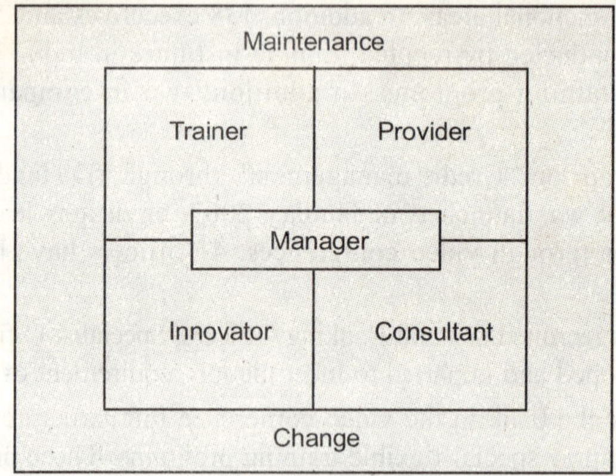

Fig. 3.11: General Trainer Roles (Bennett, 1988)

Trainer: A trainer is mainly concerned with carrying out training i.e., directly assisting the trainee to learn, supplying feedback etc. This role may involve a variety of different training methods ranging from one-to-one instruction to project work.

Provider: A provider is involved with the designing, updating, maintaining and delivering of training programs. More specifically the trainer assuming the role of a provider should be involved in undertaking TNA, establishing training objectives and possibly training or coaching trainers to deliver training.

Consultant: There are two main features to this role, analyzing organizational problems and then recommending solutions that may require training. The more detailed activities include liaison with line managers, advising training managers on training aims, objectives and policies etc.

Innovator: The primary concerns in this training role are supporting and assisting organizations to bring about effective change and to solve performance problems. These could involve the trainer in some managers on change issues, identifying where learning and educational events, such as seminars and workshops, can help managers to understand and facilitate change, advising the training functions as to its possible contribution to change process.

Manager: In this role there is concern fundamentally with planning, organizing, controlling and developing the training function. Here the role of the trainer includes setting training goals and formulating training policies and plans, contributing to the improvement of employee performances, ensuring and overseeing the development, delivery and evaluation of appropriate training activities, recruiting and developing training personnel, controlling activities against an overall training plan and budget.

A trainer assumes an innovator role when he/she emphasizes on organizational developmental perspectives and contributes to employee potential/capability development. The trainer can be said to assume a role of a consultant when he/she masters his/her role as a change agent or facilitator of change and may act as a "resource person" for developing and sharing knowledge at all levels in the organization.

A trainer needs to know, the following aspects:

- The number of participants, their position, their experience in the subject-matter
- The subject to be taught, level of coverage, skills to be developed
- The teaching provided by other trainers
- Date, time, place, arrangements and other facilities for the training
- A written summary of the entire training schedule along with the training materials (Course contents and Training materials to be supplied)
- Appropriate skills in teaching methods and in the effective use and application of audio-visual aids and presentation skills.

The following figure illustrates the trainer quadrant model based on Bennett's concept of trainer roles. This model emphasizes on four dimensions namely: organizational maintenance and organizational change dimensions in one side and the traditional and interventional approaches in the other.

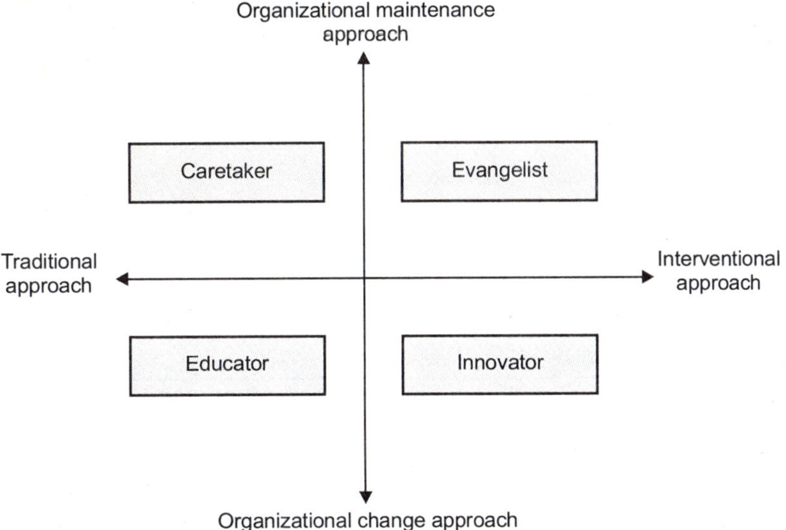

Fig. 3.12: The trainer quadrant model

Caretaker: A caretaker role of a trainer is that which has concern for a traditional as well as organizational maintenance approaches.

Evangelist: An evangelist's role of a trainer emphasizes on organizational maintenance as well as interventional approaches.

Educator: An educator role focuses on traditional training approaches to bring about change and developmental perspectives in the organization.

Innovator: An innovator emphasizes upon applying interventional approaches to bring about organizational change and development.

Beliefs of Trainers about Training

Trainer Beliefs	Impact on Training Function	Impact on Learning
1. **Training is Magical**	Lack of professionalism Lack of information increase in cost	Learning will not be predictable
2. **Training is Political**	Training as a part of Reward and Punishment System in the organization	Learning is a political tool and thereby expendable
3. **Training is Learning**	Learners experience less defensiveness More trust Mutual trust Team building	Increased productivity Increased creativity

Exhibit: Constructs of Trainer Effectiveness

Constructs of Trainer Effectiveness	Author	Field of Study
Competencies and characteristics; factors concerned with work behaviour; factors concerned with organizational characteristics; indicators of effective trainer behaviour concerned with outcomes; indicators of effective behaviour concerned with what trainers actually do	Bennett and Leduchowicz (1983)	HRD
Core instructor competencies	International Board of Standards for Training, Performance and Instruction (1988)	HRD
Performance (outcome) standards	Powers (1992)	HRD
Skills and attributes of an effective adult educator	Knowles and Associates (1984)	Adult education
Six principles of adult education practice	Brookfield (1986)	Adult education
Trainer's role	Bennett and Leduchowicz(1983)	HRD
Trainer's roles, competencies and outputs	McLagan and Suhadolnik (1989)	HRD

Adult Learning Principles in Effective Training

The field of adult learning is based predominantly on the following principles:

- Adults have a need to know why they should learn something before investing time in a learning event. Trainers must ensure that the learners know the purpose for training as early as possible.

- Adults enter any learning situation with an image of themselves as self-directing, responsible grown-ups. Trainers must help adults identify their needs and direct their own learning experience.
- Adults are *autonomous* and *self-directed.* They need to be free to direct themselves. The trainers must actively involve adult participants in the learning process and serve as facilitators for them. Specifically, they must get participants' perspectives about what topics to cover and let them work on projects that reflect their interests. They should allow the participants to assume responsibility for presentations and group leadership. They have to be sure to act as facilitators, guiding participants to their own knowledge rather than supplying them with facts. Finally, they must show participants how the class will help them reach their goals (e.g., via a personal goals sheet).
- Adults have accumulated a foundation of *life experiences* and *knowledge* that may include work-related activities, family responsibilities and previous education. They need to connect learning to this knowledge/experience base. To help them do so, trainers should draw out participants' experience and knowledge which is relevant to the topic. They must relate theories and concepts to the participants and recognize the value of experience in learning.
- Adults are *goal-oriented.* Upon being involved in a training program, they usually know what goal they would want to attain. They, therefore, appreciate the training or development program that is organized and has clearly defined elements. Trainers must show participants how the training would help them attain their goals.
- Adults are *relevancy-oriented.* They must see a reason for learning something. Learning has to be applicable to their work or other responsibilities to be of value to them. Therefore, trainers must identify objectives for adult participants before the training begins. This means, also, that theories and concepts must be related to a setting familiar to participants. This need can be fulfilled by letting participants choose projects that reflect their own interests.
- Adults are *practical,* focusing on the aspects of a lesson most useful to them in their work. They may not be interested in knowledge for its own sake. Trainers must tell participants explicitly how the training module would be useful to them on the job.
- As do all learners, adults need to be shown *respect.* Trainers must acknowledge the wealth of experiences that adult participants bring to the classroom. These adults should be treated as equals in experience and knowledge and allowed to voice their opinions freely in the training session. Adults come to a learning opportunity with a wealth of experience and a great deal to contribute. Trainers are successful when they identify ways to build on and make use of adults' hard-earned experience.
- Adults have a strong readiness to learn those things that help them cope with daily life effectively. Training that relates directly to situations faced by the participants is viewed as relevant.
- Adults are willing to devote energy to learning those things that they believe help them perform a task or solve a problem. Trainers who determine needs and interests and develop content in response to these needs are most helpful to adult learners.
- Adults are more responsive to internal motivators such as increased self esteem than external motivators such as higher salaries. Trainers can ensure that this internal motivation is not blocked by barriers such as a poor self-concept or time constraints by creating a safe learning climate.

Motivating the Adult Learner

Another aspect of adult learning is motivation. At least six factors serve as sources of motivation for adult learning:

- **Social relationships:** to make new friends, to meet a need for associations and friendships.
- **External expectations:** to comply with instructions from someone else; to fulfil the expectations or recommendations of someone with formal authority.

- **Social welfare:** to improve ability to serve mankind, prepare for service to the community, and improve ability to participate in community work.
- **Personal advancement:** to achieve higher status in a job, secure professional advancement, and stay abreast of competitors.
- **Escape/Stimulation:** to relieve boredom, provide a break in the routine of home or work, and provide a contrast to other exacting details of life.
- **Cognitive interest:** to learn for the sake of learning, seek knowledge for its own sake, and to satisfy an inquiring mind.

Guidelines for Effective Learning

There are four critical elements of learning that must be addressed to ensure that participants learn. These elements are **motivation, reinforcement, retention and transference.**

Motivation: If the trainee does not recognize the need for the information (or has been offended or intimidated), all of the trainer's effort to assist the trainee to learn would be in vain. The trainer must establish rapport with the participants and prepare them for learning; this provides motivation. This can be achieved by the following means:

- **Set a feeling or tone for the lesson:** Trainers should try to establish a friendly, open atmosphere that shows the participants they would help them to learn.
- **Set an appropriate level of concern:** The level of tension must be adjusted to meet the level of importance of the training objective. If the training material has a high level of importance, a higher level of tension/stress should be established in the training session. However, people learn best under low to moderate stress; if the stress is too high, it becomes a barrier to learning.
- **Set an appropriate level of difficulty:** The degree of difficulty should be set high enough to challenge the participants but not so high that they become frustrated by information overload. The instruction should predict and reward participation, culminating in success.
- **Feedback:** In addition, participants need specific knowledge of their learning results (*feedback*). Feedback must be specific, not general.
- **Rewards:** Participants must also see a *reward* for learning. The reward does not necessarily have to be monetary; it can be simply a demonstration of benefits to be realized from learning the material. Finally, the participant must be **interested** in the subject. Interest is directly related to reward. Adults must see the benefit of learning in order to motivate them to learn the subject.

Reinforcement: Reinforcement is a very necessary part of the training/learning process; through it, trainers can encourage correct modes of behaviour and performance from the trainees.

- *Positive reinforcement* is normally used by majority of the trainers who are particularly associated with imparting new skills to the participants. As the name implies, positive reinforcement is "good" and reinforces "good" (or positive) behaviour through encouragement, "pat on the back" etc.
- *Negative reinforcement* is normally used by trainers involved with training new skills or providing new information. It is useful in trying to change modes of behaviour. The result of negative reinforcement is *extinction* — that is, the trainer uses negative reinforcement until the "bad" behaviour disappears, or it becomes extinct.

Retention: Trainees must retain information from the training sessions in order to benefit from the learning in their real life jobs. The trainers' jobs are not finished until they have assisted the learners/trainees in retaining the information. In order for participants to retain the information taught, they must see a meaning or purpose for that information. They must also understand and be able to interpret and apply the information in their day to day job situations. This understanding includes their ability to assign the correct degree of importance to the learned material. Retention by the trainees is directly affected by their amount of practice during the learning session. Trainers should emphasize both on retention and application. After the trainees demonstrate correct (desired) performance, they should be urged to practise to maintain the desired performance.

Transference: Transfer of learning decides the effectiveness of training — it is the ability to use the training information taught in the course but in a new setting or in the real life job situations. As with reinforcement, there are two types of transfers: *positive* and *negative.*

- Positive transference, like positive reinforcement, occurs when the trainees can use the behaviour taught in the training program in their jobs.
- Negative transference, again like negative reinforcement, occurs when the trainees do not do what they are being told not to do. This results in a positive (desired) outcome.

Transference of learning is most likely to occur in the following situations:

- *Association* — trainees can associate the new information with something that they already know.
- *Similarity* — the information is similar to the material that the trainees already know; that is, it revisits a logical framework or pattern.
- *Degree of original learning* — trainee's degree of original learning is high.
- *Critical attribute element* — the information learned contains elements that are extremely beneficial (critical) on the job.

Theme Case: Changing the Role of Training at HSBC

Background: Headquartered in London, HSBC Holdings plc is one of the world's largest banking and financial services organizations. The HSBC Group's international network comprises some 223,000 staff across some 10,000 offices in 76 countries and territories in Europe, the Asia-Pacific region, the Americas, the Middle East and Africa. HSBC is marketed worldwide as 'the world's local bank'. At its core throughout the world are domestic commercial banking and financial services that fund themselves locally and do business locally. Reflecting the nature of the business and a commitment to the development of employees, there has been a strong tradition of training within the organization. HSBC currently has 15 regional training centres in operation worldwide, and a residential Group Management Training College in Hertfordshire.

Toward learning and development: The growing diversity of the financial services business, increasing competition in this sector and the sheer complexity of a global business ensures the Group continually refines its approach to 'learning and development'. A significant re-organization involving the merger of three corporate training teams took place in 2002 and a major review of training and learning activities was completed in July 2004. This review has led to better alignment with the business, a stronger commercial focus and a move to emphasize and support the learner and his or her manager in managing their learning. The department has also changed its title from 'Training' to 'Learning and Development' highlighting this change in focus.

In introducing the training review document, Graham Craddock emphasized the need to move from 'volume to value', believing 'It is essential that the learning and training function operates in areas which add greatest value to the business'. A number of senior managers have taken consultancy roles with responsibility for effective learning and development interventions for the main HSBC customer groups - emphasizing the need for greater continuity with the business.

Essential to this approach is a need to achieve greater agility and speed to market and this means different approaches to training delivery. Generally there is a commitment to move away from the training course as the primary solution to learning and development needs and to make use of alternative delivery channels to support learners — e-learning in particular is being used in many areas of the Group.

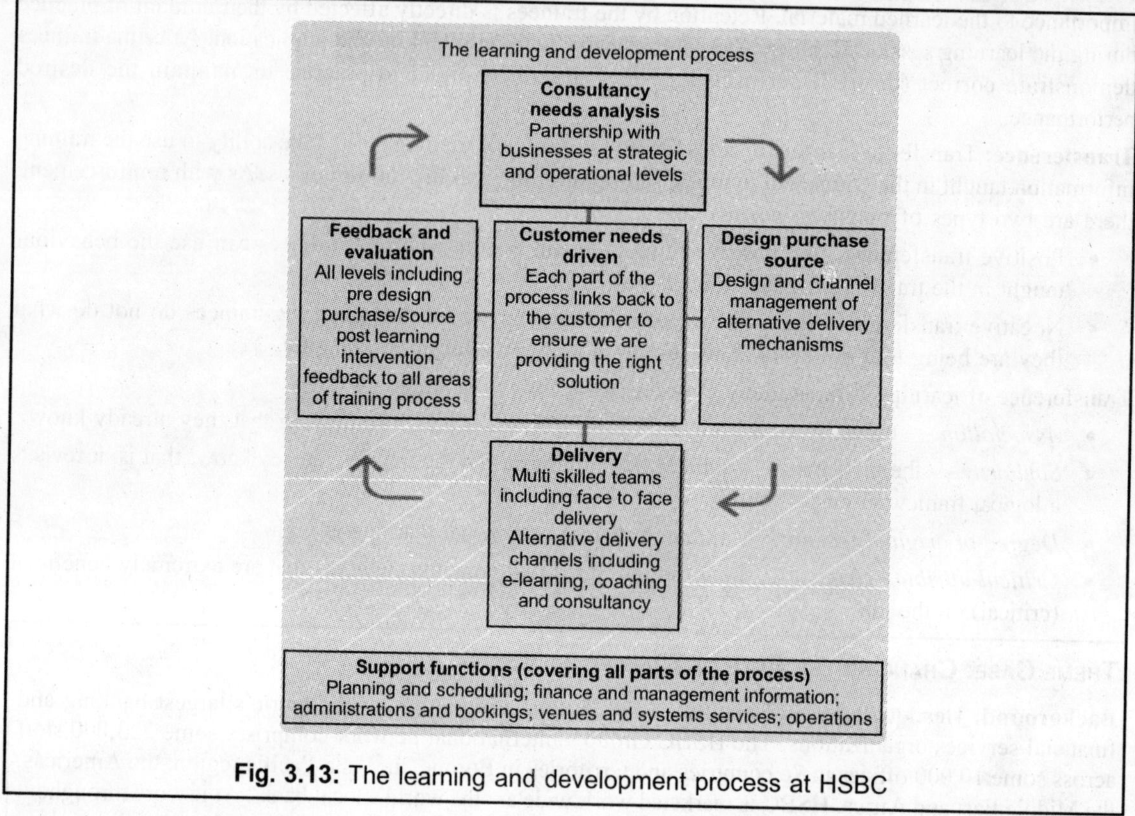

Fig. 3.13: The learning and development process at HSBC

Training Evaluation

Training Evaluation can be defined as any attempt to obtain information (feedback) on the effects of training program and to assess the value of training in the light of that information for improving further training (Hamblin, 1970).

Evaluation of training can be viewed as a method of measuring change in knowledge, skills, attitudes, job performance, costs and the quality of the training facilities. A major reason to evaluate training programs is to determine whether the training programs are accomplishing their specific training objectives. A training program that does not change employees' knowledge, skills or attitudes in the desired direction should be modified or replaced. A second reason for training evaluation is to assure that any change in the trainees' capabilities is due to the training program and not to other conditions. In order to determine that a training program is responsible for changes in trainees, it is necessary to compare the trainees' performance before and after the program with a control group.

Levels of Training Evaluation

Kirkpatrick Approach

Level	Questions
1. Reaction	Were the participants pleased with the program?
2. Learning	What did the participants learn in the program?
3. Behaviour	Did the participants change their behaviour based on what was learned?
4. Results	Did the change in behaviour positively affect the organization?

The *American Society for Training and Development*'s (ASTD) 2002 State of the Industry Report indicates the following statistics regarding companies' usage of Kirkpatrick's levels:

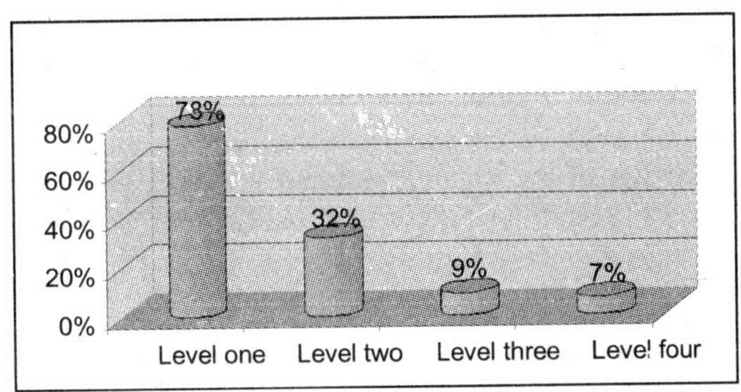

Fig. 3.14: Percentage of companies using each of Kirkpatrick levels

Nearly 92 per cent of *Training's* Top 100 companies measure training effectiveness through Kirkpatrick's Level Four (business results) and 67 per cent measure through ROI.

Calculating Training Return on Investment (ROI)

ROI is a measure of the monetary benefits obtained by an organization over a specified amount of time for a given investment in a training program. ROI can be used both to justify a planned investment and to evaluate the extent to which the desired return was achieved. ROI is calculated by making estimates or obtaining measurements of the costs and benefits associated with a training initiative. Business units can utilize this information and effectively allocate resources to improve performance and ensure organizational success.

COST BENEFIT RATIO (CBR)

CBR = (Total Benefits) / (Total Cost of Training)

A thorough ROI analysis is typically conducted for only 10 to 20 per cent of programs. Computing the ROI of training involves the following four steps:

- **Isolating the Effects of Training**—Requires identification of all key factors that impact employee performance and business outcomes. Such measurements include the performance or level of knowledge before the training initiative. Pre-training data measurements can include frequency of errors, labour hours per unit, unit of productivity, volume of lost sales, or turnover rates.
- **Converting the Effects of Training into Monetary Values**—The effects or benefits of a training program should be identified, qualified, and converted to dollars with input from management. Converting ROI data to monetary value is difficult for many HR professionals. The steps to convert effects of training into monetary value include the following: (a) Focus on the unit of measure, (b) Determine a value for the unit, (c) Calculate the change in performance data, (d) Determine an annual amount for the change, (e) Calculate the total value of the improvement.
- **Calculating the Cost of Training**—Fully loaded costs which include both indirect and direct costs should be calculated for the training program. Sample training costs include course development, loss of revenue while trainees are involved in training activities and travel time.
- **Comparing the Value of Effects to the Incurred Costs**—The ROI formula or equation uses the effects data and the incurred costs as follows:

RETURN ON INVESTMENT (ROI)

$$= \frac{\text{(Total Benefits − Total Cost of Training)}}{\text{(Total Cost of Training)}}$$

According to the *Society for Human Resources Management*, a common difficulty encountered in calculating ROI is determining the shelf-life of the training program. Changes influenced by technology, global competition, legal and regulatory agencies, employee turnover, and other factors make it increasingly difficult to accurately predict the training program's shelf-life.

Saratoga Institute Approach

Elements	Hallmarks
1. Training satisfaction	The degree to which participants are satisfied with the training they have received
2. Learning change	The actual learning that has occurred, with pre-and-post-course instruments
3. Behaviour change	The on-the-job change in behaviour as a result of the training program
4. Organizational change	Did the change in behaviour positively affect the organization?

Principles of Training Evaluation

- Evaluation specialist must be clear of the training program and also about the goals and purposes of evaluation.
- Evaluation should be continuous.
- Evaluation must be specific.
- Evaluation must provide the means and focus for trainers to be able to appraise themselves, their practices, and their products.
- Evaluation must be based on objective methods and standards.
- Realistic target dates must be set for each phase of the evaluation process.

Criteria for Training Evaluation

- Measures of reactions.
- Level of learning.
- Behaviour change patterns.
- Organizational results.

Techniques of Training Evaluation

- To use experimental and Control Groups.
- Longitudinal or Time Series Analysis.
- Sending a questionnaire to the trainees after the completion of the training program to obtain their opinions about the program's worth.
- Assess the costs benefits associated with the program, including those of needs assessment costs, salaries of training department staffs, purchase of equipments, program development costs, evaluation costs, trainers' costs, rental facilities, and trainee wages during the training period.

Impediments to Effective Training

There are many impediments, which make a training program ineffective, these are as follows:

- Management commitment might be lacking or be uneven
- Educational institutions award degrees but graduates lack skills
- Aggregate spending on training is inadequate
- Large-scale poaching of trained workers
- No help to workers displaced because of downsizing
- Employers and B Schools must develop closer ties
- Organized labour can help.

Alternative Training Evaluation RO! Methods

Alternatives to ROI are increasingly being used to measure the success of training programs. Some of these methods include the following:

- **360-Degree Appraisal Feedback Process**—This performance evaluation system uses input from all employee levels (appraisers, supervisors, and peers) to assess performance.
- **Performance-Learning-Satisfaction Evaluation**—This method uses both conceptual components and data processing to assess business results at an organizational level and financial results in terms of monetary ratios. Its creators claim the model has a 2:1 return on investment.
- **The Balanced Scorecard**—This method tracks the key elements of a company's strategy using both financial and operational measures. The balanced scorecard considers four primary questions: How does the company look to the shareholders? (Financial perspective); How do the customers see the company? (Customer perspective); At what must the company excel? (Internal perspective); Can the company continue to improve and create value? (Learning perspective).

Research also highlights other methods to creatively measure training's ROI. Such methods include the following:

- **The Success Case Method**—Demonstrates business value through credible stories that show economic impact on the company. This method relies on short, behaviour-based questionnaires which trainees complete post-training. The survey is designed to test some fundamentals about what the learning was supposed to deliver. Low success cases help the training department determine whether it is the training program or an unrelated issue that may have caused the low impact.
- **Show the Payback**—Measures the payback period of the training initiative to show how long it will take to recover the investment the organization initially made. Two major drawbacks are that such calculations ignore the opportunity cost and the time value of money.
- **Evaluate the Consequences of Not Training**—Demonstrates how not training the workforce will impact the organization in terms of competition, productivity, product marketing, and equal opportunity violations. The evaluator must identify a potential loss or problem and predict its financial or business impact while isolating how the lack of performance will have an impact, as well as the non-performance factors and their costs. Such costs are then compared to the benefits of the training program in terms of estimated costs. This method can be somewhat subjective and is not appropriate for all training programs.
- **80/20 Rule**—Estimates the soft benefits like customer satisfaction with 80 per cent accuracy using only 20 per cent of the effort. Testing and surveys can measure soft benefits like morale and increased employee satisfaction as a result of the training program.
- Merck and Company uses a unique formula, detailed below, to measure the impact of specific training programs. With this model, Merck determined that its average ROI for training programs is 84 per cent and terminated 53 programs that were not producing high enough returns.

GAIN = D x SD$ x JSI x N

Where,

D = shift in performance by average individual undergoing training expressed in standard deviations from pre-training average,

SD$ = the value in dollars of one standard deviation of performance shift,

JSI = percentage of job skills affected by training.

N = number of participants who underwent training.

Training Evaluation: Case Examples

- Johnson and Johnson focuses on trainees' change of behaviour on the job, and makes most of its training decisions based on qualitative data acquired from "worldwide employee surveys," such as six-month post-training self-reports, annual surveys and supervisor questionnaires.

Pre and post-training action plan	
Manager and trainee to complete this column before attending training	Complete this column 6 weeks to 3 months after attending training
Training:	Training:
Date:	Date:
Personal objectives	**Post-training review**
What do you want to learn by attending this training? 1. 2. 3. How will this training develop your ability to do your job? 1. 2. 3.	Comment on the degree to which the training met your objectives ☐ All objectives met by training ☐ Most objectives met by training ☐ Some objectives met by training ☐ Few objectives met by training ☐ No objectives met by training Comment on the degree to which you have used the skills you have learnt ☐ All skills learnt used on-job ☐ Most skills learnt used on-job ☐ Some skills learnt used on-job ☐ Few skills learnt used on-job ☐ No skills learnt used on-job
On-job application What barriers or issues may prevent application of these skills on the job? What strategies could be used to overcome these barriers? (Consider resources, assistance, coaching etc)	Comment on difficulties encountered in applying new skills back on the job ☐ Lack of opportunity to use skills ☐ Lack of time for use of skills ☐ Skills learnt were not relevant ☐ No supervision for skills practice ☐ Lack of coaching or feedback ☐ Other (please comment)
Sign-off	Sign-off
Manager:	Manager:
Trainee:	Trainee:

Training evaluation

Name (optional): ----------------------

Please complete this survey before you leave. Your responses will be used to evaluate this training and plan further training. Thanks for your help.

Course: **Location:** **Date:**

1. List your three main learning objectives in attending this training.
   (a)
   (b)
   (c)
2. To what extent were each of these objectives achieved? Where your expectations have not been met, why was this?
   (a)
   (b)
   (c)
3. What did you find most useful?
   (a)
   (b)
   (c)
4. What did you find least useful?
   (a)
   (b)
   (c)
5. Please list at least three words to describe the style of training delivery.
   (a)
   (b)
   (c)
6. Please rate the training in terms of the following criteria: (Circle one number only)

	Low Medium High
Your participation	1 2 3 4 5 6 7 8 9 10
Your understanding of the content material	1 2 3 4 5 6 7 8 9 10
Relevance to the content of your job	1 2 3 4 5 6 7 8 9 10
Maintained your interest	1 2 3 4 5 6 7 8 9 10
Trainer's knowledge of the subject	1 2 3 4 5 6 7 8 9 10
Creation of appropriate learning climate	1 2 3 4 5 6 7 8 9 10

7. Are there any changes you would recommend should be made to this training?

- Pfizer evaluates training programs with the classic Kirkpatrick levels of evaluation in combination with their Department of Measurement, Evaluation and Strategic Analysis. This department places great importance on business unit performance as a result of training efforts, as well as external evaluation of those efforts.
- Accenture analyzed the ROI of all their training initiatives for 261,000 employees over the history of the company to learn that the ROI of training was 353 per cent. The company used a patent-pending technique which forced out the effects of inflation, market cycle, experience, and employee level to isolate the training impact on a per person margin. Accenture determined a return of $3.53 in net benefits for every dollar invested in training.

TRAINING FEEDBACK FORM

Employee Name:

Department

Employee Code

Name of the training program attended

Dates on which the training was conducted: From Date ______ Month ______ Year ______

To Date ______ Month ______ Year ______

Venue: ______________________

How would you rate the following (on a scale of 1-4 - 1 being the lowest and 4 being the highest rating)?

Course structure

Quality of exercise	1	2	3	4
Duration of the Training program	1	2	3	4
Training environment	1	2	3	4

Course content

Handout and training aids	1	2	3	4
Training coordination and organization	1	2	3	4

Trainer feedback:

Subject knowledge/Conceptual clarity	1	2	3	4	______
Trainer created and maintained an environment for learning	1	2	3	4	______
Rate the trainers training skills and competence	1	2	3	4	______
Presentation methodology	1	2	3	4	______
Guidance and support	1	2	3	4	______

What did you like best about the course/content?

____

____

____

____

What could have been done better?

____

____

____

When you began the training

Learned much more than I expected	☐	Learned somewhat less than I expected	☐
Learned somewhat more than I expected	☐	Learned much less than I expected	☐

Do you think this Seminar/ training would help you in your current job responsibilities?

Definitely to a large extent	☐	Not sure	☐
Probably to some extent	☐	Definitely not	☐

Would you recommend this training to your colleagues?

Definitely	☐	Not certain	☐
Probably	☐	Definitely not	☐

Participant's Signature : Date Month Year

Approved by : Date Month Year

Functional Head / Supervisor

Exhibit: Training Initiatives in HDFC Bank

Skills requirement is cyclical and depends on stage in which the company's business is into. Four years ago, asset skills were relatively rare in the banking industry. Then, as foreign banks got out of many asset businesses, there were lots of people available, changing the market demand and supply. But even now, treasury skills are difficult to find as lots of people are going overseas. There is a dearth of individuals who have relevant skills to manage private and corporate banking. Down the road, there will be a shortage of generalists, as organization starts looking for individuals as solution specialist rather than product specialists. HDFC bank had thus believed in a philosophy of having the tight mix of generalists and specialists.

HDFC's induction program - Swagat - covers products and business of the bank. It is focused on developing skills and values. Four years ago HDFC started an internal employee referral program called 'Karo Sifarish'. It has become one of the company's most preferred channels and contributes significantly to talent acquisition. Earlier the focus was 100% on hard skills. Now, soft skills' training has risen from being non-existent to 30% of the training efforts. HDFC bank organizes various programs including outbound experiential learning, Open Spaces Technology, Personal Effectiveness, Leadership Excellence, art of living, Vedanta, etc. Most training programs are delivered in house, except for highly technical ones such as derivatives. The inhouse training staff comprises of 17 people. People in the smaller cities were missing out as training program was being held in larger metros. The company had started sending its trainers to the remote locations about 15 months back. The 'Back Pack Trainers' take classes after office hours and this has been much appreciated. The cost impact is minimal and the benefits manifold. HDFC Bank had also invited guest lecturers such as Bruce Carlson, CEO, Mangerial Grid and Stephen Haines, Chairman of Center for Strategic Management, to spend half a day with the company's senior management. The company has a strategic tie-up with IIM Ahmedabad for a 9 day program covering economics, quantitative, behavioural leadership, marketing, corporate communications, etc. The company sends 30 of its vice presidents every year as a part of leadership development plan.

(Courtesy Interview with Mandeep Maitra: "People Centric", Banking Frontiers, December 2006 issue, p: 4; www.bankingfrontierscom/coverstory0612_01.pdf)

Exhibit: Training Need Analysis Questionnaire

Organization's name:			
Name of staff member:			
Section:			
General			
1.	Are you a new employee or a long-standing employee of the company?		
2.	How long have you been in your **present** job?		
Confirmation of Current Duties			
3.	Do you have a duty statement for your job?	Yes	No (Go to Q 6)
4.	Is your job accurately described in the duty statement?	Yes (Go to Q 14)	No
5.A	If no, what extra duties do you do that need to be added to your duty statement?		
5.B	What duties are no longer part of your job and can be deleted from your duty statement?		
Job Analysis			
6.	Describe the tasks you regularly perform that are critical to carrying out your job effectively.		
7.	Describe the type of equipment you are required to use (for example, keyboard, machinery, tools of trade, etc.).		

8.	Do you require a high degree of technical knowledge for your job?		Yes No
9.	How do you work? Please circle		
	Alone	Part of a team	Other (specify below)
10.	If you work as part of a team, do you perform the same of different work to members of your team?		
11.	To what extent does your job require you to work closely with other people, such as customers, clients or people in your own organization? Please circle.		
	Very little	Moderately	A lot
12.	How much autonomy is there in your job, i.e, to what extent do you decide how to proceed with your work? Please circle.		
	Very little	Moderately	A lot
13.	How much variety is there in your job, i.e, to what extent do you do different things at work, using several skills and talents? Please circle.		
	Very little	Moderately	A lot
Training Needs			
14.	**To perform your current job:** What training do you still need (either on-the-job or a formal course) to perform your current job competently (e.g, Excel, bookkeeping, English as a second language, etc.)?		
15.	**To perform other jobs in the organization:** What other roles in the organization would you be interested in doing if a vacancy became available (e.g, transfer to another section, supervisor position, etc.)?		
16.	**To perform other jobs in the organization:** What training or experience would be required (e.g, machine operation, negotiation skills, occupational health and safety awareness, etc.)?		

Future Development Needs

17. What are your career aspirations?

18. What training or development do you need to help make this happen (e.g., external degree study, formal meeting procedures, leadership training, etc.)?

Recognition of Prior Learning

19. What training have you attended within the last three years? (This will help identify if any training sessions have been missed or if any refresher training is required.)

20. What training or skills have you acquired outside your current job that may be relevant to the wider organization?

Action Plan

Agreed training and development to be provided over the next 12 months:(Record the details of training courses, on-the-job experiences, buddy systems or mentor arrangements, and include the recommended dates the staff member can expect these to occur.)

Training	Date

Signature of Staff Member	:		**Date :**	
Signature of Supervisor	:		**Date :**	

Exhibit: Training Program Evaluation Form

In order to determine the effectiveness of the program in meeting your needs and interests, we need your input. Please give us your honest reactions, and make any comments or suggestions that will help us to serve you.

Name: ______________________ Date: ____________

Team/Department: ______________________ Course: ______________________

Location of the program: ____________ Instructor: ____________

How many years have you been involved in doing your current or similar job responsibilities?

____

Directions: Please check the appropriate response after each statement.

INSTRUCTOR

The instructor's...	Excellent	More than satisfactory	Satisfactory	Less than satisfactory	Poor
1. Comfort level with the subject matter appeared to be...	☐	☐	☐	☐	☐
2. Answers to my questions were...	☐	☐	☐	☐	☐
3. Clarity in responding to my questions was...	☐	☐	☐	☐	☐
4. Explanations and directions for the class exercises were...	☐	☐	☐	☐	☐
5. Effectiveness in communicating the course content was...	☐	☐	☐	☐	☐
6. Explanation on how to best utilize the job aids was...	☐	☐	☐	☐	☐
7. Checks for understanding were...	☐	☐	☐	☐	☐
8. Ability to keep the session lively and interesting was..	☐	☐	☐	☐	☐
9. Ability to use the visual/teaching aids effectively was...	☐	☐	☐	☐	☐
10. Rapport with the trainees was...	☐	☐	☐	☐	☐
11. My comfort level in asking questions was...	☐	☐	☐	☐	☐

Additional Comments:

Briefly describe the content of the program:

CONTENT

	Agree strongly	Agree somewhat	Neutral	Disagree somewhat	Disagree strongly
1. The courses in this class helped me to apply the skills and or concepts.	☐	☐	☐	☐	☐
2. The exercises/activities gave me sufficient practice.	☐	☐	☐	☐	☐
3. There was an acceptable amount of exercises/activities in this course.	☐	☐	☐	☐	☐
4. The training manual and handouts are valuable as future resources.	☐	☐	☐	☐	☐
5. The training manual and handouts were valuable as learning tools.	☐	☐	☐	☐	☐
6. I feel prepared to go out and perform the skills taught in the class.	☐	☐	☐	☐	☐
7. The Pre and Post tests in this course were accurate and fair.	☐	☐	☐	☐	☐
8. The Pre and Post tests asked questions answered in the training.	☐	☐	☐	☐	☐

What skills or specs did you have difficulty learning or understanding?

Were there areas that you felt were covered too quickly or too slowly?

TRAINING FACILITY

Rate the following items regarding the training facility:	Excellent	More than satisfactory	Satisfactory	Less than satisfactory	Poor
1. Seating arrangement	☐	☐	☐	☐	☐
2. Classroom temperature	☐	☐	☐	☐	☐
3. Lighting	☐	☐	☐	☐	☐
4. Room configuration	☐	☐	☐	☐	☐
5. Learning environment	☐	☐	☐	☐	☐
6. Overall noise level (outside the classroom)	☐	☐	☐	☐	☐

What did you like about it?

What would you improve?

OVERALL

	Excellent	More than satisfactory	Satisfactory	Less than satisfactory	Poor
1. The instructor's ability to help me learn how to use the new skills is…	☐	☐	☐	☐	☐
2. The training course's effectiveness in helping me to achieve the objectives was…	☐	☐	☐	☐	☐

What did you like about the program?

How would you describe this course to others?

What would have improved the program?

What would the ideal class size be for this course? 1–3, 3–5, 5–7 etc.

DEVELOPMENT PROGRAMS

Worker Development Program

It aims to enhance the skill and knowledge of the employees to advance in the company or to accomplish additional job responsibilities. Such programs can enable the organization to have a workforce which can make more contributions and adapt to changing situations. Among these are included on-the-job training and apprenticeship training.

Supervisory Development Program

The supervisory staff needs training most, for they form a very important link in the chain of administration in an organization. The training program for supervisors must be tailor-made so as to fit the needs of an undertaking. The training enables supervisors to cope with the increasing demands of the enterprise in which they are employed and to develop team spirit. Supervisory training aims at:

(a) Helping the present supervisors to improve their performance
(b) Helping present supervisors to prepare for greater responsibilities of the higher levels of the management
(c) Building up the security and status of supervisors
(d) Ensuring their technical and human relations competence with a view to enabling them to know and understand all about the processes operations in which their workers participate.

Exhibit: HDFC Bank uses A Comprehensive Employee Development Approach to Respond to Changing Resource Needs

Rapid growth in a burgeoning new market should be cause for celebration—unless the organization that's growing can't keep up with the demands of an expanding workforce or simplify the management of multiple databases. But Mumbai, India-based HDFC Bank wasn't about to let that happen.

Initially the premier bank in the corporate sector, HDFC Bank began its expansion into the retail market in 1995. Now, as it adds thousands of new customers each day and manages dramatic increases in its retail loan portfolio—22 per cent in 2003 alone—the bank is facing the challenges that come with rapid success.

"Today's competitive environment means that human resources [HR] must refocus away from activities that sap value from the organization and instead focus on achieving outcomes that improve company performance," says C.N. Ram, head of information technology at HDFC Bank. HDFC was already an established leader in eliminating the inefficiency traditionally associated with resource planning and management, and bank management knew just what to do.

"Due to significant growth in the number of our employees over the past few years, we could no longer handle our human capital management on Microsoft Excel spreadsheets and homegrown reports," says Ram. In addition, management understood that high growth rates might have jeopardized product quality, while tension about relative compensation levels between the sales personnel in the branch and operations could have threatened HDFC Bank's culture.

(Courtesy Interview with Mandeep Maitra: "People Centric", Banking Frontiers, December 2006 issue, p: 4; www.bankingfrontierscom/coverstory0612_01.pdf)

Management Development Program

Management Development is a systematic process of growth and development by which the managers develop their abilities to manage the organization in effective ways. It is the result of not only participation in formal courses of instruction but also of actual job experience. It is concerned with improving the performance of the managers by giving them opportunities for growth and development.

Objectives of MDPs

The objectives of management development programs are as follows:

- To overhaul the management machinery
- To improve the performance of managers
- To give the specialists an overall view of the functions of an organization and equip them to coordinate each other's efforts effectively
- To identify the persons with the required potential and prepare them for more senior positions
- To increase the morale and versatility of the members of the management group.
- To keep the executives abreast of the changes and developments in their respective specialties.
- To create the management succession which can take over in case of contingencies
- To improve the thought process and analytical abilities
- To broaden the outlook of the executive regarding his role positions and responsibilities
- To understand economic, social, technical and the conceptual issues.
- To understand the problems of human relations and improve human relation skills
- To stimulate creative thinking.

Steps in the Organization of a MDP

- Analysis of organizational development needs
- Appraisal of present management talents
- Inventory of management manpower
- Planning of individual development programs
- Establishment of development programs

Methods/techniques of MDPs

Managerial Skills	Types of Development Programs/Training Required
1. Decision-making skills	• In-Basket exercise • Business games • Case study method
2. Inter-personal skills	• Role play • Sensitivity training
3. Job knowledge	• On-the-job experience • Coaching and mentoring • Understudy
4. Organizational knowledge	• Job rotation • Multiple management
5. General knowledge	• Special courses • Special meetings • Specific readings
6. Specific individual needs	• Special projects • Committee assignments

Industry Opinion

"Besides a general management perspective and a sense of ownership at al levels, the third element or orientation of leadership is a people development perspective. For leadership at all levels, each one needs to think and act strategically and innovatively in alignment with the company's direction and do all this with a sense that the customer is the ultimate boss. Managers must focus not so much on developing a personal style or charisma but on setting an example by the practice of values, and by becoming role models so that others can act without fear." ....…Venu Srinivasan, Chairman and Managing Director, TVS Motor Company

(*Adapted from his address at the JRD Tata Corporate Leadership Award Lecture held in Delhi in February, 2005*).

(*Courtesy: Indian Management, Vol 44, Issue 4, April, 2005, p: 32.*)

Exhibit: Employee Development Worksheet

CONFIDENTIAL

NAME OF EMPLOYEE		DEPARTMENT	DIVISION
PAYROLL TITLE	WORKING TITLE	DATE HIRED	LENGTH OF TIME IN PRESENT JOB
PERIOD COVERED BY THIS EVALUATION			SUPERVISOR'S NAME AND TITLE
LENGTH OF TIME YOU HAVE SUPERVISED THIS EMPLOYEE ____________			

XYZ (Company Name)

EMPLOYEE DEVELOPMENT WORKSHEET

CHECK ONE
MORE THAN SATISFACTORY
SATISFACTORY
IMPROVEMENT NEEDED
UNSATISFACTORY

JOB RESPONSIBILITIES FOR PERIOD OF EVALUATION	COMMENTS AND OBJECTIVES	M ↓	S ↓	I ↓	U ↓

OVERALL EVALUATION

☐ MORE THAN SATISFACTORY ☐ SATISFACTORY ☐ IMPROVEMENT NEEDED ☐ UNSATISFACTORY

COMMENTS:

FUTURE PLANS: PERFORMANCE GOALS ESTABLISHED BETWEEN EMPLOYEE AND SUPERVISOR

SIGNATURE OF IMMEDIATE SUPERVISOR ________________ DATE ________

EMPLOYEE'S SIGNATURE ________________ DATE ________

(YOUR SIGNATURE INDICATES NEITHER AGREEMENT NOR DISAGREEMENT WITH THE EVALUATION, BUT IT DOES INDICATE THAT YOU HAVE READ THE EVALUATION AND IT HAS BEEN DISCUSSED WITH YOU. IF YOU WISH, YOU MAY COMMENT IN THE SPACE BELOW.)

DEPARTMENT HEAD'S SIGNATURE ________________ DATE __

Exercise Case Study: Recruitment in Hospitals

Several hospitals and large nursing homes in New Delhi, are facing an ongoing shortage of qualified doctors. Although the problem is not new, the high occupancy of the hospitals forces them to use an excessive amount of overtime to cover all shifts and weekends. The doctors keep complaining about high job stress, lack of sleep, work-life imbalance, etc. Newspaper reports several cases of suicides among doctors. Many others keep trying opening in the USA, Canada, UK and even in the Middle East. Others seeking openings in their hometowns or places near their hometowns are moving away at the first available opportunity even with lesser salaries. Still others are opening up their own clinics and earning their livelihood through private practice. Although the shortage of doctors affected all departments of medical practice, it was most acute among medicine specialists, who attended to all day to day outdoor patients.

The shortage has become so critical that even the house surgeons were unable to fill all the requests, prompting still more doctors to quit for better prospects and healthier work-life balance. Several Human Resource Directors of different private and public hospitals in Delhi met together to thrash out a strategy of attracting and recruiting doctors from all over the country to fill the vacant positions.

REVIEW QUESTIONS

Assume you were given the responsibility for developing a recruitment strategy for this consortium of health care organizations:

(a) Identify the major roadblocks you might encounter in actually recruiting these doctors.

(b) What recruitment channels would you use to find and attract qualified applicants? Why?

QUESTION BANK

1. Training programs are frequently the first items eliminated when management wants to cut costs. Why is it so? (BU 2004)
2. "Training in organizations has no value unless there is transfer of training effects". Explain.
3. What are the parameters to be used for evaluating training? Does it have any relevance to training needs identification? Give reasons.
4. Bring out the need, criteria and techniques of evaluation of training results (BU 2004).
5. The basic objective of training is to arrive at a fit between the employee and his job. Discuss.
6. What is the difference between training and development?
7. What is learning? How training leads to effective learning?
8. What do you mean by training needs analysis? Why is it important?
9. What is the difference between on the job and off the job training methods?
10. What is the importance of preparing a training schedule in delivering training?
11. How is training designed?
12. What is the role of trainers in the delivery of training?
13. What is training evaluation? How is it done?
14. Describe the importance of experiential learning in training.
15. What are the different behavioural training programs used in organizations? How are they effective in shaping the personality and attitude of employees in organizations?
16. What is development? How is it helpful for the employees?
17. What are management development programs? How do they facilitate in terms of nurturing managerial and leadership capabilities of employees in organizations?

Internet Exercises

- Suppose you are the MDP manager of a reputed IT firm. Use internet resources to find suitable management development programs for your senior executives that are being conducted by reputed B Schools or organizations like CII or AIMA.
- Go to the website www.stepconsulting.org and summarize your learnings on training and development from the same.
- Prepare a list of websites containing information on training and development and summarize their respective features to your class.

Experiential Learning and Research

- Prepare a training schedule format for a MDP program on strategic management skills for senior managers.
- Develop a questionnaire for evaluating the effectiveness of the induction program given to the freshers in the MBA course of your institute. Instrument and use this questionnaire for real life research.
- Conduct training need survey for the non-teaching staffs of your institute and build up a training program on the basis of the same.

CAREER AND SUCCESSION PLANNING

THEME CASE: RANJIT'S SUCCESS STORY

Ranjit Kumar was sitting on his chair on the **dias** and wondering how time changes so fast. Today he is being invited as a guest of honour in the alumni meet of his college from where he had done his MBA, eight years back. He had just finished his lecture on career planning and was wondering ten years back someday he was the one amongst the audience. Today he is working as the creative head of the advertisement department of a reputed FMCG company in the country with loads of responsibility and people depending on his decisions. Ranjit could still remember how naïve he was on the first few months during his student life as an aspiring MBA graduate. Yet he did his best to clear the CAT exams and get an opportunity in this premier institute to pursue his MBA. The story was a real adorable one for a simple lad like Ranjit but the most interesting one was Ranjit's transformation during the two years of study in the MBA program. Ranjit according to his friends and faculties hardly interacted with anybody, yet he was the most brilliant speaker and creative presenter in the class. Indeed none would have noticed Ranjit's talents until on the eve of the first semester, when Ranjit was sent with the college team for a management fest organized by a reputed B school. Not only Ranjit's creative talents were appreciated, but his presentation was awarded as the best presentation and first prize in the competition. Well that was the beginning. Ranjit not only became confident about what his capabilities were, he became dearer to his faculties. In the second semester he led the students committee ("Student's Professional Body") of his institute into so many creative endeavours. His dissertation project on the advertising strategy of a retail company in the city got lot of attention. Well there was no doubt that Ranjit would score brilliantly in his MBA exams and so would be his placements. He hardly had to wait one day after the end of his final exams for the news of the confirmation of his first job and that in a reputed advertisement and event management company. He worked hard under Mr. Santosh who is still regarded as one of the top "Ad Gurus" in the country and it was Mr. Santosh's mentorship that took his career to higher heights. Ranjit was the spearhead behind most of the event management and promotional campaigns organized by his company for various clients that also gave lot of reputation and recognition as a budding professional in advertisement management.

Ranjit's success according to him was mainly due to his capability of discovering his potential and his unflinching principles for hard work. His family was always supportive right from the beginning. To his teachers he is still the "good boy" with lots of brilliant ideas. His passion towards his job was his greatest strength over the years.

Note: *The name of the characters stated in the case has been kept confidential.*

What is a Career?

As revealed in the theme case, a career is the work a person does in his entire life span. A career is the sequence of jobs that an individual has held throughout his or her working life. Another definition of a career is the sequence of jobs that an individual has held throughout his or her working life. "Career Planning" therefore embraces a person's entire life—the spiritual, social, educational and vocational. It is the process by which one selects career goals and the path to these goals. So when we talk about career we generally mean:

- Career denotes all the jobs that are held during an individual's entire working life.
- It consists of a series of properly sequenced role experiences leading to an increasing level of responsibility, status, power and rewards.
- It represents an organized path taken by an individual across time and space.

- It represents decisions with respect to skill and knowledge upgradation so as to facilitate career growth and development.

Career Related Terms

The following terms are frequently discussed when we speak about careers:

Career Related Terms	Features/Hallmarks
Career Goals	The future positions, responsibilities or achievements one strives to reach as part of his/her career.
Career Path	The sequential pattern of jobs, roles and responsibilities that form a part of the career.
Career Progression	It means making progress in one's career through promotions. It is achieved through constant learning and skill development.
Career Counseling	It is the process involving guiding and advising individuals on their possible career paths and what they must do to achieve higher job responsibilities and tasks.
Mentoring	The process wherein an executive or senior employee serves as a guide, friend, philosopher and confidante to the new entrant.
Career Anchor	The basic drives that give the urge to take up a certain type of career. The best example could be like this when an aspiring marketing professional pursues an advanced diploma in advertising and sales promotions

Stages of Career

A career includes many positions, stages and transitions just as a person's life does. The various stages are as follows:

Stages of Career	Hallmarks
Exploration Stage	This stage starts after completion of formal or professional education from a college or university and involves the transition period from academics to work life. Generally this stage covers the mid twenties of an individual's life. The candidate explores relevant opportunities for a job either with the help of his/her institutions help or those from a job consultant.
Establishment Stage	This stage begins when one individual gets his/her first job. The establishment stage is more of a preparation or learning stage, where an individual accumulates experiences and learnings from his/her employer, colleagues, customers etc. Although this stage might be characterized by committing mistakes; yet it forms an integral part of the learning process of the candidate.
Mid Career	This is the stage which spans from the early or mid 30s to the 50s of an individual's age. This stage may be characterized either by steady and improved performance or may exhibit declining performance. In case the organization or the peer or support groups provide counsel, help or additional training and development-the performance may also increase leading the candidate back on his/her career track.

Contd...

Late Career	Late career can be described as a maturity stage of one's career, where an individual is characterized for attaining a relatively good position and status in the organization where he/she is being employed. The individual at this stage takes up the role of an elder statesperson.
Decline Stage	In this the individual prepares himself/herself for retirement.

Career Anchors: Career anchors can be described as the basic drives that give the urge to take up a certain type of career. Career anchors provide security and stability of career, autonomy and independence of action, and facilitate creativity, innovation and risk-taking in individuals. These are of the following types namely:

- **Technical Competence** – continuous learning and updating one's expertise in a technical or specialized area such as quality control, advertising, public relations etc.
- **Managerial Competence** – opportunities for higher responsibility, decision-making, control and influences over others.

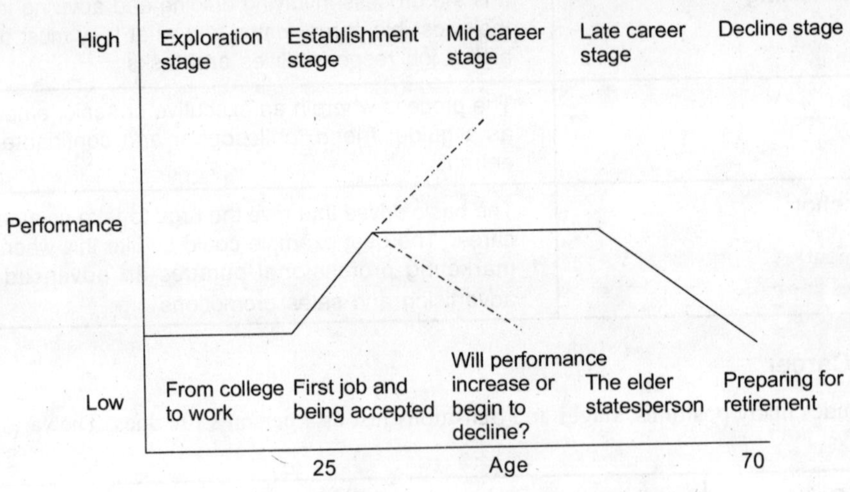

Fig. 3.15: Stages in a career

(V.S.P. Rao: "Human Resource Management, Text and Cases", 2nd Edition, Excel Books, p: 239)

What is Career Planning?

Career planning is the systematic process by which one selects career goals and the path to these goals. From the organization's viewpoint it means helping the employees to plan their career in terms of their capacities within the context of organization's needs.

Career planning is the life-long process a person goes through to learn about himself (his purpose, personality, interests, skills and talents) develop a self-concept, learn about careers, and work situations and then make a career choice based on information gathered while developing coping and social skills. It involves designing an organizational system of career movement and growth opportunities for employees from the employment stage to the retirement stage. It is in fact a managerial technique for mapping out the entire career of young employees.

The major focus of career planning is on assisting the employees achieve a better match between personal goals and the opportunities that are available in the organization. It also includes the skills a person employs in finding and keeping the job that is right for him or her. The major focus of Career Planning should be on matching personal goals and opportunities that are realistically available. A term worth defining is "**Career Path**". A Career path is a flexible line of movement through which an employee may move during employment with an organization.

Career Plan for MBA Graduate

1. Management trainee	22
2. Asst. manager	25
3. Deputy manager	30
4. Manager	35
5. Deputy general manager	40
6. General manager	45

Fig. Career plan for a MBA graduate

One can think of career planning as building bridges from one's current job/career to next job/career. Without the bridge, one may easily stumble or lose direction, but with the bridge there is safety and direction.

Theme Reading: High Career Prospects in ITES and Telecom Sectors

According to staffing company Teamlease's Employment Outlook Report for the period between January and March 2008, the two sectors have scored the best employment outlook index for the quarter. The Employment Outlook Index for the January-March 2008 had been reported to be 80 index points, a rise of two index points by the previous quarter. This index is computed as the difference in the proportion of respondents who report an increase in hiring needs over the next three months. The study had also indicated that Employment Outlook Index points of Bangalore, Chennai, Ahmedabad and Hyderabad was on the increasing side, whereas big metros like those of Mumbai, Delhi, Kolkata and even Pune saw declines.

(Courtesy: "Job Outlook high in ITES, telecom sector: Report", The Economic Times, 16th January 2008, p. 6.)

Features of Career Planning

- It is a process of developing human resources rather than an event.
- It is a continuous process due to an ever changing environment.
- It is not an end in itself but a means of managing people to obtain results.
- It is the responsibility of an organization to provide guidance and counseling to its employees in planning their careers and in developing and utilizing their knowledge and skills.
- The basic aim is integration of individual and organizational needs.

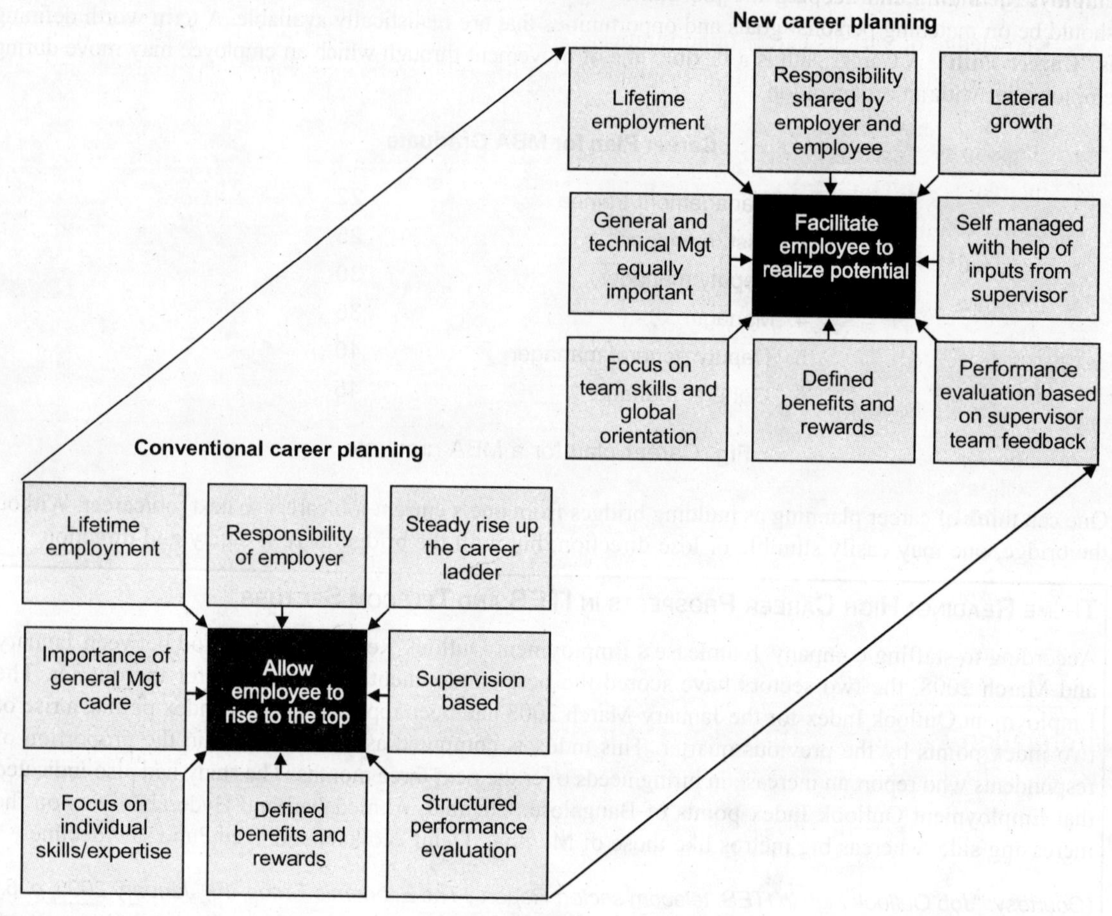

Fig. 3.16: Career planning models

(*Courtesy: Business Today, January 7–21, 1996, pp. 147–148*)

Need for Career Planning

Every employee has a desire to grow and scale new heights in his workplace continuously. If there are enough opportunities, the employee can pursue his career goals and exploit his potential fully. He feels highly motivated when the organization shows him a clear path as to how he can meet his personal ambitions while trying to realize corporate goals.

Objectives of Career Planning

The principal objectives of career planning are as follows:

- To attract and retain the right type of persons in the organization.
- To map out careers of various categories of employees suitable to their ability and willingness
- To ensure better use of human resources through more satisfied and productive employees.
- To have a stable workforce by reducing turnover and absenteeism.
- To increase the utilization of managerial reserves within an organization.
- To improve motivation and morale of employees.

Advantages of Career Planning

- Knowledge of various career opportunities
- Helps to select the career which is suitable to his lifestyle, preference, family environment and self development
- Helps to identify talented employees
- Internal promotion, up gradation and transfers boost up motivation and morale
- Lowers employee turnover
- Enhances job satisfaction
- Improves employees' performance

Relation between Career Planning and Human Resource Planning

Human Resource Planning	Career Planning
Manpower Planning provides an inventory of skills and potentials available within an organization.	Career Planning determines who (on the basis of Performance and Potential) could be groomed for higher level assignments, where, when and how (i.e. after what kind of training).
Manpower Planning provides information about the human resources available within the organization for expansion, growth and technological innovations.	Career Planning only tells as to who could succeed in case of retirement, death, resignation, etc. of existing personnel.

Information Provided by Manpower Planning for Effective Career Planning

The following are the important information provided by manpower planning for effective career planning:

- Inventory of human resources
- Manpower needs in terms of number, type, skills, levels and time
- Changes in functions and activities, two, five or ten years hence.
- Nature and extent of behavioural changes required to meet manpower needs.
- Availability of human resources within and outside the organization, training opportunities, training resources and training time.

Exhibit: Career Planning and Development Strategies in Ernst and Young (India)

The global consulting firm uses the same career development strategy in India that it uses elsewhere. Primarily, it seeks to align individual aspirations with organizational, business and functional goals, using the formal assessment system to check for skill gaps and career potential. While designing training tools, things that are given serious attention are past performance, future potential, the individual skill sets and competencies of each manager, and the need of the company. However, the firm often takes the help of professional trainers brought in from Ernest and Young Worldwide, or relevant institutions to design specific training programs for different categories and levels of managers.

Career Planning in Hyundai Motors (India)

Most executive working in Hyundai Motors (India) is middle level recruits from different industries who have been chosen on the basis of their track records – a factor who influence pervades the company's career planning and development initiative. The company aims to convert these managers into "achievers" for Hyundai, with attributes like mental toughness, professional competence and an ambition to advance.

The HR department devises interventions keeping these goals in mind. The HR functionaries are expected to look at the development process holistically. The company also conducts a 3-day process lab where the system is discussed using case studies.

Steps in Career Planning

The steps in career planning are as follows:

- Preparation of Personnel Inventory – status, duties, qualifications, age, aptitude, ability and acceptability (surplus or shortage). HR planning forms the strong foundation of this stage.
- Identifying Career Needs – (HR Manager may assist) This stage involves identifying individual career needs and assessing the potential of the candidates so as to utilize the same for identifying areas of development and growth.
- Identifying career opportunities in terms of responsibilities and positions within the organization based on individual talents and capabilities.
- Matching of Employee's Aspirations with Career Opportunities
- Formulating and Implementing Career Planning Strategies
    - Changes in the career systems by creating new career paths
    - Changing employee needs and aspirations – to help scale down unrealistic goals and/or creating new aspirations
    - Seeking new basis of integration through problem solving, negotiations and compromise
    - Training and development to meet individual and organizational needs
- Reviewing Career Plans

How to manage career planning in an organization: The career planning process can be managed in the following ways:

(*a*) ***Identifying individual needs and aspirations*:** Most individuals do not have a clear cut idea about their career aspirations, anchors and goals. The HR professionals must therefore help an employee by providing as much information as possible showing what kind of work would suit the employee most, taking his skills, experience, and aptitude into account. Such assistance is extended through workshops/seminars while the employees are subjected to psychological testing, simulation exercises etc. The basic purpose of this exercise is to help an employee form a clear view about what he should do to build his career within the company. Workshops and seminars increase employee interest by showing the value of career planning. They help employees set career goals, identify career paths and uncover specific career development activities.

(*b*) ***Analyzing career opportunities*:** Once career needs and aspirations of employees are known, the organization has to provide career paths for each position. Career paths show career progression possibilities clearly. They indicate the various positions that one could hold over a period of time, if one is able to perform well. Career paths change over time, of course, in tune with employee's needs and organizational requirements.

(*c*) ***Aligning needs and opportunities*:** After employees have identified their needs and have realized the existence of career opportunities the remaining problem is of alignment. This process consists of two steps: first, identify the potential of employees and then undertake career development programs with a view to align employee needs and organizational opportunities. Through performance appraisal, the potential of employees can be assessed to some extent. Such an appraisal would help to reveal employees who need further training, employees who can take up added responsibilities etc. After identifying the potential of employees certain developmental techniques such as special assignments, planned position rotation, supervisory coaching, job enrichment, understudy programs can be undertaken to update employee knowledge and skills.

(*d*) ***Action plans and periodic reviews*:** The matching process would uncover gaps. These need to be bridged through individual career development efforts and organization supported efforts from time to time. After initiating these steps, it is necessary to review the whole thing every now and then. This will help the employee know in which direction he is moving, what changes are likely to take place, what kind of skills are needed to face new and emerging organizational challenges. From the organizational view point, it is necessary to find out how employees are doing, what are their goals, and aspirations, whether the career paths are in tune with individual needs and serve the overall corporate objectives etc.

(*e*) ***Use of employee interest inventories*:** Assessment centres and HR departments of many organizations are frequently using employee interest inventories for managing their career paths. One such interest inventory is known as the "Strong Vocational Interest Bank (SVIB) which was first developed by K. Strong Jr. Later this interest bank was modified by G. Frederic Kuder and the new interest inventory was based on employee interests with respect to the mechanical, clerical, scientific and persuasive activities of employees in their organizations. Another inventory frequently used for measuring employee interests as well as skills is the Campbell Interest and skill Survey (CISS). It can be used not only to assist employees in exploring their career paths and career options but also to help organizations develop their employees or to reassign them because of major organizational changes. The following matrix can be used to depict combinations of employee career interests and skills.

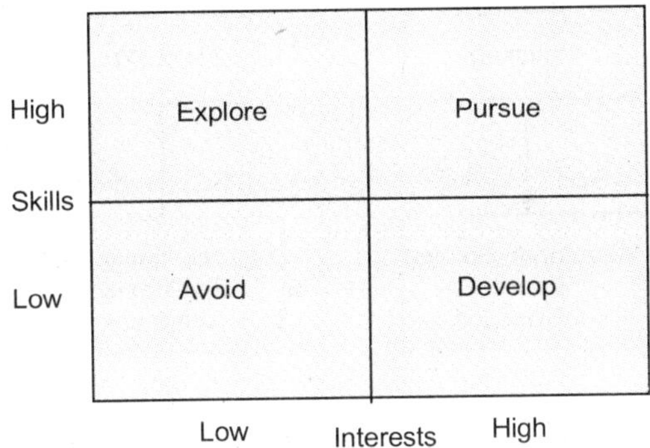

Fig. 3.17: Combinations of employee career interests and skills

Requirements of Effective Career Planning

- Top management support
- Growth and expansion
- Clear goals
- Proper selection
- Motivated and hardworking staff
- Proper age balance
- Management of career stress
- Fair promotion policy
- Adequate publicity

THEME READING: CAREER GROWTH IN IBM INDIA

IBM India is an organization which recognizes employees with leadership potential early in their career, and a structured path is carved out for them, with special developmental activities. It also focuses on leadership development at all levels and not just at the top including women's leadership and diversity leadership. Various rotational assignments are provided to employees identified as potential leaders like Blue opportunities. And these are not limited to country or region level, but exposure is provided at the global level. For example, a fresher can be identified as high potential just after 2 years in IBM, and sent on assignment to IBM headquarters in Armonk where they are exposed to the top management of corporation to gain a deeper insight into leadership skills and styles. In essence, it tries to combine the best of local and global skills and best practices.

(*Courtesy: Indian Management, Vol. 47, Issue: 1, January 2008, p. 24*)

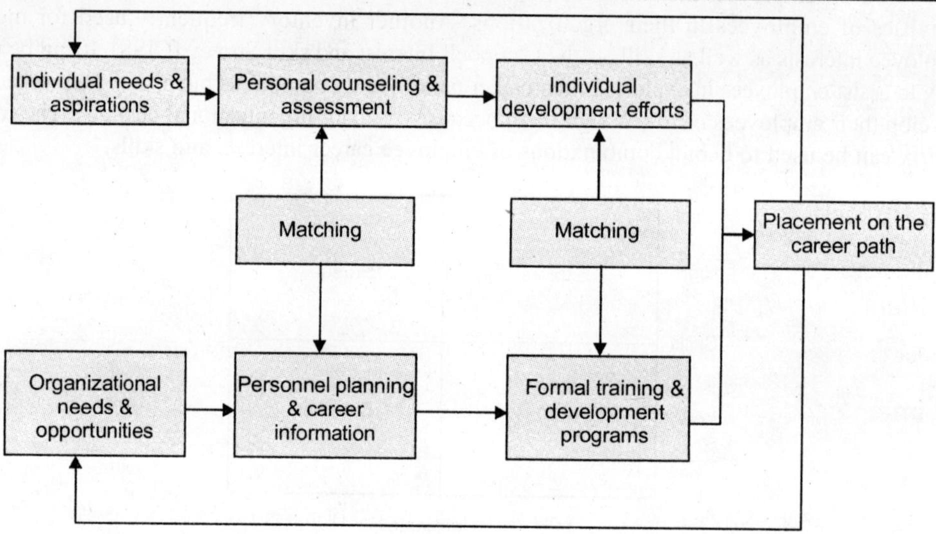

Fig. 3.18: Career planning process

Individual Career Planning	Human Resource Planning
Occupational and organizational choice ↓	The way the organization attracts, recruits and orients new talents in the organization
Job assignment choice ↓	The way the organization matches individual interest and talents with opportunities
Performance and development planning review ↓	The way the organization helps individuals perform effectively and develop capabilities
Retirement	The way the organization helps individuals prepare for satisfying secure retirement

Fig. 3.19: The career planning process and management

Effective Career Planning: Systematic career planning efforts offer innumerable benefits to both the individuals as well as to the entire organization. To ensure successful career planning, a number of steps should be taken, these include:

- **Support:** Career planning efforts must receive consistent support, commitment and assistance from the top management of the organization.
- **Goals:** The corporate goals must be laid down clearly in terms of career development opportunities in the organization.
- **Reward-performance:** Employees must be willing to expand their abilities, trainers must be willing to coach, counsel and share their knowledge with the employees. There must be appropriate rewards for people from both sides who show promise.
- **Placement:** Every effort must be made to put employees on jobs that are in tune with their capabilities. If a talented employee is put on the routine job, he will quit in frustration.
- **Career Paths:** The career paths for different types of employees must be laid down clearly. First the organization should track promotions for talented employees, seniors could be used on jobs requiring experience and judgement, juniors could be used for jobs that demand routine application of rules and procedures etc.
- **Continuous Tracking:** Career planning efforts should be carried out on a continuing basis keeping the changing needs of the employees and the organization in mind. A record of career movements of employees could be generated and maintained by the effective use and implementation of a HRIS.
- **Publicity:** Everyone should be aware of the career opportunities within the organization.

Career Planning Tools and Techniques

The popular career planning instruments used by organizations and HR departments are as follows:

Strong Interest Inventory (SII)

The SII is based on the idea that individuals are more satisfied and productive when they work in jobs or at tasks that they find interesting, and when they work with people whose interests are similar to their own. The SII measures an employee's interest in a wide range of occupations, occupational activities, hobbies, leisure activities, and types of people. These interests are compared to thousands of individuals who report being happy and successful in their jobs.

Myers-Briggs Type Indicator (MBTI)

The MBTI is the most widely used personality assessment in the world. It offers a foundation for understanding the ways people think, communicate and interact. The MBTI will assist employees in identifying occupations that will be challenging and more interesting, work environments that are satisfying, effective work relationships, and leadership and interpersonal communication styles.

Using a SWOT Analysis in the Career Planning Process

SWOT analysis, a key tool in the strategic planning process can also be applied to career planning. A SWOT analysis focuses on the internal and external environments, examining strengths and weaknesses in the internal environment and opportunities and threats in the external environment. Imagine your SWOT analysis to be structured like the table below:

INTERNAL	Employee strengths	Employee weaknesses
EXTERNAL	Opportunities in an employee's career field	Threats in an employee's career field

Fig. 3.20: SWOT analysis for employee career planning

After **SWOT analysis** an attempt should be made so as to identify the career objectives, marketing strategies and action programs needed to be taken.

Limitations of Career Planning

- Not suitable for small organizations and particularly for ownership ventures
- Not suitable for unskilled and semi-skilled jobs (like what reported for employees working in the garments industry)
- Long-term planning not feasible due to financial constraints and unfavourability of the business environment (economic conditions)
- Political intervention and union pressurization
- Careers in some sectors do not have much scope for advancement
- Technological and economic factors may lead to declining stage to some career

Exhibit: Tied Agency Career Advancement Opportunities in ICICI Prudential Life Insurance

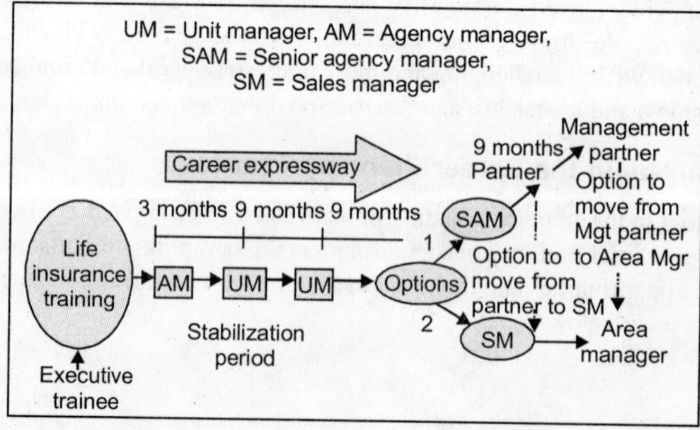

Career Advancement and Growth

Every organization has its unique career advancement and growth policy. The above figure depicts the career advancement opportunities in ICICI Prudential Life Insurance. Although for an insurance service organization, employee growth is a must but in case of the pharmaceutical giant Dr. Reddy's lab growth is not guaranteed, rather it has to be earned by self development and learning. Instead of this the company strongly advocates **nurturing meritocracy and talent development**.

Dr. Reddy's lab offers multiple job and career tracks through its internal job mart, the **'Career Centre'** and thereby continuously engage its employees through dialogue and feedback. The essence of the company's performance-management program, **PerfECT** (Performance Enhancement and Coaching Tool) further supports this career advancement initiative of the organization. The company supports its managers and transform them from bosses into coaches and mentors.

The company does not even hesitates to take risks with its talents. This is achieved by constantly challenging them with unconventional opportunities in the organization. The management trusts them through their setbacks. The company recognizes managerial and employee contributions in their accomplishments and help them to build their own careers and success.

Fig. 3.21: The motto of career advancement initiatives in Dr. Reddy's lab

Further, people have always been the strength of Dr. Reddy's, and the reason for its success. Recognizing this, the company gives great importance to providing a work culture that allows its members the space to learn, innovate, experiment and grow. It places a premium on innovation and gives its people the freedom to think differently. It also encourages individuals to take on increased responsibility and thereby contribute to the growth of the company.

***Equal Employment Opportunity in career advancement*:** For an organization like Dr. Reddy's lab the organization's reputation is well established as an equal-opportunity employer. The company believes in the philosophy of building careers rather than providing jobs to people. The management strongly advocates that a good career means different things to different people and hence it offers challenges very early on so as to make people capable for achieving any type of work related or behavioural challenges. The company realizes that learning from mistakes builds capability and by empowering its people it could facilitate holistic learning and development.

At Dr. Reddy's, career is not just about vertical growth. It is enhancing true competence of its employees. It is about taking intelligent risks with people. It is about trust and achieving breakthrough performance.

THEME READING: CAREER DEVELOPMENT THROUGH TECHNICAL LADDER IN TEXAS INSTRUMENTS

Texas Instruments (TI), winner of the Great Place to work survey in 2003 and 2004, have found an innovative strategy catering to the management development of their leaders and senior executives. Through a tool known as "The Technical Ladder", Texas Instruments provide a parallel growth track for their technical employees like engineers who get recognized for their technical contributions and receive mentoring and support to grow into technical leadership roles. TI's technical offer similar career progression, but it is the best implemented. In the last three years, over 70% of 200 patents filed from TI India have been contributed by people on the Tech ladder.

(*Courtesy: "The Parallel Track", The Economic Times, 9th January, 2008, p. 7*)

Application of Tech Ladder: As compared to a managerial role, where the employee had to worry about managing a team, possessing people management skills, resource planning and budgeting, engineers on the technical ladder can devote most of their time to solving day to day technical problems. A technical ladder has six steps and the progression moves from a member to the senior member, distinguished member, fellow and then finally senior fellow of the technical staff. Only 1% of TI employees are chosen as fellows. A fellow on the technical ladder is equivalent to the Vice president position in organization. For example, Mr. Mahesh Mehendale, the only fellow from TI India, is the one of the few people who is involved in deciding the strategic road map of the new products to come from TI. The technical ladder also had helped TI to evaluate and assess the level of innovation and differentiation that the engineer brings to the organization.

Basis of Technical Leadership Selection: The technical leadership selection at TI depends on the following criteria:

- Innovation in products leading to business impact
- How the person helps to grow the technical pool in his/her team
- How the person had contributed in order to enhance TI's image in external environment like industry and forums.

Tech Ladder as a Motivation Tool: The technical ladder also ensures not only monetary rewards for a candidate, but instills a sense of self satisfaction and recognition from the organization.

SUCCESSION PLANNING

THEME READING: SUCCESSION PLANNING IN ICICI BANK

It has to be succession planning. The institution may be 50 years old, but it views youth as its key strength. "Either you should have young people in your team or have experienced people who can think young," says K.V. Kamath, CEO, ICICI Bank. Kamath considers his "young leadership team" a global differentiator. Grooming young managers, however means having in place robust succession planning. At ICICI Bank, that's driven top down. The process runs through the organizational hierarchy, with the performance management system being the foundation of the entire process. Performance appraisal is done by a superior two levels above in the hierarchy, and the strengths and weaknesses of each individual are identified. Kamath personally knows top 150 people well – their strengths, weaknesses and skill profiles. The same runs through the entire organization to M1 level. The strategy is to build layers of competence. Once the fast trackers are identified, the bank gives differential compensation and monitors their performance. Managing and grooming "young leadership team" is not an easy task. To address soft skills and leadership development needs of young leaders, HR runs a four day leadership development capability program. This is followed by advanced e-learning modules that each of these leaders has to complete at specified time intervals. The upshot of Kamath's succession strategy: ICICI Bank has one of the youngest senior leadership teams in the world.

(*Courtesy: Jayakar, R., (2005): "Schumi in a suit", Business Today, Vol. 14, No. 6, March 27th, 2005, p. 88.*)

A succession plan is meant to ensure filling of key positions in an organization in case of possible vacancies. Succession plans can operate from within or from outside the organization. Any succession plan is essential for the survival and sustainability of an organization.

Succession planning refers to the process of developing the second line of employees, managers and executives for taking up higher roles in the organization in case of manpower requirement caused by vacancies or sudden expansion of the business. This enables organizations to rely on internal recruitments for various organizational roles rather than solely depending on external sources of hiring. This also ensures that the organization does not face a major disruption when any of its executives move out of their existing roles due to various reasons like transfer, relocation, resignation etc. The purpose of succession planning is to identify and develop people to replace current incumbents in key positions in cases of resignation, retirement, growth etc. A good succession planning system ensures smooth transition of a new incumbent into the role when the previous role holder moves out of the particular role in the organization.

Definition

Succession planning is the strategic, systematic and deliberate effort to develop competencies in potential leaders through proposed learning experiences such as targeted rotations and educational training in order to fill high-level positions without favoritism.

Succession planning is a structured process involving the identification and preparation of second line of capable employees, managers and executives to fill up possible vacancies in the organizations and support its expansion aspirations.

Elements of Succession Planning

As succession planning deals with developing future managers and leaders, it should constantly involve:

- Planning changes and habituating the same amongst the people
- Identify the potential of the existing employees and managers and utilizing the same for their further growth and development
- Ensuring continuity of leadership and executive positions
- Identifying gaps in existing talent pool

Industry Quote

"Wipro is a professionally-managed company. At any point of time and for all levels at least three people are being groomed for succession."…. *Wipro of chairman Azim Premji on the issue of succession in the company, quoted in Business Today.*

(Courtesy: Indian Management, April, 2005, Vol. 44, Issue, 4, p. 96)

Relation between Career Planning and Succession Planning

- Career planning and succession planning appear to be similar but not synonymous. Career planning is concerned with the present status of an organization's employees, whereas succession planning deals with the futuristic needs of the organization.
- Career planning covers all levels of employees whereas succession planning is generally meant for managers and higher level of executives.
- Succession plan involves identification of vacancies that are likely to occur in the higher levels and locating the probable successors. Career plans are meant for all employees in the organization.

- Succession planning facilitates continuity of the organization. Career plans help employees to realize their individual aspirations related to their career goals.
- Career planning may consist of charts showing the career paths of different categories of employees showing how they can advance up in the organization. Succession planning is purely internal to the organization and hence strictly an issue of high confidentiality to the HR department.
- Succession plan consists of developing succession charts for a particular position and they depend strictly upon the HR policies and practices of an organization.

Industry Opinion

"Bharti Airtel has a succession planning exercise for managers. We look for traits that include entrepreneurship and the ability to think big". Mr. Krish Shankar, Director, HR, Bharti Airtel.

(Courtesy: Indian Management, Vol. 47, Issue: 1, January 2008, p. 32.)

Challenges of Succession Planning

Paul C Reilly, Chairman of Korn/Ferry International, the global executive search firm and provider of leadership development solutions, believes that globally most companies are poor in their succession planning. Though in management case literature most authors frequently quote the example of organizations like GE who have mastered the art, majority of the industry captains are still in dilemma how to manage succession planning. Some of the challenges in succession planning are as follows:

- Even though corporations want to give their managers broad experiences by moving them in the career ladder in the organization, they restrain themselves in doing so by prefering to join a new organization with a better offer.
- Many companies had also been reported to suffer for taking out a member from a managerial team for his/her promotion. Although the individual selected for promotion gains, on the other hand the team without that key person suffers, as most of the time organizations do not have the right replacement.
- The size of the corporation also matters a lot. The smaller the organization, the easier it is to ensure effective leadership development and succession planning. Further high growth rate for organizations also makes it difficult for the management to cater succession planning.
- Many companies have geometric training which might not help the real cause of succession planning
- Many companies assess the top 300–400 people and put them in the right teams and help them develop leadership. If every company nurtured the top 10–15% of the managers to build future leaders, it is half the job done. Organizations must keep a regular check up on the people turnover and every manager must be given the task of retention.
- Succession planning in family run businesses is difficult and the major decisions with respect to the top management and the organization depend on the chairman or managing director positions, which are occupied by the family head.

Adapted from S. Lakshmi (2008): "The challenges of succession planning", Indian Management, Vol. 47, Issue: 1, January 2008, p. 27.

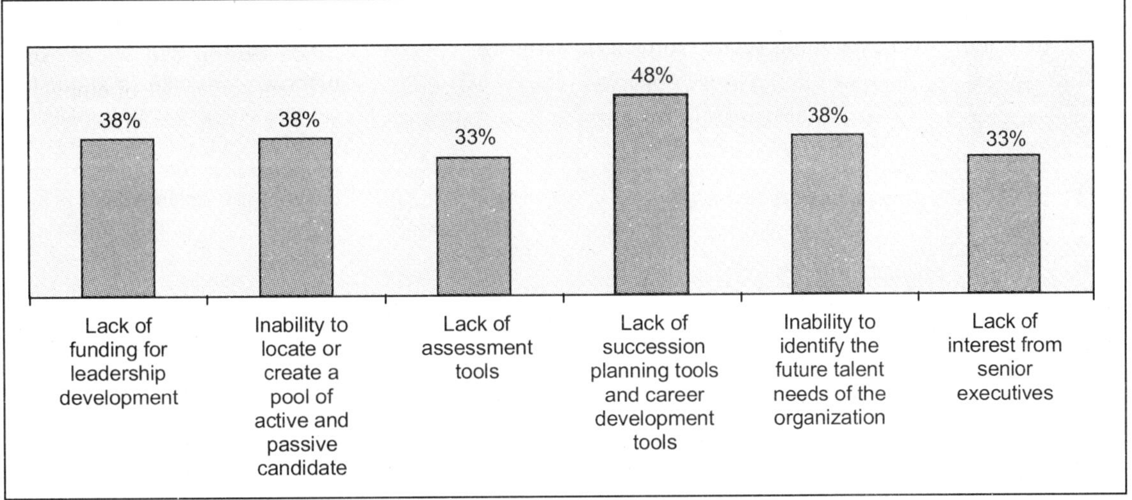

Fig. 3.22: Challenges in succession planning

(*Source: Aberdeen Group, September 2006*)

Traditional Succession Plan	The Succession Plan of the Future
Consider the key positions in today's organization and the skills required in each	Use the traditional succession plan as the staring point
Takes into consideration of the inventory of the talent existing in the organization	Emphasizes upon visualizing what the organization would look like in the next five years
Decides whether the organization has a successor for each key position	Determines what new skills the organization needs for a particular position Determines would be ready for succession
Determines where the development or coaching is required	Determines what view is required in today's perspective in terms of:· • Career management and talent retention • Management development • Recruitment and release of talents • Performance management • Knowledge management
Focuses on the initiative taken by the organization in terms of hiring new talents	Focuses on the initiative taken by the organization in terms of hiring new talents for future requirements of the organization

THEME READING: SUCCESSION PLANNING IN PRACTICE

Charlie Bell's ascension to the top spot at McDonald's within hours of Jim Cantalupo's death reflected well on an organization that had its house in order, particularly when compared – as it inevitably was – with Coca Cola's simultaneous travails. Similarly, NBC's early, orderly announcement that Brian Williams would replace network news anchor Tom Brokaw stands in stark relief of CBS's public uncertainty over Dan Rather's successor. Most important thing is that companies can do to improve succession is to bolster their leadership development and focus on those very rare people in their ranks who might one day be CEO.

"Succession planning helps the company take a strategic approach to leadership development, employee skill assessment and perhaps even more important, preserving critical organizational knowledge"

Dr Kashmira Pagdiwalla
Director (HR Operations)IBPL

"The key impediments that one faces during the succession planning exercise is about the clarity of business and business growth in the long-term, as well as designing the right structure to meet the business plans"

Rajan Dutta
President-HR
Lupin Limited

(Courtesy: Charan, R., (2005): "Do you have succession plan?" Indian Management, Vol. 44, Issue: 4, p. 26.)

Matching Succession Planning, Individual Career Plans and Organizational Career Management

Individual career plans must be matched with organizational career management systems in order to address issues ranging from retention to employee satisfaction and performance management. The succession planning system must be integrated with the organizational career management system to ensure that second line employees can move into higher roles. This would contribute to satisfying their career aspirations while fulfilling organizational talent requirements.

Industry Opinion

"Women can be a force when they work together.... At some point, all technical people step out to staff positions, but we neglect to connect out people to their profession. That's one of the more serious issues that I would like to change." **Frances Allen,** IBM Fellow Emeritus.

(Courtesy: The Economic Times, 9th January 2008, p. 7)

Exhibit: A Succession Planning Model

1. Communicate Possible Opportunities	2. Identify Who Is Interested
• Inform employees of the possible job opportunities that are anticipated over the designated time period (e.g., next three years).	• Open it up. Give employees the opportunity to indicate interest in possible job openings and willingness to participate in succession planning activities.
• Communicate what key competencies are needed for those jobs. That is, what level of demonstrated skills and knowledge is management looking for in potential candidates for these jobs?	• Clarify that participation in succession planning is not a guarantee of advancement. However, participation could help one's chances.
• Inform employees of the succession planning process that the organization intends to use (e.g., the steps in this model).	

Contd...

3. Assess Competency Readiness

- Assess individuals' readiness to assume possible job openings for which they have indicated interest.
- That is, compare the employee's present competency level to that required of the anticipated opening. Identify competencies that need development to help ready the employee for that job or occupation.
- It is advisable to use an assessment instrument that actively engages the employee as well as the supervisor in determining the employee's competency levels.

4. Prepare Development Plans

- Together with the employee, prepare an individual development plan that outlines specific activities that the employee engage in to develop needed competencies. Include a timetable with milestones for assessing progress.
- The list of activities and timetable should be reflected in the employee's EDPP.
- In addition to individual plans, it may make sense to have a group development plan applicable to core competencies for a particular occupation level that all interested employees should participate in.
- Consultation in preparing training plans and determining appropriate activities is available through the Department of Personnel's Training and Development Services.

5. Provide Development Opportunities

- Help the employee follow through with the development plan by setting up training options and providing realistic time to participate in the training activities indicated in the employee's development plan.
- The employee should also take personal responsibility to take the initiative and seek out activities that will help develop the targeted competencies. This display of initiative and follow through can show that the employee is serious about succession and may, in itself, be a key competency.
- Training options go well beyond the traditional classroom setting and do not have to be costly. Examples of development activities include: mentoring, job shadowing, task force participation, special projects/assignments, Internet and journal research, conferences, time-limited job rotations, video/audio tapes, committee participation, etc.

6. Formalize Eligibility

- For general service classified positions, employees typically must get on the appropriate job register to be formally eligible.
- Avenues to increase flexibility to formalize eligibility include:
- Use "until further notice" recruitment announce-ments so that employees can submit their application at any time
- Use desirable, not minimum qualifications
- Streamline selection procedures – avoid using complicated multiple choice exams
- Use the "in-training" program that allows bringing the employee in at a lower level with automatic advancement to the higher level
- Use competency based classification structures
- Hiring procedures could be made flexible and established by a hiring agency.

CAREER DEVELOPMENT

Career development refers to "the outcomes of actions on career plans as viewed from both individual and organizational perspectives" (Gutteridge, 1986)[2]. The outcomes desired by organizations include achieving the best match between people and jobs. Individuals' desired outcomes range from status to job flexibility to monetary rewards, depending upon the situation.

Career Development: Career development initiatives in organizations are necessary for the following reasons:

- Essential for implementing career plans
- Undertaken by individual employees and the organization to meet career aspirations and job requirements
- Every employee must accept his responsibility for development
- Career planning and organizational career planning will prove really useful if they are properly integrated

The following figure depicts a simple approach towards career development in organizations.

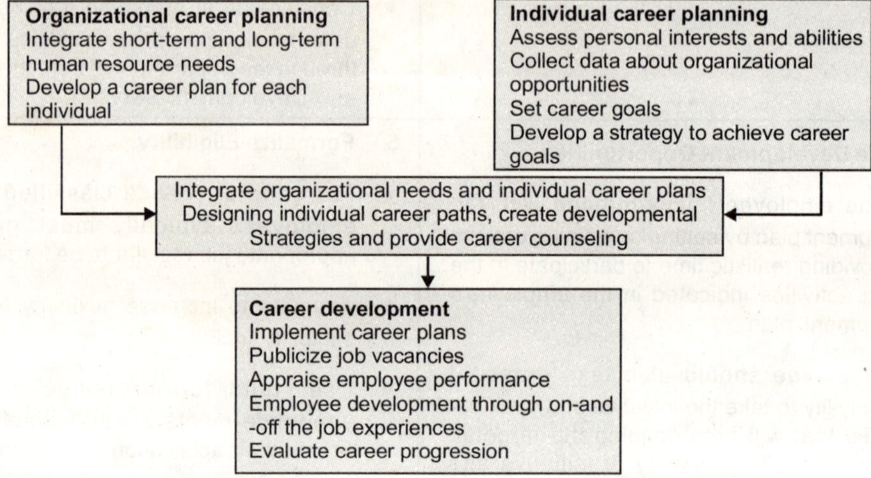

Fig. 3.23: A model of career development

Elements of Career Development

The career development process in organizations should have the following characteristic elements, namely:

- Career Need Assessment
- Developing and Publishing Career Development Opportunities
- Need-Opportunity Alignment
  - (a) Management by Objectives
  - (b) Career Counseling
- Monitoring Career Moves

Importance of Career Development

Both external and internal factors influence the need for career development. Among these factors, Slavenski and Buckner (1988)[1] list the following:

- The need to identify and forecast human resource needs
- Social and demographic trends
- The changing nature of work
- Changing types of jobs
- Multicultural work force
- Worker productivity
- Technological changes and decreasing advancement opportunities
- Organizational philosophies and practices

Employers are motivated to establish career development programs because such programs are seen as an effective response to various HR problems, because top managers prefer to promote existing employees and to ensure a good fit between the work and the worker, and because employees have expressed interest in career development as a benefit (Gutteridge, 1986)[2].

Career Management Process

The career management process provides a framework for career development practices in an organization. Each of the steps in the management process corresponds to career development strategies that help both managers and employees maximize career growth in a given organization (Slavenski and Buckner, 1988)[1]. These steps are as follows:

Hire or promote: Organizations emphasizing on this strategy focus on assessing the candidates and hiring or promoting those individuals whose skills and interests' best match with that of the job and the organization.

Orient or communicate: This step involves orienting the new employees regarding what is expected, what the organizational culture is like, and what the value systems are. Some companies establish mentoring programs to assist with this task.

Observe performance: Employee performance is measured with reference to performance expectations. Feedback is provided and development related areas are communicated.

Manage performance: Employees are rewarded for their accomplishments and achievements. Positive aspects of performance are emphasized and reinforced by reward schemes.

Develop employees: Various tools can be used for employee development, including in-service training, career planning workshops and counseling and assessment services. At this stage, managers may place employees with high potential on the "fast track".

Make selection decisions: As organizational needs arise, potential employees are recruited and the entire process starts again with a job match.

Components of Career Development Programs

Slavenski and Buckner (1988)[1] have divided career development process into three distinct phases: (1) staffing and orientation, (2) evaluation and (3) development. Each of these phases is composed of strategies from which the employer may choose to create a customized career development system.

Staffing and Orientation

This phase is composed of providing career information to the job candidate (whether internal or external) and using selection techniques so as to match potential workers with the right job. The type of career information provided may include knowledge of jobs within the organization and possible career paths for the employee. Selection techniques that are used to match employee and employment opportunity include assessment center exercises and job posting systems even for positions that are to be filled internally (a form of self-selection).

Evaluation Phase

This phase is characterized by two important aspects, namely performance review and succession planning. The purpose of performance review, from a career development perspective, is to provide feedback to employees on their skills and knowledge, both to increase job satisfaction and to help them prepare for their next job. Succession planning links information from and about individual employees to the human resource needs of the organization.

Development Phase

During the developing phase, more visible career development strategies are employed. Tools used during this phase include career discussions between employee and supervisor, career resource centers, self-assessment and career counseling, and career planning workshops.

Role of Other Support Activities

The following support activities also form an integral part of the career development programs of an organization. These include career discussions, involvement of career resource centers, career counseling, career workshops etc.

Career Discussions

Career discussions between employee and supervisor form an integral part of any career development system. Training supervisors for their career discussion role is necessary for success; even more important and difficult is convincing supervisors to apply that training.

Career Resource Centers: Career resource centers have been found to be effective if they support a larger career development system. These centers act as a concrete symbol of company support of career development and openness of information.

Self-assessment and Career Counseling

Although career counseling does exist in organizations, self-assessment is a more common tool. A trend appears to be the formal incorporation of career counseling into employee assistance programs, as career issues become more complex. Career workbooks and similar activities are currently among the most popular self-assessment tools.

Career Development Workshops

Career development workshops are frequently being used in most organizations. These workshops emphasize on teaching employees to be more empowered, enhance self-assessment capabilities, align their focus on experiencing success in their current jobs and encourage them into life career planning.

IBM's career planning workshop focuses on the interests, skills, and contributions inherent in the individual's current job. Employees study their jobs' components and learn how to make the work more challenging. In addition, participants learn how jobs evolve from business needs.

Theme Case: Employee Career Development in IBM

IBM prides itself on attracting the best and the brightest individuals and is committed to ensuring these individuals continue this momentum by not only enhancing the skills they may already have, but also by continuing to develop new skills throughout their career.

Continuing Education

IBM provides a number of ways for you to further develop your skills as an employee, including tuition refund and mentoring.

Classroom Training

Classroom training is available to employees through two educational IBM services offerings, IBM Learning Services and PBSC. Both offer a variety of courses and certifications related to technical and professional skills. Training ranges from one employee via computer to custom designed and managed corporate-wide programs.

e-learning

e-learning is a standard way of learning in IBM that is closely tied to our e-business strategy and is a complement to IBM's traditional classroom training offerings. It is a non-classroom-based learning method using technology — more specifically, the capabilities of the Internet and Intranet, Lotus Notes, and CD-ROMS — to give employees "just in time" opportunities with IBMers all over the globe. e-learning means that as an employee one is no longer limited by when and where classroom training is offered. Thus an employee can get a 24 hour-a-day, on-demand availability of the thousands of online learning offerings as provided by IBM.

Tuition Refund

When an IBMite takes approved courses on his/her own time, IBM has a policy to reimburse 100% of the required fees such as tuition ($600/course maximum), registration and text books, upon satisfactory completion of the course.

The purpose of the Tuition Refund program is to encourage employees to increase:

1. their effectiveness in the current job role
2. their potential to assume different or greater responsibilities within IBM through voluntary (vs. company encouraged/directed) participation in education programs outside regular working hours

Mentoring

The IBM Mentoring program encourages employees to share their knowledge and know-how and to be a role model for others' success. Mentoring pair's two individuals who will work together use a self-directed informal approach or a registered formal approach to achieve specific objectives for skills growth and development.

Employee Development at IBM

Employee development is so important at IBM that it is considered as a formal process known as the Employee Development Cycle (EDC). It ties together the 6 steps followed every year to ensure that the employees are developing the right skills to do their jobs related to their present needs and also with respect to that in the future.

Step 1: Establish personal business commitments

Each year, an employee and his/her manager will discuss IBM's business objectives and together detail the employees' expected contributions. When the employee succeeds, it is considered as the success of the entire organization.

Step 2: Assess employee skills/competencies

Employees bring to IBM their talent, skills, experience, education and passion to succeed. The organization emphasizes on determining the skills of employees which they require to meet IBM's business objectives, employee's current job role, and future opportunities.

Step 3: Updating individual development plan

IBM continues to offer employees a wide variety of opportunities to experience different assignments and gain relevant skills to meet both IBM's business objectives and an employee's personal career goals. IBM expects its employees to be successful and excel at what they do best.

Step 4: Complete actions on individual development plan

Executing on an individual employee development plans is the key to IBM's success. Through this an employee at IBM can gain valuable experience by shadowing an executive or by taking an interactive web-based course to expand his/her skills. The employee might need assignments on a series of projects to give him/her more project-management experience, or he/she might want to work with a mentor. IBM's initiative for career development lets employee imagination soar, and as a result the alternatives are endless at IBM.

Step 5: Review individual development plan progress with manager

Each employee and his/her manager have a job and career discussion at least twice a year — once to update your individual development plan and a second time to checkpoint on the progress the employee is making to complete the activities outlined in that plan. This is also an opportunity to discuss future career directions. If an employee is unsure what he/she might be, IBM has a career centre with professional career coaches to work with them.

Step 6: Document development results for the year

All employee efforts and focus on skill development pays off. At the end of the year, the employee goes back to those personal business commitments and document what he or she had learned, how they are using those skills, and how he/she had contributed to their success and the success of IBM.

(Courtesy: Bardsley, C.A., (1987): "Improving employee awareness of opportunity at IBM." Personnel 64, No. 4, pp. 58–63)

Problems in Career Development

Like any other process or system in an organization the career development process is also not free from hassles and problems. These are as follows:

- **Dual Career Families:** This becomes acute when both the husband and wife are working and suppose one needs to be expatriated to a foreign subsidiary for managing a project or heading an international assignment.
- **Changing Family Needs:** With organizations shifting from traditional employment practices and flexible working hours, it has become difficult for working couples to manage their career needs as well as spend quality time for each other and their families.
- **Low Ceiling Careers:** With organizations shifting towards flatter and horizontal structures, career progressions and promotion opportunities becoming lesser, many employees are being thrown towards low ceiling careers with limited growth and development opportunities.
- **Declining Career Opportunities:** Conventional jobs in sectors like manufacturing are day by day loosing their relevance and importance to jobs in the sunrise sectors such as the service sector and particularly to the IT/ITES sectors.

Role of HR to Manage Career Development Problems

In order to handle and manage the above stated problems the HR function of any organization has to play an instrumental role. This could be achieved by the following strategies, namely:

- Improving Manpower planning and forecasting systems
- Improving dissemination of career option information
- Initiating career counseling programs on regular basis
- Developing effective internal and external Assessment Centers
- Supporting educational and training programs on regular basis (e.g: Learning and Development Cells in organizations like Dell)
- Introducing more flexible reward and promotional systems

Exercise Case Study: The Frustrated Employee

Ruma negotiated hard with her new employer. The employer told her that they could not give her more in terms of remuneration since they have to take into account the pay grades and internal parity. Ruma made a face. The Human Resource Manager told her "Look Ruma, you may not be getting the remuneration you are seeking. However, please do take into consideration many other factors that go into making a job satisfactory. You would get excellent scope for developing yourself. We would train and develop you and in one year you will find that your skills would have gone up by certain notches. No wonder, in that event you would be a strong contender for being promoted to the next higher grade. Besides, the work you will be assigned just suits your personality and qualification. Further, your colleagues and boss are some of the best persons to work with. Just imagine what would happen if you do not take our offer and for a few thousand rupees. I am sure you would go and join another organization. However, there you may find the task assigned to you boring, a boss who is breathing down your neck or with less intellectual caliber, or where the scope for self-development would be far and few between. What would happen to you?" Ruma was impressed. She thought, this person makes me feel so comfortable. She agrees. She joins. She works for a year. She finds herself frustrated within this very first year with this organization. In the last twelve months neither there has been any training program, nor the task assigned to her has been really able to make use of her true potential and about her colleagues, she would not comment in public.

Review Question

Analyze the case given below in the context of the concept of psychological contract. If you were the Human Resource Manager, committed to total quality in your organization, then what you would have done?

REFERENCES

1. Slavenski, L., Buckner, M., (1988): "Career Development Programs in the Workplace," Information Series, No. 333, Columbus: ERIC Clearinghouse on Adult, Career, and Vocational Education, Centre for Education and Training for Employment, The Ohio State University.
2. Gutteridge, T.G. (1986): "Organizational Career Development Systems: The State of the Practice." In Career Development In Organizations, edited by D.T. Hall, Jossey-Bass Publishers, San Fransisco.
3. Bardsley, C.A., (1987): "Improving Employee Awareness of Opportunity at IBM," Personnel 64, No. 4, pp. 58–63
4. http://www.ericdigests.org/pre-9212/career.htm

QUESTION BANK

1. Why are some people satisfied with what is identified as a mid-career plateau while others at the same point experience career burnout?
2. What do you mean by a career? What are the various stages of career?
3. What do you mean by career path? What are the milestones of an individual's career path?
4. What is career ladder? How do they help in an individual's career?
5. Define career planning. What are the components of career planning?
6. What is career development? How do organizations cater to the challenges of career development?
7. Describe the difference between career planning and succession planning.
8. What are the problems faced in career planning and development?
9. What is succession planning? How do organizations develop succession plans?
10. What is the role of manning chart and replacement charts in succession planning?

Internet Exercises

- Go to the internet and find the list of suitable websites helpful for seeking resources and information on career planning and development and discuss the same with your friends.
- Go to the websites of various reputed organizations (Like McDonalds, Lee jeans, Tata, Sony BMG and Walmart etc.) and find out the career options in these organizations.

Experiential Learning

- Prepare your own career plan and discuss the same with your faculty or placement officer.
- Prepare a career profile for the students of your class. Collect information on the similar career profiles and after discussing with your HR faculty organize a career counselling session to facilitate the same.

EMPLOYEE COMPETENCY

What are Competencies?

Competencies are the underlying characteristics of an individual in terms of his/her knowledge, skills, attitudes, values, self-concepts, traits and motives that have casual relationship with effective/and or superior performance in a job situation. Competencies are thereby measurable human capabilities that are required for effective and successful work performance of individuals.

- **Competency:** A person-related concept that refers to the dimensions of behaviour lying behind competent performer.
- **Competence:** A work-related concept that refers to areas of work at which the person is competent.
- **Competencies:** Often referred as the combination of the above two.

Definition: Boyatzis (1982)[1] have described competency as "a capacity that exists in a person that leads to behaviour that meets the job demands within parameters of organizational environment, and that, in turn brings about desired results". Competencies have also been described as underlying characteristics that allow people to effectively perform in a job (such as knowledge, skills, abilities, motives, traits, self-concept and behaviour).

Core Competency

A core competency is a bundle of skills and technologies that enables a company to provide particular benefits to customers. It could be in the form of communication effectiveness, involvement and a deep commitment to working across organizational boundaries.

Competency Applications

- **Competency frameworks:** Competency frameworks define the competency requirements that cover all the key jobs in an organization. They comprise of generic competencies.
- **Competency maps:** Competency maps describe the different aspects of competent behaviour in an occupation against competency dimensions such as strategic capability, resource management and quality.
- **Competency profiles:** This involves a set of competencies that are requiring performing a specified role.

Underlying Characteristics of People Associated with Success on the Job

The following figure illustrates the characteristics of people associated with success on their jobs. The KSAs and behaviours of an individual are the most visible or assessable aspects that define an individual's performance in his/her workplace (they occupy the "tip of the iceberg"), whereas their attitudes, values and self image, personal traits and motives form the underlying aspects which are generally not visible or assessable, as they form the core of their behavioural patterns.

As evident from the above model behaviours, knowledge, skills and abilities (KSAs) form the top most part of the iceberg, which according to behavioural theories are the most visible aspects of an individual's characteristics. The attitudes, values, self image, individual traits and motives are the underlying components of an individual's characteristic that are difficult to uncover.

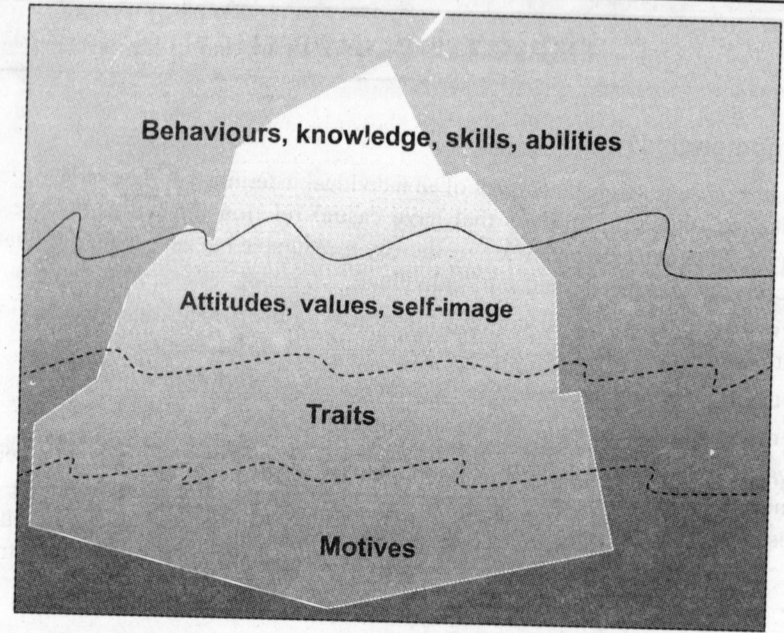

Fig. 3.24: The Iceberg model of an individual's behaviour

How do Competencies Differ from Skills and Knowledge?

Competencies only include behaviours that demonstrate excellent performance. Therefore, they do not include knowledge, but do include "applied" knowledge or the behavioural application of knowledge that produces success. In addition, competencies do include skills, but only the manifestation of skills that produce success. Finally, competencies are not work motives, but do include observable behaviours related to motives. The following figure illustrates the relationship of competency with skills, knowledge, motives and attitudes of an individual.

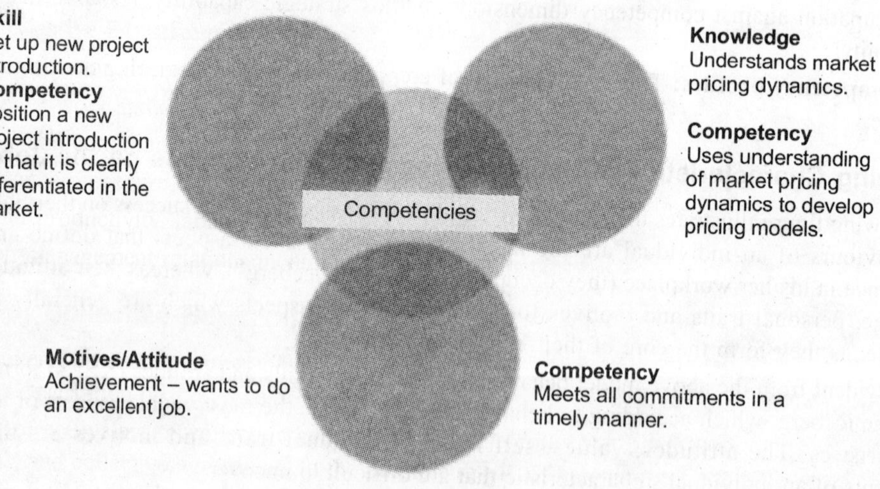

Fig. 3.25: Relation of Competency with KSAs
(Courtesy: http://www.schoonover.com/images/competency_fig1.jpg)

Integrated Human Resource Practices through Competency Development

Organizations are using competencies in virtually every human resource domain. They provide criteria that can be applied to each of the human resource practices shown below:

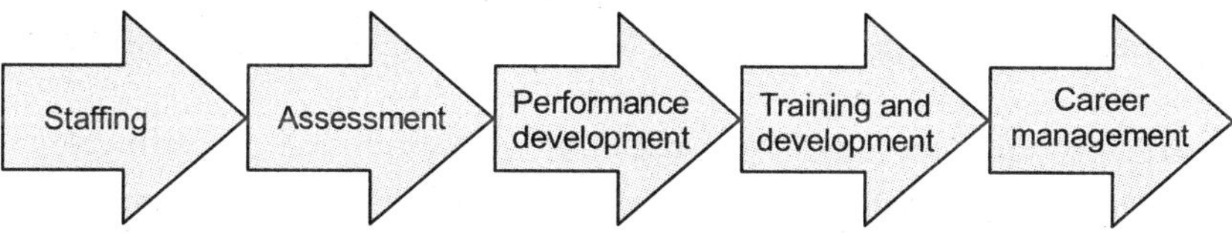

Fig. 3.26: Integrated human resource practices

Competencies are used as the "key criteria" for implementing each application. In other words, competencies are framed into a specific tool and accompanied by guidelines defining how managers and employees use the tool to produce results in each of the above areas.

Types of Competencies

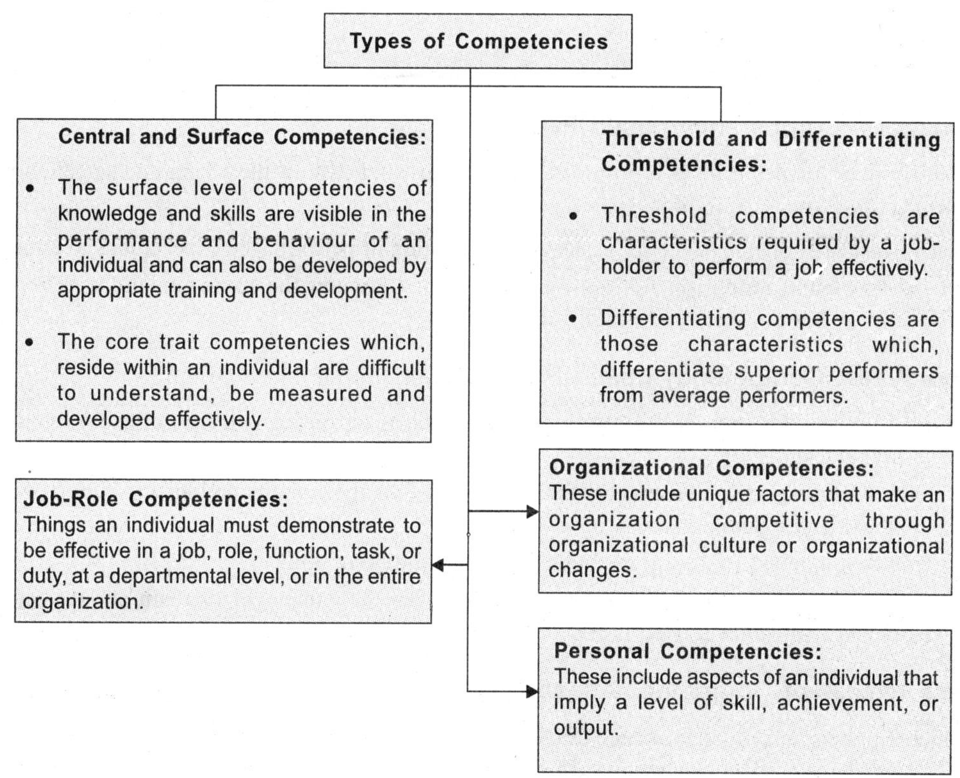

Benefits from Competency-based HR Practices

For an organization competency-based practices can:

- Reinforce corporate strategy, culture and vision.
- Establish expectations for performance excellence, resulting in a systematic approach to professional development, improved job satisfaction and better employee retention.

- Increase the effectiveness of training and professional development programs by linking them to the success criteria (i.e., behavioural standards of excellence).
- Provide data on development needs that emerge from group and/or organizational composites that are an outcome of multi-rater assessments.
- Provide a common framework and language for discussing how to implement and communicate key strategies.
- Provide a common understanding of the scope and requirements of a specific role.
- Provide common, organization-wide standards for career levels that enable employees to move across business boundaries.

Exhibit: Competencies for HR Professionals

HR competencies could be divided into five distinct domains; namely

- Knowledge of the business,
- Delivery of HR practices,
- Management of change,
- Management of culture and
- Personal credibility.

For Managers, Competency-based Practices

- Identify performance criteria to improve the accuracy and ease of the hiring and selection process.
- Provide more objective performance standards.
- Clarify standards of excellence for easier communication of performance expectations to direct reports.
- Provide a clear foundation for dialogue to occur between the manager and employee about performance, development and career related issues.

For Employees, Competency-based Practices

- Identify the success criteria (i.e., behavioural standards of performance excellence) required to be successful in their role.
- Provide a more specific and objective assessment of their strengths and specify targeted areas for professional development.
- Provide development tools and methods for enhancing their skills.
- Provide the basis for a more objective dialogue with their manager or team about performance, development and career related issues.

Business Impact of Competency-based Systems

Often leadership programs or performance development interventions are seen as important, but focused on "soft skills" that may not affect business results. One of the most important developments in human resources is the clarification of the "business value" of key programs. Some of the measurable benefits of competency-based performance development are listed below. These kinds of impacts improve talent levels, save money and improve business performance.

Assessment of Competencies

Competencies are based on an analysis of the professional role(s) and/or a theoretical formulation of professional responsibilities. Competency statements describe outcomes expected from the performance of professionally related functions, or knowledge, skills and attitudes thought to be essential to the performance of those functions.

In a competence-based assessment system, the focus is on outcomes of performance and assessment of individuals over a continuous period of time.

The key factors of a competence-based system are:

- Focus on outcomes
- Individualized assessment
- No percentage rating
- No comparison with other individual's results
- All standards (requirements) must be met
- On-going processes leading to further development
- Only "competent" or "not yet competent" judgments made.

Assessment of competences serves the purpose of:

- Measuring individual contribution to business objectives
- Measuring group/team contribution to business objectives
- Identifying potential for further development

Competence assessment may be in form of the assessment of:

- Occupation/Technical competence
- Personal/Individual competence
- General competence
- Combination of the above

The competence-based assessment may be used for:

- Certification
- Performance appraisal
- Identifying training needs
- Skills audit
- Prior learning
- Recruitment and selection
- Evaluating training

Formation of a Competency Framework

The key principles involving development of a competency framework in an organization involves the following stages, namely:

- Involving the people who will be affected by the framework
- Keeping people informed about what is happening
- Behaviours described in the competencies must be relevant to all those who will be affected by them as well as to organizational needs and intended applications

Steps in Producing a Competency Framework: The steps involved in developing a competency framework are as follows:

- Getting buy-in from key people
- Clarification of the purpose
- Planning the project

- Putting a data-gathering/-analysis team together
- Choosing analysis techniques
- Data-gathering
- Data for analysis
- Drafting the competency framework
- Validation of the draft competencies
- Revisions and finalizing the competencies
- Launching the framework

Competency Analysis and Modeling

It helps to identify and document those capabilities of employees and thereby allows an organization to use that information across a wide range of people management systems. It can be used for designing for a specific job, unit, a division, or an entire organization.

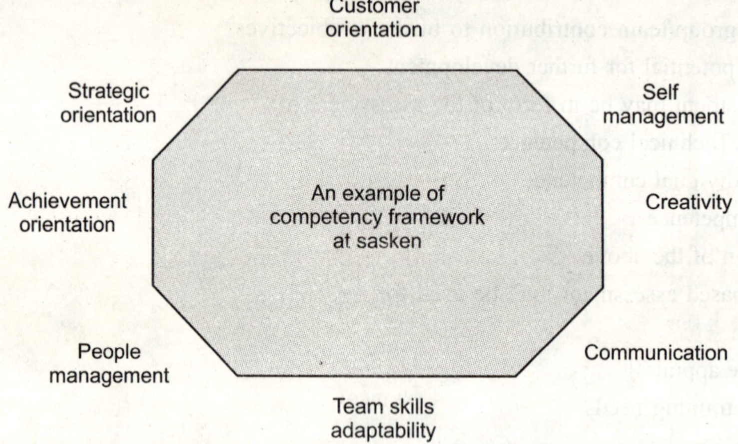

Fig. 3.27: Illustration of competency framework at Sasken

Competency Mapping

Competency mapping is a process to identify key competencies for an organization and/or a job and incorporating those competencies throughout the various processes of the organization. The steps involved in the process of competency mapping are as follows:

- Conduct a job analysis by asking incumbents to complete a position information questionnaire.
- Using the results of job analysis, a competency based job description is developed.
- Taking the competency based job description, mapping the competencies can be done.
- Taking the competency mapping one step further, one can use the results of one's evaluation to identify in what competencies individuals need additional development or training.

Competency Mapping Process: The competency mapping process consists of the following stages:

Stage1: Designing the questionnaire for data collection. While designing the questionnaire following factors are to be taken into consideration:

- Knowing the Purpose of the job
- Identifying the Critical Success Factors
- Identifying the Key Result Areas
- Breaking the KRAs into Key Activities

Stage 2: Data Collection:

- Clarity of Organization Direction
- Clarity of Organization Structure.
- Interview Job Holder.
- Interview Job Holder's Reporting Officer.
- Discuss with the Focus Group if the job are of the same family.

Stage 3: This stage involves:

- Rank Order of the list of competencies (Guided/Unguided)
- Comparing good performer and average performer with selected list of competencies.
- Use research data and assign competencies to positions.

Stage 4: Finalize role descriptions and competencies-job wise.

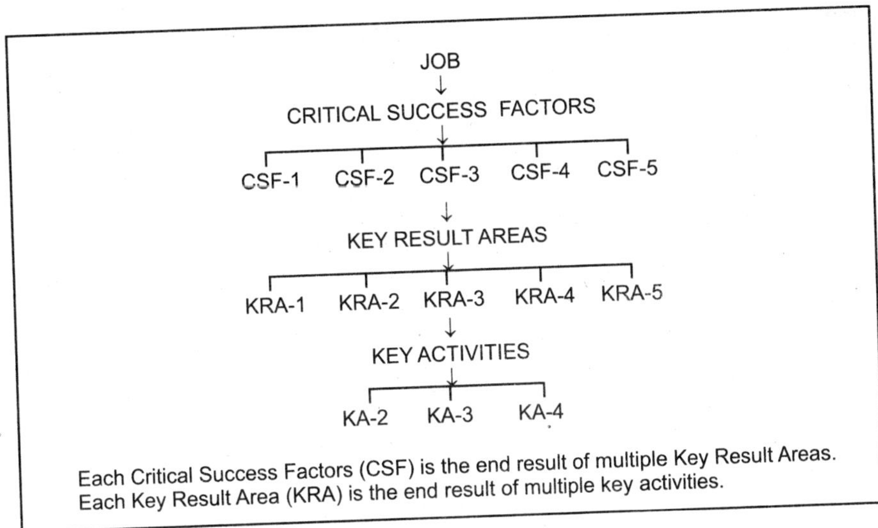

Fig. 3.28: Approach towards competency mapping

Purpose of Competency Mapping: The main purpose of competency mapping is to ensure effectiveness of an organization in terms of having a clear idea regarding the summation of the required competencies. This facilitates further:

- Gap analysis in competencies
- Role clarity
- Selection, potential identification, growth plans.
- Succession planning.
- Restructuring
- Inventory of competencies for future planning.

Approaches of Competency Mapping

The major approaches of competency mapping are as follows:

- ***Assessment Centers***: It is a mechanism to identify the potential for growth. It is a procedure specifically designed to evaluate an individual's managerial potential. Its objective is to reinforce strengths, overcome weaknesses, and exploit potential of the employees through training and development efforts. The assessors observe the behaviour of the candidates and make independent evaluation of what they have observed, which results in identifying strengths and weaknesses of the attributes being studied. Assessment center comprises a number of exercises or simulations which have been designed to replicate tasks and demands of the job. Most organizations use a combination of the following techniques to assess the strengths, weaknesses and potentials of the employees: (a) Group Discussions (b) In Tray Exercises (c) Interview Simulations/Role Plays (d) Case Studies.
- ***Critical Incident Technique***: It is a set of procedures for systematically identifying behaviours that contribute to the success or failure of individuals or organizations in specific situations. It is useful for obtaining in-depth data about a particular role or set of tasks. It involves gathering facts, content analysis and creating feedback.
- ***Interview Techniques***: The interview consists of the interaction between the interviewer and the applicant.
- ***Questionnaire***: These are written lists of questions that users fill out and return. It can be used at any stage of development depending on the questions that are asked in the questionnaire.
- ***Psychometric Tests***: It is a standardized objective measure of a sample of behaviour.

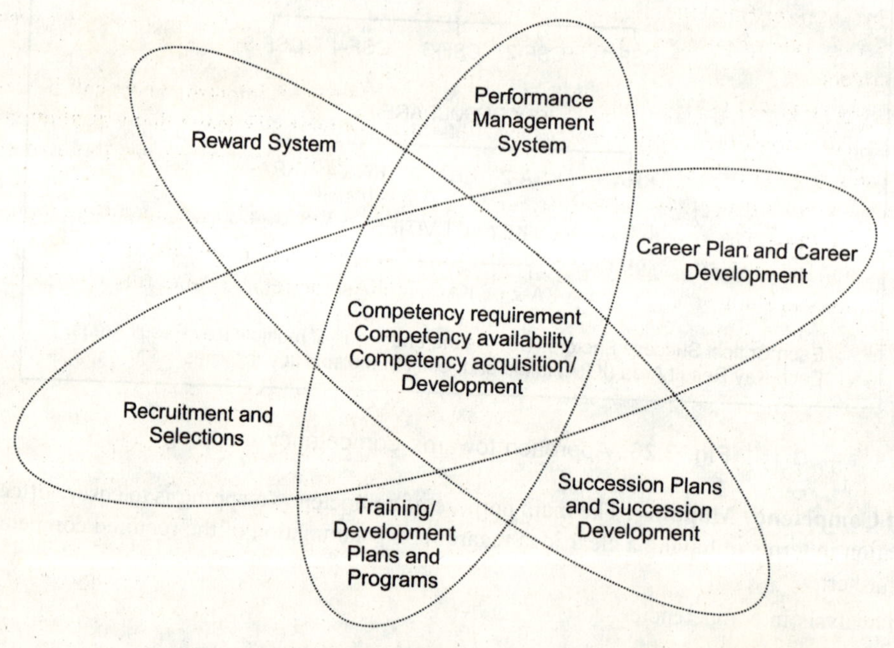

Fig. 3.29: Competency based HR practices

Competency-based HR Practices: Desired Outcomes for Organizations

- **Enhance the marketing position.** Competency-based applications can also improve the stature of an organization in terms of enhancing the employability brand of the organization.

- **Hiring effectiveness.** Competency-based efforts can have a positive effect on hiring and turnover. Improved recruiting and selection processes deliver employees who are more qualified for their new jobs.
- **Better internal placement.** Similarly, positions can be filled more effectively with properly qualified internal candidates. Employees who are ready to move up can be readily identified and promoted. Employees who want to move up but are not qualified can be steered into necessary development activities. The result is more of the right people in the right jobs.
- **Training/development efficiencies.** Organizations that train employees by title or by workgroup may be wasting a lot of productive time. Thirty-year employees may not need to be sitting next to new hires in some training class mandated by management. The goal for developing employees is just-in-time, just-as-needed. The immediate result of individual assessments is an easy win.
- **Increased productivity.** Productivity can be improved three ways. First, enhanced selection of employees results in better across-the-board performance on the job. Second, time wasted in unnecessary development activities is converted to productive work time. Third, existing employees receive the development they want and need to be more effective in their jobs.
- **Better organizational performance.** Competency-based HR applications can contribute to the overall performance of the organization, although they are hard to isolate as a direct cause. They can deliver extremely large paybacks by helping organizations identify people who can help capture market share, shorten time to market, raise the level of customer service, be more innovative, improve efficiencies and make better decisions.

Competency-based HR Practices: Desired Outcomes for Employees

- **Understanding position requirements.** Competency applications require a thorough grasp of the processes and skills/knowledge required to meet position performance standards.
- **Needed training.** Competency assessments let employees indicate, in a low-risk manner, where they need help in getting their job done. It also lets them establish where they meet qualifications and where they need not waste time in unnecessary development activities.
- **Easier to show qualifications.** When targeted business goals are not being met, the question arises whether the problem is people, processes, or uncontrollable outside factors. Competency assessments, along with the appraisal system, make it easier to show whether individual employees are properly trained and qualified.
- **Ability to prepare for the new/next job.** Performance appraisals require that an employee be in a job for a period of time before the review takes place.
- **More rational HR decisions.** Using competency assessment information, recruitment, hiring, placement, and promotion decisions are made much more objectively. Employees are hired, assessed, developed, and promoted based upon objective competencies rather than subjective preferences or unrelated factors such as seniority.
- **Assessment of competence makes it easy for the qualified worker to stand out and difficult for the unqualified worker to hide.** Competency-based HR applications help migrate the responsibility for employee qualifications from management down to the individual worker (talent volatility).

Developing a Skill Matrix

A Skill Based Matrix provides a pictorial summary of the skill areas in which employees are expected to cross-train. Each column represents a process (or step in a process) and each row is a level of difficulty. Each square is called a skill block. A group of skill blocks provide the employee with a skill path to follow.

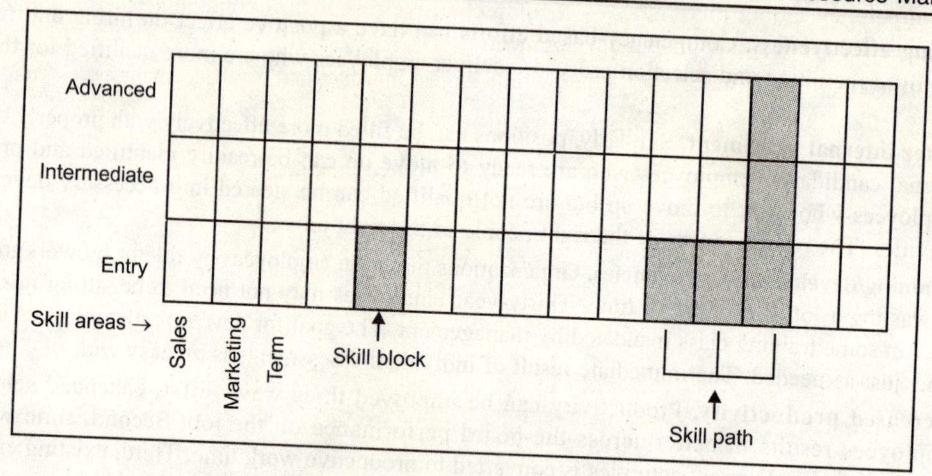

Fig. 3.30: A skill matrix

Skill Blocks: For each skill block the following information should be defined:

Knowledge Required	Activities	Standards/Certifications
Provides information on the knowledge required to perform the activities of the skill block.	Provides information on the activities performed in the skill block.	Provides standards/certifications that will result when an employee has the appropriate knowledge and successfully performs the activities in the skill block. Whenever possible this should provide quantitative information.
Examples: Knowledge of new account development technique. Knowledge of company products and services.	**Examples:** Make sales calls. Represent company at trade shows.	**Examples:** Five sales calls completed every month. One closed sale account each quarter.

Hay's Approach to Competency Model Development

Hay employs a range of methods for developing competency models but the focus is always on ensuring that the competencies will support the achievement of the organization's strategic priorities. We determine and profile the competencies associated with superior performers using distinctive Hay tools, including:

- **Behavioural event interviews (BEIs)** — in-depth, competency-based assessments of superior performers conducted by trained and certified staff and focusing on demonstrated behaviours.
- **Group BEIs** — BEIs conducted for superior performers within a focus group setting.
- **Expert panels and focus groups** — facilitated by certified consultants with employees, customers and others who have in-depth knowledge of job requirements.
- **Competency builder kits** — workshops and tools for defining current and future accountabilities, identifying required competencies and setting target levels.

- **Competency model dictionary** — a comprehensive resource of competencies customized to each organization to facilitate model development.
- **Competency model database** — the world's largest international database spanning a broad spectrum of job functions and industries.

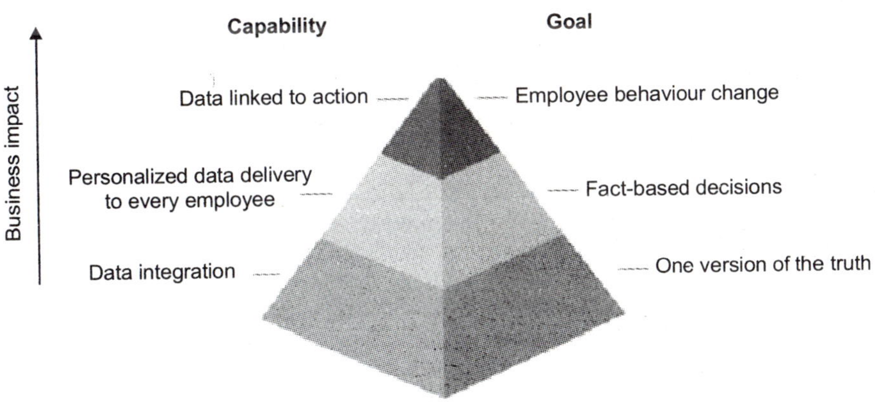

Fig. 3.31: Relation of employee capabilities and setting performance goals

Exhibit: A Knowledge and Skill Inventory

Skills	Details
Interpersonal skills and awareness	Active listening, empathy, having a range of communication styles and knowing when each style is most appropriate, sensitivity to others who are different. Being aware of others, the ability to observe, assess the styles, preferences, knowledge, skills abilities and shortcomings of others. Ability to act on these insights. Ability to delegate, give direction, appraise/evaluate, give feedback and build self-correcting mechanisms into the work design determined by observation, self-evaluation, peer evaluation in small work groups.
Networking and dynamics	Building support groups, coalitions, spheres of influence within the organization to secure results and cooperation. Determined by internship experience, and by results of career ladder moves.
Motivation and leadership	Creating compelling visions and reasons to pursue them. Understanding the dynamics of working in teams, building commitment, efficiency, productivity and satisfaction in team work. Determined by ability to engage fellow students in teamwork. Determined by success on team projects.
Organizational	Managing time, scheduling work (one's own and others) designing systems and action plans. Determined by handing in high quality work on time.
Communications	Speaking and writing, having a point and being able to get it across in a way that is clear, crisp and concise. Being convincing. Determined by presentations, written work and class participation.
Quantitative	Understanding how to use and interpret data and to use quantitative/analytical tools for decision-making and problem solving. Determined by homework, quizzes, exams and case analysis.

Contd...

Critical thinking	Developing capacity for analysis, problem solving, generalizing, questioning, and probing. Comfort with not knowing, dealing with and managing ambiguity. Determined by homework, quizzes, papers, presentations, exams and classroom participation. Determined by assessing student comfort level with ambiguous assignments
Abstract and adapt	Understanding the role of models to strip down the most essential elements from a complex business problem and model those essential interactions. Proficiency can be demonstrated by student solutions to complex model-based assignments, by independently choosing appropriate tools to solve theoretical problems, or by working as a team to adapt models from one business problem to another analogous problem.
Learning and training	Flexibility, ability to adapt, deal and move quickly when new insights or information become available. Knowing how to learn on an ongoing basis, how to/where to gather the right information. Specifically, language skills, computational skills, analytical skills and interpersonal skills. Ability to teach, how to facilitate the learning of others. Specifically, language skills, computational skills, analytical skills and interpersonal skills. Determined by exams, quizzes, papers, presentations, self-peer and professor evaluations, library research, use of internet, use of off-campus business resources.
Information technology	Word processing, spread sheet, internet, fax, attached files, Power Point, E-mail, intranet (Blackboard) etc. Determined by self and professor evaluations, exams, quizzes and demonstrated capability by examination of student project work.
Global and external awareness	Understanding issues of diversity and globalization, both the personal, legal and economic impacts. Determined by exams, papers, quizzes and observations of face-to-face interactions.
Ethical/legal environment of management	Understanding the practical, legal and ethical implications of the spirit of the law and the letter of the law, understanding one's ethical responsibilities and the consequences of shading the lines between right and wrong, fair and unfair. Absence of ethical awareness is determined by lying, cheating, free-loading, dishonest avoidance of an assignment or deadline. Presence of ethical awareness is determined by responses to case studies, by following through with commitments.
Technical knowledge	List here any specific technical knowledge not covered in the first twelve categories your course addresses.

Appendix: Using Competency Analysis for Identifying Training Needs

Competency Analysis	
Name	Date
Training Program/Course	

	A	B	C	A-B	C-B
Pre-trained ability	A				
Post-trained ability		B			
Revised pre-trained ability			C		
Change compared with initial pre-trained ability (B minus A)				A-B	
Change compared with initial pre-trained ability (B minus C)					C-B

***Please rate the following with 10 being the highest and 1 being the lowest.**

1	Aware of other people's perception and make it a point to clarify my assumptions to avoid resentment, rejection and revenge.					
2	Aware and conscious of his/her colleague's emotional state before carrying out work with them.					
3	Ability to establish rapport with colleagues and superiors					
4	Does not get intimidated when speaking with colleagues and superiors.					
5	Practice active listening when communicating with others					
6	Take into account Purpose, People and Process when attending/facilitating a meeting					
7	Involve herself/himself in the meeting as much as possible					
8	Confident in handling phone calls from internal customers					
9	Can handle properly an irate internal customer					
10	Effective in writing emails, proposals and documents in terms of form and content					
11	Can observe proper:					
	Stance Dress Code Voice Proxemics Language Gesturing					
12	Open discussion with co-worker by stating the agenda, the relevance of it and checking for acceptance.					
13	Confident in overcoming indifference in the workplace					
14	Understand the value of each internal customer					
15	Committed to serve the internal customers the best service he/she can provide.					
Totals and total movements						

Signature: ________________

REFERENCES

1. Boyatziz, R.E., (1982): "The Competent Manager, A Model for Effective Performance," John Wiley & Sons, NY.
2. M G. Jomon (2004): "Effectiveness of HRD Audit as an OD Intervention", unpublished manuscript, XIM Bhubaneshwar.

QUESTION BANK

1. Define competency. How is it different from skills?
2. What is core competency? How does it help organizations and individuals?
3. "Competency development is important for sustaining organizational competitiveness." Comment on the statement.
4. Write a note on competency development.
5. What is competency mapping? What is its importance in organizations?
6. What is skill matrix? How is it developed? State its importance.
7. What could be the competencies of a marketing manager working in a FMCG company?
8. Write a note on competency based HR practices. How does it facilitate performance improvement?
9. What is the role of competency analysis in performance management? Give suitable illustrations wherever possible.
10. Is it necessary for organizations to consider benchmarking of competencies? Give suitable reasons for your answer.
11. Majority of the human capabilities are unutilized or rather untapped. Comment on the statement.
12. Competency development is an important responsibility of HR professionals. Comment on the statement.

Internet Exercises

- Go through the following website hyperlink (http://www.assessmentspecialists.com/competency.html) and prepare a presentation for your class.
- Study the following website (http://www.developingexecutives.com/competen.htm) and discuss your learnings with your friends.
- Visit the website http://www.competencymanagement.com/ and discuss the application of competency management in practice with your friends.

Experiential Exercise

- Suppose your college is going to organize a big management fest in the next month. You are holding a leading position in the organizing team. Now how can you use the concept of competency to ensure that the capabilities of your friends are best utilized for organizing this event.
- Suppose you are working as Training and Development consultant to the Indian cricket team. How would you utilize the concept of competency management for development and utilization of the cricketing capabilities of the Indian cricket team?
- Develop a skill data bank framework of your friends in your class with respect to their soft and technical skills. You may consult your faculty. Try to use MS Excel or any other spreadsheet for the same.

PERFORMANCE MANAGEMENT

Theme Case: Woes of Ineffective Performance Management

Tom is Chief Executive Officer for a medical supply multinational. His company had just crafted a new plan to counter competitive threats. It stressed the need to cut cycle time, concentrate sales on higher-margin products and develop new markets. All in all, this was a pretty classic, very sound strategy. Four months after circulating the plan, Tom did a "walk-around" to see how things were going. He was appalled. Everywhere Tom turned, people, departments — whole business units — simply didn't "get it." First surprise: Engineering. The group had cut product design time 30%, meeting its goal to increase speed-to-market. Good. Then Tom asked how manufacturing would be affected. It turned out the new design would take much more time to make. Total cycle time actually increased. Our message is not getting through, Tom thought. Second surprise: Sales. The new strategy called for a shift — emphasizes high margin sales rather than pushing product down the pipeline as fast as possible. But just about every salesperson Tom spoke to was making transactional sales to high-volume customers; hardly anyone was building relationships with the most profitable prospects. *Sales are doing just what it's always done*, Tom thought. Worst surprise: Even his top team, the people who had helped him craft the strategy, was not sticking to plan. Tom asked a team member: "Why are you spending all of your time making sure the new machinery is working instead of developing new markets?" "Because my unit's chief goal was to improve on-time delivery," he answered. "But what about *company* goals?" said Tom. "We came up with a good plan and communicated it very clearly. But nowhere is it being carried out. Why?" The reason is poor performance management.

But what does that really mean? It means that the leaders of the company — from the CEO to the executive team to middle managers to shop-floor supervisors — did not recognize the importance of gaining clarity of goals, discussing ways to accomplish those goals, and following through to make sure behaviours were aligned with desired outcomes. Leaders at many organizations make this mistake. They assume that because they understand the objective, everyone else will too. It doesn't work that way. People don't get it.

The case is not only an example of an organization with symptoms of lack of performance planning and involvement of the human resources in showing wholehearted involvement in managing their performance. Most often, the vision of the senior leaders are not shared with those in the front line of the business. Internal communication systems lack clarity and barriers in free flow of information add to the woes of employees. Availability of true mentors, trainers and facilitators in the supervisory level had become scarce leading employees towards uncertainty and confusion at workplace. Although technology is available; hardly any of them are used in good forms or effects to improve team and individual performances. Organizations lacking a long-term and whole hearted commitment towards performance management are bound to become stagnant in doldrums, as that in the case of the aforesaid multinational.

Introduction

Performance management includes activities to ensure that goals are consistently being met in an effective and efficient manner. Performance management can focus on performance of the organization, a department, processes to build a product or service, employees, etc. Performance management can be defined as the development of individuals with competence and commitment, working towards the achievement of shared meaningful objectives within an organization which supports and encourages their achievement. Michael Armstrong have defined performance management is a strategic and integrated approach to delivering sustained success to organizations by improving the performance of the people who work in them and by developing the capabilities of teams and individual contributors. Performance assessment has a long history based on comparative judgements of human worth. In the early part of the 19th century, for example, Robert Owen used colored wooden cubes, hung above work stations, to indicate the performance of individual employees at his New Lanark cotton mills in Scotland. Various merit ratings were represented by different colored cubes which were changed to indicate improvement or decline in employee performance.

What is Performance Management?

Performance management is the process of creating a work environment or setting in which people are enabled to perform to the best of their abilities. Performance management is a whole work system that begins when a job is defined as needed. It ends when an employee leaves the organization. A **Performance Management System (PMS)** includes the following actions:

- Develop clear job descriptions (JDs).
- Select appropriate people with an appropriate selection process.
- Negotiate requirements and accomplishment-based performance standards, outcomes and measures.
- Provide effective orientation, education and training.
- Provide on-going coaching and feedback.
- Conduct quarterly performance development discussions.
- Design effective compensation and recognition systems that reward people for their contributions.
- Provide promotional/career development opportunities for staff.
- Assist with exit interviews to understand WHY valued employees leave the organization.

Aims of Performance Management

The overall aim of performance management is to establish a high performance culture in which individuals and teams take responsibility for the continuous improvement of business processes and for their own skills and contributions within a framework provided by effective leadership. Its key purpose is to focus people on doing the right things by achieving goal clarity. The various other aims of performance management are as follows:

- Empowering, motivating and rewarding employees to ensure their best efforts and performance.
- Ensuring that the employees emphasize on doing the right tasks at the right time.
- Ensuring effective alignment of individual goals along with those of the organization.
- Ensuring proactive resourcing and management of employee performance against agreed performance objectives and accountabilities.
- Facilitating the linking of job performance to the achievement of the organization's corporate strategy and service plans.
- Facilitating the alignment of individual goals and objectives with those of the tam, departments/divisional and corporate plans.
- Ensuring a systematic process and behaviours by which managers manage the performance of their people so as to deliver a high-performance organization.
- Ensuring maximization of the employee potential and capabilities.

BHARTI'S PERFORMANCE
MANAGEMENT MODEL

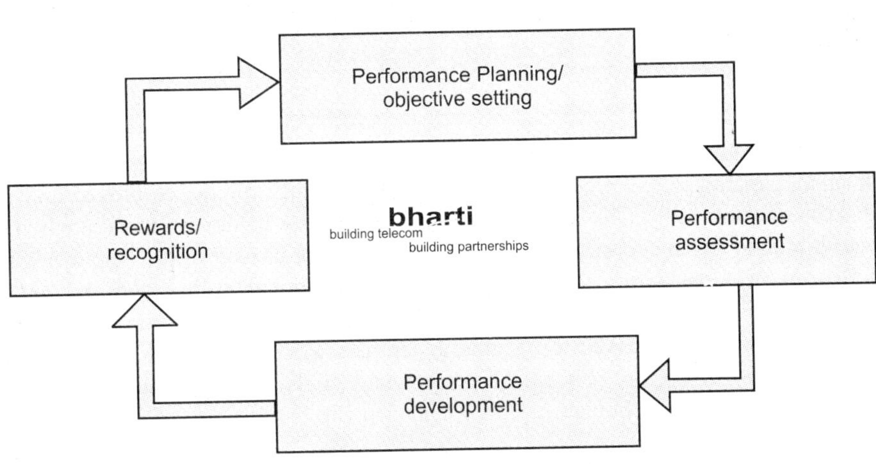

EXHIBIT: Bharti's Performance Management Model

Concerns of Performance Management

Performance Management should emphasize upon the following concerns:

- Emphasizing on front-end planning rather than back-end reviewing of performance.
- Ensuring emphasis on creating a broader definition of performance that focuses on more than narrowly defined job responsibilities.
- Emphasis on creating a constant dialogue rather than depending solely on filling performance review/evaluation forms and restricting to evaluation/rating scales.
- Focusing of the reward and recognition aspects of performance.
- Emphasis on continuous performance improvement and development.
- Ensuring the enhancement of communication at all levels of the organization
- Concern for creating value addition to stakeholder needs, interests and aspirations.
- Creating a long lasting commitment for inculcating fairness, rational and transparent performance evaluation and development.

THEME CASELET: PERFORMANCE MANAGEMENT IN INTELENET GLOBAL SERVICES

Intelenet Global Services nurtures diversity and creates an environment that empowers employees and enables them to develop into well-rounded professionals. "We have implemented a program called I-versity, which is the Internal Promotion Program for employees, designed to incorporate a growth path for employees supported by performance and strategic inputs," states Manuel D'Souza, executive VP-HR, Intelenet Global Services. Intelenet uses assessment centres to assess employees for internal promotion programmes. "Our assessment centre consists of a pool of employees that have gone through an intensive training programme. The tools are deployed by a panel of trained assessors, thus, eliminating bias and ensuring transparency," adds D'souza. Appraisal is a developmental process. Earlier, it was considered a tool for salary increment. However, with the changing mindset, the term appraisal took on a new meaning. Now, the focus has shifted to managing performance of the employee and adding value in terms of self-understanding.

Overview of Performance Management

The evolution of the concept of *performance management* as a new Human Resource Management model reflects a change of emphasis in organizations away from command-and-control toward a facilitation model of leadership. This change has been accompanied by recognition of the importance to the employee and the institution of relating work performance to the strategic or long-term and overarching mission of the organization as a whole. Employees' goals and objectives are derived from their departments, which in turn support the mission and goals of the organization.

The performance management process provides an opportunity for the employee and performance manager to discuss development goals and jointly create a plan for achieving those goals. Development plans should contribute to organizational goals and the professional growth of the employee. The planning process must also involve consideration of the emerging organizational environment. For most managers, this changing environment offers many new challenges and opportunities. Performance managers and their employees are increasingly being asked to become generalists who step outside of traditional narrowly-defined job descriptions in support of team objectives and goals. These changes are resulting in the development of new approaches to human resource management.

The performance management framework underscores the vital role of education, training and development in the envisioned future organization. In this organization, continuous learning is a prerequisite to successful job performance and organizational effectiveness. Employees must be able to *learn and facilitate others to learn*, developing effective technical and people skills in order to assume new responsibilities, and keep pace with and anticipate the changing nature of work and management practices.

The realities of the contemporary workplace will continue to challenge existing paradigms and should be considered in managing the performance of employees in a dynamic working environment.

Keys to managing performance: The principal keys to managing performance effectively are:

Achieving radical clarity around goals: Many organizations think they send clear signals, but don't. In some cases, managers subordinate broad strategic goals to operational goals within their silos. That's what happened with Tom's top team (Theme Case). Elsewhere, leaders often have too many "top" priorities — as had been seen in several case illustrations — which results in mixed signals and blurred focus. To enable effective performance management, it is important to sort and trim priorities down to a manageable number. This is true for the organization as a whole, for each department, for each team and for each individual. The first step toward effective performance management is for managers to clarify their own goals and objectives. A recent Hay Group study shows how difficult that can be. The study showed a disturbing lack of clarity on top teams (organizational clarity measures the extent to which employees understand what is expected of them and how those expectations connect with the organization's larger goals). In fact, the biggest single difference between great top teams and typical ones was in the level of internal clarity.

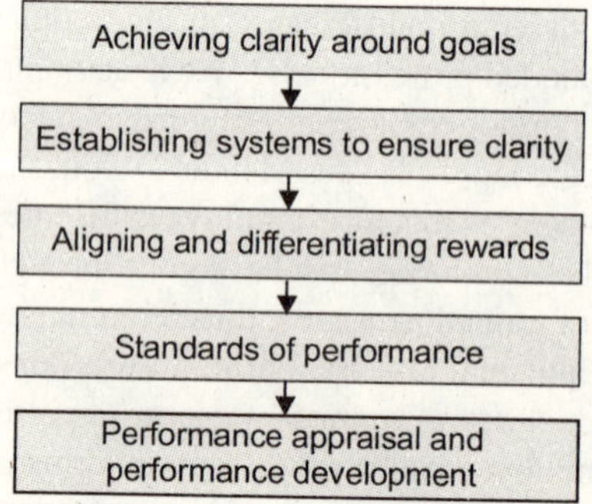

Fig. 3.32: Essentials of performance management

Establishing systems and processes to ensure clarity: Once goals are clear, organizations must create systems and processes so as to ensure that people get the right messages. These processes include: budget and planning sessions; staff and team meetings to discuss goals; performance management meetings; and talent review sessions. Dialogue drives all these processes. Each represents a "transmitter opportunity," where managers reiterate goals and monitor behaviour to ensure it's aligned with goals.

Aligning and differentiating rewards: HR managers must make sure that rewards encourage employee behaviours consistent with goals. It is common that almost everywhere managers distribute rewards more or less evenly. Lack of effective performance dialogue is a key contributor to dysfunctional reward schemes.

Standards of performance: Standards of performance are written statements describing *how well* a job should be performed. Performance standards are developed collaboratively with employees, whenever possible, and explained to new employees during their orientation or induction.

The performance standard provides a benchmark against which to evaluate work performance. While the job description describes the essential functions and the tasks to be done, the performance standard defines *how well* each function or task must be performed in order to meet or exceed expectations. Standards of performance are usually:

- Developed in collaboration with the employees who do the tasks or functions
- Explained to new employees within the first month on the job.

Performance standards may be written to different levels of complexity. The more general the applicability, the harder it is to be specific. Care should be taken so as to assess, whether the performance standards are realistic, specific, based on measurable data, observation, or verifiable information, consistent with organizational goals, challenging, clear and understandable, and dynamic.

Environmental Context of Performance Management

The effects of context variables on appraisal processes and outcomes have been the object of speculation but have not been empirically examined in the detail that these effects warrant. It is believed that context is the key to understanding appraisal in organizations.

The business environment exercises both a direct and an indirect influence on the conduct of performance assessment. Whereas legislation has specific consequences, most other environmental factors have a diffuse and often unrealized effect on performance assessment and pay structures. The main environmental factors identified as having a contextual influence on performance management include:

Business culture: At the national level, culture affects performance management through sociopolitical traditions and attitudes which determine whether performance assessment is acceptable, and to what degree. Cultural norms dictate 'acceptable' standards of performance and the management methods by which they are assured.

Legislation: In today's globalized economy, the employment relationship between workers and employing organizations is seen as a contractual matter. This relationship is expressed in formal or legalistic statements of obligation between the two, such as written employment contracts, job descriptions and performance objectives. Employers taking HR and administrative decisions on the basis of performance assessment have to be mindful of possible legal action on the following grounds:

- Validity or accuracy of assessment ratings as predictors of future performance and promotion potential.
- Validity or accuracy of ratings as measures of past behaviour.
- Statutory norms laid down by the Government and Government authorities.

General economic conditions: Prevailing attitudes towards employees and, in turn, their response to performance assessment are considerably affected by issues such as unemployment and economic conditions of the nation. Growth and shrinkage in the job market which are influenced by changes in the economic scenario of a nation is conventionally believed to be followed by changes in the behaviour of workers and employers. At times of high unemployment, workers are thought to be concerned about losing their jobs and hence more conscientious and tolerant of strict management. When suitable employees are scarce, managers must be cautious — unflattering assessments can trigger an employee's move to another organization leading to high attrition.

Industry sector: Methods of performance management vary considerably between different industrial sectors, partly as a matter of the nature of the work involved, tradition and fashion. Sales and service dominated industries, such as retail business and financial services, tend to have clear individual or team objectives which can be translated readily into performance targets. Performance-related pay (PRP) is common in this sector. In other sectors like manufacturing sector performance objectives are more diffuse and difficult to measure so that PRP is not easily justified.

Technological change: Technological change, particularly changes in information technology has a dramatic effect on the nature of supervision, and hence performance assessment. Work can be done at a distance by traveling executives, overseas affiliates or telecommuters working from home. This raises intriguing issues for performance management. Further, technology has the capability to provide extensive information and statistics regarding an individual's performance that is being recorded on a real time basis into the information system. This information not only provides a meaningful measure of job performance but also provides a clear cut picture on the areas of performance improvement and skill development.

Flexibility and diversification: In the new business environment, the traditional nature of the employment relationship has considerably changed, moving the balance of power firmly in favour of employers. Organizations in today's highly competitive era have seen job descriptions have disappeared or, at least, have been diluted, so that employees can be asked to do virtually anything required by the organization. Conversely, performance criteria have been more tightly defined, typically expressed in the form of demanding objectives: forever-moving goalposts. Performance assessment has become the crucial means of monitoring this relationship.

Employee relations: Performance management is a means of enhancing managerial control, particularly through individual performance-related pay schemes. Individualization of pay (performance based pay systems) diminishes or neutralizes the role of collective bargaining. The purpose and influence of trade unions is thereby getting day by day diluted, reducing both their effectiveness and attractiveness as an alternative focus for employee involvement.

Workforce composition: One important function of performance assessment is the identification of individual strengths and weaknesses of the employees. Strengths may indicate a potential star performer, worthy of a management career route and promotion. Assessment employed to determine development needs ultimately serves to increase a nation's human capital. This helps the organization to identify and streamline the composition of their workforce with people who are the most competent in terms of their talents and abilities.

Performance Management Process

Performance Management should be regarded as a flexible process, not as a system. The use of the term system implies a rigid, standardized and bureaucratic approach that is inconsistent with the concept itself as a flexible and evolutionary, coherent, process that is applied by managers working with their teams in accordance to the environment and text where they operate. The performance management process consists of the following stages (as revealed by the following figure).

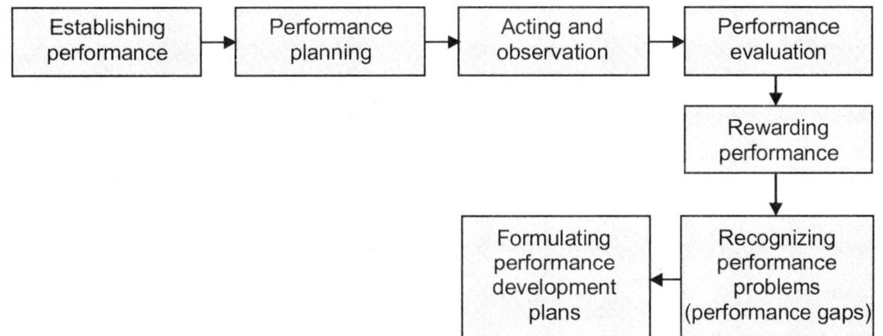

Fig. 3.33: Performance management process

- **Establishing Performance:** This stage involves the establishment of the performance objectives, competence requirements and performance related agreements with the employees and their supervisors.
- **Performance Planning:** This step involves agreeing objectives and competence requirements and agreeing upon performance related action plans, performance improvement and personal development plans.
- **Acting:** This involves carrying out various activities required to achieve objectives and plans and observing developments in the overall performance.
- **Monitoring and Evaluating Performance:** This involves checking on the progress in achieving performance objectives and evaluating the performance and achievements accomplished.
- **Rewarding:** This step involves recognizing the contribution in terms of performance accomplishments and achievements by compensation and rewards.
- **Identifying Performance Problems:** It involves identification of the bottlenecks and roadblocks of performance and also areas of improvement.
- **Performance Development Planning:** It involves planning of developmental activities so as to enhance capabilities of people and contribute to the overall performance improvement.

Performance Management Cycle

Performance Management can be described as a continuous self-renewing cycle as illustrated in the following figure. It is comprised of Planning, Acting, Monitoring, Reviewing stages. Infosys has a similar concept for their performance management system, which is known as "Corporate Performance Management (CPM)" cycle (as illustrated by the following exhibit).

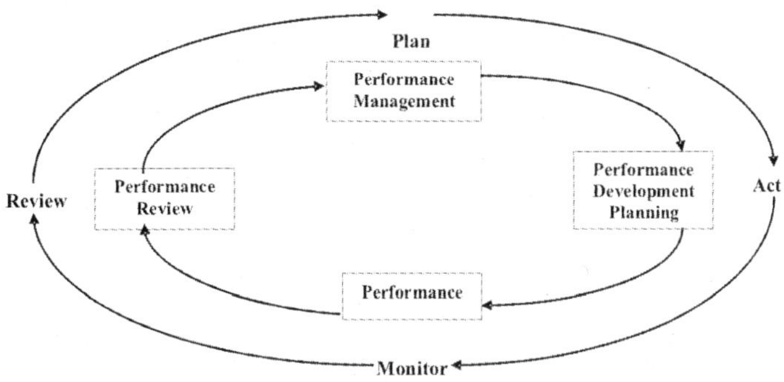

Fig. 3.34: The performance management cycle

How Performance Management Works?

The sequence of processes carried out in the performance management cycle as illustrated above follows the following sequence of activities, namely:

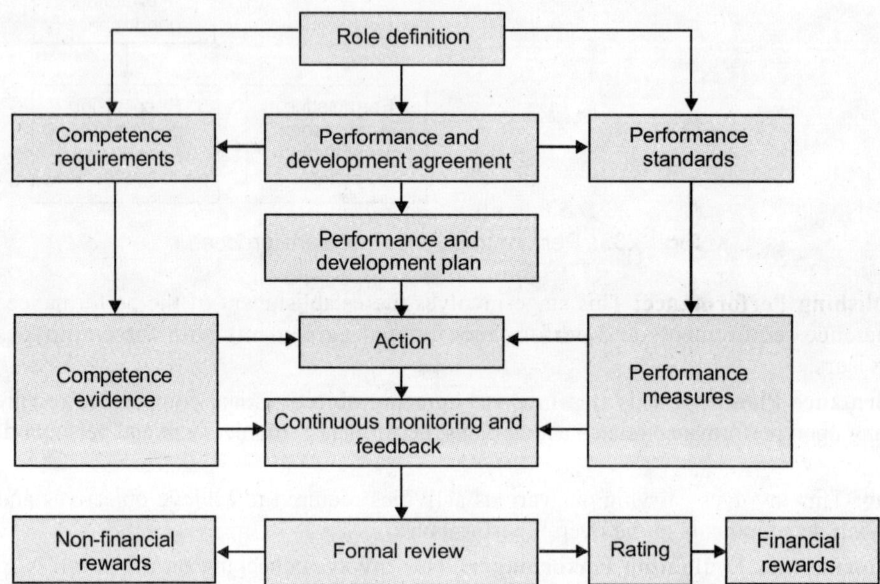

Fig. 3.35: The performance management sequence

Activities	Features
1. Role Definition	Here the KRAs and competency requirements identified and agreed upon
2. Performance Agreement	It defines performance expectations (in terms of objectives), how performance would be evaluated and competencies required to achieve the stated objectives
3. Performance Improvement Plan	It describes what individuals need to do so as to improve their performance.
4. Individual Development Plan	It describes the actions or steps individuals need to take so as to enhance their KSAs and levels of competence.
5. Managing Performance on an Ongoing Basis	It involves actions taken to implement performance agreement and performance improvement and Individual development plans.
6. Performance Review	It is the formal evaluation where a review of performance over a period occurs covering the achievements, progress and problems faced as the basis for the management of next performance cycle.

The basis upon which performance management works as a continuous process can be illustrated by the following figure:

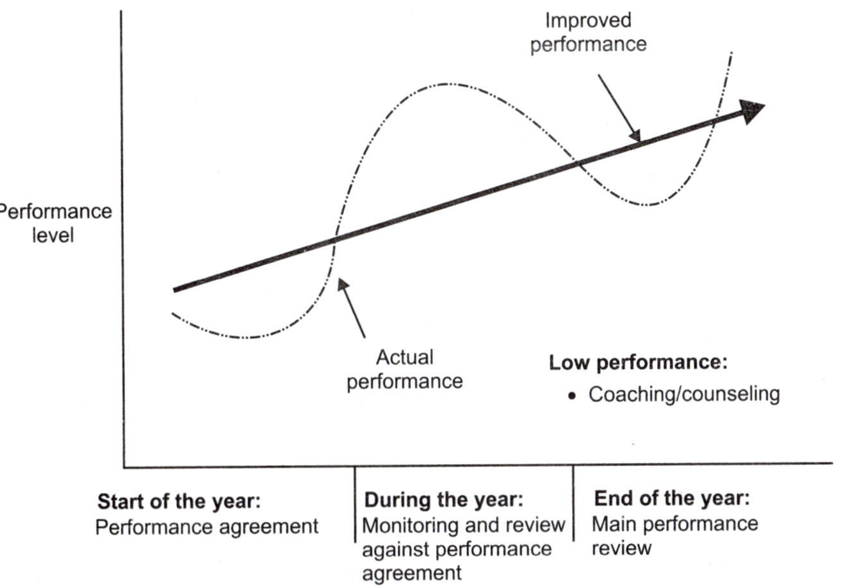

Fig. 3.36: Stages of performance management

(Courtesy: Armstrong, M., 2007: Performance Management: Key Strategies and Practical Guidelines, 3rd edition, Kogan Page Publishers, p. 18)

Who is Pesponsible for Performance Management?

Traditional Performance Management

Performance management in natural work groups usually operates according to the traditional performance management model in which the focus is on the work performance of an individual and his or her contributions to the mission of the organization, as observed and assessed by the evaluating manager. While the evaluating manager may solicit the input and involvement of the employee in each step in the process, authority and ultimate responsibility remains with the HR manager or the HR head of the organization.

Performance Management in Self Managed Teams

Performance management in self managed work team is managed by the team itself. This empowerment varies from organization to organization, or even from department to department, and also depends upon the readiness of the team members to assume those responsibilities. A fully empowered mature self managed team would decide their own jobs, set performance standards, give feedback to members about work progress, performance and team skills, appraise their own performance, and identify and support the training and development needs of the members. The organization, particularly the HR department, in this set up will provide guidelines and a framework for that performance management in terms of organizational policies and compliance regulations.

Performance Management in Cross Functional Teams

A cross-functional team typically operates without formal supervision, though it may have a team leader. Members usually report to evaluating managers in their concerned departments. These managers are often not present or be aware of what and when the team members are participating in the work of the team and may only know about the results of the team's work and the team member's performance through the reports of others, evidence of the team's products, or via customer feedback. Hence performance evaluation in this case definitely is a complexes process.

Whose Performance Should be Managed in Team Performance Evaluation?

When a team approach is in vogue, the focus of performance management is on the accomplishments of the team as well as the individual's contributions to those accomplishments. When the performance management process recognizes individual performance instead of team performance, the incentives work in favour of individual accomplishment alone, which can result in competitiveness at the expense of team interests. Many managers and supervisors have reported that team effectiveness is improved when both team and individual performance are recognized as significant and factored into the performance management process.

Performance Measures and Benchmarking

Performance Measures: Performance measures are a suite of quantifiable parameters that measure how an organization is performing over time:

- should be "mission relevant", and
- meaningful to staff and stakeholders alike, but
- not necessarily a basis for benchmarking

Benchmarking: Benchmarking is the process involving rigorously comparing an organization with similar bodies either domestically or internationally. Benchmarking provides a systematic and disciplined approach to objective comparisons with others — maintaining strengths through knowing weakness.

Definitions

Benchmarking is a method of improving business performance by learning from other companies how to do things better in order to be the "best in the class'.

"A continuous systematic process of evaluating companies recognized as industry leaders, to determine business and work processes that present the best practice and establish rational performance goals" (Kermally, S., 1997).

It does not matter which definition is being considered; all of them emphasize the fact that benchmarking practice should be a continuous, systematic process and that it should involve evaluation and measurement with a view to achieving excellence and becoming the "best in the class".

Objectives: Reputed organizations like IBM had emphasized on bechmarking for ensuring performance improvement in their organizations. The principal objectives behind these were as follows:

- To ensure that the business process goals are being set to exceed the best qualitative results achieved by world class leaders.
- To incorporate best practice throughout the organization's business process
- To reach a level of maturity where benchmarking is an ongoing process/part of the management system in all areas of the business.

Benchmarking offers the following advantages, namely:

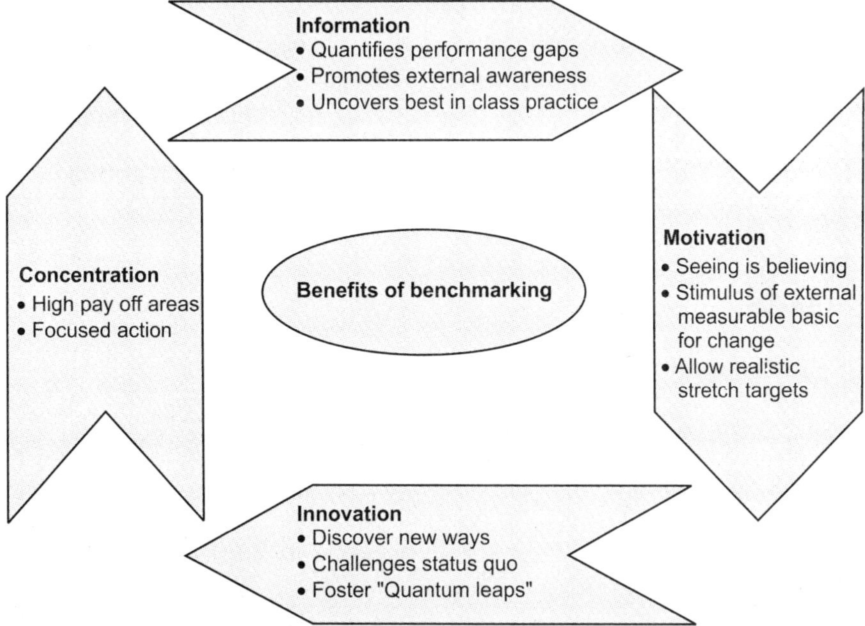

Fig. 3.37: The different benefits of benchmarking

Benchmarks could be used as a 360-degree assessment tool that offers experienced managers an in-depth look at development by assessing skills honed from a multitude of on-the-job leadership experiences. Benchmarks also helps executives identify what lessons may still need to be learned, establishes what specific work experiences need to be sought out in order to develop critical skills for success, and identifies possible problems that may stall their career.

Benefits of using Benchmarks in Performance Management

In-depth Feedback: Unlike other assessment tools, benchmarks does not emphasize administrative or communication skills—innate characteristics that usually change little through the course of a lifetime. Instead, Benchmarks goes deeper into development to assess skills learned by engaging in critical on the job experiences and how certain qualities are expressed in leadership behaviour. Further, Benchmarks assesses problems that may stall a career, helping an executive work on specific issues before an employee's career is derailed.

In-depth Development: Development is not a one-time event but rather a long-term, continuous process. Because of this, each "Benchmarks Feedback Report" is accompanied by a "Developmental Learning Guide". This guide helps the participating managers to develop an effective strategy for performance planning and improvement.

Easy to Understand: Benchmarks feedback is presented graphically— making it easy for the participating managers to assess areas of strength and areas in need of performance development.

Valid and Reliable: Benchmarks are based on research data with thousands of top executives located across the industry. Benchmarks ensure that it is reliable and valid in implementing the right performance standards in performance evaluation.

Flexibility: Benchmarks can help organizations in terms of

- Individual assessment, coaching and planning
- Complimenting an existing executive leadership development program; and
- Establishing a profile of a specific group's strengths and areas in need of performance development.

Exhibit: Performance Management Systems in Real Life Organizations

The INFYOSYS Corporate Performance Management

(*Courtesy: http://www.infosys.com/german/services/cpm/default.asp*)

Corporate Performance Management (CPM) is an approach to bring in systematic and integrated improvements in the management processes to ensure efficiency and effectiveness in strategy execution. At the core of CPM is

- A metrics-based strategic planning and execution framework that helps align strategic plans with resource allocation and strategic initiatives
- Strategic goal alignment thru enhanced communication and focusing processes/resources towards organization objectives
- A structured information based review mechanism that provides the feedback loop and connects strategic planning to operational performance measures

The INFYOSYS Approach: Most enterprises have deeply entrenched strategic planning processes; but strategy fails during execution. Executives spend ample time in making incremental improvements in processes viz. planning, budgeting and forecasting, but isolated and **siloed** implementations fail to create organization wide alignment and deliver required results.

Infosys' CPM approach focuses on incorporating best principles of corporate performance management than a mere implementation of popular frameworks, and is based on our proprietary Performance Management cycle that helps an organization to execute upon its strategies effectively and efficiently.

The INFYOSYS Performance Management Cycle: Traditional approaches to CPM are characterized by excessive reliance on popular management frameworks such as Balanced Scorecard, Six-Sigma or Activity Based Management. While these frameworks do help implement change, the applicability of these frameworks depends on the organizational context.

At Infosys, the performance management approach aims to bring systematic and integrated improvements across the performance management cycle. This holistic approach helps to identify specific areas of improvement and builds strong linkages with the existing processes of the organization.

CPM Framework at Infosys: At Infosys, we believe that a framework is as robust as the underlying principles. The CPM framework is based on following principles that the organization have derived from deep experience in successfully managing corporate performance of global corporations and advising our clients.

- Comprehensive and structured planning
- Integrated performance management processes
- Disciplined execution and review
- Information based decision-making

Contd...

- Nimble management architecture

Based on the above principles Infosys CPM framework addresses various components in the Performance Management cycle along three critical dimensions

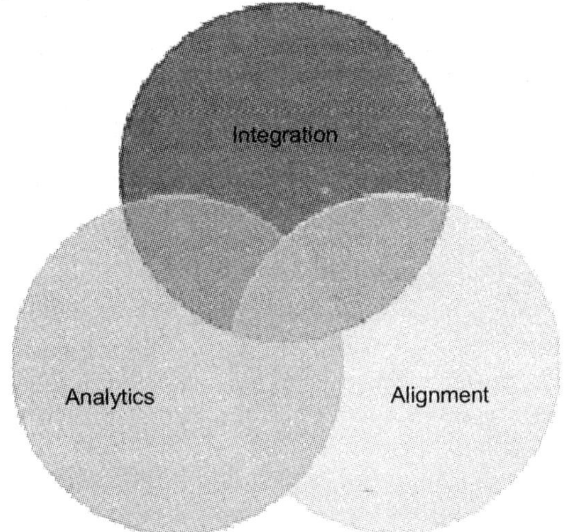

- **Integration:** Integrated planning and review builds the missing links between critical management processes like planning, forecasting, budgeting etc.
- **Alignment:** A strategy execution framework (for e.g. Balanced Scorecard) to align entire organization along the strategic objectives and create accountability by cascading key performance measures across the levels.
- **Strategic Business Intelligence:** Generate integrated business insights to aid executive decision making using right time performance analytics, scenario analysis and collaborative planning mechanisms.

Impact on Organizational Performance: Infosys' CPM approach impacts performance management processes from organizational planning (strategic planning, risk management, budgeting and forecasting, business unit planning and operational planning) to decision support processes (performance analysis and predictive business modeling) to review processes aimed at creating a closed loop of performance improvements. This ensures that the organization isn't just measuring results, but also assessing them against the articulated strategy and making course corrections where necessary – including changes in budgets – if needed. This provides the organization a unique combination of flexibility and control that is at the heart of ensuring speed and effectiveness of response to dynamic market changes.

Experiential Exercise: Performance Management Scorecard

Human resource professionals have known for years that a sound performance management process can contribute to the bottom line. From 1990 to 1993 the University of Chicago and Hewitt Associates conducted a study of 437 publicly traded companies; 205 with a performance management process and 232 without one. The study concluded that over the three-year period, companies with a performance management process had significantly greater financial returns, including return on assets, return on equity, cash flow, sales growth and shareholder return. Below is an easy to use Performance Management Scorecard to appraise the quality of an organization's current performance management process.

Applying the Scorecard

An overall rating of 3.0 indicates the current performance management process adequately measures individual performance and should be contributing to the bottom line and increasing stock value. An overall rating of less than 3.0 indicates that the performance measurement process needs an overhaul. Individual category ratings less than 3.0 show areas where organizational process could be improved and fine-tuned. Each of the categories may be weighted in importance to reflect the organization's performance capability and culture.

The selection of the categories to be rated in the scorecard is based on the following aspects:

1. **Strategic Alignment:** Studies conducted by Ernst and Young in 1998 inreputed organizations provide substantial evidence that the strategic alignment of the performance management process can have a significant impact on profitability and stock value of the company.
2. **Employee Buy-in:** To build a culture of accountability for results, the performance management process must include a plan to win over the hearts and minds of employees and gain their buy-in and support. If individuals develop their own objectives over which they have "full control" and develop their own objective measures of performance you assure personal ownership for accomplishment. High-performers thrive when they can be recognized for the value of their work. The role of the manager becomes not a taskmaster, but a coach to ensure alignment of individual objectives with key strategies and to encourage ever-improving performance. Kaplan and Norton describe this key element as a Climate for Action.
3. **Quality:** It is not sufficient just to measure what work and how much work is done but perhaps even more important to measure how well work is being done. The whole quality movement of the 80's demonstrated the significance of improvements in product quality to provide a competitive advantage. The latest generation of quality improvement initiatives, the Six Sigma process, has improved productivity and increased profits in companies such as General Electric, Allied Signal and Motorola.
4. **Degree of Difficulty:** Some judgement should be placed on the degree of difficulty to achieve an acceptable individual performance measure. Clear well-defined stretch goals can stimulate outstanding performance. In "Built to Last" Jim Collins described how BHAGs (Big Hairy Audacious Goals) can be a powerful mechanism to stimulate corporate success. Individual performance targets should be challenging, but achievable. The performance management process should have a mechanism for employee and supervisor to strike a careful balance between objectives that ensure progress, and the likelihood of achieving the objective. Unachievable performance targets set too high will be de-motivating. Performance targets that are too easy to achieve will also not be motivational and will not move the organization forward.

Exhibit: Performance Management Scorecard Please Fill in the Appropriate Rating

	Strategic alignment	Employee buy-in	Quality	"Stretch"
Rating	Degree of linkage between individual objectives with your organization's strategies and business objectives	Degree of freedom the employee has to establish achievable individual objectives and performance measures	Do performance measures include a quality component such as measurement by customers or comparison to best practices?	Degree of difficulty of performance measures i.e. "stretch"
High 5				
Above average 4				
Satisfactory 3				
Below average 2				
Poor 1				
Overall rating				

Dil Se.......

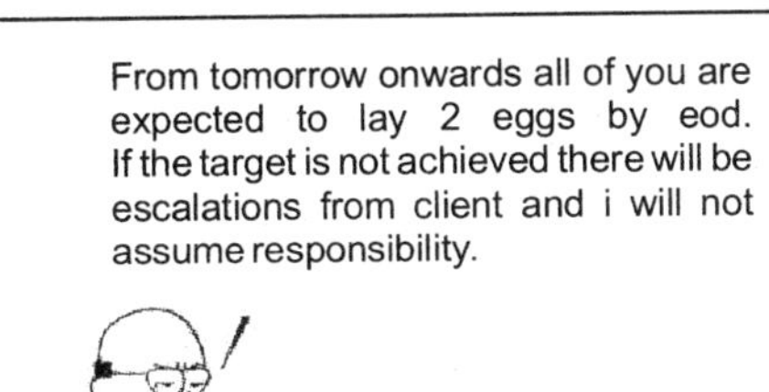

(*Courtesy: http://groups.yahoo.com/group/fun_and_fun_only/*)

REFERENCE

1. Kermally, S., (1997): "Managing Performance," Butterworth-Heinemann.

QUESTION BANK

1. Define Performance management. State its importance.
2. Describe the components of a performance management system in an organization.
3. Describe the performance management process.
4. What is performance management cycle? What are the various stages of a performance management cycle?
5. Give an example of the performance management process in a real life organization.
6. Performance management concept is a much broader concept compared to performance appraisals. Comment on the statement.
7. How can benchmarking help in performance management?
8. Distinguish between performance appraisal and performance management.

Internet Exercises

- Surf the website www.empxtrack.com and collect information regarding performance management and present the same in your class.
- Surf the website www.kpilibrary.com and enumerate your findings from the same.

Experiential Learning

- Prepare a performance development plan for employees (doctors) working in a hospital.
- Prepare a presentation on the performance management initiatives taken by a reputed organization.

PERFORMANCE AND POTENTIAL APPRAISAL

THEME READING: PERFORMANCE APPRAISAL AT PEPSI-COLA INTERNATIONAL

Pepsi-Cola International (PCI), with operations in over 150 countries, has devised a common performance appraisal system that focuses on motivating managers to achieve and maintain high standards of performance. Administrative consistency is achieved through the use of a performance appraisal system of five feedback mechanisms—instant feedback, coaching, accountability based performance appraisals, development feedback and a human resource plan. The common system provides guidelines for performance appraisal yet allows for modification to suit cultural differences. For example, the first step –instant feedback – is based on the principle that any idea about any aspect of the business or about an individual's performance is raised appropriately and discussed in a sensitive manner. The instant feedback message can be delivered in any culture; the important thing is not how it is done but that it is done.

In practice at PCI, the successful delivery of instant feedback requires same adjustment to local cultures. Americans use it because it fits the fast-paced way of doing business. In most Asian cultures, feedback may be tough and direct but is never given in public; nor; in some Asian cultures, does head-nodding during instant feedback signify agreement, only that the message has been heard. Some Latins will argue very strongly if they do not agree with the feedback, and some employees, Indian nationals, for example, will insist on a great deal of specificity. The purpose of instant feedback is always to improve business performance, not to criticize cultural styles. Using this system, PCI tries to balance the cultural and administrative imperatives of successfully managing the performance of a diverse workforce.

THEME CASE: THE CASE OF PERFORMANCE APPRAISAL IN A FAMILY OWNED BUSINESS ORGANIZATION

Frank became chief financial officer and a member of the Executive Committee of a medium sized and moderately successful family-owned contracting business six months ago. The first non-family member to hold such a position and to be included in the Executive Committee, he took the job despite a lunch-time remark by the company's CEO that some members of the family were concerned about Frank's "fit with the company culture". But the CEO (who is married to the daughter of the founder of the company) said he was willing to "take a chance" on Frank.

Soon after Frank started, the company decided for the first time to "right-size" (a euphemism for downsize) to respond to rapid changes in its business. Frank, who had been through this before when he was a senior manager in his previous company, agreed this was good for the long-term health of the 20-year-old company. He decided not to worry that family members seemed more concerned about their own short-term financial interests.

Besides, the CEO was relying on Frank to help him determine how to downsize in an ethical manner; the CEO said he trusted Frank more on this than he did the head of his personnel department, who had "been around a little too long".

On Frank's recommendation, the company decided to make its lay-off decisions based on the annual performance appraisal scores of the employees. Each department manager would submit a list of employees ranked by the average score of their last three appraisals.

If the employee had been with the company less than three years, if the score for two employees was identical, or if there was some extraordinary circumstance, the manager would note it and make a decision about where to rank the person. At some point, Frank and the Executive Committee would draw a line, and those below the line would be laid off.

As Frank was reviewing the evaluations, he was puzzled to find three departments in which the employee at the bottom of the list had "N/A" where the evaluation score should have been written. When he asked the managers to explain, they told him these employees had been with the company almost since the beginning. When performance appraisals had been instituted six years earlier, the CEO agreed to the longtime employees' request that they keep receiving informal evaluations "as they always had."

The managers told Frank they'd questioned this decision, and the CEO had told them it wasn't their problem.

When Frank raised this issue with the CEO, he responded, "Oh, I know. I haven't really evaluated them in a long time, but it's time for them to retire anyway. They just aren't performing the way they used to. The company's been very good to them. They've got plenty of retirement stored away, not to mention the severance you've convinced me to offer. They're making pretty good money, so cutting them should let us lower the line a little and save jobs for some of the younger people—you know, young kids with families just starting out. And don't worry about a lawsuit. No way they'd do that." "Do they know they're not performing well?" Frank asked. "I don't know," the CEO responded. "They should. Everybody else in the company does."

As they walked to the door, the CEO put his arm around Frank's shoulder. "By the way," he said, "you should know that you've won over the Executive Committee. They think you are a terrific fit with this company. I'm glad you talked with me today about these three employees. You got it right: This is a company that cares for its employees—as long as it can and as long as they're producing. Always has, always will." Frank left the CEO's office with the vague feeling that he had some moral choices to make. Does he have an ethical dilemma? What's the right thing to do? If he disagrees with the CEO, how does he protect his own career and the interests of his own family? What do you think?

(*Courtesy: Thomas Shanks, S.J., Executive Director of the Markkula Centre for Applied Ethics, Ref: http://www.scu.edu/ethics/dialogue/candc/cases/performance.html*)

Defining Performance Appraisal

Performance appraisal is the formal, structured system of measuring and evaluating an employee's job related behaviours and outcomes to discover how and why the employee is presently performing on the job and how the employee can perform more effectively in the future so that the employee as well as the organization can mutually benefit.

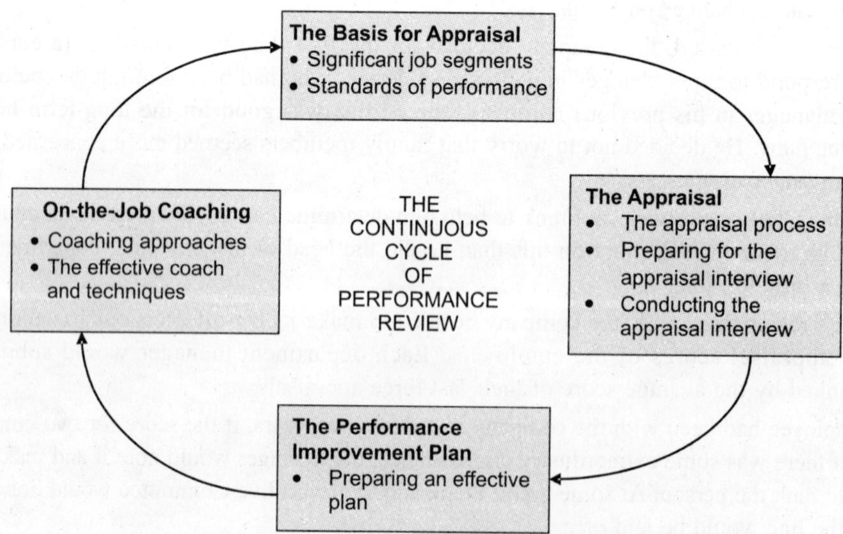

Fig. 3.38: The continuous cycle of performance review

Scott, Clothier and Spriegel have described "Performance Appraisal is the process of evaluating the employee's performance on the job in terms of requirements of the job".

Yoder has described "Performance Appraisal refers to all formal procedures used in working organizations to evaluate personalities and contributions and potential of group members".

In order to get improved performance from appraisal and coaching, a continuous process is necessary. It can be illustrated by the above figure. The first step is to clarify what is expected of the employee. This can be done by identifying significant job segments and developing standards of performance. The second step is to appraise performance and to discuss it in an appraisal interview. At the conclusion of the interview, a performance improvement plan can be developed. On-the-job coaching is necessary to help the employee improve his performance. The first step is repeated on whatever time schedule is established by the organization.

Features of Performance Appraisal

- It is a systematic process, which aims to evaluate performance of the employees on an objective and judgemental basis.
- It provides an objective description of an employee's job's relevant strengths and weaknesses.
- It aims to find out how well the employee is performing the job and tries to establish a plan for further improvement.
- The appraisal period is carried out periodically according to a definite plan.
- It can be formal or informal. The informal evaluation is likely to be more subjective and influenced by personal factors.

Objectives of Performance Appraisal

- Performance appraisal is a tool for communicating the skills, knowledge and attitudes required for the different job roles. The appraisal criteria acts as a guide to the attitudes and behaviours that the organization would like their staff in their various capacities to have.
- To enhance an organization's corporate value in the pursuit of innovative quality in the areas of **Customers, Employees, Society, Products, Technology, Management** and **Fairness.** These values are translated to performance measures that are used in the appraisal system. This enhances awareness of corporate values and promotes behaviours that are in line with the organization's values.
- To effect promotions based on competence and performance.
- To confirm services of probationary employees upon their completing the probationary period satisfactorily.
- To assess the training and development needs of employees.
- To generate adequate feedback and guidance from the immediate superior to an employee working under him.
- To decide upon a pay raise where regular pay scales have not been fixed.
- To provide inputs to system of rewards (comprising salary increments, transfers, promotions, demotions or terminations) and salary administration.
- To let the employees know where they stand in so far as their performance is concerned and to assist them with constructive criticism and guidance for the purpose of their development.
- To improve communication by providing a format for dialogue between the superior and the subordinate, and improves understanding of personal goals and concerns.
- It can be used to determine whether HR programs such as selection, training and transfers have been effective or not.
- To generate significant, relevant, free and valid information about the employees.

Need, Importance and Advantages of Performance Appraisal

- Scientific basis for judging the merit or worth of employees.
- Sound basis for promotion, demotion, transfer or termination of employees.
- Helps in distinguishing between efficient and inefficient workers.
- It reveals the defects in the selection procedure.
- Helps to know the potentials of the subordinates systematically.
- Helps correct placements.
- It helps in constructively guiding the employees.
- It prevents grievances and develops a sense of confidence.
- Protects the management against the charges of discrimination.

Table 3.2: Multiple Purposes of Performance Assessment

General Applications	*Specific Purpose*
Developmental uses	Identification of individual employee needs and aspirations Providing performance feedback Facilitating transfer and job assignments decisions Identification of individual strengths and developmental needs Forming the basis of training needs assessment
Administrative Uses/Decisions	Salary and compensation management Promotion decisions Employee retention or termination Recognition of individual performance Employee lay-offs and termination related decisions Identification of poor performance
Organizational Maintenance/Objectives	HR planning Determining organization training needs Evaluation of organizational goal achievement Information for goal identification Evaluation of HR systems Reinforcement of organizational development needs Organizational restructuring and remodeling
Documentation	Criteria for validation research Documentation for HR decisions Helping to meet legal requirements (Statutory Compliance checks)

Performance reviews can be used as a tool for day to day administrative as well as employee developmental purposes or activities. The following table depicts the comparison of two types of performance reviews.

Table 3.3: Comparison of Two Kinds of Performance Reviews

Hallmarks	*Performance Reviews for salary Administration*	*Performance Reviews for Improved Performance*
Looking	Backward	Forward
Considering	Overall performance	Detailed performance
Comparing with	Other people	Job standards and objectives
Determined by	Manager, higher management, human resources department	Manager and employee together
Interview climate	Subjective, emotional	Objective, unemotional
Factors to consider	Salary range, total money available, inflation, seniority, performance, education	Performance

Understanding Performance Appraisals

Performance appraisal has always been a hot and challenging issue for the managers across the world, HR managers as well as the line managers. The following caselets would help to discuss some of the common issues in designing and implementing a performance appraisal system.

Caselet 1

XYZ is a reputed nationalized bank which has its operations throughout India. The bank had done quite well over the years. The management is committed towards the organization's employees. The HR and administration department takes care of performance management related decisions and issues. The employees are a satisfied lot as they feel that the management is fair in terms of compensation and their performance evaluation. The HR head always made it a point to see that the appraisal system being implemented enjoyed the confidence and support of the employees. Hence there was always a feedback session after the appraisal process was over. XYZ Bank had a high turnover of employees. Even though its compensation packages were similar to those at ABC Bank, the employees were not happy as any incentive programs were not in place in their organization. ABC bank being a private organization ensured that employee contributions were recognized by a sound incentive scheme, which lacked in XYZ bank. Although XYZ bank had recently decided to introduce credit card, debit card facilities and other value added services like their private bank competitors, employees at XYZ seemed to be less interested.

Caselet 2

Premier Constructions is a 30-year-old company that has been following the traditional methods of performance appraisal. But with the changing business environment, the managing director, Amit Kumar, felt that the company should change its performance appraisal system. The company's employee strength was 1000 plus and implementing an appraisal system that catered to employees across different areas was not a simple task. The company held its monthly review meetings at which all the departmental heads and various business unit heads discussed their current problems and future strategies. These meetings provided a forum for the managers in various departments to interact with each other and identify areas of immediate improvement. The company used an innovative idea to implement the new appraisal system. They used this forum to launch and implement the new appraisal system. As a result of this initiative the change was positively accepted by the employees as they felt the new system belonged to them and the impact was immense for the management. Six months later when the company had the 1st appraisal with the new system there was a marked performance improvement for most employees as well as that for the managerial positions.

***Learnings from the Caselets*:** As evident, these caselets discuss some of the common issues in designing and implementing a performance appraisal system. One of the caselets discusses the linkage of the appraisal system with the compensation and incentive programs whereas the other not only depicts the importance of a new performance appraisal, but the broader issue of performance management and its implementation.

Performance Appraisal compared with Job Evaluation

Performance Appraisal	Job Evaluation
Performance Appraisal identifies the differences among the employees in terms of their performance.	Job Evaluation is the analysis of various jobs to know the demands which the normal performance of particular jobs make on average performance of the employees concerned.
The chief purpose of PA is to appraise the performance of individuals to take decisions like increase in pay, transfer, promotion, training etc. It also provides the employees with information regarding their strong and weak points.	The purpose of Job Evaluation is very limited i.e. to determine the worth of the job on the basis of demands made by it on the average workers

Contd...

Performance Appraisal rates the man and not the job as it is concerned with assessing the abilities of the individuals	Job Evaluation rates the jobs in the organization that will be fair and equitable. It is used as a basis of wage structure in the organization

Essentials of Effective Performance Appraisal

In order to successfully implement and execute a performance appraisal system it is essential to consider the following points:

- The employees should be made aware in terms of goals, targets and behaviour
- Performance appraisals and performance evaluations should be strictly "Job-related"
- Appraisal related decisions should be "Performance-based"
- Evaluation criteria and performance standards should be "Uniform and non-variable"
- The appraisal proceed should be "Fair, just and equitable"
- Appraisers should be honest, rational and objective in terms of executing the appraisal
- Superiors should be well trained to ensure uniformity, consistency and reliability
- Performance reports should be examined meticulously before taking any positive or negative action.
- Intra and inter-departmental consistency and uniformity should be ensured.
- There should be provision of appeals against appraisals to ensure confidence of the employees and their associations/unions.

Appraisal Formats

Over the years, many different formats and procedures have been tried to meet the above discussed issues related to appraisal systems. Commonly used performance appraisal formats include:

1. **Global ratings:** This includes "one-dimensional rating system" that uses a rater's overall estimate of performance without distinguishing between critical job dimensions (poor, fair, good, excellent).
2. **Trait-based scales:** This is a multidimensional (or graphic) approach used to measure and evaluate performance. Some commonly used traits are: loyalty, dependability, cooperation, initiative and self-confidence.
3. **Effectiveness-based systems:** This is a system based on "objective" results, representing the measurement of an employee's contribution, not an employee's activities or behaviours. Management by Objectives (MBO) is a popular example of this kind of performance appraisal format.

Timing and Frequency of Performance Appraisal

Performance appraisals should be carried out to cover specific periods, the organization deciding on the intervals. Most performance appraisal schemes are annual. Apart from this biannual evaluations are also effectively carried out as that in the case of smaller organizations. Any interval (one year or six months) is valid provided the employees (appraises) know what it is and recognize the importance of the appraisals when they occur. Ideally the whole organization should conduct appraisals within a set time, say six weeks, in order to focus attention on the process and ensure that everyone is covered roughly the same time. Spreading it out over the year is not conducive to goodwill and commitment.

Planning the Appraisal

A meaningful performance appraisal is a two-way process that benefits both the employees and the organization as a whole. The organization has to meticulously plan an appraisal strategy for this purpose:

(a) ***Before the appraisal*****:** Before the beginning of the appraisal process the organization needs to ensure the following aspects namely:

- Establish key task areas and performance goals
- Set performance goals
- Get the facts
- Schedule each appraisal interview well in advance

(b) ***During the appraisal*****:** During this emphasis is being given on the following aspects namely:

- Encourage two-way communication
- Discuss and agree on performance goals for the future
- To think about how one can assist the employee to achieve more at work.
- Record notes of the interview
- End the interview on an upbeat note

(c) ***After the appraisal*****:** This involves the following aspects, namely:

- Preparing a formal record of the performance interview discussions
- Monitor performance
- Identify areas of performance improvement

Approaches to Performance Appraisal: George Odiorne has identified four basic approaches to performance appraisals, namely:

(a) ***Personality-based systems*****:** Here the appraisal system takes into consideration of a list of personality traits that presumably are significant in the jobs of the individuals to be appraised. Such traits include those of initiative, drive, intelligence, ingenuity, creativity, loyalty and trustworthiness etc.

(b) ***Generalized descriptive systems*****:** These include qualities or actions of presumably good performers. These are described in terms of the qualities of "good performers" regarding to what extent appraises can "organize, plan, control, motivate, delegate, communicate, and make things happen".

(c) ***Behavioural descriptive systems*****:** These systems feature detailed Job Analysis and Job Descriptions, including specific statements of the actual behaviour required from successful employees.

(d) ***Result-centered systems*****:** These appraisal systems (Work-centered or job-centered systems) are directly job related. They require that manager and subordinates sit down at the start of each work evaluation period and determine the work to be done in all areas of responsibility and functions, and the specific standards of performance to be used in each area.

STAGES OF THE PERFORMANCE MANAGEMENT SYSTEM

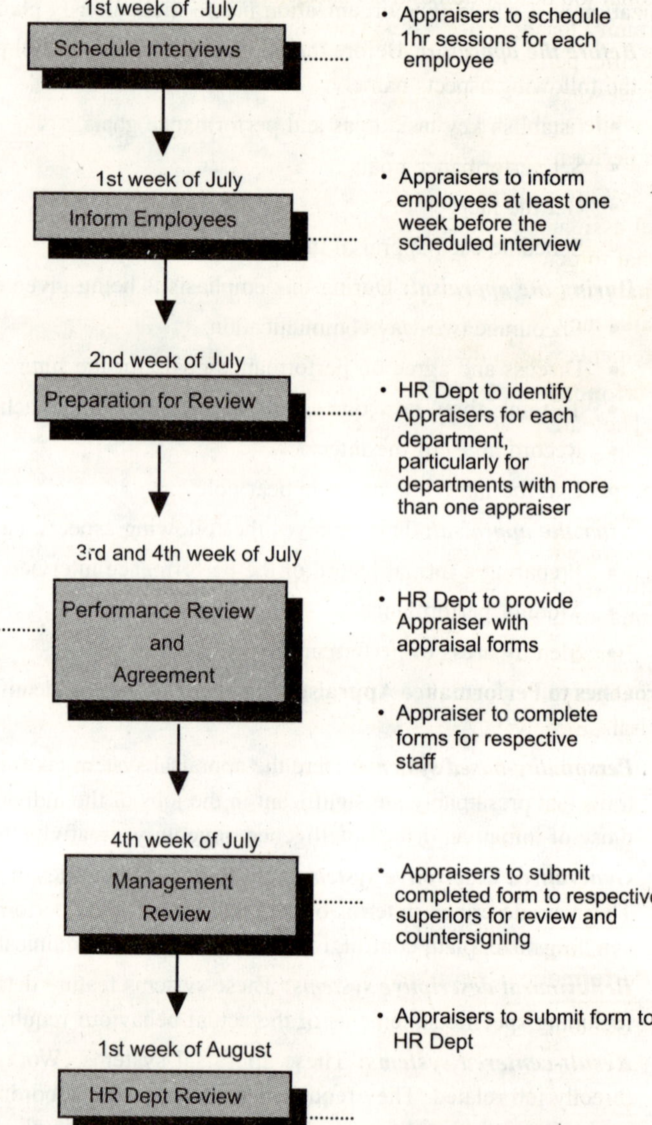

Fig. 3.39: Scheduling the appraisal process

Establishing Performance Standards

Performance Standards describe the specific duties and responsibilities for a particular job based upon the functional job description and set specific performance measures for the tasks. Standards provide a greater opportunity for more accurate communication between a supervisor and an employee if they are written to be specific, pertinent, attainable, measurable and observable. *Standards of Performance* are the conditions that exist when the work has been done in an acceptable manner. They explain *how well* the job should be done, while significant job segments describe *what* should be done. These standards become the basis on which performance is judged.

They are also an invaluable tool when writing performance evaluations, considering pay increases, special assignments and/or justification for promotions. Before conducting a performance appraisal it is essential to determine performance standards, which should be job-based and be derived from a thorough job analysis (reflected in job descriptions and job specifications). After establishment of performance standards they facilitate organizations to translate organizational goals and objectives into the respective job requirements which convey acceptable and unacceptable levels of performance to the employees.

Performance standards provide the employee with specific performance expectations for each major duty. They are the observable behaviours and actions which explain *how* the job is to be done, plus the results that are expected for satisfactory job performance. They tell the employee what a good job looks like. The purpose of performance standards is to communicate expectations. Some supervisors prefer to make them as specific as possible, and some prefer to use them as talking points with the specificity defined in the discussion with their subordinates. Managers may also expect certain behaviours (e.g. friendliness, helpfulness, courteousness, punctuality, etc.) It is often these behaviours that determine whether performance is acceptable according to organizational norms. Performance standards are:

- Based on the position, not the individual
- Observable, specific indicators of success
- Meaningful, reasonable and attainable
- Describe "fully satisfactory" performance once trained
- Expressed in terms of Quantity, Quality, Timeliness, Cost, Safety, or Outcomes

Performance standards permit managers to specify and communicate precise information to employees with respect to quality and quantity of performance in terms of outputs.

Components of Performance Standards	Features
1. Strategic Relevance	It refers to the extent to which performance standards relate to the strategic objectives of the organization, which are subsequently translated into performance standards of the employees in the organization
2. Criterion Deficiency	It refers to the extent to which performance standards represent the entire range of an employee's roles and responsibilities in the organization
3. Criterion Contamination	These involve factors outside an employee's control that can influence his/her performance
4. Reliability	It refers to the stability or consistency of a performance standard and also to the extent to which employees tend to maintain a certain level of performance over a given time.

Setting Performance Standards: The following figure depicts a three tiered model for setting performance standards. The first step involves setting performance domains, determining performance standards and identifying performance indicators.

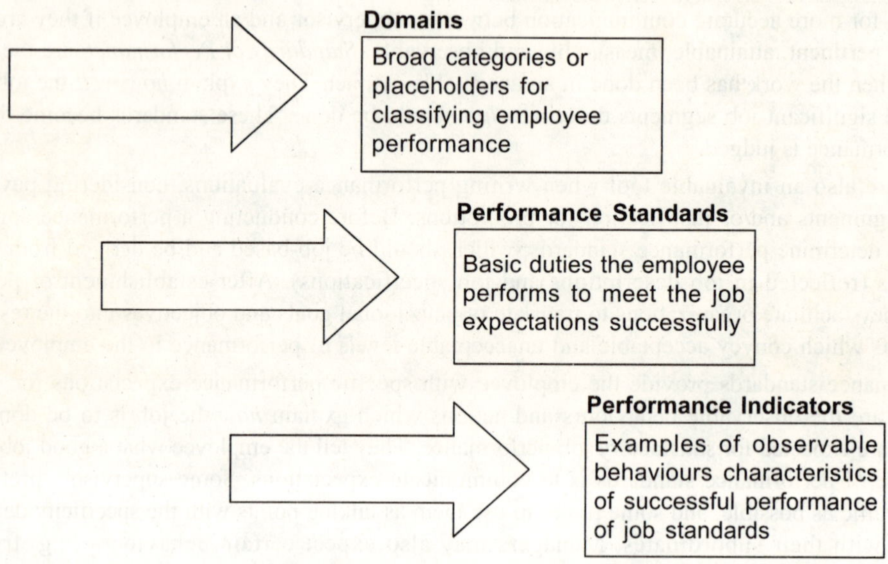

Fig. 3.40: A 3-tiered model of setting performance standards

In the first level performance domains are defined in terms of broad categories classifying employee performance. This is followed by identifying performance standards which involves basic duties the employee performs to meet the job expectations successfully. In the next level performance indicators are determined where observable behaviours of successful performance of job standards are identified. The performance standards are expressions of the performance threshold(s), requirement(s), or expectation(s) that must be met for each element at a particular level of performance. They must be focused on results and include credible measures such as:

- **Quality:** It addresses how well the employee or work unit is expected to perform the work and/or the accuracy or effectiveness of the final product. It refers to accuracy, appearance, usefulness, or effectiveness. Measures can include error rates (such as the number or percentage of errors allowable per unit of work) and customer satisfaction rates (determined through a customer survey/feedback).
- **Quantity:** It addresses how much work the employee or work unit is expected to produce. Measures are expressed as a number of products or services expected, or as a general result to achieve.
- **Timeliness:** Timeliness addresses how quickly, when, or by what date the employee or work unit is expected to produce the work.
- **Cost Effectiveness:** It addresses monetary savings or cost control. These should address cost effectiveness on specific resource levels (money, personnel, or time) that can generally be documented and measured. Cost effectiveness measures may include such aspects of performance as maintaining or reducing unit costs, reducing the time it takes to produce or provide a product or service, or reducing waste.

Following are samples of standards of performance that have been developed for segments of different jobs in a variety of organizations.

Example of Performance Standards for a Production Foreman

Significant Job Segments	Standards of Performance
1. Safety	• Monthly safety meetings are conducted in accordance with company schedules. • Safe operating procedures are followed by all employees. • Regular monthly inspections are held in the department in accordance with the approved checklist. • Action is taken within five days to correct any unsafe condition. • Monthly safety reports are submitted by the 5th of the following month.
2. Controlling costs	• Waste and scrap are kept below 2 per cent of total production. • One cost-saving improvement per month is initiated and put into operation. • Overtime costs are held to a maximum of 3 per cent of direct labour costs. • All purchases are made in the most economical manner according to a buying plan. • Overhead costs are kept within budget limitations. • Salary controls are exercised in accordance with the salary administration plan. • The ratio of productivity to costs is improved by 1 per cent every six months.
3. Developing employees	• New employees are inducted and trained in employees accordance with a definite plan. • Performance reviews are held with all employees on an annual basis. • The appraisal and performance improvement plan aspects of the performance review program are reviewed with the manager. • Discussions are held with employees at least quarterly to see that performance improvement takes place according to plan. • Responsibilities and authority are delegated to employees on a planned basis.

Example of Performance Standards for an Accounting Executive

- Researches information:
  - review contents of time-sensitive publications, accurately summarize funding information and appropriately distribute in weekly email
- Processes requests for external funding:
  - verifies accuracy of budgets and forms,
  - secures appropriate internal signatures,

- submits to finance in an accurate and timely manner
- maintains office files so that tracking the funding process is easily managed

- Monitors accounts and processes paperwork:
  - identifies charges, verifies availability of funds and obtains proper authorizations in accurate and timely manner
  - processes expenditures within five working days

Performance Appraisal Process

Managing employee performance is an integral part of the work that all managers and rating officials perform throughout the year. It is as important as managing financial resources and program outcomes because employee performance or the lack thereof, has a profound effect on both the financial and program components of any organization.

Setting Performance Appraisal Objectives and Standards: This step involves setting the objectives or targets of performance, and determining performance standards. The managers and supervisors may sit with their employees in a collaborative approach to set the performance criteria, and identify the "Key Performance Areas (KPAs)", "Key Result Areas (KRAs)" and "Key Performance Indicators (KPIs)".

Key Performance Areas (KPAs)

Key performance areas (KPAs) are those important work activities engaged in on a daily or weekly basis with a meaningful group of people in the organization. They are the things that, if employees focus on them and do them well, will produce the best results and give them the greatest success in their tasks/roles.

What are the Ways to Identify KPAs?

To determine employee key performance areas, employees must stand back and look at the totality of what they do in work or their tasks. This can easily be understood by taking an average week and thinking of the general categories of things on which they spend their time and the people with whom (or for whom) they are involved with during the tasks. These big activities can be considered or included as key performance areas.

Key Result Areas (KRAs)

"Key Result Areas" or KRAs refer to general areas of outcomes or outputs for which a role is responsible. A typical role targets three to five KRA. KRAs are also known as **key work outputs** (KWOs).

Value of KRAs

Identifying KRAs helps individuals:

- Clarify their roles
- Align their roles to the organization's business or strategic plan
- Focus on results rather than activities
- Communicate their role's purposes to others
- Set goals and objectives
- Prioritize their activities, and therefore improve their time/work management
- Make value-added decisions

Description

Key result areas (KRAs) capture about 80% of a work role. The remainder of the role is usually devoted to areas of shared responsibility (*e.g.*, helping team members, participating in activities for the good of the organization). For example, "image of the organization" is usually a very senior official's key result area, but hopefully all employees contribute to this outcome. Most roles include 3 to 5 key result areas. If individuals are accountable for more than this, they may be overloaded, or they may not be delegating effectively. Key result areas are worded using as few terms as possible with no verbs (*i.e.*, these are about results, not action) and no direction/measurement (*e.g.*, words such as "good," "increased" or "decreased"). They simply describe the areas for which one is responsible for results.

***Process*:** Individuals undertake the following steps to determine the KRAs for their roles:

- They list their main day-to-day responsibilities/activities.
- For each activity, they ask "Why do I do this?"
- They review the answers to their "why" questions, looking for common themes or areas.
- They identify their KRAs from these themes.
- They share their KRAs, preferably with those they report to, those they work along with, and those who report to them.

***Implementation*:** Individuals who identify their KRAs typically:

- Work with those they report to, those they work along with, and those who report to them to identify their KRAs so all on a team have clarity regarding outputs.
- Develop specific goals and objectives, and plans to reach them.
- Take control of their time/work management strategies

Key Performance Indicators (KPIs)

Key performance indicators (KPIs) are high-level snapshots of a business or organization based on specific predefined measures. KPIs typically consist of any combination of reports, spreadsheets, or charts. KPIs can be defined as a set of quantifiable measures that a company or industry uses to gauge or compare performance in terms of meeting their strategic and operational goals. KPIs vary between companies and industries, depending on their priorities or performance criteria. They are also referred to as "**key success indicators (KSI)**" in many organizations.

KPIs may include global or regional sales figures and trends over time, personnel stats and trends, real-time supply chain information, or anything else that is deemed critical to a corporation's success. A company must establish its strategic and operational goals and then choose the KPIs which best reflect those goals. For example, if a software company's goal is to have the fastest growth in its industry, its main performance indicator may be the measure of revenue growth year on year. A company's KPIs will be stated in its annual report. Also, KPIs will often be industry-wide standards, like "same store sales", in the retail sector.

KPIs allow goals to be observed, met and perhaps exceeded. Relatively generally formulated goal descriptions are made more concrete through the use of measurable quantities. The measurable quantities can then be allocated to the strategic goals in the perspectives and organizational units. KPIs are used by companies to better evaluate their current level of business success and to help plan for the future. KPIs add value to aspects of business operation that are difficult to quantify, like employee satisfaction or development, and are a critical piece of long-term business intelligence strategy. When establishing KPI it is important to identify metrics that are achievable.

Exhibit: Key Result Area (KRAs)/Key Performance Indicators (KPIs) for Managing Director of a Reputed Tyre Company

Mr. Raman Kumar
Managing Director and Board Member
KRAs/KPIs Performance Year FY03

Sl No.	KRAs	Key Performance Measures	Measurement Index: Base Level	Target	Exceptional Level	Weightage
1	ITL Operations	(i) PBT (Rs in mns) (ii) Gross Turnover – (Rs in mn). (iii) Net Realization from the Replacement market net of Excise (in Rs/Kg),Duty and Discount	90 17000 99.4	265 19240 107.3	360 20250 108.3	20 10 9 Total: 39
2	Strategic	Conclude Technical Tie-up and initiate effective steps for expansion of radial facilities		Q4 FY2003		10 Total: 10
3	Benchmarking	Operating Profit to Net Sales Percentage (Gap with Top 3) Sales Turn over Growth (Gap with Top 3)	4.10% 6.50%	3.10% 3%	2.60% 1%	3 3 Total: 6
4	Customer Satisfaction	Gallup Survey-Customer Survey Index	63	65	67	7 Total: 7
5	Leadership	(a) TS16949 Certification and Improvement in RPG (b) ESS Score for 2003	473 90	533 93	543 95	3 3 Total 6
					Total	68

Conducting Performance Appraisal

The first step in the process of performance appraisal also involves the setting up of the performance standards which will be used to as the base to compare the actual performance of the employees. The regulatory requirements for planning an employee's performance include establishing the elements and standards in their "**Employee Performance Appraisal Plans**" (EPAP). An EPAP outlines the specific elements and standards that the employee is expected to accomplish during the rating cycle. Performance elements and standards should be measurable, understandable, verifiable, equitable and achievable. In addition, EPAPs should be flexible so that they can be adjusted for changing program objectives and work requirements. When used effectively, these plans can be beneficial working documents that are discussed often, and not merely paperwork that is filed in a drawer and seen only when ratings of record are required. This step requires setting the criteria to judge the performance of the employees as successful or unsuccessful and the degrees of their contribution to the organizational goals and objectives. The standards set should be clear, easily understandable and in measurable terms. In case the performance of the employee cannot be measured, great care should be taken to describe the standards.

Establishing Job Expectations

The next step in the appraisal process involves setting up of employee job expectations. Once set, it is the responsibility of the management to communicate the standards to all the employees of the organization. The employees should be informed and the standards should be clearly explained to the. This will help them to understand their roles and to know what exactly is expected from them. The standards should also be communicated to the appraisers or the evaluators and if required, the standards can also be modified at this stage itself according to the relevant feedback from the employees or the evaluators.

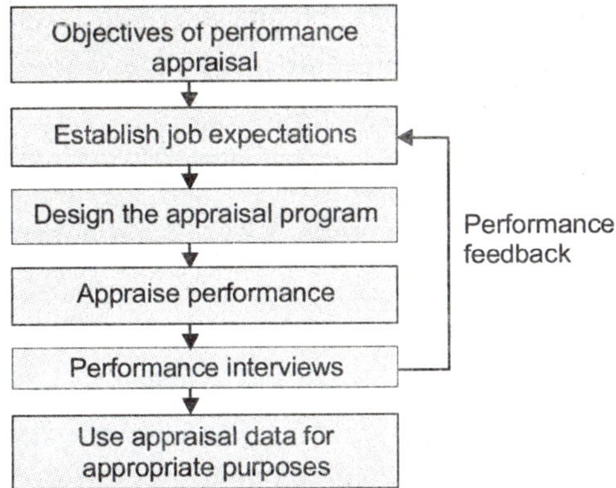

Fig. 3.41: Steps in the performance appraisal process

After communicating the KPAs, KRAs and job standards, care is taken in order to take employee opinions with respect to their job expectations and needs related to their performance. Supervisors and managers may use several documents and/or sources to assist them in determining the appropriate critical elements for their employees. To develop specific measures, the rating official must determine which of the above general measure(s) are important for a given element, and then determine how to measure it.

When specific standards are developed in addition to, or in lieu of, the benchmark standards listed below, regulation requires description at the Fully Successful level, at a minimum. However, appraisers are strongly encouraged to develop standards at additional levels so employees clearly understand their performance expectations at various levels.

PERFORMANCE ASSESSMENT GUIDE

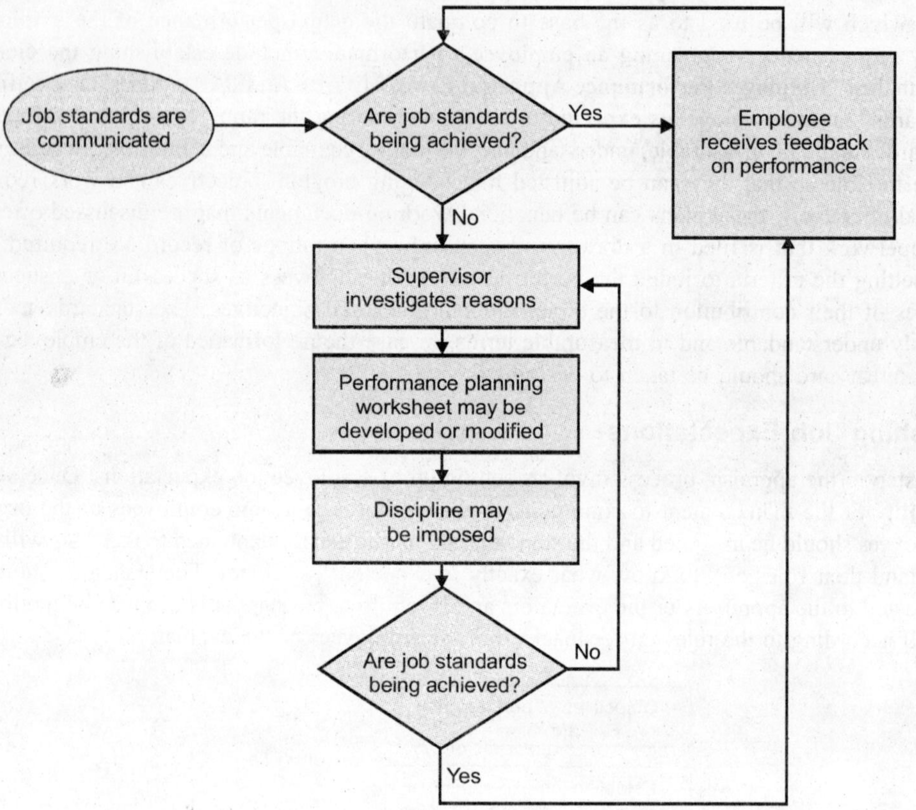

Job standards are communicated

Are job standards being achieved?

Yes

Employee receives feedback on performance

No

Supervisor investigates reasons

Performance planning worksheet may be developed or modified

Discipline may be imposed

Are job standards being achieved?

No

Yes

Fig. 3.42: Using performance standards in evaluating employee performance

Designing the Appraisal Program

This step involves a complete description and preparation of the performance evaluation schedule and developing a framework for rating employee performance. Within the context of formal performance appraisal requirements, rating means evaluating employee performance against the elements and standards in an employee's performance appraisal plan and assigning a rating of record. The rating of record is based on work performed during the entire 12-month appraisal period, including temporary assignments over 120 days.

Appraise Performances

The most difficult part of the performance appraisal process is measuring the actual performance of the employees that is the work done by the employees during the specified period of time. It is a continuous process which involves monitoring the performance throughout the year. This stage requires the careful selection of the appropriate techniques of measurement, taking care that personal bias does not affect the outcome of the process and providing assistance rather than interfering in an employees work. The actual performance is compared with the desired or the standard performance. The comparison tells the deviations in the performance of the employees from the standards set. The result can show the actual performance being more than the desired performance or, the actual performance being less than the desired performance depicting a negative deviation in the organizational performance. It includes recalling, evaluating and analysis of data related to the employees' performance.

Performance Interviews/Discussions

The result of the appraisal is communicated and discussed with the employees on one-to-one basis. The focus of this discussion is on communication and listening. The results, the problems and the possible solutions are discussed with the aim of problem solving and reaching consensus. The feedback should be given with a positive attitude as this can have an effect on the employees' future performance. The purpose of the meeting should be to solve the problems faced and motivate the employees to perform better. The rating official should discuss the completed EPAP with the employee after all required approvals are obtained. In preparation for the discussion, the rating official should ensure the following:

- All necessary approvals of the rating of record have been completed.
- Employee performance on each critical element during the rating period has been reviewed and noted, including tasks that were completed well and any areas needing improvement. Specific examples should be noted when possible.
- A private location and adequate time has been put aside to meet with the employee, including time for employee input (As a general rule, 30 minutes to one hour per employee).
- Future expectations and goals of the organization have been considered.

During the meeting, the appraiser should do the following:

- Be professional, calm and focused on performance issues.
- Begin with positive feedback on tasks the employee has done well regardless of what the final rating is.
- Go through each element and discuss items of note, both positive and negative as appropriate and assign a rating.
- Provide specific examples when possible
- Describe any changes in performance required and ensure the employee understands
- Allow for employee questions and input throughout
- Summarize the performance and assign the rating of record
- Have the employee sign and date the "Employee/Appraisee" block on the EPAP
- Sign and date the "Appraiser" block on the EPAP.

Conducting the Performance Appraisal

The activities involved before the appraisal could be summarized as follows:

BEFORE THE APPRAISAL	**Keep good records**	Both praise and criticism are most meaningful when supported by factual examples
	Review previous goals	Use previous goals to evaluate progress
	Get input from others	Seek feedback from others who work with the appraisee in areas they will have objective knowledge of and get examples where available
	Prepare carefully	Prepare in advance so that you can deliver the message that you intend to
	Prepare administrative details	• agree on a time — set aside at least one hour. Avoid postponing the appointment, and give the employee full attention. • select a location — office or conference room is best. • ask employee to prepare — ask the employee to review his/her goals, and come prepared with questions.

The activities involved during the appraisal could be summarized as follows:

DURING THE APPRAISAL	**Explain the meeting agenda**	Outline what is about to happen for the session
	Encourage communication	• listen • encourage two-way communication • ask for ideas on how they can improve their performance • ask for how they feel you can help them • ask for feedback on the appraisal section
	Stay focused	Keep the session focused on past and future performance, summarize discussion issues often to ensure agreement
	Communicating shortcomings	The employee expects and should know what he/she needs to improve
	Be open	Be versatile and open-minded if you hear things that cause you to change your opinion
	Evaluation process	• Begin with the positive things that were well done • Follow this with areas that need improvement and a plan on how to address them • Conclude with a reinforcement of your desire to help the person grow and improve
	Making promises	Don't make promises you do not have control over (e.g. salary increments, promotions, transfers etc)
	Review goals	Concentrate on a few areas— things that make a difference. Try to encourage continuation and growth in the areas of strength. Set up "smart" goals that will build strength in areas needing attention

The activities involved after the appraisal could be summarized as follows:

AFTER THE APPRAISAL	**Administration**	· Complete the paperwork required for the results of the appraisal · Make sure the appraisee signs on the bottom line · Mark the calendar on when your next appraisal session with the person will be
	Follow-up	Follow-up on agreements made during the appraisal
	Learning	Review what you have learnt about the employee, your records and systems, yourself, the appraisal process and your management style

Decision-Making: Using the Appraisal Data for Appropriate Purposes

After the previous steps, appraisers should document employee performance, both good and when improvement is needed, throughout the year. Doing this will allow the rating official to provide specific examples to the employee during progress reviews, during the rating of record, or at other times throughout the year. The next step of the process is to take decisions which can be taken either to improve the performance of the employees, take the required corrective actions, or the related HR decisions like rewards, promotions, demotions, transfers etc.

Performance Feedback

Designing effective feedback into a performance management program will improve individual and team performance and will make your organization more effective. With effective feedback processes, employees can see their progress and that motivates them to reach their performance goals successfully. Effective and timely feedback during the performance appraisal period addressing employee performance on elements and standards is an essential component of a successful performance management program. Employees need to know in a timely manner how well they are performing. They need to be told what they are doing well and if there are areas needing improvement. Feedback can come from many different sources: observation by managers and rating officials, measurement systems, feedback from peers, and input from customers, just to name a few. It will be up to rating officials to determine how best to gather the information, and from which sources, to ensure an effective rating of the employees under their supervision.

When providing feedback, appraisers should keep the following points in mind:

- Feedback works best when it relates to a specific goal, such as those established in the employee's performance appraisal plan. Basing feedback on the employee's performance against his or her elements and standards is key to providing tangible, objective and powerful feedback.
- Employees should receive information about how they are doing in as timely a fashion as possible. If they need to improve their performance, the sooner they find out about it, the sooner they can correct the problem. If employees have reached or exceeded a goal, the sooner they receive positive feedback, the more rewarding it is to them.
- Feedback should be given in a manner that will best help improve performance. Since people respond better to information presented in a positive way, express feedback in a positive manner. This is not to say that information should be sugar-coated, but present accurate, factual, and complete feedback; it is more effective when it reinforces what the employee did well and then identifies what the employee needs to do in the future to further improve his/her performance.

Exhibit: Illustration of the Steps in an Appraisal Process

Timeframe	Entity Responsible	Task
December –January	Personnel Committee	• At the December Board meeting, the Personnel Committee reviews the Performance Appraisal Process for the CEO with the Board, answering any questions and concerns.
	Board of Directors	• The Personnel Committee provides the formal Performance Appraisal Form to each Board member for completion by a specified due date. • Board members complete the form and return it to the Personnel Committee Chair. • The Personnel Committee Chair (or an assigned member of the Committee) collates Board member responses and prepares the written summary on the form. • The summary is presented as a % of the individuals responding to the particular question. The summary is presented on a Performance Appraisal Form, along with specific examples for each question. • Additional narrative responses are grouped by topic and presented as an attachment to the form.
January	CEO Supervisors	• At an All Staff Meeting, the CEO reviews the Performance Appraisal Process with all employees, answering any questions or concerns.

Contd...

		• Supervisors complete the Employee Performance Appraisal Form. Employees complete the Self-Evaluation Form. • The Program Directors and CEO review and endorse the employee appraisals, and authorize the formal meetings between supervisor and employee.
January	CEO	• Completes Self-Evaluation and provides to Personnel Committee
January	HR Committee	• Reviews summary performance appraisal and prepares a cover memo for the Board, summarizing the strengths and weaknesses, the areas requiring improvement and recommending the overall performance status.
February	Board of Directors (Executive Session as Part of regular Board meeting.	• Reviews and as necessary adjusts the CEO • Performance results as prepared by the Personnel Committee. • Formally adopts the appraisal and authorizes the Personnel Committee to conduct the performance appraisal meeting with the CEO.
February or March	Personnel Committee	Personnel Committee representatives and CEO discuss performance appraisal results (from the Board and from the E.D. self-evaluation), outline CEO goals for the new year, and confirm Professional Development Plan.
March	CEO and Personnel Committee	Present CEO goals for the new year, along with Professional Development Plan, for endorsement by the Board.
April	Board and Management	Set general directions, priorities and desired results for the new fiscal year, beginning July 1.
May	Management team and Finance Committes	• Establish the cumulative increase for the salary line for the next fiscal year budget. • Establish the merit increase ranges based on community economics and XYZ financial resources.
May	Personnel and Finance Committees	Cooperatively determine merit increase/salary adjustment for CEO, to include in budget recommendation to the Board.
June	Board of Directors	Adopts Budget and Fund Development Plan, thereby approving cumulative increase for the salary line for new fiscal year. (The Board does not approve individual salaries except for the CEO. The Board typically does not approve merit increase ranges.) Approves recommended merit increase made by Personnel and Finance Committees for the CEO, and informs CEO of merit increase and salary.
June	CEO and Supervisors	After Board approval of budget, determine merit increases for each employee and inform employee of new salary for fiscal year beginning July 1.
June	Personnel Committee and CEO Board of Directors	Present Annual Goals for the new fiscal year to the Board for approval. Review Professional Development Plan for CEO as an FYI to Board. Present E.D. goals for the new fiscal year, action plan and role of the Board.

Performance Appraisal Methods

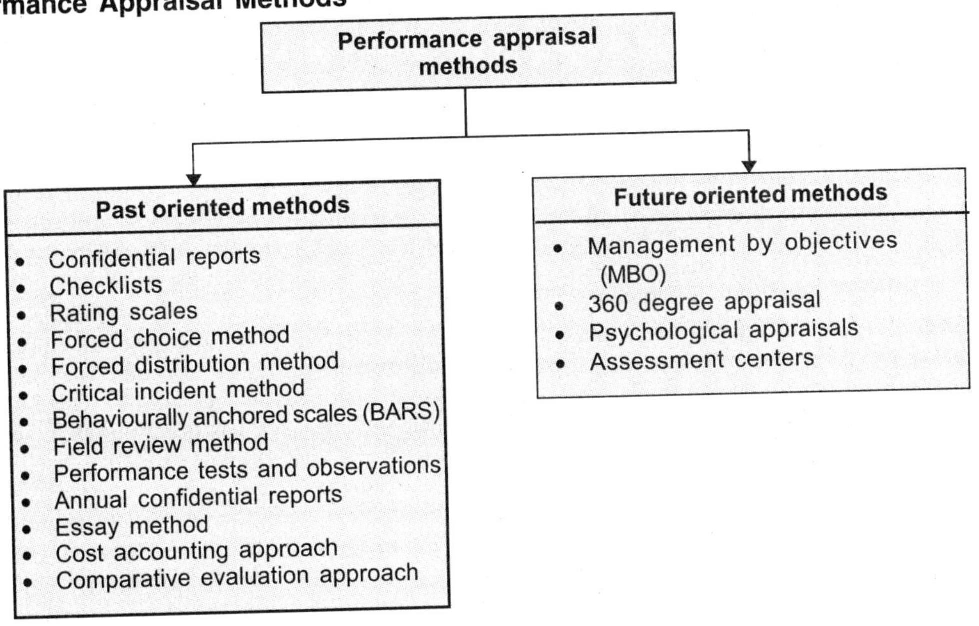

Past Oriented Methods

(a) ***Confidential Report***: It is mostly used in public sector enterprises and government organizations. It is a descriptive report prepared, generally at the end of every year, by the employee's immediate superior/supervisor. The report highlights the strengths and weaknesses of the subordinate. The report generally does not offer any feedback to the subordinate or the appraisee.

(b) ***Checklist Method***: Under this method a checklist of statements on the traits of the employee and his or her job is prepared in two columns namely; "yes" column and a "no" column. All the rater (immediate superior) needs to do is tick the option yes if the answer to the statement is positive and tick the column "no" if the answer is negative. After this, the rater forwards the list to the HR department where the actual assessment of the employee takes place. The HR department assigns certain points to each "Yes" ticked and depending on the number of "yes", the total score is arrived at. When points are allotted to the checklist, the technique is known as a ***Weighted Checklist.***

(c) ***Rating Scales***: This is the simplest and the most popular technique for appraising employee performance. The typical rating scale system consists of several numerical scales, each representing a job-related performance criterion such as dependability, initiative, output, attendance, attitude, cooperation and so on. Each scale ranges from excellent to poor. The rater checks the appropriate performance level on each criterion, and then computes the employee's total score. The number of points scored may be linked to salary increments, whereby a certain amount of point may equal a rise of some percentage. Although rating scales offer the advantage of adaptability, ready usability and cost effectiveness; the major disadvantage of the method is the involvement of the rater's biasness and so on.

(d) ***Forced Choice Method***: In this method, the rater is given a series of statements about the employees. These statements are arranged in blocks of two or more, and the rater indicates which statement is most or least descriptive of the employee. These may include statements like:

(i) Learns fast ————————> Works hard

(ii) Work is reliable ————————> Performance is a good example for

(iii) Absents often ————————> Others usually tardy

This approach is known as forced choice method because the rater is forced to select statements which are readymade. The advantage of this method is the absence of personal bias in rating. The disadvantage is that the statements may not be properly framed and may not also precisely be the descriptive of the ratee's traits.

(e) ***Forced Distribution Method*:** One of the errors in rating is leniency or the clustering of a large number of employees around a high point on a rating scale. The forced distribution method seeks to overcome the problem by compelling the rater to distribute the ratees on all points on the rating scale. The method operates under an assumption that the employee performance level conforms to a normal statistical distribution. It is assumed that the employee performance level conform to a bell-shaped curve. The major disadvantage of this method is in the assumption that employee performance levels always conform to a normal distribution curve.

(f) ***Critical Incident Method*:** This approach focuses on certain critical behaviours of an employee that makes the difference between effective and non-effective performance of a job. These events are generally noted or recorded by the superiors. One of the major advantages of this method is that the evaluation is based on actual job behaviour. Further, the approach has descriptions in support of particular ratings of an employee. Giving job-related feedback to an employee becomes also easy. This approach can also increase the chances that the subordinates would improve their performances because they learn more precisely what is expected of them. One of the few disadvantages includes those like the method depends on the recording of the incidents by the supervisor which might also be influenced by overly close supervisions.

(g) ***Behaviourally Anchored Rating Scales (BARS)*:** Behaviourally anchored rating scales are also known as Behavioural Expectations Scale. These are rating scales whose scale points are determined by statements of effective and ineffective behaviours. They are said to be behaviourally anchored in that the scales represent a range of descriptive statements of behaviours varying from the least to the most effective. A rater must indicate which behaviour on each scale best describes an employee's performance. The following table represents an example of a sales trainee's competence and application of BARS. Raters while constructing a BARS for evaluating their employee performance, take into consideration the following steps, namely:

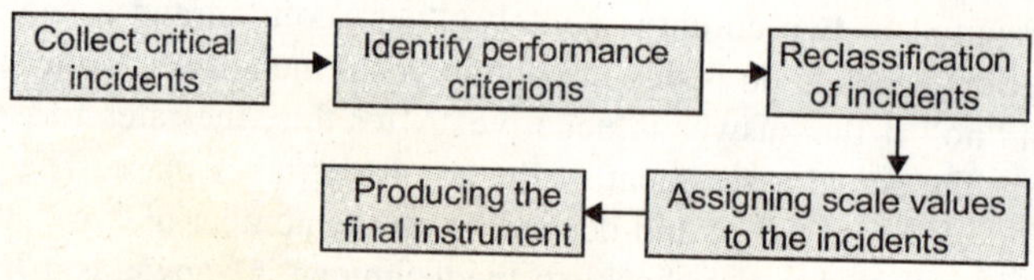

Fig. 3.43: Developing BARS

Performance	Points	Behaviour
Extremely Good	5	Can expect the trainee to make valuable contributions for increased sales and to have positive relationships with customers.
Good	4	Can expect to initiate creative ideas for improved sales.
Average	3	Can manage, with difficulty, to deliver the services in time.
Poor	2	Can expect to inform only a part of the customers about the products.
Extremely Poor	1	Can expect to take extended coffee breaks and roam around purposefully.

EABRARS: The BARS format was used to develop the **Extension Agent Behaviours and Results Anchored Rating System (EABRARS)**. Job dimensions and anchors were derived from a 1979 Extension agent job analysis commissioned by USDA and conducted by the American Institutes for Research (AIR). Nine job dimensions (5 behaviours and 4 results) were selected from the AIR analysis. Within each of these job dimensions, anchor statements were rewritten and grouped in categories from 1 to 7, according to AIR weightings. An example of the final EABRARS performance appraisal format is shown in the accompanied table.

Table 3.4: EABRARS Job Dimensions.

Behaviours
Program planning Program promotion and public relations Program implementation Program support Interpersonal and personal behaviours generally related to job
Results
Program planning Program promotion and public relations Program implementation Program support

Table 3.5: Examples of EABRARS Performance Appraisal Format

Job Dimension: Program Promotion and Public Relations Behaviours *This section includes standards for appraising the agent's behaviours in promoting programs and the Extension Service, raising funds, and using the mass media.*	
This agent can be expected to:	
7	* Conduct one of the best public information programs in the state.
	* Always get extensive media coverage for his/her programs.
6	* Constantly develop good public relations and not just at budget time.
	* Be willing to work with all groups and organizations for promotion of Extension regardless of personal feelings.
	* Communicate effectively with publicity media.
5	* Have developed a countrywide mailing list of interested individuals.
	* Make some original use of mass media.
	* Localize some of the promotional material supplied by the Extension office.
	* Make reports to advisory groups and public officials on request or as opportunities arise.
4	* Maintain communication with some local leaders, organizations, and groups.
3	* Assist with planning and implementing public relations programs even though efforts may lack consistency.
	* Insufficiently use one or more of the mass media.
2	* Make no effort to speak to community clubs or organizations.
	* Continually mention mass media that should be contacted to increase potential audiences, but do nothing about it.
	* See some parts of the program as being unimportant and thus not be concerned with them.
1	* Show disrespect for local values and customs.
	* Fail to communicate events and activities to those interested.

EABRARS represents the beginning of a new wave of performance appraisal formats that must meet legal mandates as well as serve a variety of organizational purposes in identifying, measuring, and developing human performance.

(h) ***Field Review Method*:** This is an appraisal by someone outside the assessee's own department, usually someone from the corporate office or the HR department. The outsider reviews employee records and holds interviews with the ratee his or her superior. The method is primarily used for making promotional decisions at the managerial level. Field reviews are also useful when comparable information is needed from the employees in different units or locations.

(i) ***Performance Tests and Observations*:** With a limited number of jobs, employee assessment may be based upon a test of knowledge or skills. The test may be of the paper and pencil variety or an actual demonstration of skill. The test must be reliable and validated to be useful. In order for the test to be job related, observations should be made under circumstances likely to be encountered.

(j) ***Essay Method*:** In this method, the rater must describe the employee within a number of broad categories, such as (a) the rater's overall impression of the employee performance, (b) the promotability of the employee (c) the jobs that the employee is now able or qualified to perform, (d) the strengths and weaknesses of the employee and (e) the training and development assistance required by the employee. Although this method may be used independently, it is most frequently found in combination with others.

(k) ***Cost Accounting Method*:** This method evaluates performance from the monetary returns the employee yields to his or her organization. A relationship is established between the cost included in keeping the employee and the benefit the organization derives from him or her. Performance of the employee is then evaluated based on the established relationship between the cost and the benefit.

(l) ***Comparative Evaluation Approaches*:** These are a collection of different methods that compare one worker's performance with that of his/her coworkers. Comparative appraisals are usually conducted by supervisors. As these appraisals can result in a ranking from best to worst, they are useful in deciding merit-pay increases, promotions and organizational rewards. The usual comparative forms used in this kind of evaluation are the **Ranking Method** and the **Paired Comparison Method**.

- **Ranking Method:** In this method the superior ranks his or her subordinates in the order of their merit, starting from the best to the worst. This method is subject to the halo and regency effects, although rankings by two or more raters can be averaged to help reduce bias. Its advantages include ease of administration and explanation.
- **Paired-comparison Method:** Here the appraiser compares each employee with every other employee, one at a time. For example, there are five employees namely, A, B, C, D, E. The performance of A is 1st compared with that of B and a decision is made about whose performance is better. Then A is compared with C, D and E in that order. The same procedure is repeated for other employees. The number of comparisons can be calculated with the help of a formula, namely:

  N(N–1)/2, where N stands for the number of employees to be compared.

  If there are 10 employees, the comparisons will be 10(10–1)/2 = 45. After the completion of comparison, the results can be tabulated, and a rank is created from the number of times each person is considered to be superior.

THEME READING: YARDSTICKS TO MEASURE PERFORMANCE

With shy rocketing compensation packages and employees earning never-before perks, HR managers are perhaps having a tough challenge to manage performance and reward people. Mr. Rajkumar D., Senior manager Human resources, Microland, has suggested the following means for an effective and transparent performance evaluation.

(*Courtesy: Rajkumar, D., The Economic Times, 19th March, 2008, p. 13*)

- Explain company goals and objectives to employees
- Set key result areas (KRAs) early enough in the year
- Ensure that KRAs are understood by the employees in relation to their organizational goals
- See that measurable yardsticks are created and explained at the time of implementing the KRAs.
- Both the employee and the employer should feel that the KRAs are fair, clear and measurable.
- Both employee and employer must agree upon the terms of the performance metrics used to measure the KRAs.
- Ensure that KRAs are not changed too frequently.

Future-Oriented Appraisal Methods

Industry Quotes

"We at Safexpress believe that a healthy relationship between an employer and an employee is a must if the company has to grow. This can only be achieved if the employee is sure that her/his work is being acknowledged," "An employee's growth is largely dependent on the level of motivation s/he receives from his employer," affirms Vineet Kanaujia, GM-Marketing, Safexpress. It provides her/him with a reason to give her/his best. Also, an organised appraisal system helps an individual understand her/his strengths and weaknesses. This understanding aids in the employee's development and also assists the organization in formulating a development and training schedule for the employee.

Management by Objectives (MBO)

Management by Objectives is a process whereby the superior and subordinate managers of an organization jointly identify its common goals, define each individual's major areas of responsibility in terms of results expected of him and use these measures as guides for operating the unit and assessing the contributions of each of its members.

Features of MBO

- It emphasizes participative setting of goals that are tangible, verifiable and measurable.
- MBO focuses attention on what must be accomplished (goals) rather than how it is to be accomplished (methods).
- MBO is a dynamic system which seeks to integrate the organization's need to clarify and achieve its profit and growth targets with the manager's need to contribute and develop himself.
- MBO is a systematic and rational technique that allows management to attain maximum results from available resources by focusing on achievable goals.
- MBO allows the subordinate plenty of scopes in order to make creative decisions on his own.

Key Elements of MBO

- ***Arranging organizational goals in a means-end chain:*** In a MBO system a firm's corporate goals are structured in a means-end chain. The Top management formulates a set of long-range and short-term corporate objectives for the organization as a whole. The divisional or functional managers participate in the goal-setting process to reflect their own desires and indicate the constraints to be considered. These managers then work along with their subordinates so as to formulate divisional or functional goals, which are again translated into group or individual goals.

- ***Engaging in Joint Goal-Setting:***

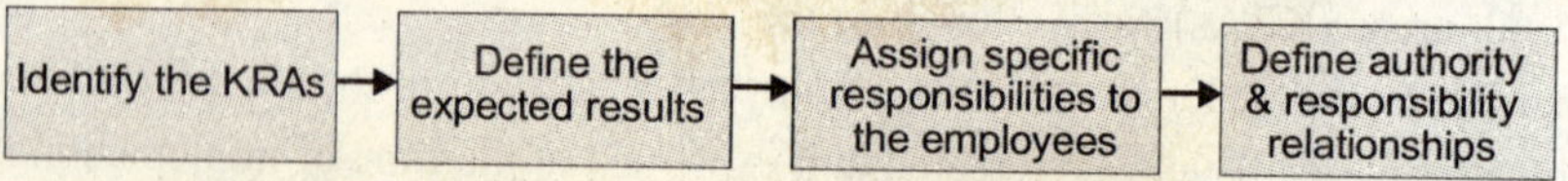

Fig. 3.44: Applying MBO in appraisals

- ***Conducting Periodic Progress Reviews:*** Performance can be periodically reviewed in order to determine progress. Supervisors and subordinates should meet regularly to review their progress towards goal attainment. These reviews should serve as built-in feedback mechanism for an MBO system.
- ***Conducting Annual Performance Criteria:*** At the end of an MBO Cycle, usually on an annual basis, the manager meets subordinate(s) to assess the employee's or the group's contribution to the organization.

Benefits of MBO

- Clearer and quantifiable/measurable Goals
- Inculcates better and effective planning
- Facilitates management control
- Facilitates objective appraisals
- Used as a motivational force
- Inculcates better employee morale
- MBO is a result-oriented, practical and rational management philosophy.

Limitations of MBO

- MBO may prove to be self-defeating in the long-run as it could be tied with a reward-punishment psychology (Pressure-oriented)
- It could be time consuming
- It could lead to increased paper work
- It could involve Goal-setting problems
- It could involve several organizational problems

Improving the Effectiveness of MBO

- Organizational commitment and support
- Training and development
- Adequate time and resources
- Taking care of necessary mechanics involved in the implementation of MBO
- Timely feedback
- Avoiding politics

360 Degree Feedback Appraisal Systems

The 360 degree feedback appraisal process is the systematic collection of performance data on an individual or group, derived from a number of stakeholders—the stakeholder being the immediate supervisors, team members, customers, peers and the self (self appraisal).

Components of 360 degree appraisals: The components of the 360 appraisal system are illustrated by the following figure.

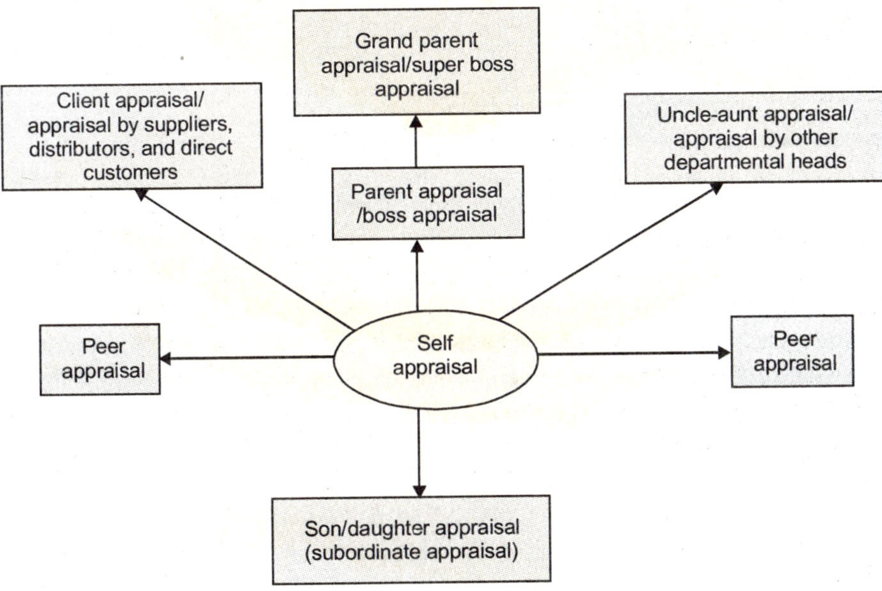

Fig. 3.45: Components of a 360 degree Feedback Appraisal System

Self appraisal: When an cmployce is being allowed to appraise himself or herself against some predefined and mutually agreed performance goals and performance standards it is known as the self appraisal. This forms the central hub of the 360 degree appraisal system.

Peer appraisal: Here an employee is being rated by his/her colleagues or employees working in the organization having similar positions and/or responsibilities.

Son/Daughter (Subordinate) appraisal: Here an employee is being appraised by his/her immediate subordinates.

Parent (Boss) appraisal: This is the most commonly used appraisal where an employee is being rated and appraised by his/her immediate supervisor.

Grandparent/Super-boss appraisal: In this appraisal the employee is being appraised by the boss's boss, who may be the divisional manager of even the general manager/vice president.

Uncle/Aunt appraisal: Here the employee is being appraised by the departmental heads of other departments of divisions of the organization with whom the employee's performance might be related.

Client appraisal: In this appraisal, the employee is being assessed by the clients with whom he/she might be regularly be dealing with. These individuals could be the customers, dealers, suppliers, distributors, vendors, any one in the value chain of the organization.

Case: 360 Degree Appraisal in Safexpress

Safexpress keeps the appraisal process absolutely transparent and objective by implementing the 360 degree appraisal policy. "This system is based on the idea that an employee's performance is not just judged by the immediate head, rather adjudged also by his/her peers and subordinates too. Evaluation is done by combining the feedback received from these people who see different aspects of an employee's performance. This process ensures that the evaluation is bias free and also increases accountability," says Vineet Kanaujia, GM-Marketing, Safexpress. The end objective is happy employees, thus resulting in happy customers. Innovation and transparency in the appraisal process helps recognise the importance of the employee's contribution to organisational success.

Steps in 360 Degree Assessment

- Identify and define the key competencies for organizational success based on the organization's vision, values and goals.
- Express the key competencies as attitudes against which participants can be assessed.
- Select the persons to be evaluated—peers, customers, subordinates, and managers.
- Compile the results. Feedback is to be kept confidential.
- Provide feedback to the individual.
- Create an action plan to improve the individual's performance.

The 360 degree performance assessment has an advantage over the traditional manager assessment process in that the individual receives feedback from multiple relevant sources. It helps foster interdependent partnership and develops team-based organizations. It facilitates greater self-development opportunities and a formalized communication links between an employee and his or her customers. It makes the employee feel much more accountable to his or her internal or external customers. By design, this method is effective in identifying and assessing interpersonal skills, customer satisfaction and team-building skills.

Strategic Data used in 360 Degree Appraisals

While the value of 360 degree feedback is often seen in terms of individual development, aggregate reporting of all recipients' results can provide valuable data for the organization as a whole. It enables leaders to

- Take advantage of under-utilized personnel strengths to increase productivity
- Avoid the trap of counting on skills that may be weak in the organization
- Apply human assets data to the valuation of the organization
- Make succession planning more accurate
- Design more efficient coaching and training initiatives
- Support the organization in marketing the skills of its members

Benefits of 360 Appraisals

- Individuals get a broader perspective of how they are perceived by others than previously possible.
- Increased awareness of and relevance of competencies.
- Increased awareness by senior management that they too have development needs.
- More reliable feedback to senior managers about their performance.
- Gaining acceptance of the principle of multiple stakeholders as a measure of performance.
- Encouraging more open feedback — new insights.
- Reinforcing the desired competencies of the business.
- Provided a clearer picture to senior management of individual's real worth (although there tended to be some 'halo' effect syndromes).
- Clarified to employees critical performance aspects.
- Opens up feedback and gives people a more rounded view of performance than they had previously.
- Identifying key development areas for the individual, a department and the organization as a whole.
- Identifying strengths that can be used to the best advantage of the business.
- A rounded view of the individual's/teams/organization's performance and what the strengths and weaknesses are.
- Raised the self-awareness of people managers of how they personally impact upon others — positively and negatively.
- Supporting a climate of continuous improvement.
- Starting to improve the climate/morale, as measured through the survey.
- Focused agenda for development. Forced line managers to discuss development issues.
- Perception of feedback as more valid and objective, leading to acceptance of results and actions required.

Limitations of 360 Feedback Appraisals

The drawbacks associated with the 360 degree feedback involve:

- Receiving feedback on performance from multiple sources can be intimidating.
- It is essential that the organization create a non-threatening environment by emphasizing the positive impact of the technique on an employee's performance development.
- Multiple Raters are less adept at providing a balanced and objective feedback than the supervisors who are sought to be replaced.
- Raters can have enormous problems separating honest observations from personal differences and biases.

Employee Self Appraisals

Employee self-appraisal, within a performance management or annual performance review system involves asking the employee to self-evaluate his or her job performance. Typically, prior to meeting with an employee, the manager will ask the employee to complete an evaluation form on his or her own, to be used as a **basis for discussion** during the annual performance review meeting. Then at the meeting, the manager and employee discuss the self-appraisal results, and negotiate final evaluations based on both the manager's perceptions and those of the employee. Self appraisals as part of performance management system can take the form of evaluating progress towards pre-defined annual objectives and performance standards, involve the employee in **rating him or her self using the same rating form the manager uses**, or even involve self-ranking.

Benefits of Self Appraisal

There are a number of benefits to **having employees self-evaluate or self appraise**, either as part of the formal performance management system, or informally. These include:

- By having employees do some sort of self evaluation before the actual review meeting, the review meetings can be shorter.
- If done properly and tactfully, encouraging employees to self evaluation or self appraise at any time during the year, including around the actual review meetings, help convey the message that the process of performance management and appraisal is a team effort, and not something the manager does to the employee. This greases the wheels of the process, making it more effective.
- Why self appraisal is an accepted and integrated part of the performance management process, it encourages employees to self evaluate throughout the year. That's exceedingly valuable, because what most managers want is employees who can do their jobs, monitor their own progress, and self-correct all year long. When that happens managers can spend far less time fire fighting or micromanaging.

Self-appraisal is an important step in making the employees feel involved in the process as the appraisee gives his perspective. Moreover, in the realm of self-managed work, a good manager should be able to identify good potential employees from the quality of goals set and self-evaluated.

Industry Opinion

"Many organizations also emphasize upon instigating "Intra-based appraisal system" which actually allows the employee to define their KRAs, like people-related, quality-related, project-related, learning-related and so forth. These are set at the beginning of the appraisal period; during the course of the year, by mutual agreement, where changes could be made to the original set of goals defined. This ensures that at the assessment stage there is a balanced set of goals that get assessed for the employee. The onus to set, change the goals rest with the employee—wherein the appropriate metrics, measures are provided," states Shrikant Kulkarni, Senior Vice-President-HR, KPIT Cummins Infosystems.

Performance Appraisal Interview

Performance appraisal interview is an important part of the appraisal process. If the interview is going to be effective, the appraiser must prepare. The purpose of the appraisal interview is to discuss performance, not personality. It is future oriented, rather than past oriented. Emphasis should be on what the employee will do in the future and not on what has been done in the past. However, a discussion of past performance is essential as the basis for the future.

Objectives to Accomplish: In the appraisal interview, there are five major objectives:

- To reach agreement on the performance of the employee
- To identify strengths
- To identify performance areas that need to be improved
- To agree on a performance improvement plan for one or more areas that need improvement
- To agree on what's expected (that is, significant job segments and standards of performance) for the next appraisal period

Preparation by the HR Manager: Before the interview takes place, the manager should make the following preparations:

1. **Decide on the best time:** The best time is when both parties are able to spend time together without interruption, so it is a good idea for the manager to suggest a time and get approval from the employee.
2. **Decide on the best place:** A private office is the best place. It may be the office of the manager or a neutral place. It should be a private place where the door can be closed and people can't look in and see what's going on. Also, it should be a comfortable place where both parties can relax.
3. **Prepare the facilities:** Arrange the furniture so that the employee will feel at ease. Perhaps the chairs should be side by side instead of across the desk from each other. If possible, have coffee or water available.
4. **Gather information and materials:** Make a complete and objective appraisal as described earlier in this chapter. Have the forms and information on hand so that they are readily available during the interview.
5. **Plan the opening:** Decide whether to talk about a current event—such as sports, politics, or weather—or to begin by stating the purpose of the interview. Use whatever approach is most natural and will create the best climate for the interview.
6. **Plan the approach:** Here are some alternatives to consider:
   (a) Begin with strengths and then discuss job segments needing improvement.
   (b) Go straight through the form, give the appraisal, and discuss one item at a time to get agreement before going ahead to the next item.
   (c) Ask the employee for his or her appraisal
7. **Give the employee appropriate advance notice:** The employee should have enough time to prepare for the interview and should clearly understand the time, place, objectives, and probable length of the interview.
8. **Plan the conclusion:** Know how and when to end the interview.

Preparation by the Employee: The employee must be given enough advance notice, as stated in item 7. In preparing for the interview, the employee should do the following:

1. Gather information related to past performance. This includes specific data on activities and accomplishments, as well as reasons why certain things weren't done or were done incorrectly.
2. Complete a self-appraisal if requested by the manager.
3. Arrange for work coverage while she is absent from the department. This is important so that the employee can concentrate on the interview and not worry about whether the job is being done properly.

Exhibit: Cause and Effect Relations in Three Types of Appraisal Interviews

Method	Tell-and-sell	Tell-and-listen	Problem solving
Role of interviewer:	Judge	Judge	Helper
Objective	- To communicate evaluation - To persuade employee to improve	- To communicate evaluation - To release defensive feelings	- To stimulate growth and development in employee

Contd...

Assumptions	-Employee desires to correct weaknesses if he knows them - Any person can improve if he so chooses - A superior is qualified to evaluate a subordinate	- People will change if defensive feelings are removed	- Growth can occur without correcting faults - Discussing job problems leads to improved performance
Reactions	- Defensive behaviour suppressed - Attempts to cover hostility	- Defensive behaviour expressed - Employee feels accepted	- Problem solving behaviour
Skills	- Salesmanship - Patience	- Listening and reflecting feelings - Summarizing	- Listening and reflecting feelings - Reflecting ideas - Using exploratory questions - Summarizing
Attitude	- People profit from criticism	- One can respect the feelings of others if one understands them	- Discussion develops new ideas and mutual interests
Motivation	- Use of positive or negative incentives or both (Extrinsic in that motivation is added to the job itself)	- Resistance to change reduced - Positive incentive (Extrinsic and some intrinsic motivation)	- Increased freedom - Increased responsibility (Intrinsic in that interest is inherent in the task)
Gains	- Success most probable when employee respects interviewer	- Develops favourable attitude to superior which increases probability of success	- Almost
Risks	- Success most probable when employee respects interviewer	- Develops favourable attitude to superior which increases probability of success	- Almost assured of improvement in some respect
Values	- Perpetuates existing practices and values	- Permits interviewer to change his view in light of the employee's responses - Some upward communication	- Both learn since experience and views are pooled - Changes is facilitated

SPECIAL APPRAISAL TECHNIQUES

Psychological Appraisals

Large organizations employ full-time industrial psychologists, who assess an individual's future potential and not past performance. The appraisal normally consists of in-depth interviews, psychological tests, discussions with supervisors and a review of other evaluations. The psychologist then writes an evaluation of the employee's intellectual, emotional, motivational and other-related characteristics that suggest individual potential and may predict future performance. The evaluation by the psychologist may be for a specific job opening for which the person is being considered, or it may be a global assessment of his or her future potential. From these evaluations, the placement and development decisions may be made to shape the individual's career.

Assessment Centers

Assessment center is a mechanism used to identify the potential for growth of individuals. Assessment centers constitute a battery of assignments and situational exercises which are competency based and are used extensively in various countries for recruitment, potential appraisal, promotion, human resource development and organizational development.

It is a procedure specifically used, designed to evaluate an employee's managerial potential. Its objective is to reinforce strengths, overcome weaknesses and exploit potential of the employees through training and development efforts. Assessment Centers (AC) are centers set up by an organization for periodic or continuous assessment of the competencies required to perform current, future likely or higher level jobs/roles/tasks. They are increasingly used to identify high fliers or fast trackers and develop leaders/competencies for the future. The assessors observe the behaviour and make independent evaluation of what they have observed, which results in identifying strengths and weaknesses of the attributes being studied. Assessment center comprises a number of exercises or simulations, which have been designed to replicate tasks and demands of the job.

Assessment centers typically involve the participants completing a range of exercises which simulate the activities carried out in the target job. Various combinations of these exercises and sometimes other assessment methods like psychometric testing and interviews are used to assess particular competencies in individuals. The theory behind this is that if one wishes to predict future job performance then the best way of doing this is to get the individual to carry out a set of tasks which accurately sample those required in the job and are as similar to them as possible. The particular competencies used will depend upon the target job but one will often find competencies such as relating to people; resistance to stress; planning and organizing; motivation; adaptability and flexibility; problem solving; leadership; communication; decision making and initiative. There are numerous possible competencies and the ones which are relevant to a particular job are determined through job analysis.

Assessees are requested to participate in "In-basket exercises", "work groups (Leaderless)", computer simulations, role-playing and other similar activities which require the same attributes for successful performance as in the actual job. After recording their observations of ratee behaviours, the raters meet to discuss these observations. The decision regarding the performance of each assessee is based upon this discussion of observations. Self-appraisal and peer evaluation are also included in for final ratings.

Assessment Centers use Multiple Methods Like

- In-Basket Exercises
- Role-plays
- Interviews
- Psychometric Tests
- Simulation Exercises

- Leaderless and Leader-led Group Discussions
- Case Studies
- Biographic Behavioural Incident Interviews (BBII)
- Simulated Incident and Assessment Technique (SIAD) etc.

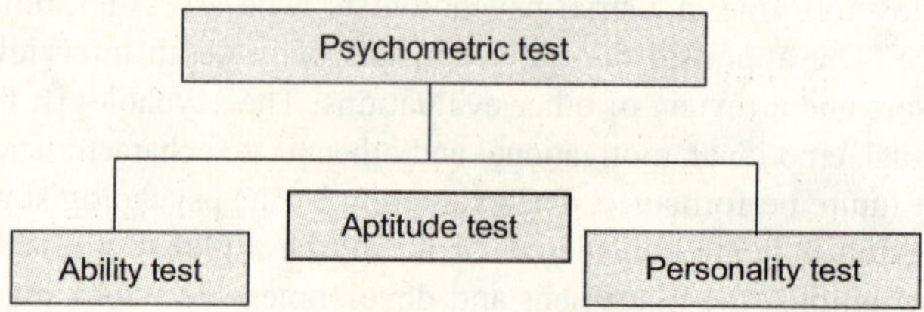

Fig. 3.46: Types of psychometric tests used in assessment centers

Type of Psychometric Test	Hallmarks
Ability Test	• It is an attempt to measure awareness, knowledge and other such aspects.
Aptitude Test	• It evaluates the verbal and numerical reasoning ability
Personality Tests	• These are those tests which are aimed at studying various dimensions of personality rather than the ability. (MBTI and 16 PF)

The characteristics of the employees assessed in a typical assessment center include assertiveness, persuasive ability, communicating ability, planning and organizational ability, self-confidence, resistance to stress, energy level, decision-making, sensitivity to the feelings of others, administrative ability, creativity, and mental alertness.

Exhibit: Organizations like appraisal-smart.com are adept in terms of providing online performance appraisal solutions to their clients

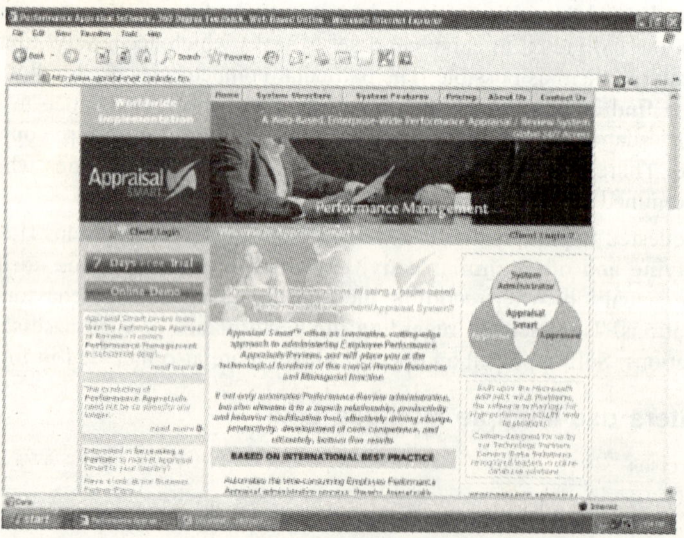

Fig. 3.47: http://www.appraisal-smart.com/index.htm

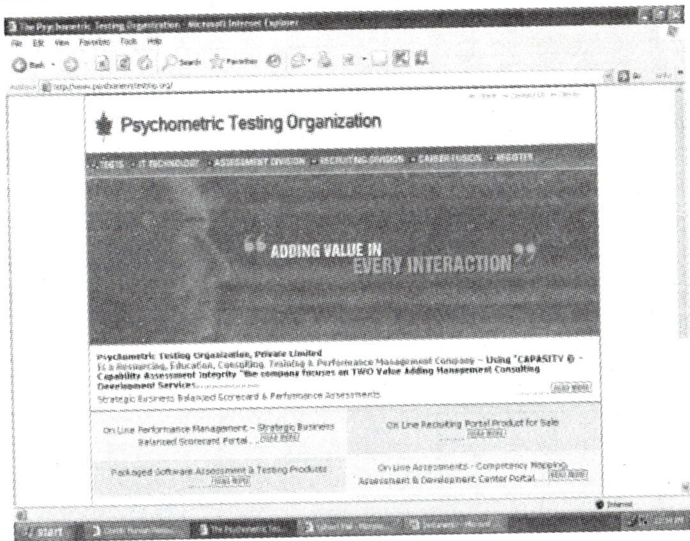

Fig. 3.48: http://www.psychometrictesting.org/

Exhibit: 360 degree feedback form template

This template allows a mixture of key skills comprising one, two, three, four, and up to six elements. The number of elements per key skill/capability varies of course, so if necessary adjust the size of the boxes in the first column accordingly to accommodate more or less elements. See the 360 degree appraisals notes for more explanation about the purpose of each column and heading, and the feedback scoring method.

Insert your own Feedback Form headings and instructions: appraisee name, date, feedback respondent name, position (if applicable) plus local instructions and guidelines for completion, etc.

Key skill/capability area	Skill/capability element	Question number	Feedback question	Feedback score
		1		
		2		
		3		
		4		
		5		
		6		
		7		
		8		
		9		
		10		

		11		
		12		
		13		
		14		
		15		
		16		
		17		
		18		
		19		
		20		
		21		
		22		
		23		
		24		
		25		
		26		
		27		
		28		
		29		
		30		

Optional section: additional feedback about the appraisee – please be constructive

Performance Appraisals for Teams

With the increased significance of Performance appraisal, challenges confronting the system are immense. One serious challenge facing the performance appraisal system relates to assessment of self-managed teams. These self-managed teams create special challenges for performance appraisal-empowered teams perform without supervisors. Another challenge is that both, individual and team performance, need to be measured. A suitable device needs to be developed in order to assess the performance of empowered teams as more and more organizations use such teams to enhance productivity. The following figure represents the various aspects of Team Appraisal.

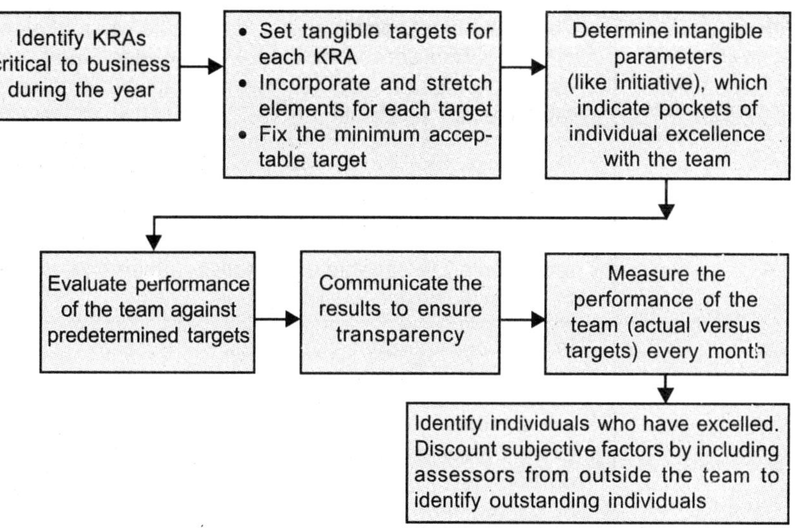

Fig. 3.49: Performance assessment for teams

The movement to a teamwork model raises a number of important issues for the performance manager. This chapter will help you to understand the issues involved, so that you can participate in making informed decisions about team performance management. Adopting a team approach to working together raises issues for performance managers in each phase of the performance management process. The University has not developed specific policies to deal with team-related performance management issues, although many departments within the University are working to resolve them in ways which meet their particular needs while remaining consistent with the organization's policies and procedures.

Errors in Performance Appraisal

Differences in perception and value systems influence the performance evaluations. Some common errors involved with the performance appraisal process are as follows:

Error Type	Hallmarks/Features
Halo Effect	This is a tendency to let the assessment of a single trait influence the evaluation of the individual on other traits too. As for example, an employee demonstrates a high degree of dependability and from this behaviour, a comparable high degree of integrity could be inferred.
Horn Effect	This is a tendency to allow one negative trait of the employee to colour the entire appraisal. This results in an overall lower rating than may be warranted.
Leniency or Constant Error	Depending upon the appraiser's own value system which acts as a standard, employees may be rated leniently or strictly. Such ratings do not carry any reference to actual performance of the employee. Some appraisers consistently assign high values to all employees, regardless of merit. This is a leniency error. The strictness tendency is a reverse situation, where all individuals are rated too severely and performance is understated.

Contd...

Central Tendency	This is the most common error that occurs when a rater assigns mainly middle range scores or values to all individuals under appraisal. Extremely high or extremely low evaluations are avoided by assigning "average ratings" to all.
Spill-over Effect	This refers to allowing past performance to influence the evaluation of present performance.
Personal Bias	Perhaps the most important error of all rises from the fact that very few people are capable of objective judgements entirely independent of their values and prejudices.
Recency Effect	In this case the rater gives greater weightage to recent occurrences than earlier performances.
Stereotyping	It is a mental picture that an individual holds about a person because of the person's age, religion, caste etc. By generalizing the behaviour on the basis of such blurred images, the rater grossly overestimates or underestimates an individual's performance.

The Halo Effect: The halo effect is the tendency of the manager to overrate a favoured employee. This can happen for a variety of reasons:

1. ***Effect of past record***: Because the person has done good work in the distant past, performance is assumed to be O.K. in the recent past, too. Good opinions tend to carry over into the current rating period.
2. ***Compatibility***: There's a tendency to rate people whom we find pleasing of manner and personality more highly than they deserve. Those who agree with us, who nod their heads when we talk, or who—even better—make notes of our words: these people get better ratings than their performance justifies.
3. ***Effect of recency***: An outstanding job done last week or yesterday can offset a mediocre performance over the rest of the year.
4. ***The one-asset person***: The glib talker, the person with an impressive appearance or an advanced degree, or the graduate of the manager's own alma mater gets a more favourable rating than the person who lacks these often irrelevant attributes.
5. ***The blind-spot effect***: This is the case where the supervisor doesn't see certain types of defects because they are just like his or her own. For example, the supervisor who loves accounting may overrate another detail person.
6. ***The high-potential effect***: We sometimes judge the person's paper record, rather than what she has accomplished for the organization.
7. ***The no-complaints bias***: Here the appraiser treats no news as good news. The employee who has no complaints and says that everything is terrific is likely to go over well.

The Horn Effect: This is the reverse of the halo effect—the tendency to rate a person lower than the circumstances justify. Some specific causes of this are these:

1. ***The manager is a perfectionist***: Because the expectations of the manager are so high, she is often disappointed and rates an employee lower than deserved.
2. ***The employee is contrary***: Here the manager vents private irritation with the employee's tendency to disagree too often on too many issues.
3. ***The oddball effect***: All the lip service to nonconformity seldom counts when appraisal time comes around. The oddball, the maverick, the nonconformist get low ratings simply because they are different.

4. ***Membership in a weak team*:** A good player on a weak team ends up with lower ratings than he would have gotten if he were on a winning team.
5. ***The guilt-by-association effect*:** The person who isn't really known well by the manager is often judged by the company he keeps.
6. ***The dramatic-incident effect*:** A recent goof can wipe out the effect of months of good work and give a person a lower rating than deserved.
7. ***The personality-trait effect*:** The employee who is too cocky, too brash, too meek, or too passive or who lacks some trait the manager associates with good employees suffers in the appraisal.
8. ***The self-comparison effect*:** The person who does the job differently from the way the manager did it when she still had that job suffers more than a person whose job the manager has never done.

Challenges of Performance Appraisal

- To create a culture of excellence that inspires every employee to improve and lend himself or herself to be assessed.
- Align organizational objectives to individual aspirations
- Clear growth paths for talented individuals
- Provide newer challenges to rejuvenate careers that have reached the plateau stage
- Forge a partnership with people for managing their careers
- Empower employees to make decisions without the fear of failing
- Embed teamwork in all operational processes.
- Debureaucratise the organization structure for ease of flow of information.

Theme Reading: Making Performance Appraisals Meaningful: Initiatives Taken by the Industry

While appraisals are still a dreaded exercise in a large number of companies because of the lack of systems and processes and the impending effect like exits, there are a handful of organizations that have managed to get out of the 360 degree feedback routine. They have, for instance, become more flexible and more democratic, and don't treat appraisals as mere rating exercises. Commenting on how appraisals have changed in the last five years, Sunder Ramachandran, Partner, WCH Training Solutions, a Delhi-based soft skills training company, says that performance appraisals have gained more acceptability in the last five years. "Earlier appraisals were seen as a tool only used by large organizations, today performance appraisals are increasingly being used by a lot of small and medium size enterprises".

Democratic Nature of Appraisals

Typically, appraisals are seen as an annual activity, but Ramachandran says that most organizations are now waking up to the need for appraising employees more frequently. So it's common now to see organizations following smaller appraisal cycles like, say, half-yearly or even quarterly. All 1,250 employees at Bangalore-based Tavant Technologies, for instance, are given a monthly one-on-one that gives a snapshot/review and feedback on their performance thus giving time and room for mid-course correction. This monthly feedback is done using templates where managers enter the required information. Apart from this, the company also has a six-monthly feedback that is done online. "This kind of regular feedback helps as employees are clear about where they are headed, rather than keeping them in the dark for 12 months," says Srini Vudumula, Vice-President, HR, Tavant Technologies.

Appraisals have also evolved to become democratic processes in quite a few companies. Sungard Offshore Services, for instance, follows the employee pick process where employees can choose a colleague to sit through his/her appraisal process to give the appraisers a different perspective of the employee's performance. Akila Krishnakumar, CEO, Sungard, says that this system brings more value to the discussion room. The employee pick is seen as an honest broker. Though he or she does not directly rate the employee, he or she could give a view that could change the way the employee is evaluated or assessed. "Employees also feel that it gives them visibility and recognition in the organization, an idea of where they stand, not just within the team, but also in the entire organization." For instance, an employee who's choosing the CEO as the 'honest broker' may be looking for recognition from the top management, but should be prepared for the fact that his or her performance will be open for viewing by the top management. Sungard has 1,200 employees in India and about 50 per cent of them opt for this programme every year. Some employees (about two-three per cent) have even opted to bring in their customers to sit through the appraisal process. Though seen as a revolutionary step, employees feel sometimes customers are able to give better feedback as they are constantly working with them, says Akila Krishnakumar.

Essential Characteristics of an Effective Performance Appraisal System

- ***Reliability and Validity***: Appraisal system should provide consistent, reliable and valid information and data, which can be used to defend the organization to appraise the employees even in case of legal challenges. Appraisals must also satisfy the condition of validity by measuring what they are supposed to measure.
- ***Job Relatedness***: The appraisal technique should measure the performance and provide information in job related areas.
- ***Standardization***: Appraisal forms, procedures, administration of techniques, ratings etc. should be standardized as appraisal decisions affect all employees of the group.
- ***Practical Applicability***: The techniques should be practically viable to administer, possible to implement and economical to undertake continuously.
- ***Legal Sanction***: Appraisals must meet the legal statutory norms and regulations.
- ***Training to Appraisers***: As appraisal is important and sometimes difficult, it would be useful to provide training to appraisers viz some insights and ideas on the rating, documenting appraisals and conducting appraisal interviews.
- ***Open Communication***: Most employees want to know how well they are performing the job. The appraisal interviews should permit both parties to learn about the gaps and prepare themselves for the future.
- ***Employee Access to Results***: Employees should receive adequate feedback on their performances. If performance appraisals are meant for improving employee performance, then withholding appraisal results would not serve any fruitful purpose.
- ***Due Process***: It follows then that formal procedures should be developed to enable employees who disagree with appraisal results. They must have the means for pursuing their grievances and having them addressed objectively.

Performance Planning for Managers

Performance planning is an essential process of determining what an employee is supposed to do in the upcoming year, ensuring everything in place so that the employee can achieve the goals and objectives set during this process.

It is important to understand that performance planning is one step in terms of achieving and implementing the overall strategy so as to improve performance and productivity of the organization.

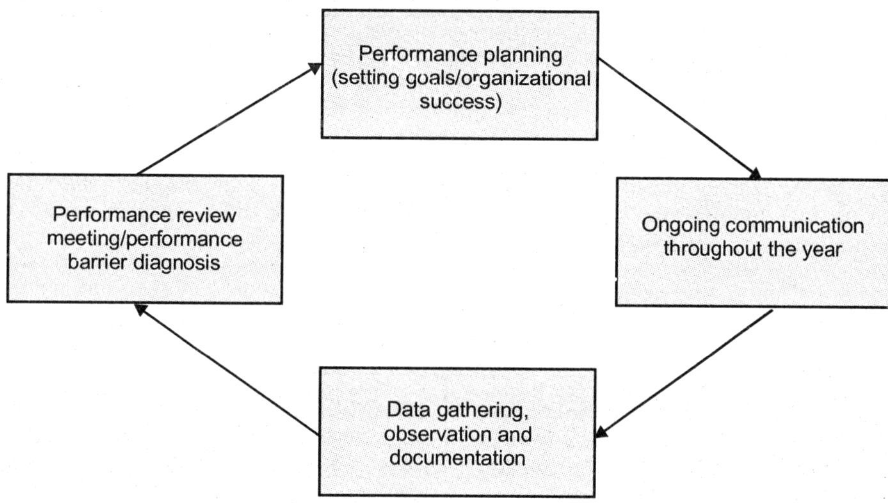

Fig. 3.50: Performance planning cycle

Performance planning is the foundation for any performance management or appraisal system. The benefits of performance planning could be as follows:

Alignment of individual and organizational needs: Each employee performance goals and objectives should be meticulously aligned with the goals and objectives of the organization or the business unit. Performance planning helps to set these goals and also ensure whether the employees are doing the RIGHT thing.

Manager-employee common understanding: Proper performance planning increases the chances the manager and the employee will understand expectations in the same way. When employees are on the same wavelength of that of their managers, they can self monitor their progress, leaving the managers to attend other strategic decision related assignments.

Reviews: Reviews or performance appraisal meetings can contribute effectively to set performance goals and objectives and also determine performance criteria for the performance evaluation process.

Optimizing performance by examining performance barriers: Performance planning is not just setting objectives. It is also an opportunity for manager and employees to identify barriers to the achievement of these goals, and create plans to remove them.

PERFORMANCE FEEDBACK FORM			
Employee Name (Last) (First) (M.I.)			Position Title
Performance Period	Discussion Date	Feedback Date	Name and Title of Supervisor
As part of our performance evaluation process, we would like you to complete and return this feedback form at your earliest convenience in the envelope provided. Please mark the item which most nearly describes the employee's performance based on your personal experience.			
Please indicate the nature and frequency of your contacts with this individual over the last year:			

EVALUATION	
Interpersonal and Communication Skills: The individual's behavioural characteristics toward clients, customers, and peers. Listens well, makes contributions, and keeps others informed. — Outstanding skills for this job. — Very desirable skills for this job. — Skills satisfactory for this job. — Skills questionable for this job. — Skills unsatisfactory for this job.	**Client/Customer Service:** The ability to serve the customer/client in a competent manner. Has a clear understanding of how to utilize the resources properly and realistically to accomplish tasks. — Very competent; understands and uses proper resources. — Competent and usually uses proper resources. — Understands resources, but does not always use them. — Limited knowledge of available resources/ sometimes demanding. — Does not understand or utilize proper resources.
Courtesy: The polite attention an individual gives other people. — Inspiring to others in being courteous and very pleasant. — Always very polite and willing to help. — Agreeable and pleasant. — Sometimes tactless, argumentative. — Blunt; discourteous; antagonistic.	**Responsiveness:** Responds to tasks or requests in a cooperative and timely manner. — Extremely cooperative; completes all tasks/ requests in a timely manner. — Cooperative and usually completes tasks/ requests on time. — Accommodates tasks/requests as best he/ she can. — Gets to tasks/requests at his/her own convenience. — Uncooperative; continuously delays completion of tasks/requests.
Problem Solving: The ability to work independently and to make good judgement/ decisions with amount of information available. — Exceptionally keen and alert when solving problems. — Usually quick to solve problems. — Solves problems with little help from others. — Requires help with solving problems. — Slow to "catch on."	**Teamwork:** Willingness to help others, to resolve problems quickly, and get along with co-workers; maintaining a positive, supportive work environment; promoting a "can do" attitude to achieving goals. — Exceptional team player—always goes the extra mile. — Outstanding team player—always willing to help. — Is a good team player. — Uncooperative; prefers working alone. — Cannot/will not work in a team environment.

Comments: (accolades and/or areas for improvement)

FEEDBACK		__ Summarize my comments with those of others.
PROVIDED BY	(PLEASE PRINT NAME	____________________
		My feedback may be shared with the individual.
Signature____________________		
Date _______		

Outcomes of Performance Appraisal

Developing Employees

The process of performance management provides an excellent opportunity to identify developmental needs. During planning and monitoring of work, deficiencies in performance become evident and can be addressed. Areas for improving good performance also stand out, and action can be taken to help successful employees improve even further. Developing employees is more than just training employees. Developing employees covers all efforts to foster learning, which happens on the job every day. When organizations focus on developing their employees' capacity to perform rather than just training them, employees will be able to adapt to a variety of situations, which is vital for the survival, well-being, and goal achievement of individuals as well as organizations. Employee development can be either formal or informal.

One effective means of identifying formal training for an employee is establishing an **Individual Development Plan (IDP)**, as follows:

The Individual Development Plan 1-2-3 Process

1. **Self-Assessment:** The employee reviews prior job experience, training, education and other developmental experiences to provide concrete information regarding current strengths and skills. This could include a review of past applications for employment and past training records. The employee reviews the standards for work performance to determine core competencies necessary for the job and past performance evaluations for indications of areas needing improvement and identifies core skills specific to that need. This could also involve employee assessing their personal career goals and determines both short and long term steps toward achieving the goals.
2. **Discussions and Collaboration:** In order to obtain mutual commitment between the supervisor and the employee, open discussion and collaboration is necessary. The employee and supervisor mutually agree to discuss the results of the self-assessment and draft IDP prepared by the employee. The discussion includes both perspectives of organizational needs, job requirements, the employee's strengths and developmental needs, financial limitations, timing and learning opportunities that the supervisor will actively support. The supervisor should coach the employee by giving open and constructive feedback, identifying challenging assignments, discussing career paths in the organization and reasonable timeframes for meeting the objectives of the IDP.

The supervisor and employee then should sign a completed IDP based on mutual agreement or final decisions of the supervisor.

3. **Implementation and Follow-up:** The employee ensures that any necessary procurement or training request forms are prepared and monitors work that is assigned to best accomplish the IDP's developmental experiences. The employee reports on completion of items in the IDP. The supervisor and the employee meet periodically throughout the year to review and update the IDP.

Informal Employee Development Initiatives

While managers have a large influence over formal training, they have even greater impact on creating a climate for **informal** employee development, which can take a wide variety of forms:

- **Feedback** is a natural part of the monitoring process of performance management, but specific and timely feedback to employees about their performance against established expectations also provides the foundation for discussing developmental needs.
- **Job rotations and special assignments** can stretch and challenge employees and broaden their understanding of the organization.
- **Coaching and counseling** provides individualized advice and instruction.
- **Mentoring** helps employees clarify career goals, understand the organization, analyze strengths and developmental needs, build support networks, and deal with roadblocks.
- **Using the manager as an informal teacher** acknowledges that managers consciously teach employees through their own model, habits, and system of values.
- **Learning teams** can form to meet regularly to focus on improving performance.
- **Self-development** includes a broad collection of techniques and approaches, demonstrations at other organizations.

Although these informal developmental strategies cost very little, they have potentially big payoffs in terms.

Exhibit: Performance Plan and Review

Employee Name (please print)____________________

Employee Code____________________

Department/Unit____________________

Position Classification____________________

Leader/Manager/Supervisor____________________

Performance Evaluation period __________ to __________.

The performance plan and review is a formalization of ongoing discussion, agreed upon performance objectives and appraisal of outcomes. People work more effectively if they understand performance expectations and are involved in setting goals and objectives. The Performance Plan and Review is a cumulative summary of discussions that have occurred throughout the year between the manager and the employee where performance feedback has regularly been provided so staff can continue to develop, enhancing opportunity for personal and professional growth and development.

DEFINITION OF PERFORMANCE LEVELS

Below Expectations: Performance is **consistently** below the standards of performance required and defined for reasons **other than** lack of experience and/or development. ***HR manager should be contacted for advice and guidance.***

Needs improvement: Performance is below the standards of performance required and defined **for reasons of lack of experience and development**. A development plan will be established to support the growth of the employee.

Meets expectations: Performance is solid, effective and consistently meets the performance standards required and defined.

Exceeds expectations: Performance is **consistently** above the standards of performance required and defined and contributions are well beyond normal job expectations for the period.

Where to go for assistance: *HR manager/executives are available to meet with staff and leaders/managers to ensure there is an understanding of the performance plan and review process.* If there are concerns or questions, the HR manager is available for advice and assistance by contacting extension.

Performance Plan and Review

Provide comments and feedback on performance on the following areas:

- Leadership Competencies
- Professional/Management Skills
- Human Relations skills (i.e., communication, team work)
- Service Responsiveness

Successes and Achievements - *Outline achievements during the past year including comments on goals and objectives.*

Identify Area(s) of Development

Overall Appraisal for the period ______________ **to** ______________ **:**

☐ Below Expectations ☐ Needs Improvement ☐ Meets Expectations ☐ Exceeds Expectations

Employee's Comments:

______________________________ ______________________________

Employee Signature ***Leader/Manager Signature***

Goals and Objective (PMA)

(Once completed, separate for review and attachment to the following PPR)

Goals and objectives for the next ______ months.			
	Time frame	√	*Comments*

Employee Signature ***Supervisor/Manager Signature***

EXHIBIT

BHARTI TELE-VENTURE LIMITED

Existing Performance Review and Development Plan (PRDP)

(______________) to (______________)

Name: ____________________ **Designation:** ______________ **E.Code:** ______________

Department: ______________ **Date of Joining:** __________ **Band:** ______________

Career Progression Form:

	From	To	Position and Level	Department/Business
Career progression at Bharti				
	Duration	**Year**	**Subject/Topic/Area**	**Conducted by**
Training and development at Bharti				

Section I (a): PERFORMANCE PLANNING					
KRAs to be established at the beginning of the year (Weightage: 60% task related KRAs, 40% Competency / Performance Indicators					
TASK FACTORS	**Sl no.**	**KRAs/Targets**	**Measures/Formula**	**Weightage**	**Time Frame**
	1	**Service Provisioning**	Error free service provisioning: 95% Activation time 30 M TS/SEF: 90%	**15%** (7.5) (7.5)	**Date**
	2	**Documentation**	To ensure documentation is complete - Documents with correct data: > 95% - Documents with wrong data: < 05%	15% (7.5) (7.5)	
	3	**Archiving**	Archiving for all documents	**10%**	
	4	**Reduce activation time**	Average activation time per account: < = 20 min	**10%**	
	5	**Accuracy in bill delivery**	Errors in bill delivery: < = 1%	**10%**	
COMPETENCY	**Sl no.**	**Competencies**	**Measures**	**Weightage**	**Time Frame**
	1	**Planning and organizing**	Observation and assessment	**10%**	
	2	**Problem solving and analysis**	Observation and assessment	**10%**	
	3	**Hard work and commitment**	Observation and assessment	**10%**	
	4	**Initiative and drive**	Observation and assessment	**10%**	

Appraiser's Signature and date **Appraiser's Signature and date**

Section I (b): MID TERM REVIEW	
1st Quarter Review – Feedback (Signature of appraiser)	**Realignment of KRAs./Targets, if any** (Signature of appraiser)
Half-Yearly Review – Feedback (Signature of appraiser)	**Realignment of KRAs./Targets, if any** (Signature of appraiser)
3rd Quarter Review – Feedback (Signature of appraiser)	**Realignment of KRAs./Targets, if any** (Signature of appraiser)

Section I (c): ANNUAL PERFORMANCE ASSESSMENT					
	S. No.	Key Result Areas	Self Appraisal	Appraiser's ratings	
				% Achieved	Ratings
Task and Competencies Performance Factors					

Section I (c): ANNUAL PERFORMANCE ASSESSMENT (continued)					
	S. No.	Key Result Areas	Self Appraisal	Appraiser's ratings	
				% Achieved	Ratings
	1.	Planning and organizing		99%	(99/100)*10 = 9.9%
	2.	Problem solving and analysis		96%	(96/100)*10 = 9.6%
	3.	Initiative and drive		105%	(105/100)*10 =10.5%
	4.	Hard work and commitment		100%	(100/100)*10 =10%
		Total			40% out of 40%

Section II: OVERALL RATINGS and COMMENTS

OVERALL SCORE = Total score from section – I(c) = __ %

Overall Rating based on final score

4	3	2	1
Exceptional contributor (> = 15%)	**Significant contributor (100%–114%)**	**Contributor (85%–95%)**	**Partial contributor (< = 84%)**

Appraiser's Report and Feedback Provided

Appraiser's signature

Section III: DEVELOPMENT PLAN and REVIEWER'S COMMENTS

To be filled up by the appraiser after discussion with appraisee

Development Needs	Inputs	Time Frame
For Existing Role:		
For Career Development:		

Inputs: training, coaching/mentoring, special assignments, reading, job rotation, job enrichment/job enlargement/enhancement

Appraisee's signature **Appraiser's signature**

Reviewer's Comments

Reviewer's signature

SAMPLE PERFORMANCE APPRAISAL FORM FOR A MANAGER

Name of Appraisee **Designation:**
Department: **Service Start Date:**
Appraisal Period From: ___________ **to** ___________ **Purpose of Review:** ***Confirmation***
Annual Review

Name and Designation of Appraiser:
Nature of Relationship:

XYZ Company seeks corporate value of higher significance, pursuing **innovative quality** in the areas of **Customers, Employees, Society, Products, Technology, Management** and **Fairness**

The purpose of this evaluation is to communicate clearly to the individual evaluated how well he/she is meeting expectations for a person at his/her level. *You are required to support your rating with comments in the spaces provided for each category. For statements that do not apply to the person being evaluated, please mark, "Not Applicable" (NA). Comments should be specific (including examples) and explanatory. If your evaluation and recommendations cannot be adequately covered in the space provided, you should prepare an attachment to this appraisal form. This form should be reviewed by the next level of authority, before discussion with the person being evaluated.

*Please refer to the goals set during the previous appraisal period, as you conduct your assessment.

Performance for each category is graded into the following:

Outstanding Consistently	5 points	Performance is exceptional and far exceeds expectations. Consistently demonstrates excellent standards.
Very Good	4 points	Performance is consistent and exceeds expectations.
Good	3 points	Performance is consistent. Clearly meets job requirements.
Fair	2 points	Performance is satisfactory. Meets minimum requirements of the job.
Needs Improvement	1 point	Performance is inconsistent. Meets requirements of the job occasionally.
Unsatisfactory	0 point	Performance does not meet minimum requirements of the job.

PART-I CUSTOMERS		Outstanding	Very good	Good	Fair	Needs improvement	Unsatisfactory	Not applicable
Customer focus	1. Places high priority on achieving customer satisfaction (both internal and external customers)	5	4	3	2	1	0	NA
	2. Displays effective negotiation skills with both suppliers, customers and internal staff	5	4	3	2	1	0	NA

Contd...

PART-II	EMPLOYEES	Outstanding	Very good	Good	Fair	Needs improvement	Unsatisfactory	Not applicable
Staff training and welfare	3. Demonstrates an interest in the career development of staff within the department	5	4	3	2	1	0	NA
	4. Is pro-active in training new hires and less experienced staff	5	4	3	2	1	0	NA
Interpersonal/facilitation of team work	5. Strives to develop good relations with other departments	5	4	3	2	1	0	NA
	6. Ensures team work and co-operation amongst staff	5	4	3	2	1	0	NA
	7. Displays effective interpersonal skills	5	4	3	2	1	0	NA

COMMENTS

		Outstanding	Very good	Good	Fair	Needs improvement	Unsatisfactory	Not applicable
Communication skills	8. Communicates and presents information effectively	5	4	3	2	1	0	NA

PART-III SOCIETY									
Cost consciousness	9.	Actively promotes practices that save company resources and minimize wastage	5	4	3	2	1	0	NA

PART-IV PRODUCTS AND SERVICES									
Job knowledge/ technical skills	10.	Keeps current about industry developments	5	4	3	2	1	0	NA
	11.	Displays a high level of technical competence in job area	5	4	3	2	1	0	NA

Work attitude	12.	Displays commitment to personal and career development	5	4	3	2	1	0	NA
	13.	Plans and organises work effectively	5	4	3	2	1	0	NA
	14.	Is pro-active and displays initiative	5	4	3	2	1	0	NA

COMMENTS

			Outstanding	Very good	Good	Fair	Needs improvement	Unsatisfactory	Not applicable
Quality mindset	15.	Ensures that work performed in the department is accurate and of high quality	5	4	3	2	1	0	NA
Safety	16.	Ensures careful work habits that comply with safety requirements in his department	5	4	3	2	1	0	NA

PART-V TECHNOLOGY								
Process improvement	17. Seeks to continually improve processes and work methods	5	4	3	2	1	0	NA

PART-VI MANAGEMENT								
Decision making	18. Exhibits sound judgement when making decisions	5	4	3	2	1	0	NA

Problem solving	19. Helps resolve staff problems on work-related matters	5	4	3	2	1	0	NA
	20. Handles problem situations effectively	5	4	3	2	1	0	NA

COMMENTS

		Outstanding	Very good	Good	Fair	Needs improvement	Unsatisfactory	Not applicable
Goal orientation	21. Sets realistic goals and is responsible for meeting them	5	4	3	2	1	0	NA
Leadership /motivation	22. Is a positive role model for subordinates	5	4	3	2	1	0	NA
	23. Motivates staff to perform better in all areas	5	4	3	2	1	0	NA
	24. Delegates responsibilities to subordinates effectively	5	4	3	2	1	0	NA
	25. Ensures staff receive timely feedback	5	4	3	2	1	0	NA

PART-VII	FAIRNESS							
Integrity	26. Demonstrates integrity and good work ethics in the company's best interest	5	4	3	2	1	0	NA
Dependability/ responsibility	27. Demonstrates ability to assume and discharge responsibility	5	4	3	2	1	0	NA
	28. Is adaptable and willing to accept new responsibilites	5	4	3	2	1	0	NA

COMMENTS

EVALUATION

	Formula	Score
Total score	$\frac{\text{Total scores} \times 100\%}{\text{Number of questions answered} \times 5}$	

GRADING

90%–100%	**Outstanding** Performance is exceptional and far exceeds expectations. Consistently demonstrates excellent standards in all job requirements.
76%–89%	**Very Good** Performance is consistent, and exceeds expectations in all situations.
60%–75%	**Good** Performance is consistent. Clearly meets essential requirements of job.
45%–59%	**Fair** Performance is satisfactory. Meets requirements of the job.
31%–44%	**Needs Improvement** Performance is inconsistent. Meets requirements of the job occasionally. Supervision and training is required for most problem areas.
0%–30%	**Unsatisfactory** Performance does not meet the minimum requirements of the job.

GROWTH AND DEVELOPMENT

(i) List the appraisee's strengths

____

____

____

(ii) List the areas for improvement

____

____

____

(iii) What specific plans of action, including training, will be taken to help the appraisee in their current job or for possible advancement in the company?

____

____

____

ACHIEVEMENT

(i) Describe the appraisee's areas of additional responsibilities and/or other work-related achievements

____

____

____

REVIEW WITH STAFF: My immediate superior and I have discussed my performance review.

(   ) I agree with the appraisal

(   ) I disagree with the appraisal

COMMENTS

____

____

____

____

____

Signature of Employee Date

RECOMMENDATIONS

- ☐ Termination
- ☐ Extension of probation
- ☐ Suitable for confirmation (w.e.f. __________)
- ☐ Normal increment of S$_____
- ☐ No salary increment ____________________
- ☐ Consider for merit increment
- ☐ Transfer to other types of work
- ☐ Ready for promotion
- ☐ Has potential for promotion, but not ready
- ☐ Others:____________________

OTHER REMARKS

Signature of Appraiser

Date

HUMAN RESOURCE DEPARTMENT'S USE

Present Salary: ____________________ Date of Last Increment: ____________

New Salary: ____________________ Effective Date: ____________

COMMENTS

Signature of Managing Director

Date

BALANCED SCORECARD A TOOL FOR HOLISTIC PERFORMANCE MANAGEMENT

Introduction

Measuring organizational success is a continuous challenge for both managers and researchers. While financial measures were in wide use for many years, new frameworks have emerged in recent years that extend organizational perspectives beyond traditional financial measures. Among them, the 'Balanced Scorecard' is one of the most popular.

What is Balanced Scorecard?

A new approach to strategic management was developed in the early 1990s by Drs. Robert Kaplan (Harvard Business School) and David Norton. They named this system the 'balanced scorecard'. Recognizing some of the weaknesses and vagueness of previous management approaches, the balanced scorecard approach provides a clear prescription as to what companies should measure in order to 'balance' the financial perspective.

The balanced scorecard is a ***management system*** (not only a measurement system) that enables organizations to clarify their vision and strategy and translate them into action. It provides feedback around both the internal business processes and external outcomes in order to continuously improve strategic performance and results. Kaplan and Norton describe the innovation of the balanced scorecard as follows:

"The balanced scorecard retains traditional financial measures. But financial measures tell the story of past events, an adequate story for industrial age companies for which investments in long-term capabilities and customer relationships were not critical for success. These financial measures are inadequate, however, for guiding and evaluating the journey that information age companies must make to create future value through investment in customers, suppliers, employees, processes, technology, and innovation".

Scope of Balanced Scorecard

The balanced scorecard seeks to measure a business from the following perspectives:

- **Financial perspective**—this will be familiar to business managers and measures such as financial ratios, debtors or cash flow common.
- **Customer perspective**—seeks to measure aspects directly impact on customers such as the time taken to deal with calls, customer surveys, complaints or competitive rankings.
- **Internal business perspective**—looks at the impact of internal processes on the business - how long is spent prospecting? How much rework is required? How successful are we when tendering for new business?
- **Innovation and learning perspective**—how much revenue comes from new ideas? How many employee suggestions are there? How do we train staff?

The components of the balanced scorecard as described above can be illustrated by the following figure:

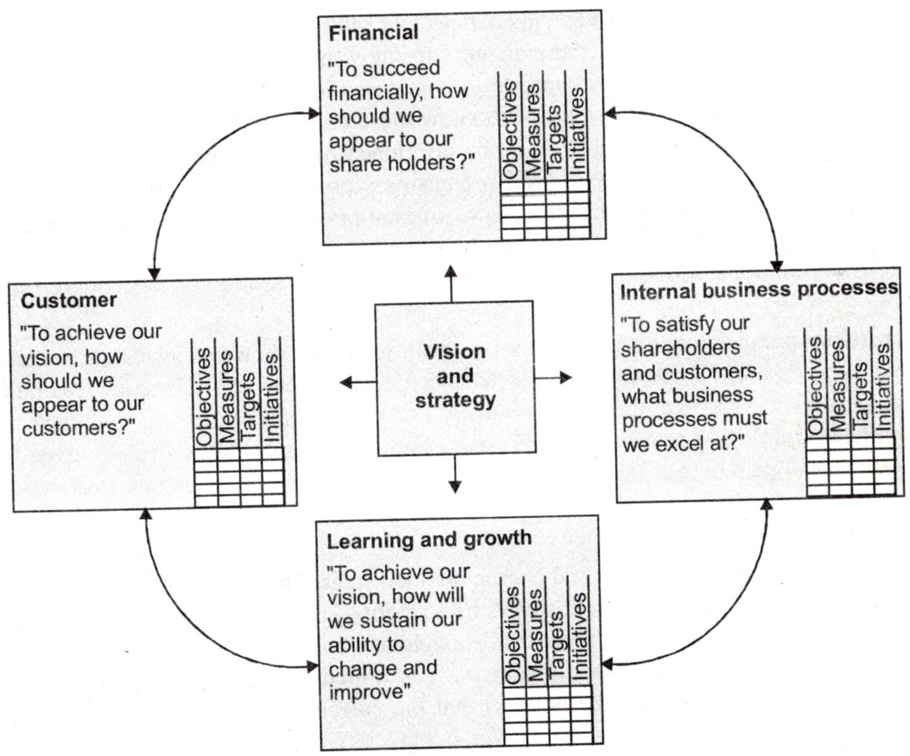

Fig. 3.51: Components of balanced scorecard

The specific measures within each of the perspectives will be chosen to reflect the drivers of that business. The method can facilitate the separation of strategic policymaking from the implementation, so that organizational goals can be broken into task oriented objectives which can be managed by front-line staff. It can also help detect correlation between activities.

Perspectives of Balanced Scorecard

The balanced scorecard suggests that we view the organization from four perspectives, and to develop metrics, collect data and analyze it relative to each of these perspectives:

1. **The learning and growth perspective:** This perspective includes employee training and corporate cultural attitudes related to both individual and corporate self-improvement. In a knowledge-worker organization, *people* — the only repository of knowledge — are the main resource. In the current climate of rapid technological change, it is becoming necessary for knowledge workers to be in a continuous learning mode. Government agencies often find themselves unable to hire new technical workers, and at the same time there is a decline in training of existing employees. This is a leading indicator of 'brain drain' that must be reversed. Metrics can be put into place to guide managers in focusing training funds where they can help the most. In any case, *learning and growth constitute the essential foundation for success of any knowledge-worker organization.* Kaplan and Norton emphasize that 'learning' is more than 'training'; it also includes things like mentors and tutors within the organization, as well as that ease of communication among workers that allows them to readily get help on a problem when it is needed. It also includes technological tools; what the Baldrige criteria call "high performance work systems." One of these, the Intranet, will be examined in detail later in this document.
2. **The business process perspective:** This perspective refers to internal business processes. Metrics based on this perspective allow the managers to know how well their business is running, and whether its products and services conform to customer requirements (the mission). These metrics have to be carefully designed by those who know these processes most intimately; with our unique missions these are not something that can be developed by outside consultants. In addition to the strategic management process, two kinds of business processes may be identified: (a) mission-oriented processes, and (b) support processes. Mission-oriented processes are the special functions of government offices, and many unique problems are encountered in these processes. The support processes are more repetitive in nature, and hence easier to measure and benchmark using generic metrics.
3. **The customer perspective:** Recent management philosophy has shown an increasing realization of the importance of customer focus and customer satisfaction in any business. These are leading indicators: if customers are not satisfied, they will eventually find other suppliers that will meet their needs. Poor performance from this perspective is thus a leading indicator of future decline, even though the current financial picture may look good. In developing metrics for satisfaction, customers should be analyzed in terms of kinds of customers and the kinds of processes for which we are providing a product or service to those customer groups.
4. **The financial perspective:** Kaplan and Norton do not disregard the traditional need for financial data. Timely and accurate funding data will always be a priority, and managers will do whatever necessary to provide it. In fact, often there is more than enough handling and processing of financial data. With the implementation of a corporate database, it is hoped that more of the processing can be centralized and automated. But the point is that the current emphasis on financials leads to the "unbalanced" situation with regard to other perspectives. There is perhaps a need to include additional financial-related data, such as risk assessment and cost-benefit data, in this category.

How Balanced Scorecards Work

To obtain a satisfactory overview of performance, the scorecard will require a mix of lagging and leading (forward looking) measures. Financial measures tend to be lagged and consequently, the measures chosen for the other perspectives will need to include leading measures. In general, outcome measures tend to be lagged, for example, current market share is the result of past decisions and consequently is a lagging measure. Thus the challenge in designing a Balanced Scorecard is to choose driver measures which lead changes in the outcome measures in the non-financial perspectives and which ultimately drive the financial measures. Once the firm's objectives have been agreed and the appropriate outcome and driver measures chosen for each of the perspectives, firm and managerial performance is assessed by comparing actual attainment on each measure with the target set for that measure.

Objective	Measure	Target	Actual

Exhibit: Building a Balanced Scorecard: The Process

Kaplan and Norton described a typical plan that they used to create balanced scorecards for multiple organizations. It essentially comprised of four steps that were further broken down into a total of ten tasks. In addition to achieving the objective of developing a balanced scorecard that was useful for measuring and managing corporate performance, this plan was also intended to ensure that senior managers and middle-level managers in the organization committed themselves to the overall initiative. The four steps and ten tasks are listed here.

Step 1: **Define the Measurement Architecture**

Task 1: Select the appropriate organizational unit

Task 2: Identify SBU/corporate linkages

Step 2: **Build Consensus around Strategic Objectives**

Task 3: Conduct first round of interviews

Task 4: Synthesis session

Task 5: Executive workshop: First round

Step 3: **Select and Design Measures**

Task 6: Subgroup meetings

Task 7: Executive workshop: Second round

Step 4: **Build the Implementation Plan**

Task 8: Develop the implementation plan

Task 9: Executive workshop: Third round

Task 10: Finalize the implementation plan

(Source: Adapted from Kaplan R S and Norton D P (1996), Translating Strategy into Action – The Balanced Scorecard, Harvard Business School Press.)

A Balanced Scorecard measures the progress of an organization toward its strategic goals by translating their vision and objectives into tactics and measures across a balanced set of perspectives. It helps the organization to capture the expectations of customers and measures the company's ability to meet them. It also facilitates to translate the organizational Strategy, Mission and Vision into tangible measures for use by decision makers through to line workers. A BSC is the culmination of a sophisticated data gathering and analysis process and system that can and would drive the process of change in an organization.

Components of the Balanced Scorecard

Perspectives: Four top-down perspectives on enterprise performance (Financial, Internal Business Process, Innovation and Learning, Customer).

Objectives: What the company needs to do to accomplish its strategy; one guideline is to have up to sixteen measurable objectives.

Metrics: Actionable and tangible measurements which support achieving objectives; this is what makes it real.

Targets: Performance level expectations set against the strategic plan. For each metric, set a goal or plan so progress against the objective can be evaluated.

Exhibit: Components of the Balance Scorecard (Financial Perspective) in a tyre company

Financial				
"To succeed financially how should we appear to our shareholders"	**Objectives**	**Measure**	**Target**	**Initiatives**
	To achieve turnover of Rs. 1850 mn by FY05 To reduce the gap in PBT with industry leader to less than 1% from current 4.4%	- Sales turnover - PBIDT	- To achieve turnover of Rs 1850 mn by FY05 - PBIDT of Rs 1500 mn (FY05) - Decrease in conversion cost from Rs 25/Kg to 21/Kg in the Bhopal Plant and from Rs 28/Kg to Rs 25/Kg in the Mysore Plant	- Developing acceptable 1000-20 lug. tyres - Increasing number of sales offices from 180 to 220. - 7 day work week to be introduced in Rs the Bhopal Plant - Reduction in conversion cost from Rs 25 to Rs 18/Kg - Waste reduction, fuel efficiency - Power consumption reduction

Creating a Balanced Scorecard

The process of creating a balanced scorecard starts with the business strategy, and progressively breaks that strategy into tactical measures. Balanced scorecard measures should be used not only to assess the "health" of the organization but to also to challenge the organizational strategy to ensure that it is the most effective one for the company. The following are the steps involved in developing a balanced scorecard, namely:

- The balanced scorecard puts vision and strategy at the center of performance measurement.
- The definition of a clear strategy, mission and vision is critical to the balanced scorecard building process.

- If the strategy isn't clearly defined, there is no way to measure performance against that strategy.
- A balanced scorecard will not give you a strategy but it will inform you quickly if the strategy of the company isn't working.
- The balanced scorecard helps align the organization's strategic objectives across the entire organization, at all levels.
- The strategy is used to establishes the organization's objectives, which are then used to define the measures.
- The measures pull people at all levels towards the overall strategy.
- The measures will then indicate whether the strategy is being fulfilled effectively.

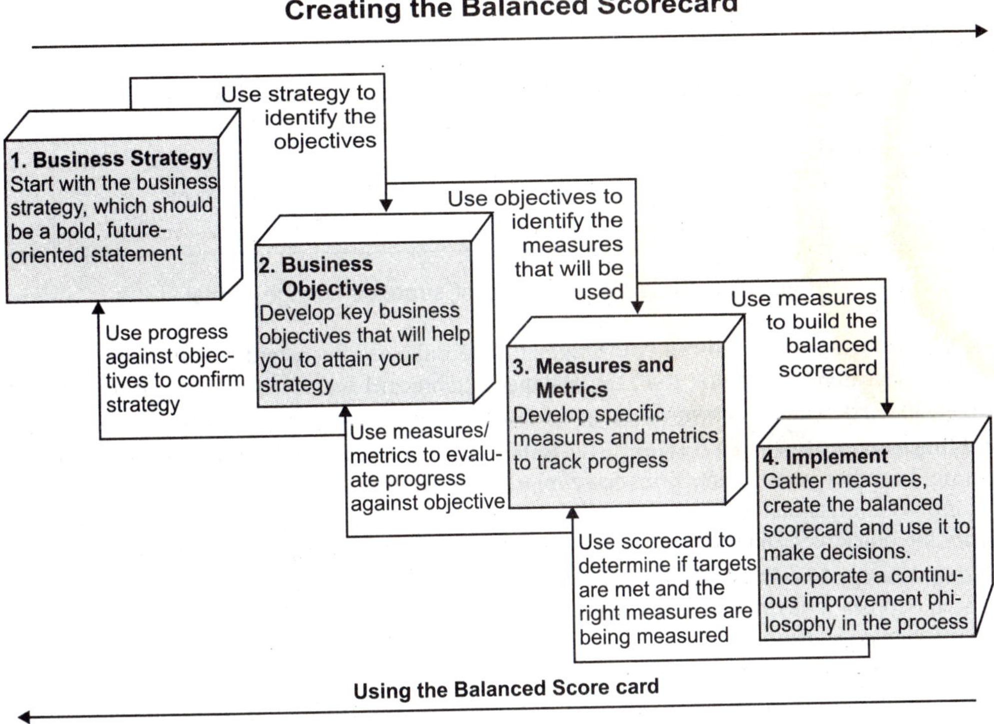

Fig. 3.52: Developing a balanced scorecard

Benefits from Adopting the Balanced Scorecard

There are several benefits from implementing a Balanced Scorecard. These are as follows:

Role in strategic management process: Balanced Scorecard could play a pivotal role in the strategic management process. As it requires the management of an organization to clarify and obtain consensus on the strategic objectives of the firm, it can assist in the communication of the chosen strategy, consequently aligning the efforts both of individuals and of departments. In this role, there is a clear link between the Balanced Scorecard and management by objectives (MBO).

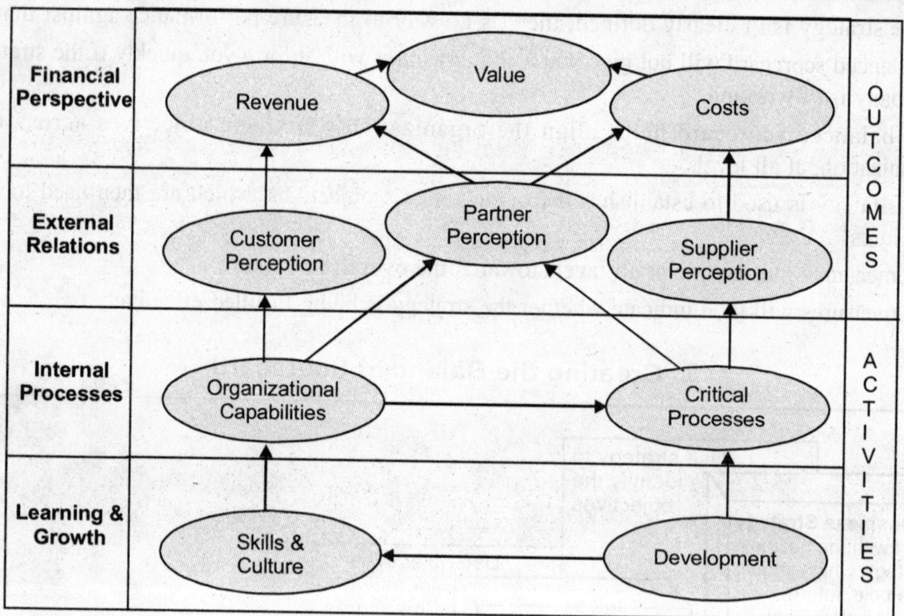

Fig. 3.53: Simplified example of strategic linkage model

Tool for performance measurement: Originally the Balanced Scorecard was seen as a useful tool for performance measurement. In this role, the Balanced Scorecard was seen as integrating financial/non-financial, internal/external and leading/lagging information on firm performance in a coherent fashion.

Enabling corporate restructuring: The Balanced Scorecard could be used to assist in corporate restructuring. In recent years, many firms have migrated away from a traditional hierarchical structure to a flatter, team-based organizational structure. The Balanced Scorecard can support such changes, as it can help clarify the objectives and the critical success factors for the newly formed teams.

Linking strategy to critical success factors: Apart from the communication and co-ordination roles of the Balanced Scorecard in strategic implementation, the Balanced Scorecard can be used to link strategy to specific critical success factors in the customer, internal business process and growth/learning perspectives. By setting both short and long-term targets for driver and outcome measures and by comparing actual attainment against target, feedback is obtained on how well the strategy is being implemented and on whether the strategy is working.

Role in investment appraisal processes: Building on the Balanced Scorecard's use as a strategic management tool, it has been suggested that the Balanced Scorecard can play a role in the investment appraisal process. Traditional methods of investment appraisal such as discounted cash flow do not cope well with investments which generate indirect rather than direct financial returns. Examples of these include investments which enhance the future 'flexibility' of a firm or investments in the firm's infrastructure, such as an enhanced management information system. The Balanced Scorecard can assist management's investment appraisal decisions as it provides managers with a mechanism to incorporate the strategic aspects of the investment into the appraisal process. This could be achieved by using a weighting system developed from a firm's Balanced Scorecard measures to evaluate new projects. An index score would be calculated for each investment opportunity and projects would then be ranked and selected based on this score.

Linkage to compensation system: If the Balanced Scorecard is to be taken seriously by employees, the compensation system must be linked to the employee's attainment (or otherwise) of their individual targets on each perspective. In line with the ideas of controllability and cascaded scorecards, a portion of senior management's compensation should be linked to the attainment of financial targets such as profitability, cash-flow or economic value added, whereas junior management's targets will most likely be linked to operational measures in the customer and internal business perspectives. While the logic of linking the compensation system to the Balanced Scorecard is obvious, there are a number of practical difficulties in creating this linkage.

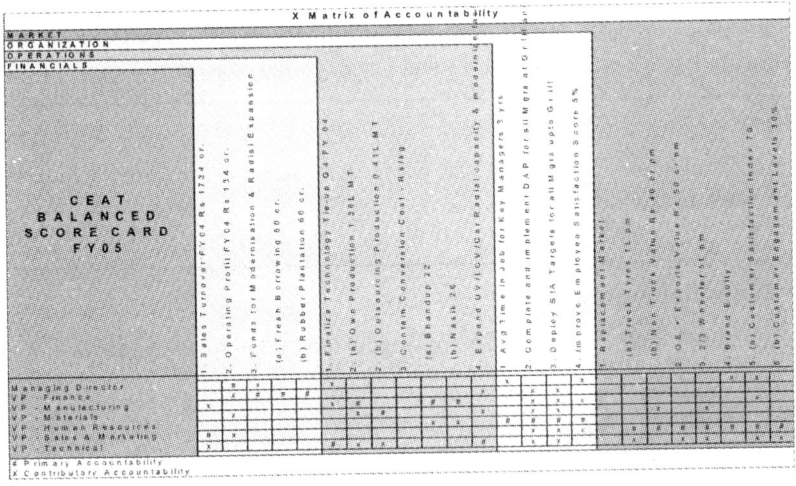

Fig. 3.54: Balanced scorecard in a tyre company

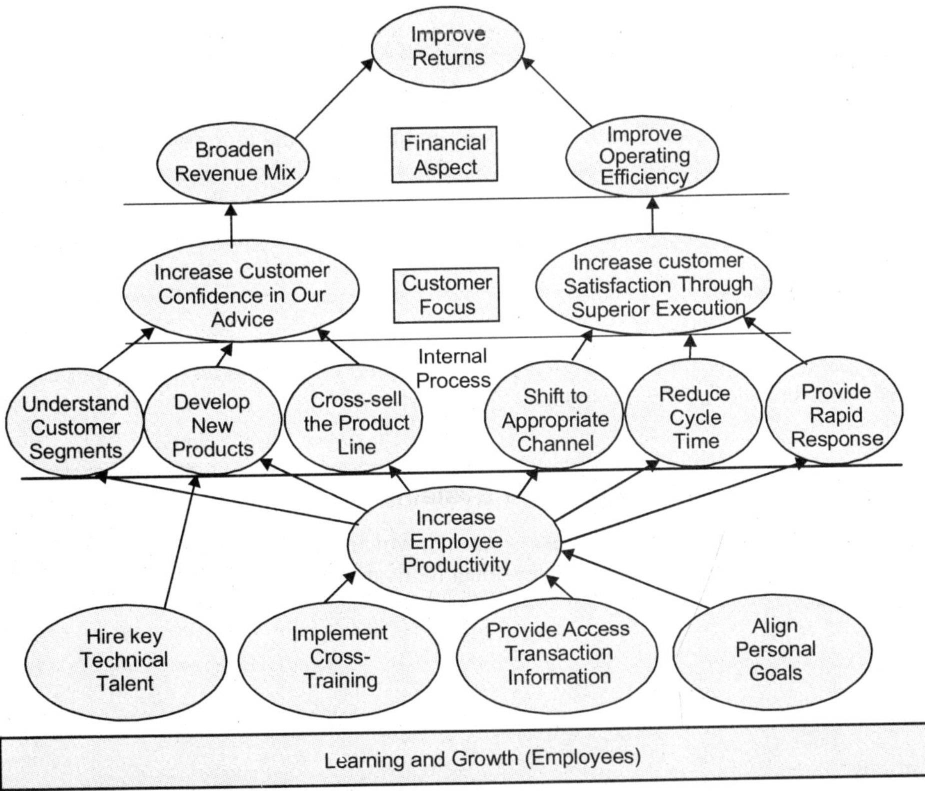

Fig. 3.55: Importance of strategic mapping in developing a balanced scorecard (Meghna, H., "The HR Scorecard", HR Folks International, www.hrfolks.com)

POTENTIAL APPRAISAL

The potential appraisal is a future-oriented appraisal by which the potential of an employee to occupy higher positions and to assume higher responsibilities is evaluated. The potential appraisal can help the extension staff to know their strengths and weaknesses and can motivate them to further develop their skills. Thus the potential appraisal helps in planning overall career development of employees. Some of the techniques used for the appraisal are self-appraisals, peer rating, the management by objectives (MBO) approach, psychological test and simulated work exercises, case analyses and leadership exercises.

Industry Opinion

"Potential Appraisal is an important area because people have to be prepared to take up responsibility"…. Mr. PV. Nayak, Director, Glaxo India.

(*Courtesy: Business Today, January 7–21, 1996, p. 245*)

Objectives of Potential Appraisal

The objective of potential appraisal is to occupy higher positions in the organizational hierarchy and undertake higher responsibilities.

Potential appraisals are required to:

- Inform employees about their future prospects
- Help the organization chalk out of a suitable succession plan
- Update training efforts from time to time
- Advise employees about what they must do to improve their career prospects

Potential Appraisal in Philips

Philips had adopted the potential appraisal system where it uses a five point grading scale – excellent, very good, good/adequate, weak and sufficient – to evaluate employees on the four broad attributes of conceptual effectiveness, operational effectiveness, interpersonal effectiveness and achievement motivation. Philips had emphasized on identifying star performers at the junior level by using performance data to chart out the highest level a manager can reach and thereby makes full utilization of the capabilities of a particular employee in the organization.

Industry Opinion

"A potentially good manager must display certain behavioural characteristics which transcend his job." Mr. G. Sridhar, Vice President, Cadbury India.

(*Courtesy: Business Today, January 7–21, 1996, p. 247*)

Criteria for Effective Potential Appraisal Systems

Potential appraisal system is a managerial process through which the conceptual effectiveness, interpersonal effectiveness, operational effectiveness and achievement motivation levels of appraisees are uncovered. These criteria are as follows:

Conceptual effectiveness	Interpersonal effectiveness
Vision Business orientation Sense of reality Entrepreneurial/intrapreneurial orientation	Network directedness Negotiating power Personal influence Verbal behaviour Empathy
Operational effectiveness	**Achievement motivation**
Result orientation Individual effectiveness Initiative Risk taking and control	Drive Self development and learning Professional ambition Innovativeness Stability

Fig. 3.56: Criteria used for potential appraisal system

Steps to be Followed While Introducing a Good Potential Appraisal System

The following are some of the steps required to be followed while introducing a Potential Appraisal System:

(a) ***Role descriptions:*** Organizational roles and functions must be defined clearly. A good potential appraisal system would be based on the clarity of roles and functions associated with different roles in the organization. This requires extensive job descriptions to be made available for each job. These job descriptions should spell out the various functions involved in performing the job effectively.

(b) ***Qualities required:*** Based on Job Descriptions, the roles to be played by employees should be prepared (i.e. Technical, managerial jobs and behavioural dimensions)

(c) ***Rating mechanisms:*** Besides listing the functions and qualities, the potential appraisal system must list mechanisms of judging the qualities of employees such as: rating by others, Use of various psychological tests and games, technical knowledge and skills and performance appraisal records maintained.

(d) ***Organizing the system*:** Once the functions, the qualities required to perform these functions, indicators of these qualities, and mechanisms for generating these indicators are clear, the organization is in an effective position so as to establish and operate a potential appraisal system.

(e) ***Feedback*:** If the organization believes in the development of human resources it should attempt to generate a climate of openness. Such a climate is required for helping employees to understand their strengths and weaknesses and to create opportunities for development. A good potential appraisal system should provide an opportunity for every employee to know the results of assessment and should also help in order to understand the qualities actually required for performing the role for which the employee thinks he or she has the requisite potential.

Exercise Case Study: The Woes of a Telephone Operator

Rashmi was a telephone operator in a large Public Sector Undertaking (PSU). She was a graduate in Commerce and had learned the technique of operating a telephone board while on the job. The problem with Rashmi was that her job with the PSU was contractual. She kept responding to advertisements for employment in the newspapers but, as luck would have it, she could not manage to get a permanent job in any good organization. Frustrated she requested a distant uncle of hers to use his influence and provide her with a good job. This uncle of hers was politically well connected and he managed to use his political clout to get Rashmi a permanent job in another PSU. However, since there was no vacancy for the post of telephone operator in this PSU, Rashmi was assigned the job of private secretary to one of the Deputy

Manager in this new organization. At the time of performance appraisal, at the end of one year, Rashmi was shocked to hear from her immediate boss that her performance has been atrocious throughout the year. She was officially communicated that she would continue to be under probation till she has substantially improved in her performance to be confirmed in the post of private secretary.

Review Questions

Examine what went wrong in the performance appraisal process of Rashmi. Was there any fundamental flaw in the process itself ? Please justify your answer with relevant conceptual linkages.

REFERENCES

1. Thornton, G.C., Byham, W.C. (1982): "Assessment centers and managerial performance," Academic Press, New York.

QUESTION BANK

1. What are the different methods of performance appraisal? Which type of appraisal is most suitable for executive cadre and for non-executive cadre of employees?
2. "Behaviourally anchored rating scales are a milestone achievement in the performance measurement process". Comment.
3. What are the conditions required for developing new capabilities among employees?
4. Performance appraisal systems may be built on a relative or absolute judgement basis. Discuss what these two bases are and the relative merits and disadvantages of each.
5. Explain why performance management is important in accomplishing organizational goals. (BU July/ August 2005).
6. What is BARS? Why might BARS be better than trait-oriented measures of appraising the employee performance?
7. What is performance evaluation? Discuss the methods and limitations associated with the performance evaluation process.
8. Discuss the significance of performance appraisal. Discuss the important methods of appraisal with their merits and demerits.
9. Bring out the methods of performance appraisal. Explain them in detail. (BU 2003).
10. Bring out the difference between performance appraisal and job evaluation. Why is not job evaluation conducted as regularly as performance appraisal? (BU July/August 2005).
11. Outline the sequence of steps that should be taken to make performance counseling more effective. (BU 2001).
12. Who are the raters of employee performance? What are the common raters' problems? How can they be overcome?
13. "Effectiveness of performance management system depends on the performance appraisal system." Discuss how would the choice of an appraisal system affect the performance management system of a company. What other factors would play an equally significant role?
14. "Managerial acceptance of any particular performance appraisal system depends upon how well they understand the purpose of that particular way of appraising performance". Comment.
15. Critically evaluate various methodologies for planning individual performance. Which of them, according to you is most effective and why?
16. Evaluate the significance of performance appraisal. What are its key objectives?
17. What is self-appraisal? How can it help in enhancing managerial effectiveness?

Internet Exercises

- Study the article from titled "Performance appraisal is a boon not a bane" from the following web resource (http://www.deccanherald.com/Content/Jul22008/avenues2008070176412.asp) and discuss with your friends.
- Search for a sample performance appraisal form uploaded in the Internet and discuss the same in your class.
- Study the website http://www.performance-appraisal.com/intro.htm and discuss your learnings with your friends.
- Surf the following hyperlink (http://www.businessballs.com/performanceappraisals.htm) and analyze the performance appraisal templates mentioned in the website.

Experiential Learning

- Enumerate the various extra curricular skills and capabilities of your friends in the class and make a plan how these could be useful for their future career. You may consult your faculties for the same.
- How can you apply the concept of performance appraisal in improving your class performance? You can discuss the same with your class teacher.

The following exercise is for working HR professionals/managers/executives. This exercise would aim to evaluate whether the Performance Appraisals (Reviews) of your organization are working effectively?

Read each statement below and give your organization points based on the following scale: Doesn't apply = 0 points; Sometimes occurs = 1 point; Frequently occurs = 2 points.

1. ___ In the past five years you have changed, reformatted, or completely revamped the appraisal process within your organization.
2. ___ Once appraisals are filed away, people pay little attention to the process.
3. ___ You have to use tactics of force to get appraisals completed (threatening directives, withholding increases, posting the names of tardy supervisors, etc.).
4. ___ Supervisors frequently complain about the bureaucratic nature of the process and wasted time required for paperwork.
5. ___ Each year a substantial number of employees see the process as unfair and are even demoralized.
6. ___ Marginal performers have a track record of being rated generously, having the effect of creating an impediment to discharge.
7. ___ Because of inconsistencies in approach, appraisals have little value as a screening tool for promotion applicants.
8. ___ Appraisal ratings are inflated en masse, making the linkage to a "pay for performance system" ineffective.
9. ___ Supervisors' and employees' alike go through the motions, putting little heart into the process.
10. ___ Dissatisfied employees take up human resources staff time with bias, complaints, and rating appeals.

Scoring

Add up the number of points you have from each question. What is your score?

0-5 People seemingly are very satisfied with your process. You are a very rare company as only 5% of organizations report such success.

6-10 Warning: There may be substantial problems in your present rating system. Many in your company are unhappy and depressed about the process. It's time to investigate abolishing performance appraisals altogether.

11-20 Beware: It's definitely time to look at alternatives to the traditional appraisal model your company is using.

COMPENSATION MANAGEMENT

Theme Case: TCS Signals Variable Pay Squeeze

TCS, India's largest software, exporter, is affecting a small across-the-board cut in employee salaries based on the company's performance in the third quarter, a move reflecting caution amid tough times for the IT/ITES industry. A top company officer confirmed the move, while stock market analysts commented that revenue growth has not met internal targets and employees can't expect a big wage in the 2008–2009 financial years.

The news came like a shocking experience for Vijay, a software engineer working for Dell in Bangalore. It seemed the inevitable downfall was there knocking right at the doors. This was not only the case for IT professionals and techies in Bangalore, the entire nation's IT sector were worried with the news. For a company like TCS, Vijay said to his friend working in Infosys, "Things are unexpected! Aren't they for an organization like TCS". Amit who was working in the same sector was seen commenting, "This can spread a strong signal to the IT professionals like all of us that the next few months could be tough for us". Indeed Amit and Vijay's concerns was not baseless, because for an organization like TCS which had worked diligently over the years with a philosophy of "***Passion for excellence in its workforce practices"*** the news was unexpected. Infact TCS is the organization which has constantly believed and cherished with a HR philosophy emphasizing upon "creating HR practices that shape the organization's competencies and its workforce to continuously innovate in a volatile and dynamic industry".

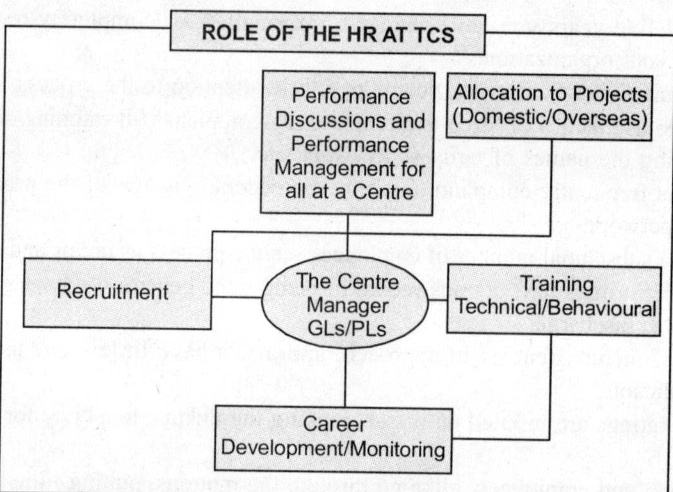

Fig. 3.57: Role of HR at TCS

For an organization like TCS which has nurtured the sensitive breed of IT professionals, and the well it had grown to and sustained at the number one position could expect this was a question which most market watchers had asked themselves a hundred times with the news.

Over the years, TCS has developed an unbreakable bond with sound HR practices in an environment that defies traditional roles and responsibilities. The role of HR in TCS, evidently is that of a facilitator. In TCS HR had been the catalyst which initiates and institutionalizes processes whether it be recruitment or even career development initiatives in the organization. The role of HR at TCS had been described as one of the most proactive HR practices in the nation where HR is considered as an integral part of the strategic objective of the organization. Recent records have shown that TCS had reported a 5% quarter-on-quarter growth in revenues and 6.7% rise in the net profit for the October-December 2007, in line with market expectations.

Information from reliable sources have indicated that TCS has shaved off a portion of its variable pay linked to the company performance, effectively reducing an employee's salary by about 1.5% for the January-March 2008 quarter.

The management of TCS seemed to be quite oblivious of the commotion created by this news. This can be reflected by the following statement made by S. Padmanabhan, Executive Director and Head of Global Human Resources, TCS in an interview with a reputed business daily.

"*We undertake a review of variable pay every quarter and this time, we decided to make an adjustment. We will revisit in April*".

Company resources on had indicated that TCS has reduced the variable portion linked to company performance in the last two years. The top management of TCS in this regard was of the opinion that the outsourcing sector had been facing macroeconomic challenges which had to be factored in the quarterly review of the company. The variable pay related to individual performance has not been touched was one of the latest announcements by the HR department of TCS.

(Courtesy: The Economic Times, 30th JANUARY, 2008, Page, 1)

Introduction

"If you pick the right people and give them the opportunity to spread their wings and put compensation and rewards as a carrier behind it - you almost don't have to manage them".

-Jack Welch

Compensation is any form of payment given to the employees in exchange for the work they perform. Financial payment made at or near place where work is performed is called "***Direct Compensation***" (e.g: Wages, Salaries, Overtime Pay, and Commissions/Incentives and Bonuses). Compensation is a systematic approach to providing monetary value to employees in exchange for work performed. Compensation may achieve several purposes assisting in recruitment, job performance and job satisfaction.

Remuneration is the compensation an employee receives in return for his or her contribution to the organization. An employee's standard of living, status in the society, motivation, loyalty, and productivity depends upon the remuneration he or she receives from an organization.

How is Compensation Used?

Compensation is a tool used by management for a variety of purposes to further the existence of the company. Compensation may be adjusted according the business needs, goals and available resources.

Compensation may be used to:

- Recruit and retain qualified employees.
- Increase or maintain morale/satisfaction.
- Reward and encourage peak performance.
- Achieve internal and external equity.
- Reduce turnover and encourage company loyalty.
- Modify (through negotiations) practices of unions.

Compensation Trends in India

India's transition to a market driven economy began in 1991 with the introduction of liberalization (pro-market economic reforms). Prior to 1991, the Government was (and still is) the biggest employer and job creator, accounting for over 85% of post-matriculation (High School) jobs. Pay was largely determined by high-level agreements between employee unions and the Government and was largely guaranteed in nature. Compensation packages were low on cash and high on fringe benefits such as accommodation, cars and subsidized loans. Variable pay was largely restricted to top and senior management in few private sector enterprises. Grading systems were largely industry-wide and salary progression was purely determined by length of service.

Current Trends

Productivity gains (4% in 2003–04), fast growth in real wages (40% over the last 5 years), a booming but extremely competitive economy, simplification of tax rules and emergence of knowledge-based industries such as Information Technology and Outsourcing Services, Healthcare etc. are key factors that have influenced compensation in India post liberalization. Compensation is now characterized by a Total Cost of Employment approach, a rapid movement to flexible benefits, and increasing levels of variable pay (variable pay now forms about 7% – 35% of fixed pay). Grade structures have become organization specific and salary progression is driven by market forces and individual performance. Average salary increases over 2003–04 ranged from 5% – 20%.

Essentials of the Compensation System

(a) ***Fairness or equity:*** The most important objective of any pay system is fairness or equity. Equity has three dimensions, namely:

- **Internal equity:** It ensures that more difficult jobs are paid more and jobs of similar nature and difficulty are paid equally.
- **External equity:** It ensures that jobs are fairly compensated in comparison to similar jobs in the industry and other rival companies.
- **Individual equity:** It ensures equal pay for equal work that is; each individual's pay is fair in comparison to others doing the same or similar jobs.

(b) ***Attract talents:*** Compensation needs to be high enough to attract talented people. Since many firms compete to hire the services of competent people, the salaries offered must be high enough to motivate them and attract towards an organization.

(c) ***Retain talents:*** If compensation levels fall below the expectations of the employees or are not competitive, employees may quit the organization in frustration. Hence many firms include compensation plans as an integral part of the employee retention plan of the organization.

(d) ***New and desired behaviour:*** Pay should reward loyalty, commitment, experience, risk taking, initiatives and other desired behaviours.

(e) ***Control costs:*** The cost of hiring people should not be too high. Effective compensation management ensures that workers are neither overpaid nor underpaid.

(f) ***Comply with legal rules*:** Compensation programs must invariably satisfy Government rules and regulations regarding minimum wages, bonus, allowances, benefits etc.

(g) ***Ease of Operation:*** The compensation management system should be easy to understand and operate.

Compensation Policy

The aim of compensation statement is to set down the organization's policy with regard to salary. It is the responsibility of all concerned to implement the compensation policies and to explain the same fully to their subordinates. A compensation policy should aim:

- To recognize the value of all, jobs in relation to each other within the organization.
- To take account of wage rates paid by companies of similar size, product and philosophy.

- To ensure stable earnings.
- To enable individuals to reach their full earning potential as far as reasonably practicable.
- To ensure employees' share in the company's prosperity as a result of increasing efficiency.

Exhibit: Rewards and Benefits at IBM

Whether an employee is joining **IBM** as a fresh graduate or a seasoned professional, the company believes that everyone who works at IBM should feel valued and appreciated. That is why IBM offers a total compensation package that includes both cash compensation and benefits.

Cash compensation: IBM's compensation package aims to attract, retain and motivate high-performing people. As such, IBM offers a cash compensation structure that will recognize its employee's specific skills and business expertise. Its compensation structure takes different forms to reflect individual performance levels. It includes base pay, fixed bonuses, allowances, or other payments relevant to the local market. Performance bonus and sales incentives may also be included in the total cash compensation, and are used to ensure that IBMites are paid competitively within the market.

Performance bonus: Another principle IBM follows is to attract, motivate and retain the most talented employees by offering a performance bonus package. If one candidate is a regular employee, he/she will have some portion of his/her annual compensation tied directly to business results. This is to ensure that employee to receive the appropriate recognition and rewards.

Global recognition program: This is the pinnacle of sales excellence within IBM! IBM wants its employees to know that the company values its employee contributions and appreciate their leadership initiatives. IBM's global recognition program is designed to bring out the best, and encourage employees to inspire and motivate others.

Employee stock purchase plan: Since 1958, IBM has offered stock purchase plans because the company had believed in the value of employee ownership. All regular employees, including IBMers who are regular part-timers, are eligible to participate in the plan if they choose. The overall philosophy followed here is "let's grow the company together!"

Healthcare, well-being and personal benefits: IBM offers a range of personal benefits such as medical schemes, dental schemes, health screening, wellness programs, retirements and insurance programs. An IBMite may even be able to include his/her spouse/partner and dependants under his/her coverage for greater peace of mind. The company tries to be as flexible as possible, so that its employees can choose what is appropriate for their personal needs.

Flexibility and work-life balance: IBM is committed to creating a workplace culture and environment in which its employees can balance career with their personal priorities. The company offers a number of programs, ranging from staggered work hours to working from home to part time regular work, which gives its employees the opportunity to achieve a better work/life balance.

Additional programs: An IBMite may find that many of the benefits at IBM are designed to make life a little easier and a lot more fun! IBM offers employees various discounts for goods and services – IBM Personal Computer Purchase, Housing Assistance Purchase Plan, Car Purchase Assistance Plan, Child Care Services, Mobile Phone Plans, Fitness Centers, and Educational courses. Employees are also automatically eligible to join the company's many recreational, social and cultural clubs, and events.

Staggered working hours: If any IBMite would prefer to work from home or start later in the day, he/she is allowed to do so at IBM. IBM gives its employees the flexibility to manage their work hours, so that they could effectively meet the needs of their personal life.

WAGE THEORIES

Wage is the payment for labour or services to a worker, especially remuneration on an hourly, daily, or weekly basis or by the piece. Real wages depend on the price level, as well as on the nominal or money wages.

Economic theories abo ıt wages: Many theories have been advanced to explain the nature of wages. The first of them was the subsistence theory of wages, also called the "iron law of wages," of which David Ricardo was one of the main exponents. According to this theory the demand for labour depends on:

1. Productivity of labour
2. Technology
3. Demand for the product
4. The price of capital input

The shift in demand for labour again depends on two elements, namely:

- The industries demand as a whole represent the market demand for labour.
- An industry is collection of firm.

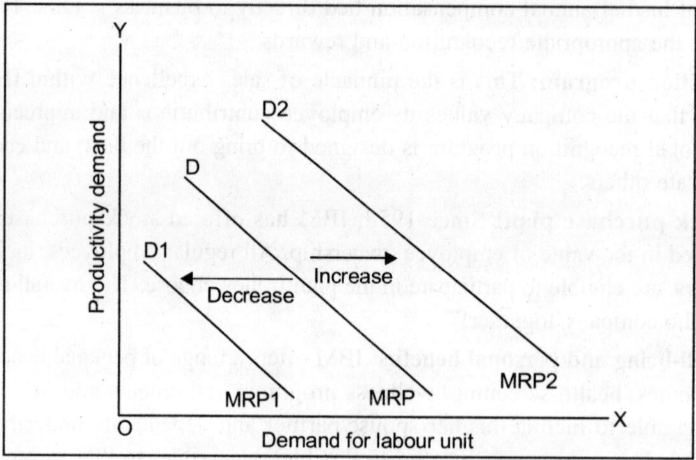

Fig. 3.58: Shift in the demand for labour

Modern wage theory of wage: Wage is a price of productive labour. The marginal productive theory, indeed, provides fairly satisfactory explanation of wage determination but its main shortcoming is that it does not consider the supply aspect of labour and concentrate on demand side. The modern theory of wages is an extension of this theory in more logical and rational way. Here, the wage rate is determined by the interaction of the forces of demand for and supply of labour in given market situation.

Importance of the Compensation System

(a) ***Pay dissatisfaction and its impact on employee performance*:** The following figure illustrates the impact of pay dissatisfaction on employees in an organization. Pay dissatisfaction can lead to job dissatisfaction, high absenteeism and increasing turnover rates.

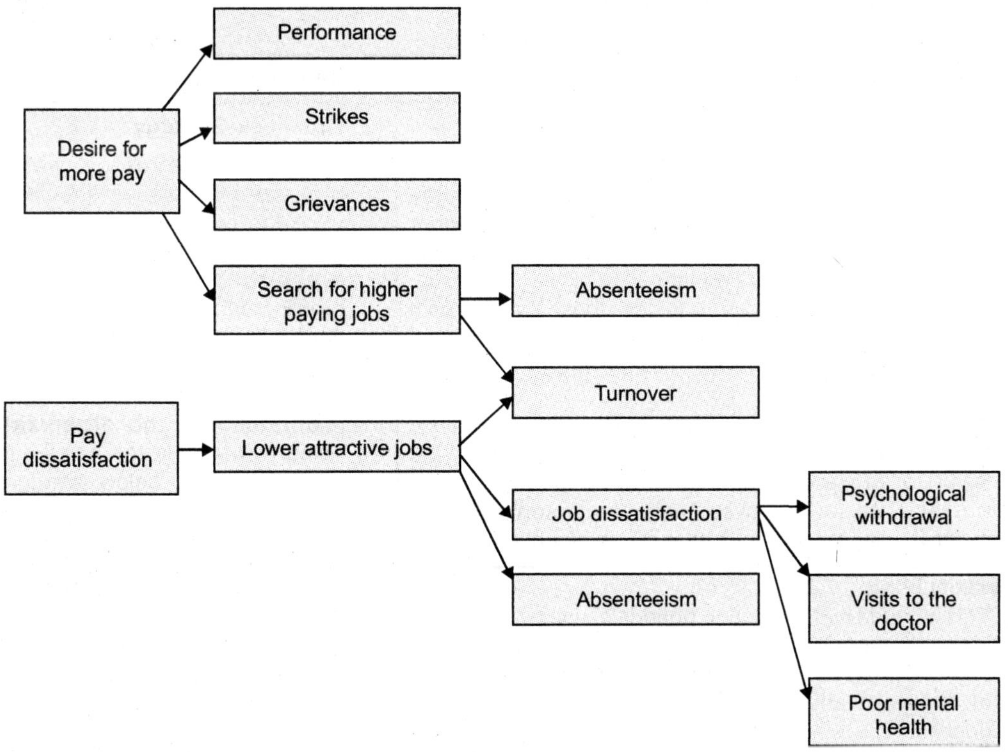

Fig. 3.59: Pay Dissatisfaction and its impact on employee performance

(b) ***Motivation and performance model*:** This model depicts the relation between employee goals and impact of rewards in performance improvement.

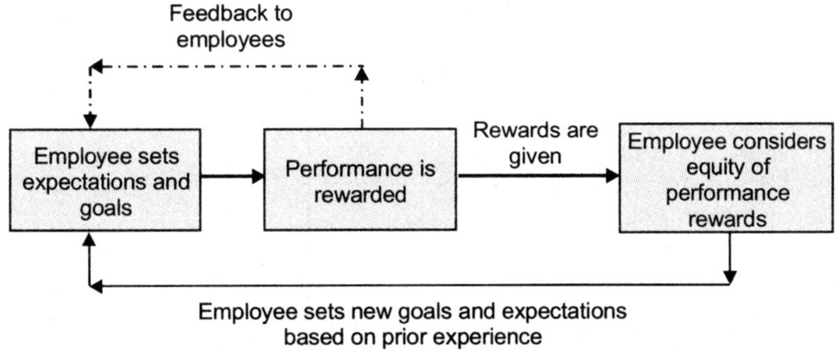

Fig. 3.60: Motivation and performance model

Factors Influencing the Employee Remuneration System: The factors influencing employee compensation strategy are as follows:

External Factors	Internal Factors
1. **Labour Market** • ***Demand for and supply of labour*** influence wage and salary fixation. A low wage rate may be fixed when the supply of labour exceeds the demand for it. A higher wage will have to be paid when the demand exceeds supply, as in case of skilled labour. • ***Going rate of pay:*** Going rates are those that are paid by different units of an industry in a locality and by comparable units of the same industry located elsewhere. • ***Productivity:*** Productivity levels of labour also influence wage fixation. It can arise due to increased effort of the worker, or as a result of the factors beyond the control of the worker such as improved technology, sophisticated machines and equipment, better management and so on.	1. **Business Strategy** The overall strategy which an organization pursues should determine the remuneration to its employees. Where the strategy of the organization is to achieve rapid growth, remuneration should be higher than what the competitors pay. Where the strategy is to maintain and protect current earnings (due to declining profitability of the organization), remuneration level needs to be average or even below average.
2. **Cost of Living** This criterion matters during periods of rising prices, and is forgotten when prices are stable or falling. A rise in the cost of living is sought to be compensated by the payment of dearness allowances, where basic pay remains undisturbed.	2. **Job Evaluation and Performance Appraisal** • Job evaluation helps to establish satisfactory wage differentials among jobs. • Performance Appraisals help award pay increases to employees who exhibit improved performance.
3. **Labour Unions** The presence or the absence of labour organizations often determine the quantum of wages paid to the employees.	3. **The Employee** Several employee-related factors interact to determine his or her remuneration. These include performance, seniority, experience, potential etc.
4. **Labour Laws** • Payment of Wages Act, 1936 • Minimum Wages Act, 1948 • Payment of Bonus Act, 1965 • Equal Remuneration Act, 1976 • Payment of Gratuity Act, 1972	
5. **Society** Remuneration is paid to employees is reflected in the prices fixed by an organization for its goods and services.	
6. **The Economy** While it is possible for some organizations to thrive a recession, there is no question that the economy affects remuneration decisions. As for example, a depressed economy will probably increase the labour supply. This in turn, should serve to lower the going wage rate.	

THEME READING: INDUSTRY TRENDS IN COMPENSATION

Prior to the 1991 economic reforms, government restrictions mandated that monthly salaries for senior executives could be no more than Rs 15,000 (about $320 in today's dollars). The government relaxed this policy in 1993 and 1994, and today there are few restrictions on remuneration at the top end of the scale. Most companies are now allowed to create appropriate compensation packages for their managing director and directors within the limit of 5% (if there is only one director) or 10% (if there are multiple directors) of the firm's net profits.

Although pay in India is considerably lower than in Western countries (and even some developing nations), shortages of skilled workers (especially in IT) have led to dramatic pay inflation. This is due to a combination of factors, including rationalization and re-evaluation, entry of more multinational companies (increased demand for certain types of skilled labour), and global worker shortages. Salaries in some sectors of the economy climbed at a staggering 40 percent annually during the mid-1990s. Since then, the Asian financial crisis and the IT slowdown have caused the economy to cool off, with the job market following suit. Consequently, pay increases have slowed markedly over the past few years, although average salary increases continue to significantly outplace the inflation rate of 6–7%.

Table 3.5: Average Salary Increase (%) for Management in India, 2000–2001

Industry	*2000 (%)*	*2001 (%)*
Information Technology	25.9	10.0
Hotels	19.8	19.8
Diversified	17.8	19.5
Consumer Products	17.1	15.5
Engineering	15.8	14.0
Pharmaceuticals	13.8	14.9
Others	14.5	15.2
Overall	17.1	16.0

(*Source: Watson Wyatt Worldwide*)

Recent investigations from MA FOI and OMAM reveal a different perspective in compensation trends in India.

Table 3.6: Recent Trends in Compensation Hikes in Various Sectors

Sector	*MA FOI*			*OMAM*		
	Senior	*Middle*	*Junior*	*Senior*	*Middle*	*Junior*
IT	30–40%	20–25%	15–20%	15%	18%	16%
ITES	30–40%	20–25%	15–20%	20%	18%	18%
Financial services	20%	15%	10–12%	14%	15%	15%
Retail	30–35%	20%	15%	17%	18%	18%
Pharma	30–35%	20%	15%	15%	16%	15%

(*Courtesy: Adapted from Business Today, Col. 14, No. 13, July 3rd, 2005, p. 51*)

COMPONENTS OF REMUNERATION

Wages

Wages represent hourly rates of pay, and salary refers to the monthly rate of pay, irrespective of the number of hours put in by an employee. Wages and salaries are subject to annual increments. They differ from employee to employee, and also depend upon the nature of the job performed, seniority levels and merit of the individual. Under the **Workmen's Compensation Act, 1923**, "wages for leave period, holiday pay, overtime pay, bonus, attendance bonus, and good conduct bonus" also form an integral part of wages. Further, under the **Payment of Wages Act, 1948**, "retrenchment compensation, payment in lieu of notice and gratuity payable on discharge also constitutes the wages of individuals." In wages the term **"Allowances"** includes amounts paid in addition to wages over a period of time including holiday pay, overtime pay, bonus, social security benefits etc. The wage structure in India can be broadly examined under the following heads:

(a) ***Basic Wage*****:** The basic wage in India corresponds with what has been recommended by the Fair Wages Committee (1948) and the 15th Indian Labour Conference (1957). The various awards by wage tribunals wage boards, pay commission reports and job evaluations also serves as guiding principles for determining the "Basic Wage". While deciding the Basic wage, the following criteria may be considered, namely: (i) Skills need of the Job (ii) Experience needed (iii) Difficulty of work-mental as well as physical (iv) Training needed (v) Responsibilities involved (vi) Hazardous nature of the Job.

(b) ***Dearness Allowances (DA)*****:** It is the allowance paid to the employees in order to enable them to face the increasing dearness of essential commodities. It serves as a cushion, a sort of insurance against the increase in price levels of commodities. Instead of increasing wages every time-there is a rise in price levels; DA is paid to neutralize the effects of inflation. DA in India is linked to three factors, namely: **The Index factor (All India Consumer Price Index/AICPI), The Time Factor and The Point Factor.**

(c) ***House Rent Allowance (HRA)*****:** Housing is one of the most burning issues in metropolitan cities. Rising prices of residential premises and high rentals is a bane of big metropolitan cities. To attract and retain talent, employers offer to meet part of the rental costs of the employee in the form of **House Rent Allowance (HRA).**

(d) ***Conveyance Allowance*****:** It includes any allowance granted to meet the **cost of travel on tour** or on transfer, any allowance, whether, **granted on tour or for the period of journey** in connection with transfer, to meet the ordinary daily charges incurred by an employee on account of absence from his normal place of duty; any allowance granted to meet the **expenditure incurred on conveyance in performance of duties** of an office or employment of profit.

(e) ***Transport Allowance*****:** It is the allowance granted for commuting between place of residence and the place of duty.

Incentives

Also known as "payments by results", incentives are paid in addition to wages and salaries. Incentives depend upon productivity, sales, profit, or cost reduction efforts. There are (i) individual incentive schemes, and (ii) group incentive programs. Individual incentives are applicable to specific employee performance. Where a given task demands group effort for completion, incentives are paid to the group as a whole. The amount is later divided among the group members on an equitable basis.

Fringe Benefits

These include such employee benefits such as provident funds, gratuity, medical care, hospitalization, accident relief, health and group insurance, canteen, uniform, recreation and the likes.

Provident Fund

PF is a fund paying benefits to the company employees who are fund members upon the termination of their employment. Contributions paid into the fund by both the employees and the employers are invested in accordance with the pre-determined condition of amount and risks.

Gratuity

Gratuity can be a sizeable portion of an employee's retirement benefits. An employee is eligible to receive gratuity if he/she have had put in at least five years of service with the employer. The **Payment of Gratuity Act of 1971** makes it mandatory for any organization employing more than 19 employees to provide the benefit. Gratuity is payable 15 days per year of service on the salary at the time of exit with a monetary ceiling of Rs. 3,50,000. As per accounting standards, it is mandatory to reflect this Liability in the Annual Accounts. This Liability is required to be valued by an Actuary. Contribution to the fund up to 8.33% of annual wage-bill is allowed as tax deduction.

Payment of Gratuity involves (1) Gratuity shall be payable to an employee on the termination of his employment after he has rendered continuous service for not less than five years, (a) on his superannuation, or (b) on his retirement or resignation, or (c) on his death or disablement due to accident or disease : Provided that the completion of continuous service of five years shall not be necessary where the termination of the employment of any employee is due to death or disablement :

Perquisites

These are allowed to executives and include company car, club membership, paid holidays, furnished house, employee stock option schemes and the like. Perquisites are offered so as to retain competent executives and talents in an organization.

Non-Monetary Benefits

These include challenging job responsibilities, recognition of merit, growth prospects, competent supervision, comfortable working conditions, job sharing and flexi-time.

Delighting Employees with e-Rewards

Many organizations are frequently using services offered by websites like those of www.giftcertificates.com/business to delight their employees in the organization. In US and Canada, employers using SuperCertificate®

Fig. 3.61: e-rewards schemes

Rewards can simply choose the amount to give, and the advantage is that on the other side the recipients can get the fun of choosing a gift certificates related to hundreds of popular stores, airlines, hotels, theaters, restaurants and more.

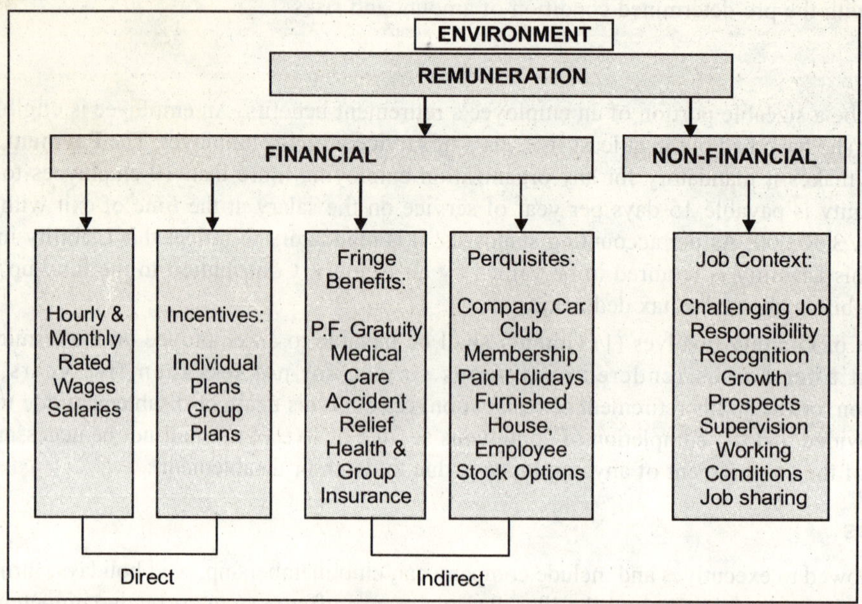

Fig. 3.62: Components of employee remuneration

Wage Policy in India: Minimum Wage, Fair Wage and Living Wage

Minimum Wage

Minimum wage is that wage which must invariably be paid whether the company, big or small, makes profit or not. It is the bare minimum that a worker can expect to get for services rendered by him. The 15th Indian Labour Conference 1957 formally quantified the term "minimum wage" as:

- In calculating the minimum wage— the standard working class family should be taken to comprise three consumption units for one earner, the earnings of women, children and adolescents being disregarded.
- Minimum food requirements should be calculated.
- Clothing requirements should be estimated on the basis of per capita consumption.
- In respect to housing, the rent corresponding to the minimum area provided for under government Industrial Housing Scheme should be taken into consideration in fixing minimum wage.
- Fuel, lighting and other miscellaneous items of expenditure should constitute 20% of the total minimum wage.

Fair Wage

It is the wage, which is above the minimum wage, but below the living wage. According to the committee on fair wages, 1948, fair wage should be determined taking the following factors into consideration:

- The productivity of labour
- The prevailing rates of wages in the same or similar occupations in the same region or neighboring regions.

- The level of national income and its distribution.
- The place of the industry in the economy of the nation
- The employer's capacity to pay.

Living Wage

According to the committee on fair wages, the living wage is the highest among the three. It must provide (i) basic amnesties of life, (ii) efficiency of worker, and (iii) satisfy social needs of workers such as medical, education, retirement etc. Living wage is a dynamic concept, which grows in line with the growth of the national economy.

Bonus

Starting as an adhoc and ex-gratia payment, bonus was claimed as dearness allowance during the World War II. Under the Payment of Bonus Act, 1965, it secured the character of a legal right.

Bonus refers to an extra payment given to the workers beyond the normal wage of individuals. It is argued that bonus is a deferred wage payment which aims at bridging the gaps between the actual wage and the need based wage. It is also said that bonus is a share of the workers in the prosperity of the organization. The third argument is that bonus is primarily a share in the surplus in the organization.

Payment of Bonus Act, 1965

- 60% of the surplus (67% in the case of foreign companies) should be allocated for the payment of bonus.
- Salary for the purpose of bonus means Pay + DA.
- Employees drawing up to Rs 1,600 are eligible for bonus. If the amount of salary is beyond Rs 700 and up to Rs 1,600 it would be taken as Rs 700 for the purpose of bonus payment.
- Employees dismissed for fraud, theft etc. are disqualified for bonus.
- Minimum bonus payable is 4% of the salary or Rs 40 whichever is higher.
- If the available surplus is not adequate to pay the minimum bonus it can be set off up to a maximum period of 4 years.
- If an employee is below 15 years of age the bonus payable is 4% of the salary or Rs 25 whichever is higher.

Methods of Wage Payment Systems

***Time Wage System*:** In this system, the worker is paid on the basis of the time spent on the work irrespective of the amount of work done. The basis of this time may be hour, day, week or month.

***Guaranteed Time Rates*:** In this system, the payment is at the time rates, but adjusted to the cost of living. This system also includes merit awards for personal qualities, skill, ability, punctuality etc.

***Piece Rate System*:** Here the workers are paid at a stipulated rate per piece or unit of output. In this system, the worker is paid according to the number of pieces completed or the volume of work done by him.

Type of Piece Rates	Hallmarks
Straight Piece Rate	Here the payment is made on the basis of a fixed amount per fixed units produced without regard to the time taken i.e. Earnings = No. of units × rate per unit.
Piece Rate with Guaranteed time rate	In this system, employees are paid minimum wages on the basis of time rates.
Differential Piece Rate	In this scheme, the rate per piece is increased, when the output level is increased.

Determining Pay: Organizational Approaches

Once the organization has completed an internal job evaluation and obtained wage survey data, it needs to translate this information into pay rates for each class of job in the organization. This process involves interpretation of wage survey results, the merging of the job evaluation with the survey data, and considerations of the organization's pay related policy. In this regard there are three fundamental options available for organizations, namely: to match, lead, or lag behind the market level pay ranges. Many organizations start this exercise by developing the wage curve.

The Wage Curve

The relationship between the relative worth of the jobs and their wage rates can be represented by means of a graphical representation known as the "Wage Curve". The wage curve may indicate the rates currently paid for jobs within an organization, the new rates resulting from job evaluation, or the rates for similar jobs currently being paid by rival organizations within the industry. A curve may be constructed graphically by preparing a scatter-diagram consisting of a series of dots that represent the current wage rates in the market or that in the industry. The following figure illustrates a wage curve. In an organization generally the wage curve helps to assign pay rates to various job grades that come out as outcomes of job evaluations.

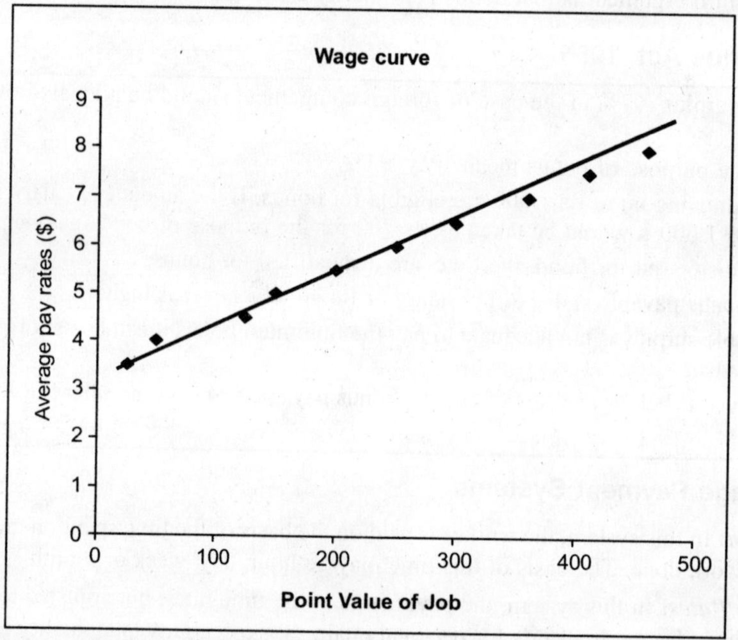

Pay grades: From an administrative point of view, it is preferable to group jobs into **Pay Grades** and to pay all jobs within a particular grade the same rate or rate range. When the classification system of job evaluation is used, jobs are grouped into grades as part of the evaluation process. When the point and factor comparison systems are used, however, pay grades must be established at selected intervals that represent either the point or the evaluated monetary value of these jobs. The graph in the following figure, illustrates a series of pay grades designated along the horizontal axis at 50-point intervals.

Rate ranges: Although a single rate may be created for each pay grade, it is often common to provide a range of rates for each pay grade. The rate ranges may be the same for each grade or proportionately greater for each successive grade as depicted by the following figures. Rate ranges constructed on the later basis provide a greater incentive for employees so as to accept a promotion to a job in a higher grade.

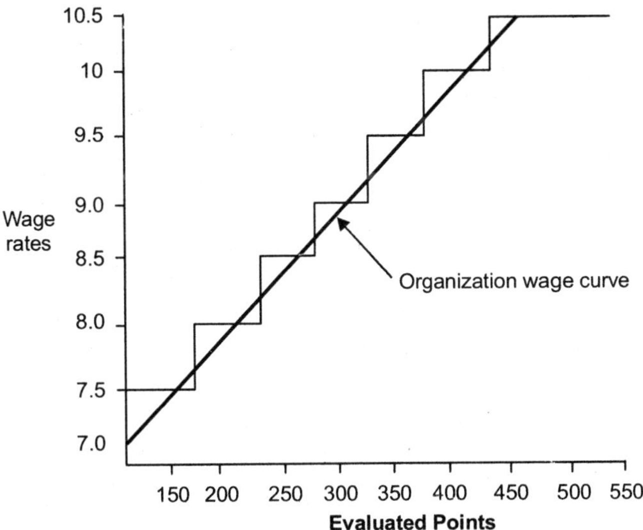

Fig. 3.63: Single rate structure

Rate ranges generally are divided into a series of steps that permit employees to receive increases up to the maximum rate for the range on the basis of merit or seniority or a combination of the two. Most compensation structures provide for the ranges of adjoining pay grades to overlap. The purpose of the overlap is to permit an employee with experiences to earn as much as more than a person with less experience in the next higher job classification. The final step in setting up a wage structure is to determine the appropriate pay grade into which each job should be placed on the basis of job requirements without regard to the performance of the employee in that job. Performance of employees who exceed the requirements of a particular job may be acknowledged by merit increases within the grade range or by promotion to a job in the next higher pay grade. Organizations might pay their employees above the maximum of the pay range when employees have high seniority or promotional opportunities are scarce. Wages paid above the range maximum are called **"Red Circle Rates.**"

Matching Organizational Pay Ranges with Market Rates

As mentioned above, the organizational pay options could be three fold in terms of matching, leading or lagging behind the market pay rates. According to these the respective pay policies could be as follows:

(a) ***Matching the Competition Policy*:** By setting the organization's pay levels at the market rate, the organization attempts to keep its labour cost comparable to those of its business rivals in the market. Such an approach tends to neutralize pay as a factor in attracting, retaining and motivating employees while ensuring that labour costs are also competitive.

(b) ***Lead Policy*:** This means paying a higher wage rate as compared to that of the market rate or that of the organization's business rivals. It is a strategy meant to attract higher-quality employees while maximizing the satisfaction of the employees who are already there in the organization. These organizations have labour costs that represent a small proportion of the cost of production or have higher levels of productivity which ultimately makes the policy affordable.

(c) ***Lag Policy*:** This is an approach where organizations set their pay rates below those of their competitors. Although this policy might appear to be ineffective in terms of attracting and retaining employees, yet organizations like those of the public sector enterprises frequently use this approach and provide additional benefits to their employees in the form of employment security, superior benefits (e.g., leave benefits) or an enjoyable work environment.

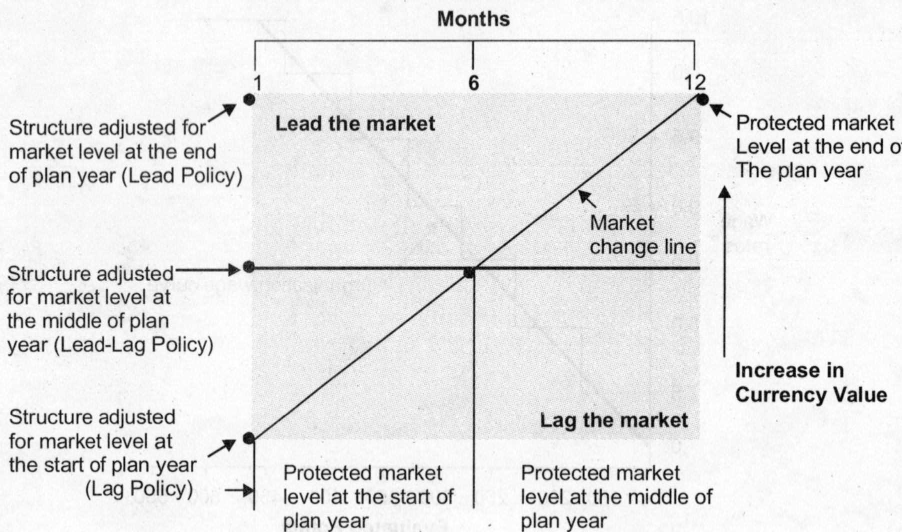

Fig. 3.64: Pay policies over time: Lag, match and lead pay structures

Incentive Plans

Incentive plans envisage a basic rate usually on time basis applicable to all employees and incentive rates payable to the more efficient among them as extra compensation for their meritorious performance in terms of time, cost and quality. The incentive rates may take the form of bonus or premium. Bonus means payment to employees of the entire benefit accruing from savings in cost, time, improvement in quality etc. Premium benefits accruing to the firm as the result of higher output or better quality will be shared equally or on some agreed basis between the management and the workers.

Features: The characteristics of incentive plans are as follows:

- Minimum wages are guaranteed to all workers
- Incentives by way of bonus etc. are offered to efficient workers for the time saved
- A standard time is fixed and the worker is expected to perform the given work within standard time. The standard time is set after making time studies for the performance of a specific job.

Common Incentive Plans

Profit Sharing and Stock Options Plan

Profit sharing is a scheme whereby employers undertake to pay a particular portion of net profits to their employees on compliance with certain service conditions and qualifications. The purpose of this profit sharing schemes had been mainly to strengthen the loyalty of the employees to the organization by offering them an annual bonus provided they are on the service rolls of the firm for a definite period of time. The share of the profit can be given in cash or in the form of shares in the company, which is known as **Employees' Stock Option Plan (ESOP).** The IT sector made ESOPs quite popular in the early part of this decade. ESOPs have emerged as an important tool to keep talents from **splilling** over.

Industry Opinion

"Our ESOP scheme has been a tremendous success, both in terms of HR and organizational growth. Today, we are one of those rare IT companies where the attrition rate is a very low 2%. In fact, we are probably one of its kind in the industry with 22.32% of the company being held by employees." C.K. Shastri, Managing Director, Intense Technologies.

(Courtesy: Bajpai, V., (2008): "Quick guide to ESOPs", Dare, Vol. 2, Issue: 06, March, 2008, p. 62)

Exhibit: SBI All Set to Open ESOP Locker for Staff

Bankers in India's state owned banks often considered poor cousins of their counterparts in the new age private and foreign banks in terms of remuneration package, may soon shed that tag. The government has approved a proposal for a stock option plan for staffers of the country's largest bank, State Bank of India, marking a first in the Indian banking industry and perhaps for any state owned company. SBI, which is readying for a rights offering of over Rs 16000 crore this fiscal, may well be in a position now to unveil an Employee Stock Option Plan aggregating up to 0.7% of its capital base of Rs 526 crore. By offering stock options, the belief is that employees could be far more motivated which could reflect on the performance of their organizations.

(Courtesy: The Economic Times. 14th January, 2008, p. 1)

Team Based Pay

Team pay links payments to members of a formally established team to the performance of that team. The rewards are shared among the team members with respect to a specific formula as specified by the company policy or on an adhoc basis in the case of exceptional performance achievements. Individual rewards in this case are influenced by assessments of their contributions for achieving team goals and objectives. The basic objectives of team based pay are as follows:

- To provide incentives and other means of recognizing team contributions in organizations.
- To clarify what teams are expected to achieve by relating rewards to the attainment of predetermined and agreed targets and standards of performance.
- To convey the message that one of the organization's core values is effective teamwork.

Team based pay and individual pay: Some organizations focus on paying team bonuses only. A minority pay individual bonuses as well, which are often related to an assessment of the competence of the individual, thus, it is thought, providing encouragement to develop skills and rewarding them for their contributions.

Exhibit: Sales/Operations Staff Incentive Chart of an IT Company

MARCH 2006

Incentive Slabs	Sales Achieved Kgs	Incentive per Kg	Amount Payable
		INR	INR
On Published Rate	87,292	0.50	43646.00
On 5% Incentive	63,498	0.25	15874.50
More than 5% Incentive	105,145	Nil	-
Total Upliftment	255,935		59520.50

INCENTIVE PAYABLE

Sales Manager	25%
Sr. Sales Executive	15%
Sr. Sales Officer	15%
Co-ordinator	5%
Supervisor Operations	10%
Executive Operations	5%
Trainee – Operations and Sales	5%
Trainee – Operations	5%
Trainee – Operations	5%
Admin	5%
Admin	5%
Total	100%

Approved

Signature
(Head Sales/HR)

Exhibit: Trends in the Use of ESOPs

The downturn in the stock markets appears to have prompted some companies, which had so far shied away from rewarding employees through stock options. Around a dozen companies have granted ESOPs in the last 2 months. The list includes Yes Bank, Godrej Consumer Products, Network 18, Axis Bank, Kashyap Technologies, Dalmia Cements, Strides Arcolab, Jindal Stainless and Edel Weiss Capital. Tarun Gulati, Vice President, ESOP Direct, a Pune based ESOP Consultancy firm commented, "For a company that is confident of its growth but is going through a depressed stock price due to a market downturn, a low market presents a fantastic opportunity to grant ESOPs at an attractive prices to the employees.

(*Courtesy: Naithani, A., (2008): "Companies grant ESOPs as markets slowdown", The Economic Times, 15th July, 2008, p. 8.*)

Exhibit: ESOP at

Infosys Technologies Ltd's board has allotted 78,920 equity shares of Rs 5 to the optionees pursuant to the exercise of the options granted to the employees under the company's 1999 stock option plan

(*Courtesy: http://www.ciol.com/content/news/2005/105051605.asp*).

FRINGE BENEFITS

The term fringe benefit refers to the extra benefits provided to the employees in addition to the normal compensation paid in the form of wage or salary.

The main features of "Fringe Benefits" are as follows:

- They are supplementary forms of compensation apart from the wage or salary given to the employees.
- They are provided to all employees based on their membership in the organization.
- They are indirect forms of compensation because they are usually extended as a condition of employment and are not directly related to employee performance.
- They help to raise the living conditions of the employees and contribute to enhance the quality of work life (QWL) in organizations.
- They may be statutory or voluntary. PF is a Statutory Fringe Benefit whereas transport facilities, group insurance scheme are voluntary Fringe Benefits.

Need for Fringe Benefits

Most organizations in India have been extending fringe benefits to their employees due to the following reasons:

- To satisfy employee needs and aspirations
- To satisfy Trade Union demands
- Employers prefer fringe benefits to pay-hikes
- Fringe benefits serves as the basis for providing social security and improving QWL
- Fringe benefits help to improve human relations in organizations.

Objectives of Fringe Benefits

- To create and improve sound employee and industrial relations
- To motivate employees by identifying and satisfying their unsatisfied needs
- To provide security to employees against social risks like old age benefits and maternity benefits
- To protect the health of the employees and to provide safety to the employees against accidents
- To promote employee welfare
- To create a sense of belongingness among employees and to retain them.
- To meet the requirements of various statutory legislations and compliance checks.

Types of Fringe Benefits

A. Payment for time not worked: This includes (a) hours of work, (b) Paid holidays, (c) Shift premium, (d) Holiday pay; and (e) Paid vacation.

B. Employee Security: This includes benefits such as ***(a) Retrenchment Compensation:*** The **Industrial Disputes Act 1947,** provides for the payment of compensation in case of any lay-off and retrenchment. ***(b) Lay-off Compensation:*** In case of lay-off, employees are entitled to lay off compensation at the rate equal to 50% of the total of the basic wage and dearness allowances for the period of their lay off except for weekly holidays. Lay off compensations can normally be paid up to 45 days in a year.

C. Safety and Health: To protect the employees against accidents, unhealthy working conditions and to protect the worker's productive capacity.

D. Workmen's Compensation: In addition of safety and health measures, provision for the payment of compensation has also been under Workmen's Compensation Act, 1923. The Act is intended to meet the contingency of invalidity and death of a worker due to an employment injury or an occupational disease specified under the act at the sole responsibility of the employer.

E. Health Benefits: These include (i) Sickness Benefits, (ii) Maternity Benefits, (iii) Disablement Benefits (iv) Dependent's Benefits (v) Medical Benefits etc.

F. Voluntary Arrangements: These include providing health maintenance services, emergency cares, on the job treatment care for minor complaints, health counseling, medical supervision in rehabilitation, accident and sickness prevention, health education programs, extension of medical benefits to employee family members and retired employees.

G. Welfare and Recreational Facilities: These include: (i) Canteens, (ii) Consumer Stores/Societies, (iii) Credit Societies, (iv) Housing Facilities like staff quarters, (v) Legal Help and counseling, (vi) Employee counseling, (vii) Welfare organizations and welfare officers, (viii) Holiday homes and company guest houses, (ix) Educational Facilities for employees and their children, (x) Transportation facilities, (xi) Parties, picnics, social gatherings and celebrating festivals, (xii) Miscellaneous activities like organizing sports, cultural programs, setting up of clubs, community service activities, Leave Travel Concessions (LTCs), performance awards etc.

H. Old Age and Retirement Benefits: These include providing (i) Employee Provident Funds (PFs), (ii) Pension Schemes, (iii) Deposit linked Insurances, (iv) Gratuity, (v) Medical benefits.

Appendix: Sample Compensation Policy of an Organization

Objective: To provide for a uniform, stable and reasonably competitive compensation structure for all employees.

Grades and Designations: To rationalize the compensation policy, positions are classified into grades. The grades and respective designations are as below:

GRADE	DESIGNATION
Executives	M.D, C.O.O, President, Sr. V.P, V.P
M-10	Sr. General Manager
M-9	General Manager
M-8	Dy. General Manager
M-7	Sr. Manager
M-6	Manager
M-5	Dy. Manager
M-4	Asst. Manager
M-3	Executive
M-2	Sr. Officer
M-1	Officer
GET	Graduate Engineer Trainee
Tr. Officers	Trainee Officers

Basic Scale: The basic scale would be as per the terms of employment and revisions from time to time.

Grade	Designation	Basic Pay Structure
M-1	Officer	2000-125-2125-125-2250-125-2375-125-2500-125-2625-125-2750-125-2875- - -
M-2	Sr. Officer	3000-175-3175-175-3350-175-3525-175-3700-175-3875-175-4050-175-4225- - -
M-3	Executive	4000-225-4225-225-4450-225-4675-225-4900-225-5125 -225-5350-225-5575- - -
M-4	Asst. Manager	5000-275-5550-275-5825-275-6100-275-6375-275-6650 -275-6925-275- - -
M-5	Dy. Manager	6000-325-6325-6650-325-6975-325-7300-325-7625-325 -7950-325- - -
M-6	Manager	9000-375-9375-375-9750-375-10125-375-10500-375 -10875-375-11250- - -
M-7	Sr. Manager	11275-425-11700-425-12125-425-12550-425-12975 -425-13400- - -
M-8	Dy. General Manager	15000-500-15500-500-16000-500-16500-500-17000 -500-17500- - -
M-9	General Manager	17000-600-17600-600-18200-600-18800-600-19400 -600-20000-600- - -
M-10	Sr. General Manager	24000-700-24700-700-25400-700-26100-700-26800 -700-27500- - -

House Rent Allowance (HRA): Management staff not provided with any type of company accommodation i.e. either company owned or leased, will be paid house rent allowance at 40% of basic salary.

Conveyance Allowance: Management staff not provided with company car will be paid conveyance allowance as follows:

Grades	Allowance (Rs. per month)
M-1 to M-4	500
M-5	800
M-6	1500
M-7	2000
M-8	2500
M-9 to M-10	3000

Education Allowance: Management staff will be entitled to education allowance as follows:

Grades	Allowance (Rs. per month)
M-1 to M-10	Rs. 200/-

Medical Allowance: Management staff will be paid medical allowance @ 8.33% of basic salary per month.

LEAVE TRAVEL ASSISTANCE

Eligibility

- Management staff will be entitled to LTA **on completion of one year of service** subject to confirmation of services. However, pro-rata LTA will be paid at the time of FandF even if 1 year is not completed.
- LTA will be calculated on a calendar year basis (i.e. January to December every year) and on pro-rata basis for the part of the year.

***Quantum of LTA*:** The LTA will be paid at the rate of one month's basic salary per year.

For claiming LTA with tax deduction at source:

- No leave will be required for claiming LTA with tax deduction.
- An application to be made to HR Department for claiming LTA in the prescribed format.

For claiming LTA to avail income tax exemption:

- A **minimum of six days Leave** should be availed for claiming LTA.
- LTA should be claimed in the prescribed form.
- Approval of Leave must be attached at the time of claiming LTA.
- Any two journeys (LTA) can be claimed for tax exemption in a block of four years beginning from January 2002. LTA for self and family is admissible for tax exemption.

***Quantum of exemption under the IT Act*:** Quantum of Exemption – The amount of LTA for self and family permissible under the Income Tax Act for exemption is as follows:

- For journeys performed by Air: Economy fare of Indian Airlines by the shortest route to the place of destination.
- For journeys performed by Rail: Airconditioned first class rail fare by the shortest route to the place of destination.
- For journeys performed by Road: The amount equivalent to airconditioned first class rail fare, for the distance of journey by the shortest route, as if the journey had been performed by rail.

***Documents Required for Claiming Exemption*:** The following documents must be produced along with the prescribed LTA claim form:

Mode of travel	Documents
Rail	Photocopies of railway tickets
Air	Original Jacket of used tickets
Road	By own vehicle: Petrol bills
	By hired car: • Bill of the operator • Proof indicating the places visited

Advance for LTA: An advance for LTA can be availed for booking tickets by making an application to HR Dept. together with a copy of the approved leave application. The advance will be paid up to 70% of entitlement. The balance amount shall be paid on production of travel tickets within seven days of completion of the journey, failing which the advance will be recovered from the salary.

Accumulation of LTA: Accumulation of unavailed LTA is allowed up to two years within the block of four years specified under the Income Tax Rules. However, the fourth year's **LTA cannot** be carried forward to the next block for accumulation purposes. The current block is for the period of calendar year 2002–2005.

Telephone allowance: Telephone allowance will be paid as under:

Grades	Allowance (Rs. per month)
M-1	200
M-2	300
M-3	400
M-4	500
M-5	600
M-6	800
M-7	1000
M-8	1200
M-9 to M-10	1500

Soft Furnishing Allowance: Soft furnishing allowance will be paid as under:

Grades	Allowance (Rs. per month)
M-1 to M-2	200
M-3	400
M-4 to M-5	600
M-6 to M-7	800
M-8 to M-10	1000

Book and Periodicals Allowance: Books and periodicals allowance will be paid as under:

Grades	Allowance (Rs. per month)
M-1 to M-4	nil
M-5	200
M-6	400
M-7	600
M-8	800
M-9 to M-10	1000

Drive Allowance: Driver allowance will be paid as under:

Grades	Allowance (Rs. per month)
M-1 to M-7	nil
M-8	1500
M-9 to M-10	2000

Petrol allowance: Petrol allowance will be paid as under:

Grades	Allowance (Rs. per month)
M-1 to M-7	nil
M-8	2500
M-9 to M-10	3000

Ex-gratia: Management staff will be paid Ex-Gratia @ 8.33% of basic salary per month.

Exhibit: Increment Letter

Date: 26.05.2008

Mr. Suman Das
XYZ [P] Ltd.
Bangalore Branch,

Dear Mr. Suman,

The Company is pleased to inform you that your base salary has been revised to Rs._________. w.e.f. _________. The detailed Pay Structure is annexed as a part of this letter. (Annexure I (II)).
All the other terms and conditions of your appointment remain unchanged. We appreciate the efforts put in by you and expect that you would continue to do so in the future.

Yours sincerely,

For ***XYZ [P] Ltd.***

Authorized signatory
[Name]
[Designation]

Encl.: Annexure: - Terms and Conditions (Annexure I (II))

Enclosure

1. Your annual compensation package consists of a gross of Rs. ____________/- Salary ***(Rupees __________________ only.)*** per annum, Your annual Salary Break up is as follows:- Basic: Rs. ________/-, HRA: Rs. ___________/-, Medical: Rs. _________/-, Conveyance: Rs. _________/- (**Annexure II**), with effect from the date of your joining. Income Tax /Professional Tax will be deducted each month according to the Income Tax rules as/if applicable. Each employee will be expected to take care of his/her tax planning on an individual basis. Rs. ____________/annum is your fixed salary. ***(From Annexure I, Terms and Condition of Employment).***

Please understand that this letter spells out some of the terms and conditions of employment and that the other service rules of the company, as currently in force and as amended from time to time will be applicable to you.

I have read, understood and agree to abide by the aforesaid terms and conditions of employment.

Signature of the employee: Date:

[Name]

[Desig]

Appendix: Employee satisfaction survey with respect to pay and reward systems

You are required to state your agreement or disagreement with respect to the following statements by rating in the following manner:

1 = strongly agree, 2 = agree, 3 = disagree, 4 = strongly disagree

Statements	Your rating
1. Employee contributions are adequately rewarded in my organization	
2. Pay increases occur fairly	
3. My perception regarding my pay is that, it does not take into consideration of my performance	
4. My pay is equitable to that in other organization	
5. My pay is not equitable to those of other working in same position in this organization	
6. The compensation policy of my organization is being reviewed for modifications	
7. Pay-grade decisions are being made rationally and fairly	
8. The management communicates well regarding the pay decisions with the employees	
9. I know how my job position has been graded	
10. Employees get feedback on their performance	
11. Employees in this organization are clear regarding what they are expected to achieve	
12. Employees are rewarded for their contribution in this organization	
13. The organization follows a performance based pay system	
14. Employees in this organization are aware regarding their progression plans	
15. The incentives are given on timely basis	
16. My organization is transparent in its incentive schemes	
17. The benefit package is well as compared to other organizations	
18. Employees are being given choice and freedom to choose the benefits according to their needs	
19. Employees are not clear regarding the pay policy of the organization	
20. Payment of salary is being done on timely basis every month	
21. The management clarifies employee doubts regarding income tax planning	
22. My organization regularly deducts professional tax and meets other statutory regulations of the state	
23. My organization provides PF scheme	
24. Pension scheme is provided by my employer	
25. Life and health Insurance schemes are provided by my employer	

QUESTION BANK

1. What factors determine the pay structure decision? What methods can be used to ensure pay satisfaction and also ensure its motivation potential for employees?
2. How can managers use the organization's reward system to encourage workplace safety? (BU July/ August 2005).
3. What are the different kinds of compensation systems in practice in Indian companies today? Give examples under each of the classified systems.
4. Bring out the procedure for fixing salary for monthly-rated employees in an organization. (BU 2004).
5. How are wages determined in an industry? Also discuss the role and functions of the "Wage Board".
6. Briefly describe the various components of a compensation package.
7. Discuss the popular myths about pay and compensation. Explain the reality.
8. Define compensation. How is it used in organizations?
9. What are the components of a compensation system?
10. Write a brief note on the compensation trends in India.
11. What is compensation planning? What are the objectives of compensation planning?
12. What do you mean by compensation policy? What are the hallmarks of compensation policy?
13. What do you mean by rewards? Classify rewards with suitable examples.
14. What is employee stock option plan (ESOP)? How is it used by organizations?
15. Define fringe benefits. Why are they used? Classify fringe benefits.
16. What is the importance of the remuneration system in an organization? How is it managed?
17. What are the industry trends in today's compensation?
18. What are the components of remuneration? How are they used in organizations?
19. What are provident funds, gratuity and employee pension? What are the state regulations with respect to provident funds, gratuity and employee pension?
20. Classify wages. How wages are different from salaries?

Internet Exercises

- Use internet resources for preparing a presentation on latest trends in compensation. Take the help of your faculty for fine tuning your presentation.
- What types of software packages are available in the market to streamline the compensation management system in an organization? Use internet resources to prepare a suitable presentation.

Experiential Learning

- Use a MS Excel spreadsheet to prepare a monthly salary sheet for the employees working in your institute. You may take the permission of your departmental head/principal for doing the same.
- Prepare a format using MS Excel spreadsheet to calculate tax deductions of your faculties working in your department.

PERFORMANCE AND SKILL BASED PAY SYSTEMS

THEME CASE: PERFORMANCE BASED PAY SYSTEMS AND FLEXIBLE BENEFITS IN PRICE WATERHOUSE COOPERS

Introduction

Price waterhouse coopers (PWC) is the world's largest multi-professional services firm, with 16,000 employees in the UK and 125,000 worldwide PWC considers itself engaged in the "war of talent". It recruits hundreds of graduates each year, and seeks to attract the best. To meet its employees' requirements, PWC had adopted a total reward policy – replete with a competitive reward package, flexible benefits, genuine work/life choices, flexible working and a strong emphasis on personal development, advancement and recognition. PWC head of reward and recognition, Sasha Hardman believes that "PWC is seeking to bring together and maximize the effectiveness of teams of people with different and complementary skills, ideas and experience which will produce better solutions for its clients".

Pay: PWC seeks itself as a meritocracy and aims to pay for performance. Its reward strategy is market driven and output focused, with a strong emphasis on the total package. Employees of PWC are paid on the basis of a combination of performance based pay (PBP) and market rates. Pay for non-managerial employees at PWC is more structures than that for other grades. Most new recruits are institute pass-outs on a 3-year training contract while they qualify as professionals in their respective disciplines. These management trainees are paid at a particular staring rate, which varies from region to region and later as they progress, PWC provides opportunities for differentiation and pay hikes depending on their performance and contributions to the organization.

Flexible benefit plans: One of the most important features contributing to PWC's employment practices success could be due to its flexible benefit plans it had instrumented successfully over the years. The benefit programs at PWC had been tailor made to suit their own personal needs. PWC mainly tried to enhance its staff awareness of the value of their total remuneration package and the value of their benefits in particular. The company was also seeking to introduce a leading edge approach to its reward programs. By giving staff flexibility in implementing the reward and benefits, the company ensured that this initiative enhanced the psychological commitment of its employees as well as it contributed to enhance the overall employability image of the organization.

The company provides all its employees with certain minimum benefits irrespective of their capabilities or positions in the organization which are known as the core benefits. The core benefits include those of standard holiday entitlements of 20 days a year and up to a further 10 days more on request, insurance cover for self and dependants etc. This is illustrated by the following table.

Table 3.7: Employee Benefits at PWC

Benefits	***Insurance Benefits***
Pensions	Pet insurance
Company car	Travel insurance
Retail vouchers	Dental insurance
Health screening	Private medical insurance
Permanent health and life insurance	Critical illness cover
Childcare vouchers	Personal accident insurance

Many benefits offer advantages because PWC's superior buying power means that a benefit is cheaper than it would be if the employee bought it in the open market (example: Retail vouchers, childcare vouchers). At PWC, even a newly recruited management trainee can request for a company car.

PERFORMANCE AND SKILL BASED PAY SYSTEMS

The objective of the development of performance based pay system is to create favourable environment for better motivation of employees and support achievement of organizational goals. Through performance based pay schemes employees are transmitted the message – what results and effort is especially expected from them.

Pay Reforms: The Move to Performance Based Pay (PBP)

Traditionally wages and pay have been determined through government regulation, minimum wage determination, negotiation with unions, decisions of arbitration or labour courts and the individual contract of employment. The factors or criteria which have influenced pay and pay increases include profit (but generally unrelated to individual or group performance), job evaluation, seniority, cost of living, manpower shortage or surplus, negotiating strength of the parties and skills. Performance measures such as productivity or profit related to the performance of a group have been of less importance in determining pay increases. Though skills have been reflected in pay differentials, pay systems have been seldom geared to the encouragement of skills acquisition and application. Industrialized countries have built their competitive advantage not around low wages, but around clusters of competitive industries in which high earnings and standards of living have been sustained through improved technology, productivity and quality.

In this context, the major concern for employers and organizations to negotiate pay systems had been to:

- Achieve a strategic business objective
- Ensure flexibility in the variable component of pay that could absorb downturns in business and reduce labour costs
- Ensure that pay systems are oriented towards achieving better performance in terms of productivity, quality, profit, etc.
- Ensure that pay systems are being capable of enhancing workers' earnings through improved performance
- Ensure that pay systems are being able to reward and recognize good performance without increasing labour costs and also attract competent staff
- Ensure that variable pay incentives could be used achieving higher employee engagements.

The objective of the development of **performance based pay system** had been to create favourable environment for better motivation of employees and support achievement of organizational goals. Through performance based pay schemes employees are transmitted the message – what results and effort is especially expected from them. In the course of creating performance based salary system the jobs where performance based salaries are advisable to implement are singled out.

Types of PBP Schemes

The types of schemes which fall within the description of performance pay are varied. Broadly speaking, they consist of schemes designed to share or distribute the financial results of enterprise performance with or to employees. In essence, performance pay is based on paying the worker for his or her value, rather than the value of the job. Such schemes fall into four broad categories:

- Individual-based schemes are based on individual performance, such as incentive schemes and sales commissions
- Profit-sharing scheme which applies to all or most of the employees
- Gain-sharing schemes are measured by a predetermined performance formula, applicable to all or groups of employees. The performance measure may be profit or some other objective such as productivity
- Employee share ownership schemes.

Basis of PBP

The basis of PBP systems in organizations are as follows:

Consolidated pay increases: Scope is provided for consolidated pay progression within pay brackets attached to grades or levels in a graded pay structure. Such increases are permanent.

Cash bonuses (Variable pay): Alternatively or additionally, high levels of performance or special achievements may be rewarded by cash bonuses which are not consolidated and have to be reearned. Individuals may be eligible for such bonuses when they have reached the top of the pay bracket for their grade or when they are assessed as being fully competent, having completely progressed along their learning curve.

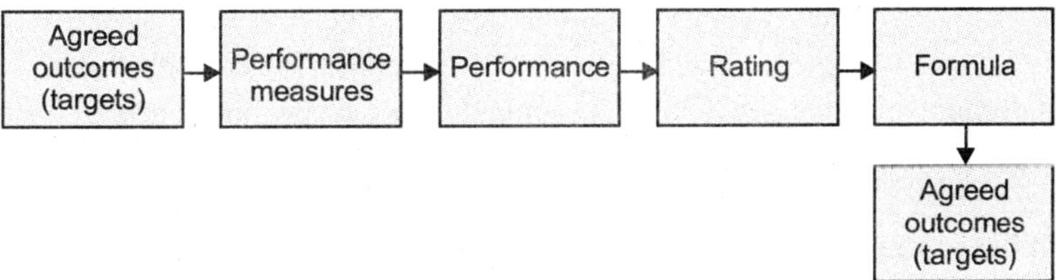

Fig. 3.65: Performance based pay

SKILL BASED PAY

What is Skill-based Pay?

Skill-based pay refers to a pay system in which pay increases are linked to the number or depth of skills an employee acquires and applies and it is a means of developing broader and deeper skills among the workforce. Skill-based pay provides employees with a direct link between their pay progression and the skills they have acquired and can use effectively. Such increases are in addition to, and not in lieu of, general pay increases employees may receive. The pay increases are usually tied to three types of skills:

- horizontal skills, which involve a broadening of skills in terms of the range of tasks
- vertical skills, which involve acquiring skills of a higher level
- depth skills, which involve a high level of skills in specialized areas relating to the same job.

Skill-based pay differs in the following respects from traditional pay systems which reflect skills differences in a structure consisting of rates of pay for unskilled, semiskilled and skilled workers:

- Skill-based pay is a person-based and not a job-based, system. It rewards a person for what he/she, rather than the job, is worth. Job worth is reflected in a basic rate of pay for minimum skills, but pay progression is directly linked to skills acquisition (rather than to general pay increases applicable to all).

- It rewards (and therefore emphasizes) a broad range of skills which makes the employee multi-skilled and therefore flexible.
- It positively encourages skills development.
- A skill-based pay system may not necessarily reflect how well the skill is used, as this falls within the performance component of pay.

Introducing a Skill-based Pay System in an Organization: Introducing a skill-based pay system requires several steps to be taken and several issues to be addressed:

- The skills requirements of the enterprise should be analyzed
- The availability of resources for training should be ascertained
- The jobs to be covered by the scheme should be identified
- The individual jobs have to be grouped into 'job families' on the basis that in each 'family' the skills needs are similar. The skills within each job family and the tasks needed to perform the job should be analyzed
- The above will lead to an identification of the skill blocks or levels. The skill level is the pay grade relative to the competence to use particular skills, and the skill block is the training input which has to be completed to the satisfaction of the certifying authority in order to gain entitlement to the extra pay
- Training modules have to be formulated
- The way in which certification is obtained that the skill has been acquired should be agreed upon.
- The criterion for extra payment is not acquisition of the skill, but its application
- The period during which the skill should be applied before a new one is acquired should normally be decided on, as the skill should benefit the employer who should receive a return on the investment made.

Problems in Skill-based Pay: There are several problems associated with the introduction of skill-based pay which should not be underestimated. They can be extremely costly with respect to:

- the extra payment involved
- training costs
- the fact that some skills may be paid for but used infrequently
- the possibility that unusable skills may be acquired unless the system is properly administered
- the fact that it is not always easy for an employer to anticipate accurately what skills will be needed in a few years' time.

Factors for the Success of a Skill-based Pay System

Some of the circumstances which contribute to the success of skill-based pay are:

- the organization's commitment to continuous training and development
- the value attached by the organization to personal growth and encouragement of a learning orientation
- dismantling strong bureaucratic hierarchies and narrow job demarcations
- participative management practices, independent and cooperative forms of work.

Appropriate Industries Relevant for a Skill-based Pay System

Skill-based pay systems are most appropriate to enterprises which depend on a high level of skills, and in which labour costs represent a relatively small portion of total costs, unlike in labour intensive industries. Though such pay systems have been commonest in manufacturing organizations, they are applicable to service industries as well though the objectives may differ. In banks and airlines, for example, skill-based pay can be used to encourage people to work in areas where manpower is most needed at a given point of time due to customer flows. Skill-based pay is particularly consistent with knowledge-based work.

Advantages of a Skill-based Pay System

Among the advantages of skill-based pay are the following:

- It contributes to job enlargement and enrichment by breaking down narrow job classifications.
- Flexibility is increased by encouraging the performance of multiple tasks. It enables job rotation, and filling of temporary vacancies due, for instance, to absenteeism. It therefore contributes to a leaner workforce.
- It enhances productivity and quality through better use of human resources.
- It facilitates technological change, which may meet with resistance in a purely job-based system.
- The higher pay levels, continuous training, and job enlargement through the broadening of skills, tend to reduce staff turnover.
- Elimination of unnecessary jobs can result from a workplace having broad, rather than narrow, skills. It also reduces the need for supervision.
- Job satisfaction is engendered through employees having greater control over the planning and implementation of their work.
- Broadening of skills leads employees to develop a better perspective of operations as a whole.
- It is an incentive for self-development.
- It provides employment security through skills enhancement.
- It reduces the need to look to promotion to higher levels (which are always limited) as the only way to enhance earnings, and it facilitates the planning of an employee's career development path.
- Since the reward flows from the application of a skill and it does not reduce opportunities for others to similarly increase their skills and earnings, there is likely to be less competition among individuals.
- Since the pay increases on account of skills are linked to a measurable standard, the criticism of subjectivity often associated with performance appraisals and individual-based performance-related pay, is avoided.

Contribution Related Pay

Contribution related pay is a process for making pay decisions which are based on assessments of both the outcomes of the work carried out by individuals and the inputs in terms of competence and competency which have influenced these outcomes. It focuses on what people in organizations are there to do, i.e., to contribute by their skill and efforts to the achievement of their organizational or team goals. The following model depicts the contribution related pay model:

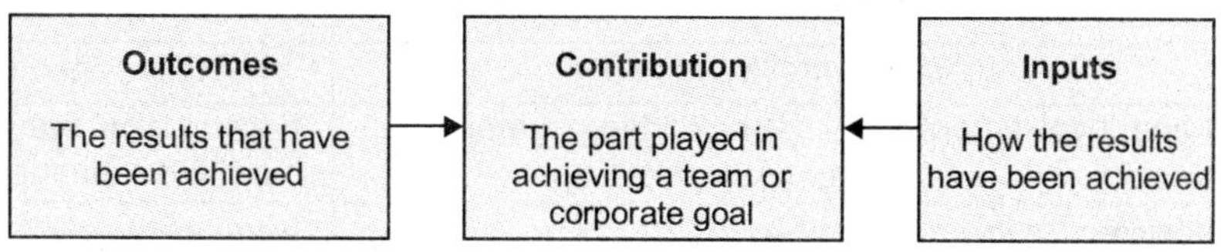

Fig. 3.66: Contribution pay model

Basis: Contribution related pay rewards people for both their performance (outcomes) and their competence (inputs).

Pay Awards: Pay awards can be made as consolidated pay increases but in some schemes there is also scope for cash bonuses.

Exhibit: Infosys Pays 100% Variable Salary

Call it an attempt to prevent employee churn or being one-up on biggest competitor TCS. Infosys Technologies, India's second biggest software exporter, has not fiddled around with the variable pay of employees for the October-December 2007 quarter. "For Q3, it is 100% average payout," an Infosys spokesperson told TOI through an e-mail, in response to a questionnaire addressed to Infosys HR director TV Mohandas Pai. According to the company spokesperson, the percentage of variable pay at Infosys ranges from nearly 10% of total compensation at the entry level to 50% (of total compensation) at senior-level roles.

The variable payouts are mostly done on a quarterly basis. However, some part of the variable pay is paid on a monthly basis too. Only for very senior roles, the variable payout takes place on a half-yearly basis. The monthly payout of the variable pay varies from 45% to 90% of the variable component, the spokesperson added. Infosys—which added over 11,600 employees during October-December 2007—has more than 88,000 employees in over 40 offices worldwide. While announcing its Q3 results, the company had allayed fears of a talent shortfall in the industry. Pai had then even said that collective efforts of industry majors "have resulted in better depth and breadth of talent availability in the market".

Exhibit: PBP Versus Contribution Related Pay

Hallmarks	PBP	Pay for Contribution
Organizing philosophy	Formula, systems	Processes
HR approach	Instrumentalist, people as costs	Commitment, people as assets
Measurement	Pay for results	Multidimensional, pay for results and how they are achieved
Measures	Financial goals	Broad variety of strategic goals
Focus of measurement	Individual	Multi-level; business, team
Design	Uniform merit pay and/or individual bonus approach throughout the organization	Diverse approaches using wide variety of reward methods to suit the needs of individual groups
Time scales	Immediate past performance	Past Performance and contribution to future goals
Performance assessment	Performance appraisal-past review and rating focus; top down and quantitative	Performance management mixed model-past review and future development; partnership approach, quantitative and qualitative
Pay linkage	Fixed formula, matrix	Looser, more flexible linkages
Administration	Controlled by HR	Owned/operated by users
Communication and involvement	Top down, non-transparent, imposed	Face to face, transparent, high involvement
Evaluation of effectiveness	Act of faith	Regular review and monitoring against clearly defined success criteria
Change over time	All or nothing	Regular incremental modification

(*Source: Armstrong, M., and Brown D., (1999): "Paying for contribution", Kogan Page*)

Theme Reading: Fixed vs Variable Pay: The Right Ratio

The trend of variable pay is not new, but it was not implemented by many companies earlier. The concept was first introduced during the early 1980s when an individual's earning was divided into two portions—fixed and variable pay packages. The move was most likely triggered by the increasing sense of competitiveness, both for more business as well as for better talent.

Fixed pay is sufficient for an employee to live comfortably. The variable pay was originally designed as a huge incentive for an employee to exceed expectations; thus increasing profitability of the organization and in turn being rewarded. Most companies today have fixed and variable components in their salary i.e. some amount of the pay comes to the individual at the end of every month and another component will only be payable in case the person or the company is able to achieve certain milestones. The percentages (fixed vs variable) vary according to the years of experience and the more senior a person is, the more his/her compensation becomes variable.

"The reason why this has been adopted is because companies need to keep their top 20 per cent happy with salaries that are higher than the market and this is not possible unless they have a variable component in the salary. Only then organisations will be able to reward people based on their performance and market dynamics, and not on the years of experience that they have," explains Gautam Sinha, CEO, TVA InfoTech.

This has now become a common practice in the IT industry and even when companies announce salary hikes there are differentials in the amounts that are awarded to people.

Says Manoj Tandon, Assistant Vice-president, CSC India, "At senior levels we have the concept of variable pay. The idea is that the fixed component is there to do the job, whereas the variable component is for going beyond the job. We are gradually introducing variable pay to lower levels as well. There are two aspects to it—one is that employees should not feel confused, and the second and the most important part is that people at various levels should gradually adapt to it and enhance their performance accordingly to reap benefits".

The ideal ratio: The ratio of fixed to variable pay depends on the level of the employee in an organization and the responsibility attached to his job. "The ratio of fixed to variable component, as a norm, varies based on the role an employee plays. As a rule, the hunters i.e. employees engaged in sales activities, usually have a larger variable than the farmers i.e. employees in execution roles. In the Indian conditions, for the sales portfolio the ratio of fixed to variable can be as much as 60:40, while in countries like the US it could be as much 30:70," says Sreenivas Chakravarthy, Vice-president, People Department, Aditi Technologies.

For non-sales roles, most companies normally follow an 80:20 ratio depending on the person meeting his or her objectives. However, a role that determines profitability of either a business unit or an organization might warrant a ratio of as much as 60:40.

Popular thumb rule ensures that the variable pay is directly proportional to the level or responsibilities—owing to the contribution an employee is able to make to the revenues or growth of the organization. The exception comes for stand-alone roles like sales where your existence directly affects top-line revenues.

The ratio of the variable component varies based on the role an employee plays **Sreenivas Chakravarthy** Vice-president, People Department Aditi Technologies	A company can design the best plan, but if employees do not understand it, the plan will fail **Gautam Sinha** CEO TVA Infotech

Individual vs Job Based Pay Systems

Compensation design has been changing to meet the environmental challenges of the new millennium. The bureaucratic "Job-based Pay (JBP) approach" used in determining pay is no longer the only game, nor it would be the major format used to design pay systems in the near future. Instead, the new designs would be "People or Individual based". There are several variants of Individual or People Based Pay, such as "Skill-Based Pay (SBP)", "Knowledge Based Pay (KBP)", "Credential Based Pay", Feedback Based Pay" and "Competency Based Pay".

From Job-based Pay to Skill-based Pay Systems

Skill-based pay (SBP) is a rapidly spreading pay innovation that compensates for the range, depth and types of employee skills, rather than for the jobs employees perform. A recent study of the prevalence of SBP reported that more than half of the Fortune 1000 manufacturing and service companies in the U.S. were using SBP to compensate at least some of their employees and were expecting increased usage of SBP in their companies in the next two years. Indeed, many of the best known examples of SBP plans are in unionized establishments, such as General Motors, Ford Motor Co., ATandT, Corning, Maxwell House, Trico Products, Inland Bar and Structural Company, and Volvo.

Table 3.8: SBP and JBP Compared

Factors	*JBP*	*SBP*
1. Pay structure	Based on job performance	Based on ability to perform
2. Employer's focus	Job carries wage; employee linked to job	Employee carries wage; employee linked to skills
3. Employee focus	Job promotion to earn greater pay	Skill acquisition to earn greater pay
4. Procedures required	Assess job content; value jobs	Assess skills; value skills
5. Advantages	Pay based on value of work performed	Flexibility; reduced workforce
6. Disadvantages	Potential personal bureaucracy; inflexibility	Potential personnel bureaucracies; cost controls

What is Broadbanding?

Broadbanding is the grouping of jobs with similar duties, responsibilities, and on the basis of the levels of accountability. Broadbands are created based upon the job analysis process of examining the body of work being performed in an organization. Broadbands widen salary ranges in order to facilitate organizational flexibility, encourage individual career development and market competitiveness. The use of broadbanding also reduces the number of job classifications and excessive job grades.

Definition

In a broadband pay structure, the numbers of pay grades are consolidated into fewer, but broader, pay ranges. In broadbanding, the spread of the pay ranges is wider and there is less overlap with other pay ranges. Broadbanding is defined as a strategy for salary and pay structures that consolidate a large number of pay grades into a few "broadbands". Organizations using broadbanding practices typically have only one-third as many salary grades as do firms using traditional pay practices. This normally translates to seven to fifteen grades for their entire workforce, from entry-level clerk to the CEO. Broadbanding applications vary significantly. Some organizations include all of the positions in the company, while others limit its use to narrower categories, such as professionals or executives.

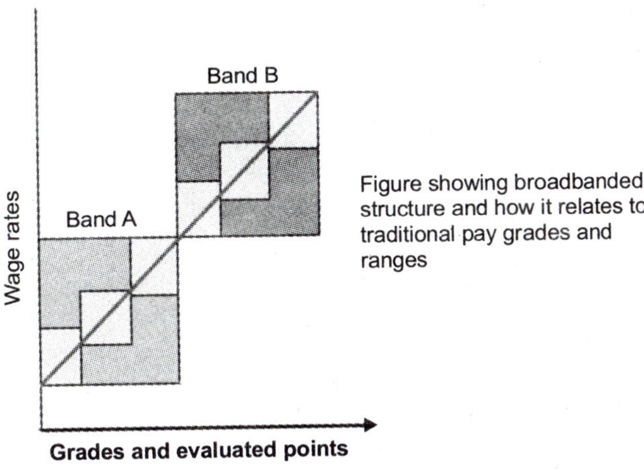

Fig. 3.67: Broadbanded pay structure

Broadbanding evolved because organizations want to flatten their hierarchies and move decision-making closer to the point where necessity and knowledge exist in organizations. In flattened organizations, fewer promotional opportunities exist so the broadbanding structure allows more latitude for pay increases and career growth without promotion. Traditional salary ranges have maximums that exceed their minimums by about 35% for non-exempt jobs and by about 50% for exempt and management jobs. With broad banding, the ranges are often 100% to 150% in width.

Why Firms Use Broadbanding?

Frequently the initial motivation of using broadbanding had been to simplify the compensation administration process. The features that attract firms to broadbanding include:

Efficiency: Broadbanding is used as a way to simplify an organization's salary administration process. By having fewer grades, organizations expect to spend less time evaluating jobs and defending grade placement decisions.

Flexibility: Organizations have realized that having fewer pay grades enhances the ability of the organization to transfer employees between jobs. Since fewer grades exist, employees are less likely to view the transfer as a demotion (instead of going from grade 32 to grade 31, the move is within Band G). The increased flexibility that the organization can gain is useful, particularly when it is going through rapid change or downsizing.

Decentralization: Broadbanding also facilitates decentralization and institutionalize the organizational restructuring programs so as to enhance their efficiency.

Performance Focus: Braodbanding enables the pay system in an organization to be more performance based.

Development of Skills: Broadband pay structures encourage the development of broad employee skills, because non-managerial jobs are appropriately valued and skill development is rewarded. Additionally, a broadband pay structure is not as sensitive to changing market pricing conditions, so they cost less to administer and manage over time. They also provide serious non-promotional income opportunities for employees.

Broader scope: Broadband classifications are broad in scope and describe the general body of work, not the specific duties that belong to all of the jobs included within that classification. The broadband classification description documents the job's duties and responsibilities as well as the knowledge and skills essential to the classification.

Benefits of Broadbanding

- Broadbanding has been successfully implemented in large, hierarchical organizations which attempted to flatten their organizations and remove levels of management. For example, organizations that had eight levels of management could eliminate four levels, widen the salary ranges of the remaining four levels, and simply slot each manager into one of those ranges.
- With broadbanding, a manager can more easily encourage his/her employees to broaden their skills and abilities. This is valuable to organizations because employees with broad skills and abilities are critical for the success in a total quality/continuous improvement environment.
- Broadbanding brings into play a performance-based salary structure wherein compensation is based on job complexity, responsibilities and skills. This approach values the role of employees and lays emphasis on skill enhancement to perform the job successfully.
- Employees are paid on the basis of the skills they develop rather than just the individual work they perform. Management rewards employees for substantial capability improvement with salary increases, thus encouraging them to broaden their skills and abilities.
- By focusing on performance and rewarding employees for their competencies, the accent shifts to individual career growth as opposed to mere promotional advancement.
- The grouping of numerous jobs in a single salary range with large midpoint differentials creates more income opportunities for employees.
- Management can easily capture appropriate market pay differentials and become nimbly responsive to the dynamic business environment.

GROUP INCENTIVE PLANS

Group incentive plans enable employees to share the benefits of improved efficiency realized by major work teams and mainly aim to encourage a cooperative rather than individualistic spirit among the employees involved in the team. Many organizations have included group incentive schemes as a part of their performance based pay strategy. The components of such group incentive plans are as follows:

Scanlon plan: Scanlon plan is a bonus incentive scheme using employee and management committees so as to gain the cost reduction improvements in the organization. The main objective behind the Scanlon plan is to ensure involving the employees and all the teams in the organization to offer ideas and suggestions to the management so as to enhance the productivity of the organization. This scheme demands good management, leadership, trust and respect between the work teams and the managers and when properly implemented can bring about drastic improvements in productivity and improved quality in the organization. The following model depicts the Scanlon plan model commonly practiced in organizations.

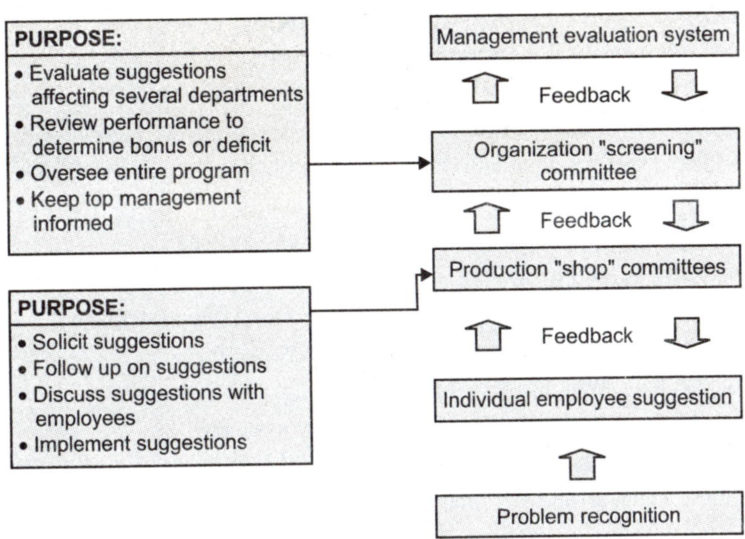

Fig. 3.68: Scanlon plan suggestion process

According to Scanlon plan, effective employee participation, which includes the use of committees, is crucial for the success of the scheme. As depicted in the given model, the shop and screening committees play a crucial role in the success of the Scanlon plan. Financial incentives under the Scanlon plan scheme are offered to the members of these committees on the basis of an established formula, which is based on increases in employee productivity.

Rucker plan: Rucker plan or share-of-production plan (SOP) is a bonus incentive plan based on the historic relationship between the total earnings of hourly employees and the production value created by the employees. It uses a far less elabourate participatory structure as compared to the Scanlon plan. The financial incentive in the form of bonus is based on any improvement in the historic relationship between the total earnings of hourly employees and the production value that they create.

Improshare: This is a gain sharing program under which bonuses are based upon the overall productivity of the work team. The concept was first developed by Mitchell Fain an industrial engineer. Improshare bonuses are based on the overall productivity of the work team and the output is measured by the number of finished products that a work team produces in a given period of time. Both production (direct) employees as well as non production (indirect) employees are involved in this bonus scheme.

Earnings-at-risk plans: These are incentive plans which involve placing a portion of the employee's base pay at risk, but giving the opportunity to earn income above the base pay when goals are met or exceeded. The main objective of this scheme is to ensure that employees should not expect substantial rewards without assuming some risk for their performance. These plans allow employees to recapture lower wages, or reap additional income above full base pay when quality; service or productivity goals are met or exceeded.

Team incentives: These are compensation plans where all team members receive an incentive bonus payment when production or service standards are met or exceeded. This incentive scheme seeks to establish a psychological commitment and a sense of belongingness in the team and also to the organization as a whole. The contribution of individual employees depends on the group or team level coordination. They tend to reduce employee complaints over individual or narrow interests and constantly encourage cross-training and acquiring of new interpersonal skills.

QUESTION BANK

1. Define pay. What are the objectives of pay?
2. What led organizations to move towards performance based pay systems?
3. What is performance based pay systems? What are the challenges and problems associated with this pay system?
4. What are the benefits of having a performance based pay system?
5. Classify performance based pay system.
6. What is the relevance and importance of performance based pay systems?
7. What are the guidelines for performance based pay systems?
8. What is skill based pay? Why are they important?
9. What are the problems associated with skill based pay systems?
10. What are the factors contributing to the success of skill based pay systems?
11. What are the disadvantages and advantages of having a skill based pay system?
12. What is variable pay? How are they used in today's organizations?
13. What is broadbanding? How is it used in compensation management?

Internet Exercises

- Surf the following link (http://www.ilo.org/public/english/dialogue/actemp/papers/1998/srspaysy.htm) with respect to the International Labour Organization (ILO) and read the materials on PBP systems.
- Read the article titled "Performance pay: poison, placebo or panacea?" from the following hyperlink (http://www.wisenet-australia.org/issue54/mbrown.htm) and discuss the same with your friends.

Experiential Exercises

- How has been the PBP system been applied to our Indian Cricket team? Discuss with your friends.
- How PBP could be used by academic institutions for motivating the research scholars? Develop your own framework defining the same.

CHAPTER 4

EMPLOYEE SAFETY AND HEALTH MANAGEMENT

THEME CASE: EMPLOYEE HEALTH AND SAFETY AT BP

BP is one of the world's largest energy companies, providing its customers with fuel for transportation, energy for heat and light, retail services and petrochemicals products for everyday items.

Occupational Health and Safety Practices at BP

BP recognizes that the health and safety of its workforce and communities is affected by its operations and that meeting the organization's corporate goal of no harm to people requires continuous effort, everyday. Health, safety and environmental issues are integral parts of BP's operating management system and the company continues to develop practices that set expectations of HSE performance in BP. For example, in the area of health management, guidelines will cover industrial hygiene, asbestos, fitness to work, health impact assessment, medical emergency management, health promotion and wellness. Healthy performance is achieved through healthy people, in healthy plants, implementing healthy processes that promote healthy decisions.

Managing and Maintaining a Healthy Workforce

In its health management initiative, BP has aimed to have healthy employees, healthy plants and healthy processes in its operations. BP had always believed that a healthy company would be a productive company, capable of sustaining high performance over longer periods of time. The company's priorities are to comply with regulations and its own policies; to act consistently across the various levels and branches of the organization and to communicate effectively about health with employees and contractors.

Managing Health Programs

BP manages its health programs by identifying relevant risks and taking action to mitigate them. These include risks could be from the physical working environment issues such as noise, temperature and air quality; risks of infectious diseases such as malaria, travel-related illnesses or HIV/AIDS; psychological and social factors such as stress or fatigue; and exposure to chemicals. In order to achieve consistency in the health and safety standards applied across BP, the management uses a **Healthmap process** in which businesses identify their key health risks and put mitigation plans in place. A **Healthmap** can cover the whole range of health issues and, through a systematic process, identify and prioritize health issues relevant to a particular site or unit. The company has set targets for **Healthmaps** to be completed for each of its locations and their quality assured, by the end of 2009.

To assist health management in BP, the company has appointed a director of health standards, who sits on the health leadership team of the safety and operations function. A pilot was conducted using the safety and operations audit process to review health in BP facilities. Findings of this study were applied to train safety auditors and improve the health and safety improvement process.

In order to ensure that the company's health management compares well with best practices among companies, the management of BP has commissioned a benchmarking survey to examine health performance indicators used by other companies in the energy industry and beyond. During 2007, BP completed work on plans to manage the risk of a pandemic including processes to protect staff, ensure continuity of its business and support the essential infrastructure.

Working with Others on Health Issues

BP works closely with many other companies and organizations in initiatives and programs to promote healthy living in the workforce and communities. In 2007, this work included taking a leading role in developing a series of industrial hygiene courses designed to develop the skills necessary to assess and control health risks. This involved working with other energy companies and pharmaceutical businesses to clarify the requirements of the hygiene courses around the world. BP developed partnerships with a group of well respected and acknowledged subject matter experts (SMEs) to develop comprehensive safety training materials for the courses. The materials were produced by the University of Wollongong in Australia with support from the International Occupational Hygiene Association.

BP also chaired the Human Factors group of the Energy Institute which is working on projects such as workforce involvement in health and safety issues and the investigation of accidents and incidents. BP remains an active member of the Global Business Coalition on HIV/AIDS, TB and malaria. As a co-chair of the joint health committee of the International Petroleum Industry Environmental Conservation Association (IPIECA) and the International Association of Oil and Gas Producers (OGP), BP is taking a leading role in its work to bring greater consistency to health performance indicators used in the energy industry. During 2007, health was covered as a key agenda item at the European Workers' Council meeting.

BP's Health and safety committees: BP'sentire European workforce of around 37,000 employees is covered by two **BP works councils**, while over ten per cent of its US employees are represented by the United Steelworkers Union.

The European Works Council covers approximately 32,600 employees from the refining and marketing, gas power and renewables and integrated supply and trading businesses, as well as the centralized functions and regions. HSSE forms part of the business update given at every meeting of the European Works Councils. HSSE is a mandatory item on the agenda of each of the plenary meetings of the European Works Council.

Think Healthy, Act Healthy is a preventive and remedial health awareness program initiated by BP as a community development initiative. It was set up in 2006 by a clinician at the Cascade/St Ann's Community Medical Clinic, in response to the local health issues associated with obesity, hypertension and diabetes. At the heart of the program is a nine-month self help process that provides local people with instruction on diet, food preparation and community-based exercise. Think Healthy, Act Healthy is all about taking action to change one's lifestyle. Participants attend twice-weekly exercise classes and are encouraged to do 'exercise home work'. Program coordinators provide encouragement and advice. The benefits of the program are regularly assessed by measuring body mass index (BMI), blood pressure, the demand for medication and diabetes indicators.

(*Courtesy: www.bp.com/*)

WHAT IS SAFETY?

By the term safety one generally refers to the freedom from the occurrence or the risk of injury or loss to an individual working in an organization. Industrial safety or employee safety refers to the protection of workers from the danger of industrial accidents and occupational health hazards.

What is Health?

WHO has defined health as "a state of complete physical, mental and social well-being and not merely the absence of disease or infirmity?" Industrial health refers to "a system of public health and preventive medicine which is prevalent within the industries". Hence it is evident that the features of industrial health involve the following components namely:

- Preservation and maintenance of physical and mental health
- Preservation and maintenance of social well-being
- Preservation and maintenance of working environment which promotes health
- Prevention of working conditions causing accidents, pollution and health hazards
- Protecting workers from risks and other occupational health hazards
- Creating and designing a work environment with the right equipments and tools that suits employee health and mental well-being.

What is Accident?

Accidents can be described as unplanned and uncontrolled events in which an action or reaction of an object, a substance, an individual or any occupational health hazard results in personal injury.

Causes of Accidents

Accidents are caused by a combination of circumstances and events, usually resulting from unsafe work acts, and unsafe work environment or both. The main causes of accidents are as follows:

A. Unsafe Conditions:
   - Improper use and maintenance of machines, tools and equipments
   - Defective machines and equipment
   - Hazardous procedures in, on or around machines or equipments
   - Unsafe storage-congestion, overloading
   - Improper illumination-glare, insufficient light
   - Improper ventilation
   - Use of hazardous chemicals.

B. Unsafe Acts:
   - Throwing and dumping of materials
   - Working at unsafe speeds (too fast or too slow)
   - Making safety devices inoperative
   - Using unsafe procedures in loading, placing, mixing or combining
   - Lifting improperly
   - Lack of individual attention and care
   - Lack of awareness
   - Lack of training.

Impact of Accident Prevention: Accident prevention activities help to:

- Reduce unsafe conditions
- Reduce unsafe acts through selection and placement
- Reduce unsafe acts through postures and propaganda
- Reduce unsafe acts through training
- Reduce unsafe acts through incentive programs and positive reinforcement
- Reduce unsafe acts through top management commitment
- Reduce unsafe acts by emphasizing safety measures
- Reduce unsafe acts by establishing a safety policy
- Reduce unsafe acts by setting specific loss control goals
- Reduce unsafe acts by conducting safety and health inspections
- Reduce unsafe acts by monitoring work overload and stress.

Types of Accidents

Accidents can be broadly classified in the following ways, as depicted by the following figure:

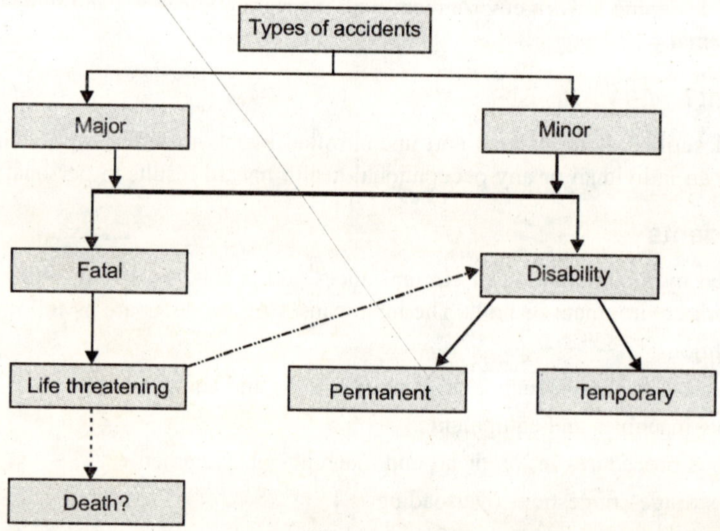

Fig. 4.1: Types of accidents

Accident Rates

Accidents are described in terms of frequency, severity and incidence. Organizations generally maintain frequency, severity and incidence records of accidents.

(a) ***Accident Incidence Rate***: It is ratio of recordable injuries to the number of employee exposure hours.

$$\textbf{Accident Incidence Rate} = \frac{\text{Number of recordable injuries} \times 1 \text{ million}}{\text{Number of employee exposure hours}}$$

(b) ***Accident Severity Rate***: The accident severity rate reflects the hours actually lost due to injury of the employees. It recognizes that not all injuries are equal.

$$\textbf{Accident Severity Rate} = \frac{\text{Total hours charged} \times 1 \text{ million}}{\text{Number of employee hours worked}}$$

(c) ***Accident Frequency Rate***: The accident frequency rate is similar to the incidence rate except that it reflects the number of injuries per million hours worked rather than per year.

$$\textbf{Accident Frequency Rate} = \frac{\text{Number of disabling injuries} \times 1 \text{ million}}{\text{Number of employee hours worked}}$$

Principles for Avoiding Accidents

The following principles can enable the management of an organization to understand the causes and consequences of accidents and to introduce suitable safety measures and/or devices. These include:

- The occurrence of an injury invariably results from a complete sequence of factors that leads to the accident. The accident is caused or permitted directly by an unsafe act of an employee and/or mechanical or physical hazard.
- The unsafe acts of employees are responsible for a majority of accidents.
- The employee who suffers a disability/injury by an unsafe act has had an average of over 300 narrow escapes from serious injury that might have resulted from the very same unsafe act.
- The occurrence of an accident that results in an injury is largely preventable.
- Four basic methods are available for the prevention of accidents-engineering revision, persuasion and appeal, personal adjustment and discipline.
- The methods most valued in accident prevention are analogous to the methods required for the control of quality, cost and quantity of production.
- The supervisor is the key person in industrial accident prevention.
- The humanitarian incentive for preventing accidental injury is supplemented by a realization of two powerful economic factors, namely: (a) A safe establishment is efficient productively, and an unsafe establishment is inefficient (b) The direct employer costs of industrial injuries for compensation claims and for medical treatment are $1/4^{th}$ of the total which the employer must bear.
- Safety should be driven internally, not externally.
- Safety incentive programs should focus on processes rather than outcomes.
- Behaviour is dictated by activators and motivated by consequences.
- When people feel empowered, their safe behaviour spreads to other situations.

Need for Safety

- ***Cost Saving***: Two types of costs are incurred by the management when an accident occurs. There are direct costs, in the form of compensation payable to the dependants of the victim if the accident is fatal and medical expenses incurred in treating the patient if the accident is non-fatal.
- ***Increased Productivity***: Safety promotes productivity.
- ***Moral***: Safety is important on humane grounds. This is why managers must undertake accident prevention measures so as to minimize the suffering of injured workers and their families as a result of accidents.

- ***Legal*****:** This is meant for compliance with laws covering occupational health and safety guidelines given by statutory compliance norms.

Fig. 4.2: A safety drill in a factory

Occupational Health and Safety Programs

Occupational health and safety programs deal with the prevention of accidents and with minimizing the resulting loss and damage to persons and property. These programs are based on five principles namely:

- Industrial accidents and disease result from a multiplicity of factors, but these have to be traced to their root causes which are usually faults in the management system.
- The most important function of a health and safety program is to identify the potential hazards, provide effective safety facilities and equipment, and take prompt remedial action.
- Health and safety are the concern of the top management.
- Managers and supervisors must be made fully accountable for the health and safety performance in the areas they control.
- All employees should be given thorough and continuing guidance in safe methods of work.

In order to apply these principles, an organization needs to:

- Develop health and safety policies
- Set up an organization required to maintain health and safety
- Prepare and implement health and safety programs.

Elements of health and safety programs: A comprehensive industrial health and safety program should include:

- A professional staff of physicians and nurses.
- Adequate facilities for emergency care and injuries sustained in the course of work and for the conduct of pre-employment and post-employment medical check-ups.
- Proper first aid treatment for occupational injuries and diseases.

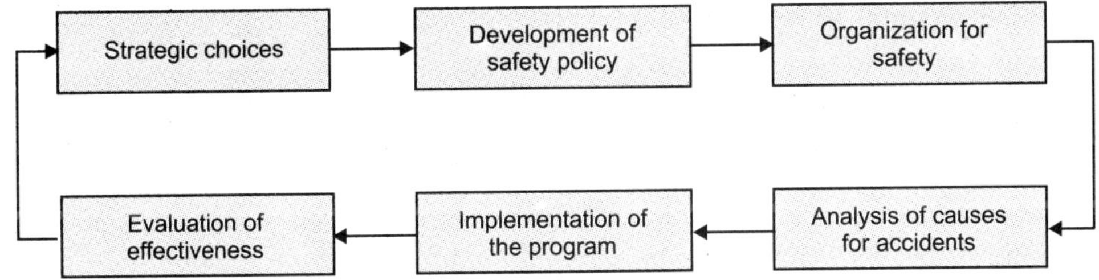

Fig. 4.3: Elements of health and safety programs

- A careful post-employment medical examination of those who are exposed to particular occupational hazards.
- Reasonable first-aid treatment of employees for non-occupational ailments.
- Information and educational services, which aim at promoting the health of employees.
- The maintenance of adequate and confidential medical records.
- Cooperation of the organization's medical officer with those who are responsible for accident prevention and control of environment with a view to achieving an integrated employee health program.
- Cooperation with public health authorities in implementing mass inoculation program and other measures for the prevention of communicable diseases.
- Advice on and supervision of, with provision and maintenance of satisfactory sanitary conditions in the factory premises.

The following facts should be given due consideration in any safety organization program:

- Safety programs must have top management approval, sanction and support.
- Responsibility for safety must rest with the supervisory personnel.
- Safety must be given equally important consideration in the elimination of mechanical and personal hazards
- Provision must be made for prompt action in the elimination of mechanical and personal hazards
- A definite safety program must be developed so as to educate all employees in safety and to secure their active cooperation in the effort to eliminate accidents.
- Safety must be included in all phases of planning, purchasing, supervision and operation.

Role of a Safety Officer/Manager/Supervisor

Organizations should emphasize upon appointing the responsibility of monitoring the safety practices to a trained manager/supervisor. Many organizations hire experienced people for the position of a safety officer/ manager. The roles and responsibilities of the safety manager are as follows:

- To lay down health and safety policies, rules and procedures.
- To advise on safety equipment and protective clothing
- To carry out safety audits and inspections
- To investigate accidents
- To maintain safety records and statistics
- To liaise with Government and Non-government organizations dealing with safety and health practices of employees at the workplace.

A Systems Approach to Safety

Any comprehensive and systematic approach to safety begins with the organizational commitment. This effort should be coordinated from the top to involve all members of the organization and be reflected in their actions and work. Once commitment is made to organizational safety, planning efforts must be coordinated, with duties assigned to supervisors, managers, safety specialists and personnel specialists. The focus of any systematic approach to safety is continued diligence of the workers, managers and other members of the top management of the organization.

Safety Education and Training

Safety education for all levels of management and for employees is a vital ingredient for any successful safety program. Education in this context refers to the development of proper perspective and attitudes towards safety. Training on the other hand, is more concerned with immediate job KSAs and work methods. Safety training of employees, as it is often conducted, has apparently been more effective in arousing safety consciousness than in teaching safe job skills. Group training is helpful in maintaining employee awareness of safety but does not become effective until the employee knows the hazards of his job and the means of avoiding them.

Top and middle management require education in the fundamentals of safety and the need for an effective accident prevention program. The supervisors must understand their key role in the safety effort, namely, that they are primarily responsible for preventing accidents. They must conduct safety training programs for their employees who are directly under their supervision. Apart from these, periodical safety meetings should also be organized from time to time at the shop floor level.

Exhibit: Safety Initiatives at Tisco

TATA STEEL

Tata Steel has determined that it will be among the safety leaders of the world. The Company's leaders consistently urged its employees to build the safety habit into their everyday work culture and behaviour. National safety day and a plethora of activities designed to propagate the message are consistently used by the company towards this goal. In this perspective, TISCO considers safety is of paramount importance and an area where the company has now launched an extremely focused campaign. The 34th National Safety Day celebration was therefore celebrated with great zeal and enthusiasm across the company, including the Tubes Division on March 4, 2005. To reinforce the significance of maintaining safety standards, a one day in-house training-cum-safety talk was organized at Jamadoba Colliery on January 22, 2005 for all Safety Committee Members of the Colliery. The training program focused on two key aspects—identification of unsafe acts, unsafe practices and unsafe conditions, and the correct procedure of roof bolting and checking.

Safety Awareness Programs

Effective safety awareness programs have the following features:

- To use records to identify the most common unsafe acts that lead to accidents.
- To establish committees and ensure participation by all departments within the company.
- To communicate about safety in a variety of ways e.g: posters, pamphlets, demonstrations at departmental meetings.
- To instruct supervisors as how to communicate, demonstrate and train employees in the safe use of equipments.

- To use incentives, rewards and positive reinforcement to encourage safe behaviours
- To encourage widespread communication and enforcement of safety rules.

Safety Audit

The safe operation of industrial plants is the responsibility of the top management and senior managers. To effectively discharge this responsibility, there is need for laying down a broad safety policy as well as a comprehensive program to ensure its implementation. Safety Audit is a useful technique used to undertake a systematic critical appraisal of the effectiveness of an organizations' safety program. Such a periodic review provides an independent assessment of the correctness of the basic direction as well as identifies the specific areas for action to improve the program. It is a tool used for ensuring that the plant operation and maintenance procedures match the design intent and standards.

Exhibit: Safety Initiatives at Aditya Birla Group

At Aditya Birla Group, the **Corporate Safety, Health and Environment Cell** offers technical support to the group with functional responsibility for safety, health and environment. The Cell's activities include implementation of a uniform corporate safety, health and environment policy across the group, maintaining contact with concerned statutory authorities, supporting business / unit managements in ensuring adherence to local legislation and organizing need based training programs for employees.

This initiative is headed by *Mr. Satish Karnik*, Corporate Safety, Health and Environment Cell.

Exhibit: Awards for Excellence in Safety Initiatives: The BHEL Story

Bharat Heavy Electricals Ltd. (BHEL) has bagged the safety initiative award, initiated by the Institute of Engineers, for implementing innovative safety and quality procedures and practices. The company has also established its commitment towards the environment in and around its manufacturing plants, besides ensuring that its products, systems and services also meet such requirements. The company has also received the national safety award from the Ministry of Labour for outstanding achievements in terms of the longest accident-free period and lowest accident frequency rate at its works.

EMPLOYEE HEALTH

Various issues on "Employee Health" can be discussed under the following broad headings namely, physical health, mental health, noise control, stress management, AIDS, alcoholism, drug abuse and management of workplace violence.

Management of Physical Health

A typical organization renders the following health services to its employees:

- Pre-hiring medical check-up for all employees.
- Periodical physical, check-up of all employees. Regular medical check-up of executives to detect early signs of tension, ulcers, diabetes etc.
- First aid treatment following an accident.
- Treatment of minor complaints such as cough, fever and headaches.
- Rehabilitation and job placement of seriously injured workers.
- Control of occupational health hazards.
- Provision of healthy sanitary facilities, such as supply of potable water, disposal of wastes and garbage etc.
- Special examination of eyes, teeth, ears.
- Cooperation with family physicians, local hospitals, clinics as well as with specialists.
- Special care of employees working in painting, welding and foundry sections where the risk of health hazard is more.
- Maternity and child welfare, including family planning.
- Adequate ventilation, good lighting, tree planting and good residential quarters.

Management of Mental Health

A mental health service is generally rendered in the following ways:

- Psychiatric counseling
- Cooperation and consultation with outside psychiatrics and specialists
- Education of company personnel in the nature and the importance of mental health
- Development and maintenance of an effective human relations program.

Noise Control

Noise control at the workplace is a critical issue for employee health. It can be achieved (a) at the source of the noise, (b) through enclosures, (c) by absorption or (d) by ear protection.

Exhibit: Metrics Used for Tracking Safety and Health by Hindustan Coca Cola Beverages Pvt. Ltd.

Lost Time Incident Rate (LTIR): It can be defined as the number of lost time incidents (number of incidents)/ 100 FTEs working 40 hrs per week, 50 weeks per year. LTIR can be calculated as:

LTIR = Total no. of LTI × 200,000/Number of hours worked by FTEs

Lost Time Injury Severity Rate (LTISR): It is the measure of injury severity/100 FTEs working 40 hours per week, 50 weeks per year.

LTISR = Number of work days lost × 200,000/Number of FTEs.

Total Incident Rate (TIR): It is the number of medical treatment cases per 100 FTEs.

TIR = Number of medical treatment cases × 200,000/Number of FTEs.

Lost Time Incident Costs (LTIC): It is the sum of all costs incurred by the company in handling the lost time injuries.

Illustration of Metrics Calculation: If monthly recorded data for a plant are like:

Number of hours worked by FTEs = 100000 (as per HR records)

Number of lost time incidents = 2 (as per monitoring logsheets)

Number of workdays lost = 10 (as per HR records/monitoring logsheets)

Medical treatment cases (including LTI) = 4 (monitoring logsheet)

Hospital Bill for LTI = Rs 5000 (as per finance records)

Then the safety metrics for the plant is estimated as:

TIR = $4 \times 200000/100000$ = 8

LTI = $2 \times 200000/100000$ = 4

LTISR = $10 \times 200000/100000$ = 10

LTIC = Rs. 5000

(Courtesy: Hindustan Coca Cola Beverages Pvt. Ltd., Bidadi Industrial Area, Bangalore)

Exercise Case Study: D'Souza Electronics

D'Souza Electronics produces a line of electronic equipment; including components of mobile phones, pocket FM radios etc that can be held in one's hand. In the final assembly of this plant, 34 employees work on an assembly line, using parts from parts bins. Each employee performs a different operation and then passes the assembly to the next person. The last two steps on the line are inspection and boxing. Inspection includes an operational test of each recorder. If a recorder fails inspection, it is placed at a bench where another employee reworks. If the stack of recorders at the bench grows too large for the benchworker to handle, one of the regular assemblers is assigned overtime benchwork to reduce the backlog.

A recent Job satisfaction survey showed that the assembly employees are reasonably satisfied. They have a friendly group, and the assembly design encourages conversation because there are seven employees on each side of the line facing each other. Turnover and absenteeism are considered normal by the management. The employees are organized by a national labour union, but none of them appears to be active in the union. There are four racial minority and several ethnic minorities in the group.

QUESTIONS FOR DISCUSSION

1. How favourable is the QWL for the assembly workers? Discuss.
2. Do you recommend any changes in the assembly jobs? Discuss.
3. What steps can be taken to further improve the productivity of the assembly workers?

QUESTION BANK

1. What do you mean by safety? What are the elements which disrupt industrial safety?
2. Define accident. Classify accident. What are the common causes of industrial accidents?
3. Write a note on accident prevention and management.
4. What is accident rate? State the principles influencing organizations to avoid accidents.
5. What do you mean by occupational health and safety? How are they managed in organizations?
6. What are health and safety management programs? What are the components of such programs used in organizations?
7. What are safety awareness programs? How can they be useful in organizations?

8. What is safety audit? How are they useful?
9. What are the components of employee health?
10. How can QWL contribute to enhance the state of occupational health and safety in organizations?

Internet Exercises

- Visit the websites of reputed organizations and prepare a presentation on various safety and health management initiatives taken by these organizations.

Experiential Learning

- Prepare a training program schedule for health and safety management in a garment factory.
- As a HR manager working in an IT company what issues with respect to employee health should you be aware of ? Discuss with your friends and prepare a presentation on the same.

EMPLOYEE WELFARE

Theme Case: Employee Welfare Committee of TSMC

Taiwan Semiconductor Manufacturing Company (TSMC) was founded on February 21, 1987, at Hsinchu Science-Based Industrial Park, Taiwan. TSMC views its role as a responsible corporate citizen seriously. The Company is committed to both community service and maintaining strong shareholder relationships. TSMC's Board of Directors (the Board) is comprised of experienced businessmen and distinguished scholars. The Board upholds the financial integrity and management wisdom of TSMC. Sir Tom Bonfield (formerly CEO and Chairman of the Executive Committee, British Telecommunications) and Professor Lester Thurow of M.I.T joined TSMC as independent directors in 2002. In addition, Professor Michael Porter became a Supervisor. An Audit Committee was established in 2002 to oversee the integrity of TSMC's financial and audit systems, while a Compensation Committee was established in September 2003 to review and recommend issues related to employee compensation.

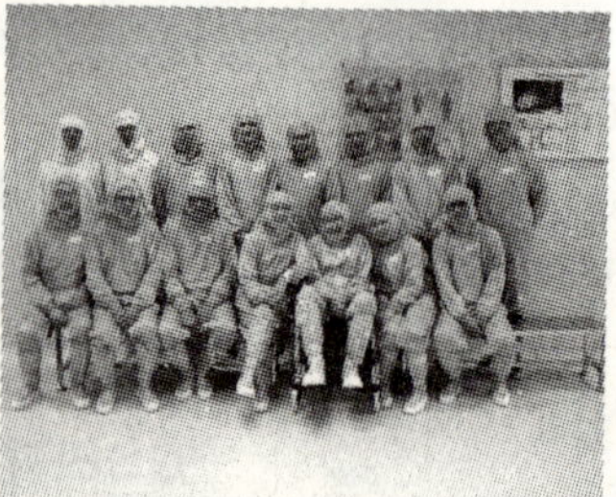

Fig. 4.4: TSMC campus

Targets

Aiming at the welfare within the company, TSMC's Employee Welfare Committee has been undertaking quality and diverse activities.

Actions Taken by the Organization

1. **Annual Events and Festival:** With an attempt to enhance the interaction and affinity between employees and the company, the Employee Welfare Committee holds annual events, including annual "Sports Day", a prize-draw in their annual "Evening Parties" and "Family Day", etc. Concerts and other entertaining activities are also held on important holidays, such as Chinese New Year, Moon Festival, or Christmas, etc.
2. **Quality Programs of Culture and Art for Families:** The Employee Welfare Committee arranges high quality and diverse programs of culture and art, which enrich the leisure time of the employees. Activities cover family film entertainment, jogging, three-on-three basketball games, dance parties and festivals of culture and art. Work and social seminars, such as music, travel, tension alleviation, and financial management are also held to broaden the minds of employees. In addition, the employees of TSMC can always access the customized art-performing programs, which are specifically arranged for TSMC's employees, through their online order system.
3. **Colourful Club Activities:** More than forty clubs have been assisted or registered under the name of TSMC's Employee Welfare Committee. Activities are vigorous in various clubs, including Hwei-Hsin Club, Mountain Climbing Club, Tai-Chi Quan Club, Aerobics Club, Flower Arranging Club, and so on. Diverse Clubs allow the employees with the same interests to enjoy happy moments together while at the same time increasing personal networks within the working community.
4. **Contracted Stores and On-site Service:** With the hope of satisfying all aspects of employees' lives, the Employee Welfare Committee signed contracts with stores and institutes within the neighborhood, including banks, laundry service, household appliances company, and a travel agency, etc. It also requested these contracted stores and institutes to offer their services in TSMC's on-site service area, which enables nine-to-five office workers to manage their financial affairs and to shop for daily necessities without taking time off.
5. **Health and Fitness Center:** According to different space requirements of each fab, the Employee Welfare Committee established diverse and well-rounded facilities for entertainment, including the gym, basketball courts, badminton courts, tennis courts, aerobic rooms, table tennis rooms and a children's play area. Reservation for these facilities can be made on the website of TSMC athletic park, which allows the employees to browse through the facilities provided and to make reservations on line.
6. **TSMC Children Center:** Founded in March 1999, TSMC Children Center was the first government-registered nursery under the name of an enterprise in Hsinchu Science Park. The establishment of the TSMC Children Center aimed to offer pre-school education for the children of TSMC's employees. The Children Center provides quality pre-school education and consultation services and has been one of the most welcomed welfare facilities in TSMC.
7. **Innovation of TSMC Children Center:** TSMC Children Center installed a real-time video system in every classroom. The employees can easily access the real-time video system through the intranet network to see if their children are doing well in class. With the help of an email system in the office, the communication between the center and the employees is direct and immediate. The Children Center also set up a website under the website of the Employee Welfare Committee. Latest information regarding pre-school education, educational concepts, and parental skills is provided for the employees. The function of parental education has been added to the original purpose of pre-school education.

   ***Personnel Structure*:** The personnel structure of the TSMC Children Center consists of one director, one administrative assistant, and eight qualified teachers with backgrounds in pre-school education. These ten professional and experienced staff create a pleasant environment for 100 children to learn and grow. Apart from the effort of the teaching staff, the professional services are provided by the in-house specialists in related sections, comprising medical care, security, environmental protection, general management, and so on. All these sections have focus on one main objective and that is to create a secure, healthy, and clean environment for children to learn.

***The Number of Class and Children*:** TSMC Children Center consists of four classes, 100 children in total. The target children are pre-school infants, ranging from 2 to 6 years of age. The service time of TSMC Children Center is from 7:00 a.m. to 8:00 p.m., Monday to Friday, and is tailor-made for the schedule of the employees in TSMC.

***Social Responsibility*:** TSMC Children Center serves as one example for enterprises that intend to establish similar daycare centers for their employees. The important experience of TSMC Children Center can be passed on and shared with other enterprises. With the ideal of liberal education, TSMC Children Center adopts the holistic educational approach, which is acknowledged by academic institutes of pre-school education. As an institute of pre-school education, TSMC has become the best choice for departments of early childhood care and education, to learn teaching approaches and perform internship.

TSMC Children Center has been offering internship for the students of early childhood education in National Hsinchu Teachers College. Through offering hands-on experience of pre-school education, the Children Center can assist the training of pre-school education teachers.

Results: The Employee Welfare Committee of TSMC has been striking for the objective of providing high quality and diverse welfare measures for their employees. The promotion and innovation of welfare in the Employee Welfare Committee can serve as a reference and a benchmark for other enterprises in Taiwan. TSMC Children Center is also highly praised by the government and academic institutes of early childhood education. It is granted by the Council of Labour Affairs, Executive Yuan every year and was rated as the nursery of the highest caliber. In 2002, TSMC Children Center stood out in the comprehensive evaluation of public and private nurseries in Hsinchu City and won three prizes, including childcare and education, sanitation and health care, and was deemed to be excellent in their overall evaluation.

(*Courtesy: http://csr.moea.gov.tw/en/cases/cases_content.asp?cs_ID=1111*)

WHAT IS LABOUR WELFARE?

Labour welfare relates to taking care of the well-being of workers by employers, trade unions, governmental and non-governmental institutions and agencies. Welfare includes anything that is done for the comfort and improvement of employees and is provided over and above the wages. Welfare helps in keeping the morale and motivation of the employees high so as to retain the employees for longer duration. Employee welfare includes monitoring of working conditions, creation of industrial harmony through infrastructure for health, industrial relations and insurance against disease, accident and unemployment for the workers and their families.

According to ILO, labour welfare can be defined as a term, which is understood to include such services, facilities, and amenities as may be established in or in the vicinity of undertakings to enable the persons employed in them to perform their work in healthy, congenial surroundings and to provide them with amenities conducive to good health and high morale.

Merits and Demerits of Welfare Measures

Merits	Demerits
1. Providing both statutory as well as non-statutory facilities to the employees.	1. The concept of labour welfare implies "do-gooding"

Contd...

Merits	Demerits
2. Employee welfare facilities facilitate in order to help, motivate and retain employees.	2. Welfare is provided by the state services, hence the concept of it in private organizations might seem to be a duplication of the same which already exists.
3. Employee welfare activities help to reduce employee dissatisfaction with their management and also help to develop loyalty amongst the employees towards the organization.	3. Organizations might perceive labour welfare in a way that the private affairs of the employees and their off-the-job interests should not be the concern of their employers.
4. Employee welfare facilitates to remove and minimize social evils, such as alcoholism, gambling, drug addiction.	
5. It helps to raise the image of the organization and often acts like a marketing tool for the organization to attract talents.	
6. Employee welfare may not directly increase productivity, but it may add to the general feelings of satisfaction with the organization and cut down labour turnover.	

Objectives of labour welfare: Labour welfare has the following objectives:

1. To provide better life and health to the workers
2. To make the workers happy and satisfied
3. To relieve workers from industrial fatigue and to improve intellectual, cultural and material conditions of living of the workers.

Features of labour welfare: The basic features of labour welfare measures are as follows:

1. Labour welfare includes various facilities, services and amenities provided to workers for improving their health, efficiency, economic betterment and social status.
2. Welfare measures are in addition to regular wages and other economic benefits available to workers due to legal provisions and collective bargaining.
3. Labour welfare schemes are flexible and ever-changing. New welfare measures are added to the existing ones from time to time.
4. Welfare measures may be introduced by the employers, government, employees or by any social or charitable agency.
5. The purpose of labour welfare is to bring about the development of the whole personality of the workers to make a better workforce.

The very logic behind providing welfare schemes is to create efficient, healthy, loyal and satisfied labour force for the organization. The purpose of providing such facilities is to make their work life better and also to raise their standard of living. The important benefits of welfare measures can be summarized as follows:

- They provide better physical and mental health to workers and thus promote a healthy work environment.
- Facilities like housing schemes, medical benefits, and education and recreation facilities for workers' families help in raising their standards of living. This makes workers to pay more attention towards work and thus increases their productivity.
- Employers get stable labour force by providing welfare facilities. Workers take active interest in their jobs and work with a feeling of involvement and participation.

- Employee welfare measures increase the productivity of organization and promote healthy industrial relations thereby maintaining industrial peace.
- The social evils prevalent among the labours such as substance abuse, etc are reduced to a greater extent by the welfare policies.

Types of Labour Welfare Activities

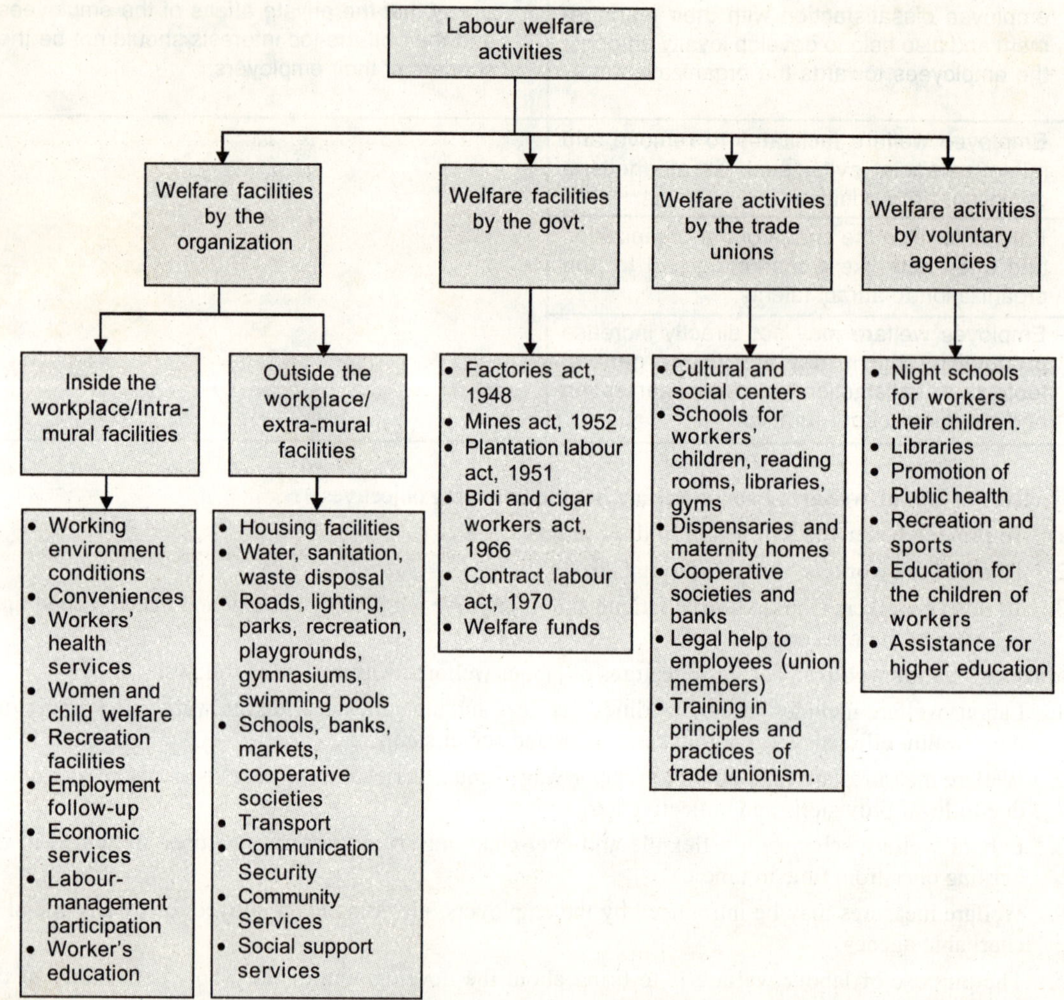

Extra-mural Labour Welfare Activities

These activities are commonly known as benefit programs. They consist of providing social security, medical coverage, insurance, housing facilities, water, sanitation, waste disposal, roads, lighting, parks, recreation, playgrounds, gymnasiums, swimming pools, schools, banks, markets, cooperative societies, transport, Communication facilities: Postal, telegraph, telephone and internet, community development services etc.

Intra-mural Labour Welfare Activities

Intra-mural activities or services include those of providing working environment conditions, conveniences, workers' health services, women and child welfare, recreation facilities, employment follow-up, economic services, labour-management participation, worker's education etc.

Statutory Measures

Statutory welfare measures are those laid down by government through enactment of legislative laws. Benefits like those of provident funds, welfare funds, pension schemes, insurance coverage, ESI schemes etc. come under the purview of statutory measures.

Statutory Provisions

- ***Statutory provisions as under the Factories Act, 1948***
- ***Labour Welfare Officer***: Schedule 49 of Factories Act, 1948 provides that in every factory wherein 500 or more workers are employed, the employer should appoint at least one welfare officer. The duties of the labour officer includes, those of:
  - Supervision of safety, health and welfare programs, working of joint committees, granting leaves with wages and redressing worker grievances.
  - Worker counseling in their personal and family problems, adjusting to work environment and understanding employee rights and privileges.
  - Advising management in matters of formulating welfare policies, apprenticeship training programs, complying with statutory compliances and developing fringe benefits and facilitating worker education.
  - Liaisoning with workers so that they may appreciate need for harmonious IR in the organization, resolve disputes, understand limitations under which they operate and interpret company policies effectively.
  - Liaisoning with the management so as to appraise the later about workers' viewpoints on organizational matters.

Welfare Provisions: Chapter V of the Factories Act provides for welfare facilities like adequately screened washing facilities for the use of male and female workers, for drying of wet clothes, resting places, first aid boxes or cupboards. It also stipulates that no adult worker should be allowed to work for more than 48 hours a week. It also indicates that women workers are not to be employed during night or between 7 pm and 6 am (though exceptions can be made). No child below 14 years of age is allowed to be employed in any factory.

Non-statutory Provisions: Non-statutory benefits, also called voluntary benefits, include loans for house building, education of children, leave travel concessions, fair price shops, loans for purchasing vehicles etc.

Mutual Welfare Schemes

These are those facilities agreed to by mutual consultation between the employee representatives (unions) and the employers. These schemes could be in the form of paid vacations, leaves etc.

Approaches to Labour Welfare

The various approaches to labour welfare are as follows:

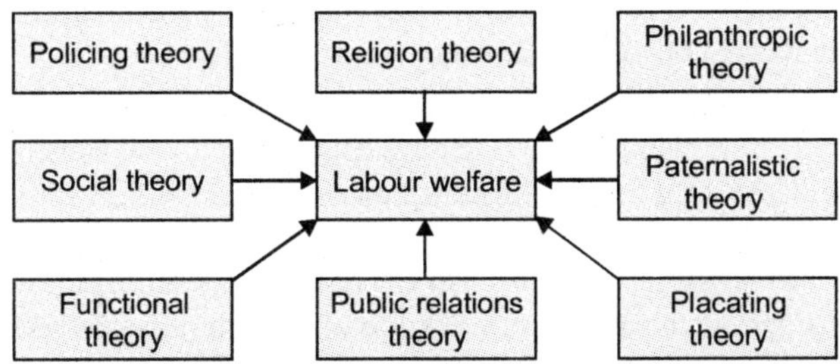

Fig. 4.5: Various theories of labour welfare

Labour Welfare Theories	Features/Hallmarks
Functional Theory	This theory assumes that employee welfare is a part of the personnel/HR function of the organization. In this regard, organizations depute a labour welfare officer or manager to manage the welfare activities in the organization.
Social Theory	This theory assumes that organizations take benefits, resources and raw materials from the society for producing their products and services and by providing labour welfare activities in their organization and outside the organization (Extra Mural Activities) they are showing their concern for the development and well being of the society.
Policing Theory	This theory assumes that organizations provide ample opportunities for owners and managers of capital to exploit workers in unfair ways like by compelling employees with long working hours, by paying low wages, by not improving the quality of life at the workplace. The statutory norms and legislations provided by the state with respect to welfare activities acts as a stringent measure to prevent these unfair activities towards the workforce.
Religion Theory	From the investment perspective, the religion theory implies that by committing towards welfare activities the management could reap the benefits of employee loyalty and trust in the near future. On the other hand, from the atonement perspective the religion theory implicates that it is the moral responsibility of the management to be concerned for the well being of the employees.
Philanthropic Theory	This concept mainly proposes that labour welfare should provide good working conditions, rest rooms, drinking water facilities, common rooms, canteens etc. that would contribute to improve the standard of living and well being of the employees in the organization.
Paternalistic Theory	According to this theory, the social responsibility and the responsibility of an employer of an organization with respect to the employee welfare is conceived as a "paternalistic duty or responsibility" towards the society and the employees who are being employed in the organization.
Placating Theory	Placating theory considers that labour welfare initiatives taken by an organization are like appeasement and its works for the management particularly when the workers are organized and violent in terms of charting their demands from the management.
Public Relations Theory	This concept assumes that labour welfare can create a good corporate image and enhance the employability brand of the organization.

Concepts of Labour Welfare

Labour welfare can be described in terms of three dimensions namely the holistic welfare initiatives, social and relative welfare programs taken by the organization.

Holistic Concept of Labour Welfare: The "holistic" concept of labour welfare can be described as the achievement of desirable state of existence involving physical, mental, moral and emotional well-being of the working class. One case could be cited here to illustrate holistic labour welfare. In the Peenya Industrial Area of Bangalore, the Peenya Industrial Association (PIA) which is a professional body/association comprising of the membership of almost all big/large, medium/small enterprises in the area had catered all feasible initiatives in the Peenya area so as to improve the quality of work life of the enterprises working in this part of the city of Bangalore. This includes conducting special training and induction programs for workers from various expertise and capabilities, counseling programs, entrepreneurial development programs, providing financial assistance to sick units and needy workers, extending insurance schemes and facilitating loans to needy employees, improving the condition of the roads, drainage, lighting of the roads (done in association with BESCOM and the state Government authorities) and also ensuring the preservation of the greenery of the area.

Social component of labour welfare: The social concept of labour welfare involves the well being of an individual and the harmonious relationship established with the community and even his/her own family, working groups, superiors, subordinates etc.

Relative concept of labour welfare: Labour welfare could be considered as a more or less relative term; relative to the time, place and even the individual(s) concerned. Hence taking this into consideration labour welfare should be described in terms of a dynamic and flexible concept. Thus the concept of labour welfare may vary from place to place, industry to industry and even country to country.

Principles of Labour Welfare: The various principles of labour welfare are as follows;

1. **Adequacy of Wages:** High wage alone cannot create a healthy and desirable working environment in an organization. A combination of adequate wages, welfare activities and the right working environment is essential for job satisfaction of employees in an organization.
2. **Social Responsibility:** The organization or the industry in which the employees are being employed have the responsibility and obligation in terms of taking care of the well being and welfare of the employees.
3. **Efficiency:** Organizations should perceive that by contributing to employee welfare they can motivate their employees, which can also contribute to enhance the efficiency of the employees as well as that of the entire organization.
4. **Re-personalization:** This emphasizes the development of human personality as the principal objective welfare activities in the organization.
5. **Totality of Welfare:** The need and the importance of employee welfare must be felt and practiced at all levels of the organization.
6. **Integration and Coordination:** Coordinated approach is crucial in order to achieve a successful welfare program for the organization. At the same time care should be taken so as to integrate all the subsystems of the organization along with the fundamental welfare initiatives taken by the organization.
7. **Participation:** For the success of any welfare initiatives in an organization it is essential for employee participation from all levels of the organization.
8. **Responsibility:** For the success of any welfare initiatives both the employer as well as the employees should be mutually responsible. The trade unions should also take the responsibility of emphasizing upon labour welfare initiatives rather than focusing on their vested political interests.
9. **Accountability:** Management of any organization should be critical with respect to the accountability of labour welfare initiatives taken by them. The management representative should be given the authority to take necessary decisions in order to ensure accountability of the welfare activities.
10. **Timeliness:** Employee welfare measures must be provided on a timely basis as and when required on a priority basis, otherwise this could lead to decrease the effectiveness of the HR function in terms of increased cost and wastage. In this regard the management of any organization should emphasize upon proper planning and control.

EMPLOYEE WELFARE FUNDS

Labour welfare refers to all the facilities provided to labour in order to improve their working conditions, provide social security and raise their standard of living. Majority of labour force in India is working in unorganized sector. In order to provide social security to such workers, Government has introduced Labour Welfare Fund to ensure assistance to unorganized labours. Five different welfare funds, which are governed by different legislations, are administered by Ministry of Labour. The purpose of these welfare funds is to provide housing, medical care, educational and recreational facilities to workers employed in beedi industry and non-coal mines and cine workers. The five legislations governing welfare funds are as follows:

- The Mica Mines Labour Welfare Fund Act, 1946
- The Limestone and Dolomite Mines Labour Welfare Fund Act, 1972
- The Iron Ore, Manganese Ore and Chrome Ore Mines Labour Welfare Fund Act, 1976
- The Cine Workers' Welfare Fund Act, 1981

Schemes under welfare funds provide assistance with respective to the following:

- Public health and sanitation
- Housing
- Recreational (including standard of living)
- Social security
- Educational facilities
- Water supply
- Transportation
- Medical facilities (prevention of diseases)
- Social security
    - Group Insurance Schemes for Beedi and Cine workers
    - Social Security under Mine Workers Welfare Fund
- Family welfare

The welfare funds are raised by government by imposing cess on manufactured beedis, feature films, export of mica, consumption of limestone and dolomite and consumption and export of iron ore, manganese ore and chrome ore. An explanation of the cess levied under different legislations is given below:

- Beedi Workers Welfare Cess Act, 1976 provides for levy of cess by way of excise duty on manufactured beedis from Re. 1/- to Rs. 5/- per thousand manufactured beedis. This is presently Rs. 2 per 1000 beedis with effect from 28th June 2000.
- The Cine Workers Welfare Cess Act, 1981 provides for duty of cess, at such rate not being less than one thousand rupees and not exceeding twenty thousand rupees, on every feature film submitted to the Chairman, Central Board of Film Certification. This is Rs. 20,000 per feature film of Hindi and English and for regional films it is Rs. 10,000 per film with effect from 20th April 2000.
- The Iron Ore, Manganese Ore and Chrome Ore Mines Labour Welfare Cess Act, 1976 provides for levy and collection of cess on Iron Ore, Manganese Ore and Chrome Ore between 50 p to Re. 1/-, Re. 1/- to Rs. 6/- and Rs. 3/- to Rs. 6/- respectively.
- The Limestone and Mines Labour Welfare Fund Act, 1972 provides for the levy and collection of cess on Limestone and Dolomite as a duty of excise at such rate not exceeding one rupee per metric tone of limestone and dolomite. The rate of cess on Limestone and Dolomite is Re.1/- with effect from 27th December 2000.
- Mica Mines Labour Welfare Fund Act, 1946, provides for levy and collection of cess on all mica exported as duty of Customs not exceeding 6.25% ad valorem. This is 4.5% ad valorem on export with effect from 1st November 1990.

The Employees State Insurance (ESI) Act, 1948

The ESI Act has been passed to provide for certain benefits to employees in case of sickness, maternity and employment injury and to make provisions for related matters. As the name suggests, it is basically an 'insurance' scheme i.e. employee gets benefits if he is sick or disabled.

ESIC: Employees State Insurance Corporation (ESIC) has been formed to supervise the scheme under section 3 of the Act. The corporation supervises and controls the ESI scheme.

No dismissal or punishment during period of sickness

- Section 73 of the Act provides that no employer shall dismiss, discharge or reduce or otherwise punish an employee during the period employee is in receipt of sickness benefit or maternity benefit.
- He also cannot dismiss, discharge or otherwise punish employee when he is in receipt of disablement benefit or is under medical treatment or is absent from work due to sickness.
- This gives protection to employee when he is in receipt of sickness benefit or maternity benefit. Employer cannot take disciplinary action against employee in such cases. This provision is grossly misused by employees.

Applicability of ESI Scheme

- The scheme is applicable to all factories [Section 1(4)]. The Appropriate Government can also make it applicable to any other industrial, commercial, agricultural or other establishments, by issuing notification and giving 6 month notice. [Section 1(5)].
- ESI Act can be made applicable to 'shops' also. However, since Government has to provide for hospitals and medical facilities, the Act can be made applicable to different parts of state at different dates.
- Thus, if a factory is at a place where ESIC is unable to provide medical facilities, ESI Act may not be made applicable to the area.
- Government can exempt a factory or establishment or persons or class of persons from provisions of ESI Act, if the employees are getting better medical facilities [e.g. if Government is convinced that the factory itself is providing very good medical facilities e.g. like TISCO].

Benefits under ESIC

The promulgation of Employee's State Insurance Act, 1948 envisaged an integrated need based social insurance scheme that would protect the interest of workers in contingencies such as sickness, maternity, temporary or permanent physical disablement, and death due to employment injury resulting in loss of wages or earning capacity. The act also guarantees reasonable good medical care to workers and their immediate dependants. The section 46 of the Act envisages following six social security benefits:-

(a) Medical Benefit

(b) Sickness Benefit(SB)

1. Extended Sickness Benefit (ESB)
2. Enhanced Sickness Benefit

(c) Maternity Benefits (MB)

(d) Disablement Benefit

1. Temporary Disablement Benefit (TDB)
2. Permanent Disablement Benefit (PDB)

(e) Dependant's Benefit(DB)

(f) Funeral Expenses

An interesting feature of the ESI Scheme is that the contributions are related to the paying capacity as a fixed percentage of the workers wages, whereas, they are provided social security benefits according to individual needs without distinction.

Pensioners' Medical Scheme (E.S.I.C.- PMS): The Standing Committee of the ESI Corporation, in its meeting held on 13th Dec., 2005, has approved certain medical facilities to the pensioners of the E.S.I.C. under the name and style of "The E.S.I.C. Pensioners' Medical Scheme, 2006" which shall come into force w.e.f. 1st April, 2006. The Scheme is optional and contributory in nature. Pensioners opting for this scheme shall pay contribution in advance for a minimum period of six months at the following rates:-

Pay Range	Pension/Family Pension	Rate of Monthly Contribution
Pay up to Rs. 3000	Up to Rs. 1500	15
Rs. 3001 to Rs. 6000	Rs. 1501 to Rs. 3000	40
Rs. 6001 to Rs. 10000	Rs. 3001 to Rs. 5000	70
Rs. 10001 to Rs. 15000	Rs. 5001 to Rs. 7500	100
Rs. 15001 and above	Rs. 7501 and above	150

Employee welfare w.r.t. the Employees' Provident Fund and Miscellaneous Provisions Act, 1952:

Coverage for Employers

- Establishments employing 20 or more persons and engaged in any of the 180 industries/Classes of Businesses specified.
- Cooperative Societies, employing 50 or more persons and working without the aid of power.
- Establishments not coverable statutorily can come under the coverage of the Act statutorily.
- An establishment continues to be covered under the Act, irrespective of the fall in the employment strength.
- Since the Act applies on its own force to the establishments, the employers are required to file the particulars in the specified format for registration and allotment of business number.

Duties of Employer

- Enroll all categories of employees including the employees engaged by or through contractors and also piece rated, hourly rated employees.
- Remit the contributions and administrative charges before the 15th of the following month.
- File the initial returns of Form 9, Form 3(P.S.), form 5A.
- File the monthly returns in Form 12A, Form 5, Form 10 and Challans for remitting the dues.
- Maintain the contribution card in respect of each employee in Form 3A and submit the annual returns in Form 3A and 6A after reconciliation with Challans and form 12A.
- The employer has to ensure that statutory dues in respect of contractor's employees are remitted and returns filed.
- Employer should attest the form No.2 and the claims forms submitted by the member/legal heirs/ nominees.
- Make available all relevant records for inspection of visiting officials with due authorization.

For Employees (New entrants)

- Enrolment: An employee is eligible for membership from the day he joins the covered establishment.
- If the employee's emoluments exceed Rs. 6,500/- per month, he has the option to join the Scheme(s) with the consent of employer.
- Declare previous employment details, if any, in Form No. 11 to the employer.
- On becoming a member of the Schemes file details in Form No. 2 (family particulars/nominations) through the employer.
- Rate of contribution payable by a member shall be @ 12% of his emoluments.
- A member can contribute statutorily over and above the prescribed rate.

Employee Gratuity: The Payment of Gratuity Act, 1972

Gratuity is payable if there is c***ontinuous service of 5 yrs*** (not necessary in case of death or disablement). It is payable under the following conditions, namely:

- On termination due to superannuation or retirement
- Resignation, death or disablement due to accident or disease
- In case of death, the amount will be paid to nominee or legal heir

Calculation of Gratuity: Gratuity can be calculated by the following formula:

$$\text{Gratuity} = \frac{\text{Monthly rate of wage last drawn}}{26} \times 15$$

Mode of Payment of Gratuity

- In ***cash*** or ***DD*** or ***bank cheque***
- Payment by ***postal money order*** if amount is ***less than Rs.1000*** if employee desires
- *Maximum amount payable is Rs.3,50,000*

Employees' Provident Fund Scheme (Employee Provident Fund Miscellaneous Provisions Act, 1952): The central government may, by notification in the official gazette, frame a scheme to be called Employees Provident Fund Scheme for employees or class of employees of establishments to which the Act applies. Obligation of employee involves to contribute to the PF at the rates specified in the Act, furnish to the employee particular about himself or his nominee. The rights of the employers is to deduct the contribution payable to the worker from their wages for the period for which the contribution is payable.

Exhibit: Employee Welfare and Human Rights Policy in Premier Foods

As a major employer, Premier Foods is aware of its responsibility to its employees and our policy on employee welfare and human rights sets a minimum standard to which all of the group companies adhere in order to meet their moral, legal, ethical and humanitarian responsibilities.

Our policy incorporates the standards set out in the Ethical Trading Initiative Base Code and is encapsulated within our Ethical Assurance Policy Statement of Principles. We conduct audit activity across our own sites as well as our supply chain for compliance with the Ethical Assurance Policy through which we also manage ethical standards in our supply chain. Human resources and investment in people we recognize that our employees are our single most valuable asset and we strive to be an employer of choice in the areas in which we operate through the ongoing development of our employer brand. We promote career development and the group provides its employees with access to relevant training and development schemes through in-house training, educational assistance, participation in National Vocational Qualification Schemes and encouraging professional memberships. Our aim is to ensure that we have a highly trained and motivated workforce, capable of meeting the highest standards required by customers and investors.

Equal opportunities: We are committed to equal opportunities in all areas of our business, with people gaining promotion on merit. We recruit, train, promote and retain skilled and motivated people irrespective of sex, age, marital status, disability, sexual orientation, race, religion, ethnic or national origin.

Whistle blowing: In line with our commitment to promote a culture of openness and responsibility within our business we welcome the reporting of genuine and serious grievances, or alleged breaches of company policy. No employee will suffer as a consequence of notifying such alleged breaches in accordance with the Whistle Blowing Policy.

Bullying and harassment: In line with our core values we believe that every employee should be treated with the same respect and dignity and we are committed to providing a working environment that is free from bullying and harassment. We will not tolerate bullying or harassment in the workplace either as a management style or between work colleagues and will take disciplinary action against any employee who is proven to have bullied or harassed others.

Disciplinary actions: Our reputation and success as a business relies on the ability of our employees to assume responsibility and maintain acceptable standards of conduct in the work environment. The aim of the disciplinary process is to be corrective rather than punitive, setting reasonable standards of performance and behaviour to ensure consistency and fairness of treatment for all employees. This objective, however, needs to be balanced with our responsibility to protect the safety of all employees and the reputation of the business and serious misconduct or persistent failure to comply with corporate standards is not tolerated.

Brian Carlton

Date: March 2008

Human Resources Director

QUESTION BANK

1. Define labour welfare. What are the merits and demerits of labour welfare?
2. What is the purpose of labour welfare in organizations?
3. What are the characteristic features of labour welfare in organizations?
4. Classify labour welfare activities with suitable illustrations.
5. What is the difference between extra mural and intra mural labour welfare activities? Give examples wherever possible.
6. What constitute the quality of work life (QWL)? Give some suggestions to improve QWL of assembly line workers in India.
7. What kind of employee welfare action decisions is available to an organization where there is (a) surplus and (b) shortage of labour?
8. Design a questionnaire (consisting of 15 questions/items) for assessing the job satisfaction level of the shop floor employees.
9. What is participative management? What are the ways of ensuring participative management? What are the ethical issues involved in participative management? (BU July/August 2005).
10. Bring out the benefits of employee socialization. (BU 2002).
11. Would you rather work for an organization where everyone knows what others are earning, or would you prefer an organization where this information is kept secret? Why?

Internet Exercises

- Visit the websites of reputed companies and prepare a presentation on the various welfare activities taken in the IT/ITES sector.

Experiential Learning

- What are the various welfare activities taken in a public sector enterprise? Study such an organization and prepare a presentation on the same.

ABSENTEEISM, LEAVE MANAGEMENT AND ATTRITION

Staff meeting to improve time management...

It appears that everyone else is late.

(*Courtesy: With permission received from Mr. John Ditchburn*)

THEME CASE: EYE ON ATTENDANCE – AN EMPLOYEE RELATIONS CASE STUDY

"Well, look there, Robin decided to come in today only five minutes late, instead of 10," Beverly whispers to Anna as Robin rushes in at 8:05 a.m. "May be I should sleep in more often. Chris doesn't seem to care if she's late all the time. This has been going on for six months and he's done nothing about it." Anna, tired of hearing Beverly complain about her friend Robin, decides to bring the issue up to their supervisor, Chris.

"Since my office is not in direct view of her area, I've only noticed Robin coming in late once or twice," Chris responds to Anna. "I can't address this issue with her based on hearsay that she's late every day." Chris agrees to pay more attention to Robin's tardiness. He recalls that her job performance has been satisfactory, so this appears to be the only issue of concern at this time.

Over the next week, Chris notices that Robin is between five and 15 minutes late on four out of five days. He is shocked that this has been happening without him noticing. On Friday, Robin rushes in at 8:10 a.m. Chris immediately calls her into his office (in front of Anna and Beverly) and tells her that this has to stop – if she is late for work one more time, she will be terminated. Robin leaves Chris's office in tears, speechless. Alone in his office, Chris ponders the brief, uncomfortable interaction that just took place. He decides to call the employee relations consultant for his area.

Following a conversation with his department's ER consultant, Chris decides to acknowledge his poor handling of the interaction with Robin and arranges a time early the next week to meet with her privately. At the meeting, he states that although their previous conversation did not go so well, he is concerned about her tardiness and needs to address it more professionally. He describes what he has observed and explains how his observations supported information he received from others regarding her tardiness. Chris asks Robin for her perspective and then just listens. Robin describes problems with her daycare provider and personal issues she was facing recently with a divorce. She says she feels overwhelmed just to get up in the morning, and making it to work on time is becoming more and more difficult.

Chris empathizes with Robin's life concerns, but refocuses the conversation on the need for her to be to work on time and the problems it causes when she is late – others needing to cover her phone, division among the staff, and reduced morale in the work area. Chris states he expects Robin to be at work at 8 a.m. everyday, and he will review her attendance in two weeks. If her prompt attendance is satisfactory, he will review again in 30 days. He understands that all staff may have reasonable cause to be a few minutes late on rare occasions, and he tells Robin she may discuss any special circumstances with him directly. Chris then offers the employee assistance program to help robin work through her personal issues and refers her to work-life programs for childcare resources. Chris follows up this meeting in writing.

WHAT IS ABSENTEEISM?

Absenteeism is a habitual pattern of absence from a duty or obligation. Absenteeism means an individual remain absent without any information or intimation to his superior. Whether it is one day or more, the issue of absenteeism and unscheduled leave has always been of importance to businesses interested in their bottom line. Absenteeism can occur at mass level also. Normally, 6–8 % absenteeism is found in all industry. If it beyond consecutively, then the matter is serious.

Absence from the duty in the following cases—should be included in absenteeism.

- If employee is on CL/SL/EL—should be include in absenteeism
- If employee in on Official Duty—should be include in absenteeism
- Without Pay—should be include in absenteeism

Absenteeism in India

Absenteeism in Indian industries is not a new phenomenon. It is the manifestation of a decision by employees not to present themselves at their place of work, at a time when it is planned by the management that they should be in attendance. Many research reports reveal that there has been a phenomenal increase in absenteeism in some industrial sectors. The absenteeism becomes a problem to organizational management particularly when employees absent from their work environment without giving sufficient notice and by justifying their stand by furnishing fake reasons.

The reasons for absenteeism are many. The factors contributing to absenteeism from work includes individual and environmental factors. These consists of sickness, accidents, occupational diseases, poor production planning (flow of work), bad working conditions and inadequate welfare conditions, lack of trained labourers, insecurity in employment, process, rigid control system, lack of supervisory support, lack of interest, lack of cohesive and cordial culture and so on. The individual reasons may vary from organization to organization depending upon the organizational climate, employee's attitude and influence of external organizational factors (market forces, social activities that influence the industrial culture prevailing in geographical zone etc.).

For Blue Collar Employees:

Absenteeism means—absence from his duty or work. This could be in the form of:

- **Unauthorized absenteeism**—without any information or intimation to his line manager or supervisor.
- **Authorized absenteeism**—with information or intimation to his line manger or supervisor by taking prior leave applications.
- **Absenteeism on the work:** It is caused in both conditions where work could not be completed in that particular day as per the organization's target which was supposed to be completed within the time frame specified.

For White Collar Employees:

- Unauthorized absenteeism is same
- Authorized absenteeism can be called as on leave because maximum white collar employees can perform or complete his work on any other day also.
- As far as legal is concerned, only unauthorized absenteeism shall be counted or as per standing order of the company.

LEAVE APPLICATION FORM	
Name:	Designation:
Department:	No of days:
	From:
	To:
Reason	Total no of days
Leave sanctioned	Leave not sanctioned
Signature of the applicant	Date:
Signature of the authorized signatory	Date:

Fig. 4.6: Sample leave application

Cost of Absenteeism

Absenteeism is detrimental to any organization irrespective of any industry. The cost of absenteeism can be evaluated by using the following formula:

Calculation about Annual Cost of Absenteeism per year in an organization is given as

__________ × __________ = __________

(# work days lost per year) * (cost per work day) = (Annual cost)

For example, there are 180 employees are working in an organization, where on an average 1 employee remain 3 time absent in a year. Employee's average salary is 170 per day.

Total employees = 180

Average work days lost per year = 180 (employees) * 3 (days in year) = 540 days

Average salary per employee = 170

Annual cost of absenteeism per year = 540 days * 170 (salary per day) = Rs 91800

To calculate an organization's absenteeism rate the following approach can be suggested:	
a. Number of employees in the company/department:	100
b. Average monthly salary per person (or expected pay):	\$3,200
c. Benefits (estimated 35% of monthly salary):	\$1,120
d. Total monthly compensation:	\$4,320
e. Average number of workdays missed in the month:	4
Total cost of absenteeism annually:	\$691,200
Average cost of absenteeism per day:	\$1,899

Guidelines for Absenteeism Management

There are two types of absenteeism, each of which requires a different type of approach.

1. **Innocent Absenteeism:** Innocent absenteeism refers to employees who are absent for reasons beyond their control; like sickness and injury. Innocent absenteeism is not culpable which means that it is blameless. In a labour relations context this means that it cannot be remedied or treated by disciplinary measures.
2. **Culpable Absenteeism:** Culpable absenteeism refers to employees who are absent without authorization for reasons which are within their control. For instance, an employee who is on sick leave even though he/she is not sick, and it can be proven that the employee was not sick, is guilty of culpable absenteeism. To be culpable is to be blameworthy. In a labour relations context this means that progressive discipline can be applied.

For the large majority of employees, absenteeism is legitimate, innocent absenteeism which occurs infrequently. Procedures for disciplinary action apply only to culpable absenteeism. Many organizations take the view that through the process of individual absentee counseling and treatment, the majority of employees will overcome their problems and return to an acceptable level of regular attendance.

Managing absenteeism through time keeping and monitoring employee movements

Inputs of time keeping

Employee code number: Whenever an employee joins the organizations as a trainee; probation; permanent he/she is allotted a code No. _________ which shall be referred in all the official transactions in addition to his name.

Shift working: All the operations has a system of general shift working for 8 hours in a day, each area has got separate timings match to their functional requirements. The time will be notified to the employee concern at their respite departments.

Attendance register: At all the departments they should maintain a attendance register, for all the employees for marking attendance. The personnel concerned shall comply with all statutory formalities and forward the particulars after closing the wage period to HRD corporate for necessary payment of salary.

Weekly off: As per statutory obligations, that whenever an employee works for six days at a stretch he/she is entitled for a rest day i.e. 7th day otherwise calls weekly of. In case of emergency operations personnel could work continuously however in any case it should not be postponed beyond the 10th day.

Additional duty: Due to exigencies of work load or to take care of absenteeism, the office or operations might engage employee beyond the scheduled employee hours, whenever employees are advised to work additional duty due to production schedule or any other valid reasons, such employee shall be given compensatory off in some other working day.

Employee movement passes/punch cards: Whenever an employee intends to leave the premises or sent on official work before schedule ending or the shift, he/she shall be allowed in writing to leave the premises by the authorized official, the same is called employee movement pass/punch cards.

Exhibit: Policy Manual: Role of the Attendance System for Managing Absenteeism

Attendance should be marked daily according to the rules prescribed from time to time for the organization. Employees who are required to sign the attendance register should be made to mark the time of reporting for duty. Employee who is required to punch time card can also get cards punched in the time clock at the time of reporting for duty and at the time of leaving duty. All employees should be made to report to their place of work punctually at the specified time in the manner directed by the management from time to time.

No employee should be accepted on duty if he is late by more than 10 minutes on any day or comes late for more than 3 times in a calendar month and he may be shut for that day and treated as absent with consequent deductions of salary as per the provisions of the payment of wages Act 1936 under section 9. Expect in those case where in the interest of the work he has been allowed to work under written permission of an authority not below the cadre as notified/authorized by the management from time to time.

An employee who is absent from duty without prior or post factor sanctioned leave shall be liable for deduction of wages for the period of his absence in accordance with the provisions of the payment of wages for the period of his absence in accordance with the provisions of the payment of wages Act 1936 under section 9.

If an employee, although present in his place of work fails to do his assigned work or part thereof and/or refuses to carry out his work or part thereof slows down the place of work, he/she shall be deemed to be treated as absent for the whole day.

Identity badge: Every employee excluding (Casual/Temporary/Apprentice) will be issued an Identity Badge or other means of identifications.

Every employee shall take utmost care to ensure against loss or theft of the Identity Badge. Loss or theft of the Badge shall be immediately notified in writing to the issuing authority. Replacement of Badge shall be at employee expenses as may be specified by the management. Employee shall be also responsible for obtaining fresh badge, where the old one becomes indisputable. Every employee shall wear Identity Badge in a conspicuous position on his dress and hold the same in his custody while on duty as directed by the management from time to time. The Badge shall be shown on demand to the security personnel or any other authorized officials by the management.

LEAVE CARD RECORD

		Leave		
Employee Code: ________		EL	CL	SL
Name: ________	Eligibility as on 1/1/20			
Designation ________	Balance B/F			
Date of Joining: ________	Total Eligibility			
Date of Confirm: ________				

		Leave Period		Earned Leave		Casual Leave				Spl Occasion Leave				
S. no.	Reason of Leave	From	To	Availed	Balance	Availed	Balance	Availed	Balance	Sick Leave	LWP	Employee Signature	Approval (Immediate Senior)	Signature of HR

Fig. 4.7: Sample leave card record

Identifying Excessive Absenteeism

Attendance records should be reviewed regularly to be sure that an employee's sick-leave days are excessive compared to other employees. If a supervisor suspects that an employee is excessively absent, this can be confirmed through reviewing the attendance records.

If all indications show that an employee is excessively absent, the next step is to gather as much information as possible in order to get a clearer picture of the situation. The employees' files should be reviewed and the employee's immediate supervisor should document all available information on the particular employee's history.

Exhibit: Absenteeism and Shift Duty Tracking: The Coca Cola Way

Many organizations like Hindustan Coca Cola Beverages Pvt Ltd. use their shifting schedules for managing absenteeism. Any leaves taken by the employees are reflected in the "Employee Shift" databases and necessary actions are taken by the HR department for replacement and deputation of a worker for a particular work. At the Bidadi plant in Bangalore, the production is done in four work shifts. These are as follows:

Name of the Shift	Timings	Breaks/Recess
A Shift	7 hrs to 15 hrs	Breakfast: 8–8.30 am; Tea: 10.30–10.45 am, Lunch Break: 12.30–14.00 (on rotation basis)
B Shift	15 hrs to 23 hrs	Tea: 16.00–16.15; Dinner: 19.30–21.00 (on rotation basis)
C Shift	23 hrs to 7 hrs	Snacks fast: 24.00–24.30; Tea: 5–5.30 am
General Shift	9 hrs 18 hrs	Lunch: 13.30–14.00 hrs

(Courtesy: Hindustan Coca Cola Beverages Pvt. Ltd., Bidadi Plant, Bangalore.)

Managing Absenteeism: Organizational Approaches

Individual communication: After all available information has been gathered, the supervisor should individually meet with each employee whom has been identified as having higher than average or questionable (or pattern) absences. This first meeting should be used to bring concerns regarding attendance to the employee's attention. It is also an opportunity to discuss with the employee, in some depth, the causes of his or her attendance problem and possible steps he or she can take to remedy or control the absences. Employee's responses in this regard should be noted carefully. The HR department may take the initiative to formally inform the employees with high absenteeism records, either communicating officially or through their respective supervisors.

Proof of illness: Sometimes it is helpful in counseling employees with excessive innocent or culpable absenteeism to inquire or verify the nature and reasons of their absence. HR department should take care in terms of verifying the cause of absence by making it mandatory to submit proof of illness from concerned and recognized medical authorities as and whenever required.

Counseling innocent absenteeism: Innocent absenteeism is not blameworthy and therefore disciplinary action is not justified. It is obviously unfair to punish someone for conduct which is beyond his/her control. Absenteeism, no matter what the cause, imposes losses on the employer who is also not at fault. The damage suffered by the employer must be weighed against the employee's right to be sick. The procedure an employer may take for innocent absenteeism is as follows:

1. Initial counseling(s)
2. Written counseling(s)
3. Reduction(s) of hours and/or job reclassification
4. Discharge

Initial counseling: Presuming that supervisors have communicated attendance expectations generally and have already identified an employee as a problem, it is essential that supervisors should now continue to monitor the effect of these efforts on the employee's attendance. If the absences are intermittent, focus should be given on meeting the employee each time he/she returns to work. If absence is prolonged, managers should keep in touch with the employee regularly and stay updated on the status of his/her condition.

Written counseling: If the absences persist, managers should meet with the employee formally and provide him/her with a letter of concern. If the absenteeism still continues to persist then the employee should be given a second letter of concern during another formal meeting. This letter would be stronger worded in that it would warn the employee that unless attendance improves, termination may be necessary.

Reduction(s) of hours and/or job reclassification in case of medical reasons: In case of identification of any serious medical problems, the employee may be given the option to reduce his/her hours to better fit his/her personal circumstances. If the nature of the illness or injury is such that the employee is unable to fulfil the requirements of his/her job, but could for example benefit from modified work, counsel the employee to bid on jobs of such type if they become available.

Discharge: Only when all the previously noted needs and conditions have been met and everything has been done to accommodate the employee can termination be considered. An arbitrator would consider the following in ruling on an innocent absenteeism dismissal case.

Corrective Actions for Culpable Absenteeism

As already indicated, culpable absenteeism consists of absences where it can be demonstrated that the employee is not actually ill and is able to improve his/her attendance. Presuming that managers have communicated attendance expectations generally, have identified the employee as a problem, have met with him/her as part of the attendance program, made individual recommendations on the specific absenteeism known and have offered counseling as appropriate, with no improvement despite the positive efforts, disciplinary procedures may be appropriate.

The procedures for corrective/progressive discipline for culpable absenteeism are generally the same as for other progressive discipline problems. The discipline should not be prejudicial in any way. The general procedure is as follows: [Utilizing counseling memorandum]

- Initial Warning(s)
- Written Warning(s)
- Suspension(s)
- Discharge

Attendance Management Programs

An attendance management program can be split into three basic parts:

1. Development of information/communication systems
2. Information testing
3. Taking appropriate group action

Leave Management Systems: Many organizations have perceived the importance of institutionalizing leave management systems/softwares in their organizations. An illustration of such software is given below:

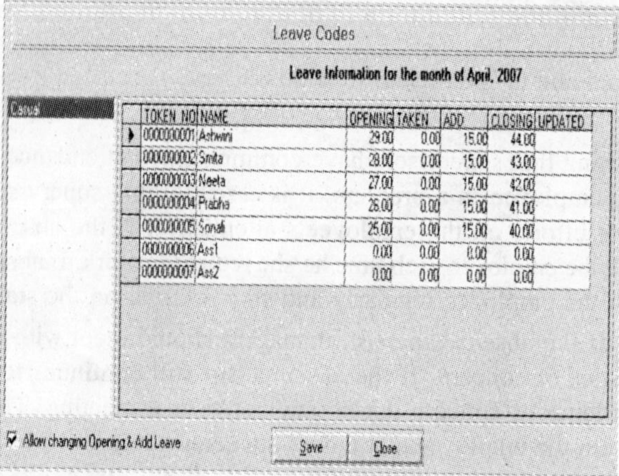

TOKEN NO	NAME	OPENING	TAKEN	ADD	CLOSING	UPDATED
0000000001	Ashwini	29.00	0.00	15.00	44.00	
0000000002	Smita	28.00	0.00	15.00	43.00	
0000000003	Neeta	27.00	0.00	15.00	42.00	
0000000004	Prabha	26.00	0.00	15.00	41.00	
0000000005	Sonali	25.00	0.00	15.00	40.00	
0000000006	Ass1	0.00	0.00	0.00	0.00	
0000000007	Ass2	0.00	0.00	0.00	0.00	

Fig. 4.8: Leave management software

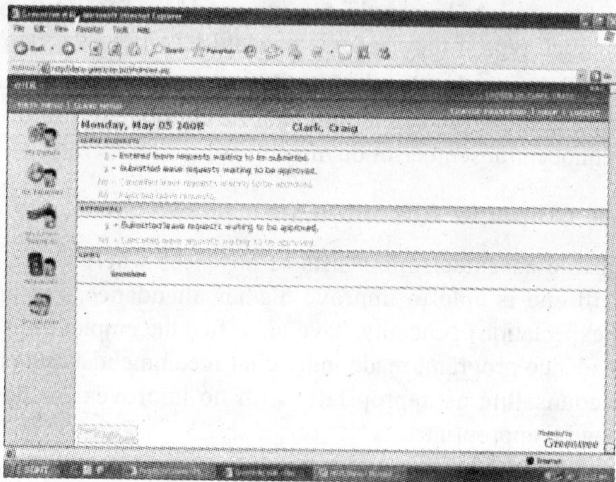

Fig. 4.9: Illustration of a leave management system

Arbo-Planning: ArboPlanning is a new trend emerging in today's HRM in terms of battling absenteeism due to sickness. Now-a-days in European countries like Holland, employers have to pay up to a maximum of 2 years of wages if an employee is unable to work. More and more employers think that if an employee remains sick, their managers are responsible for a "**Back to work program**".

About ArboPlanning

- Founded in 2000
- Working for 77 companies
- The companies have +/– 70000 employees, 90% working in health care (2004) Operating in the whole of Holland
- 2 back offices
- Doctors appointments on the location of the client

ArboPlanning is a fast growing certified ARBO service and is part of the **MetaPlanning Group**. The group operates independently from insurance companies, banks and other conglomerates. Among its clients there are hospitals, other health care organizations and also International call centers, service organizations and a chain of fashion shops.

Because the ArboPlanning approach is universal it can also be implemented in other countries with a different juridical system where companies have the same problems with absenteeism due to sickness. ArboPlanning can advise his clients about setting up an absenteeism policy by doing a quick scan on topics like health, safety and well being in the company, and helps the client with achieving the goal of limiting the risks and diminishing the costs of absenteeism due to sickness.

In the Netherlands ArboPlanning started working according to the guidelines given by the Gatekeepers law and the ARBO rules. There is a meticulous medical examination at the 5th week of sickness and a report on the possibilities for any form of work is obtained. (If the employee is fit to do his or her own jobs a notice of total work capability will be send). The employer and the employee can try to find alternatives inside the company or, if that is not a possibility, discuss outplacement. In all this, ArboPlanning acts as an adviser, not only on medical issues but also on reorganization issues. The consultant can offer an absenteeism coach, who will train the manager in dealing with all the issues.

ATTRITION AND EMPLOYEE RETENTION IN ORGANIZATIONS

Theme Reading: Managing Attrition in the Indian Information Technology Industry

The year 2004–2005 was another successful year for the Information Technology (IT) industry in India with total software and services revenues recording a high of $22 billion for the year 2004–2005. The employee base also showed a whopping increase to cross the one million mark in the year 2005. However, despite the growth in the overall employee base, companies were struggling to retain their existing employees. Analysts observed that managing attrition in the industry was important because skilled professionals formed the crux of this knowledge-intensive industry. What's more, the cost of recruitment and training was a huge expense for most IT firms.

Table 4.1: Revenue Distribution of Nasscom Member Firms (n = 405) by Geographic Region, in 1997

Region	*Revenue ($M)*	*Number*
Mumbai	539.8	86
Bangalore	323.6	84
New Delhi	152.9	72
Noida and Gurgaon	132.9	23
Chennai	130.9	34
Hyderabad	62	21
Other	115.3	85

(*Source: CMU Software dataset*)

Table 4.2: Industry Concentration: Computer Software

Industry group	***No. of firms***	***Total assets (millions of rupees)***	***Firms with asset size more than Rs. 300 mil***	***Total revenue (millions of rupees)***	***Firms with more than Rs. 500 mil in revenue***	***Industry revenue concentration of 4 largest firms***
Custom Programming	31	3224	2	6240.3	5	72.3%
Prepackaged Software	26	3228	6	5070.0	7	39.6%
Custom Designing	11	1562	3	2596.0	3	32.1%
Core Industry	68	8114	11	13906.3	15	53.4%

(Source: Chakraborti, C., Dutta, D.,(2006): "Indian Software Industry: Growth Patterns, Constraints and Government")

Initiatives: Handling the menace of attrition was therefore very important to IT companies. Attrition affected the quality of service and also led to higher Training and Development expenditure, affecting the overall performance of the organization. IT companies in India were taking steps to counter the rising levels of attrition.

Companies were beginning to realize the importance of factors other than salary with which to motivate their employees to stay. A healthy work environment, continuous employee learning, work-life balance, recognition and corporate brand building were some of the key initiatives taken up by IT companies in recent years to manage attrition. In 2004, Infosys Technologies Limited devised a policy of taking security deposits from fresh graduates who joined the company at the entry level to discourage them from leaving the company during the training period whereas Wipro Technologies Ltd started a matchmaking service for its employees. The purpose of this service was to help employees chose their life partners within Wipro in the hope that if employees picked spouses from the same company, they could spend more time together, say while traveling/dining etc. thereby improving the work-life balance.

Trends in attrition: Liberalization of the Indian economy in 1991 paved the way for the growth of the IT industry. The most prominent players in the Indian IT industry by the mid-1990s were Tata Consultancy Services (TCS), Infosys, Wipro, Satyam Computer Services Limited (Satyam), Polaris Software Labs (Polaris), and Patni Computer Systems Limited (Patni). By 1995 there was a new trend of 'poaching' of employees by rival IT firms. Poaching necessarily meant luring skilled employees of a rival company by offering better pay and fringe benefits. Over the years, more and more software professionals were also immigrating to foreign countries, particularly to the US. By late 1998, the Y2K problem was hanging over companies across the globe and software services from Indian IT service companies were increasingly in demand. In 1999, of the total number of H1-B visas given to foreign workers by the US, half were to Indian IT professionals. The average starting yearly salary in computer software jobs, in that year was $ 60,000 - nearly 10 times the average salary for a computer professional in a comparable job in India. The employee turnover in 1999–2000 in Indian IT companies was around 15–20% with the cost of replacing an employee running at over 120% of the salary per employee.

Exhibit: Major Problems for Indian Software Firms

Problem	Export	Domestic
Manpower shortage/skills	57	32
Employee attrition	44	27
Physical infrastructure	12	12
Commercial infrastructure	24	17
Quality certification	11	6
Finance/capital	20	14
Marketing access	42	17
Lack off government support	10	11
Tariffs and other barriers	11	8

Note: *The firms were asked to indicate their top three problems.*

(*Source*: *CMU Software dataset — CMU Survey of Indian Software Industry. N = 104*)

Combating attrition: Experts are of the view that since the IT industry thrives on individuals with a vital knowledge base, the industry should help employees develop their knowledge base further in addition to giving them appropriate monetary and other compensation in order to retain talent. Combating attrition involves management of people and a thorough understanding of the human psyche. High levels of employee turnover occur due to a combination of various workplace environment influences and personal choices made by the employees. In 2003, a National Association of Software and Service Companies (NASSCOM) survey identified some of the major drivers of attrition.

Recruitment: Effective recruitment strategies can help organizations in employee retention. Companies following the traditional methods of recruitment observed that a major drawback of the traditional selection processes was either a poor response or a mismatch between company goals and individuals' expectations.

Compensation and rewards: Incentives to employees play a vital role in motivating and retaining them in the organization. Compensation and rewards in the IT industry have long included a basic pay component along with a bonus pay when the company made higher profits. Later firms initiated performance based pay that rewarded the employee based on his contribution to the overall company profits.

Table 4.3: Software Professionals: Comparative Salaries, 1997

Designation	***United States ($ per annum)***	***India ($ per annum)***
Programmer	32,500 — 39,000	2,200 — 2,900
System Analyst	46,000 — 57,500	8,200 — 10,700
Programmer Analyst	39,000 — 50,000	5,400 — 7,000
Network Administrator	36,000 — 55,000	15,700 — 19,200
Database Administrator	54,000 — 67,500	15,700 — 19,200
Help—desk Support Technician	25,000 — 35,000	5,400 — 7,000
Software Developer	49,000 — 67,500	15,700 — 19,200

Note: *Converted at exchange rate of Rs. 41.50/US$.*

(Source: INFAC, Mumbai)

Organization Culture: Studies and surveys analyzing the psyche of the employee have found that the work environment has a major impact on the behaviour of an employee. An effective retention strategy would involve acknowledging the employee as the internal customer and aligning the organizational strategies with employee needs and wants.

Work Life Balance: Employees differentiate a good employer from any other employer through the feeling of 'wellbeing' that is generated at the workplace. A balance between work and the personal goals and wants of an employee contributes positively to the retention of employees.

Learning and Growth: The dynamic nature of technology requires the IT industry to upgrade its operations frequently. So, another way to retain employees is to help them update their knowledge from time to time through training programs.

Leadership: Surveys also identified poor leadership as one of the reasons for employee attrition. It was observed that leaders incapable of motivating and guiding employees pushed employees to change jobs frequently. Wipro initiated the 'Wipro Leaders' qualities survey in 1992.

Emerging Challenges: By 2004, most Indian IT companies started positioning themselves as global firms. Many companies already had offices in foreign countries. For instance, Infosys had development centres in Canada, China and the Czech Republic.

Employee Turnover

Turnover is the process in which employees leave the organization and have to be replaced. Many organizations have found that turnover is a costly problem. The various types of turnover are as follows:

Types of Turnover	Hallmarks
Involuntary	Terminations for poor performance or work rule violations
Voluntary	Employee leaves by choice
Functional	Lower performing or disruptive employees leave the organization
Dysfunctional	Key individuals and high performers leave at critical times
Uncontrollable	Occurs for reasons outside the impact of the employer
Controllable	Occurs due to factors that could be influenced by the employer like: poor QWL, lack of training and development, career growth etc.

Definition of Attrition

Attrition measures the amount of recurring revenue lost during a particular time frame, expressed on a monthly/annualized basis. Attrition can be measured in many different ways. The nomenclature used to describe the measurement tool and methodology can vary widely. Gross attrition is the absolute of employee or human capital losses without the inclusion of any offset or reduction activity such as price increases, acquisition or other "add backs" to the employee or human capital base. Net attrition is the result of offsetting "like employee" gains from the gross attrition losses.

Attrition Rate

The attrition rate has always been a sensitive issue for all organizations. Calculating employee turnover rate is not that simple as it seems to be. No common formula can be used by all the organizations. A formula had to be devised keeping in view the nature of the business and different job functions. There is no standard formula to calculate the attrition rate of an organization. This is because of certain factors as:

- Many firms may not include attrition of freshers who leave because of higher studies or within three months of joining.
- In some cases, attrition of poor performers may also not be treated as attrition.

Calculating attrition rate Attrition rates can be calculated using a simple formula

Attrition [(No. of attritions x 100)/(Actual Employees + New Joined)] /100.

What makes employees leave their organizations?

Staff attrition (or turnover) and absenteeism represent significant costs to most organizations. Many organizations appear to accept them as part of the cost of doing business—a sign of increasing job mobility and decreasing staff loyalty perhaps, a matter to be regretted but just 'one of those things.' They add a sum in their budgets for 'temp staff' and 'recruitment' and forget about it. Employees do not leave an organization without any significant reason. There are certain circumstances that lead to their leaving the organization. The most common reasons can be as follows:

Job is not what the employee expected to be: Sometimes the job responsibilities don't come out to be same as expected by the candidates. Unexpected job responsibilities lead to job dissatisfaction.

Job and person mismatch: A candidate may be fit to do a certain type of job which matches his personality. If he is given a job which mismatches his personality, then he won't be able to perform it well and will try to find out reasons to leave the job.

No growth opportunities: No or less learning and growth opportunities in the current job will make candidate's job and career stagnant.

Lack of appreciation: If the work is not appreciated by the supervisor, the employee feels demotivated and loses interest in job.

Lack of trust and support in coworkers, seniors and management: Trust is the most important factor that is required for an individual to stay in the job. Non-supportive coworkers, seniors and management can make office environment unfriendly and difficult to work in.

Stress from overwork and work life imbalance: Job stress can lead to work life imbalance which ultimately many times lead to employee leaving the organization.

Compensation: Better compensation packages being offered by other companies may attract employees towards themselves.

New job offer: An attractive job offer which an employee thinks is good for him with respect to job responsibility, compensation, growth and learning etc. can lead an employee to leave the organization.

Key Attrition Factors

- Inability to use ones' competencies
- Lack of challenge
- Boss and his management style
- Lack of scope for growth in terms of salary, status and other factors
- Lack of role clarity
- Job stress or role stress
- Lack of independence or freedom and autonomy
- Lack of excitement and innovation in the job.

Fig. 4.10: Key Attrition Factors

(Courtesy: Rao, T.V., 2006: "Old pillars of people management", Indian Management, vol. 45, issue: 6, p. 79)

Exhibit: Wake up Call

(*Courtesy: "Are your employees leaving you?", The Economic Times, 7th January, 2008, p. 8*)

- Textile, handicraft marine and leather industries are among the worst affected by attrition problems.
- The textile sector (Rs. 75,000 crore) faces estimated 10 lakh job losses. Layoffs in the seafood processing industry could cross 50,000 in this year.
- Training has emerged as the most effective solution to tackle this problem.

Attrition Rates in Asia

In Asia, organizations faced an overall attrition rate of 16% in 2005. Attrition rate was 14% in 2004 and 10% in 2003.

According to Hewitt's Attrition and Retention Study Asia Pacific 2006, the no.1 reason for this growing attrition rate is compensation unfairness. 21% of the organizations who took part in the survey said that their employee left the organization because they got offers from other organizations offering better pay packages. The no. 2 reason was less growth opportunities and no. 3 reason was role stagnation. The study also revealed that the top retention strategy being used by the organizations in Asia was to pay above the industry standards, providing opportunities to employees to learn new skills, and provide work life balance.

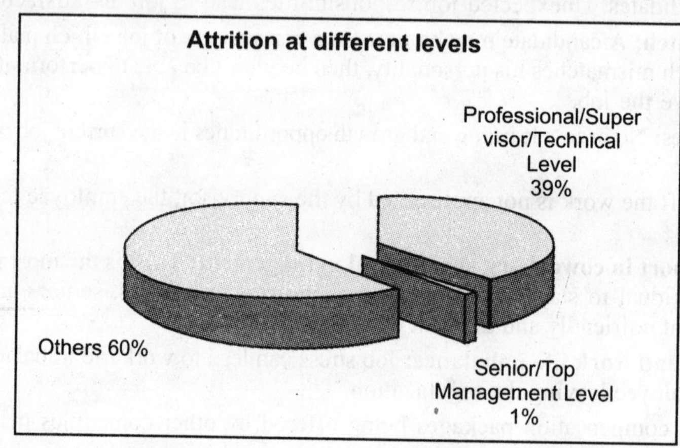

Fig. 4.11: Attrition at different levels (according to Hewitt's attrition and retention study Asia Pacific, 2006)

According to the employees, attrition at the professional/supervisor/technical level was the highest (39%) and lowest at the senior/top management level (1% approximately).

Theme Reading: Attrition in India

In India, the average attrition rate in the BPO sector is approximately 30–35 per cent. It is true that this is far less than the prevalent attrition rate in the US market (around 70 per cent), but the challenge continues to be greater considering the recent growth of the industry in the country. The US BPO sector is estimated to be somewhere around three decades old. Keeping low attrition levels is a major challenge as the demand outstrips the supply of good agents by a big margin. Further, the salary growth plan for each employee is not well-defined. All this only encourages poaching by other companies who can offer a higher salary. An attrition rate in call (or contact) centres has become legendary. Indeed, the attrition rates in some Indian call centres now reach 80%. This is an extreme figure but the average attrition rates in Indian call centres are up around 30–40%.

The attrition rate has crossed 20 per cent in the manufacturing sector while the services sector is facing 40 per cent attrition, according to an ASSOCHAM study. The ASSOCHAM Business Barometer Survey on "Attrition Problem in a Growing Economy" revealed that maximum attrition is taking place among employees in the age group of 26–30 years, while those with an experience of 2–4 years were job-hopping the most, the survey covering 160 HR heads noted. The survey found that women employees were less prone to job changing compared to men as for every 10 men leaving jobs there were only two women crossing over.

Table 4.4: Attrition Rates (Source-Times News, New York)

Countries	***Attrition Rates***
US	42%
Australia	29%
Europe	24%
India	18%
Global Average	24%

The following figure depicts the attrition rates in different sectors in India:

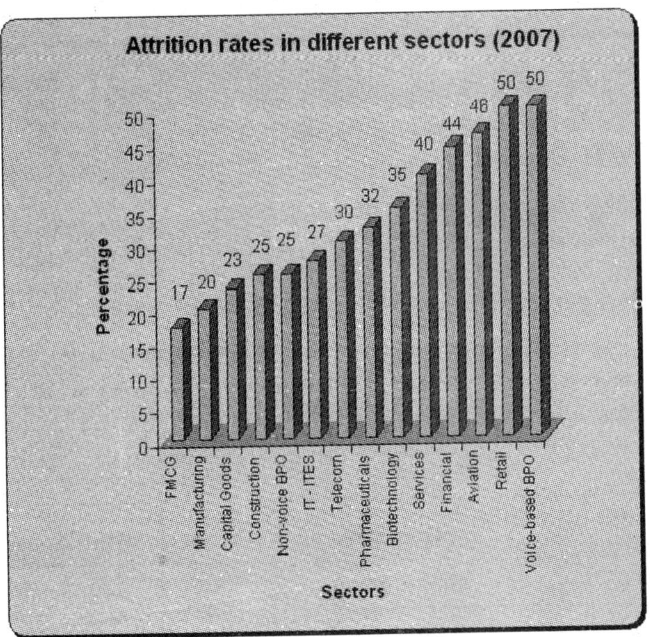

Fig 4.12: Attrition rates in different sectors in India (2007)

Attrition Rates in Indian FMCG Sector

The Indian FMCG sector demonstrated a steady rise in the attrition rate over the past three years. The attrition rate was 9.8 % in 2004. It moved up to 10.8% in 2005. In 2006, the attrition rate became 17%. The major companies in FMCG sector are Asian paints, Britannia, Colgate, Cadbury, HLL (HUL), ITC, Marico, Nestle, P&G, Palmolive, Pepsi, Reckitt Benckiser, etc.

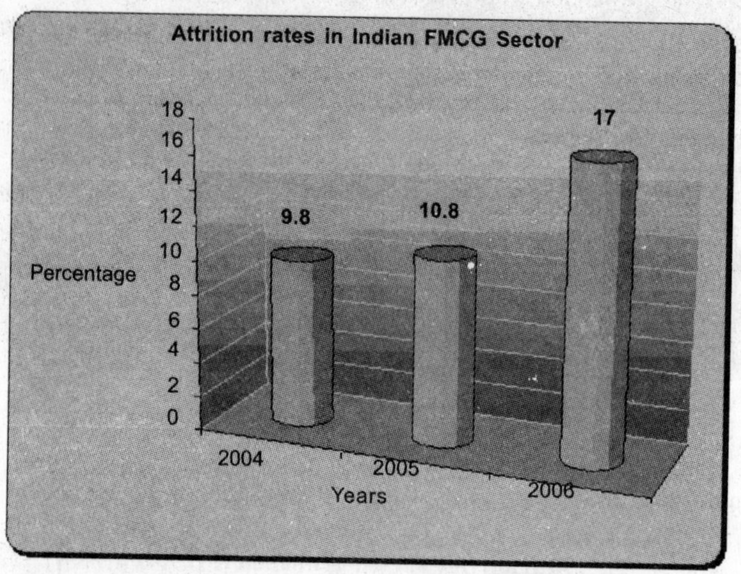

Fig. 4.13: Attrition rates in Indian FMCG sector

Attrition Rates in the IT Sector

Almost every sector in India is facing high rates of attrition these days. A recent study revealed that employees leave either because of compensation reasons or due to better growth opportunities. According to NASSCOM, Indian IT-ITES industry recorded US$ 39.6 billion in revenues in 2006–07. The revenue of US$ 49–50 billion has been projected in 2007–08 at a growth rate of 24–27 per cent. The IT industry's contribution to GDP was 4.8 per cent in 2005–06. Though the IT/ITES sector is booming, it is constantly facing high attrition rates of 25%–30%. Even the big brands are also facing the same problem. Below are the details of attrition rates of various players in IT sector. According to the survey conducted by BES and Data Quest, Sierra Atlantic recorded highest attrition rate (29%) followed by Kanbay with 25% and Accel Frontline with 20 per cent.

Rank	Company	Attrition rate (FY 06)
1	Sierra Atlantic	29%
2	Kanbay	25%
3	Accel Frontline	20%
4	Sasken	19%

5	Nucleus	18%
6	Geometric	18%
7	Flextronics	18%
8	HCL Infosys	16%
9	Induslogic	16%
10	NIIT Technologies	15%
11	Cybage	15%
12	Wipro	13%
13	Hexaware	13%
14	Computer Sciences Corp	12%
15	Infosys	10%
16	TCS	9%
17	Interra	9%
18	RMSI	8%
19	Cadence	8%
20	Aztecsoft	6%

**BES Survey 2006 Source: DQ-IDC*

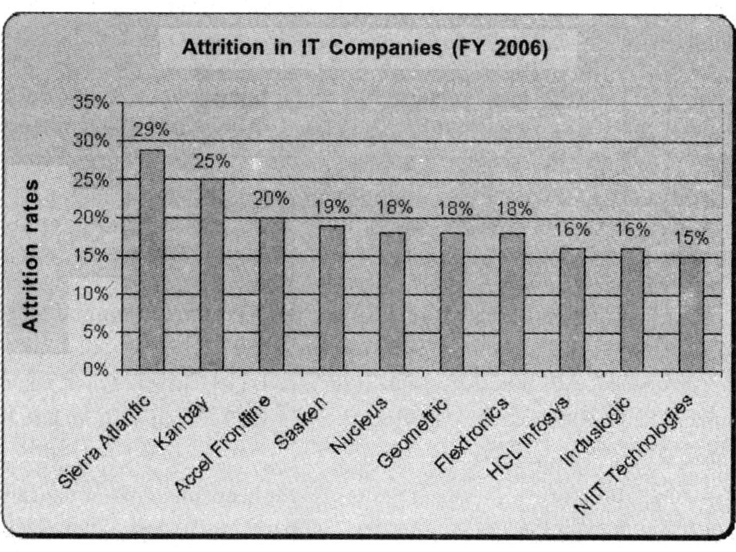

Fig. 4.14: Attrition in IT companies (FY 2006)

How to calculate attrition rate?

The formula and correct logic behind calculation of **ATTRITION RATE** could be depicted as:

[(No. of attritions x 100)/(Actual Employees + New Joined)] /100.

Illustration 1

Actual employees (opening BAL)	No. of people left (attritions)	No. of employees joined	Total employees (current headcount)
150	20	25	155

Solution:

So according to the formula, (attrition can be depicted as [(20 × 100)/(150 + 25)]/100; which comes to 0.1142 i.e. 11%.

Now, as the company had 150 employees previously and now 25 had joined so it employee strength becomes 150 + 25 = 175

Now, if we calculate 11.42% of 175 i.e. 175 × 0.1142 = 20

This clearly shows that 175 – 20 = 155, which is the current headcount and at the same time it can be said that the attrition is 11.42% (which shows that 20 employees out of 150 and 25 more joined which makes count to 175).

Thus it can be said that, in terms of numbers, attrition rate is calculated as "The total number of resigns per month (Whether voluntary or forced) divided by (Total Number of employees at the beginning of the month plus total number of new joiners minus total number of resignations) multiplied by 100".

Illustration 2

The following record shows the information regarding an organization's employees. Calculate the attrition rate using the given information.

Actual employees (opening BAL)	No. of people left (attritions)	No. of employees joined	Total employees (current headcount)
100	50	0	50

Solution:

This is the **special** case where we are considering attritions only keeping into mind that nobody has joined in particular month.

So according to the formula: Attrition is given as [(50 × 100)/(100)]/100; which comes to 0.5 i.e. 50%.

Now as the company had 100 employees previously and now 0 joined so it makes 100 + 0 = 100.

Now if we calculate 50% of 100 i.e. 100 × 0.5 = 50.

This clearly shows that 100 – 50 = 50, which is the current headcount and at the same time we can say that the company's attrition is 50% that shows that the company has lost 50 employees out of 100 and as 0 has joined it makes the count to 50.

If calculating in monetary terms, it includes the following:

1. Costs due to a Person Leaving
2. Recruitment Costs

3. Training Costs
4. Lost Productivity Costs
5. New Hire Costs
6. Lost Sales Costs

Theme Case: Crisis in Nipha Exports

Last week, Rakesh Shah, Director of Kolkata based Nipha Exports, a manufacturer of agricultural tillage tools and cotton processing machines, registered for a paid service on a prominent recruitment portal that allows his company to access CVs of potential candidates to hire, and made a startling discovery, 23 of his middle to senior executives, from the post of the sales manager to the GM Works had posted their CVs on the said portal. While none of them may be leaving anytime soon now, thanks to this revelation, even small exporters like Nipha Exports can no longer sit back and relax. People like Mr. Shah have come to understand that they can no longer afford to take the loyalty of their employees for granted. And after the rupee's appreciation against the dollar and prospects of declining volumes looming large, exporters like Mr. Shah and particularly those exporting engineering goods to the US are doubly cautious about how they could retain their key talents. "With the boom in software and infrastructure, qualified engineers now have alternative career options, unlike before," says Mr. Shah, who is also the Chairman of the Engineering Export Promotion Council (EEPC).

(Courtesy: Vikas Kumar, P. Chatterjee, Sachin, D., Tapash Talukdar,"Are your employees leaving you", The Economic Times, 7th January, 2008, p. 8).

Employee Retention

Retention starts with recruitment. Early departures arise from the wrong recruitment process. Here are a few ways to ensure how to hire the right talent for a particular job.

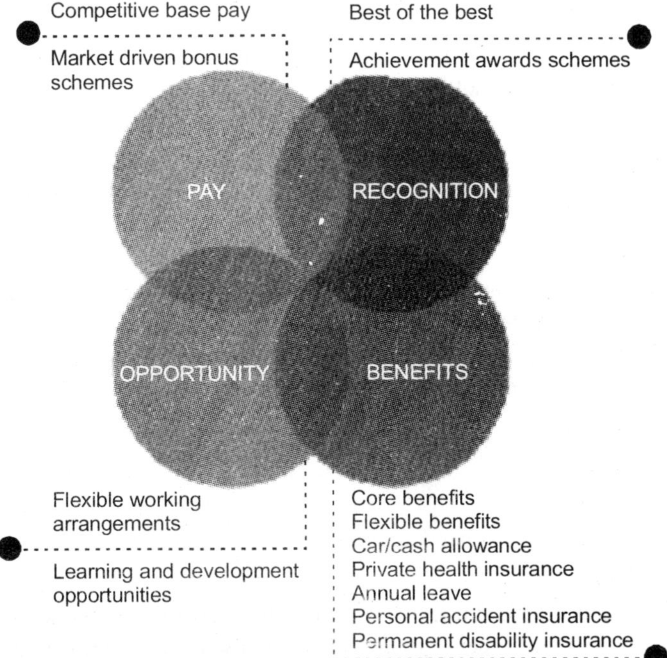

Fig. 4.15: Approach towards employee retention

Hiring appropriate candidates: Hire candidates who are actually suitable for the job. For this the employer should understand the job requirements clearly. Don't hire under qualified or clearly overqualified candidates.

Providing realistic job preview at the time of hiring: Mostly employees leave an organization because they are given the real picture of their job responsibilities at the time of joining. Attrition rate can be reduced if a right person is hired for a right job. Realistic preview of the job responsibilities can be given to the employment seekers by various methods like discussions, trial periods, internships etc.

Clearly discussing what is expected from the employee: Before joining the organization, tell the candidate what is expected from him. Setting wrong expectations or hiding expectations will result in early leaving of employees.

Discussing what the expectations of the employees are: Ask employees what they expect from the organization. Be realistic. If their requirements can be fulfilled only then promise them. Or tell them before hand that their requirements cannot be fulfilled. Don't show them an unrealistic picture.

Ensuring culture fit: Try to judge individual's capability to adapt to the organization's culture. A drastic change in the culture may give a culture shock to the candidate.

Referrals: According to the research, referred candidates stay longer with the organization. There is a fear of hampering the image and reputation of the person who referred the candidate.

Compensation: Compensation constitutes the largest part of the retention process. The employees always have high expectations regarding their compensation packages. Compensation packages vary from industry to industry. So an attractive compensation package plays a critical role in retaining the employees. Compensation includes salary and wages, bonuses, benefits, prerequisites, stock options, bonuses, vacations, etc. While setting up the packages, the following components should be kept in mind:

Growth and career: Growth and development are the integral part of every individual's career. If an employee cannot foresee his path of career development in his current organization, there are chances that he'll leave the organization as soon as he gets an opportunity. The important factors in employee growth that an employee looks for himself are:

- **Work profile:** The work profile on which the employee is working should be in sync with his capabilities. The profile should not be too low or too high.
- **Personal growth and dreams:** Employees responsibilities in the organization should help him achieve his personal goals also. Organizations cannot keep aside the individual goals of employees and foster organizations goals. Employees' priority is to work for themselves and later on comes the organization. If he's not satisfied with his growth, he'll not be able to contribute in organization growth.
- **Training and development:** Employees should be trained and given chance to improve and enhance their skills. Many employers fear that if the employees are well rained, they'll leave the organization for better jobs. Organization should not limit the resources on which organization's success depends. These trainings can be given to improve many skills like:
  - Communications skills
  - Technical skills
  - In-house processes and procedures improvement related skills
  - C or customer satisfaction related skills
  - Special project related skills

Need for such trainings could be recognized from individual performance reviews, individual meetings, employee satisfaction surveys and by being in constant touch with the employees.

Quality of Work Life

The success of any organization depends on how it attracts recruits, motivates, and retains its workforce. Organizations need to be more flexible so that they develop their talented workforce and gain their commitment. Thus, organizations are required to retain employees by addressing their work life issues. The elements that are relevant to an individual's quality of work life include the task, the physical work environment, social environment within the organization, administrative system and relationship between life on and off the job. The basic objectives of a QWL program are improved working conditions for the employee and increase organizational effectiveness. Providing quality work life involves taking care of the following aspects:

- **Occupational health care:** The safe work environment provides the basis for the person to enjoy working. The work should not pose a health hazard for the person. The employer and employee, aware of their risks and rights, could achieve a lot in their mutually beneficial dialogue.
- **Suitable working time:** Organizations are offering flexible work options to their employees wherein employees enjoy flexi-timings for dedicating their efforts at work.
- **Appropriate salary:** The appropriate as well as attractive salary has always been an important factor in retaining employees. Providing employees salary at par with the other counterparts of above that what competitors are paying motivates them to stick with the company for long.

QWL consists of opportunities for active involvement in group working arrangements or problem solving that are of mutual benefit to employees or employers, based on labour management cooperation. People also conceive of QWL as a set of methods, such as autonomous work groups, job enrichment, and high-involvement aimed at boosting the satisfaction and productivity of workers. It requires employee commitment to the organization and an environment in which this commitment can flourish.

Providing quality at work not only reduces attrition but also helps in reduced absenteeism and improved job satisfaction. Not only does QWL contribute to a company's ability to recruit quality people, but also it enhances a company's competitiveness. Common beliefs support the contention that QWL will positively nurture amore flexible, loyal, and motivated workforce, which are essential in determining the company's competitiveness.

Support: Lack of support from management can sometimes serve as a reason for employee retention. Supervisor should support his subordinates in a way so that each one of them is a success. Management should try to focus on its employees and support them not only in their difficult times at work but also through the times of personal crisis. Management can support employees by providing them recognition and appreciation.

Feedback: Managers can also provide valuable feedback to employees and make them feel valued to the organization. The feedback from supervisor helps the employee to feel more responsible, confident and empowered. Top management can also support its employees in their personal crisis by providing personal loans during emergencies, childcare services, employee assistance programs, counseling services, et al. Employers can also support their employees by creating an environment of trust and inculcating the organizational values into employees. Thus employers can support their employees in a number of ways as follows:

- By providing feedback
- By giving recognition and rewards
- By counseling them
- By providing emotional support

Organizational Environment

Maintaining a conducive organizational environment is not about managing retention. It is about managing people. If an organization manages people well, retention will take care of itself. Organizations should focus on managing the work environment to make better use of the available human assets.

People want to work for an organization which provides

- Appreciation for the work done
- Ample opportunities to grow
- A friendly and cooperative environment
- A feeling that the organization is second home to the employee
- Organization environment includes
- Culture
- Values
- Company reputation
- Quality of people in the organization
- Employee development and career growth
- Risk taking
- Leading technologies
- Trust

Types of Environment Employees Seek in an Organization

- **Learning Environment:** It includes continuous learning and improvement of the individual, certifications and provision for higher studies, etc.
- **Support Environment:** Organization can provide support in the form of work life balance. Work life balance includes:
  - Flexible hours
  - Telecommuting
  - Dependent care
  - Alternate work schedules
  - Vacations
  - Wellness

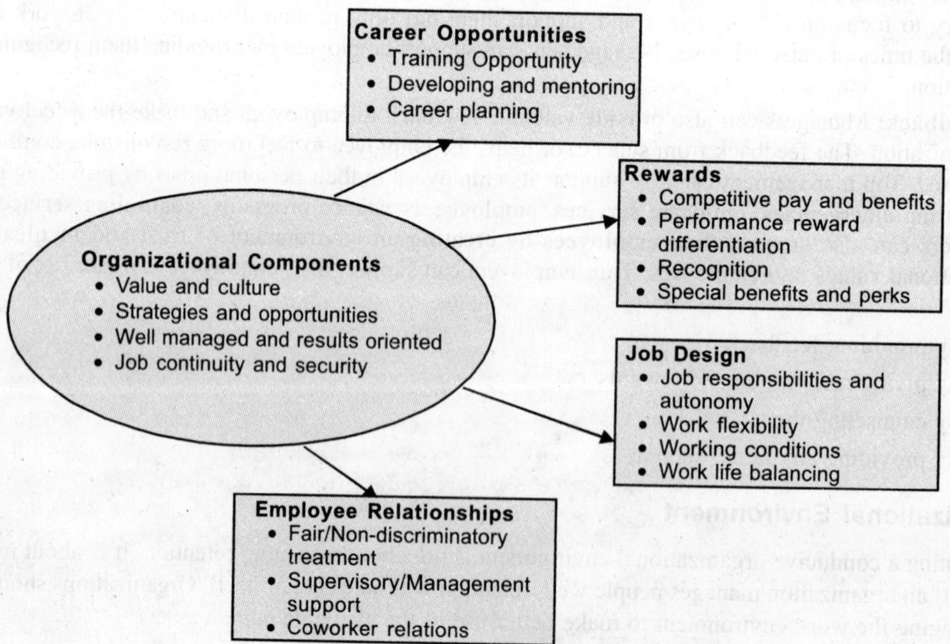

Fig. 4.16: Retention determinants

Work Environment: It includes efficient managers, supportive coworkers, challenging work, involvement in decision-making, clarity of work and responsibilities and recognition. Lack or absence of such environment pushes employees to look for new opportunities. The environment should be such that the employee feels connected to the organization in every respect.

Communication between employee and employer: Communication is a process in which a message is conveyed to the receiver by the sender. The message may be or may not be in a common format or language that both the sender and receiver understand. So there is a need to encode and decode the message in the process. Encoding and decoding also helps in the security of the message. The process of communication is incomplete without the feedback.

Employers and their key drivers to attract and retain talents: an Indian experience

The following table describes the "Key Drivers" in Indian organizations so as to attract and retain talent.

Employers	Key Driver to Attract and Retain Talent
Procter and Gamble India	• Early responsibilities in career • Flexible and transparent organizational culture • Global opportunities through a variety of exposure and diverse experiences • Performance recognition
American Express (India)	• Strong global brand • Value-based environment • Pioneer in many people practices
NTPC	• Learning and growth opportunities • Competitive rewards • Opportunity to grow, learn and implement • Strong social security and employee welfare performance-oriented culture
Johnson and Johnson	• Strong values of trust, caring fairness and respect within the organization • Freedom to operate at work • Early responsibility in career • Training and learning opportunities • Visible, transparent and accessible leaders • Competitive rewards • Innovative HR programs and practices
Glaxo Smith Kline Consumer Healthcare	• Performance-driven Rewards • Its belief in "Growing our own timber" • Comprehensive development and learning programs • Flat organization, where performance could lead to very quick progression • Challenging work context • Competitive rewards • Exhaustive induction and orientation program
Tata Steel	• Organization philosophy and culture • Job stability • Freedom to work and innovate

Contd...

Colgate Palmolive India	• Company brand • Open , transparent and caring organization • Management according to the managing with respect to guiding principles • Training ad development programs • Structured career planning process • Global career opportunities
Wipro	• Company's brand as an employer • Early opportunities for growth • High degree of autonomy • Value compatibility • Innovative people program
Indian Oil Corporation	• Company brand image • Work ethics • Learning and growth opportunities • Challenging work assignments • Growing organization
TCS	• The group brand equity • Strong corporate governance and citizenship • Commitment to learning and development • Best in people practices • Challenging assignments • Opportunity to work with fortune 500 clients

Industry Opinion

"We follow the GE way when identifying Global leaders from a local talent pool." ....Mr. K. Ramkumar, Group Head—HR, ICICI Bank.

THEME CASE: EMPLOYEES RETAINED IN THE IPL WAY

A Bangalore based reputed IT Company which has taken over two firms and is spread across several offices in different locations of the city found a new way to knit together employees—an IPL-style cricket tournament, complete with jazzy team names, auctions and cheerleaders.

"I knew only 10% of my colleagues till 4 weeks ago. Now I know 300, says Arun Menon, global head, services, Bangalore, of 31 infotech. That happened as he took part in Sunday afternoon matches.

For the company's HR division, it was a challenge to make all employees feel they were part of the same organization. The company, which provides IT solutions, has 200 employees each at its Infantry Road and Hosur Road offices, 30–40 each at its Whitefield and Dickenson Road, and another 30–40 at its BPO in HSR Layout. The head count includes 400 employees from two acquired companies—Command International and Datacons. Cricket, the IPL way, it was felt, would integrate all 600 employees. And so followed the matches played over about four weeks.

"Had it been traditional cricket, employees would have created teams among their departments. So we borrowed the IPL idea. This way, no one would know who would be in their team", said Menon. All the better to bond. One of the rules was for every team to include two girls, who had to bat. IPL-like, the teams have cheerleaders too besides a "transfer policy"—a good player can be bought. Eight teams were put up for auction for which there were 16 participants. Once the team names were sold, the players were up for auctions, from about 175 employees. The employees were split into various categories based on their cricket skills, including the women. The owners of each team then bid for the players and created their teams.

From among the 600 programmers, sales management, support administration, HR and BPO employees, 200 were involved. The finals of the cricket matches, titled "Tenacity 2000", happened on Sunday, climaxing a show that spanned two and half months.

M S Chandrashekar, executive VP of the company and "sponsor" for the event said, "About 200 employees signed on, including 25 regular cricketers. Interacting through the matches will help us in understanding what to expect from another person and how to support him or her".

(Courtesy: Phandis, R., (2008): "IPL in our own backyard", Bangalore Mirror, July 14th, 2008, p. 4.)

Theme Reading: Importance of E-SAT Surveys

According to Mr. Rajkumar D., Senior manager-Human resources, Microland, employee retention becomes a daunting task for most organizations as their HR managers often fail to forsee the pitfalls of conducting 360 degree Employee satisfaction (E-SAT) surveys. Many of the HR managers tend to conduct the survey through an online portal or an external agency. However many of them fail to realize that if the program is poorly designed it eventually results into helping their organizations nowhere. Mr. Rajkumar had pointed out five common problems faces by HR managers with respect to this issue. These are:

- E-SAT surveys are done by the HR department only, where most HR managers treat E-SAT more as an administrative activity rather than a serious research contributing to organizational development.
- Most of the E-SAT surveys do not have well-defined objectives.
- Selection of questions in such surveys are quite often misguided
- There might not be an adequate employee participation (that's one of the most common syndromes hampering the research)
- Most often organizations emphasize upon implementing a too high-profile task force to handle the project rather than empowering the team leaders and senior officers.

(Courtesy: Rajkumar D.,: " Eliciting it right", Economic Times, 9th January, 2008, p. 8)

Industry Opinions

"We revamped job composition and offered more responsibility to convince people that the best could rise." .....Ganesh Shermon, Group Vice President (Personnel), Arvind Mills.

"Money is one-third of what is critical for employee retention. An employee is fired by the opportunities offered." ....Jude Coelho, Vice President, Kotak Mahindra Finance.

(Courtesy: Business Today, Jan 7–21, 1996, pp. 127–128)

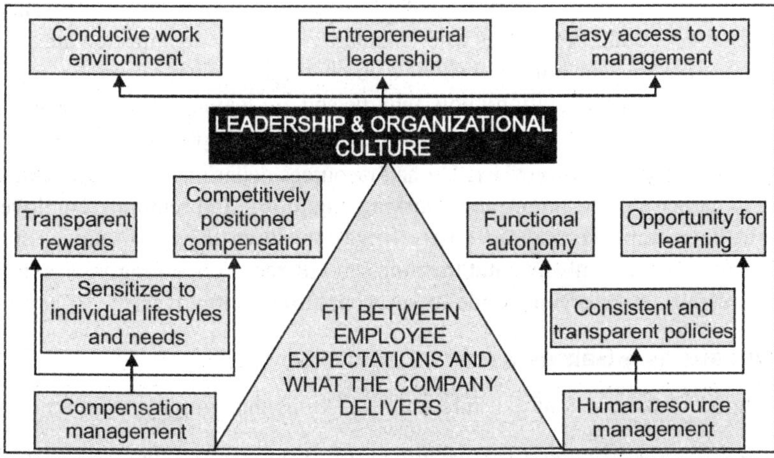

Exhibit: How Kotak Mahindra Retains its Employees (Courtesy: Business Today, Jan 7–1, 1996, p.128)

THEME READING: RETENTION STRATEGIES OF BHARTI AIRTEL

Most companies are worried of attrition amidst rising demand for the talent, today. India's largest mobile operator with over 20,000 employees, Bharti Airtel, is gearing up to the challenge to retain its employees even as companies across sectors are eyeing the telco's highly trained and efficient workforce. Bharti Airtel president and CEO, Mr. Manoj Kohli on this issue commented, "We have a multi-tier leadership development at Airtel. All senior leaders in turn get to further enhance their skills at institutions such as IIMs, ISB, NCR and CCL of the United States. We also have a system in place where our top leaders are coached on employee management by big executives from other sectors who are some of the country's biggest achievers".

According to Mr. Kohli, Airtel had taken this calculated risk of having a huge headcount and the company being such a large player had facilitated it. The company's focus had been to retain their employees not detain them like what most organizations tend to do in the name of employee retention. Even if someone wishes to quit, he/she is send off with a positive heart, which means that these individuals still continue to remain the brand ambassadors of Airtel wherever they go or join. The company is confident with respect to the retention of its top level executives, as it provides them bright career prospects and better offers. Airtel had also outlined the organization's vision beyond 2010 and hence it strongly believes that its employees feel more enriched and have added reasons to stay with the organization.

Mr. Kohli strongly believes that, at Bharti Airtel, the attrition rate is perhaps the lowest when compared to other companies. The company had been doing its best to retain the soul of a small company that makes Airtel the home away from home for its employees. Almost all its promotions for new posts had been from within and as a result the internal talent pool had always been motivated to deliver higher pursuits for the organization.

(Courtesy: Joji Thomas Philips (2208): "Airtel attrition rate lowest among telcos", The Economic Times, 10th July, 2008 issue, p. 6.)

Importance of Exit Interviews in understanding why employees leave organizations

Exit interviews might help organizations to understand why employees leave their organizations or identify factors influencing the dissatisfaction of the employees.

What is an Exit Interview?

An exit interview is typically a meeting between at least one representative from a company's human resources (HR) department and a departing employee. (The departing employee usually has voluntarily resigned vs. getting laid off or fired.) The HR rep might ask the employee questions while taking notes, asks the employee to complete a questionnaire, or both. Employees who voluntarily leave the organization are sources of valuable information. They can give you an honest feedback about the organization, voice complaints, offer a constructive criticism or let the organization know why he/she are leaving. This is most beneficial for the employer as it is an eye-opener and a significant review to see how the company is doing.

What is the purpose of an exit interview: Human resources departments conduct exit interviews (also called exit surveys) to gather data for improving working conditions and retaining employees. However, a hidden purpose is to help employers avoid costly litigation down the road, caused by "disgruntled" employees. In other words, your comments and the notes an HR rep takes during your exit interview might be used against you in court, should you decide to sue your former employer.

Exit Interview Questions - Samples

Listed below are samples of the types of exit interview questions that employers commonly ask departing employees.

- What is your primary reason for leaving?
- Did anything trigger your decision to leave?
- What was most satisfying about your job?
- What was least satisfying about your job?
- What would you change about your job?
- Did your job duties turn out to be as you expected?
- Did you receive enough training to do your job effectively?
- Did you receive adequate support to do your job?
- Did you receive sufficient feedback about your performance between merit reviews?
- Were you satisfied with this company's merit review process?
- Did this company help you to fulfil your career goals?
- Do you have any tips to help us find your replacement?
- What would you improve to make our workplace better?
- Were you happy with your pay, benefits and other incentives?
- What was the quality of the supervision you received?
- What could your immediate supervisor do to improve his or her management style?
- Based on your experience with us, what do you think it takes to succeed at this company?

Exit Interviews: Reality Bites

Understanding why employees leave is almost as important as understanding why they stay. Some would say it is even more important. An employee's real reasons for leaving can be revealed in exit interviews. Interviews that are conducted by the human resources department or other company employees at time of resignation may or may not produce accurate and legitimate answers. Most departing employees are reluctant to reveal important demotivators because they do not want to burn their bridges. They may not want to offend the management at that sensitive time of saying good-bye.

An experienced third party, a consultant or firm that specializes in conducting these sensitive interviews and collecting a wealth of invaluable inputs, can often accomplish effective and productive exit interviews. The information gathered in this process can guide corporate management in making changes that will reduce future turnover, as well as potentially solve other problems in the organization.

Exhibit: Sample Exit Interview Record Format

Employee Name__________________	Termination Date:
Employee ID # __________________	Eligible for Rehire
	[ ]Yes [ ] No
Job Title __________________	Job Code __________________

Reason for Termination

Voluntary		**Involuntary**
[ ] Another Position	[ ]	Attendance
[ ] Personal Reasons	[ ]	Violation of Company Policy
[ ] Relocation	[ ]	Lay Off
[ ] Retirement	[ ]	Reorganization
[ ] Return to School	[ ]	Position Eliminated
[ ] Other __________________	[ ]	Other __________________

Employee Comments:

Interviewer Comments:

Employee's Signature____________________________ **Date**

Interviewer's Signature____________________________ **Date**

Exercise Case

John is the CEO of a large organization experiencing high turnover. His Human Resources staff was spending more and more time recruiting, hiring and training replacements. As soon as they got them trained, they would be gone in six months. Customers were upset and complaints were increasing.

John decided to explore the main reasons people were quitting. He identified new strategies and tactics such as creating an emerging leaders program, providing training for managers, and improving their employee recognition program. As a result, they are now attracting better talent and more importantly, have retained their best people. The Human Resource Department is happier because they are not spending all their time conducting training.

Few businesses realize how much employee turnover impacts their bottom line. It takes $7,000 – $14,000 to replace a typical employee. Replacing a key manager costs the same as buying a new Honda. In the healthcare arena, it costs up to $185,000 to replace a critical care nurse. The question then arises, how can a business survive when the cost of turnover and recruitment runs into the millions of dollars each year?

(*Courtesy: http://searchwarp.com/swa349124.htm*)

QUESTIONS FOR DISCUSSION

1. Analyse the above case by applying HR concepts
2. How can HR managers ensure employee engagement at their workplace?

QUESTION BANK

1. What are exit interviews? How are they useful for developing people retention strategies in organizations?
2. Define absenteeism. What are the common causes of absenteeism?
3. What strategies can be applied for coping absenteeism?
4. What is absenteeism rate? How is it calculated?
5. What are the factors contributing to absenteeism?
6. What is attrition? What are the factors causing attrition?
7. Write a note on strategies used by organizations to cope attrition.
8. What is employee retention? How can talents be retained?
9. Enumerate the people retention strategies of reputed organization known to you.

Internet Exercises

- Surf the website http://www.highretention.com/ and collect relevant information regarding evolving retention strategies.
- Visit the following hyperlink (http://searchwarp.com/swa349124.htm) and comment on the concept of PRIDE highlighted in the stated article.
- Use the following hyperlink (http://www.cpiworld.com/en/cms/?296) and present your learnings from the same.

Experiential Exercises

- Using MS Excel prepare a format for recoding the leaves taken by the employees in an organization. You may do the project in your own institute taking permission from your principal.
- "Young professionals would prefer a career to a lucrative job", Discuss this topic in an open forum inviting your faculties to judge the performance of the participants.
- **Debate:** Discuss the following topic in an open forum, "Talent Volatility is an opportunity for today's organizations".

CHAPTER 5

EMPLOYEE DISCIPLINE

THEME CASE: A LIFE THREAT

The Incident: *A visibly upset male employee cornered a female employee in her office, and said quietly and slowly that she* ***will pay with her life*** *for going over his head to ask about his work. The male employee then stared at his coworker with his hands clenched rigidly at this side before leaving the office and slamming the door behind him. The female employee, fearful and shaken, reported this to her supervisor, who immediately reported the incident to the director of Employee Relations.*

Response: The agency's response plan calls for involvement of Employee Relations, Security and the Employee Assistance Program (EAP) in cases involving threats. Immediately following the report to the response team, the **Security Officer** contacted the female employee to assist her in filing a police report on the threat and to discuss safety measures that she should be taking. The victim was also referred to the **EAP**, where she received brief counseling and educational materials on handling severe stress.

An investigation was immediately conducted by an investigator from **the Office of Inspector General**. In her statement, the female employee repeated what she had reported to the supervisor earlier about the threat. In his statement, the male employee stated that, on the day in question, he had been upset about what he felt were some underhanded activities by the female employee and his only recollection about the conversation was that he made a general statement like *You'll pay* to her. He stated that this was not a threat, just an expression. The investigation showed that the employee had several previous incidents of intimidating behaviour which had resulted in disciplinary actions.

Resolution: After reviewing the results of the investigation, the supervisor proposed a removal action, finding that the female employee's version of the incident was more credible. In his response to the proposed notice, the employee brought in medical documentation that said he had a psychiatric disability of Post Traumatic Stress Disorder, which caused his misconduct, and he requested a reasonable accommodation. The deciding official consulted with an agency attorney and employee relations specialist who explained that nothing in the Rehabilitation Act prohibits an agency from maintaining a workplace free of violence threats of violence. Further, they explained that a request for reasonable accommodation does not excuse employee misconduct nor does it shield an employee from discipline. The deciding official determined that removal was the appropriate discipline in this case. The employee did not appeal the action.

EMPLOYEE DISCIPLINE

The maintenance of harmonious relations within an industry depends on the extent of promotion and maintenance of discipline in the organizations. No organizations can grow and prosper without effective disciplinary system. Some common disciplinary issues caused by problem employees include absenteeism, tardiness, productivity deficiencies, pilfering, alcoholism, insubordination, misuse of equipments and other company resources, and negligence. The goal of discipline is behaviour modification, that is, to modify unacceptable behaviour and misconduct.

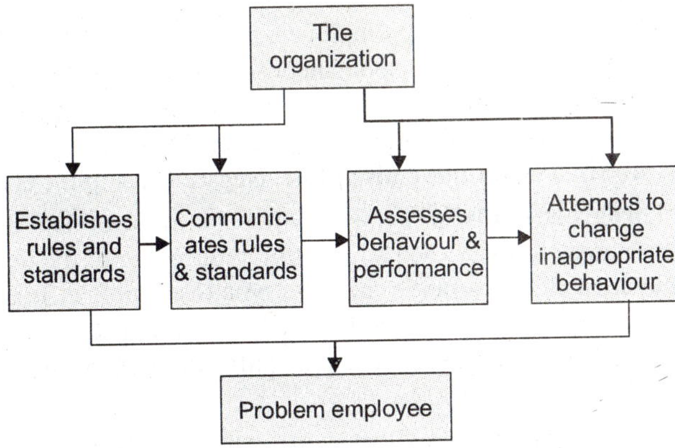

Fig. 5.1: Identifying a problem employee

What is Discipline?

In a wider perspective, discipline means orderly and systematic behaviour. Organizations in order to achieve operational efficiency frame certain codes of behaviour, contracts or statutes, norms for their employees to ensure productivity and organizational efficiency. The establishment of disciplinary activities as depicted by the above figure not only is limited with formulation and establishment of these rules and standards, it extends in the form of communicating these rules and standards to all employees and using the same for assessing the behaviour and performance of the employees engaged in the organization. Any deviation from these desired behaviours leads to disciplinary actions or interventions.

Discipline management process: The discipline management process can be described as a cyclical process comprising of the following steps:

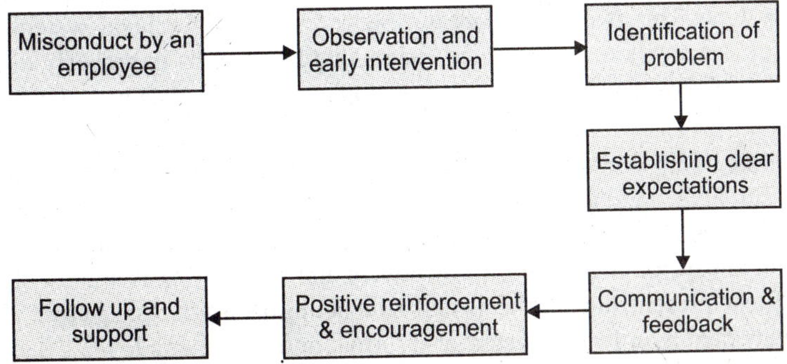

Fig. 5.2: Discipline management process

As evident in the above figure the disciplinary procedure starts with the observation/identification of the misconduct of an employee. It is followed up by early interventions from the managerial side followed by a thorough analysis of the problem. In 1990 Walter Kiechel proposed the "Red Hot Stove Rule" to administer discipline in an organization. The manager then involves an interactive session with the "problem employee" and communicates clear expectations of ideal behaviour from the employee and makes an attempt to reinforce the same by instrumenting positive reinforcement and encouragement. This is followed by constant support and feedback.

Disciplinary Systems

There are many systems available for disciplining employees. Disciplines are typically classified as **Positive and Negative Disciplines**. When an individual spontaneously abides with the organizational norms, it is known as **positive or constructive discipline**. It is achieved through education, development and training on an on-going basis. But when an employee is compelled to behave in a desired way under threat or fear of punishment, it is termed as **negative or punitive discipline**. Negative discipline is enforced by punishment.

Another system, called **progressive discipline**, is very popular in the organizational context. It requires the employer to constantly progress through each step before proceeding to the next. This is very limiting. Frequently, the facts and circumstances warrant a different type of discipline. It is better to craft a system that ensures that managers and supervisors have the flexibility to administer verbal warnings, suspensions, or terminations based upon the seriousness of the particular incident in question, regardless of the employee's prior disciplinary history.

A better system provides managers and supervisors with flexibility and can be referred to as a "**corrective discipline**" system. Corrective discipline is ideally suited to solve continual performance problems, rather than isolated ones. Such a system allows the manager or supervisor to select the type of discipline based upon the facts and circumstances of the particular situation. However, this flexibility does not relieve the manager or supervisor of the responsibility to ensure that similarly situated employees are treated similarly. It is then the responsibility of the human resources department to review discipline for consistency.

Corrective Discipline

The purpose of discipline is to assist employees in changing their performance, attendance, or behaviour. This requires that the employees have adequate information about their current performance, attendance, or behaviour versus the desired performance, attendance, or behaviour. When disciplining or terminating an employee, a manager can decrease his/her legal risk if he/she can show that the erring employee had been previously warned and/or counseled without any improvement in behaviour or performance, making clear to the employee what he/she was doing wrong and what was being required to do in order to meet the company's expectations were not done. This is a good employment practice, and the legal system will generally give great weight to such evidence when an employee claims that he/she was improperly discharged. There are four general types of disciplinary actions available when employees fail to meet expected levels of performance or conduct.

1. **Verbal counseling:** This is generally the first step of the disciplinary actions taken against an erring employee. An employee might receive several verbal warnings before progressing to the next step of the disciplinary procedure. However, for a serious problem, managers might skip this step. Verbal warnings should always be done calmly, objectively and privately. It is a good idea to have a second manager or officer present during the verbal counseling as a witness. Verbal counseling sessions should be documented by a formal memo or informal note in the employee's personnel file.
2. **Written warning:** This step is generally preceded by a verbal warning. The manager or supervisor should meet with the employee and his representative (if applicable) as in a verbal counseling

session, but the employee should be given and allowed to review a formal written warning. As with verbal counseling, a second manager can be present as a witness. The written warning should have a place for the employee to sign, acknowledging that he or she has received the warning, regardless of whether he or she agrees with the contents of the warning. If the employee refuses to sign, another manager or supervisor should be called as a witness to observe that the employee has been presented with the warning and refused to sign it, and that witness should sign the warning. An adequate written warning should include, at a minimum, the following elements:

- The date of the warning
- The employee's name
- The name of the manager or supervisor administering the warning
- A statement depicting the details of the misconduct or inadequate performance of the employee
- The date of the misconduct or poor performance (if appropriate)
- A signature line for the manager or supervisor
- A signature line for the employee
- A signature line for a witness, if the employee refuses to sign
- A formal "action plan," depending upon the nature and severity of the offense.

Components of a Formal Disciplinary Action Plan

A formal disciplinary action plan may include the following additional elements, namely:

- A statement of the policy, rule, or practice that was violated.
- The steps which the employee agrees to follow in order to correct the problem or meet the desired level of performance, attendance, or behaviour.
- Any commitments of assistance or support that the manager or supervisor has made.
- The time frame to be followed in achieving the goal of improved performance, attendance, or behaviour.
- The consequences that will occur if the performance, attendance, or behaviour is not improved within the specified time frame.

3. **Suspension:** This may range from one day to two weeks or more, depending upon the circumstances, and is almost always unpaid. In unusual circumstances, some employers will place employees on one day of paid "decision-making" leave, as a way of encouraging the employee to think about the future of his employment. Paid suspensions, however, can be perceived as a "reward" for poor behaviour, and may therefore have an adverse effect. For this reason, most employers prefer unpaid suspensions. Some employers will progress immediately from the first suspension to termination for the next offense, while others will attempt to correct the employee's performance or behaviour with multiple suspensions of increasing length (e.g., 1-day, 3-day, 5-day, 10-day, etc.). As a general rule, each suspension should be longer than the last, with termination as the final result.
4. **Termination:** Before terminating an employee, a manager should review the personnel file and all relevant documents in order to determine if the termination is appropriate — and defensible in a subsequent lawsuit — given the facts and circumstances. In addition, he should also ensure that similarly situated employees have been treated similarly in the past. Some behaviour warrants automatic dismissal. These include those of:

- Violent behaviour or threats of violence
- Drug and alcohol use on duty
- Carrying a weapon on company property

- Disregarding safety rules and regulations
- Theft, destruction of company property, or falsifying documents
- Insubordination
- Abandonment of job (no call, no show for three consecutive days).

5. **Other forms of discipline:** In addition to the steps outlined above, it is worthwhile to explore other forms of discipline, such as demotion, transfer, and reduced raises or bonuses. Many employees can be very satisfactorily managed by economic concerns, such as bonuses and raises.

Theories of Disciplinary Powers

Managers or employers derive their disciplinary power presumably from two theories, namely:

- **Institutional Theory:** According to this theory employers being the heads of an organization assume highest responsibility to look after the interests of the employees and the discipline of the organization as a whole.
- **Contractual Theory:** This theory considers that employers' disciplinary powers arise from the contract of employment which subjects employees to subordination and thereby vest employers with the necessary authority to ensure discipline and harmony in the organization.

Impact of Disciplinary Problems

Poor handling of disciplinary actions may cause serious problems to the organization. The various problems arising out of indiscipline could be summarized as follows:

- Increase in the number of cases to arbitration thereby enhancing the cost both in terms of arbitration and work stoppages.
- Increase in the cost of training and recruitment for high labour turnover. Failure to handle or manage disputes and grievances may add to this problem.
- Increase in frequent work disruptions resulting in loss of production, loss of man days etc.
- Increase in hostility and loss of self respect and degradation of organizational culture.

Categorizing Performance and Disciplinary Problems

Performance and disciplinary problems can be categorized into four distinct types:

- **Type 1 Situations** where the employee's quality and/or quantity of work is unsatisfactory.
- **Type 2 Situations** where personal problems, off the job, are influencing the employee's work performance, e.g., alcoholism, drug abuse, financial or family problems.
- **Type 3 Situations** where there has been a deliberate violation of the law or established company rules or regulations, e.g., through theft, fighting, falsification of records, conflict of interest, harassment or safety infractions (for an example and an attempt to correct it).
- **Type 4 Situations** where there have been repeated minor violations of company rules, regulations, or performance problems that have not responded to non-disciplinary corrective action, e.g., minor safety infractions, incidental insubordination, uncorrected tardiness or continued poor quality workmanship.

A clear distinction has to be made between types 1 and 2 and types 3 and 4. The first two involve unsatisfactory work performance; the second two involve violations of rules, regulations, or the law, or behaviour that is organizationally unacceptable and known by the employee to be so.

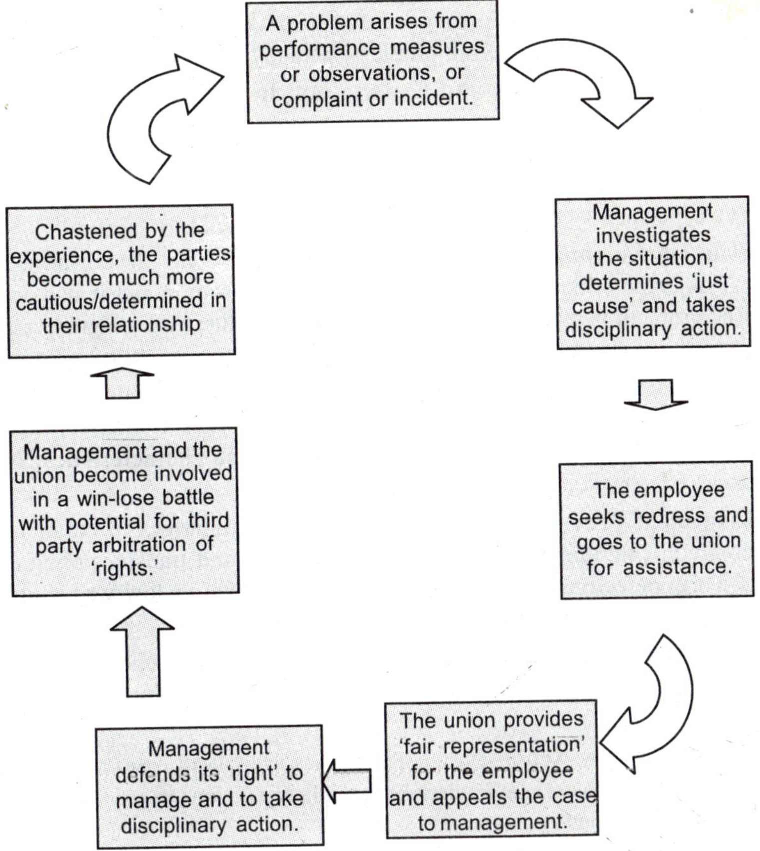

Fig. 5.3: The vicious cycle of discipline

The above figure locates the four types of problems in the larger context of diagnosis and problem solving. Inputs—performance measurement, behavioural observation, complaints and incidents—provide a basis for determining the type of problem. Depending upon the input and the type of problem, a manager (ideally in concert with the union) would use very different strategies or corrective actions.

Analyzing Type 1 Situations: Performance Problems

Performance evaluation provides the primary source of information on Type 1 problems. Not only is valid and reliable performance information important for determining whether a problem actually exists, it is also essential for finding solutions that avoid the adversarial of traditional punitive measures. Behavioural observations, complaints, and incidents are other potential indicators of problems. Analysis of all of this information provides the basis for determining the cause of the problem. Once the cause is determined, potential solutions can then be developed. Poor performance originates either from management and organization-centred causes or from employee-centred causes.

A. Managerial and Organizational Shortcomings

1. **Lack of Effective Leadership:** Absence of effective leadership results in poor management in areas of direction, guidance, instructions etc. which in turn leads to employee indiscipline. Sometimes lack of

interest of the top management also leads to this problem. In many cases the supervisors of the organization may not be even properly trained to understand and solve the problems of their subordinates in a proactive way, before problems actually creep up at the workplace.

2. **Lack of Understanding of Roles and Expectation:** In many instances management fails to tell subordinates what their roles are and what is expected of them. Performance problems arise when the performance expectations of individual employees differ from those of the organization, or when, in the absence of clearly defined standards and objectives, the employee simply does not perform to management's expectations, however poorly defined they might be.
3. **In Appropriate Job Assignment:** Poor performance may occur when the organization makes a poor job assignment. This is more likely to occur in a growing organization, but it also occurs in more stable situations. The problem lies in promoting, transferring, or otherwise assigning an employee to a job to which he/she is not fitted because of a lack of training, personal skill, background, or experience.
4. **Job Design:** In many instances poor performance arises because of the design of the job. Employees will be motivated to perform well in jobs that offer variety, a challenge, responsibility, and an opportunity for personal growth. In the absence of these characteristics, less than optimum performance can be expected.
5. **Unfair Management Practices:** Management sometimes indulges in unfair practices like wage discrimination, non-compliance with promotional policies and transfer policies, discrimination in allotment of work, defective handling of grievances, payment of low wages, delay in payment of wages, creating low QWL etc.
6. **Communication Barriers:** Communication barriers along with absence of upward communication, lack of humane and understanding approach on the par of superiors result in frustration and leads to indiscipline.
7. **Non-Uniform Disciplinary Actions:** Management has to treat all cases of indiscipline in a fair and equitable way. But management may undertake disciplinary actions in a discriminating way, leading to violent protests from various quarters.
8. **Divide and Rule Policy:** Many managers may often divide the employees into employee groups, get the information from different groups about others and encourage the spying activity.
9. Inadequate attention to personnel problems and delay in solving personnel problems also creates frustration among individual workers.

B. Employee-Centred Causes

The most common employee-centred causes are the following:

1. **Lack of Interest:** Obviously, if an employee is to perform properly, he/she must be interested in the type of work that needs to be done.
2. **Personality:** An employee's personality may be a major cause of poor performance. Because personality traits are often very difficult to change, it may be necessary to assign the individual to a position more in keeping with his/her personality.
3. **Limited Capabilities**. All employees are limited in their capabilities to carry out certain organizationally required functions, and problems will arise when they are required to perform tasks that are beyond their capabilities.
4. **Victimization and** excessive pressures on the work also may lead to grievance and dissatisfaction at the workplace.

Dealing with Type 2 Situations: Personal Problems

Most personal problems arise for two reasons:

- **Health and stress problems:** The levels of stress associated with working in the modern organization can severely affect a person's health and lead to personal problems such as alcoholism and absenteeism.
- **Family and personal problems:** Family and personal problems are major outside sources of unsatisfactory performance. Almost everyone has family or personal troubles that affect their work performance at some time during their care. Employees have parents, children, or brothers and sisters who face various crises, such as sickness or death. Similarly, there are personal problems related to finances, life-style and relationships that will be significant enough to affect an employee's commitment and motivation.

Employee Assistance

In many cases, the employee's problem can be corrected or alleviated only with professional help. Many companies and unions deal with personal problems using employee assistance programs (EAPs) that operate confidentially and refer employees to professional social workers, counselors or trained coordinators.

Taking Disciplinary Action in Type 3 Situations

For dealing with performance and personal issues and collabouration between labour and management in type 1 and type 2 situations, management will be required to take some disciplinary action in some type 3 situations. The reasons will usually be similar to those that would lead to criminal or civil action in society. Some of the prominent causes are:

- theft of property belonging to the company, fellow employees, suppliers or customers, falsification of documents essential to the company's operation,
- sexual or other forms of harassment,
- willful violation of company rules and regulations concerning safety, operating methods, procedures and so on,
- willful and malicious destruction of property belonging to the company, fellow employees, suppliers, or customers.

In each of these type 3 situations, the test of whether discipline is justified is whether:

- the employee deliberately carried out the act,
- the employee knew or should have known that what he or she was doing was wrong,
- the rule or regulation was reasonable, and
- the discipline that is contemplated is appropriate to the seriousness of the offence.

Taking Disciplinary Action in Type 4 Situations

Type 4 problems are the most difficult to analyze and deal with, because they arise out of type 1, 2 and 3 problems. Type 4 problems are:

- Type 1 problems that have not responded to management taking all the appropriate and corrective action to try to solve the performance discrepancy. The employee has not been prepared to recognize his/her responsibility in solving the problem. Consequently, the quantity or quality of the work is still unsatisfactory.
- Type 2 problems for which the employee has been provided with appropriate assistance and support to deal with a personal problem, but the personal problem still results in performance shortcomings.
- Type 3 problems in which continued minor violations and infractions have led to a culminating incident, and, as a consequence, management is required to discipline the employee.

Implementing a New Approach for Managing Discipline

Organizations that have implemented non-punitive discipline methods (discipline without punishment) have experienced improvements in labour relations and grievance rates. Although non-punitive methods are a step in the right direction, these innovations cannot achieve the potential of the new approach described here for reasons that have already been discussed.

The following figure shows that the New Approach to Performance and Discipline Management (NAPDM) is a four-phase process. To be successful, it requires collabouration between management and labour in:

- Undertaking a joint assessment of the impact of current practices on employee relations,
- Developing new policies and procedures for diagnosing problems and taking the appropriate action,
- Training shop stewards and supervisors in the new approaches,
- Communicating the new approaches to employees,

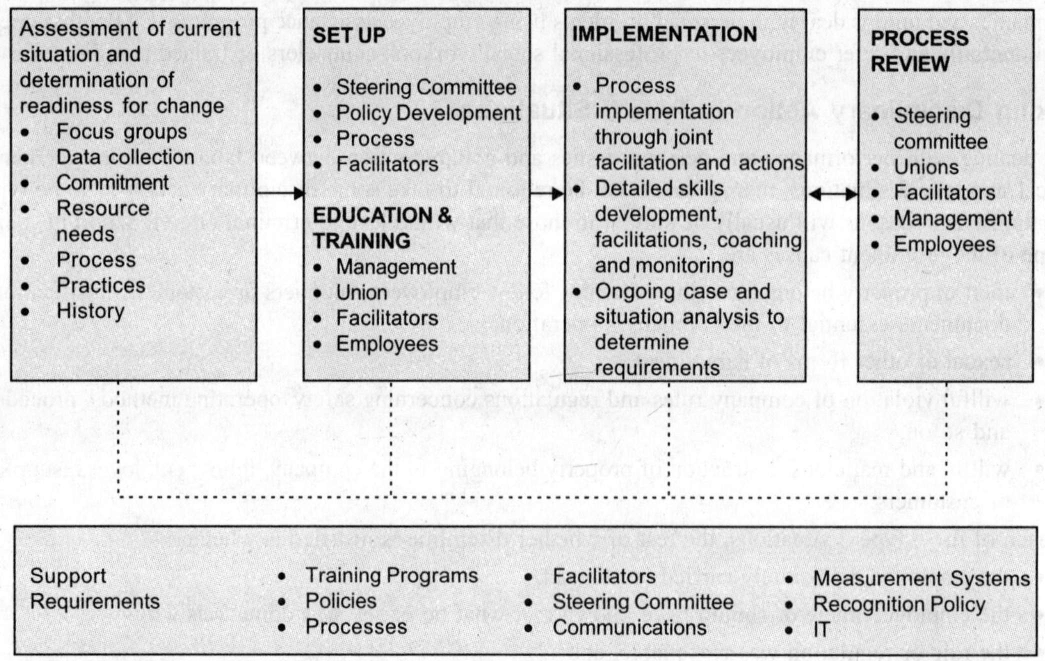

Fig. 5.4: A new approach to performance and discipline management (NAPDM)

Whistleblowing, a new approach for managing organizational discipline

Whistleblowing can be described as an innovative practice in an organization where an individual or group of individuals (**whistleblowers**) are being given the responsibility to report misconduct to their employers or entities that have the power and presumed willingness to take corrective action against the same. The misconduct may be a violation of a law, rule, regulation and/or a direct threat to public interest, such as fraud, health/safety violations, and corruption. One famous whistleblower is Jeffrey Wigand, who exposed the Big Tobacco scandal, revealing that executives of the companies knew that cigarettes were addictive and approved the addition of carcinogenic ingredients to the cigarettes.

Definition of a whistleblower: Most whistleblowers are *internal whistleblowers*, who report misconduct to a fellow employee or superior within their company. *External whistleblowers*, however, report misconduct to outside persons or entities or government agencies. In these cases, depending on the information's severity and nature, whistleblowers may report the misconduct to lawyers, the media, law enforcement or watchdog agencies, or other local, state, or federal agencies.

Steps for Creating a Whistleblowing Culture

Create a policy that coerces and strictly handles indiscipline: A policy about reporting illegal or unethical practices should include:

- Formal mechanisms for reporting violations, such as hotlines and mailboxes
- Clear communications about the process of voicing concerns, such as a specific chain of command, or the identification of a specific person in the organization, such as an ombudsman or a human resources professional
- Clear communications about bans on retaliation

In addition, a clear connection should exist between an organization's code of ethics and performance measures. For example, in the performance review process, employees can be held accountable not only for meeting their goals and objectives but also for doing so in accordance with the stated values or business standards of the organization.

Endorsement and Support from the Top Management: The Top management, starting with the CEO, should demonstrate a strong commitment to encouraging whistleblowing. This message must be communicated by line managers at all levels, who are trained continuously in creating an open-door policy regarding employee complaints.

Publicize the Organization's Commitment: To create a culture of openness and honesty, it is important that employees hear about the discipline policy regularly. Top management should make every effort to talk about the commitment to ethical behaviour in memos, newsletters, and speeches to company personnel. Publicly acknowledging and rewarding employees who pinpoint ethical issues is one way to send the message that management is serious about addressing issues before they become endemic.

Investigation and Follow Up: Managers should be required to investigate all allegations promptly and thoroughly, and report the origins and the results of the investigation to a higher authority. For example, at IBM, a long-standing open-door policy requires that any complaint received must be investigated within a certain number of hours. Inaction is the best way to create cynicism about the seriousness of an organization's ethics policy.

Assess the Organization's Internal Whistleblowing System: Care should be taken so as to find out employees' opinions about the organization's culture vis-à-vis its commitment to ethics and values.

The following figure depicts a model illustrating how whistleblowing works in organizations:

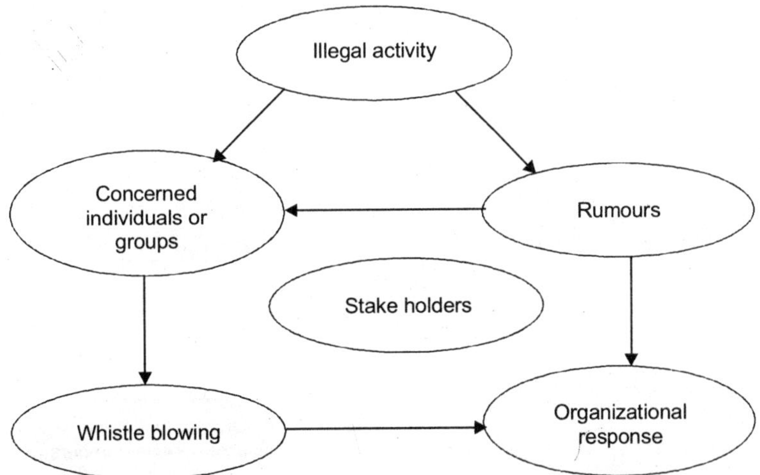

Fig. 5.5: A model depicting how whistleblowing works in organizations

The four factors have organizational and individual dependence. The unclear part would be why only some employees act as whistleblowers. One obvious reason would be the availability of the information. The sensitive information would be available only to a selected few or understanding the issues in the information is possible only by particular individuals. The second reason which points at the organizational dependence and culture would be the issue of conformity. Employees at large feel that the information or the illegal activity is part of the organizational functioning and tend to avoid making bold moves to correct them. Considering both of these factors, we can generalize to a certain level that whistleblowers have a high level of moral responsibility, guts and concern for the organization and society at large.

In the organizational context, some of the activities which the employees feel are misdemeanors will be exposed in the form of rumors in the organization. Interestingly trade unions, opposition parties and social activists are whistleblowers in this context and whistleblowing is considered an essential part of their effective functioning. In the other case, where the whistleblower comes across serious manipulations or illegal activity, the reaction is of a different type due to two reasons. Either the employee has first hand information of the activity and goes through a variety of decision-making challenges, or the response is difficult and may be against a set system.

In the whole process the various stakeholders play a major role. The managers, other employees and the society at large can be seen as major stakeholders. The whistleblowers are often treated as traitors by the organization. Other employees tend to treat them as outcasts and blame the whistleblowers for putting the organization in a difficult position.

Exhibit: TCS Shows Doors to Techies with Fake CVs

The IT-BPO industry is becoming increasingly alert on fake biodatas. India's largest IT service providers, TCS has recently asked close to 20 employees at its Kolkata centre to leave after the company, during the background verification, found that these employees used fudged resumes,to get job. TCS is not the only firm doing this. Earlier Infosys had asked close to 100 employees to leave in the FY'07 due to discrepancies found in the resumes. Same goes for Satyam and Wipro Technologies.

(Courtesy: Business Standard, July 14th 2008, p. 5.)

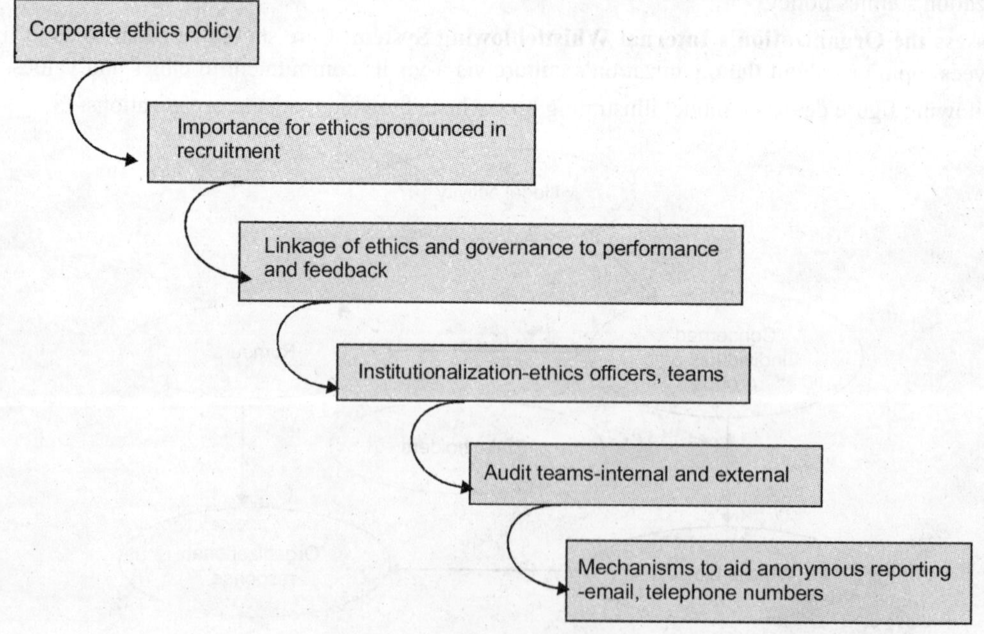

Fig. 5.6: Managing whistleblowing

Managing Whistleblowing: As employees or former employees, it is important to make sure that certain aspects are taken into consideration before whistleblowing. Whistleblowers should confirm whether the practice followed in the organization will cause harm to an individual or the general public if uncorrected, make sure that the facts in hand are reliable and not mere rumors, be fairly certain that by bringing the matter before an outside group the problem can be corrected and harm avoided.

QUESTION BANK

1. What is discipline? What are the various types of discipline?
2. Describe in brief the discipline management process.
3. Write a note on disciplinary systems.
4. What is corrective discipline? What is its significance?
5. What are the impacts of disciplinary problems in employee performance?
6. Categorize performance and disciplinary problems.
7. Describe the vicious cycle of discipline.
8. Describe the various discipline management initiatives taken by organizations.
9. What is whistleblowing? How could it be useful for discipline management?
10. Describe how whistleblowing works in organizations. How could they be managed by managers?

Internet Exercises

- Use the following hyperlink (http://www.vault.co.in/nr/hottopiclist.jsp? ch_id=402&nr_page =13&cat_id=1082) and discuss the issues described in the website in your class.
- Read the article titled "Avoiding a Hostile Workplace: Fairness in Employee Discipline" and discuss your view points in the class. The article is available in the website, http://contentdig.com/business/ethics/avoiding-a-hostile-workplace—fairness-in-employee-discipline.html

Experiential Exercises

- Discuss in an open forum whether whistle blowing concept could be implemented in academic institutions.
- Design a discipline management record database using a spreadsheet to control student class participation and attendance in the class.

GRIEVANCE MANAGEMENT

THEME CASE: GRIEVANCE MANAGEMENT: BEST PRACTICES AT MARRIOTT INTERNATIONAL

Marriott

Marriott International, Inc., is a leading lodging company of the world. Marriott consistently makes it to the Fortune's Best Employer's List in the industry. Retaining employees in the hospitality industry is vital as the cost of recruiting and training new employees is very high. Marriott operated in an industry where every day counted and weekends and holidays generated more business than weekdays. Customer service had to be provided on a 24/7/365 basis. The implication was that employees had to go through a hectic work schedule; an average work week lasted more than 50 hours. With the increasing work load due to rising customers in the late-1990s, several key managers at Marriott left.

They wanted to devote more time to their personal lives and their jobs at Marriott were not helping the cause. There was increase in the number of grievance related cases and workplace conflicts. Facing this challenge, Marriott launched a new program called Management Flexibility in February 2000 on a pilot basis at three of its hotels. The aim was to assist Marriott's managers in balancing their professional and personal lives, without negatively affecting customer service or the company's financials.

Employee relations: Empowerment is the cornerstone of employee relations in the "Marriott way". Marriott has numerous examples of how their Associates (employees) feel empowered. It is the employees who decide when to give a fruit basket or other complimentary items to guests. There is a high degree of pride in the unique relationships they form with their guests. Marriott employees feel empowered because they know that fair treatment is a cornerstone of the organization's philosophy. This is what J W Marriott, Jr, current Chairman and CEO has to say, " I want our Associates to know that there really is a guy named Marriott who cares about them…" as he is affectionately called, makes sure these are not empty words. Each manager has to give an undertaking of fair treatment.

There is a process of escalation of employee grievances (Speak Out process), right up to him. Indeed, as the current HR Manager found out, getting a call from the CEO's office to enquire about an employee grievance is not surprising. Considering that Marriott employs over 150,000 employees globally, this is a strong example of the emphasis placed on fair treatment. And for employees too shy to write to the CEO, there is always the option of anonymously calling up the Integrity hotline, a 24 by 7 toll free number.

If fairness ensures that employees are not penalised for doing the right thing, communication processes are what ensures that employees know what the right thing is. This is what Bill Marriott says in his blog (http://www.blogs.marriott.com), "Many years ago, Marriott did something revolutionary at the time for hotels. We not only began asking guests about their stays, what they liked and didn't like, but we also took that information and created databases and tracking mechanisms so we knew how each hotel was doing".

Grievance Redressal System

By the mid-1990s, Marriott had a comprehensive complaint resolution system in place, known as the Guarantee of Fair Treatment (GFT), to ensure that employee grievances were addressed.

Under GFT, complaints passed through successive stages in Marriott's hierarchy, starting with the immediate superior, depending on whether or not the said employee was happy with the redress response given at each stage. However, given the decentralized nature of Marriott's operations, and with managers handling several tasks, resolution of complaints through GFT did not quite produce the desired results.

It, therefore, decided to try new methods of complaint resolution while continuing with GFT. These methods included mediation, a toll free hotline and peer-review.

The Benefits Reaped

Marriott's efforts over the decades to develop an employee-friendly work place earned it widespread recognition in the hospitality industry. The awards it received for 'the best place to work' were testimony. The company reaped benefits like higher employee satisfaction and less turnover. Employee satisfaction could be gauged from the 2003 Associate Opinion Survey, in which 90% of employees surveyed expressed great pride in working for Marriott.

(Courtesy: www.blogs.marriott.com, www.marriott.com)

What is Grievance?

Grievance means any type of dissatisfaction or discontentment arising out of factors related to an employee's job which he thinks is unfair. A grievance is a sign of an employee's discontentment with his job or his relationship with his colleagues. Grievances generally arise out of the day-to-day working relations in an organization. An employee or a trade union protests against an act or policy of the management that they consider as violating employee's rights.

A grievance arises when an employee feels that something has happened or is happening to him who he thinks is unfair, unjust or inequitable. In an organization, a grievance may arise due to several factors such as:

- Violation of management's responsibility such as poor working conditions
- Violation of company's rules and regulations
- Violation of labour laws
- Violation of natural rules of justice such as unfair treatment in promotion, etc.

Sources of Grievances: Various sources of grievance may be categorized under three heads: (i) management policies, (ii) working conditions and (iii) personal factors

1. Grievance resulting from management policies include:
   - Wage rates
   - Leave policy
   - Overtime
   - Lack of career planning
   - Role conflicts
   - Lack of regard for collective agreement
   - Disparity between skill of worker and job responsibility
2. Grievance resulting from working conditions include:
   - Poor safety and bad physical conditions
   - Unavailability of tools and proper machinery
   - Negative approach to discipline
   - Unrealistic targets
3. Grievance resulting from interpersonal factors include:
   - Poor relationships with team members
   - Autocratic leadership style of superiors
   - Poor relations with seniors
   - Conflicts with peers and colleagues

It is necessary to distinguish a complaint from grievance. A complaint is an indication of employee dissatisfaction that has not been submitted in written. On the other hand, a grievance is a complaint that has been put in writing and made formal.

Grievances are symptoms of conflicts in industry. Therefore, management should be concerned with both complaints and grievances, because both may be important indicators of potential problems within the workforce. Without a grievance procedure, management may be unable to respond to employee concerns since managers are unaware of them. Therefore, a formal grievance procedure is a valuable communication tool for the organization.

Benefits of Grievance

The grievance process creates stability in day-to-day employee relations because it gives the employee a sense of assurance during the life of the collective agreement that there is a mechanism to resolve issues rather than letting them continue. Without a grievance process in place, a workplace dispute could escalate unnecessarily. Additionally, the grievance process plays an important role in creating a sense of democracy in the workplace by allowing employees to raise issues without fear of reprisal by the employer. Furthermore, by employees voicing their concerns through this process, the employer is able to focus on problem areas and bring about solutions. This reinforces strong labour relations, improved morale and increased productivity overall.

Types of Grievance

There are different types of grievances: individual, group and policy. They differ in their intent as well as in their processes.

Individual Grievance

An individual grievance is a complaint brought forward by a single employee in which a decision made affects that specific employee. For example, an employee who has applied for a vacancy within the organization may grieve the fact that she was unsuccessful at securing that position. She may feel that she is the most qualified and therefore should be appointed, as per the collective agreement. A grievance is filed to contest the decision of the hiring department. The onus will be on the hiring department, with the assistance of Human Resources, to present the facts supporting decisions made in the hiring process.

Group Grievance

A group grievance is a complaint brought forward which concerns more than one employee grieving the same alleged violation. In this case, the facts surrounding the alleged violation are the same in all cases. A group grievance involves the "effect of management action on two or more employees" under the same collective agreement. Any settlement of a group grievance would apply to all employees identified with the grievance.

Policy Grievance

A policy grievance is a dispute involving a question of general application or interpretation of any article of the collective agreement rather than the direct management action involving a particular employee. For example, the process by which a position is posted may be viewed by the union as a violation of the collective agreement and therefore they wish to challenge it. These types of grievances are initiated at the final step of the grievance procedure and arise directly between the employer and the union.

Roles in the Grievance Process

Each participant in a grievance process has a defined role as well as specific obligations, responsibilities and privileges. They are as follows:

The Employee: An employee may use the grievance procedure without prejudice to his/her employment should (s)he feel there has been a violation of the specific terms of the collective agreement. However, prior to launching an individual or group grievance, the supervisor outside the bargaining unit must be provided an opportunity to be made aware of the issue and have an opportunity to resolve it. If the issue remains unresolved, the employee may bring the issue to the union to assess and to decide whether or not to pursue a grievance.

The Supervisor/Manager: The Supervisor/Manager has a right to exercise his/her management rights subject to the provisions of the collective agreement. If an employee brings forward an alleged violation of the collective agreement, the supervisor/manager must meet with that employee to discuss the issue within the time frame specified in the collective agreement. The supervisor/manager has a responsibility to fully investigate the issue and respond back to the employee on the findings and a decision. The supervisor/manager is responsible for keeping and presenting accurate and up-to-date records of circumstances relating to the grievance and the employee's work history and performance record.

The Union Representative: The union representatives play a dual role within an organization. They are first an employee with role responsibilities that must be completed and subject to supervision and policies/procedures as any other employee. Secondly, the union representative has privileges, duties, and responsibilities as a representative of the union. They serve as advisors to employees about the collective agreement and will support and represent them when there is a dispute related to the collective agreement. To accomplish this second role, union representatives are allowed time, with permission, to tend to problems that may arise with members, and to represent them during the grievance process.

Rights of the Union Representative: A union representative has the right to observe and, if necessary, to protest the employer's actions. The only legal avenue of protest is through the grievance procedure. If the union representative disagrees with the employer's decision or action, the union representative must honour the decision or action and pursue the dispute through the grievance process.

Representation Rights: Union representation is at the employee's discretion and is allowed at any meetings where disciplinary action is imposed.

Grievance Procedure

Grievance procedure is a formal communication between an employee and the management designed for the settlement of a grievance. The grievance procedures differ from organization to organization.

- Open door policy
- Step ladder policy

Open door policy: Under this policy, the aggrieved employee is free to meet the top executives of the organization and get his grievances redressed. Such a policy works well only in small organizations. However, in bigger organizations, top management executives are usually busy with other concerned matters of the company. Moreover, it is believed that open door policy is suitable for executives; operational employees may feel shy to go to top management.

Step ladder policy: Under this policy, the aggrieved employee has to follow a step by step procedure for getting his grievance redressed. In this procedure, whenever an employee is confronted with a grievance, he presents his problem to his immediate supervisor. If the employee is not satisfied with superior's decision, then he discusses his grievance with the departmental head. The departmental head discusses the problem with joint grievance committees to find a solution. However, if the committee also fails to redress the grievance, then it may be referred to chief executive. If the CEO also fails to redress the grievance, then such a grievance is referred to voluntary arbitration where the award of arbitrator is binding on both the parties.

Grievance Procedure in the Indian Industry

The 15th session of Indian Labour Conference held in 1957 emphasized the need of an established grievance procedure for the country which would be acceptable to unions as well as to management. In the 16th session of Indian Labour Conference, a model for grievance procedure was drawn up. This model helps in creation of grievance machinery. According to it, workers' representatives are to be elected for a department or their union is to nominate them. Management has to specify the persons in each department who are to be approached first and the departmental heads who are supposed to be approached in the second step. The Model Grievance Procedure specifies the details of all the steps that are to be followed while redressing grievances. These steps are:

STEP 1: In the first step the grievance is to be submitted to departmental representative, who is a representative of management. He has to give his answer within 48 hours.

STEP 2: If the departmental representative fails to provide a solution, the aggrieved employee can take his grievance to head of the department, who has to give his decision within 3 days.

STEP 3: If the aggrieved employee is not satisfied with the decision of departmental head, he can take the grievance to Grievance Committee. The Grievance Committee makes its recommendations to the manager within 7 days in the form of a report. The final decision of the management on the report of Grievance Committee must be communicated to the aggrieved employee within three days of the receipt of report. An appeal for revision of final decision can be made by the worker if he is not satisfied with it. The management must communicate its decision to the worker within 7 days.

STEP 4: If the grievance still remains unsettled, the case may be referred to voluntary arbitration.

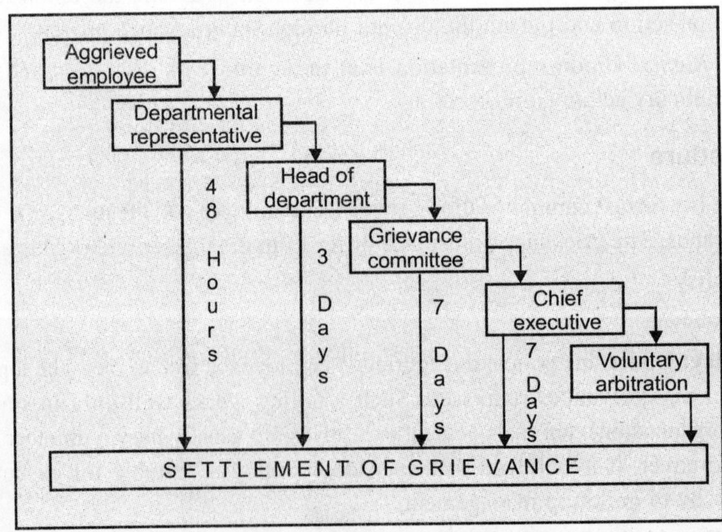

Fig. 5.7: Settlement of grievance

Theme Reading: E-grievance Management Through Grievanceware™

Grievanceware is a grievance management application designed to manage the grievance process from complaint through arbitration. It is:

Web-based: A web-based system means that a software application can be accessed through an Internet browser.

Search friendly: Users have the ability to conduct quick searches to find information on grievances, employers, collective agreements and members among all other stored information.

Auto-email notification: Local executive, union representatives and employer's representatives can be automatically notified by email regarding approaching due dates and step changes.

Supporting document management: Documents, files, and images can be uploaded and shared as a part of correspondence and meeting information. Documents can be shared with the employer or maintained in a private repository. In both cases the system provides a centralized database of all documentation.

Permissions and accesses: Grievanceware provides three main views of the Grievance data be collected, Local View (master view), Employer View (specific to grievance), Union Rep View (summarizing Grievances going to Grievance Committee). Union Locals, as Masters of their data will manage all access to the system, providing access to there Stewards, and if they choose providing restricted access to the Employer and the Union Representatives where required.

Management of grievance costs and expenses: By using this software one can allocate costs and expenses to any individual grievance. The costs and expenses can be categorized, and then reports can be generated show costs by grievance, costs by category and costs by collective agreement.

Reports: Grievanceware reports in list and graphical formats. Locals and employers can extract customized reports based on submitted criteria.

Exercise Case Study

Sherron Watkins opened up the accounting scandal at Enron. Watkins was concerned about the fraud accounting practices and the partnership between the CEO, CFO and other executives who were duping the company. Watkins, knowing that informing the CFO who happened to be her boss about the wrong practices would be a job terminating move, approached the Chairman to voice her concern. As Watkins puts it, "CEO Jeffrey Skilling, Fastow and other executives "did dupe Ken Lay and the board," she said." Mr. Skilling and Mr. Fastow (CFO) are highly intimidating. I think they intimidated a number of people into accepting" the partnerships (CNN). The initial response of the Chairman was just to ask an agency to make an enquiry and in response CFO demanded for firing Watson and seizing her computer. Before Enron finally filed for bankruptcy, Watson again informed the Chairman about the pathetic state of affairs at Enron. Lay ignored the advice of Watson and paved way for one of the most humiliating falls. Watson quit the job after the scandal and believes that some of her colleagues still hate her as they believe that if the organization was given enough time it would have corrected the mistakes by itself. Ironically, as the Time reports, the notepads of Enron, had the inspiring quote of Martin Luther King Jr, which reads "Our lives begin to end the day we become silent about things that matter." !

(*Source-CNN, Feb. 12, 2002 and Time, Dec. 22, 2002 by Richard Lacayo and Amanda Ripley*)

QUESTIONS FOR DISCUSSION

1. How would you analyze the given case?
2. What would have been your approach if you were a part of the top management of this organization?

QUESTION BANK

1. Define grievance. What are the sources of employee grievance?
2. What are benefits of having a grievance management system in the organization?
3. Classify grievances with suitable examples.
4. Describe the roles of various parties involved in the grievance management process.
5. Write short note on the following: (a) Grievance procedure (b) Open door policy (c) Step ladder policy
6. Write a note on grievance procedure followed in the Indian industry.
7. What do you mean by grievance redressal? How is it managed?
8. What is e-grievance management? How it helps today's organizations?

Internet Exercises

- Go through the following internet resources and discuss the same with your team members. The web address is www.hr.ecu.edu.au/er/html/**grievance_management**_homepage.cfm

EMPLOYEE AND INDUSTRIAL RELATIONS

Theme Reading: ER in Unilever India

Devarajan Harish, Head-Employee relations, India, reveals why working for Unilever is so rewarding.

"I am currently responsible for employee relations in Hindustan Lever Ltd, India (GBP 1.6 billion with 40,000 employees). My key focus is to sustain the high-performance culture by nurturing a willing, committed and productive workforce.

Unilever has been true to its promise. I have in the last ten-plus years benefited from cross-functional, cross-business, cross-cultural, cross-continental exposure. Each assignment has been more challenging than the last and in the bargain I've learnt, contributed and grown. In addition, I am grateful for the opportunity to work alongside some of the best professionals in an organization that has a record of outstanding performance and genuinely believes in the key contribution of people development efforts.

I am very proud of my contribution to the process of building an enterprise culture in Unilever, starting with the initial phase of defining and communicating it. I derive energy and a sense of satisfaction from collective achievement. I thrive on the opportunity to create positive mindsets and build capabilities amongst individuals and teams to achieve outstanding results. Unilever has provided a never-ending flow of challenging assignments which have provided exposure to different businesses, people, cultures and places.

Unilever's people are our most important asset. In Human Resources (HR), you'll support and develop those people, enabling them to deliver outstanding business performance".

Unilever's HR Practices: An eye on the future

Unilever India's culture is about empowering its employees, both in order to contribute to its business objectives and to achieve an employee's own personal and career goals. The company also keeps an eye on the future, with its **'leadership behaviours'** initiative aiming to identify the next generation of leaders.

The company's overall HR function is aimed to devise and implement strategies and policies so as to ensure that the company has the right people with the right skills. Within that, there are numerous options for an individual employee. For example, it could be covering culture change, leadership development, strategic talent management, coaching and skills development or alignment of reward with performance.

For effective ER Unilever India aims to have

- Strong interpersonal and leadership skills.
- The ability to see the big picture while delivering on day-to-day goals.
- A real interest in how people drive business.
- The strength and integrity to take tough decisions.
- An interest in coaching and developing people

LABOUR MARKET

Labour market: A labour market is defined as a pool of all potential workers who compete for jobs. It also includes the employers who compete for workers. Labour markets are based on the supply and demand of labour in a country or a specific location that are able and willing to work.

Labour force: Labour force includes all persons classified either as employed or unemployed during a specified period of time, usually a day or a week. Labour force can be categorized as self-employed, wage and salary earners, casual workers and unemployed.

Casual workers: Casual workers are those workers who are generally employed by small entrepreneurs on daily or weekly basis on a low wage rate. They are not entitled to any paid holiday leave or paid sick leaves.

Unemployed persons: The persons in the labour market who are without work, that is, without paid employment or self-employment and are currently either available for work or are seeking any work are considered to be unemployed.

Labour force participation rate: It is the number of persons in the labour force as a percentage of the working-age population. The working-age population is the population above a certain reference age like 15 years old and over or 15–64, etc.

Labour Market in India

The Indian labour market can be categorized into three sectors:

- Rural workers , who constitute about 60% of the workforce
- Organized of the formal sector, that constitutes about 8% of the workforce; and
- Urban unorganized or informal structure which represents the 32% of the workforce.

The chart below describes the estimated increase in the number of labours from 1977–78 to 2004–05. The labour force has grown from 276.3 million to 385.5 million between 1977–78 and1993–94 showing an annual growth rate of 2.1%. During the year 1999–2000, the workforce was estimated to be 407 million. In 2004–05 the labour market consisted of 430 million workers and has grown up to 500 million in 2006.

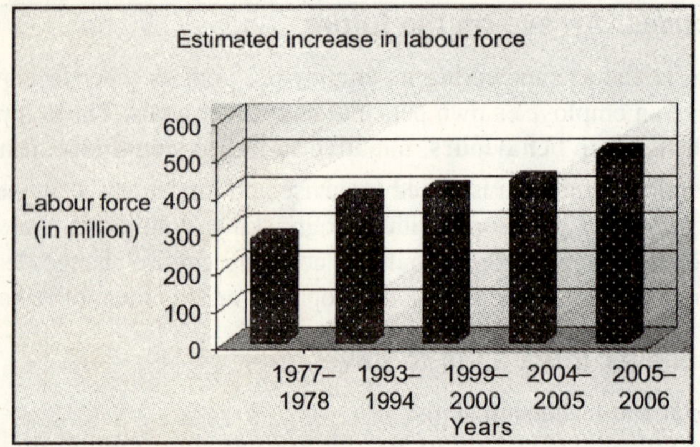

Fig. 5.8: Estimated increase in labour force (1977 to 2006)

Table 5.1: Category of Labour

Sl. No	***Category of labour***	***Self employed***	***Wage and salary earners***	***Casual workers***	***Un-employed***	***Total (%)***
1	Rural males	53.96	8.7	35.63	1.71	100
2	Rural females	57.75	3.05	39.5	1.05	100
3	Urban males	39.59	39.81	16.09	4.51	100
4	Urban females	42.78	31.37	20.14	5.71	100
5	Rural persons	54.94	6.73	36.86	1.47	100
6	Urban persons	40.22	38.13	16.9	4.75	100
7	Total persons	51.68	13.68	32.44	2.2	100
8	Total males	50.23	16.77	30.56	2.44	100
9	Total females	54.81	7.01	36.49	1.69	100
10	Urban share: Males	20.43	61.56	13.65	47.91	25.93
11	Urban share: Females	10.91	62.59	7.71	47.2	13.98
12	Urban share: Persons	17.24	61.73	11.54	47.74	22.15

Organized and Unorganized Labour

In India, a major chunk of labour force is employed in the unorganized sector. The unorganized/informal employment consists of causal and contributing family workers; self employed persons in unorganized sector and private households; and other employed in organized and unorganized enterprises that are not eligible either for paid, sick or annual leave or for any social security benefits given by the employer.

According to the results of the National Sample Survey conducted in 1999–2000, total workforce as on 1.1.2000 was of the order of 406 million. About 7% of the total workforce is employed in the formal or organized sector (all public sector establishments and all non-agricultural establishments in private sector with 10 or more workers) while remaining 93% work in the informal or unorganized sector. The NSS 55th round, 1999–2000 also covered non-agricultural enterprises in the informal sector in India. As per that survey, there were 44.35 million enterprises and 79.71 million workers employed thereof in the non-agricultural informal sector of the economy. Among these 25.01 million enterprises employing 39.74 million workers were in rural areas whereas 19.34 million enterprises with 39.97 million workers in the urban area. Among the workers engaged in the informal sector, 70.21 million are full time and 9.5 million part times. Percentage of female workers to the total workers is 20.2 per cent.

The table below describes major employment trends for the organized and unorganized sector for the years 1983, 1987–88, 1993–94 and 1999–2000. It is evident that throughout this period a large portion of the workforce in India is found to be employed in the unorganized sector. Out of 397 million workers in 1999–2000, it is estimated that 369 million workers (nearly 93 per cent) are employed in the unorganized segment of the economy whereas only 28 million workers (7 per cent) are engaged in the organized sector. The share of unorganized employment in the economy has displayed remarkable steadiness over the years. The share of informal employment has risen from 92 per cent (nearly 276 million out of 300 million) in 1983 to 93 per cent in the 1999–2000. It is clear that employment opportunity in the organized sector has remained more or less stagnant, showing only a marginal increase from 24 million in 1983 to 28 million in 1999–2000.

The largest numbers of informal workers are in agriculture. In fact, 98.84 per cent of the employment in agriculture is informal. In the non-agricultural sector, the highest numbers of informal employees are in retail trade, construction, land transport, textiles etc.

Table 5.2: Estimates of Population, Labour Force, Employment and Unemployment (in million)

Items	*1983*	*1988*	*1994*	*1999–2000*
Estimated population	718.21	790	895.05	1004.1
Labour force	308.64	333.49	391.94	406.05
Employed	302.75	324.29	374.45	397
Unemployed	5.89	9.2	7.49	9.05
Unemployment rate (as % of labour force)	1.91	2.76	1.96	2.23
Employment in organized sector	24.01	25.71	27.37	28.11
Employment in unorganized sector	278.74	298.58	347.08	368.89

Thus, the unorganized sector plays a vital role in terms of providing employment opportunity to a large segment of the working force in the country and contributes to the national product significantly. The contribution of the unorganized sector to the net domestic product and its share in the total NDP at current prices has been over 60%. In the matter of savings the share of household sector in the total gross domestic saving mainly unorganized sector is about three fourth. Thus unorganized sector has a crucial role in our economy in terms of employment and its contribution to the National Domestic Product, savings and capital formation.

What is Employee Relations?

The term employee relations refer to the competitive and cooperative relationships that arise out of the employment of labour by an organization. In employee relations the two parties who are normally involved include the employer and the employees who work in a particular organization. The objective of the employer is to ensure the maximization of organizational efficiency and profitability. Whereas the employees on the other hand seek to achieve job security, better income, good working conditions, benefits and most importantly job satisfaction from their employers.

Employee relations systems exist at different levels. Regardless of the levels at which the system operates, an industrial relations (IR) system can be viewed as having the following components, namely:

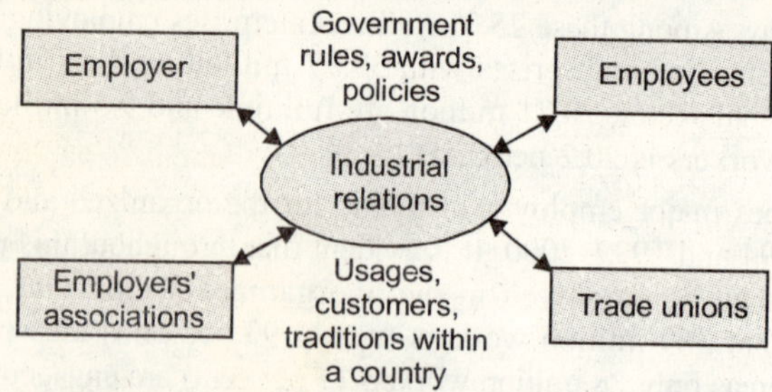

Fig. 5.9: Components of industrial relations

Industry Opinion: "From organizing a simple celebration in the department to a mega company wide celebration, people here have ample opportunities to enjoy, learn and grow. Be it the Music Club, Quiz or a Social Initiative Volunteering, at Dr. Reddy's its more than just work. It is all about how profound a person you become over the years." **Ms. Deepti Varma,** *Corporate Centre, Dr. Reddy's Lab.*

Legislations Governing: Employee Relations in India

Employment relations in India are governed by labour legislations as those of the Workmen's Compensation Act, 1923. However, the Industrial Disputes Act, 1947 is considered as the most important and the most litigated of all the labour legislations passed in India. It has a major impact on the employment relations and the act has been applied for more than five decades. However, in today's perspective, four important pieces of legislation have played a major role in shaping employment relations in India. These are as follows:

1. The Workmen's Compensation Act, 1923
2. The Industrial Disputes Act, 1947
3. The Industrial Employment (Standing Orders) Act, 1946 and
4. The Trade Unions Act, 1926

The Workmen's Compensation Act, 1923

This act has been well received by the Indian workforce in the employment relations. Due to the poverty of the workers and the complexity of industry, the workers aspire for protection from accidents at the workplace. This legislation has emphasized that the employer should provide adequate safety devices to reduce accidents at the workplace. Further, the employer has to provide medical treatment to the injured employees in case of any accident during work. This act ensures provision for the payment by certain classes of employers to their workmen of compensation for injury by accident. Compensation should be paid to the workmen who sustain personal injuries by accidents arising out of and in the course of their employment. Injuries by accident also include occupational diseases contracted in the course of employment. Under this act, the state government may appoint any person to be a commissioner for workmen's compensation. Every such commissioner is deemed to be a public servant. An injured workman has to make an application to the commissioner for workmen's compensation, who settles the claim.

The Industrial Disputes Act, 1947

The Industrial Disputes Act, 1947 is an act to make provision for the investigation and the settlement of industrial disputes and for certain other purposes. The law relating to industrial disputes in India is also known as "industrial law". Industrial disputes are disputes, which are related to an industry. Industrial law was developed due to the awakening of workers of their rights and duties. Employment relations include a complex relationship between workers, employers, concerned authorities and the government. These relationships mostly deal with the determination of terms of employment, wages, conditions of workmen, conditions of labour and workplace.

The Industrial Disputes Act has seven chapters dealing with various matters connected with industrial disputes. Various authorities under the Act including the Board of Conciliation, Industrial Tribunal and Labour Courts take part in the settlement of disputes.

The Industrial Employment (Standing Orders) Act, 1946

The Industrial Employment (Standing Orders) Act, 1946 was passed in order to make the employers in industrial establishments to formally define conditions of employment under their jurisdiction. This Act provides for preparation of draft standing orders and the certification of these standing orders by the certifying officer. The standing doers have to cover the following for the purpose of certification:

- Classification of workmen for example: whether permanent, temporary, apprentices, probationers or badlis (Casual).
- Manner of intimating workmen-periods and hours of work, holidays, pay-days and wage rates.
- Shift working
- Attendance and late coming
- Conditions of and procedure in applying for and the authority which may grant leave and holidays
- Requirement to enter premises by certain gates and liability to search
- Closing and reopening of sections of the industrial establishment and temporary stoppages of work and the rights and liabilities of the employer and workmen arising there from.
- Termination of employment and the notice thereof to be given by employer and workmen.
- Suspension or dismissal for misconduct and acts or omissions which constitute misconduct.
- Mans of redress for workmen against unfair treatment or wrongful exactions by the employer or his agents or servants.
- Any other matter which may be prescribed.

Trade Union Act, 1926

The overall objective of this act was to provide for the registration of trade unions and to define law relating to registered trade union. According to section 2(h) of the Trade Union Act, 1926, "Trade Union" means any combination, whether temporary or permanent, formed primarily for the purpose of regulating the relations between the workmen and the employers or between workmen and workmen, or between employers and employers or for imposing restrictive conditions on the conduct of any trade or business and includes any federation of two or more trade unions. However, the act does not affect any agreement between partners in relation to their business or agreement between an employer and employee in relation to employment in their own business or any agreement related to the sale of goodwill of business. The Act also provides for registration of the trade union under section 4.

Exhibit: Managing Employee Relations the I-Vantage Way

Employee Relationship Management (ERM) has taken on a new meaning with companies, especially in the IT sector, going all out to pamper their employees and keeping them in good humour. Stopping the exodus of employees is the final goal and is achieved through some lucrative sops.

To strengthen the relationship between the management and the employees, Hyderabad-based i-Vantage India has introduced a new initiative called Maitree's Karma Yatra. Launched as part of the company's human resources initiative, the Yatra's main objective is to promote ERM effectively in the organization. i-Vantage, a leading provider of outsourced IT-enabled solutions, believes the HR initiative will help the overall development of the organization and the employees as well.

Born from personal one-on-one interaction with Yatris (employees) at i-Vantage and ADP India DS (a division of the Fortune 3000 company ADP), with professionals of other companies, and from the man on the street, Karma Yatra is a three stage process—Karma Yatri (employee), Karma Nivas (employee's home) and Karma Bhoomi (workplace) over a period of three years. The process aims in culminating in an overall growth of the Yatri, instilling a sense of fulfillment, whether at work or at home or life in general.

New learning: This HR initiative has made the company and its employees understand the essence of team spirit, self-learning and the advantage of taking charge of oneself, believes Maheshwari. Adds Rajesh Agarwal, "Our initiative has helped us build skills and competencies on par with international standards; this is a leading edge." ERM is all about effective organizational communications, which can build employee confidence, trust and loyalty, enabling managements to realize the potential of the skills and knowledge within the organization. It is a powerful business tool that enables employees to do their job better. The emerging discipline of ERM allows organizations to identify, differentiate, interact and personalize the relationship with their employees, providing much of the same benefits as a successful customer relationship solution.

THE LABOUR RELATIONS PROCESS

The labour relations process can be described in the form of a sequential process comprising of four steps, namely:

- Workers' desire for collective representation
- Unionization and its campaign
- Collective Bargaining Stage (negotiations leading to a contract between the management and the representatives of the union/employees)
- Administration of the Collective Bargaining Agreement.

These sequential steps are illustrated by the following figure:

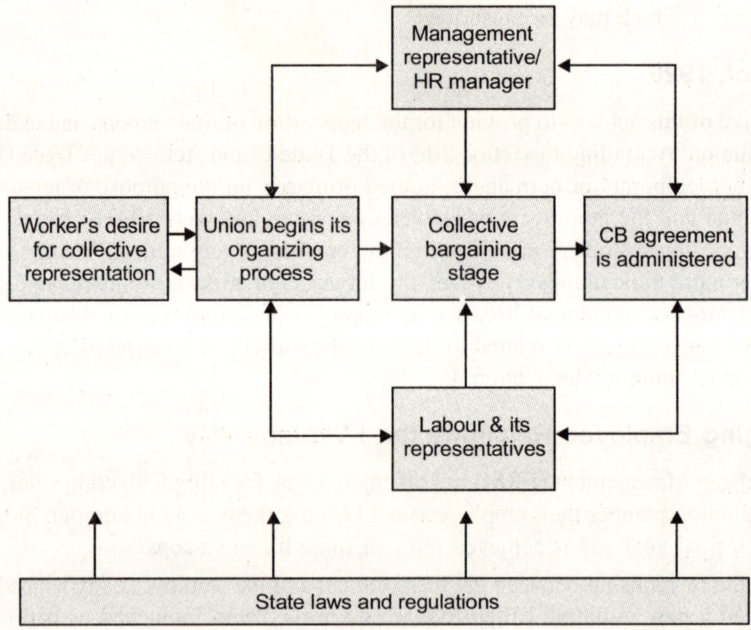

Fig. 5.10: Stages in the labour relations process

EXHIBIT

Exhibit: Coca Cola: Human Rights Statement and Workplace Rights Policy

Human Rights Statement

The reputation of the Coca Cola Company is built on trust and respect. The company's employees and its global business partners know that Coca Cola is committed to earning their trust with a set of values that represent the highest standards of quality, integrity, excellence, compliance with the law and respect for the unique customs and cultures in the communities where the company operates.

Coca Cola has always endeavoured to conduct business responsibly and ethically. As an responsible organization the company respects international human rights principles aimed at promoting and protecting human rights, including the united nations declaration of human rights and the international labour organization's declaration on fundamental principles and rights at work, and actively participates in the united nations global compact.

Acknowledgement of these international principles is consistent with the company's dedication to enriching the workplace, preserving the environment, strengthening the communities where it operates and engaging with the stakeholders to pursue progress toward these goals.

In all the workplaces and the communities in which the company operates, Coca Cola believes that a serious commitment to human rights is fundamental to the way it conduct the business. The company treats its employees with dignity, fairness and respect, and the management is guided by the shared values of integrity, collabouration and accountability.

The company's commitment is formalized and manifested through various policies including the workplace rights policy, the code of business conduct and also the environmental governance and management systems. While these policies apply to The Coca Cola Company and all of the entities that it owns or in which it holds a majority interest, the company is committed to working with and encouraging all the independent bottling partners to uphold the values and practices that these policies drive.

The Coca Cola company and its bottling partners jointly understand that the true measure of a well-managed business is not just weather it is financially successful, but how it achieves that success. As this system facilitates the company to do business around the world touching so many different and distinct local cultures, the management of Coca Cola knows that it's not enough to be profitable, they must also be responsible. This is best achieved in Coca Cola's unique business system when the company and bottlers work together toward its shared goals.

Coca Cola have expressed these shared goals in a global framework for good corporate citizenship and local accountability called Citizenship @ Coca Cola. The framework consists of a commitment to embrace a shared set of principles across the global system and is designed to measure and drive improvement in four areas of operation: workplace, marketplace, community and environment. The company expects the individual companies that belong to its system to accept the accountability to live up to this commitment and apply these principles to every facet of their local operations.

Through its Supplier Guiding Principles Program, Coca Cola works with its direct suppliers to ensure that they uphold laws and regulations in the workplace and conduct their business ethically and responsibly.

WORKPLACE RIGHTS POLICY OF COCA COLA

Coca Cola values the relationship it has with its employees. The success of its business depends on every employee in the company's global enterprise. The company is committed to fostering open and inclusive workplaces that are based on recognized workplace human rights, where all employees are valued and inspired to be the best they can be.

The Coca Cola Company's workplace rights policy is guided by international human rights standards, including the universal declaration of human rights, the international labour organization's declaration on fundamental principles and rights at work and the united nations global compact.

The Workplace Rights Policy applies to The Coca Cola Company and all of the entities that it owns or in which it holds a majority interest. The company is committed to working with and encouraging its independent bottling partners to uphold the principles in this policy and to adopt similar policies within their businesses. The policy includes the following components:

- Freedom of Association and Collective Bargaining
- Forced Labour
- Child Labour
- Discrimination
- Work Hours and Wages
- Safe and Healthy Workplace
- Workplace Security
- Community and Stakeholder Engagement

Freedom of Association and Collective Bargaining: The company respects the employees' right to join, form or not to join a labour union without fear of reprisal, intimidation or harassment. Where employees are represented by a legally recognized union, the company is committed to establishing a constructive dialogue with their freely chosen representatives. The company is committed to bargaining in good faith with such representatives.

Forced Labour: The company prohibits the use of all forms of forced labour, including prison labour, indentured labour, bonded labour, military labour or slave labour.

Child Labour: The company adheres to minimum age provisions of applicable laws and regulations. The company prohibits the hiring of individuals that are under 18 years of age for positions in which hazardous work is required. The company's prohibition of child labour is consistent with International Labour Organization standards.

Discrimination: The company values all employees and the contributions they make and has a long-standing commitment to equal opportunity and intolerance of discrimination. Coca Cola is dedicated to maintaining workplaces that are free from discrimination or physical or verbal harassment on the basis of race, sex, colour, national or social origin, religion, age, disability, sexual orientation, political opinion or any other status protected by applicable law. The basis for recruitment, hiring, placement, training, compensation and advancement at the Company is qualifications, performance, skills and experience.

Work Hours and Wages: The company compensates employees competitively relative to the industry and local labour market. Coca Cola operates in full compliance with applicable wage, work hours, overtime and benefits laws. It offers its employees opportunities to develop their skills and capabilities and provide advancement opportunities where possible.

Safe and Healthy Workplace: The company provides a safe and healthy workplace. Employees and the members of the top management are dedicated to maintaining a productive workplace by minimizing the risk of accidents, injury and exposure to health risks.

Workplace Security: The company is committed to maintaining a workplace that is free from violence, harassment, intimidation and other unsafe or disruptive conditions due to internal and external threats. Security safeguards for employees are provided as needed and will be maintained with respect for employee privacy and dignity.

Community and Stakeholder Engagement: The company recognizes its impact on the communities in which it operates. Coca Cola is committed to engaging with stakeholders in those communities to ensure that the company is listening to, learning from and taking into account their views. Where appropriate, Coca Cola is committed to engaging in dialogue with its stakeholders on workplace rights issues related to the business and within the company's sphere of influence. The management believes that local issues are most appropriately addressed at the local level. Coca Cola is also committed to creating economic opportunity and fostering goodwill in the communities in which it operates through locally relevant initiatives.

Guidance and Reporting for Employees: The Coca Cola company creates workplaces in which open and honest communications among all employees are valued and respected. Coca Cola is committed to following all applicable labour and employment laws wherever we operate.

(Courtesy:http://www.coca-colaindia.com/about_us/corporate-governance/workplace_rights.asp)

WORKPLACE BULLYING

Bullying is usually seen as acts or verbal comments that could 'mentally' hurt or isolate a person in the workplace. Sometimes, bullying can involve negative physical contact as well. Bullying usually involves repeated incidents or a pattern of behaviour that is intended to intimidate, offend, degrade or humiliate a particular person or group of people.

What are examples of bullying? While bullying is a form of aggression, the actions can be both obvious and subtle. It is important to note that the following is not a checklist, nor does it mention all forms of bullying. Examples include:

- spreading malicious rumors, gossip, or innuendo that is not true
- excluding or isolating someone socially
- intimidating a person
- undermining or deliberately impeding a person's work
- physically abusing or threatening abuse
- removing areas of responsibilities without cause
- constantly changing work guidelines
- establishing impossible deadlines that will set up the individual to fail
- withholding necessary information or purposefully giving the wrong information
- making jokes that are 'obviously offensive' by spoken word or e-mail
- intruding on a person's privacy by pestering, spying or stalking
- assigning unreasonable duties or workload which are unfavourable to one person (in a way that creates unnecessary pressure)
- under work - creating a feeling of uselessness
- yelling or using profanity
- criticizing a person persistently or constantly

- belittling a person's opinions
- unwarranted (or undeserved) punishment
- blocking applications for training, leave or promotion
- Tampering with a person's personal belongings or work equipment.

It is sometimes hard to know if bullying is happening at the workplace. Many studies acknowledge that there is a "fine line" between strong management and bullying. Comments that are objective and are intended to provide constructive feedback are not usually considered bullying, but rather are intended to assist the employee with their work.

How can bullying affect an individual? People who are the targets of bullying may experience a range of effects. These reactions include:

- shock
- anger
- feelings of frustration and/or helplessness
- increased sense of vulnerability
- loss of confidence
- physical symptoms such as
  - inability to sleep
  - loss of appetite
- psychosomatic symptoms such as
  - stomach pains
  - headaches
- panic or anxiety, especially about going to work
- family tension and stress
- inability to concentrate, and
- low morale and productivity.

How can bullying affect the workplace? Bullying affects the overall "health" of an organization. An "unhealthy" workplace can have many effects. In general these include:

- increased absenteeism
- increased turnover
- increased stress
- increased costs for employee assistance programs (EAPs), recruitment, etc.
- increased risk for accidents/incidents
- decreased productivity and motivation
- decreased morale
- reduced corporate image and customer confidence, and
- poorer customer service.

What can an employer do? The most important component of any workplace prevention program is management commitment. Management commitment is best communicated in a written policy. Since bullying is a form of violence in the workplace, employers may wish to write a comprehensive policy that covers a range of incidents (from bullying and harassment to physical violence).

A workplace violence prevention program must:

- Be developed by management and employee representatives.
- Apply to management, employee's, clients, independent contractors and anyone who has a relationship with the company.
- Provide clear examples of unacceptable behaviour and working conditions.
- State in clear terms of the organization's view toward workplace bullying and its commitment to the prevention of workplace bullying.

INDUSTRIAL RELATIONS

The term 'Industrial Relations' comprises of two terms: 'Industry' and 'Relations'. "Industry" refers to "any productive activity in which an individual (or a group of individuals) is (are) engaged". By "relations" we mean "the relationships that exist within the industry between the employer and his workmen." Hence it can be said that, the term industrial relations explain the relationship between employees and management which stem directly or indirectly from union-employer relationship.

Industrial relations are the relationships between employees and employers within the organizational settings. It looks at the relationship between management and workers, particularly groups of workers represented by a union. Industrial relations are basically the interactions between employers, employees and the government, and the institutions and associations through which such interactions are mediated.

The term industrial relations have a broad as well as a narrow outlook. Originally, industrial relations were broadly defined to include the relationships and interactions between employers and employees. From this perspective, industrial relations cover all aspects of the employment relationship, including human resource management, employee relations and union management (or labour) relations. Now its meaning has become more specific and restricted. Accordingly, industrial relations pertains to the study and practice of collective bargaining, trade unionism, and labour management relations, while human resource management is a separate, largely distinct field that deals with non-union employment relationships and the personnel practices and policies of employers.

The relationships which arise at and out of the workplace generally include the relationships between individual workers, the relationships between workers and their employer, the relationships between employers, the relationships employers and workers have with the organizations formed to promote their respective interests, and the relations between those organizations, at all levels. Industrial relations also includes the processes through which these relationships are expressed (such as, collective bargaining, workers' participation in decision-making, and grievance and dispute settlement), and the management of conflict between employers, workers and trade unions, when it arises.

Industrial Relation System

An industrial relation system consists of the whole gamut of relationships between employees and employees and employers which are managed by the means of conflict and cooperation. A sound industrial relations system is one in which relationships between management and employees (and their representatives) on the one hand, and between them and the state on the other, are more harmonious and cooperative than conflictual and creates an environment conducive to economic efficiency and the motivation, productivity and development of the employee and generates employee loyalty and mutual trust.

THEME READING: INDUSTRIAL RELATIONS AT BATA INDIA LTD., BATAGANJ, PATNA

The industrial relations at Bataganj unit at Patna of Bata India Ltd. have all along been cordial and peaceful. For good harmonious and workable industrial relations, the management believes in regular dialogue with the recognized union only and not with splinter groups. The Bata Mazdoor Union which represents the entire workforce is affiliated to INTUC and its own constitution. Leadership of the union is decided on the basis of annual election by sector ballot. The following joint committees (comprising of equal number of representative of the employees and the management) are functioning responsibly in order to contribute to peaceful industrial relations in the plant. These are as follows, namely:

- Works committee
- Unit emergency production committee
- Canteen committee
- Welfare committee
- Safety committee
- Joint Management Council

The concern for effective industrial relations at Bata stems out from its concern for people. The company firmly believes that giving its people the right encouragement yields in comparable rewards. With the advent of the modern technology the organization has given every emphasis to the effectiveness of its man management systems. Care is taken by the managers so that every opportunity is being given to the people so that they could grow along with the organization. It is a Bata policy to provide equal opportunity so as to promote on merit and to stimulate its people into thinking globally.

Employee welfare is woven into the fabric of the company's philosophy. Proper housing, medical facilities, a clean and cheerful environment where children can thrive and prosper are some of Bata India's perspectives.

(Courtesy: Organization study done by Syed Ghulam Sarwar in Bata India Ltd.)

Scope of Industrial Relations

The concept of industrial relations has a very wide meaning and connotation. In the narrow sense, it means that the employer, employee relationship confines itself to the relationship that emerges out of the day to day association of the management and the labour. In its wider sense, industrial relations include the relationship between an employee and an employer in the course of the running of an industry and may project it to spheres, which may transgress to the areas of quality control, marketing, price fixation and disposition of profits among others. The scope or industrial relations are quite vast. The main issues involved here include the following:

1. Collective bargaining
2. Machinery for settlement of industrial disputes
3. Standing orders
4. Workers participation in management
5. Unfair labour practices

Perspectives of IR

IR has three types of perspectives, namely:

Unitary Perspective: In unitarism, the organization is perceived as an integrated and harmonious system. A core assumption of unitary approach is that management and staff, and all members of the organization share the common objectives, interests and purposes; thus working together, hand-in-hand, towards the achievement of the shared mutual goals. Furthermore, unitarism has a paternalistic approach where it demands loyalty of all employees towards the organization and the management as a whole. Trade unions are deemed as unnecessary and conflict is perceived as disruptive. From employee point of view, unitary approach means that:

- Working practices should be flexible. Employees should be business process improvement oriented, multi-skilled and ready to tackle with efficiency whatever tasks are required.

- If a union is recognized, its role is that of a further means of communication between groups of staff and the company. The union if exists should contribute to enhance the working conditions in the organization and should encourage the employees in the achievement of the same.
- The emphasis is on establishing good relationships and sound terms and conditions of employment between the management and the employees.
- The management should help in terms of empowering individuals in their roles and emphasizes team work, innovation, creativity, discretion in problem-solving, quality and improvement groups etc.
- Employees should feel that the skills and expertise of managers supports their endeavours in productivity and creative inputs.

From employer point of view, unitary approach means that:

- Staffing policies should try to unify effort, inspire and motivate employees.
- The organization's wider objectives should be properly communicated and discussed with staff.
- Reward systems should be so designed as to foster to secure loyalty and commitment.
- Line managers should take ownership of their team/staffing responsibilities.
- Staff-management conflicts—from the perspective of the unitary framework—are seen as arising from lack of information, inadequate presentation of management's policies.
- The personal objectives of every individual employed in the business should be discussed with them and integrated with the organization's needs.

Pluralistic-Perspective: In pluralism the organization is perceived as being made up of powerful and divergent subgroups - management and trade unions. This approach sees conflicts of interest and disagreements between managers and workers over the distribution of profits as normal and inescapable. Consequently, the role of management would lean less towards enforcing and controlling and more toward persuasion and coordination. Trade unions are deemed as legitimate representatives of employees. Conflict is dealt by collective bargaining and is viewed not necessarily as a bad thing and if managed could infact be channeled towards evolution and positive change. Realistic managers should accept conflict to occur. There is a greater propensity for conflict rather than harmony. They should anticipate and resolve this by securing agreed procedures for settling disputes.

The implications of this approach include:

- The firm should have industrial relations and personnel specialists who advise managers and provide specialist services in respect of staffing and matters relating to union consultation and negotiation.
- Independent external arbitrators should be used to assist in the resolution of disputes.
- Union recognition should be encouraged and union representatives given scope to carry out their representative duties.
- Comprehensive collective agreements should be negotiated with unions.

Marxist Perspective: This view of industrial relations is a by product of a theory of capitalist society and social change. Carl Marx argued that:

- Weakness and contradiction inherent in the capitalist system would result in revolution and the ascendancy of socialism over capitalism.
- Capitalism would foster monopolies.
- Wages (costs to the capitalist) would be minimized to a subsistence level.
- Capitalists and workers would compete/be in contention to win ground and establish their constant win-lose struggles would be evident.

This perspective focuses on the fundamental division of interest between capital and labour, and sees workplace relations against this background. It is concerned with the structure and nature of society and assumes that the conflict in employment relationship is reflective of the structure of the society. Conflict is therefore seen as inevitable and trade unions are a natural response of workers to their exploitation by capital.

Industrial Harmony

Industrial harmony is all about ensuring a peaceful and healthy relationship between the workers/trade unions and their employers. In ensuring a healthy relationship in the manufacturing and services sectors, union leaders have a huge responsibility. In the recent context it seems that severe politicization of trade unions had actually weakened the cause and the noble objectives of forming trade unions.

In this context, the present National Council of Labour may, through a consensus, provide fresh guidelines to promote collective bargaining, including the vexed question of the determination of bargaining agents. It is necessary to evaluate the impact of *bandhs* or *hartals* on the common man. It is the old story of a foreign business leader with appointments fixed, landing in India to find that there was either a sudden *bandh* or a holiday to honor a dead VIP. The Kerala High Court has held that enforcing a *bandh* is illegal, and the Election Commission is also seized of the matter. Let us refer the case of TISCO, an organization which had successfully evaded political pressure and had successfully achieved industrial harmony over the years.

Exhibit: The Milestones in Industrial Harmony in TISCO

1915–18: Daily wages, free medical facility and welfare department of the company established.

1919: Works Committee is set up

March 5, 1920: Firing on workers by English officials.

March 20, 1920: End of strike. Leave with pay, Workers' Provident Fund scheme and Worker's Accident Compensation implemented.

1928: Departmental strikes become general strike. Netaji Subhas Chandra Bose is third President of Labour Association. Honourable agreement reached. Maternity benefit implemented.

1934: Profit sharing given for the first time in India.

December 9, 1938: Labour Association registered in the name of Tata Workers' Union.

1942: Tata Steel employees through representation of leaders of Tata Workers' Union join Quit India movement.

1948: Supervisory and Technicians unit set up in Tata Workers' Union.

January 8, 1956: Comprehensive Agreement between Tata Steel and the Tata Workers' Union broke new ground in collective bargaining and workers' participation in management.

1959: A new agreement is signed between TWU and Tata Steel to implement a new wage structure.

1965 ...1970...1975...1999...2001: Agreements continue to strengthen bonds of industrial harmony of Tata workers and the management.

(Courtesy "Mil ka Pathhar" by Mr M S Singh "Manas, Tata Workers' Union)

India and the ILO

India is a founder member of the International Labour Organization, which came into existence in 1919. At present the ILO has 175 members. A unique feature of the ILO is its tripartite character. The membership of the ILO ensures the growth of tripartite system in the member countries. At every level in the Organization, Governments are associated with the two other social partners, namely the workers and employers. All the three groups are represented on almost all the deliberative organs of the ILO and share responsibility in conducting its work. The three organs of the ILO are:

- International Labour Conferences: General Assembly of the ILO – Meets every year in the month of June.
- Governing Body: Executive Council of the ILO. Meets three times in a year in the months of March, June and November.
- International Labour Office: A permanent secretariat.

The work of the Conference and the Governing Body is supplemented by Regional Conferences, Regional Advisory Committees, Industrial and Analogous Committees, Committee of Experts, Panels of Consultants, Special Conference and meetings, etc.

International Labour Conference

Except for the interruption caused by the Second World War, the International Labour Conference has continued, since its first session in 1919 to meet atleast once a year. The Conference, assisted by the Governing Body, adopts biennial programme and budget, adopts International Labour Standards in the form of Conventions and Recommendations and provides a forum for discussing social economic and labour related issues. India has regularly and actively participated in the Conference through its tripartite delegations.

ILO and Child Labour

ILO's interest in child labour, young persons and their problems is well-known. It has adopted a number of Conventions and Recommendations in this regard. In India, within a framework of the Child Labour (Prohibition and Regulations) Act, 1986 and through the National Policy on Child Labour, ILO has funded the preparation of certain local and industry specific projects. In two Kanor projects, viz. Child Labour Action and Support Programmes (CLASP) and International Programme on Elimination of Child Labour (IPEC), the ILO is playing a vital role.

ILO's Concept of Decent Work

The concept of decent work is being propagated by the ILO. It encompasses four strategic objectives –

- **Promotion of Rights at Work** — It calls for renewed attention to ILO's standards, as well as a fresh look at complimentary means and instruments for achieving this goal.
- **Employment** — Creation of greater employment and income opportunities for women and men as a means to reduce poverty and inequality.
- **Social Protection** — This section emphasises expansion of social security schemes.
- **Social Dialogue** — This emphasises examining ways of strengthening the institutional capacity of ILO constituents as well as their contribution to the process of dialogue.

The concept of decent work emphasises that the quantity of employment should not be divorced from quality of work and stresses that a social and economic system should be evolved to ensure basic security and employment without compromising workers' rights and social standards in a highly competitive world.

Although India agrees that the four strategic objectives are necessary for decent work, this has no meaning unless we can provide an opportunity to work. Therefore, employment generation should be the focus of the all ILO programmes and activities. The basic requirement of decent work should be to first ensure work to any potential worker and then all other elements of the decent work concept will automatically follow. This stand of India was appreciated by other nations as well. India also made it clear in the meetings of the ILO that the concept of decent work has to be fixed keeping in mind the conditions of work in the social, economic and cultural context of each country. It cannot be made applicable uniformly to every country.

India's Future Stands on Linkages Issue

India had expressed its concerns for continuing to adhere to the stand that all matters related to international labour standards are to be agitated only in the relevant forum of the ILO and that the comparative advantage of countries, particularly developing countries, must in no way be put into question. India will continue to reject the use of labour standards for protectionist purposes and any attempt to link labour standards with trade will be vehemently opposed invariably, even if isolated by other countries.

Labour Reforms in India

Labour reform in India, in the context of the liberalization and globalization, has much been apprehended and misinterpreted. The issue has been a touchy one ever since the liberalization era began in the early 1990s. This is because of the enormity and uniqueness of the subject, and also due to the initial approach the government and industry adopted to address it.

In the hurry to reform and keep up with the globalization trend set in motion by the General Agreement on Tariffs and Trade/GATT (now replaced by the World Trade Organization), the immediate focus was on the **retrenchment of 'surplus workers'** and the **closure of 'sick' public and private sector units**. The immediate reactions from the workforce and trade unions were to resist this initiative. Massive rallies were organized in protest, and the government was called a puppet in the hands of the developed countries.

***Initiatives taken by the Tata Group*:** The Tatas were the pioneers in introducing a number of 'firsts' in the field of labour welfare. The group felt that unless a worker's welfare needs were met, there would be no profits for industry and no progress for the nation. Well ahead of any Indian legislation on this front, several benefits — the eight-hour working day, free medical aid, provident fund, gratuity, leave with pay, maternity leave, accident compensation, etc. — were incorporated by the Tatas into their workplace culture.

Positive Viewpoint Towards Reforms

One of the positive sides of labour reforms has been the focus on social welfare, which is primarily the responsibility of any industry. The Tatas are now considering labour reforms very carefully, with a view to ease the social burden of their employees and at the same time preserve the equilibrium of job security.

The Indian industry is going through a crucial phase of restructuring as competition increases. Countries such as China, where labour is cheap and labour disputes comparatively fewer, are posing serious threats to Indian organizations. With high productivity and mass production, China is a good example for Indian labour to emulate in terms of costs and productivity. Given the Indian track record of getting financial help from outside for development, the trade and economic policies of the government come under closer scrutiny from world bodies such as the International Monetary Fund, the Asian Development Bank and the WTO. Thus, it becomes inevitable for reforms of many kinds: economic and fiscal, market, law, and labour.

Two-fold benefits: From the industry perspective it is essential to have labour reforms in both organized and unorganized sectors. In the present scenario, there would be more industries coming up in India, and it naturally follows that this would create more employment opportunities. If prompt and correct measures are taken up in terms of interventions and transparency, then both the industry and the labour community would benefit.

Labour reform is not just about facilitating the closure of a sick industrial unit or about laying off employees. The core issues of labour reforms centre on a few major points namely: wage policy, employment security, labour redundancy, industrial relations, labour market information and human resources development. These issues can be solved by liberalizing existing labour legislations, enacting a flexible exit policy, 'rightsizing', reforming trade unions, by continuously retraining and updating workforce skills, worker participation in management, and by good and clean corporate governance. Government, industry, trade unions, industry associations, economists, sociologists, constitutional experts, intellectuals, institutes of management and social sciences, and the media, all of these should be involved in the labour reform process. A holistic and multi-disciplinary approach is required to solve the problems relating to labour reforms.

Cooperation required: All three parties — government, industry and trade unions — are equally responsible when it comes to putting effective labour reforms in place. One such case could be cited here, is that of Tata Tea. This company has been undertaking a lot of welfare measures for its employees and their children, measures that are beyond the scope of any legal requirement. These activities are costing Tata Tea a lot, and at a time when the tea industry is passing through a serious crisis.

Case evidence: The Tata Tea management had requested its unions to cooperate with the company to increase productivity. This would have helped both the company and its workers, but the union leaders were not agreeable to the idea. Because of their adamant nature the company and its employees suffered. This sort of irrational and destructive approach is detrimental to India's industry and economy. This kind of old-order trade unionism has to go.

Requirements for Effective Labour Reform Initiatives

- Two of the major impediments in bringing about desired labour reforms include the anti-labour stand in the management mindset, and labour prejudices.
- Good and clean corporate governance is a vital necessity of labour reforms.
- Attention towards human resource development.
- Worker training and education. The worker education models adopted by the Productivity Council of India, etc. need a thorough revamping.
- There is tremendous labour potential in the rural sector. This has to be tapped by industry, with a renewed focus on unorganized labour.
- The media has been covering labour reforms and related issues for long. A media-relations strategy should be worked out to highlight issues relating to the subject.

While India is labour intensive, it also boasts top-notch intellectual capital. The country's human talent and rich economic capital investment potential make it highly suited for industrial development.

Socio-economic and Technological Perspective of Industrial Relations

Industrial relations (IR) is the relationship which exists between an employer and an employee/s, employees and employees, employer and trade union/s, as representative/s of workmen/staff, employer and employer, and employer and the state, as a third party. Industrial relations in countries, sub-regions and regions, have been influenced by a variety of circumstances and actors such as political philosophies, economic imperatives, and the role of the State in determining the direction of economic and social development, the influence of unions and the business community, as well as the legacies of colonial governments. There are several factors which influence IR issues, but the scope of this present discussion would be limited with the socio-economic and technological perspectives.

Impact of Sociological Factors

The industry is a part of the society. Organizational goals cannot be separated from the society. Hence IR should be a matter of social understanding between the employer and the employees. The contemporary practices of an organization on safety, health and welfare, selection process, job placement, training, promotion, motivation, compensation and performance management have direct bearing on the IR of a company. Sociological factors like values, customs, and educational background shape the culture of a community in which the industry operates. This is why, organizations like TISCO have since its inception included in the memorandum of understanding (MoU) social responsibilities for the development of the community in which it operates (Jamshedpur and its adjacent areas). Today, responsible and progressive employers have taken up social responsibilities as the part of organizational functioning.

An important sociological factor influencing today's IR is the changes occurring in workforces, to varying degrees, in both industrialized market economies and developing economies. Many countries have witnessed the emergence of workforces with higher levels of education and skills than before which need to be managed in a manner different from the way in which employees, especially blue collar employees, have hitherto been managed. The skills of an employee are, therefore, an issue on which the interests of employers and employees converge, and the "development" of the employee is now of greater mutual advantage to employers and employees. Hence the greater need than before for cooperative and participative forms of IR. The increasing number of temporary and part time employees in the rapidly expanding service industries, some of which experience peak periods (hotels, airlines, shops) require a flexible labour force.

Exhibit: The Tisco and Telco Case

During the 1960s Telco, Jamshedpur took up a drive as part of its community development efforts to develop a nearby village situated behind the Telcoworks, where some of the company's workers used to reside. The village, namely, Chotagovindapur was renamed as Govindapur and developed as a modern, clean and ideal village where social amenities like sewing classes for women, school for children, medical dispensary, and library were provided by Telco. Besides Telco developed the infrastructure e.g., road, lighting and provided housing loan for house construction.

In Tisco, it is said that as a part of its organizational strategy, the management makes efforts to influence the worker's mind at his very residence. This is one of the most significant reasons why there is a very high level of belongingness amongst the employees of the company. This is also reflected in peaceful work environment in the company. Tisco did not have a major work stoppage for more than 50 years. Workers are partners in progress in Tisco. The trade unions have a positive approach to the organizational growth.

Impact of the Economic Environment

The global market economy has forced the Indian entrepreneurs as well as the workers and their representatives to own up the business and join hands to work for higher productivity. Trade unions also realize that the classical confrontational and agitational approach is dysfunctional in today's environment. They collabourate and cooperate with the management in understanding the difficulties confronting the management in the wake of the downturn in the business environment. They also have understood that the old militant approach can prove to detrimental to the cause of labour in the wake of the entrepreneurs' struggle for existence in the highly competitive environment. As a result, there was less number of strikes and manpower losses due to workers' direct agitational actions.

Exhibit: The BHEL Case

During the early 1980s, BHEL suffered due to scarcity of business orders. Employees including executives were worried over the impending loss of jobs that the company might envisage as a part of organizational strategy for downsizing. All the employees geared themselves to meet the challenge by being effective on the job. The management took steps to obtain business orders through International biddings and changing internal methods or working to meet the customers' demands of delivery time and quality standards. IR was absolutely proactive and highly participative.

The changing economic and business environment has forced the government ever since 1980 to change its policies on the industry and trade to make business competitive. Gradual liberalization of the "License Raj"/controls has forced Indian business to take a more positive approach to manage business. People are looked upon as power centres, and centre-staged due to the realization that they drive all the other sources of production. Investing on people through proper training, compensation and care is in the best interest of the organization.

Globalization has led employers to push for less regulation of IR, less standardization of the employment relationship, and a greater focus on the workplace as the centre of gravity of IR. Employers as well as some governments are viewing IR from a more strategic perspective, *i.e.*, how IR can contribute to and promote workplace cooperation, flexibility, productivity and competitiveness. It is increasingly recognized that how people are managed impacts on an enterprise's productivity and on the quality of goods and services, labour costs, the quality of the workforce and its motivation.

Impact of Technology

An important development which has shifted attention to workplace relations is technology. On the one hand, technology management is possible only through people, and the way they are managed and trained affects the success of such transfer. Technology is also displacing traditional jobs and creating new jobs requiring different skills. Further information technology, the limits of which are not known in terms of its potential to effect change, is exerting a tremendous impact on the structure of organizations, the nature and location of work and the way it is organized. This has resulted in management effected less by command and supervision, and more through emphasis on cooperation, information-sharing and communication, and with a more participative approach to managing people. Modern technology now makes it possible for aspects of work to be performed outside the enterprise, for example from home, and even outside national borders. Part time work is increasing particularly due to the influx of more females into employment and their preference in some cases for part time work. Developing countries are also feeling the impact of these changes.

Industrial Relations in the Information and Communications Technology Sector

The information and communications technology (ICT) sector is growing in economic and employment terms, but the nature of industrial relations in the sector is largely unknown.

There are many factors that help explain this:

- Many software and services firms are very young and it usually takes some time before bargaining structures emerge;
- Many employees consider themselves more or less as "professionals" and would arguably not even consider joining a union. Instead they prefer to negotiate their own terms of employment;
- The internal organization of these firms often resembles a partnership more than a traditional organization with a strict hierarchy;
- Many employers in the sector are unenthusiastic about unions and collective bargaining.

THEME READING: LABOUR UNREST AT HONDA MOTOR

On July 25, 2005, the management of the Honda Motorcycle & Scooter India (Private) Limited, (HMSI), a wholly-owned subsidiary of Honda Motor Company Limited (HMCL), encountered violent protests from workers that disrupted production at their plant in Gurgaon. HMSI workers were severely beaten up by the police, and newspapers and TV channels gave wide coverage to the violence of the action. The protest followed six months of simmering labour unrest at the HMSI factory in which the workers also resorted to job slowdown (since December 2004 when the workers' demand for an increase in wages was rejected by the HMSI management).

With their demands being rejected by the management, the workers tried to form a trade union and this resulted in a confrontation with the management. Fifty workers of the production team were suspended and four others dismissed in May 2005. Apparently there was a show of strength between the management and the workers.

While the management alleged that the workers were resorting to 'go-slow' tactics and were threatening not to return to work until their colleagues had been reinstated, the workers alleged that the management was using pressure tactics such as victimization of active union members and a 'lock-out' o break the back of the union.

On July 25, 2005, the workers of the plant were demanding reinstatement of the suspended employees when some workers allegedly attacked policemen on the plant premises.

This led to police intervention and a violent tussle ensued between the police and the workers in which workers protesting peacefully were also beaten up. The police were reported to have overreacted and it was alleged that they had been overzealous in protecting the interests of the HMSI management, even without any direct request from the company's management.

EXERCISES

Case Study: An Employee Relations Problem

Karen Smith has been employed in your department for six years. During her tenure she has been a valuable employee, although during the past two years you've observed a drop in her work performance due to tardiness and absenteeism. The whole department is aware that Karen is facing many problems at home, and her coworkers have covered for her and even completed work for her when necessary, but they are beginning to complain.

Although you had hoped that Karen's issues would improve and she would return to being the dependable employee you once knew, you must confront her about the work piling up.

When you meet with her the next morning and begin the discussion of her work performance, she starts to cry and tells you her husband has been abusive, her son is taking drugs, and she's been battling alcoholism and depression. You try to help her talk through these issues. You suggest that she visit the Employee Assistance Program and see her physician, and by the end of the meeting, she seems better. She leaves your office and starts a one-week vacation that you've just granted so she can begin to deal with these issues.

You feel she is taking steps to improve her situation. You realize that you never really did discuss her work performance, but you're confident that she'll be fine once she takes your advice.

Questions for Discussion

1. What did this supervisor do right?
2. What could this supervisor have done better?

QUESTION BANK

1. "With the mergence of knowledge workers, traditional concepts of industrial relations and trade unions are loosing their relevance". Respond to this statement with necessary arguments.
2. Write a note on the Indian labour market depicting the latest trends.
3. What do you mean by organized and unorganized labour? Explain with relevant examples.
4. Write a note on the status of women employment in India.
5. What is employee relations? What are the components of ER?
6. Write an essay on the ER scenario in India.
7. What are the stages of labour relations process?
8. What is workplace bullying? What is its impact on employee relations in organizations?
9. Define Industrial relations. What is its importance?
10. What do you mean by the IR system? What is its scope? Describe the perspectives of IR.

Internet Exercises

- Study the website www.labour.nic.in/ir/welcome.html and share your learnings with your friends in the class.
- Visit the ILO website (www.ilo.org/) and collect important information on latest IR practices.

Experiential Exercises

- If there is a nearby industrial estate close to your institute, conduct a small research to identify what are the various ER/IR practices used in the industry.
- "Is IR necessary for today's organizations?" Conduct a debate on the given topic in your class.

TRADE UNIONS

THEME CASE: A PLANT MANAGER'S WOES

ABC Motors is a part of the ABC group of industries which had its presence in India for more than 50 years. Although the main business of the company been manufacturing iron and steel, over the years the company had diversified its business into various products and services such as telecommunications, electronic goods, consultancy services, watches, tea etc. ABC motors is one successful sister concern of the group that had its record of manufacturing high quality vehicles both for Indian and International customers. Recently the management had decided to launch a new family car meant for the middle class Indian customers that would cost approximately Rs 1 lakh on road. The company had acquired land in the XYZ state in India and the project ever since its inception was flamed up with controversy. First of all there was a strong resistance from the local farmers who were against the setting of the plant and accused the state Government for forcibly acquiring their agricultural land and lease-selling the same at throw away prices to a private organization like that of ABC Motors. The entire issue turned out into a political drama, with the opposition party leader Mrs. Sabita Bose directly supporting the villagers into an organized protest against the government and ABC group. Yet amidst all these turmoil, ABC motors started its operations in time and by August 2008 the company was ready to launch its product into the market.

With the launching of the product knocking at doors, Mr. Ramesh, the Plant manager was tensed how things would shape. After finishing an urgent meeting in the company head office, Mr. Ramesh was returning to the plant on the company car. There was a road blockage on the highway leading to the plant site. The blockage was made by the trade union supported by the party of Mrs. Bose. Ramesh found that in the cue of vehicles standing on the highway two trucks were also meant for his organization's plant and they were supposed to deliver important components needed for the manufacturing of the car.

TRADE UNIONS

A trade union can be described as the representative body comprised of the employees working in an organization formed on a continuous basis for the purpose of securing diverse range of benefits and well being of the employees as well as that for the organization.

Objectives of Trade Unions

Trade unions are formed to protect and promote the interests of their members. Their primary function is to protect the interests of workers against discrimination and unfair employment practices. Trade unions are formed to achieve the following objectives:

Representation: Trade unions represent individual workers when they have a problem at work. Unions offer their members legal representation. Normally this is to help people get financial compensation for work-related injuries or to assist people who have to take their employer to court.

Negotiation: Negotiation is where union representatives, discuss with management, the issues which affect people working in an organization. There may be a difference of opinion between management and union members. Trade unions negotiate with the employers to find out a solution to these differences. Pay, working hours, holidays and changes to working practices are the sorts of issues that are negotiated. In many workplaces there is a formal agreement between the union and the company which states that the union has the right to negotiate with the employer.

Voice in decisions affecting workers: The economic security of employees is determined not only by the level of wages and duration of their employment, but also by the management's personal policies which include selection of employees for lay offs, retrenchment, promotion and transfer. Intervention of unions in such decision-making is a way through which workers can have their say in the decision-making to safeguard their interests.

Member Services: During the last few years, trade unions have increased the range of services they offer to their members. These include:

- **Education and training** — Most unions run training courses for their members on employment rights, health and safety and other issues. Some unions also help members who have left school with little education by offering courses on basic skills and courses leading to professional qualifications.
- **Legal assistance** — As well as offering legal advice on employment issues, some unions give help with personal matters, like housing, wills and debt.
- **Financial discounts** — People can get discounts on mortgages, insurance and loans from unions.
- **Welfare benefits** — One of the earliest functions of trade unions was to look after members who hit hard times. Some of the older unions offer financial help to their members when they are sick or unemployed.

Functions of Trade Unions

Trade unions perform a number of functions in order to achieve the objectives. These functions can be broadly classified into three categories:

- Militant functions
- Service and support functions

Militant Functions: Onc sct of activities performed by trade unions leads to the betterment of the position of their members in relation to their employment. The aim of such activities is to ensure adequate wages secure better conditions of work and employment get better treatment from employers, etc. When the unions fail to accomplish these aims by the method of collective bargaining and negotiations, they adopt an approach and put up a fight with the management in the form of go-slow tactics, strike, boycott, gherao, etc. Hence, these functions of the trade unions are known as militant or fighting functions. Thus, the militant functions of trade unions can be summed up as:

- To achieve higher wages and better working conditions
- To raise the status of workers as a part of industry
- To protect labours against victimization and injustice

Service and Support Functions: Another set of activities performed by trade unions aims at rendering help to its members in times of need, and improving their efficiency. Trade unions try to foster a spirit of cooperation and promote friendly industrial relations and diffuse education and culture among their members. They take up welfare measures for improving the morale of workers and generate self confidence among them. They also arrange for legal assistance to its members, if necessary. Besides, these, they undertake many welfare measures for their members, e.g., school for the education of children, library, reading-rooms, in-door and out-door games, and other recreational facilities. Some trade unions even undertake publication of some magazine or journal. These functions of trade unions can be summed up as:

- To take up welfare measures for improving the morale of workers
- To generate self confidence among workers
- To encourage sincerity and discipline among workers
- To provide opportunities for promotion and growth
- To protect women workers against discrimination

Importance of Trade Unionism

Trade unions help in accelerated pace of economic development in many ways as follows:

- by helping in the recruitment and selection of workers.
- by inculcating discipline among the workforce.
- by enabling settlement of industrial disputes in a rational manner.
- by helping social adjustments. Workers have to adjust themselves to the new working conditions, the new rules and policies. Workers coming from different backgrounds may become disorganized, unsatisfied and frustrated. Unions help them in such adjustment.

Trade unions are a part of society and as such, have to take into consideration the national integration as well. Some important social responsibilities of trade unions include:

- promoting and maintaining national integration by reducing the number of industrial disputes.
- incorporating a sense of corporate social responsibility in workers achieving industrial peace.

Reasons for Joining Trade Unions

The important forces that make the employees join a union are as follows:

Greater Bargaining Power: The individual employee possesses very little bargaining power as compared to that of his employer. If he is not satisfied with the wage and other conditions of employment, he can leave the job. It is not practicable to continually resign from one job after another when he is dissatisfied. This imposes a great financial and emotional burden upon the worker. The better course for him is to join a union that can take concerted action against the employer. The threat or actuality of a strike by a union is a powerful tool that often causes the employer to accept the demands of the workers for better conditions of employment.

Minimize Discrimination: The decisions regarding pay, work, transfer, promotion, etc. are highly subjective in nature. The personal relationships existing between the supervisor and each of his subordinates may influence the management. Thus, there are chances of favouritisms and discriminations. A trade union can compel the management to formulate personnel policies that press for equality of treatment to the workers. All the labour decisions of the management are under close scrutiny of the labour union. This has the effect of minimizing favouritism and discrimination.

Sense of Security: The employees may join the unions because of their belief that it is an effective way to secure adequate protection from various types of hazards and income insecurity such as accident, injury, illness, unemployment, etc. The trade union secure retirement benefits of the workers and compel the management to invest in welfare services for the benefit of the workers.

Sense of Participation: The employees can participate in management of matters affecting their interests only if they join trade unions. They can influence the decisions that are taken as a result of collective bargaining between the union and the management.

Sense of Belongingness: Many employees join a union because their coworkers are the members of the union. At times, an employee joins a union under group pressure; if he does not, he often has a very difficult time at work. On the other hand, those who are members of a union feel that they gain respect in the eyes of their fellow workers. They can also discuss their problem with' the trade union leaders.

Platform for Self Expression: The desire for self expression is a fundamental human drive for most people. All of us wish to share our feelings, ideas and opinions with others. Similarly the workers also want the management to listen to them. A trade union provides such a forum where the feelings, ideas and opinions of the workers could be discussed. It can also transmit the feelings, ideas, opinions and complaints of the workers to the management. The collective voice of the workers is heard by the management and give due consideration while taking policy decisions by the management.

Betterment of Relationships: Another reason for employees joining unions is that employees feel that unions can fulfill the important need for adequate machinery for proper maintenance of employer-employee relations. Unions help in betterment of industrial relations among management and workers by solving the problems peacefully.

TRADE UNIONS IN INDIA

General Background

Development of modern industry, especially in the Western countries, can be traced back to the 18th century. Industrial development in India on Western lines however commenced from the middle of the 19th century. The first organized Trade Union in India named as the Madras Labour Union was formed in the year 1918. Since then a large number of unions sprang up in almost all the industrial centers of the country. Similarly, entrepreneurs also formed their organizations to protect their interests. In 1926, the Trade Unions Act was passed by the Indian Government. The Act gave legal status to the Registered Trade Unions. The Registrars of Trade Unions in different states were empowered to register the Trade Unions in their respective states. These registered Trade Unions (Workers and Employers) are required to submit annual statutory return to the Registrar regarding their membership, General Funds, Sources of Income and Items of Expenditure and details of their assets and liabilities, which in turn submit consolidated return of their state in the prescribed **proformae** to Labour Bureau.

Growth of Trade Unions

Trade Union in India is the primary instrument for promoting the union of **trade union movement** and championing the cause of **working class** in India. The **Madras Labour Union** was the first organized **Trade Union in India** followed by a large number of **trade unions** in the Indian industrial centers. The Indian government passed the **Trade Unions Act** in 1926, which legalized the registered **Trade Union in India**. The Act also gives protection to these trade unions against certain civil and criminal cases.

Trade Unions Act, 1926

Trade Unions Act, 1926 provides for the registration of the Trade Unions with the Registrars of Trade Unions of their territory. Any seven or more members of a trade union by submitting their names to the registrar of trade unions and otherwise complying with the provisions of the Act with respect to registration may apply for the registration of the Trade Union under the Trade Unions Act. The Act gives protection to registered trade unions in certain cases against civil and criminal action.

Significant Trade Unions in India

There are at present many **Trade Unions** in India which regulate the aspirations of the **working class**. The **All India Trade Union Congress** (AITUC) is the oldest **Trade Union in India** and till 1945 it remained the central **trade union organization in India**. Some others are like –

- **All India Bank Officers Confederation**— AIBOC is the premier organization of Bank Officers in India. This **Trade Union in India** stands apart from the others as it is organized purely on a political lines.
- **All India State Government Employees Federation**— AISGEF is a **trade union organization** representing state employees and teachers of different states in India.
- **Center of Indian Trade Unions** — CITU is one of the major **Trade Union in India**, opposing imperialistic intentions and patronizing interest of the **working classes**.
- **Hind Mazdoor Sabha** — HMS is a progressive **Trade Union in India** that prefers to refrain from political control.

- **National Confederation of Officer's Association** —NCOA represents the managerial and supervisory staff of the Indian government owned public enterprises.
- **Trade Union International** — TUI forms a part of the structure of **World Federation of Trade Unions**, representing the public employees, telecommunication employees, health services, financial sector employees and municipal employees of different countries of the world.

The **Trade Union in India** is engaged in protesting against the attacks on trade union right, right to strike, right to collective bargaining, reduction of social security, closure of industrial units and massive retrenchment of workers, and the endangering growth of unemployment.

Phases of Trade Union Movement in India

The trade unionism in India developed quite slowly as compared to the western nations. Indian trade union movement can be divided into three phases.

The first phase (1850 to 1900): During this phase the inception of trade unions took place. During this period, the working and living conditions of the labour were poor and their working hours were long. Capitalists were only interested in their productivity and profitability. In addition, the wages were also low and general economic conditions were poor in industries. In order to regulate the working hours and other service conditions of the Indian textile labourers, the Indian Factories Act was enacted in 1881. As a result, employment of child labour was prohibited.

The growth of trade union movement was slow in this phase and later on the Indian Factory Act of 1881 was amended in 1891. Many strikes took place in the two decades following 1880 in all industrial cities. These strikes taught workers to understand the power of united action even though there was no union in real terms. Small associations like Bombay Mill-Hands Association came up by this time.

The second phase (1900 to 1946): This phase was characterized by the development of organized trade unions and political movements of the working class. Between 1918 and 1923, many unions came into existence in the country. At Ahmedabad, under the guidance of Mahatma Gandhi, occupational unions like spinners' unions and weavers' unions were formed. A strike was launched by these unions under the leadership of Mahatma Gandhi who turned it into a Satyagraha. These unions federated into industrial union known as textile labour association in 1920. In 1920, the first national trade union organization (The All India Trade Union Congress (AITUC)) was established. Many of the leaders of this organization were leaders of the national movement. In 1926, Trade union law came up with the efforts of Mr. N N Joshi that became operative from 1927. During 1928, All India Trade Union Federation (AITUF) was formed.

The third phase (Post 1947): The third phase began with the emergence of independent India (in 1947). The partition of country affected the trade union movement particularly Bengal and Punjab. By 1949, four central trade union organizations were functioning in the country:

1. The All India Trade Union Congress,
2. The Indian National Trade Union Congress,
3. The Hindu Mazdoor Sangh, and
4. The United Trade Union Congress.

Trade unions in India (Present scenario): At present there are twelve Central Trade Union Organizations in India:

1. All India Trade Union Congress (AITUC)
2. Bharatiya Mazdoor Sangh (BMS)
3. Centre of Indian Trade Unions (CITU)
4. Hind Mazdoor Kisan Panchayat (HMKP)
5. Hind Mazdoor Sabha (HMS)

6. Indian Federation of Free Trade Unions (IFFTU)
7. Indian National Trade Union Congress (INTUC)
8. National Front of Indian Trade Unions (NFITU)
9. National Labour Organization (NLO)
10. Trade Unions Coordination Centre (TUCC)
11. United Trade Union Congress (UTUC) and
12. United Trade Union Congress - Lenin Sarani (UTUC - LS)

Table 5.3: Number and Membership of Workers' Unions by Major Industry Divisions for the Year, 2002

Code	*Industry Division*	*No. of Unions submitting returns*	*Membership*		
			Men	*Women*	*Total*
1		2	3	4	5
A	Agriculture, Hunting, Forestry	310	683094	389589	1072686
		(4.0)	(13.5)	(20.9)	(15.5)
B	Fishing	24	10021	5162	15183
		(0.3)	(0.2)	(0.3)	(0.2)
C	Mining and Quarrying	181	153097	28467	181564
		(2.3)	(3.0)	(1.5)	(2.6)
D	Manufacturing	2798	1365258	355979	1721237
		(36.2)	(27.0)	(19.1)	(24.9)
E	Electricity, Gas and Water	214	320712	16086	336798
		(2.8)	(6.3)	(0.9)	(4.9)
F	Construction	430	415568	144107	559675
		(5.6)	(8.2)	(7.7)	(8.1)
G	Wholesale and Retail Trade repair of motor vehicles, motor cycles and personal and household goods	239	122854	6840	129694
		(3.1)	(2.4)	(0.4)	(1.9)
H	Hotels and Restaurants	96	19439	719	20158
		(1.2)	(0.4)	(0.0)	(0.3)
I	Transport, Storage and Communication	1286	1125413	66740	1192153
		(16.6)	(22.2)	(3.6)	(17.2)

Contd...

J	Financial, Inter-mediation	733	195831	34845	230676
		(9.5)	(3.9)	(1.9)	(3.3)
K	Real Estate, Renting and Business Activities	392	248433	568390	816823
		(5.1)	(4.9)	(30.5)	(11.8)
L	Public Administration and Defence, Compulsory Social Security	263	127406	21842	149248
		(3.4)	(2.5)	(1.2)	(2.2)
M	Education	69	5496	20697	26193
		(0.9)	(0.1)	(1.1)	(0.4)
N	Health and Social Work	92	35182	10237	45419
		(1.2)	(0.7)	(0.5)	(0.7)
O	Other Community, Social and Personal Service Activities	597	231085	193768	424853
		(7.7)	(4.6)	(10.4)	(6.1)
P	Private, House Holds with Employed Persons	10	745	405	1150
		(0.1)	(0.0)	(0.0)	(0.0)
Q	Extra-Territorial Organizations and Bodies	-	-	-	-
	TOTAL	**7734**	**5059634**	**1863873**	**6923507**

N.B. Figures in brackets indicate percentages to total.

Workers Trade Unions in Public Sector

State wise statistics pertaining to the number of Workers' Unions submitting returns and their membership in Public Sector separately for State Sphere and Central Sphere for the year 2002 is given in statement 3.3. It may be seen from the statement that public sector accounted for 33.3 per cent of unions and 32.9 per cent of the membership in total workers unions submitting returns. Out of 2576 unions submitting returns in the Public sector 717 (27.8 per cent) unions were in the Central Sphere. Membership of Trade Unions in the State Sphere and Central Sphere was 13,40,340 persons and 9,34,359 persons respectively.

Employers Unions

State wise number of Employers' Unions on register submitting returns and their membership are given in statement 4.1. In 2002, out of 189 registered Employers Unions, 78 unions (i.e. 41.3%) had submitted returns. All the employers, trade unions submitting returns were State Unions. These unions had a membership of 49,815 persons. Out of which 42,535 (85.4%) were men and remaining 7,280 (14.6%) were women. The average membership per employers union was 639.

Finances of Trade Unions

General Funds

Information relating to financial position of registered Trade Unions submitting returns (i.e. Opening Balance, Income, Expenditure and Closing Balance) for the year 1991 to 2002 are presented in Statement 5.1. During 2002 all the 7,812 Trade Unions submitting returns had an income of 66.61 Crores against which an expenditure of Rs. 56.84 Crores were reported.

Table 5.4: Percentage Distribution of Income of Workers' and Employers' Unions by Sources During 2002

	Sources of income	*Percentage of income*			
		Workers' unions		*Employers' unions*	
Sl. No.		*Central unions*	*State unions*	*Central unions*	*State unions*
1	2	3	4	5	6
1	Contribution from members	42.6	57.6	-	23.7
2	Donations	18.1	19.0	-	15.9
3	Sale of periodicals, books etc.	1.4	1.4	-	0.0
4	Interest on investments	10.1	6.5	-	14.9
5	Income from miscellaneous sources	27.7	15.4	-	45.4
	All sources	100.0	100.0	-	100.00

Trade Union International (TUI)

Trade Union International (**TUI**) forms a part of the structure of World Federation of Trade Unions. It represents the Public Employees, Telecommunication Employees, Health Services and Allied Employees, Financial Sector Employees and Municipal Employees of different countries of the world. The World Federation of Trade Unions (**WFTU**) was established in Paris on 3 October, 1945. The constitution of WFTU provided the formation of industry-wise TUIs. Accordingly **TUI** of Public and Allied Employees was formed. **TUI** is an autonomous body but WFTU & TUIs cooperate with each other. The constitution of **TUI** is framed in accordance with that of WFTU. The policy of **TUI** is also in conformity with that of WFTU.

Principal Activities

The Trade Unions International Takes an Active Part

- in all questions interesting the personnel of the public services in the professional, economic and social field, and priorities are: the safeguarding of full employment, the improvement of the conditions of work and remuneration, labour, hygiene and safety, the prevention of negative effects of the introduction of new techniques and technologies, the securing of the necessary vocational training and further training as well as the end of any discrimination against working women and youths.
- in all questions concerning the public services, their utilization, their developments, their means, their role especially with a view to preventing the social character of public services from being destroyed

by projects of massive privatizations, and in order to achieve that the financial, material, and human resources which are being wasted in the armament race are employed in favour of socially useful expenditure, of the development of public services, for the well-being and for raising the living standard of the population.

- in all questions concerning public employees' unions, their development, their struggles, the organization of their activities, principally for : the intensification of international solidarity between public employees' unions who authentically represent the interests of the employees, without considering their international affiliation, the increased participation of the trade unions in the struggle for peace and disarmament, for guaranteeing trade union rights and liberties, for the rights of man, against racism and militarism.

Changing Role of Trade Unions

The role of trade unionism in India has been significantly changing over the years. One example that could be cited is that of the case in Mumbai, where almost all the textile mills in the city closed because of the unreasonable demands made by trade unions under Datta Samant. India has the advantages of (a) growing both long staple and short staple cotton and (b) a huge domestic market. But battling militant trade unions, on the one hand, while coping with price controls imposed by unimaginative governments and textile quotas imposed by foreign governments, on the other, proved too much for our textile industry. The textile industry did not have the necessary financial and managerial resources, and it failed to modernize and remain competitive in terms of quality and cost. So ultimately it declined and became terminally ill.

Trade unions are a legitimate system for organizing workers and to voice their rights and grievances. Without them companies would become either too paternalistic or too dictatorial. Responsible unions help to create a middle path in the relationship between management and labour while maintaining the responsibilities of the former and the dignity of the latter.

Fortunately today, workers have become better informed and aware of the economic forces that impact their industry. The media has helped to create much greater economic awareness. So it is not so easy to mislead them. Managements too have become more sensitive and skilled in handling relationships with employees. This is true of even family-owned and managed businesses. TVS in the South is a prime example of how a large family-managed industrial group has successfully managed its relationship with employees through enlightened management. There are more such examples in other parts of the country.

As the skill levels and educational qualifications of employees advance, the role and significance of trade unions tend to diminish. This is because (a) employees are able to represent their own case and (b) managements are more sensitive to the needs of individual employees, whose intellectual skills become almost uniquely valuable. This is already happening in the sunrise industries based on brainpower such as IT and telecommunications. Another phenomenon in these modern industries is that employees have greater opportunity and tendency to move from one company to another, not only because of better terms of employment but also because of their yearning to learn new skills. This phenomenon is facilitated by the fact that there are plenty of employment opportunities in IT and it is a young industry. That is why one does not notice any union flags in the Silicon Valley of India/Bangalore's Electronic City.

The privatization or corporatization of many public services such as electricity and water supply has accelerated this shift. Hopefully the same shift in the character and role of trade unions will happen in India — even in places like Kerala and West Bengal, as employment starts to move to more intellect-based activities and public sector industries are privatized. Responsible trade union leaders with a long-term vision will adapt their policies to suit the new realities.

COLLECTIVE BARGAINING

Collective Bargaining is the process whereby workers organize collectively and bargain with employers regarding the workplace. In various national labour and employment law contexts collective bargaining takes on a more specific legal meaning. In a broad sense, however, it is the coming together of workers to negotiate their employment. Collective bargaining is specifically an industrial relations mechanism or tool, and is an aspect of negotiation, applicable to the employment relationship.

A collective agreement is a labour contract between an employer and one or more unions. Collective bargaining consists of the process of negotiation between representatives of a union and employers (represented by management, in some countries by employers' organization) in respect of the terms and conditions of employment of employees, such as wages, hours of work, working conditions and grievance-procedures, and about the rights and responsibilities of trade unions. The parties often refer to the result of the negotiation as a *Collective Bargaining Agreement* (CBA) or as a *Collective Employment Agreement* (CEA).

Exhibit: Industry Opinion

"Today, the unions have taken a pragmatic stand. They appreciate need for modernizing workplaces in this era of competition. There's no ideological opposition on several counts any more. Even the Left has had to effect some change in postures with regard to the changing environs," says Mr Shantha Raju, General Secretary, All India Bank Officers Confederation (AIBOC).

Bargaining Form and Tactics

A collective bargaining process generally consists of four types of activities—distributive bargaining, integrative bargaining, attitudinal restructuring and intra-organizational bargaining. Distributivc bargaining: It involves haggling over the distribution of surplus. Under it, the economic issues like wages, salaries and bonus are discussed. In distributive bargaining, one party's gain is another party's loss. This is most commonly explained in terms of a pie. Disputants can work together to make the pie bigger, so there is enough for both of them to have as much as they want, or they can focus on cutting the pie up, trying to get as much as they can for themselves. In general, distributive bargaining tends to be more competitive. This type of bargaining is also known as conjunctive bargaining.

Integrative Bargaining

This involves negotiation of an issue on which both the parties may gain, or at least neither party loses. For example, representatives of employer and employee sides may bargain over the better training programme or a better job evaluation method. Here, both the parties are trying to make more of something. In general, it tends to be more cooperative than distributive bargaining. This type of bargaining is also known as cooperative bargaining.

Attitudinal Restructuring

This involves shaping and reshaping some attitudes like trust or distrust, friendliness or hostility between labour and management. When there is a backlog of bitterness between both the parties, attitudinal restructuring is required to maintain smooth and harmonious industrial relations. It develops a bargaining environment and creates trust and cooperation among the parties.

Intra-organizational Bargaining

It generally aims at resolving internal conflicts. This is a type of maneuvering to achieve consensus with the workers and management. Even within the union, there may be differences between groups. For example, skilled workers may feel that they are neglected or women workers may feel that their interests are not looked after properly. Within the management also, there may be differences. Trade unions maneuver to achieve consensus among the conflicting groups.

Characteristics of Collective Bargaining

- It is a group process, wherein one group, representing the employers, and the other, representing the employees, sit together to negotiate terms of employment.
- Negotiations form an important aspect of the process of collective bargaining i.e., there is considerable scope for discussion, compromise or mutual give and take in collective bargaining.
- Collective bargaining is a formalized process by which employers and independent trade unions negotiate terms and conditions of employment and the ways in which certain employment-related issues are to be regulated at national, organizational and workplace levels.
- Collective bargaining is a process in the sense that it consists of a number of steps. It begins with the presentation of the charter of demands and ends with reaching an agreement, which would serve as the basic law governing labour management relations over a period of time in an enterprise. Moreover, it is flexible process and not fixed or static. Mutual trust and understanding serve as the by products of harmonious relations between the two parties.
- It is a bipartite process. This means there are always two parties involved in the process of collective bargaining. The negotiations generally take place between the employees and the management. It is a form of participation.
- Collective bargaining is a complementary process i.e. each party needs something that the other party has; labour can increase productivity and management can pay better for their efforts.
- Collective bargaining tends to improve the relations between workers and the union on the one hand and the employer on the other.
- Collective bargaining is continuous process. It enables industrial democracy to be effective. It uses cooperation and consensus for settling disputes rather than conflict and confrontation.
- Collective bargaining takes into account day to day changes, policies, potentialities, capacities and interests.
- It is a political activity frequently undertaken by professional negotiators.

Essentials of Collective Bargaining

Collective bargaining generally includes negotiations between the two parties (employees' representatives and employer's representatives). Collective bargaining consists of negotiations between an employer and a group of employees that determine the conditions of employment. Often employees are represented in the bargaining by a union or other labour organization. The result of collective bargaining procedure is called the collective bargaining agreement (CBA). Collective agreements may be in the form of procedural agreements or substantive agreements. Procedural agreements deal with the relationship between workers and management and the procedures to be adopted for resolving individual or group disputes. This will normally include procedures in respect of individual grievances, disputes and discipline. Frequently, procedural agreements are put into the company rule book which provides information on the overall terms and conditions of employment and codes of behaviour. A substantive CBA deals with specific issues, such as basic pay, overtime premiums, bonus arrangements, holiday entitlements, hours of work, etc. In many companies, agreements have a fixed time scale and a collective bargaining process will review the procedural agreement when negotiations take place on pay and conditions of employment.

The collective bargaining process comprises of five core steps:

1. **Prepare:** This phase involves composition of a negotiation team. The negotiation team should consist of representatives of both the parties with adequate knowledge and skills for negotiation. In this phase both the employer's representatives and the union examine their own situation in order to develop the issues that they believe will be most important. The first thing to be done is to determine whether there is actually any reason to negotiate at all. A correct understanding of the main issues to be covered and intimate knowledge of operations, working conditions, production norms and other relevant conditions is required.
2. **Discuss:** Here, the parties decide the ground rules that will guide the negotiations. A process well begun is half done and this is no less true in case of collective bargaining. An environment of mutual trust and understanding is also created so that the collective bargaining agreement would be reached.
3. **Propose:** This phase involves the initial opening statements and the possible options that exist to resolve them. In a word, this phase could be described as 'brainstorming'. The exchange of messages takes place and opinion of both the parties is sought.
4. **Bargain:** Negotiations are easy if a problem solving attitude is adopted. This stage comprises the time when 'what ifs' and 'supposals' are set forth and the drafting of agreements take place.
5. **Settlement:** Once the parties are through with the bargaining process, a consensual agreement is reached upon wherein both the parties agree to a common decision regarding the problem or the issue. This stage is described as consisting of effective joint implementation of the agreement through shared visions, strategic planning and negotiated change.

Levels of Collective Bargaining

Collective bargaining operates at three levels:

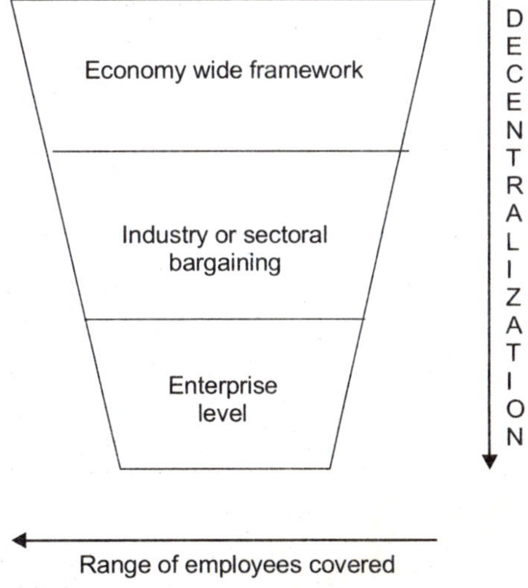

Fig. 5.11: Framework of collective bargaining

- **National Level Bargaining:** Economy wide (national) bargaining is a bipartite or tripartite form of negotiation between union confederations, central employer associations and government agencies. It aims at providing a floor for lower-level bargaining on the terms of employment, often taking into account macroeconomic goals.

- **Sector or Industry Level Bargaining:** Sectoral bargaining, which aims at the standardization of the terms of employment in one industry, includes a range of bargaining patterns. Bargaining may be either broadly or narrowly defined in terms of the industrial activities covered and may be either split up according to territorial subunits or conducted nationally.
- **Company/Enterprise Level Bargaining:** The third bargaining level involves the company and/or establishment. As a supplementary type of bargaining, it emphasizes the point that bargaining levels need not be mutually exclusive.

Types of Collective Bargaining	Features/Hallmarks
1. Plant level CB	• Here negotiations and agreements are settled between the management and the union representatives. • Scope of collective bargaining is confined to the micro-level problems with no involvement of other unions in other organizations or industries.
2. Industry level CB	• Here organizations in a particular industry who face similar IR problems follow this type of CB. • Agreements/contracts signed at this level is applicable for all organizations in the industry and also various unions coming under the purview of the industry.
3. National level CB	• Here the common problems of all workers cutting across the industries, regions, and even sectors are discussed between representatives of National Trade Unions and representatives of industry and business community. • Eg: (a) 1951-Agreement between INTUC and management to "rationalize work practices" (b) 1956-Agreement between Trade unions (HMS) and Indian Tea Planter's Association on bonus for plantation workers.

Scope of Collective Bargaining: The scope of collective bargaining is as follows:

- Wages fixation, increments and bonus payments
- Hours of work and overtime
- Terms and conditions of work, safety, welfare and health care.
- Grievance procedure
- Labour productivity, labour standards and modernization
- Union-management relations including worker participation

Features of Collective Bargaining

There are several essential features of collective bargaining, all of which cannot be reflected in a single definition or description of the process:

- It is not equivalent to collective agreements because collective bargaining refers to the process or means, and collective agreements to the possible result, of bargaining. Collective bargaining may not always lead to a collective agreement.
- It is a method used by trade unions to improve the terms and conditions of employment of their members.

- It seeks to restore the unequal bargaining position between employer and employee.
- Where it leads to an agreement, it modifies, rather than replaces, the individual contract of employment, because it does not create the employer-employee relationship.
- The process is bipartite, but in some developing countries the state plays a role in the form of a conciliator where disagreements occur, or where collective bargaining impinges on government policy.

Components of Collective Bargaining

- Statutory support by Legislative measures (Acts)
- Existence of employees representatives – the unions
- Recognition of union by employer as the bargaining agent
- Existence of industrial disputes
- Threat of economic force in the form of "lock out" or "strike" to settle industrial dispute
- Negotiation
- Finalization of agreement
- Implementation of agreement

Process of Collective Bargaining

The collective bargaining process has the following phases, namely:

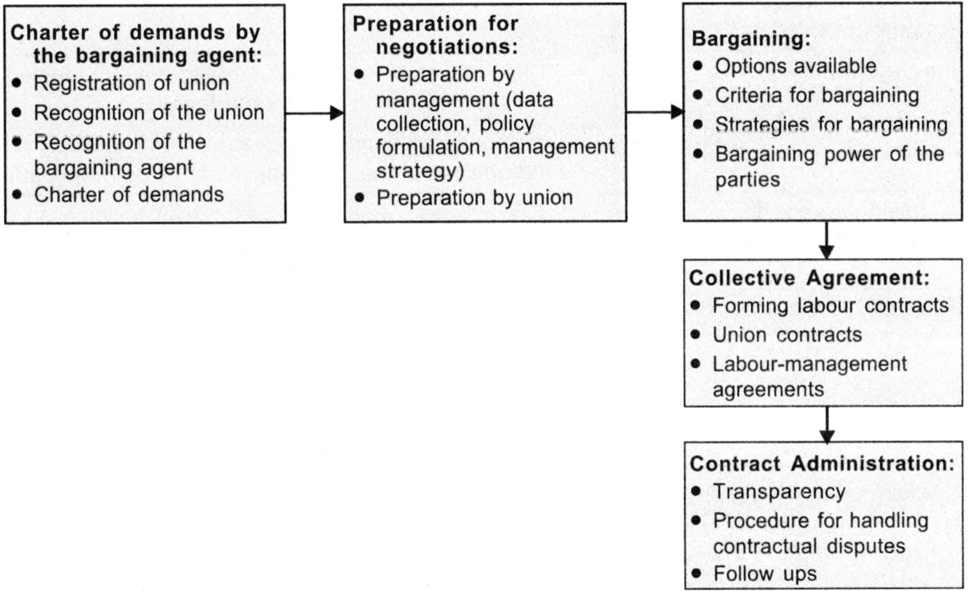

Fig. 5.12: The steps in the collective bargaining process

Charter of demands by the bargaining agent: The charter of demands is generally prepared by the bargaining agent i.e. the trade union. In case of multiple unions, the unit level charter of demands is prepared by a "Joint Action Council" which consists of the representatives of all the participating unions. In case of collective bargaining done at the industrial level, the association of such unions is involved with preparing the charter of demand.

Preparation for negotiations: This stage is characterized by the preparation from the side of the management as well as from the side of the union concerned.

- ***Preparation by the Management*:** This involves three stages, namely: collection of data with respect to employee performance, labour standards, productivity, absenteeism records, turnover records etc along with external data with respect to current state of the economy, sales forecast, industry trends etc. the next stage involves policy formulation based on the data and assessing the expectations of the employees/unions. This is subsequently followed by management strategy formulation with respect to prioritization of demand, stand on the unions and decisions with respect to industrial disputes like those of strikes, lockouts etc.
- ***Preparation by Unions*:** The unions may also collect information related to the problem being bargained with the management from industry sources and may thereby develop strategies or action plans depending on their respective negotiation power, market conditions, public support and other relevant factors influencing the bargaining process.

Bargaining Stage: The bargaining stage is perhaps the most prolonged stage of the collective bargaining process. It starts with the process of identifying the various **options available** during/for the bargaining process. This may involve issues such as identifying the criteria for rejection of all demands, criteria for temporary suspension of negotiations, identifying areas or potential for counter demands. Once the options for the bargaining process are sorted out, the **criteria for the bargaining process** are identified with respect to both the management and the bargaining agent. The next stage involves identifying the relevant **strategies for the bargaining process**. This may involve the following:

Types of Collective Bargaining Strategies	Features/Hallmarks
1. Intra-organizational	• This involves the strategies for preparing for the negotiation between the management and the union. • Intra-organizational bargaining aims to broadly lay down the outlines of the demands made by both the parties.
2. Attitudinal structuring	• This strategy mainly emphasizes on building an ongoing relationship between the unions and the management instead of an **adhoc** arrangement or agreement.
3. Distributive bargaining	• This approach is based on the “gain/loss” philosophy.
4. Interactive bargaining	• Here the objective of this bargaining strategy is to facilitate each party to prosper taking in to considerations needs and aspirations of both the union as well as objectives of the management.

The success of the bargaining stage also depends on the bargaining power of both the intervening parties in terms of the control or influence of the management on the employees and the unions and on the other hand side the ability of the unions to convene an issue to the management. The bargaining power of the union may considerably vary depending on their membership, representation, political influence, competition from other rival unions, styles, objectives and motives of negotiation etc.

Contract Administration and Implementation

Once the collective agreement is documented and signed by the bargaining parties implementation of the contract becomes crucial for the success of the bargaining process. This depends on factors like those of:

- Maintaining transparency in any sort of interventions
- Creating procedures for handling contractual disagreements and disputes
- Ensuring follow up and feedback on the implementation of the agreement

Factors Important for the Success of Collective Bargaining

Pluralism and the Freedom of Association

A pluralistic outlook involves the acceptance within a political system of pressure groups (e.g. religious groups, unions, business associations, political parties) with specific interests with which a government has dialogue, with a view to effecting compromises by making concessions. Pluralism implies a process of bargaining between these groups, and between one or more of them on the one hand and the government on the other. There can, therefore, be no meaningful collective bargaining without the freedom of association accorded to both employers and workers.

Trade Union Recognition

The existence of the freedom of association does not necessarily mean that there would automatically be recognition of unions for bargaining purposes. Especially in systems where there is a multiplicity of trade unions, there should be some pre-determined objective criteria operative within the industrial relations system to decide when and how a union should be recognized for collective bargaining purposes. The accepted principle is to recognize the most representative union, but what criteria is used to decide it and by whom may differ from system to system.

Support of Labour Administration Authorities

Support by the labour administration authorities is necessary for successful collective bargaining. This implies that they will:

(i) Provide the necessary climate for it. For instance, they should provide effective conciliation services in the event of a breakdown in the process, and even provide the necessary legal framework for it to operate in where necessary, *e.g.* provision for the registration of agreements.
(ii) Will not support a party in breach of agreements concluded consequent to collective bargaining.
(iii) As far as is practicable, secure observance of collective bargaining agreements.
(iv) Provide methods for the settlement of disputes arising out of collective bargaining if the parties themselves have not so provided.

Good Faith

Collective bargaining is workable only if the parties bargain in good faith. If not, there will be only the process of bargaining without a result *viz.* an agreement. Good faith is more likely where certain attitudes are shared among employers, workers and their organizations *e.g.* a belief and faith in the value of compromise through dialogue, in the process of collective bargaining, and in the productive nature of the relationship collective bargaining requires and develops.

Proper Internal Communication

Both the management and union should keep their managers and members respectively well informed, as a lack of proper communication and information can lead to misunderstandings and even to strikes. Sometimes managers and supervisors who are ill-informed may inadvertently mislead workers who work under them about the current state of negotiations, the management's objectives and so on. In fact, it is necessary to involve managers in deciding on objectives and solutions, and such participation is likely to ensure greater acceptance - and therefore better implementation - by them.

Negotiation in Industrial Relations

Collective bargaining and negotiations are often used synonymously. But in reality negotiation is actually considered to be a part of the collective bargaining process. Negotiation has been described by Walton and McKersieas as "the deliberate interaction of two or more complex social units which are attempting to define or redefine the terms of their interdependence". Gottschalk had defined negotiation as "an occasion where one or more representatives of the two or more parties interact in an explicit attempt to reach a jointly acceptable position on one or more divisive issues". In industrial relations, negotiation is used a process for resolving conflict between two or more parties whereby both or all modify their demands to achieve a mutually acceptable compromise.

Prerequisites for Negotiation

The requirements for an effective negotiation process are as follows:

- There should be mutual dependence between the conflicting parties.
- Some interests must be shared and others opposed.
- On party should not have, or be unwilling to use, coercive power in the conventional "command and control" strategy.

Process of Negotiation

During negotiation, the conflicting parties involved move from their ideal position to a settlement point that is mutually acceptable. The position of this settlement point depends on the relative bargaining strength and skills of the negotiator. Here one of the parties might have to move more or less as compared to the other one. The process of negotiation may be illustrated by the following figure:

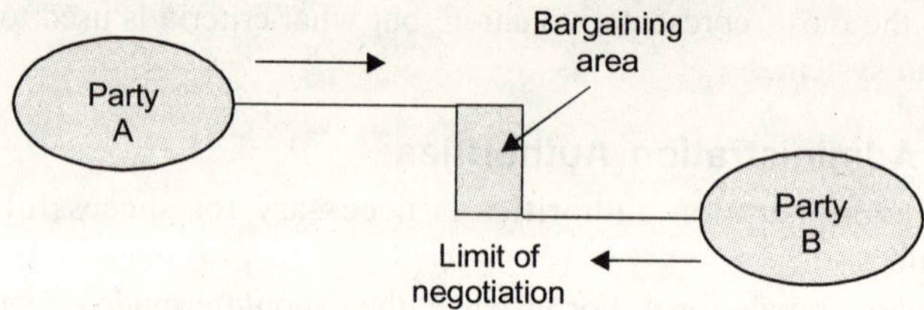

Fig. 5.13: Negotiation process

QUESTION BANK

1. "With the mergence of Knowledge Workers, Trade unions are loosing their relevance". Respond to this statement with necessary arguments.
2. In what ways do organized unions constrain strategic choices of managers? (BU July/August 2005).
3. Discuss collective bargaining as a method of managing employee relations.
4. "The role of trade union movement has changed due to globalization and privatization". Discuss. (BU 2002).
5. Review the changes in the concept of IR and their effects on HRM.
6. Identify and discuss the factors that make unionization attractive to employees. Are these factors different today than they were 50 years ago? (BU 2004).
7. Are union free plants desirable? Yes or no – discuss. Illustrate your answer with five examples. (BU 2004).
8. Discuss briefly the growth and development of Employee's Associations and their functions in India.

Internet Exercises

- Visit the website www.labourbureau.nic.in and collect the latest information on trade union movement in India.
- Read the article titled "Trade union? India's BPO workers say 'no'" given in the following hyperlink: www.rediff.com/money/2005/sep/26bpo.htm and share it with your friends.

INDUSTRIAL DISPUTES

THEME CASE: MRS. BOSÉ AND ABC BANK

Mrs. Bose joined ABC Bank as a clerk after her M.Com, in 1968. She was aspiring for promotion to the officer's post. She completed CAIIB to which certain weightage is given in promotion. After getting the eligibility service in 1976, she applied for the officer's post in the bank under the promotion quota.

She could not get the promotion as her score in the written test was quite low. But at that time she was transferred to her native place. She tried for officer's post several times but could not succeed. She was vexed with her trials. But very soon she was elected to the office of President of local branch of Bank Employees Union. Since then she has become a problem to the management. She could solve a number of problems of the members of her union.

Consequently almost all the clerks of the branch joined the union. However, she has been continuing her trials for officer's post; she was not given the promotion in 1980 though she got more than the minimum score in the written test on the ground that her interview score was less than the minimum. Infect, the confidential of the branch manager regarding her trade union activities worked against her. With this failure, she decided not to make any further trials and activised the trade union activities. Furthcr, she started a business of dealership in automobiles. She succeeded in diverting the deposits of the business community in her bank to other banks by her growing business contacts.

The management has decided to promote her to the officer cadre based on the recommendation of the new branch manager. One day Mrs. Bose received an appointment letter for the officer's post and the news of the same spread like a rapid fire in her office and the other branches of her bank. While Mr. Bose's union was celebrating their victory - the rival union decided to go on for a protest sensing unfair dealings! The management of the bank was aghast with the twinaround of the new crisis.

Introduction

Industrial disputes and conflicts have been a source of major concern because of the disruption they cause to planned economic development in a Country like ours and the losses involved for everyone concerned i.e. workers, owners, and the public. The hidden costs of strikes and the effect on industries with forward and backward linkages are difficult to measure. Conflict is inevitable in industrial society and it should be handled carefully to ensure the viability of the organization, to remove the discontentment among workmen and to avoid hardship to the society. Industrial Disputes Act 1947, defined industrial dispute as "any dispute or difference between employers and employers or between employees and employees or between employers and employees which is connected with the employment or non-employment or the terms of employment or with the conditions of work of any person".

So as evident in the above definition, dispute can occur in any of the following two ways, namely:

- Between individuals
- Between groups

Nature of Conflicts in Organizations Leading to Industrial Disputes

Organizational conflicts can be due to several reasons. Conflicts leading to industrial disputes in organizations can be broadly classified as follows:

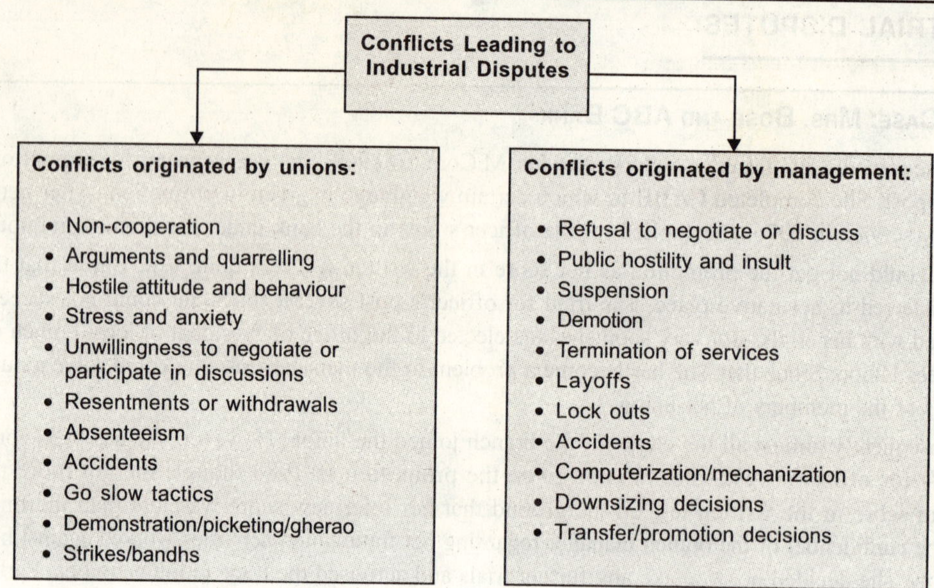

Fig. 5.14: Conflicts leading to industrial disputes

Causes of Industrial Disputes: There are various factors leading to industrial disputes in organizations. These can be represented by the following table:

Causes of Industrial Disputes	Features
Economic factors	Compensation, Incentive schemes, Benefits, Bonus etc
Social factors	Impact of Globalization, Privatization and Liberalization, Poor QWL, Poor work environment, poor hygiene, unemployment, economic recession, bureaucratic management, red tapism, illiteracy in workers etc
Political factors	Political unrest caused by inter party rivalry and violence, Political influence on trade unions, Unstable state and central governments
Psychological factors	Attrition rates in the industry, loss of job, increasing job dissatisfaction
Market influences	Competition, New Products, Products/services offered by MNCs, Recession of the industry
Technological factors	Fear of loss of jobs caused by automation, mechanization and computerization, rapid technological changes
Legal factors	Changing legislations, lack of legal help and support for the workers etc.

The causes of industrial disputes can be broadly classified into two categories: economic and non-economic causes. The economic causes will include issues relating to compensation like wages, bonus, allowances, and conditions for work, working hours, leave and holidays without pay, unjust layoffs and retrenchments. The non-economic factors will include victimization of workers, ill treatment by staff members, sympathetic strikes, political factors, indiscipline etc.

Wages and allowances: Since the cost of living index is increasing, workers generally bargain for higher wages to meet the rising cost of living index and to increase their standards of living. In 2002, 21.4% of disputes were caused by demand of higher wages and allowances. This percentage was 20.4% during 2003 and during 2004 increased up to 26.2%. In 2005, wages and allowances accounted for 21.8% of disputes.

Personnel and retrenchment: The personnel and retrenchment have also been an important factor which accounted for disputes. During the year 2002, disputes caused by personnel were 14.1% while those caused by retrenchment and layoffs were 2.2% and 0.4% respectively. In 2003, a similar trend could be seen, wherein 11.2% of the disputes were caused by personnel, while 2.4% and 0.6% of disputes were caused by retrenchment and layoffs. In year 2005, only 9.6% of the disputes were caused by personnel, and only 0.4% was caused by retrenchment.

Indiscipline and violence: From the following table, it is evident that the number of disputes caused by indiscipline has shown an increasing trend. In 2002, 29.9% of disputes were caused because of indiscipline, which rose up to 36.9% in 2003. Similarly in 2004 and 2005, 40.4% and 41.6% of disputes were caused due to indiscipline respectively. During the year 2003, indiscipline accounted for the highest percentage (36.9%) of the total time-loss of all disputes, followed by cause-groups wage and allowance and personnel with 20.4% and11.2% respectively. A similar trend was observed in 2004 where indiscipline accounted for 40.4% of disputes.

Bonus: Bonus has always been an important factor in industrial disputes. 6.7% of the disputes were because of bonus in 2002 and 2003 as compared to 3.5% and 3.6% in 2004 and 2005 respectively.

Leave and working hours: Leaves and working hours have not been so important causes of industrial disputes. During 2002, 0.5% of the disputes were because of leave and hours of work while this percentage increased to 1% in 2003. During 2004, only 0.4% of the disputes were because of leaves and working hours.

Miscellaneous: The miscellaneous factors include those of intra Union Rivalry, charter of Demands, work load, standing orders/rules/service conditions/safety measures, non-implementation of agreements and awards etc.

Table 5.5: Percentage Distribution of the Causes of Disputes

Causes of disputes	*2002*	*2003*	*2004*	*2005*
Wages and allowances	21.3	20.4	26.2	21.8
Personnel	14.1	11.2	13.2	9.6
Retrenchment	2.2	2.4	0.2	0.4
Layoff	0.4	0.6		0.2
Indiscipline	29.9	36.9	40.4	41.6
Violence	0.9	1	0.9	0.4
Leave and hours of work/shift working	0.5	1	0.4	
Bonus	6.7	6.7	3.5	3.6
Inter/Intra union rivalry	0.4	0.6	0.4	0.4
Non-implementation of agreements and awards etc.	3.1	1	1.1	0.9
Charter of demands	10.5	8.8	5.7	7.1
Work load	0.5	0.4	0.7	1.1
Standing orders/rules/service conditions/safety measures	1.8	1	2.4	0.2

Types of disputes in organizations: Industrial disputes can be broadly categorized in the following ways:

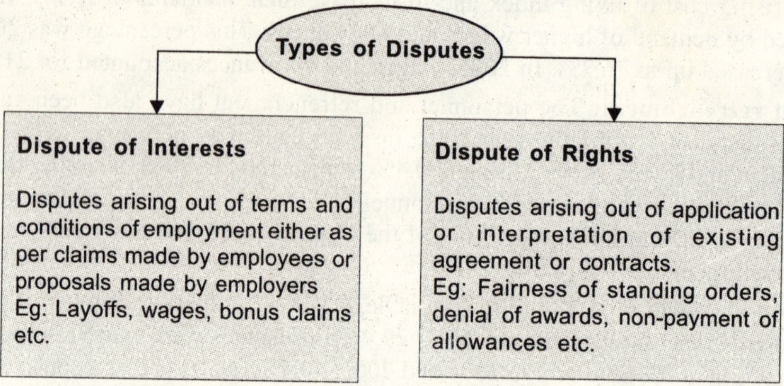

Fig. 5.15: Types of disputes in organizations

STRIKES

A strike is a very powerful weapon used by trade unions and other labour associations to get their demands accepted. It generally involves quitting of work by a group of workers for the purpose of bringing the pressure on their employer so that their demands get accepted. When workers collectively cease to work in a particular industry, they are said to be on strike.

According to Industrial Disputes Act 1947, a strike is "a cessation of work by a body of persons employed in an industry acting in combination; or a concerted refusal of any number of persons who are or have been so employed to continue to work or to accept employment; or a refusal under a common understanding of any number of such persons to continue to work or to accept employment". This definition throws light on a few aspects of a strike. Firstly, a strike is a referred to as stoppage of work by a group of workers employed in a particular industry. Secondly, it also includes the refusal of a number of employees to continue work under their employer.

In a strike, a group of workers agree to stop working to protest against something they think is unfair where they work. Labours withhold their services in order to pressurize their employment or government to meet their demands. Demands made by strikers can range from asking for higher wages or better benefits to seeking changes in the workplace environment. Strikes sometimes occur so that employers listen more carefully to the workers and address their problems.

Causes of strikes

Strikes can occur because of the following reasons:

- Dissatisfaction with company policy
- Salary and incentive problems
- Increment not up to the mark
- Wrongful discharge or dismissal of workmen
- Withdrawal of any concession or privilege
- Hours of work and rest intervals
- Leaves with wages and holidays
- Bonus, profit sharing, provident fund and gratuity
- Retrenchment of workmen and closure of establishment
- Dispute connected with minimum wages

Types of Strikes

1. **Economic Strike:** Under this type of strike, labours stop their work to enforce their economic demands such as wages and bonus. In these kinds of strikes, workers ask for increase in wages, allowances like traveling allowance, house rent allowance, dearness allowance, bonus and other facilities such as increase in privilege leave and casual leave.
2. **Sympathetic Strike:** When workers of one unit or industry go on strike in sympathy with workers of another unit or industry who are already on strike, it is called a sympathetic strike. The members of other unions involve themselves in a strike to support or express their sympathy with the members of unions who are on strike in other undertakings. The workers of sugar industry may go on strike in sympathy with their fellow workers of the textile industry who may already be on strike.
3. **General Strike:** It means a strike by members of all or most of the unions in a region or an industry. It may be a strike of all the workers in a particular region of industry to force demands common to all the workers. These strikes are usually intended to create political pressure on the ruling government, rather than on any one employer. It may also be an extension of the sympathetic strike to express generalized protest by the workers.
4. **Sit Down Strike:** In this case, workers do not absent themselves from their place of work when they are on strike. They keep control over production facilities. But do not work. Such a strike is also known as 'pen down' or 'tool down' strike. Workers show up to their place of employment, but they refuse to work. They also refuse to leave, which makes it very difficult for employer to defy the union and take the workers' places. In June 1998, all the Municipal Corporation employees in Punjab observed a pen down strike to protest against the non-acceptance of their demands by the state government.
5. **Slow Down Strike:** Employees remain on their jobs under this type of strike. They do not stop work, but restrict the rate of output in an organized manner. They adopt go-slow tactics to put pressure on the employers.
6. **Sick-out (or sick-in):** In this strike, all or a significant number of union members call in sick on the same day. They don't break any rules, because they just use their sick leave that was allotted to them on the same day. However, the sudden loss of so many employees all on one day can show the employer just what it would be like if they really went on strike.
7. **Wild Cat Strikes:** These strikes are conducted by workers or employees without the authority and consent of unions. In 2004, a significant number of advocated went on wild cat strike at the City Civil Court premises in Bangalore. They were protesting against some remarks allegedly made against them by an Assistant Commissioner.

LOCKOUTS

A lockout is a work stoppage in which an employer prevents employees from working. It is declared by employers to put pressure on their workers. This is different from a strike, in which employees refuse to work. Thus, a lockout is employers' weapon while a strike is raised on part of employees. According to Industrial Disputes Act 1947, lockout means the temporary closing of a place of employment or the suspension of work or the refusal by an employer to continue to employ any number of persons employed by him.

A lockout may happen for several reasons. When only part of a trade union votes to strike, the purpose of a lockout is to put pressure on a union by reducing the number of members who are able to work.

For example, if a group of the workers strike so that the work of the rest of the workers becomes impossible or less productive, the employer may declare a lockout until the workers end the strike. Another case in which an employer may impose a lockout is to avoid slow downs or intermittent work-stoppages. Occupation of factories has been the traditional method of response to lockouts by the workers' movement.

PICKETING

When workers are dissuaded from work by stationing certain men at the factory gates, such a step is known as picketing. If picketing does not involve any violence, it is perfectly legal. Pickets are workers who are on strike that stand at the entrance to their workplace. It is basically a method of drawing public attention towards the fact that there is a dispute between the management and employees.

The purpose of picketing is:

- to stop or persuade workers not to go to work
- to tell the public about the strike
- to persuade workers to take their union's side

GHERAO

Gherao in Hindi means to surround. It denotes a collective action initiated by a group of workers under which members of the management are prohibited from leaving the industrial establishment premises by workers who block the exit gates by forming human barricades. The workers may *gherao* the members of the management by blocking their exits and forcing them to stay inside their cabins. The main object of *gherao* is to inflict physical and mental torture to the person being *gheraoed* and hence this weapon disturbs the industrial peace to a great extent.

Fig. 5.16: A picketing campaign

Prohibition of Strikes and Lockouts

Employees are prohibited from striking according to the section 22 of Industrial Disputes Act, 1947. Employees, who are working in a public utility service, cannot go on a strike without giving a notice of strike within the six weeks before striking. They cannot go on strike either within fourteen days of providing the strike notice or before the expiry of the date of strike specified in any such notice. The same rule applies to the employers. Employers who are carrying on a public utility service cannot lockout any of their employees without giving them a prior notice within six weeks before the lockout or within the fourteen days of giving such a notice. Moreover, the notice of strike or lockout is to be given in a prescribed manner showing the number of persons involved in the strike/lockout.

A notice should be issued on the day on which the lockout is declared just to intimate the appropriate authorities about the lockout. The employer is supposed to report the number of notices of strikes received by him to the appropriate government or the authority prescribed by the government within the five days of receiving such notices.

Illegal Strikes and Lockouts

A strike or a lockout is illegal if it is declared in noncompliance with the section 22 (as defined above) of Industrial Disputes Act 1947, that is, if the notice period is not served or if the strike is held within the fourteen days of issuing the notice of strike. If a strike or lockout has already taken place and is being referred to a Board, the continuance of such a strike or lockout is not illegal provided it is in compliance with the provisions of Act. Moreover, a lockout declared in consequence of an illegal strike or a strike declared in consequence of an illegal lockout shall not be deemed to be illegal.

Penalty for illegal strikes and lockouts

A workman who is involved in an illegal strike can be penalized with imprisonment for a term extendable to a month or with a fine or fifty rupees or both. In similar way, an employer who initiates and continues a lockout is punishable with imprisonment extendable to a month or with a fine of one thousand rupees or both. According to Section 25 of Industrial Disputes Act 1947, no person should provide any sort of financial aid to any illegal strike or lockout. Any person who knowingly provides such a help in support of any illegal strike or lockout is punishable with imprisonment for a term which may extend to six months, or with fine which may extend to one thousand rupees, or with both.

Important Aspects of Industrial Dispute

The two most important components of the statistics on Industrial Disputes are: the maximum number of workers affected directly or indirectly on any day during the entire period of the work-stoppage and secondly, the number of man days lost which is obtained by adding up the actual resultant absences caused directly or indirectly by the work-stoppages, in each shift of the potential working day (excluding weekly-off and other scheduled holidays when the establishments would have otherwise remained closed even if no work-stoppages had taken place). The other components are (i) the number of disputes, (ii) duration of a dispute, (iii) wages lost and (iv) the value of production loss.

STATE-WISE MAJOR CONTRIBUTORS TO MANDAYS LOST DUE TO WORK STOPPATGES DURING THE YEARS 2003 AND 2004

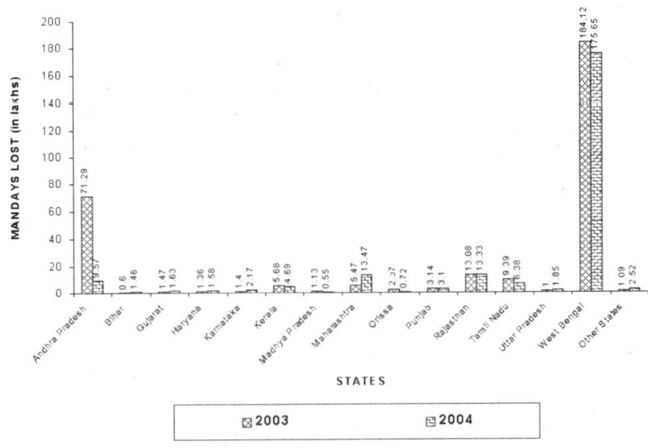

Fig. 5.17: State-wise major contributors of man days lost due to work-stoppages

TRENDS IN INDUSTRIAL DISPUTES AND THE RESULTANT MAN DAYS LOST IN INDIA

Industrial Disputes in the Public and Private Sectors of both Central and State Spheres: The number of disputes; workers involved and man days lost in Public Sector constitutes 10.3; 76.7 and 7.6 per cent respectively of the all India total number of Disputes, Workers involved and man days lost. Similarly Private Sector constituted 89.7; 23.3 and 92.4 per cent respectively during the year 2004.

Industrial Disputes in the Central and State Spheres on All India Basis: On all India basis, it is the State Sphere, which has the highest proportion of disputes and man days lost i.e., 92.2 and 93.1 per cent respectively as compared to the Central Sphere which constituted only 7.8 and 6.9 per cent respectively. The number of workers involved is higher in the Central Sphere (77.9 %) than in State Sphere (22.1 %).

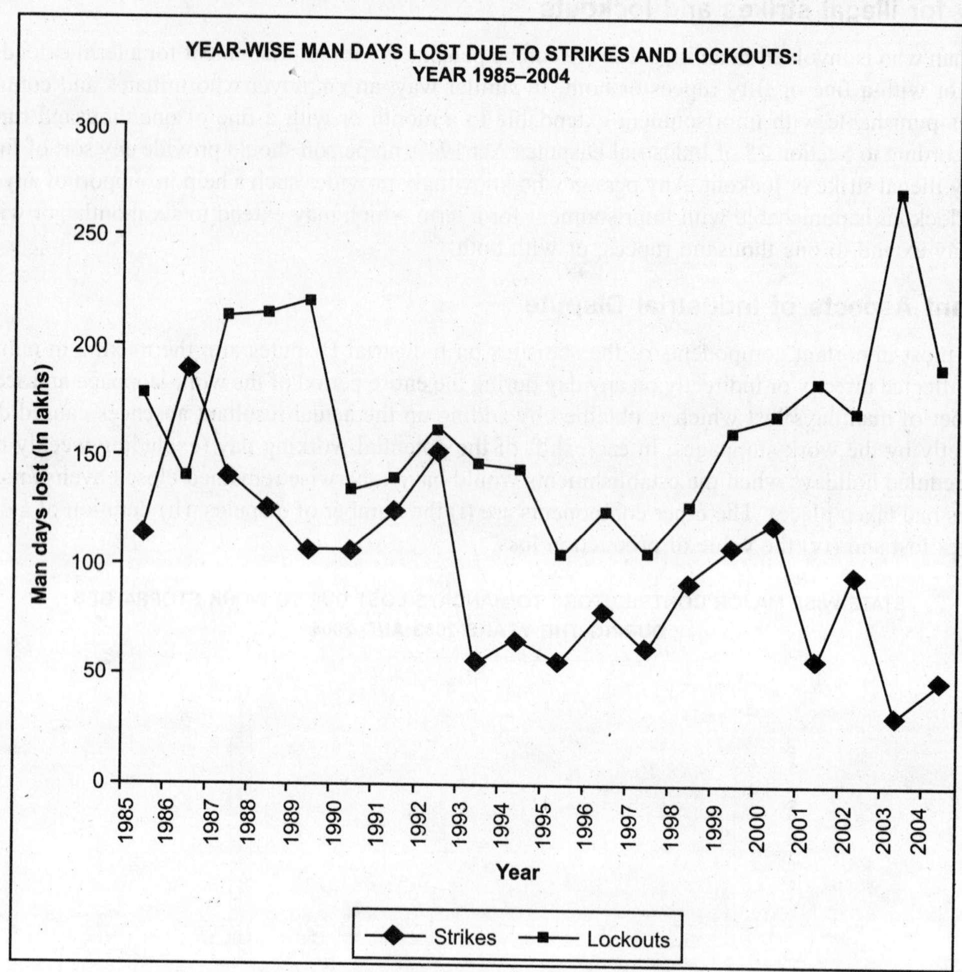

Fig. 5.18: Year-wise man days lost due to strikes and lockouts in India

Industrial Disputes in 2004 vis-a-vis 2003: Table A-II shows the number of strikes and lockouts during 2003 and 2004 in different sectors and spheres. The number of strikes reported during 2004 was 236 (47 in public and 189 in private sectors) which were lower by 7.5 % than the previous year. The number of lockouts, (241 comprised of 2 in public sector and 239 in private sector) registered a decrease of 18.9 % as compared to the previous year. Thus the total number of disputes (477) reported during 2004 were less by 13.6 % as compared to the number of disputes during the year 2003.

Time-loss due to Industrial Disputes in 2004 vis-a-vis 2003: During 2004 as compared to 2003, the time-loss due to Strikes accounted for an increase of 234.33 per cent whereas Lockouts registered a significant decrease of 100.00 per cent in the Central Sphere, while in the State Sphere the time-loss due to Strikes registered an increase of 17.28 per cent and Lockouts decreased by 8.55 per cent during the same period. Average time-loss per dispute decreased from 54,811 man days in 2003 to 50,034 man days in 2004. In the case of strikes it increased considerably from 12,572 to 20,461 man days and for lockouts it decreased from 91,077 to 78,994 man days per dispute.

STRIKES and LOCKOUTS DUE TO INDUSTRIAL DISPUTES

Year	No. of Strikes and Lockouts						
	Central Sphere	State Sphere	Public Sector	Private Sector	Strike	Lockout	Total
1993	272	1121	359	1034	914	479	1393
1994	249	952	316	885	808	393	1201
1995	285	781	343	723	732	334	1066
1996	316	850	381	785	763	403	1166
1997	384	921	448	857	793	512	1305
1998	231	866	283	814	665	432	1097
1999	129	798	165	762	540	387	927
2000	109	662	125	646	426	345	771
2001	115	559	139	535	372	302	674
2002	66	513	63	516	295	284	579
2003(P)	102	500	108	494	309	293	602
2004(JAN.-APR.)(P)	41	66	42	65	90	17	107

WORKERS INVOLVED IN STRIKES AND LOCKOUTS (IN THOUSANDS)							
Year	Central Sphere	State Sphere	Public Sector	Private Sector	Strike	Lockout	Total
1993	513	441	565	389	672	282	954
1994	490	356	523	323	626	220	846
1995	700	289	725	264	683	307	990
1996	478	461	606	333	609	331	939
1997	624	358	618	363	637	344	981
1998	955	334	901	388	801	488	1289
1999	549	761	553	758	1099	212	1311
2000	1139	279	1147	271	1044	374	1418
2001	379	308	428	260	489	199	688
2002	360	720	347	733	900	179	1079
2003(P)	1,121	706	1,110	717	1,023	804	1827
2004(JAN.-APR.)(P)	325	29	310	43	344	10	353

Table: Number of Closures and Workers Affected by Industrial Disputes

NUMBER OF CLOSURES AND WORKERS AFFECTED THEREIN

DURING 1985–2004 BY SPHERES						
Year	Central Sphere		State Sphere			
	No. of Units	Workers Affected	No. of Units	Workers Affected	Total No. of Units	Workers Affected
1985	4	821	180	19638	184	20459
1986	2	21	234	28006	236	28027
1987	3	3400	195	15749	198	19149
1988	4	1568	255	12518	259	14086
1989	-	-	239	6921	239	6921
1990	-	-	154	4967	154	4967
1991	3	537	247	24553	250	25090
1992	-	-	187	12422	187	12422
1993	3	79	490	25579	493	25658
1994	-	-	228	21394	228	21394
1995	-	-	183	14495	183	14495
1996	1	102	203	11288	204	11390
1997	2	150	152	12794	154	12944
1998	-	-	175	13386	175	13386
1999	1	21	158	15686	159	15707
2000	2	333	136	11571	138	11904
2001	6	826	145	10773	151	11599
2002	2	32	211	9993	213	10025
2003(P)	2	453	109	7432	111	7885
2004(JAN-MAY)(P)	0	0	49	6758	49	6758
- = NIL						
(P) = PROVISIONAL						
Source: Labour Bureau, Shimla						

Table: Man Days Lost Due to Strikes and Lockouts

Year	MAN DAYS LOST DUE TO STRIKES AND LOCKOUTS (IN MILLIONS)						
	Central Sphere	State Sphere	Public Sector	Private Sector	Strike	Lockout	Total
1993	1.2	19.1	2.29	18.01	5.61	14.69	20.30
1994	0.59	20.4	1.32	19.67	6.65	14.33	20.98
1995	3.86	12.43	4.79	11.5	5.72	10.57	16.29
1996	1.2	19.09	3.15	17.13	7.82	12.47	20.28
1997	1.41	15.56	2.18	14.79	6.3	10.68	16.97
1998	7.25	14.81	7.58	14.49	9.35	12.71	22.06
1999	0.87	25.91	1.18	25.61	10.62	16.16	26.79
2000	10.04	18.72	10.68	18.08	11.96	16.8	28.76
2001	1.19	22.57	2.02	21.74	5.56	18.2	23.77
2002	0.83	25.75	0.8	25.78	9.66	16.92	26.58
2003(P)	6.74	22.96	6.76	22.93	3.17	26.53	29.70
2004(JAN-APR)(P)	0.32	0.89	0.31	0.9	0.87	0.34	1.22

(P) = PROVISIONAL

Source: Labour Bureau, Shimla

Table: Number of Disputes by Sectors and Spheres during 2003 and 2004

Sphere	Strikes/ Lockouts	Public sector		Private sector		Total	
		2003	2004	2003	2004	2003	2004
1	2	3	4	5	6	7	8
I– Central Sphere	Strikes	35	36	8	1	43	37
	Lockouts	3	0	0	0	3	0
	Strikes and Lockouts	38	36	8	1	46	37
II– State Sphere	Strikes	21	11	191	188	212	199
	Lockouts	0	2	294	239	294	241
	Strikes and Lockouts	21	13	485	427	506	440
Total Central and State sphere	Strikes	56	47	199	189	255	236
	Lockouts	3	2	294	239	297	241
	Strikes and Lockouts	59	49	493	428	552	477

Management of Industrial Disputes

Industrial dispute resolution is an issue of great strategic importance for organizations in terms of maintaining industrial harmony and peace. These initiatives can be classified as:

- Labour legislations and administrations of the state
- Statutory machinery for resolving disputes
- Non-statutory measures

Fig. 5.19: A trade union rally

Labour Legislations and Administrations of the State

State intervention in industrial relations is essentially a modern development. With the emergence of the concept of welfare state, new ideas of social philosophy, national economy and social justice sprang up with result that industrial relation no longer remains the concern of labour and management alone. In all the countries, over a period of time, the state has assumed power to regulate industrial relations.

- It is the state which is now the most significant element in determining the legal environment within which industrial relations operate.
- The state operates as an actor within industrial relations performing a number of distinct roles.
- The distinct role that state performs are broadly, categorized fall into five categories, namely:
    - Firstly, it acts as a third party regulator promoting a legal framework which establishes general ground rules for union-management interaction, particularly in the procedure for collective bargaining.
    - Secondly, and additionally, as a means of supporting and underpinning collective bargaining or as a supplement to it the law can be used establish minimum standards while collective bargaining exploits particular advantages to secure higher standards whenever it can.
    - The third well established function in many countries is the provision of state service for conciliation, mediation and arbitration with a view to facilitating the settlement of industrial disputes.
    - A fourth aspect of the role of the state that has become increasingly important is that of a direct and primary participation as a major employer in the public sector. In this respect, it influences the pattern of industrial relations by its own behaviour and example.

- A fifth role that the state has come to play in many countries is that of a regulator of incomes. As a result, direct and active state involvement in the industrial relations has become much more pronounced in recent years.

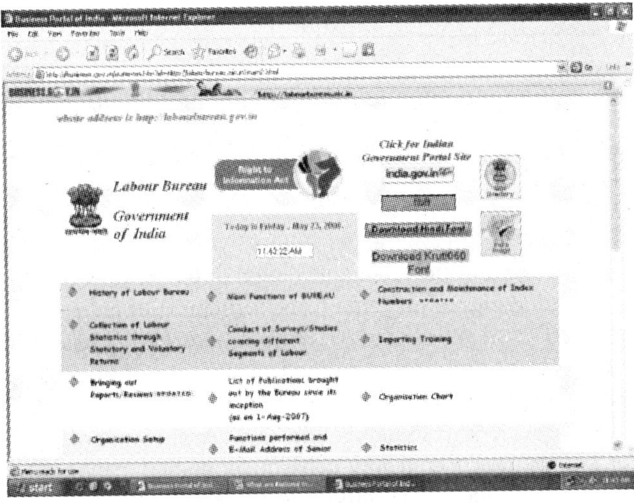

Fig. 5.20: Labour bureau website

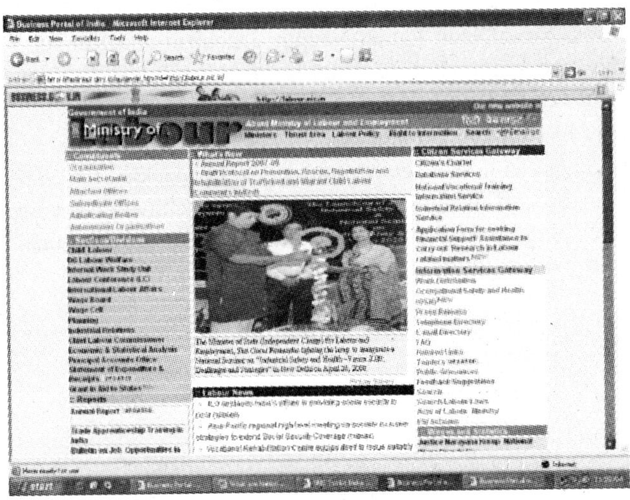

Fig. 5.21: Business portal of India

(a) Role of Department of Labour in Industrial Dispute: The Departments of Labour in the States and Regional Labour Commissioners (Central) collect the basic information in respect of the work stoppages in the State and Central Spheres respectively on account of strikes and lockouts. They collect the required information from the units under their jurisdiction on uniform lines laid down for the purpose whenever such occurrence of a work-stoppage becomes known either directly or from the police records as per the practice in vogue in different States/areas. This information is collected on a voluntary basis and furnished by the aforesaid authorities in consolidated monthly returns and submitted to the Labour Bureau in each succeeding month.

(b) Role of the Local Offices of Central Government: The labour commissioner appoints regional officers to represent the central government in each state.

(c) Industrial Tribunals: Industrial tribunals are set up in different regions of India. Presently there are eight Tribunals who deal with industrial disputes.

(d) State Government Agencies: Labour ministry of each state government has its regional offices set up at each district attached to the collectorate as state labour officers, whose jobs are to ensure implementation of the state legislations and intervene to settle industrial disputes in the region.

The Organization of Chief Labour Commissioner (Central Industrial Relations Machinery /CIRM):

The Organization of the Chief Labour Commissioner (C) known as Central Industrial Relations Machinery was set up in April, 1945 in pursuance of the recommendation of the Royal Commission on Labour in India and was then charged mainly with duties of prevention and settlement of industrial disputes, enforcement of labour laws and to promote welfare of workers in the undertakings falling within the sphere of the Central Government. Combining the former organizations of the Conciliation Officer (Railways) and Supervisor of Railway Labour and the Labour Welfare Advisor, it started with a small complement of staff comprising Chief Labour Commissioner (C)) at New Delhi, 3 Regional Labour Commissioners at Bombay, Calcutta & Lahore and 8 Conciliation Officer and increased gradually consequent upon expanding labour legislation's in the Post-independence period, increased industrial activity in the country and growing responsibilities of the Organization.

Presently there are 18 regions each headed by a Regional Labour Commissioner (C) with Headquarters at Ajmer, Ahmedabad, Asansol, Bangalore, Bombay, Bhubaneshwar, Chandigarh, Cochin, Calcutta, Guwahati, Hyderabad, Jabalpur, Madras, New Delhi, Patna, Nagpur, Dhanbad and Kanpur. Out of these, 14 regions have been placed under the supervision of three zonal Dy. CLCs (C) and 4 regional offices are supervised directly by Headquarters office of CLC(C).

CIRM is headed by the Chief Labour Commissioner (Central)[CLC (C)]. It is entrusted with the task of maintaining good industrial relations in the Central sphere. At the headquarters, CIRM has a complement of 25 officers who perform line and staff functions. In the field, the machinery has a complement of 253 officers and their establishments are spread over different parts of the country with zonal, regional and unit level formations as presented in the organogram.

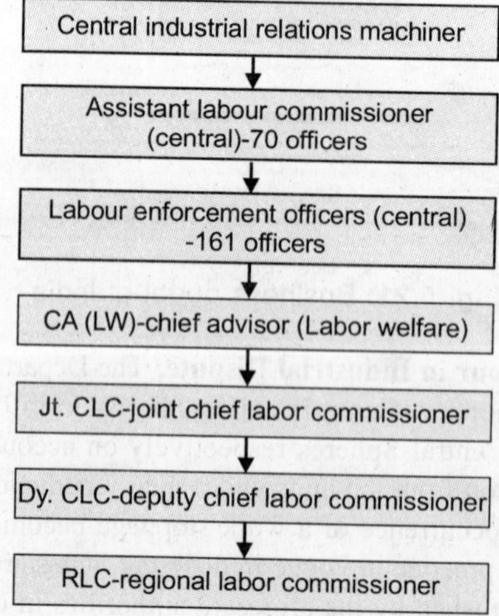

Fig. 5.22: Organogram of the organization of chief labour commissioner

During the year 2001–2002 the CIRM intervened in 630 threatened strikes and its conciliatory efforts succeeded in averting 622 strikes which represents a success rate of 98.7%. The machinery handled the Industrial Disputes during the year 2001–2002 as given in the following table:

Table 5.6: Industrial Disputes Intervened by CIRM During the Year 2001–2002

No. of disputes received by CIRM	No. of disputes which were considered unfit for intervention by CIRM	No. of disputes which were settled without holding formal conciliation proceedings	No. of disputes which formal C.P. were held	No. of disputes in which conciliation proceeding led to the settlement of disputes	No. of disputes in which conciliation proceedings ended in failure	No. of disputes pending with the CIRM on the close of the year
12388	13	2860	8303	764	4372	4085

Objectives of the CLC(C) Organization

- Promotion of peaceful and harmonious Industrial Relations in the Central Sphere through prevention and settlement of Industrial disputes in the Industries for which Central Govt. is the appropriate Govt.
- Verification of the Trade Union's Membership.
- Enforcement of labour laws in central sphere.

Specific Functions of CIRM

The CIRM administers the Labour Laws in the industries for which the Central Govt. is the 'appropriate Government' under that Act. Its functions therefore are:

- Prevention and settlement of industrial disputes
- Enforcement of Labour Laws
- Verification of membership of Trade Unions
- Enforcement of Awards and Settlements
- Conduct of inquiries into the breaches of Code of Discipline
- Promotion of Works Committees and Workers' Participation in Management
- Collection of statistical information
- Defense of court cases and writ petitions arising out of implementation of labour laws.

Regulations under the Industrial Disputes Act, 1947

This act applies to workers carrying out manual, unskilled, technical, operational or supervisory work and does not apply to workers earning more than Rs. 1,600 per month carrying out managerial work. In addition, the worker must have had continuous service of at least one year.

It provides for the conciliation and adjudication of industrial disputes by Conciliation Officers, a Board of Conciliation, and Courts of Inquiry, Labour Courts, Industrial Tribunals and a National Industrial Tribunal. Each has a different jurisdiction or purpose, except for Conciliation Officers, whose jurisdiction is more general. Industrial disputes include cases of unfair dismissal. Unfair dismissal following sexual harassment has been argued in a number of cases, to amount to an unfair labour practice as listed in item 5 of Schedule 5.

Industrial disputes are considered by conciliation officers at their discretion (in the case of public utilities, conciliation may sometimes be mandatory), and will only be considered by the other bodies if the dispute is referred by the appropriate Government. No reference can be made under the Act to Conciliation Boards, Labour Courts or Industrial Tribunals, unless the dispute has first been the subject of a decision of a Grievance Settlement Authority. However, provision is made for voluntary reference of disputes for arbitration (see ss. 2A-7B, 9C, 10, 10A and 12.).

Industrial disputes are the disputes which arise due to any disagreement in an industrial relation. The term 'industrial relation' involves various aspects of interactions between the employer and the employees; among the employees as well as between the employers. In such relations whenever there is a clash of interest, it may result in dissatisfaction for either of the parties involved and hence lead to industrial disputes or conflicts. These disputes may take various forms such as protests, strikes, demonstrations, lock-outs, retrenchment, dismissal of workers, etc.

Some of the important causes of an industrial dispute are:

- Demand for higher wages and allowances.
- Demand for payment of bonus and determination of its rate thereof.
- Demand for higher social security benefits.
- Demand for good and safer working conditions, including length of a working day, the interval and frequency of leisure and physical work environment.
- Demand for improved labour welfare and other benefits. For example, adequate canteen, rest, recreation and accommodation facility, arrangements for travel to and from distant places, etc.
- Besides, poor personnel management; conflicting legislative measure or government policies; and psychological factors such as denial of opportunity to the worker for satisfying his/ her basic urge for self-expression, personal achievement and betterment may also result in labour problems.

In India, the Industrial Disputes Act, 1947 is the main legislation for investigation and settlement of all industrial disputes. The Act enumerates the contingencies when a strike or lockout can be lawfully resorted to, when they can be declared illegal or unlawful, conditions for laying off, retrenching, discharging or dismissing a workman, circumstances under which an industrial unit can be closed down and several other matters related to industrial employees and employers.

The Act is administered by the Ministry of Labour through its Industrial Relations Division. The Division is concerned with improving the institutional framework for dispute settlement and amending labour laws relating to industrial relations. It works in close coordination with the Central Industrial Relations Machinery (CIRM) in an effort to ensure that the country gets a stable, dignified and efficient workforce, free from exploitation and capable of generating higher levels of output. The CIRM, which is an attached office of the Ministry of Labour, is also known as the Chief Labour Commissioner (Central) [CLC(C)] Organization. The CIRM is headed by the Chief Labour Commissioner (Central). It has been entrusted with the task of maintaining industrial relations, enforcement of labour laws and verification of trade union membership in central sphere. It ensures harmonious industrial relations through:-

- Monitoring of industrial relations in Central Sphere;
- Intervention, mediation and conciliation in industrial disputes in order to bring about settlement of disputes;
- Intervention in situations of threatened strikes and lockouts with a view to avert the strikes and lockouts;

- Implementation of settlements and awards.

The basic objectives of the Act are:-

- To provide a suitable machinery for the just, equitable and peaceful settlement of industrial disputes.
- To promote measures for securing and preserving amity and good relations between employers and employees.
- To prevent illegal strikes and lockouts.
- To provide relief to workers against layoffs, retrenchment, wrongful dismissal and victimization.
- To promote collective bargaining.
- To ameliorate the conditions of workers.
- To avoid unfair labour practices.

Exhibit: International comparisons (Doing Business Data, De Jure indicators) Labour Legislation in India and Comparator Countries

Country	Difficulty of hiring (1)	Rigid hours (2)	Restrictions to retrenchment (3)	Compensation for dismissal (4)	Rigidity of employment (5)
India	33	20	90	79	48
Comparator's Average	27	45	48	87	40
High Income Countries Average	22	49	24	41	32
World Average	35	50.6	37.9	56	41
World Median	31	60	40	46	41

(Source: Doing Business 2004 http://rru.worldbank.org/DoingBusiness/)

Statutory Machinery of Resolving Industrial Disputes in India

As per Industrial Dispute Act, 1947, the following are considered as statutory machinery for resolving Industrial disputes in India:

- Works committee
- Mediation and Conciliation
- Investigations
- Conciliation officers
- Board of conciliation
- Voluntary arbitration
- Adjudication (compulsory arbitration): (a) Labour Courts (b) Industrial Tribunals (c) National Tribunals

Works Committee

In any Industrial Establishment in which 100 or more workmen are employed or have been employed in the preceding 12 months, the Government may, by general or special order, require the employer to constitute a **Works Committee**, consisting of representatives of the employers and the workmen engaged in the establishment.

The number of representatives of workmen on such Committee shall not be less than the number of representatives of the employer. The representatives of workmen shall be chosen in the prescribed manner from amongst the workmen, engaged in the establishment and in consultation with the Trade Union. It is the duty of the Works Committee to promote measures for securing and preserving amity and good relations between the employer and workmen and, to that end, to comment upon matters of their common interest and endeavour to compose any material difference of opinion in respect of such matters. Their task is only to smooth away friction that may arise between the workmen and the management in day-to-day work. They cannot decide any alteration in the conditions of service by rationalization. Even if the workman's representatives on the Works Committee agree to a scheme of rationalization, that is not binding either on the workers or on the mills. [S.3 of Industrial Disputes Act, 1947]

Mediation and Conciliation

Under the Industrial Disputes Act 1947, effective conciliation machinery has been provided which can take cognizance of the existing as well as apprehended dispute, either on its own or on being approached by either of the parties to the dispute. The Act further makes conciliation compulsory in majority of disputes. As per ILO conciliation is defined as "the practice by which the services of neutral third party are used in a dispute as a means of helping the disputing parties to reduce the extent of their differences and to arrive at an amicable settlement or agreed solution." Conciliation is not "judicial" but "administrative" in character. It must start working within 14 days of reporting and must put their efforts and result in a report to the Govt. stating reasons if the conciliation has failed.

***Conciliation Officers*:** Labour officers can act as conciliation officers for establishments having less than 20 workers. The labour commissioner, Additional Labour Commissioner or Deputy Labour Commissioner can also act as conciliation officers for establishments having more than 20 workers.

***Board of Conciliation*:** This is a higher forum formed on adhoc basis. This is not a permanent body like conciliation officers. Board of conciliation consists of equal number of representatives from either side, presided over by an independent person appointed by the government. The board must complete the assignment within two months and submit its report to the government.

***What are Conciliation Proceedings*:** Conciliation Proceedings refer to any proceedings, held by a conciliation officer or board. Conciliation proceedings are therefore the machinery or means of promoting the settlement of disputes.

Investigation: Section 6 of the Act empowers the government to constitute a court of inquiry, for inquiring into any matter pertaining to an Industrial Dispute. The procedure of the court of inquiry has also been prescribed by Section 11. While the report of the court is not binding on the parties, many time it paves the way for an agreement.

Court of Enquiry

The Industrial Disputes Act, 1947 provides the procedure for a court of enquiry and its proceedings are quasi-judicial in nature as per sections 193 and 228 of the Indian Penal Code (1980). This has been set up by the government so as to facilitate voluntary settlement of industrial disputes. It must submit its report or recommendations within six months.

Voluntary Arbitration

Voluntary arbitration is a part of the infrastructure of resolving the industrial dispute in the industrial adjudication. Section 10 of the Act provides for the provision for resolving the industrial dispute by way of arbitration, which leads to a final and binding award. However, in India arbitration is not a preferred way of resolving industrial disputes.

Voluntary arbitration is a binding, adversarial dispute resolution process in which the disputing parties choose one or more arbitrators to hear their dispute and to render a final decision or award after an expedited hearing.

Voluntary arbitration implies that the two contending parties, unable to compromise their differences by themselves or with the help of mediator or conciliator, agree to submit the conflict/ dispute to an impartial authority, whose decisions they are ready to accept. In other words, under voluntary arbitration the parties to the dispute can and do they refer voluntarily and dispute to arbitration before it is referred for adjudication. This type of reference is known as "voluntary reference", for the parties themselves volunteer to come to a settlement though an arbitration machinery.

The essential elements in voluntary arbitration are as follows:

- The voluntary submission of dispute to an arbitrator.
- The subsequent attendance of witnesses and investigations.
- The enforcement of an award may not be necessary and binding because there is no compulsion.
- Voluntary arbitration may be specially needed for disputes arising under agreements.

Adjudication

Adjudication means a mandatory settlement of industrial disputes by labour courts, industrial tribunals or national tribunals under the Act or by any other corresponding authorities under the analogous state statutes. Adjudication is the legal process by which an arbiter or judge reviews evidence and argumentation including legal reasoning set forth by opposing parties or litigants to come to a decision which determines rights and obligations between the parties involved. Three types of disputes are resolved through adjudication:

- Disputes between private parties, such as individuals or corporations.
- Disputes between private parties and public officials.
- Disputes between public officials or public bodies.

By and large, the ultimate remedy of unsettled dispute is by way of reference by the appropriate government to the adjudicatory machinery for adjudication. The adjudicatory authority resolves the industrial dispute referred to it by passing an award, which is binding on the parties to such reference. There is no provision for appeal against such awards and the same can only be challenged by way of writ under Articles 226 and 227 of the constitution of India before the concerned High Court or before the Supreme Court by way of appeal under special leave under Article 136 of the constitution of India.

Constitution and Functioning of Labour Courts, Industrial Tribunals and National Tribunals

The Industrial Disputes Act, 1947 provides for setting up of labour courts, industrial tribunals and national tribunals.

Labour Courts

Under S.7 of the Industrial Disputes Act 1947, Central and State Governments may establish one or more Labour Courts for the adjudication of industrial disputes relating to any matter specified in the Second Schedule of the Act. The matters in the Second Schedule include wrongful dismissal and all matters not within the jurisdiction of industrial tribunals. Note, however, that under S.10 of the Act, the government may refer a matter to the Labour Court, even if it falls within the jurisdiction of an Industrial Tribunal, if it is likely to affect more than 100 workmen.

Labour Courts and Industrial Tribunals are set up by the Central Government and the State Government or the Administrations of Union Territories for dealing with matters which fall in the Central and the State sphere respectively. It is, however, open to the Central Government to refer a matter in relation to which it is the appropriate Government to a Labour Court or a Industrial Tribunal constituted by the State Govt.

Labour Courts deal with matters pertaining to discharge and dismissal of workmen, application and interpretation of Standing Orders, propriety of orders passed under Standing Orders, legality of strikes of lockouts etc.

Labour Courts also deal with applications for determination of workers' dues under Section 33(c) (2) of the Industrial Disputes Act and other miscellaneous matters. The appropriate Government may refer its order relating to layoff, retrenchment or closure to a tribunal for adjudication on its own motion or on an application made by the employer or a workman.

Industrial Tribunals

The Industrial Tribunal was constituted under the Industrial Disputes Act 1947. Industrial Tribunals deal with collective disputes such as wages, hours of work, leave, retrenchment, and closure as well as all matters which come under the jurisdiction of Labour Courts. This is a one man court who is the President. President is a serving or retired High Court Judge. Matters coming under third schedule if the Industrial Dispute Act, 1947 are referred to this tribunal. An Industrial Tribunal shall consist of one person to be appointed by the appropriate Government and the person shall not be qualified for appointment as such unless:

- He is or has been a judge of a High Court;
- He has for a period of not less than three years been a District Judge or an Additional District Judge.

In addition to the president, two assessors can also be appointed by the Government if found necessary. The appropriate Government, by a notification in the Official Gazette, may constitute one or more Industrial Tribunals for the adjudication of industrial disputes, relating to any matter specified in the Second or Third Schedule and for performing such other functions as may be assigned to them under this Act.

The Industrial Tribunal is assisted by a Secretary in the cadre of Senior Superintendent and other staff members are drafted from Labour Department.

The matters, falling within the jurisdiction of the Industrial Tribunals, are as follows:

1. Wages, including the period and mode of payment;
2. Compensatory and other allowances;
3. Hours of work and rest intervals;
4. Leave with wages and holidays;
5. Bonus, profit sharing, provident fund and gratuity;
6. Shift working, otherwise than in accordance with the standing orders;
7. Classification by grades;
8. Rules of discipline;
9. Rationalization;

10. Retrenchment of workmen and closure of establishment; and
11. Any other matter that may be prescribed.

National Tribunals

The Central Government may, by notification in the Official Gazette, constitute one or more National Tribunals for adjudication of industrial disputes which, in the opinion of the Central Government, involve questions of national importance or are of such a nature that industrial establishments in more than one State are likely to be interested in, or affected by such disputes.

The National Tribunal shall consist of one person only, to be appointed by the Central Government and a person shall not be qualified for appointment as such unless he is or has been a Judge of a High Court. The Central Government may, if it thinks fit, appoint two persons as assessors to advice the National Tribunal in the proceeding before it.

Now 17 CGIT have been set up by the Central Govt. which as follows:

Sl. No.	Location	No. of CGIT-cum-Labour Court
1.	Mumbai	2
2.	Dhanbad	2
3.	Asansol	1
4.	Bangalore	1
5.	Kolkata	1
6.	Chandigarh	1
7.	Jabalpur	1
8.	New Delhi	1
9.	Kanpur	1
10	Lucknow	1
11.	Jaipur	1
12.	Nagpur	1
13.	Bhubaneshwar	1
14.	Chennai	1
15.	Hyderabad	1

According to the Industrial Disputes Acts, 1947 the Central Government is the appropriate Govt. for investigation and settlement of Industrial disputes in regard to the departmental undertakings of the Central Govts., major ports, mines, oil fields, cantonment boards, banking and Insurance Companies, LIC Industrial Finance Corporation of India Limited, the Oil and Natural Gas Corporation Ltd., the Indian Airlines, Air India, the Airport Authority of India and all air transport services under the Industrial Disputes Act. In relation to other industrial establishments the State Govt. is the appropriate Govt.

Arbitration

Arbitration is a legal technique for the resolution of disputes outside the courts, wherein the parties to a dispute refer it to one or more persons (the "arbitrators", "arbiters" or "arbitral tribunal"), by whose decision (the "award") they agree to be bound. It is more helpful, however, simply to classify arbitration as a form of binding dispute resolution, equivalent to litigation in the courts, and entirely distinct from the various forms of non-binding dispute resolution, such as negotiation, mediation, or non-binding determinations by experts. Arbitration is, today, most commonly used for the resolution of commercial disputes, particularly in the context of international commercial transactions.

Compulsory Arbitration is a non-binding, adversarial dispute resolution process in which one or more arbitrators hear arguments, weigh evidence and issue a non-binding judgement on the merits after an expedited hearing. The arbitrator's decision addresses only the disputed legal issues and applies legal standards. Either party may reject the ruling and request a trial de novo in court.

Compulsory arbitration is one where the parties are required to accept arbitration without any willingness on their part. When one of the parties to an industrial dispute feels aggrieved by an act of the other, it may apply to the appropriate government to refer the dispute to adjudication machinery. Such reference of a dispute is known as "compulsory" or "involuntary" reference, because reference in such circumstances does not depend on the sweet will of either the contending parties or any party to the dispute. It is entirely the discretion of the appropriate govt. based on the question of existing dispute, or on the apprehension that industrial dispute will emerge in particular establishment.

Under compulsory arbitration, the parties are forced to arbitration by the state when:

a. When there is a national emergency which requires that the wheels of production should not be obstructed by frequent work-stoppages.
b. The parties fail to arrive at a settlement by a voluntary method
c. The country is passing through a grave economic crisis
d. There is a grave public dissatisfaction with the existing industrial relations
e. Public interest and the working conditions have to be safeguarded and regulated by the state.
f. Compulsory arbitration leaves no scope for strikes and lockouts; it deprives both the parties of their very important and fundamental rights.

Advantages and Disadvantages of Arbitration

Parties often seek to resolve their disputes through arbitration because of a number of perceived potential advantages over judicial proceedings:

- when the subject matter of the dispute is highly technical, arbitrators with an appropriate degree of expertise can be appointed
- arbitration is often faster than litigation in court
- arbitration can be cheaper and more flexible for businesses
- arbitral proceedings and an arbitral award are generally secret
- because of the provisions of the New York Convention 1958, arbitration awards are generally easier to enforce in other nations than court judgements
- in most legal systems, there are very limited avenues for appeal of an arbitral award

However, some of the disadvantages of arbitration can be that:

- consumers and employees usually do not know in advance that they have been forced into mandatory binding pre-dispute arbitration by purchasing a product or taking a job
- if the arbitration is mandatory binding pre-dispute arbitration, the individual must, in advance, give up his or her right to access the courts and have a judge or jury decide the case
- the parties need to pay for the arbitrators, which adds an additional layer of legal cost that can be prohibitive, especially in small consumer disputes
- a recovery of attorneys' fees is usually unavailable, making it difficult or impossible for consumers or employees to get legal representation

- the arbitrator depends on the corporation for repeat business, so there is an inherent incentive to rule against the consumer or employee
- there are very limited avenues for appeal, which means that an erroneous decision cannot be overturned
- although usually thought to be speedier, when there are multiple arbitrators on the panel, juggling their schedules for hearing dates in long cases can lead to delays
- in some legal systems, arbitral awards have fewer enforcement remedies than judgements
- arbitrators are generally unable to enforce interlocutory measures against a party, making it easier for a party to take steps to avoid enforcement of an award, such as the relocation of assets offshore
- rule of applicable law is not binding, and arbitrators not subject to overturn on appeal may be more likely to rule according to their personal ideals
- large corporations may exert inappropriate influence in consumer disputes, pressuring arbitrators to decide in their favour or lose future business

Drafting an Arbitration Agreement

Before signing an **Arbitration Agreement** the following must be properly addressed:

- Applicable law to arbitration
- Location of arbitration
- Number of arbitrators
- Language of arbitration
- Discovery procedure
- Limitation to arbitration powers
- Interim measures/Provisional remedies
- Privacy
- Rules applicable
- Appeal and enforcement
- Be aware of local peculiarities
- Survival after termination of the main agreement.

The arbitration agreement should be modified as applicable under different circumstances.

Exhibit: Sample Performa of Agreement of Reference to a Common Arbitrator

AGREEMENT OF REFERENCE TO A COMMON ARBITRATOR

THIS AGREEMENT is made at ... this ... day of .... between Mr. A of .... residing at .... hereinafter referred to as the Party of the First Part and Mr. B of .... residing at .... hereinafter referred to as the Party of the Second Part.

WHEREAS by an Agreement (Building contract) dated the ... day of ... entered into between the parties here to the Party of the First Part entrusted the work of constructing a building on his plot of land situated at... to the Party of the Second Part on the terms and conditions therein mentioned.

AND WHEREAS the Party of the Second Part has commenced the construction of the building according to the plans sanctioned by the... Municipal Corporation and has completed the construction to the extent of the 1st floor level.

AND WHEREAS the Party of First Part has made certain payments to the Party of the Second Part on account but the Party of the Second Part is pressing for more payments which according to the Party of the First Part the As not bound to pay and, therefore the work has come to a standstill.

AND WHEREAS disputes have therefore arisen between the parties hereto regarding the interpretation of certain provisions of the said agreement and also regarding the quality of construction and delay in the work.

AND WHEREAS the said agreement provides that in the event of any dispute or difference arising between the parties the same shall be referred to arbitration of a common arbitrator if agreed upon or otherwise to two arbitrators and the arbitration shall be governed by the provisions of the Arbitration and Conciliation Act, 1996.

AND WHEREAS the parties have agreed to refer all the disputes regarding to the said contract to Mr... Architect, as common arbitrator and have proposed to enter into this agreement for reference of the disputes to the sole arbitration of the said Mr..........

NOW IT IS AGREED BETWEEN THE PARTIES HERE TO AS FOLLOWS

1. That the following points of dispute arising out of the said agreement dated... are hereby referred to the sole arbitration of the said Mr... for his decision and award.
2. The points of dispute are:-
   (a) Whether the Party of the Second Part has carried out the work according to the sanctioned plans and specifications.
   (b) Whether the Party of the Second Part has delayed the construction.
   (c) Whether the Party of the Second Part is overpaid for the work done up to now.
   (d) Whether Party of the First Part is bound to make any further payment over and above the payments made up to now for the work actually done.
   (e) All other claims of one party against the other party arising out of the said contract up to now.
3. The said Arbitrator shall allow the parties to file their respective claims and contentions and to file documents relied upon by them within such reasonable time as the Arbitrator may direct.
4. The said Arbitrator shall give hearing to the parties either personally or through their respective Advocates but the Arbitrator will not be bound to take any oral evidence including cross examination of any party or person.
5. The said Arbitrator shall make his Award within a period of four months from the date of service of a copy of this agreement on him by any of the parties hereto provided that, the Arbitrator will have power to extend the said period from time to time with the consent of both the parties.
6. The Arbitrator will not make any interim award.
7. The Arbitrator will have full power to award or not to award payment of such costs of and incidental to this arbitration by one party to the other as he may think fit.
8. Subject to the provisions of the Arbitration and Conciliation Act 1996 the award will he binding on the parties hereto.
9. The Arbitration shall subject to what is herein provided be governed by the provisions of the Arbitration Act.

IN WITNESS WHEREOF the parties have put their respective hands the day and year first herein above written.

Signed by the within named
Mr. A ... in the presence of

Signed by the within named

Mr. B... in the presence of

Non-Statutory Machinery of Resolving Industrial Disputes

Code of Discipline

Indian Labour Conference held in New Delhi in July 1957, formulated a "code of discipline" for Indian industries after thorough discussions. The code was developed for the purpose of maintaining discipline both in public and private sector industries. Following are the salient features of this:

Mutual agreement between management and unions

- There shall be no strike or lockout due notice.
- No unilateral action on industrial matter.
- Industrial disputes must be settled at appropriate level utilizing existing machinery.
- Affirm faith in democratic principles.
- Bind themselves to settle disputes/grievances by mutual negotiations or through voluntary arbitration.
- Neither party take the line of coercion, intimation or "go-slow tactics".
- Avoid litigation, "sit-down" and "stay-in" strikes or lockouts.
- Promote constructive cooperation.
- Agree to establish mutually accepted procedure for settling grievances and do not resort to arbitrary actions.
- Educate management personnel and workers in regards to their duties, responsibilities and obligations.

Agreement on the part of the management

- Do not increase workload unilaterally.
- Discourage unfair labour practice like discrimination, coercion, victimization etc.
- Take prompt actions for redressal of grievances and implementation of settlements and awards.
- Publicize Code of Discipline in local language and display the same promptly.
- Follow laid down sequential steps in disciplinary action taking like warning, suspension, etc.
- Take disciplinary actions against officers/management staff who are found guilty of precipitating indiscipline among workers.
- Recognize trade union according to criteria evolved at the 16th session of Indian Labour Conference held in May 1958.

Agreement on the part of the trade unions

- Do not encourage physical duress.
- Do not permit rowdyism and violent demonstrations.
- Do not allow members to engage in any union activity during working hours.
- Discourage unfair labour practices such as "go-slow" damage, carelessness etc.
- Take prompt action to implement awards and settlement.
- Display at a prominent place the "code of discipline" for the knowledge of workers.
- Take actions against office bearers of unions who are found violating Code of Discipline.

Ratification of Contracts

Ratification of contract means, after days and months of industrial disputes in the form of *bandh*, picketing and *hartals*, when any trade union decides to break the strike and allow the workers to return back to the work after signing an agreement (ratification agreement) with the management of the organization. One such recent case could be cited here is that of Goodyear tyres.

The Goodyear Tyre Case

With ratification of a new three-year master contract a foregone conclusion, union (steelworker union) workers and Goodyear management had mutually agreed to get on with the task at hand-returning the financially ailing tyre maker to profitability. The contract basically mirrors the BF Goodrich-Michelin national agreement, which Goodyear until now had refused to sign. Each of the local unions approved the contract, which passed by a two-to-one margin.

A key issue in the strike was Goodyear's threat to close two plants. Goodyear as the news is, would still close the Tyler, Texas, plant, eliminating 1,100 jobs. The plant would remain open until the end of 2007, however, and buyout packages would be made available to the terminated workers to ease their economic pain. Further Goodyear agreed not to outsource to low-wage countries the work done at the Tyler plant.

A second key issue was retiree health care, for which a fund had been established. Hourly wage rates remained in place for the current employees, a third of whom had faced drastic pay cuts. However, a two-tier pay scale put new hires at a lower rate of pay.

Regardless of what the Goodyear workers settled for through this ratification contract, they went back to work with a heightened level of class consciousness. With workers at Ford, GM and Chrysler facing similar and possible strikes, both the Goodyear and Alcoa workers cheered their supportive auto workers with the comment that "We've got your back".

Industrial Tripartite Committees (ITCs)

ITCs have been constituted with the view to promote the spirit of tripartism. These tripartite bodies provide a forum whereby the social partners through dialogue can appreciate the problems of industries and workers affected by Economic Reforms. These Committees are non-statutory Standing Committees meetings of which are convened as and when required. Government's proactive role has successfully harmonized the interest of the employers and the workers resulting in a change of attitude from confrontation to that of cooperation. There are 8 ITCs, one ITC each on

1. Cotton Textiles Industry
2. Jute Industry
3. Road Transport Industry
4. Electricity Generation and Distribution Industry
5. Engineering Industry
6. Sugar Industry
7. Chemical Industry, and
8. Plantation Industry

In 2003, meetings of the Industrial Tripartite Committees on 'Road Transport', 'Jute Industry' and 'Cotton Textiles industry' were held on 10th April, 25th August and 15th December, respectively. In 2002 and 2005, meetings of the Tripartite Industrial Committee on Plantation Industry were held on 3rd April, 2002 and 26th August, 2005 respectively.

Exercise Case Study: Union Relations

Mary, a union shop steward in the food service department of Patterson Memorial Medical Centre, was on her regularly scheduled day off at home. She was called by her supervisor and told to talk to three union members and instruct them to attend a meeting called a "Quest for Quality Interaction Committee" meeting which was to be held on company time. The Quest for Quality program was a high priority at Patterson Memorial Medical Centre for improving the quality of patient care at the facility and the food service department was responsible for improving nutritional care. The union had objected to the implementation of the Quest for Quality program which called for all employees to work in teams (such as quality circles) on projects to improve quality. The union opposed the project because they felt that employees were being asked to collect and analyze data and perform decision-making functions which were the responsibility of management. Since the employees were not paid extra for serving on these teams, the union told employees they could attend the meeting if their jobs were threatened, but they should do so under protest and then file a grievance afterward.

Management's position regarding the union's objection was that quality was everyone's job, not just management's. This program is designed to improve the quality of care to patients — not just to make work for the food service workers. Since the union employees are "front line" workers, they would know best how to make improvements to improve patient care. Additionally, since quality improvement is everyone's job every day, there is no extra compensation warranted in this situation.

On the day in question, in a three-way conversation with the three employees, Mary told them that she would not order them to attend the Quest for Quality meeting, although she had been asked by her supervisor to instruct them to go to the meeting. She told them to follow the union guidance, as indicated above. Since the supervisor who called Mary wanted to avoid a confrontation with the employees, she did not order the employees to attend the meeting but relied on the union shop steward to issue the order. When Mary failed to order the employees to attend the meeting, the Director of Food Service suspended her for two weeks. Mary immediately filed a union grievance against the food service director asserting that the two week suspension was inappropriate and unjust.

As part of the negotiated agreement, both sides were required to meet monthly to discuss any grievances that may have been lodged by either side. At the next monthly meeting, neither the union nor management would budge on the issue so they could not come to an agreement on the grievance. As a result, both sides agreed to submit the grievance to binding arbitration.

The union position was that the company had no authority to discipline Mary on her day off for failure to give what it termed was a "management function". The union pointed out that it was unfair that the employer refused to order the employees directly to attend the meeting but then expected the union shop steward to do so. The union argued that while it is not unusual to call upon a union shop steward for assistance in problem solving, the company had no right to demand that she replace supervisors or management in giving orders and then discipline her for refusing to do so.

Management's position was that the opposition of the union to the Quest for Quality meetings put the employees in a position of being unable to attend the meetings without direction from the union shop steward and that employees would be looked upon as going against the union if they went to the meeting on their own. Management indicated that Mary was given the job assignment of directing the employees to attend the meeting because the union had openly and strongly opposed the program and that employees would not willingly go to the meeting without union consent. Her failure to follow that job assignment constituted insubordination and just cause for her suspension.

Nonetheless, the union contended that the arbitrator must examine the nature of the order when deciding whether the insubordination was grounds for discipline. As to the nature of the order in this case, the employer had to demonstrate that the order was directly related to the job classification and work assignment of the employee disciplined. The refusal to obey such an order must be shown to pose a real challenge to supervisory authority.

Management countered with the assertion that the union had set up an environment where the employees were put in a no-win situation and it was difficult for management to issue the order without a confrontation with the employees. As such, it was the union's responsibility to correct the situation and direct the employees to attend the meeting.

Mary did not dispute the fact that she failed to follow the orders given to her by her supervisor, but pointed out that she was not on duty at the time and that the task being given to her was not because of her job with the company but because of her status as a union shop steward.

Management indicated that the task was given to her because the union had openly opposed the quality meetings and the meeting was that day — and she was the on-site union official. She was called when she was not on duty, because it was a union problem and she was the only one who could remedy the problem.

QUESTIONS

1. As the arbitrator, do you think the employer had just cause to discipline the employee? You must fully defend your position, no matter what you decide.
2. If the union's opposition to the Quest for Quality program encouraged the employees to not participate in the program, should the union be held responsible for directing the employees to attend? Why or why not?
3. As the arbitrator you have a captive audience and, after you make your decision, you can provide guidance to both parties. If you were to give advice to both parties on what they could have done to avoid this problem in the first place, what advice would you give to them?

QUESTION BANK

1. What is industrial dispute? Explain the statutory and non-statutory methods of resolving the disputes. (BU July/August 2005).
2. What is the statutory machinery available in India to resolve industrial disputes? (BU 2002).
3. Supreme court has declared that the "Government staff cannot go on strike". Comment on the pros and cons on the judgement? (BU 2003).
4. Do you think the proposed amendments to the Industrial Disputes Act, Factories Act and Trade Unions Act, will affect the workers' interest? Discuss. (BU 2003).
5. Discuss the historical foundation of the struggle between employers and employees. How does it help or hinder industrial relations climate in organizations?

Internet Exercises

- Go through the website www.**india**labourarchives.org/ and share your findings with your friends in the class.
- Surf the website www.indiastat.com/india and collect important information on Industrial Disputes in India.

Experiential Exercise

- You are an Industrial Relation Officer of a manufacturing unit. One fine morning when you reached your factory office you found 200 workers shouting slogan against the management. On enquiry you found out that the workers are at strike and there is loss of production in the plant. What options are available to you to resolve the strike?
- You are the HR director of a large cotton spinning mill. A couple of days ago in a serious fire in one of your plants, five workers have been seriously injured. Now all the employees have gathered outside your chamber and demanding compensation for the mishap. You are about to address the gathering. Assume the role and present the same to your class.

Chapter 6

e-HUMAN RESOURCE MANAGEMENT

Theme Reading: Accenture's HR Management System

For Accenture, India is one of the most happening centres bubbling with action and driving major innovations. This can be gauged from the fact that some of its new technology and management initiatives are being first developed and deployed in India and later replicated in other parts of its global operations spread across 40 integrated development centres in 30 countries.

One such is **Abacus**, a HR management system. Accenture India has successfully deployed this across its delivery centres in the country and is now poised to implement it in other centres across the world. For a large enterprise that has about 16,000 plus employees in India of the 1,23,000 plus globally, a streamlined technology-driven HR has made a world of difference.

The Head of Human Resource, Accenture India, Mr. Rahul Varma, told that Abacus has been developed in India on the NET platform and provides an integrated HR management functionality.

Right from forecasting of resource requirements to candidate selection to monitoring efficiencies of resources among other issues, the software handles it all. In effect, it is like an ERP system for HR management. Manufacturing and marketing companies have been traditionally using supply chain management technologies that have brought about significant efficiencies. Give the complexity HR brings to the table in a knowledge-driven industry, Accenture India has taken a cue from the traditional industry and developed Abacus, Mr. Varma said.

Abacus enables companies to manage its human resource better, right from prospective candidates applying for a job online to employees quitting, covering the entire spectrum within the enterprise. Most large companies have bits and pieces of technology that are laced together to function as a system in HR management environment. Abacus seeks to eliminate all of this by providing a uniform integrated system that helps manage its resources as if they were all present at one place.

"Accenture in India has registered significant growth from being a 200-people organization to 16,000 plus and we continue to recruit at a hectic pace and the flow is steady. Therefore, HR is a critical part of meeting the multiple objectives of an enterprise that is now serving more than 170 clients through several delivery centres".

IT is playing a key role in managing the employee lifecycle, right from a prospect's application to training and development, performance management, promotion, and incentives. Even a referral has the advantage of tracking the movement of a candidate's interview status. The best part is, it aligns with business objectives and goals of the Company and CEO. This software is complemented by an engagement portal that tracks the work progress, Mr. Varma said.

Electronic (E) Human Resource (HR) Perspective to Organizational Effectiveness

"e-HR refers to the broad access to human resources data, tools and transactions available directly on the web in most workplaces today. It describes the "net effect" of the explosion in web technologies and the dramatic impact this growth has had on the way employees now receive employment-related information through integrated self-service applications. It also includes the variety of new technologies available that help connect multiple systems, tools and databases, both inside and outside organizations" (Watson Wyatt Research Report - The Net Effect). Much has been written in the past several years about HR acting as a strategic partner. HR leaders have been told repeatedly that they must earn a "seat at the table" with top management in order to play a significant role in the development of organizational strategies and business success. But, while many HR leaders have become active participants in strategy sessions occurring in boardrooms around the world, they are continually hindered by the need to think and act strategically, while still overseeing the time-consuming administrative aspects of day-to-day HR. It is clear that HR must find a way to relieve itself of administrative burdens (without abdicating their administrative role) in order to maximize its contribution to business strategy.

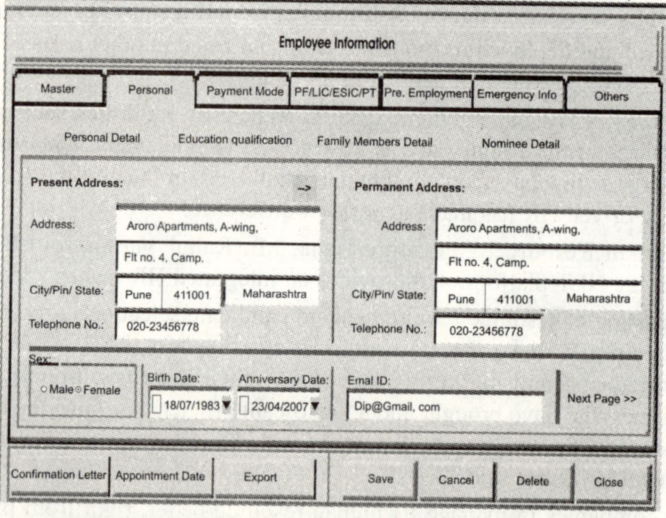

Fig. 6.1: An e-HR application showing employee information in a company

Technological change is a key driver for HR transformation, providing the foundation to support HR's growing strategic focus. In particular, Web and Internet technologies have already given workers direct access to each other, to HR, and to business information with such ease and intelligence that every worker can contribute more directly to business results.

Although great strides have been made in recent years to use technology to simplify HR, technology until now offered only partial solutions to HR's challenges. Consider the employee self-service model that evolved throughout the 1990's. Developed in part due to employee and manager complaints about the impersonal and inefficient services offered by outsourced solutions of the early 1990's, self-service has proven to be extraordinarily popular.

What is e-HRM?

Electronic Human Resource Management System (e-HRM System) is a web-based solution that takes advantage of the latest web application technology to deliver an online real-time human resource management solution. It is comprehensive but easy to use, feature-rich yet flexible enough to be tailored to your specific needs.

A recent research report on e-HR people management strategies is associated with a nearly 2% increase in a company's market value. e-HR helps maximize a company's progress toward a knowledge economy and increased shareholder value.

Peculiarities of e-HRM

The e-HRM business solution excels in the following capabilities:

- modularity
- the solution can be accessed and used in a web browser
- security of data, protected levels of access to individual modules, records documents and their component parts
- parametric and customizability
- access to archived records and documents
- user-friendly interface
- connectivity with the client's existing information system (payroll accounting, ERP, attendance registration, document systems...)
- multi-language support

Features of e-HRM

- Web based HRM application
- Customizable work flow flexibility
- Access control and multi site capability
- Online leave application, auto routing and approval capability
- Integrated with Time Management System
- Integrated with Payroll System
- Web reporting features using Crystal Report and other report generating applications

Benefits

- Gradual implementation
- Adaptability to any client
- Collection of information as the basis for strategic decision-making
- Integral support for the management of human resources and all other basic and support processes within the company
- A more dynamic workflow in the business process, productivity and employee satisfaction
- A decisive step towards a paperless office
- Lower business costs
- Easy and fast to deploy
- Multi site consolidation of information online and real time
- Cost savings in IT infrastructure by using the Internet
- Reduce IT capital expenditure through centralization and eliminate equipment duplication in multi site configuration
- Eliminate data duplication and maintain data integrity

How e-HRM works?

Venkateswaran et al. had proposed a model describing how e-HRM works in an organization. The following figure illustrates how this works:

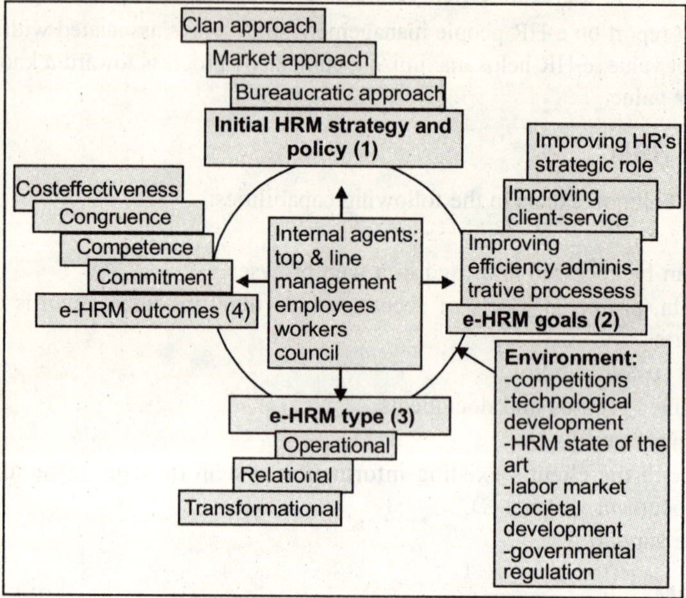

Fig. 6.2A: Model of e-HRM

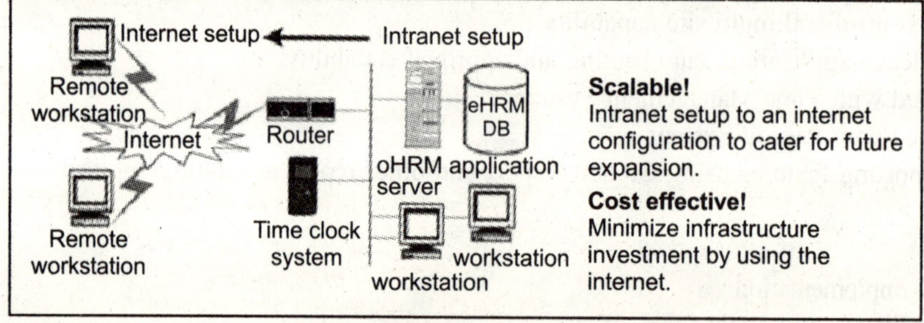

Fig. 6.2B: Model of e-HRM

e-HR Softwares

By using Virgo, an organization can ensure that its business is supported by a business information systems platform that will evolve and change as the organization develops its business or respond to marketplace changes.

Virgo

Virgo is designed from the ground up to support all products and services that clients may provide, and to provide whole-of-business reporting and online analysis. Virgo Recruitment is a comprehensive business solution for multi-facetted Recruitment and Consultancy Services Firms. Virgo provides complete end-to-end, whole-of-business functionality to support everything from strategic discussions on pre-market diversification and Tender Response processing, through to pre-sales, order entry and processing, order fulfilment, payroll and invoicing, etc.

Furthermore, being based on web technologies Virgo fully supports remote users such as clients, candidates, mobile consultants, affiliates, etc.

Virgo integrates with the Accounting and Finance system of your choice, meaning that you do not need to change accounting system, and that your finance and accounting department can use the accounting system of choice. Virgo supports:

- Project-based consulting, training, out-placement, management services, team-based consulting, etc.;
- Temporary and contract placements across all industries and niche markets;
- Shift-based placements across all industries and niche markets including nursing and health, human services, aged care, childcare, hospitality, retail, etc.;
- Call centres and help-desk;
- Permanent and Executive Search;
- Miscellaneous items such as sale of licensed intellectual property, research documents, standard fixed-price services, etc.

Virgo Provides

- End-to-end, fully integrated order processing that spans all operational processes, as well financial reporting and operational controls;
- Integrated Activity and Performance Management and Reporting;
- Integrated Payroll and Accounting systems—either our offering, or your preferred products;
- Multiple business entities with integrated support for divisions, departments, branches, teams, and projects supported by performance monitoring and exception-based control;
- Inherited Skills and attributes recorded against clients, client divisions and branches, order types, job types, and personnel that are defined once and included automatically in the integrated Skills Search and Select processing;
- Customizable workflows, business processes, security, etc.;
- Automated notification of all events;
- Diary, Business Development Schedules (call planning), etc.;

Low-cost/no-cost enhancements that support your specific competitive.

Adrenalin

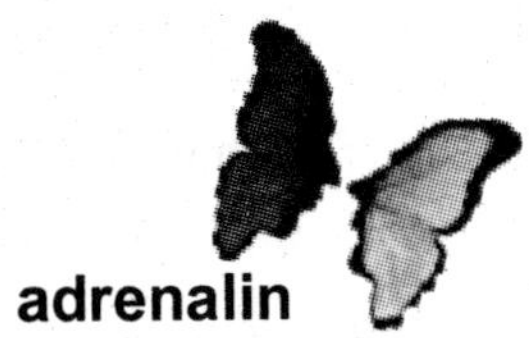

"It transforms"
Human Capital Alignment Software

Adrenalin, one of India's most chosen human capital management software, aids the CEO of an organization in alignment, streamlining the organization vision with HR. The software empowers people to multiply their performance dramatically through a web-based software application. Adrenalin transforms people and working, departments and mind-sets, productivity and profits. Business leaders can now seamlessly align human resources with business results. It facilitates people and processes to work seamlessly and maximize productivity. Performance and efficiency can now be showcased more effectively with the help of Adrenalin. Adrenalin is developed and marketed by Adrenalin eSystems Ltd., a group company of Polaris Software Lab Ltd.

Salient Benefits of Adrenalin

- Stimulates employee alignment
- Creates a performance culture
- Aids better planning, better decisions
- Delivers significant cost savings
- Improves administrative responsiveness and efficiency
- Enables greater employee satisfaction, fuels organizational productivity

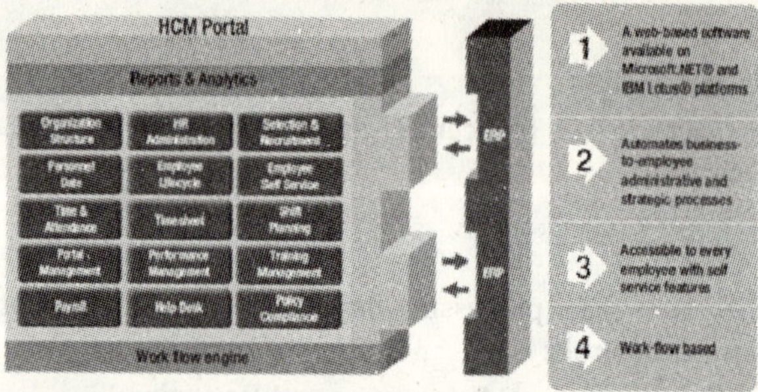

Fig. 6.3: Illustration depicting how Adrenalin works

(*Courtesy: http://www.myadrenalin.com/india/ET-adva.asp*)

Adrenalin has been successfully implemented in several reputed Indian organizations like Hero Honda. Adrenalin provides the users with a good workflow system. The system has the flexibility to address business rules of various employee levels as well as departments. This gives our employees flexibility in their routine work. This was the comment made by Mr. Umesh Malhotra, Manager-IT, Hero Honda Motors. The benefits acclaimed by Hero Honda by using Adrenalin were as follows:

- The online HR, administrative, claim and reimbursement processes have reduced the process time and follow up. Accuracy of data has also helped in quickening processes.
- With processes going online, the company has moved closer being a paper less office.
- The system provided flexibility to employees, while bridging the gap between distributed teams.
- With the Travel and Expense module, status of requests and approvals can easily be available and the team can focus on their work instead of worrying about the expenses.
- Increased profitability, by providing a high value for money solution, streamlining all financial and administrative tasks which has freed up time for productive work.

(*Courtesy: http://www.myadrenalin.com/india/*)

The HR and IT Partnership

HR professionals in this new age, need to become facilitators of change, people who help deliver competitiveness and profitability. HR's new positioning and needs portend interesting times for Information Technology. Companies are realizing that they must reduce costs and increase the contributions HR makes to the bottom line. As HR searches for business practices that benefit the bottom line, it is likely to reach far beyond back-office automation systems towards the cutting-edge technology in Human Capital Management. HR needs IT's help-not only to automate recurring processes but also to speed recruitment, to improve employee development, performance management and succession planning.

IT systems are what will drive the HR function forward. In effect, the following changes need to occur if HR is going to make the transition to a strategic role within the organization:

- Reengineer all employment processes using IT automation wherever practical, ensuring that the end result provides added customer value without mounting the workload for line managers.
- Reengineer the role of HR, shifting away from the routine of running employment processes, and toward employment process design and audit.
- Recognize the effect on the role of the line manager, and successfully deploy the line manager's use of HR information in planning and managing people.

IT helps in improving employee access to HR information. It also delivers value in areas such as applicant tracking, recruiting, competency management, training administration and performance management.

THEME READING: e-HR PRACTICES AT SATYAM

The Human Resources function in Satyam is a strategic support function. All the geographical locations have there own dedicated HR representatives who help the Strategic Business Units in their day-to-day functioning. They are in turn supported by Corporate HR operating from Hyderabad. In Satyam all the sub-functions of HR like Recruitment, Training, Associate Relations, Compensation and Benefits make use of Information Technology (E-mail, Intranet, Software tools etc.) in their everyday operations.

E-mail: E-mails in an organization like Satyam has supplanted the hard copy internal memo and taken over external communications in the initiative of the organization so as to make it a paper less office. For example, the recruitment team most often receives applications via e-mails. e-mail is also one of the best ways to keep in touch with associates, and it overcomes constraints of space, time and organizational hierarchies.

Access to company information system: In Satyam employees get the advantage of having direct access to information like that of their payroll information, Tax computations and annual salary statements etc.

Intranet advantage: Satyam has been able to effectively integrate HR contents into a company-wide Intranet—rather than a stand-alone HR site- to provide a seamless and intuitive medium for its employees to interact with the company and amongst themselves in a comfortable, relevant and logical way. The benefits can be seen as increased information sharing and improved employee motivation and morale. Moving HR function onto the company Intranet has improved service to internal customers, and helped the organization to interact with its associates more effectively, and this has reduced many routine administrative costs. Associates with a HR question use the Intranet to access the information they want, when and where they need it.

e-Training and e-Learning: Satyam Intranet is also used for training and communicating with associates (e-training and e-learning). The Intranet has enabled information and learning for use in conjunction with existing training process. It has also enabled disseminating information organization-wide and provides a forum which supports communication and discussions and collabourative activities directly amongst teams and individuals. The Intranet is searchable and associates can quickly find matters on the subjects they are looking for. In Satyam, one of the ways of measuring effectiveness of training is through an online survey on the Intranet. Associates can access course materials, monthly and annual training calendars, calendars of external training institutions through the Intranet.

e-Library Facilities: Browser-based Library information has offered immediate savings in administration and distribution. Only one copy needs to be prepared and updates can be implemented universally and instantaneously. Indexes and cross-references within and between documents have become 'live' and meaningful with the use of web-technology. Books can be searched across locations, abstracts can be read and books can be reserved online. One can even find out the associate who has borrowed the book.

Online Climate and Employee Satisfaction Surveys: Organizational Climate surveys are conducted in Satyam via the Intranet which ensures that it is not geographically constrained and a large number of associates are covered in a short period of time. There is an **online feedback mechanism** wherein an associate either anonymously or if he/she so wishes, by his/her name send a grievance or feedback to a particular department. New associates are encouraged to browse through the Intranet and familiarize themselves with policies, procedures and other departments on the Intranet.

(*Courtesy: Roshan Joseph, Gautam Ghosh, "**The HR and IT Partnership at Satyam:** Reaching out to people"*, Satyam Technology Centre, Bahadurpally, Hyderabad-500043)

e-Recruitment

The buzzword and the latest trends in recruitment is the "e-Recruitment". Also known as "Online recruitment", it is the use of technology or the web based tools to assist the recruitment process. The tool can be either a job website like naukri.com, the organization's corporate website or its own intranet. Many big and small organizations are using Internet as a source of recruitment. They advertise job vacancies through worldwide web. The job seekers send their applications or curriculum vitae (CV) through an e-mail using the Internet. Alternatively job seekers place their CV's in worldwide web, which can be drawn by prospective employees depending upon their requirements.

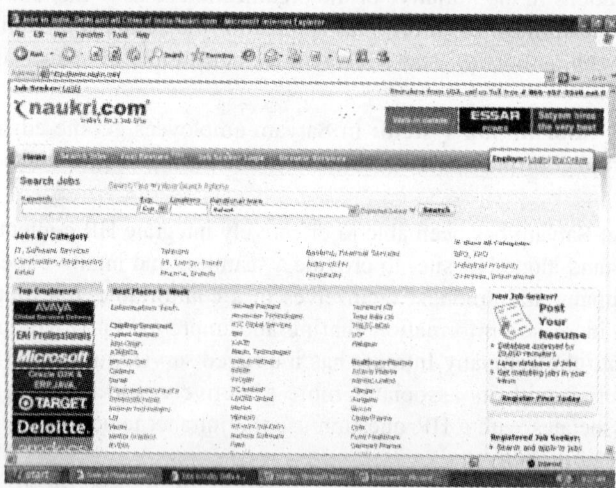

Fig. 6.4: Illustration of a job website

The various kinds of e-recruitment that an organization can use is:

- **Job portals** – i.e. posting the position with the job description and the job specification on the job portal and also searching for the suitable resumes posted on the site corresponding to the opening in the organization. Job sites provide a 24*7 access to the database of the resumes to the employees facilitating the just-in-time hiring by the organizations. Also, the jobs can be posted on the site almost immediately and is also cheaper than advertising in the employment newspapers. Sometimes companies can get valuable references through the "passers-by" applicants. Online recruitment helps the organizations to automate the recruitment process, save their time and costs on recruitments.

- **Creating a complete online recruitment/application section in the companies own website:** Companies have added an application system to its website, where the 'passive' job seekers can submit their resumes into the database of the organization for consideration in future, as and when the roles become available.

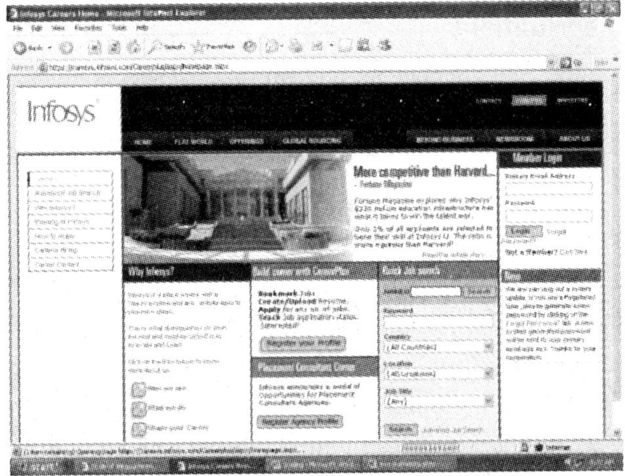

Fig. 6.5: Online recruitment in the Infosys website

- **Resume Scanners:** Resume scanner is one major benefit provided by the job portals to the organizations. It enables the employees to screen and filter the resumes through pre-defined criteria's and requirements (skills, qualifications, experience, payroll etc.) of the job.

Online recruitment techniques involve features such as:

- Giving a detailed job description and job specifications in the job postings to attract candidates with the right skill sets and qualifications at the first stage.
- E-recruitment should be incorporated into the overall recruitment strategy of the organization.
- A well-defined and structured applicant tracking system should be integrated and the system should have a back-end support.
- Along with the back-office support a comprehensive website to receive and process job applications (through direct or online advertising) should be developed.

Advantage and Disadvantage of e-Recruitment

There are many benefits – both to the employers and the job seekers but the e-recruitment is not free from a few shortcomings. Some of the advantages and the disadvantages of e-recruitment are as follows:

Advantages of e-Recruitment

- Lower costs to the organization. Also, posting jobs online is cheaper than advertising in the newspapers.
- No intermediaries.
- Reduction in the time for recruitment (over 65 per cent of the hiring time).
- Facilitates the recruitment of right type of people with the required skills.

- Improved efficiency of recruitment process.
- Gives a 24 × 7 access to an online collection of resumes.
- Online recruitment helps the organizations to weed out the unqualified candidates in an automated way.
- Recruitment websites also provide valuable data and information regarding the compensation offered by the competitors etc. which helps the HR managers to take various HR decisions like promotions, salary trends in industry etc.

Disadvantages of e-Recruitment

Apart from the various benefits, e-recruitment has its own share of shortcomings and disadvantages. Some of them are:

- Screening and checking the skill mapping and authenticity of million of resumes is a problem and time consuming exercise for organizations.
- There is low internet penetration and no access and lack of awareness of internet in many locations across India.
- Organizations cannot be dependant solely and totally on the online recruitment methods.
- In India, the employers and the employees still prefer a face-to-face interaction rather than sending e-mails.

Industry Opinion

"HCL is pioneer in the usage Web 2.0 in its recruitment process and 5–7% of its total recruiting is done through this". Mr. Ravi Shankar, Global Head, Talent Management Group, HCL Technologies.

(Courtesy: Bajpai, V., (2008): "Innovative Hiring Strategies", Dare, Vol. 2, Issue 10, July 2008, p. 55.)

e-Performance Management

In Satyam, the performance appraisal process was automated in a case where associates from a Strategic Business Unit along with two assessors for each associate filled the appraisal form online. The data was processed and transferred to HR at the headquarters electronically.

In Satyam associates use an online Performance Management System that draws upon a concept called **Numeric Management**. This concept uses a framework that objectively captures and manages business concerns. At a very fundamental level all business concerns can be expressed in numbers, and the manager's role is one of manipulating "reality" to achieve the "desired" state on the specified number. This method enables managers to capture various business phenomena objectively to arrive at decisions.

Wipro offers an integrated end-to-end Performance Management Solution. This solution is based on global people processes drawn from best practices and helps organizations streamline their performance evaluation processes. Wipro's e-Performance Management solution not only helps you establish the best practices in Performance Management, like 360 degree appraisal, MBO, etc., but enables reduced Performance Management cycle time without compromising on the sub-processes which are so critical to your HR values, like Work Planning Conference, Work Plan establishment, Development plans and Objective setting, Interim Review, Overall evaluation, Detecting Performance deficiencies, Tracking, Documentation and Archiving.

The various features of this e-performance management system involves the following characteristics:

- Align employee objectives to the business goals. Enable strategic Performance Management through Management by Objectives (MBO).
- Measure and Assess employee performance periodically and provide feedback and support to achieve quantitative, qualitative and process targets.

- Evaluate and track Hi-Performance and achievers based on Competency driven practices.
- Enable online Reward and Recognition

The following model depicts how this e-performance system works:

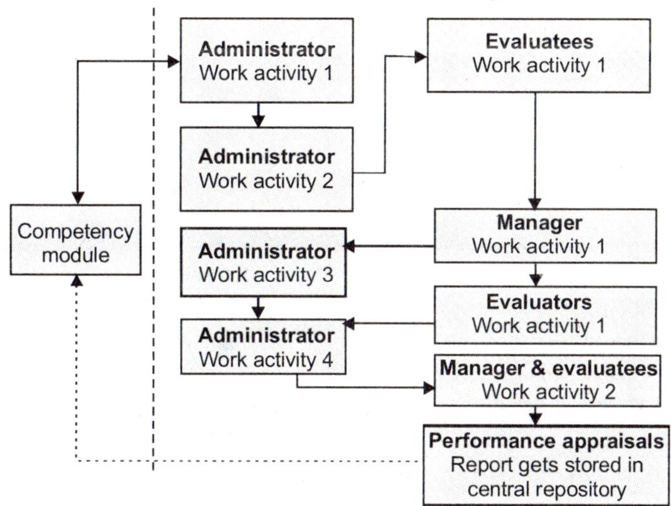

Fig. 6.6: Wipro's e-Performance management solutions

PeopleSoft Enterprise e-Performance Management System

With Oracle's PeopleSoft e-Performance, you can increase your business success by driving and fostering employee engagement with business objectives in a clear process. This process enables you to identify, plan, observe, improve and reward performance. E-Performance is a Web-deployed performance management solution that streamlines the appraisal aspect of the development business process, from goal planning and coaching to performance assessments and rewards. Managers, employees, and HR administrators can collabourate on performance evaluations and goals, review performance history, and monitor and manage the overall performance process. Workflow notifications keep all interested parties up-to-date throughout the performance cycle.

Benefits

- PeopleSoft e-Performance management system drives business results by directly linking employee performance and rewards with the organization's financial and business objectives.
- Goal linking capabilities drive alignment among missions, initiatives, and departmental or individual goals.
- Leverage Profile Management data by incorporating job-, industry- or organization-specific content into performance documents as performance criteria.
- Compare performance ratings and outcomes to job requirements, and then trigger learning to close gaps.
- Multi-document functionality enables multi-rater and 360 degree feedback.
- Support unique sets of business rules and approval processes for different organizations within your enterprise.
- Tailor the application for any workforce group, region, or individual.

- Drive the employee development process with workflow in an easy-to-use, Web-based environment.
- Construct high-quality feedback for employees more frequently, while simultaneously reducing the risk associated with non-standardized assessments.
- Real-time graphical reports ensure visibility into the process.

View Performance Documents

Document Details

Cynthia Chandler, Clerk-Accounting
Performance Document: 01/01/2004 - 01/01/2005

Performance Document Details

Employee: Cynthia Chandler **Job Title:** Clerk-Accounting
Document Type: Performance Document **Period:** 01/01/2004 - 01/01/2005
Manager: Betty Locherty **Status:** Completed
Template Name: Non-collaborative

Document Progress

Step		Status	Due Date	
Review Self Evaluation	○	Not Started	01/11/2005	
Review Manager Evaluation	✔	Completed	01/21/2005	View

Fig. 6.7: Oracle's PeopleSoft e-Performance management system

Knowledge Bank: One of the main features of the Various organisational in branch like that of Satyam Intranet, which many associates find useful, is the **Knowledge Bank Repository**. The Knowledge Repository on the Intranet has many merits in terms of contributing to the organization's success. The **Knowledge Base** is a database of experiences and collection of knowledge captured within functions and projects. It contains information that helps avoid re-inventing the wheel and repeat mistakes, tools methods etc. The Knowledge Base also contains the project information base and a closed project base. Discussions are organized around questions and the posts are archived monthly.

e-Journals/Magazines: The electronic in-house magazine run by the associates connects associates across the organization. User-friendly applications like **'Classifieds'** on the Intranet helps associates in locating people, houses, things etc.

Vision compass: Vision Compass, a software product developed and marketed by Satyam Computers Limited draws upon the philosophy of Numeric Management and provides a framework for operationalising Numeric Management within an organization.

QUESTION BANK

1. What is e-HRM? What are its peculiarities?
2. What are the characteristic features of e-HRM? What are the potential benefits of e-HRM?
3. How does e-HRM work in organizations?
4. What is human capital management system? Give examples.
5. Give examples of some e-HR applications known to you.
6. What is e-recruitment? How is it managed? What are its merits and demerits?

7. Write short notes on: (a) Job Portals (b) Resume Scanners.
8. What is e-performance management? State its peculiarities.
9. What are the potential benefits of e-performance management systems?
10. "e-HRM can empower today's line and staff managers" Comment on the statement.

Experiential Exercises

- Debate on the following topic in your class: "Will e-HRM make the job of HR professionals redundant?"
- "Advancement in IT and e-HR" prepare a paper on the given topic and present the same in your class.

Internet Exercises

- Compare the following job portals: naukri.com, monster.com, jobsahead.com and prepare a presentation on their merits and demerits.
- Compare any two company websites which allow uploading candidate CVs in their websites.

HR AND ITS CONTRIBUTION TO BUSINESS ETHICS AND CSR

Theme Reading: Best Practice @ Wipro

Azim Premji is one of those billionaires whose heart is as gargantuan as his wealth. And he is shoveling in considerable amounts of the latter to fulfil the call of the former. The Azim H. Premji Foundation (AHF), which focuses only on primary education, is funded entirely out of his personal wealth. Its annual spend: Rs. 25 crore. This is addition to Wipro's contribution of Rs. 3 crore every year. Premji firmly believes that "the education system should foster creativity rather than rote learning." Since 2000, this literary mission has financed 7000 schools in Karnataka, Andhra Pradesh, Tamil Nadu, Himachal Pradesh, Madhya Pradesh, Punjab and Rajasthan. More than 18 lakh young students and 29000 teachers have benefitted from this program. The mission was recently extended to Uttaranchal at the invitation of the state government. Wipro and AHF say that they will go to other states if the government is willing to work with them to improve the education system. To ensure that this who run the systems have a stake in it, Wipro and the foundation which put in 50% of the cost, insist that their partner organizations cough up the rest. Wipro employees are also encouraged to participate in the company's literacy mission. Premji's business acumen helped India become a knowledge powerhouse. Now, the call of his conscience may well help create the base to sustain this comparative advantage.

(Courtesy: Venkatesha Babu (2005): "Get, set, Grow", Business Today, Volume 14, No. 6, March 27th, 2005, p. 78.)

Introduction

Organizations and industry captains have now a days recognized the importance of corporate social responsibility (CSR). While there is no agreed-upon definition, the World Business Council for Sustainable Development defines CSR as the business commitment and contribution to the quality of life of employees, their families and the local community and society overall to support sustainable economic development. Simply put, the business case for CSR—establishing a positive company reputation and brand in the public eye through good work that yields a competitive edge while at the same time contributing to others—demands that organizations shift from solely focusing on making a profit to including financial, environmental and social responsibility in their core business strategies.

Corporate Social Responsibility: Emerging Trends

As the concept of CSR becomes more widely accepted and integrated in business, it is helpful in this discussion to understand that the development of CSR in organizations is in transition. The first generation has demonstrated that companies can contribute to society without risking commercial success. Today, the second generation is developing more fully as CSR gradually becomes an integral part of companies' long-term business strategies. Finally, the third generation addresses significant societal issues, such as poverty and clean up of the environment.

Table 6.1: Old and New Organizational Ethics

Old Ethics	*New Ethics*
Do the minimum as required by statutory laws and regulations	Do the right thing
Keep a iow profile	Show that right things are being done
Downplay public concerns	Seek to identify and address public concerns
Reply to shareholders enquiries when necessary	Be responsible to stakeholders
Communicate on need-to-know basis	Communicate openly
Make decisions on the bottom line and laws alone	Integrate all the above in decision-making

Exhibit: CSR in Sony

The core responsibility of the Sony Group to society is to pursue the enhancement of corporate value through innovation and sound business practices. The Sony Group recognizes that its businesses have direct and indirect impact on the societies in which it operates. Sound business practices require that business decisions give due consideration to the interests of Sony stakeholders, including shareholders, customers, employees, suppliers, business partners, local communities and other organizations. The Sony Group will endeavor to conduct its business accordingly.

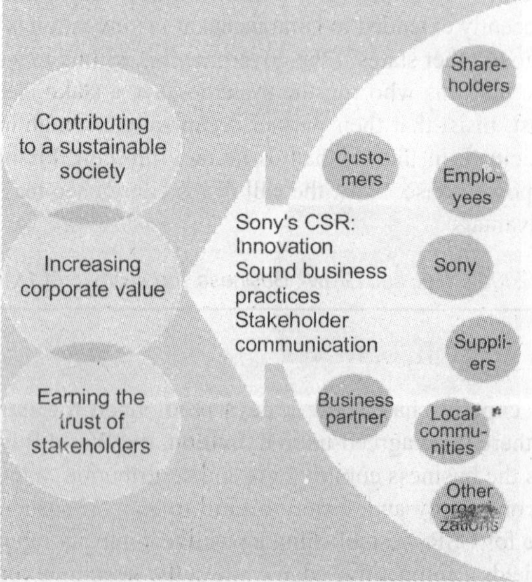

Fig. 6.8: Model of CSR in Sony

(*Courtesy: http://www.sony.net/SonyInfo/Environment/about/index.html*)

Initiatives taken by Sony India: Taking its commitment towards the enhancement of scientific literacy forward, Sony India had organized the Sony Science Show in Delhi from November 19 – 21, 2007. Aimed at fourth graders (nine years), the Science Show held at Apeejay School, Sheikh Sarai had an audience of over 7000 students from 28 participating schools.

(Courtesy: http://www.sony.co.in/section/community?site=hp_en_IN_i)

Making the Business Case for CSR

In recent years, intangible assets—company values, human and intellectual capital, reputation and brand equity—have become increasingly important to organizations. Companies that exhibit good corporate citizenship are likely to gain a competitive edge. Below are just a few examples of today's CSR success factors that are fast becoming the primary measures of an organization's credibility.

Reputation and Brand Enhancement

Company reputation and brand are greatly influenced by public perception. For example, in the largest global survey of the public's expectations, the *Millennium Poll on Corporate Social Responsibility* documented that over 25,000 individuals across 23 countries on six continents revealed they form their impressions of companies by focusing on corporate citizenship and two out of three people want companies to go beyond making money and contribute to broader society goals.

Accountability and Transparency

Open, reliable and regular reporting of a company's performance—known as accountability and transparency are important aspects of an organization's CSR initiatives. Organizations need to have a proactive stance on employee treatment by prohibiting child labour, forced labour and discrimination and protecting freedom of association for workers.

Risk Management

Managing investor confidence is another factor supporting the business case for CSR. Today, the financial community is examining organizations' CSR report cards and their risk profile. The rapid rise of socially responsible investment illustrates that corporate citizenship is becoming a key measure that investors consider when aligning ethical concerns with publicly held corporations.

The Talent War

CSR influences a company's competitive advantage today through two key value drivers: (1) company reputation and brand; and (2) human capital. HR leaders have begun to assume leadership roles to address both areas. In addition, the talent war is evidenced by an influx of "best places to work" awards (e.g., *Fortune* magazine's "100 Best Companies to Work For," www.fortune.com/fortune/fortune 500). By applying for and winning these awards, HR leaders can gain invaluable exposure for their organizations and use the award as a key feature in recruiting campaigns. Thus, a strong argument for CSR is talent management in both the short and the long-term.

Exhibit: CSR in Syndicate Bank

Syndicate Bank has pioneered in social change and development of the nation. Being a responsible corporate social citizen, the Bank has recognized promoting social and economic transformation through direct humanitarian action and sustainable development in the country. Some of the bank's initiatives in the field of corporate social responsibility are as follows:

- Undertaking ponds cleaning work where the bank and its sponsored RRBs had undertaken cleaning and clearing of 115 ponds/tanks infested with shrubs and plants to conserve water.
- Organized painting competition in different parts of the country like Bangalore, Mysore, Hubli, Mangalore, Hyderabad, Mumbai during November and December 2007.
- Sponsored Mobile Mammography Projects.
- Sponsored social activities of hospital trust (Karunashraya).
- Sponsored cost of ashram building project of Mathruchaya.
- Sponsored micro credit summi.
- Sponsored 37th senior national and state carrom championship.
- Donated to corpus fund of the Karnataka Parents' Association for mentally retarded citizens.
- Displayed road direction boards, messages, parking boards, traffic umbrellas, solar reflector etc.

(Courtesy: Syndicate Bank Annual Report, 2007–2008, pp. 32–33.)

HR Challenges for Achieving CSR

The HR function of the organization plays an immense role to ensure CSR in majority organizations. Among the challenges is that social and/or environmental impact differs across industries, complicated by the fact that the term CSR has different meanings to different industry sectors in different parts of the globe. The HR challenges could be in the form of:

- Network with other HR professionals to learn about their organizations' CSR initiatives (ideas and information about programs; what worked and lessons learned).
- Explore partnering with other organizations (e.g., cosponsor a community event).
- Contact local business organizations, such as the Chamber of Commerce, to learn what events they sponsor and how the company may contribute.
- Solicit employee suggestions regarding CSR initiatives.

HR's Leadership Role

With company reputation, viability and sometimes survival at stake, one of the critical roles of HR leadership today is to spearhead the development and strategic implementation of CSR throughout the organization and promote sound corporate citizenship. Attracting and retaining competent people is one of the primary business reasons for CSR. Many HR leaders are already looking ahead to the future. According to the *SHRM® 2004–2005 Workplace Forecast*, key HR trends are (1) demonstrating HR's return on investment; (2) HR's role in promoting corporate ethics; and (3) building people management and human capital components into key business transactions. HR leaders need to emphasize upon:

- Increasing spending on learning and training initiatives.
- Changing company policy as a response to environmental issues.
- Changing company policy as a response to grassroots pressure to change specific business practices.
- Increasing involvement in social programs.

Theme Case: HR's Role in CSR: Coca Cola Bangalore Plant's Success Story

The HR leaders in Coca Cola Bangalore plant in Bidadi had played an instrumental role in order to involve all the plant employees and workers in promoting the CSR drive for the organization. This is a remarkable achievement for organization as big as that of Coca Cola where the plant at Bidadi, Bangalore employes around 500 employees working in three shifts of eight hours each. The Bidadi plant has a manufacturing capacity of 70,000 cases everyday (where one case contains 24 bottles of 300 ml if it is a glass bottle and if it is a 2 ltr plastic bottle case, each case contains 9 bottles) and the requirement for water is obviously quite high. The company uses Calvary river water supplied to the plant for its production. The water is processed, filtered and throughly tested before using the same for the production process.

As the region had typically been affected by drinking water problems particularly during the dry months, the company and its HR professionals had played an instrumental role in terms of enhancing the awareness of the local villagers on the importance of water conservation in the region.

In this regard the mission and vision statements of the plant are ample proofs of the company's concern for water conservation in the region.

Plant mission statement: "We the team of the HCCBPL, Bidadi, shall ensure efficient and effective use of water during manufacturing process in our plant by continuously improving the infrastructure, monitoring and controlling".

Plant vision statement: "Efficiently reduce, reuse, recycle and recharge water as a responsible corporate citizen".

The Coca Cola employees ably led by their HR heads had taken initiatives not only to conduct rain water harvesting awareness programs at the various village schools but had also been instrumental in conducting several meetings and presentations on the same with the local farmer communities.

Employees at the Bidadi plant use the word "WATER" itself as a hallmark of the organization's responsibility in water conservation and spreading the awareness of the same amongst people. Here the word "WATER" means:

W = **W**atch

A = **A**ct

T = **T**reasure

E = **E**conomize

R = **R**echarge, **R**educe, **R**euse, **R**ecycle

Coca Cola's "Water-Check Dam" initiative had been a special success in the nearby villages and rural areas in the Ramnagar Taluk. This entire project had been pioneered by the employee of Coca Cola with the guidance and able leadership of their HR heads. The organization had invested in constructing check dams in various parts of the Ramnagar Taluk of rural Bangalore with total rain water harvesting (RWH) potential of 11000 lts. Coca Cola's RWH program was inaugurated in the association of mentally challenged school on the World Water Day by the Director General of Police, Karnataka. Very recently the company had also successfully completed the second phase of its "MY WATER" project in various schools of Bangalore with TERI. Apart from these the company had frequently conducted free health and blood donation camps at various parts of rural Bangalore district. One of the noteworthy initiatives taken by Coca Cola was the tree plantation drive in the surrounding areas of the plant and nearby villages. The HR department of the company had also been instrumental in enhancing the civic amenities in the nearby villages. These had been achieved by donating water tanks, supply pumps to local farmers and dust bins to nearby villages.

(Courtesy: Hindustan Coca Cola Beverages Pvt. Ltd., Bidadi Plant, Bangalore.)

Status of CSR in the Organization

HR leaders can influence three primary standards of CSR—ethics, employment practices and community involvement—that relate either directly or indirectly to employees, customers and the local community, as outlined below. By considering these three CSR standards, HR leaders can then identify the CSR stage of their organization before making decisions to develop and implement CSR initiatives (Figure 3).

- *Ethics*—Ethical standards and practices are developed and implemented in dealings with all company stakeholders.
- *Employment Practices*—Human resource management practices promote personal and professional employee development, diversity at all levels and empowerment. Employees are valued partners, with the right to fair labour practices, competitive wages and benefits and a safe, harassment-free, family-friendly work environment.
- *Community Involvement*—The company fosters an open relationship that is sensitive to community culture and needs and plays a proactive, cooperative and collabourative role to make the community a better place to live and conduct business.

Evaluating CSR

Evaluating CSR initiatives in the organization, consideration of ethical principles, implementation and employer brand will assist HR leaders in determining how or why CSR initiatives can be further improved.

Table 6.2: Evaluating CSR Initiatives

Principle	*Implementation*	*Employer Brand*
How is CSR distinguished from corporate philanthropy and donations	How can CSR best be embedded in corporate management objectives and incentives	Why are talented people attracted to work for the organization
How far down the supply chain does responsibility extend	How can HR get all employees involved in and committed to CSR	How can HR ensure a culture and work environment for superior performance
What is the distinctive corporate contribute to the poverty/sustainable livelihood issue	How can HR assess and report on softer, less defined areas	How can HR ensure managers nurture the CSR initiative and this culture

Role of the HR Function

HR leaders can use a checklist to track the HR scorecard on CSR as initiatives are developed and implemented over time. This may include issues like those of:

- Creating a strong organizational culture around core company values.
- Scanning the environment to identify potential threats (e.g., competition for talent within the organization's industry sector).
- Building personal and professional capability of the workforce (e.g., expand intellectual capital within the organization and in collabouration with other organizations).
- Including ethical concerns in staff performance measures.
- Supporting participative decision-making.
- Ensuring highest standards in workplace health and safety.
- Encouraging active engagement in community activities

Equal Employment Opportunity

Equal opportunity employment refers to the approach of the employers to ensure the practice of being fair and impartial in the employment process.

Discrimination in employment: Discrimination refers to the any kind of prejudice, biasness or favouritism on the basis of disability, race, age, sex, sexuality, pregnancy, marital status in employment. No person should be treated less favourably than any other on the basis of the specified issues above. Many countries (like South Africa) have already implemented Equal Opportunity Act, making it against the law to treat anybody unfairly.

Diversity in workforce: With the globalization and the increasing size of the organizations going global, the diversity in the workforce is increasing i.e. people from diverse backgrounds, educational background, age groups, race, gender, abilities and cultures etc. come together to work for one organization and common objectives. Therefore, it is the responsibility of the employer to create an equality-based and discrimination-free working environment and practices.

Equal opportunity: It means treating people equally and fairly irrespective of their race, religion, sex, age, disability etc. Giving women an equal treatment and access to opportunities at the workplace is also an important aspect of this issue.

Equal employment opportunity or anti discriminatory working principles help to realize and respect the actual worth of the individual on the basis of his knowledge, skills, abilities and merit. And the policy should cover all the employees of an organization whether permanent or temporary, contractual etc.

Equal employment opportunity is necessary to ensure:

- To give fair access to the people of all development opportunities.
- To create a fair organization, industry and society.
- To encourage and give disadvantaged or disabled people a fair chance to grow with the society.

Gender Issues in Equal Employment Qpportunities in Organizations

The steady increase in the number of working women in organizations had major social, economic and organizational consequences. As in one side we see organizations like Pepsi Co. being ably headed by India born Ms. Indra Nooyi, whereas in case of a garment factory in the Peenya industrial estate, Bangalore, it could just be another day of harassment and abuse for a woman worker. In fact many sociologists have attributed the sudden spurt in the strength of working women had led to more sex/gender related issues to jobs and careers. Additionally, the selection and promotion criteria that employers use can discriminate against women. Even some cases have been identified where women are being still not allowed to enter certain jobs or job fields. The following problems can be cited so as to state the issues affecting organizations:

The glass ceiling effect: The glass ceiling effect can be described as those discriminatory practices that have prevented women and other protected–class members from advancing to top management positions in organizations or getting promoted to executive level jobs.

Glass walls and glass elevator: Another related problem is that women have tended to advance to senior management in a limited number of support areas, such as HR and corporate communications. Because these jobs tend to pay less than jobs in sales, marketing, operations or finance, the overall impact has been in terms of reducing women's career progression and income. Limits that keep women from progressing only in certain fields have been referred to as "glass walls" or "glass elevators."

Breaking the glass: Organizations could emphasize on the following strategies for the effectiveness of their business:

- Establishing formal programs for women and racial/ethnic individuals
- Providing career rotation opportunities into operations, marketing and sales for individuals who have shown talent in various functional areas like, finance, marketing HR etc.

- Increasing top management and board of directors membership to include women and individuals of colour.
- Establishing clear goals for retention and progression of protected and minority class individuals and holding managers accountable for achieving these goals.
- Allowing for alternative work arrangements for employees, particularly those balancing work/family responsibilities.

Sexual Harassment Issues and Workplace Relationships

With the increase in the number of working women, many organizations have reported with cases involving close personal relationships between colleagues of the opposite gender and most importantly sexual abuses and harassments.

Impact of romantic relationships: When work based friendships bloom into romance and off-the-job intimate relationships organizations face the dilemma whether they should have a watch dog policy to monitor these individuals under disciplinary codes of conduct or leave them as they are until these relationships are off-the-job and do not interfere into performance of other employees in the organization.

Sexual harassment issues: Sexual harassment has become a major concern for most organizations. It can be in either ways where men could be harassing women or a woman boss harassing a male subordinate and even in case of same sex harassments. The following figure illustrates various roles of individuals in organizational sexual harassments.

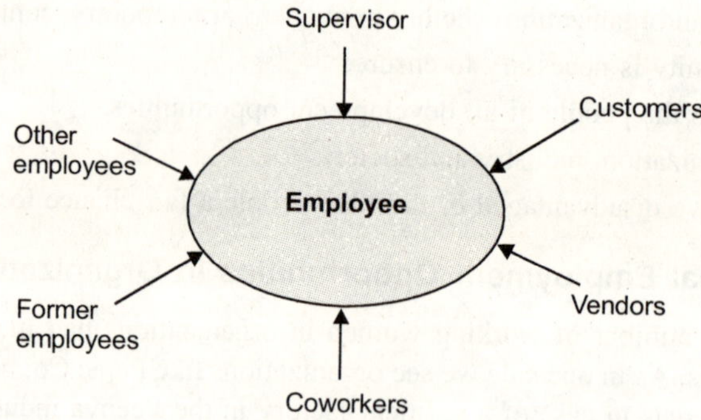

Fig. 6.9: Potential sexual harassers

Types of sexual harassment: The following table illustrates the various types of sexual harassments:

Types of sexual harassment	Features
Quid Pro Quo	• It is the harassment in which employment outcomes are linked to the individual grating sexual favours. • Here the employee might be told that he/she might get promotion or get a desirable work assignment but only if the employee submits to granting some sexual favours to the supervisor. • They are less prevalent as compared to hostile environment sexual harassments.
Hostile environment	• It exists when an individual's work performance or psychological well-being is unreasonably affected by intimidating or offensive working conditions. • They are more prevalent, partially because the standards and consequences are more varied.

***Managing sexual harassments*:** Sexual harassment can't be prevented alone neither by an employer, legal authority nor any trade union, rather a holistic approach has to be initiated in organizations, as depicted by the following figure:

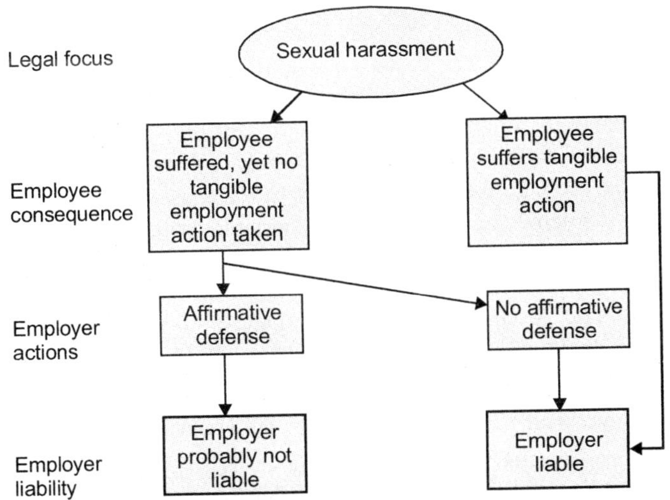

Fig. 6.10: Sexual harassment liability determination model

In this regard the general initiatives taken by organizations involve those of:

- Establishing sexual harassment policy
- Communicating the policy regularly
- Training employees and managers on avoiding sexual harassments
- Investigating and taking actions when complaints are lodged and reported
- Legal support and help
- Prompt actions preceded by investigations and enquiries
- Legal actions against offenders

Exhibit: Equal Employment Opportunity Policy of WIPRO

Wipro's policy is that employees and job aspirants are considered for employment solely on the basis of their qualifications and competencies. Wipro's hiring policy is geared to ensure that Wipro hires employee's without regard to their race, colour, religion, national origin, citizenship, age, sex, marital status, ancestry, physical or mental disability, medical condition, veteran status or sexual orientation.

Exercise Case Study 1: Ethics and HRM, A Case of a junior marketing executive

Mr. Vijay Srivastava, a recent MBA passout of a reputed B School in Pune, was selected by ION Insurance Company Pvt Ltd. as a junior marketing executive in the Pune division. He was put on a rigorous training program of two months at the company HQ at Mumbai, followed by a probation period of one year. He was deputed into a sales area of Pune region where 15 more experienced marketing executives were competing hard to achieve their quarterly targets set for all of them. Vijay could achieve the target in the first two quarters. In the third quarter the market throughout the country was going through a recessive trend in terms of the products and services marketed by ION Insurance Co.Pvt Ltd. Till the last week of the third quarter, he still had a gap of few thousands in his sales target. On the second last day of the third quarter, while having snacks in a nearby restaurant, he met Mr. Sudhakar Wagle, a management consultant whole had been the former regional marketing head of ION Insurance Company Pvt. Ltd. Mr. Wagle said that he was aware of the potentials of Vijay and offered him Rs 60,000 as loan to Vijay to show on sales and cross his sales target. He said "Young man these are the ways. Go ahead." With this Vijay could have become eligible for Rs 6,000 bonus for achieving his target and a possible promotion on completion of his one year of service with ION. Vijay, who was under pressure of losing the job for not achieving the target, was in a dilemma and finally opted for the offer given by Mr. Wagle. In the very next month he resigned from ION Insurance and joined Mr. Wagle's company as a Business Development Officer and Trainee Consultant.

Questions for Discussion

1. What are ethical or unethical HR-issues depicted in the given case?
2. Was Vijay justified in choosing the career path offered by Mr. Wagle? Was it fair for Mr. Wagle to poach his ex-employer for a talented employee like Vijay?
3. What would have you done as the HR manager of ION Insurance Company Pvt. Ltd., if you were in this situation?

QUESTION BANK

1. What is corporate social responsibility? Why should organizations be concerned on CSR?
2. What are the emerging trends in CSR?
3. How can an organization benefit from CSR?
4. What are the HR challenges for achieving CSR?
5. What is the role of HR in evaluating the effectiveness of CSR?
6. What is the role of HR as a change agent in CSR?
7. Write a note on HR and business ethics.
8. Write short notes on: (a) Equal Employment Opportunity (b) Glass Ceiling Effect
9. What initiatives should HR departments take to manage problems related to sexual harassment issues and workplace violence?

Internet Exercises

- Download the article from the following hyperlink (www.indianet.nl/CSRIndia_CREMfinal.pdf) and discuss the same with your friends.
- Visit the following hyperlink (http://www.itcportal.com/sets/echoupal_frameset.htm) with respect to ITC and discuss your findings.

Experiential Exercises

- Plan and organize an activity from your class that would help the surroundings of your institution have an impact on the place where it is being located.
- "CSR is an investment with long term benefits in mind". Use this topic and invite your friends for presenting their views.

HR AUDIT, REVIEWS AND DUE DILIGENCE

Theme Caselet: Ramesh's Woes

Ramesh is a well known business man in Mysore. He owns a number of small engineering plants at Mysore. His businesses were doing quite well and Ramesh was happy as were his friends and well wishers. But fate had something else for him. The last six months was itself the evidence how things change quickly in business. Ramesh did never expect that his only closest relative his uncle would expire suddenly of a heart attack. And Ramesh being the only relative of his uncle would have to take care of his garments factory in Bangalore. It was a bolt from the blue. Ramesh had absolutely no clue what was the situation of his uncle's business, its legal obligations and other issues. Being the only survivor in his uncle's family Ramesh had to take charge of things. The first month was absolutely hastle free. But in the month of February, when Ramesh sent his financial advisor to check the financials at his uncle's factory lots of problems were identified.

- Most of the employees were working in the factory without any formal appointment orders.
- The contractual workers not paid regularly and the company had a lum sum Rs 3 lakhs due in this regard.
- There were some irregularities in the records concerned with PF statements of the permanent staffs.
- Irregularity was also found in the accounts of some senior supervisors who had taken personal loans from the company.

Next day when Ramesh personally talked with the factory manager, he came to know that in his uncle's time all issues related to manpower were decided either by his uncle or the factory manager himself. The company did not take any consultation of any HR expert in terms of taking care of the aforesaid issues. Ramesh thought "It's high time to change things".

Definitions

HR Due Diligence is the most detailed service and is aimed at valuing the contribution of the HR function to the success of the business in a purchasing, outsourcing or market testing environment.

HR Reviews involve an in-depth approach to meeting specific objectives and terms of reference. While this is a comprehensive review, the methodology is guided by the objectives and is usually aimed to increase the strategic alignment, effectiveness and efficiency of the HR function.

HR Audit is a 'snapshot' review that uses a systematic approach to identify any major areas of improvement in the HR function. This is often used as input into the HR planning process.

Components of HR Due Diligence

The HR due diligence practice encompasses the following components:

HR Compliance Audits: Audit of HR practices, compliance against legislation, internal policy and procedure as well as review of general HR practices.

Investment Due Diligence on Human Resources: Review of HR practices in association with valuations for investment, funding, listings and trade sales. Generally, due diligence refers to the care a reasonable person should take before entering in an agreement or transaction with another party. HR due diligence study involves the process of checking the accuracy of information related to an organization's HR contained in a company public statement, such as a prospectus, before recommending that company to others.

Business Assurance Assessment: Review of practices associated with business assurance and business continuity.

HR Policy and Procedure Review/Assessment: Review of HR policy and procedures in the context of legislation, industry best practice and 'fit for purpose' assessments.

Circumstances Influencing Due Diligence Review

The due diligence study involves a multifaceted process of evaluating the feasibility of licensing, investment opportunities, and acquiring technology of an organizations by evaluating the accuracy of information related to an organization's HR contained in a company public statement, such as a prospectus, before recommending that company to others. While the process is seemingly straight forward there are circumstances that may present confounding issues when a firm decides to conduct their own due diligence review, such circumstances may include:

Circumstances	Hallmarks
Resources	Internal company demands and projects may strain a firm's resources or personnel and limit the effectiveness and integrity of the due diligence process.
Expertise	Depending on the complexity of the due diligence review, companies may not have the internal expertise to fully evaluate and integrate its manufacturing, marketing activities and third-party relationships. The Due Diligence study would be able to facilitate the understanding of these areas and integrate these disciplines for proper HR valuation.
Confidentiality	When a company that is the subject of a HR due diligence review does not want their employees to be aware of a pending business relationship the depth of the review may be limited. Using a third party intervention can facilitate a meaningful in-depth review of the effectiveness of an organization's human resources.
Conflict of Interest	When two firms have common technologies or interests or knowledge the depth of the due diligence process may be limited by concerns of either firm acquiring proprietary information. The Due Diligence review offers an understanding of these concerns and would facilitate organizations to develop a plan so as to accommodate such circumstances.
Bias(es)	Employees of a firm may introduce their own biases into the due diligence review. While such biases are not usually deliberate they usually surface as a result of a conflict. These conflicts may result from a disagreement with senior management regarding the technology; a perception that the technology does not fit with the company's core technology; or personal conflict with the new technology.

Confidentiality Issues

Strategic restructuring negotiations - and especially merger negotiations - necessarily entail the potential partners sharing sensitive, confidential or proprietary information with one another. For example, the due diligence process asks each party to disclose lawsuits, debts, and other obligations; staff integration negotiations will usually involve sharing salary information for all employees; development staff may compare donor lists to determine the extent of overlap, and staff programmatic reviews may reveal unique service components or approaches.

Most commonly, human resource due diligence is an in-depth analysis of the management team, staff, structure, issues, and managerial capacity of a potential partner. In hostile takeovers in the corporate world, the acquiring firm may even go so far as to do a secret assessment of talent of a potential acquisition using investigative reporting tactics, business intelligence methods, and research into the leadership of a potential target.

The value of an HR due diligence is often underestimated while the people dimension is critical for the merger success. During a due diligence, our HR professionals provide strategic business support and advise on the following areas: Culture, Executive compensation and "golden parachute" contracts, Collective bargaining agreements and potential change of ownership liabilities, Defined benefit and defined contribution pension plans, Postretirement benefits, Retention and severance plans, Health and welfare insurance structure and reserves , HR functional structure and service delivery, HRIS, Employment litigation, etc.

During merger negotiations and integration, attention and energy must be devoted to the real people issues. Human due diligence will help organizations to focus attention on what will become the core of an integration plan.

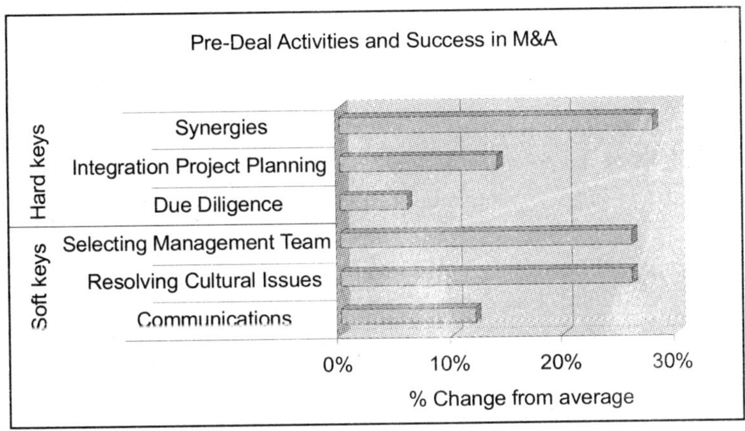

Fig. 6.11: Pre-deal activities and success in M&A

Objectives of HR Due Diligence

The primary objectives of HR due diligence are as follows:

- Identify any potential deal breakers
- Uncover any significant liabilities which can be brought to the negotiating table
- Assess the potential costs and risks (such as huge cultural differences) and strategy required to contain them
- Identify and prioritize HR issues that need to be dealt during the integration
- Identify and prioritize HR issues that need to be dealt during the post-integration.

Elements that are reviewed in human due diligence for non-profits can include:

Employment Relations Issues and Practices: Does the potential partner have solid HR policies, procedures, and employment relationship practices?

Motivation of workforce: Is the workforce of the partner generally satisfied, engaged and connected to each other and the mission of the agency?

Appropriate rewards systems: Are the rewards system in the potential partner equitable, internally and externally? Are rewards tied to performance? Are people accountable for the work that they do?

Respect: Do management and staff respect each other? Is there respect for the board by the staff, and for the staff by the board? Are the clients spoken of and treated with respect?

Managerial competence: How competent is the management team of the potential partner? Should some, or all, of the existing team serve on the management team of the new organization?

Internal training and development functions: What are the existing internal training and staff development resources and functions within each partner? How has this been dealt with, or not dealt with? What will be the training needs in the new organization, both immediately post-merger and over the long-run?

Feedback and learning mechanisms: This is beyond performance appraisal. What mechanisms exist for staff to get feedback on their performance and on the effectiveness of programs and resources? Is learning a core value within the organization?

Alignment internally: Is the staff internally aligned and connected to each other? How much resistance will be encountered during integration?

Connection to a community: What is the level of connection to the local community in terms of reputation? What is said about the partner? What is the reputation?

Connection to mission: Do the individuals in the organization, staff, management, and board feel connected to the mission?

Skill sets: What skills, educational backgrounds, competencies are brought by staff? How replaceable or irreplaceable are the skills of the potential partner?

Organizational capacity: Is the organization geared for growth? Do they have the resources, capacity and flexibility to survive a major organizational transition?

Succession planning: The existence of a succession plan is a good indicator of how well the organization thinks about the future. Has there been any thinking about succession planning on the senior staff or board level?

Key Areas to be Covered in HR Due Diligence

Elements of HR due diligence tend to be determined by the level of HR functioning within the merging entities. If the HR systems are primarily transactional in nature, then the process will focus on risk management issues, recruitment systems, record keeping, record retention, workplace safety, aligning compensation systems, benefits integration, and any potential outstanding employee relationship claims.

On a higher, more strategic level, HR due diligence can, and should, deal with issues related to corporate culture, talent retention, training and development integration, career management, employee communication strategies, compensation issues in transition, stay pay, promotional opportunities, workforce composition, past change management initiatives, and finally the interface of technology and people issues.

Strategic Importance of HR Due Diligence

Regulatory Strategy: From a regulatory perspective the HR due diligence review provides all of the traditional regulatory services to an organization like managing the statutory compliance regulations, permits and so on. While interacting with regulatory authorities and the compilation of documents for submission to such authorities (like pollution control board) is the primary responsibility of this study. This ultimately facilitates the HR department to work effectively with regulatory bodies and thereby help them to develop a comprehensive organizational regulatory strategy.

Mergers and Acquisitions: With respect to mergers and acquisitions, the HR due diligence study provides assistance to organizations in identifying information related to an organization's human capital and their performance and also facilitates the management to take vital decisions related to statutory compliance checking and management.

Contribution to OD: Depending on where a firm is in the development and growth continuum, the area of OD is one of the major stumbling blocks for small and medium size enterprises. A proper due diligence study particularly with respect to their HR due diligence enables them to integrate the people related capabilities with the basic technology associated with the product and at the same time effectively understand and manage the regulatory approval pathway (That is integrating people, logistics and regulatory requirements), which is critical for their organizational development and growth.

Reassurance activities and programs: HR due diligence reviews also facilitates the management to organize "Reassurance Activities" in the form of a special package of programs so as to assist investors be constantly informed with the developments in the organization. These include how the human resources of the company have established check and control systems with respect to their performance evaluation and development and so on. Further this could also help the Board of Directors of the organization to be more accountable especially when the firm has failed to meet objectives.

How HR/OD Consultants can help in HR Due Diligence?

Depending on access to relevant senior management and key HR information (such as culture or climate surveys) HR/OD Consultants can address important questions such as:

- Retention issues—what is the likelihood that key senior management are at risk of leaving the organization? Does the organization have retention issues in relation to staff critical to business operation? What is the typical cost of hiring? Benchmark turnover statistics.
- HR management—do HR policies and procedures generally meet standard legal compliance and provide a sound framework for managing staff?
- Culture and values—How adaptable and resilient is this organization? Are its staff likely to 'hit the ground running' post-deal? Is the culture likely to have a positive or detrimental impact on expected value/benefit realization of the acquisition? If merging two organizational cultures, different are they and what are the likely implications?
- Industrial relations environment—What is the current level of unionization and to what extent is this likely to pose any risks post-deal?

Appendix: Human Resource and Cultural Due Diligence (and HR Audit) Checklist

Sl. No.	Table of Contents	Put a tick (√) mark
1.	**Company Organization and Management:**	
	(a) **Organization Structure:**	
	(i) Mission Statement	
	(ii) Functional Reporting relationships	
	(iii) Position responsibilities	
	(iv) Administrative reporting relationships	
	(v) Interface with union representatives, government agencies, etc.	
	(vi) Regional/plant personnel functions (not reporting to corporate)	
	(b) **Scope of department responsibilities and authority:**	
	(i) Key sub functions	
	(ii) Ad hoc tasks and responsibilities	
	(iii) Policy-making capabilities	
	(iv) Bargaining unit negotiations	

Contd...

	(c) **Profiles of key management:**	
	(i) Personal profiles (names, positions, education, etc.)	
	(ii) Skills and talents	
	(iii) Attitudes toward achievement	
	(iv) Historical data on experience and background	
	(v) Areas of responsibility	
	(vi) Intention to continue after merger/acquisition	
	(vii) Compensation history (cash, equity and deferred arrangements)	
	(viii) Contractual arrangements	
	(ix) Personal, non-contractual arrangements	
	(d) **Employee payroll records**	
	(e) **Payroll history**	
	(f) **Physical office arrangements/sufficient space**	
	(g) **Human resource operating budget:**	
	(i) Allocations	
	(ii) Performance to plan	
	(iii) Historical	
	(iv) Planning process	
2.	**Considerations**	
	Internal and external reputation of department management	
	(b) Type and strength of management control:	
	(i) Centralization	
	(ii) Formality	
	(iii) Participative decision-making	
	(iv) Autonomy	
	(c) Leadership qualities	
	(d) Necessity for additional management following acquisition	
	(e) Competency and adequacy of current management	
	(f) Adequacy of department staff members	
	(g) Lines of succession	
	(h) Morale, work climate and motivation levels	
	(i) Level of work commitment	
	(j) Team orientation	
	(k) Compatibility of management styles between companies	
	(l) Attitude of company management toward risk	
	(m) Authority structure and degrees of responsibility at each hierarchical level	
	(n) Inter and intra-departmental conflict	
	(o) Formal vs. informal organizational structure	
3.	**Data Sources**	
	(a) Organization charts	

Contd...

	(b) Position descriptions (c) Compensation records (d) Personnel files (e) Management contracts (f) Personnel policies and procedures manual (g) Operations (policy) manuals (h) Operations budget (i) Human Resource information systems (i) Management reports (turnover, FTE, merit increases, absence, etc.)	
	General Human Resource Programs	
1.	**Evaluation Factors** (a) Existence of employee development (training) programs: (i) 1st and 2nd line supervisors (ii) Managers (iii) Degree of company commitment (iv) All employees (v) Program documentation (b) EEO/Affirmative action program (c) Management succession program (d) Employee education programs (i) Annual costs (ii) Reimbursement scope (iii) Level of employee participation (iv) Employee scholarships (v) Eligibility (e) Safety programs (See Section 10) (f) Communication programs: (i) Computer networks (ii) "Hot Line" telephone (iii) House organs/newspapers/employee publicity (iv) Quality circles and the like (v) Employee orientation practices (vi) Attitude surveys (g) Community relations/public relations programs/scholarship funds (h) Policies and procedures (i) Compensation practices (See Section 5) (j) Benefit programs (See Sections 6, 7, 8) (k) Relocation allowances (l) Computerized data sources and information (m) Use of outside consultants (n) Employee Assistance (EAP) and Grievance Programs	

Contd...

2.	**Employee services** (i) Physical fitness programs (ii) Recreation (iii) Social programs (iv) Parking (v) Credit union Employee food services: (i) In-house facilities (cafeteria, eating areas, etc.) (ii) Neighbourhood restaurants	
3.	**Considerations** (a) Quality and professionalism of employee programs (b) Fairness of application and eligibility (c) Degree o mechanization and /or computerization (d) Comprehensiveness of company policies (e) Staffing vs. use of outside services	

HR AUDIT

Introduction

Like financial audits, HR audits are designed to assess management activities, identify policy and practice weaknesses, perform due diligence, benchmark best practices, and to quantify and evaluate outcomes. The Human Resources (HR) Audit is a process of examining policies, procedures, documentation, systems and practices with respect to an organization's HR functions. The purpose of the audit is to reveal the strengths and weaknesses in the organization's human resources system, and any issues needing resolution. The audit works best when the focus is on analyzing and improving the HR function in the organization. The HR audit itself is a diagnostic tool, not a prescriptive instrument. It is most useful when an organization is ready to act on the findings, and to evolve its HR function to a level where its full potential to support the organization's mission and objectives can be realized.

What is an HR Audit?

An HR audit is a means by which an organization can measure where it currently stands and determine what it has to accomplish to improve its human resources function. It involves systematically reviewing all aspects of human resources, usually in a checklist fashion, ensuring that government regulations and company policies are being adhered to. HR auditing activities include:

1. **Quantifying and measuring HR functions and outcomes:** A critical element HR audits is the determination of current and potential outcomes of the organization with respect to its HR function.
2. **Comparing activities and results to standards and goals:** Like financial audits, HR audits compare activities and results to external and internal standards and to expected and budgeted goals.
3. **Reviewing structural, organizational, and cultural issues:** The effectiveness of various employment policies, practices and procedures is determined by a number of external and internal factors. HR audits help to identify and assess these factors.
4. **Assessing the employment brand:** Like product branding, employment branding influences customers' (employees') desire and willingness to buy the product (becoming and staying an employee). HR audits help to assess the organization's employment brand.

5. **Inspecting employment posters, notices, and facilities:** HR auditing activities inspect and review employment practices with respect to compliance with various state and local employment laws.
6. **Inspecting employee personnel files:** HR auditing activities inspect a random selection of personnel files and records.
7. **Assessing HR management and employment practices:** Using enhanced softwares and IT packages, (like the latest version of ELLA®) HR audits can review and assess various HR management and employment practices areas, including those of:
   - Recruitment, selection and hiring
   - Application forms
   - Reference checking and responding
   - Immigration related issues
   - Employee handbooks and procedural manuals
   - Positive employee relations
   - Diversity, inclusion and workplace discrimination
   - Affirmative Action-Pay Equity
   - Sexual harassment
   - Drug-free workplace
   - Job performance management
   - Retention issues
   - Conflict resolution
   - Discipline, terminations and downsizing
   - Leaves of absence
   - Wage and hour issues
   - Unemployment insurance
   - Workplace safety
   - Ethics and governance
   - Strategic HR decisions, procedures and processes

HR audit serves as an examination on a sample basis of practices and systems for identifying problems and ensuring that sound accounting principles are followed. Similarly, an HR audit serves as a means through which an organization can measure the health of its human resource function.

The Audit Process

The HR audit process is conducted in different phases. These phases are as follows:

Pre-audit information: This phase involves the acquiring and review of relevant HR manuals, handbooks, forms, reports and other information. A pre-audit information request is forwarded to the client who compiles the necessary information for review by auditors.

Pre-audit self-assessment: The self-administered yes/no questionnaire asks a number of questions about current HR policies and practices. The completion of this self-administered questionnaire allows auditors to identify key areas for focus during the HR audit.

On-site review: This phase involves an on-site visit at the client's facility interviewing staff regarding HR policies and practices. A very in-depth HR audit checklist is completed in this regard.

Records review: During the on-site visit, a separate review is conducted of HR records and postings. Employee personnel files are randomly examined as well as compensation, employee claims, disciplinary actions; grievances and other relevant HR related information are checked.

Audit report: The information gathered is used to develop an HR audit report. The audit report categorizes action needs into three separate areas. The areas that are urgent and important (UI), not urgent needs but important (NUI), not urgent but not important needs (NNI), and important opportunities needs (IO). As a result of this scheme of classification, managements can prioritize their steps.

The Critical Areas

The comprehensive HR audit covers all areas of HR management like recruitment practices, training and development, compensation and benefits, employee and union relations, health, safety and security, miscellaneous HR policies and practices-welfare, strategic HR issues, manpower planning/budgeting. Besides classifying needs in each of the above areas, the HR audit also cites relevant laws, cases and research to support the recommendations.

Preparation for an Audit

Auditor engagement: If any external firm/consultant is carrying out the audit, it is preferable to set terms in writing defining and agreeing on scope. If the firm uses internal resource it is better to appoint them formally with clarity on scope and select persons who are unbiased or those who are not high on the oragnization's hierarchy. Documents, manuals, handbooks, forms and reports auditor must have access to relevant information contained in employee files and other confidential documents of the organization. Auditors must be given unrestricted access to records, once they sign agreement for confidentiality.

Data gathering: Completion of a self-assessment questionnaire significantly expedites the audit process and allows for better audit planning.

On-site access: The on-site portion of the audit is the most critical.

Using Audit Findings

Organizations generally have three options for dealing with audit results.

- Use the HR audit as a blueprint or action plan for addressing HR needs.
- Address as many needs as possible using the organization's internal expertise and resources.
- Contract out those need areas where internal expertise and resources are not available or do not fit in the core competencies of the organization.

Characteristics of a HR Audit

An HR audit is much like an annual health check. It can perform the same function for the organization. An audit is a means by which an organization can measure where it currently stands and determine what it has to accomplish to improve its HR functions. It involves systematically reviewing all aspects of human resources, usually in a checklist fashion, ensuring that the government regulations and company policies are being adhered to. The necessary traits of an HR audit are as follows:

- The HR audit needs to be undertaken as a proactive, creative exercise with open participation by members of the function plus a representative sample of an organization's employees.
- The HR audit is an essential step towards improving departmental credibility and overall quality goals. It is therefore, a check on the compliance with legislative and company procedures.
- The HR audit usually covers three parameters, namely, the HR policies and practices, the HR professionals and the HR department.
- The HR audit should cover three areas:
  - Identifying current HR practices and procedures
  - Analyzing the cost and effectiveness if time and resource allocation with respect to HR activities
  - Reviewing client's satisfaction and expectations.

Importance of HR Audit

- To ensure the effective utilization of an organization's human resources.
- To review statutory compliances with a myriad of administrative regulations.
- To instill a sense of confidence in management and the human resources function that it is well managed and prepared to meet potential challenges.
- To maintain or enhance the organization's and the department's reputation in the community.
- To perform a "due diligence" review for shareholders or potential investors/owners.

What does HR Audit Entail?

An HR audit principally aims to evaluate the effectiveness of the following aspects of the HR functions in an organization, namely:

- Evaluation of legal and statutory compliances
- Compensation/salary administration
- Employment/recruiting
- Orientation
- Terminations
- Training and development
- Employee relations
- Communications
- Files/record maintenance/technology
- Policies and procedures (including employee handbook)
- Communications

In this regard it can be mentioned that, an HR audit should have three aspects, namely:

Aspects of HR Audit	Hallmarks
Systems audit	Reviews the various paper flow, the procedures and controls with respect to the HR function in the organization. It includes all HR-related forms, records and files, whether held manually or in the Information systems
Operations audit	Reviews how efficiently these HR systems are applied in practice.
Climate audit	Reviews what employees perceive regarding the HR functions

The HR audit also serves to educate HR professionals on the latest trends and best practices used by their peers and industry counterparts. The HR audit can give those responsible for employee relations some reassurance that legal risks have been managed and minimized, thus freeing them to focus on more creative aspects of their jobs that can add value to the employer's bottom line.

How to Conduct HR Audits?

Consensus building stage: Most Human Resources professionals are well aware of the issues that create the greatest legal risks. Hiring, firing, benefits, wage and hour compliance, employee handbooks and illegal discrimination are the most common areas where lawsuits arise. In order to assess the degree of exposure that a company has, the management of an organization must first be familiar with the legal requirements in each of these areas. Other legal obligations arise from state and local laws as well. The Human Resources professional must also have at least a basic familiarity with the employer's obligations under those laws.

Acquiring legal knowledge: A HR professional can conduct an HR audit even if he/she does not have the necessary legal knowledge himself/herself. There are commercial HR audit tools available that can guide a HR professional through a self-audit. In addition, there are service providers (Consultants) who can also perform an audit for a fee.

Implementing and conducting the audit: After assuming a knowledge of the substantive law, the next step in conducting an audit is to gather information on the operating environment and procedures with respect to the functioning of various HR practices and functions in the organization. In this regard, HR professionals are guided in this process by a checklist (which might be in print, on software, or web-based).

Analyzing the audit information: The next step involves analyzing the HR-related information. After the information in the checklist is processed, the next step involves analysis of the organization's employment practices and policies so as to determine whether the company is in compliance with the applicable laws. The net result of the HR audit should be some sort of a **scorecard, or a list of action items** that would need attention on the strategic perspective.

Taking actions/interventions: The audit report should provide both a snapshot of the company's strengths and also a roadmap for how to correct its weaknesses. If actions or interventions are being taken so as to correct the deficiencies, the audit would have its effectiveness.

HR ACCOUNTING

Theme Reading: Valuing Human Resources at Infosys

In the financial year 1995–96, Infosys Technologies (Infosys) became the first software company to value its human resources in India. The company used the Lev and Schwartz Model and valued its human resources assets at Rs 1.86 billion. Infosys had always given utmost importance to the role of employees in contributing to the company's success. Analysts felt that **human resources accounting (HRA)** was a step further in Infosys' focusing on its employees. Narayana Murthy (Murthy), the then chairman and managing director of Infosys, said: "Comparing this figure over the years will tell us whether the value of our human resources is appreciating or not.

For a knowledge intensive company like ours, that is vital information. The concept of HRA was not new in India. HRA was pioneered by public sector companies like Bharat Heavy Electronics Ltd. (BHEL) and Steel Authority of India Ltd. (SAIL) way back in the 1970s.

However, the concept did not gain much popularity and acceptance during that time. It was only in the mid-1990s, after Infosys started valuing its employees, that the concept gained popularity in India. By 2002, HR accounting had been introduced by leading software companies like Satyam Computers and DSQ Software, as well as leading manufacturing firms like Reliance Industries.

HRA enabled companies to understand whether the skill sets of their human capital was appreciating or not. R. Krishnaswamy, an actuarial accountant, said, "The value can be used internally by an organization to make comparisons from unit to unit, from year to year, as well as within its industry".

HRA in Practice at Infosys

Infosys' HRA model was based on the present value of the employees' future earnings with the following assumptions:

- An employee's salary package included all benefits, whether direct or otherwise, earned both in India and in a foreign nation.
- The additional earnings on the basis of age and group were also taken into account.

To calculate the value of its human assets in 1995–96, all the 1,172 employees of Infosys were divided into five groups, based on their average age. Each group's average compensation was calculated. Infosys also calculated the compensation of each employee at retirement by using an average rate of increment.

HRA - The Benefits and Hurdles in Infosys

The benefits of adopting HRA were manifold. It helped an organization to take managerial decisions based on the availability and the necessity of human resources. When the human resources were quantified, it gave the investors and other clients true insights into the organization and its future potential. Proper valuation of human resources helped organizations to eliminate the negative effects of redundant labour.

This, in turn, helped them to channelize the available skills, talents, knowledge and experience of their employees more efficiently. By adopting and implementing HRA in an organization, the following important information could be obtained:

- Cost per employee
- Human capital investment ratio
- The amount of wealth created by each employee
- The profit created by each employee
- The ratio of salary paid to the total revenue generated
- Average salary of each employee
- Employee absenteeism rates
- Employee turnover rate and retention rate

Aspects of HR Accounting

Human assets accounting or human resource accounting (HRA) stands for the process involving the measurement and reporting of the cost and value of people as organizational resources.

"Human Resource Accounting (HRA) is basically an information system that tells management what changes are occurring over time to the human resources of the business. HRA also involves accounting for investment in people and their replacement costs, and also the economic value of people in an organization," says P K Gupta, the director of strategic development-intercontinental operations, of Legato Systems India. The current accounting system is not able to provide the actual value of employee capabilities and knowledge. This indirectly affects future investments of a company, as each year the cost on human resource development and recruitment increases. Experts point out that the information generated by HRA systems can be put to use for taking a variety of managerial decisions like recruitment planning, turnover analysis, personnel advancement analysis and capital budgeting, which can help companies save a lot of trouble in the future. The various costs incurred in HRA are as follows:

Table 6.3: Acquisition Costs

Costs	*Definition*
Recruiting	Originates with the search for human resources. Included in this is advertising, publicity, mailing etc. Costs corresponding to rejected candidates are applied to the contracted candidates
Selection	Corresponds to the selected personnel.
Contracting	Begins once the selected personnel is inducted and placed
Placing	Includes a variety of administrative costs, produced by the necessity of suiting the new employee to his/her job.

Table 6.4: Learning Costs

Costs	*Definition*
Training	This is derived from complimentary training for adjusting the candidate with the job. Greatest cost is incurred when the employee is unproductive.
Orientation	This is hardly estimable and refers to familiarizing the new employee with the HR policy, products and services of the organization, and the organization in general.
Promotion	Originates every time an employee changes his/her job whether in the same category or the other. This normally is a relevant part of the total cost.
Improvement	Maintains and improves the real potential capacity of each employee. It forms an important component of the historical costs.

Exit Costs

***Concept*:** Exit costs can be classified into the three categories of lost efficiency prior to separation, job vacancy cost during the new search and termination pay.

***Treatment*:** It is difficult to put a value on lost efficiency prior to separation. Productivity per employee seems to be the most adequate measure. However, this measure (generally calculated by means of a ratio) is not problem-free. If this loss is expressed according to the productivity ratio, the same problems arise that were discussed in previous points (except for the estimated wasted return percentage that, in this case, becomes unnecessary). Regarding termination pay, accounting normally refers to this as indemnities.

QUESTION BANK

1. What is HR due diligence? What is its importance?
2. What are the components of HR due diligence? What are the circumstances that might influence a HR diligence review?
3. "Due diligence reviews are highly confidential and the confidentiality of the same should be strictly managed". Comment on the statement.
4. What are the objectives of HR due diligence? What are their strategic implications for an organization?
5. What could be the role of HR/OD consultants in due diligence studies?
6. Define HR audit. What are its components?
7. Describe the HR audit process. How would you prepare for a HR audit?
8. What are the characteristic features of a HR audit process?
9. State the importance and benefits of HR audit.
10. How should managers conduct HR audits?
11. What are the various factors influencing a HR audit process?
12. What is HR accounting? How is it different from HR audit?
13. Describe the cost elements of human resources and mention how are they incorporated for human resource accounting.
14. Write a note on training and selection cost analysis.

Internet Exercises

- Visit the Pricewaterhouse Coopers website (http://www.pwc.com/Extweb/service.nsf/docid/92D80C64553BDF0FCA257209000201F6) and collect information regarding their expertises on conducting HR due diligence for their clients.
- Study the following hyperlink (http://www.lapiana.org/sr/tips/diligence/key_areas.html) and collect relevant information on HR due diligence and discuss the same with your friends.

Experiential Exercises

- "HR audit is an essential element to ensure the success of a HR plan" organize a discussion session in your class on the given topic.

HUMAN RESOURCE OUTSOURCING

Industry Quote

"Outsourcing isn't about moving jobs. It's about the flexibility to put resources in the right places at the right time."....... Lucent Vice president, Dave Ayers, quoted in Business Week

(Courtesy: Indian Management, April 2005, Vol. 44, No. 4, p. 96)

HRO what is it?

Human Resource Outsourcing (HRO) has been a topic of debate and immense interests in high profile organizations over the years. HRO has been utilized as a tool for multiple occasions like those of merger, acquisition, divestiture, turnaround and growth.

Definition

Human Resource Outsourcing HRO is a momentous strategic HR initiative. It helps organization to focus on internal resources towards doing what they do best and simultaneously helps to control the bottom lines.

Why Human Resource Outsourcing?

HR is an essential partner in developing and executing organizational strategy as is evident HR is something that is really critical to an organizations functioning. Human Resources (HR) responsibilities includes all the related functions that work towards employee well-being in the organization including payroll, benefits, hiring, firing and keeping up to date with state and federal tax laws. The recent competitive challenges of the global marketplace are creating demand for expert human resource outsourcing HRO providers in order to manage non-value adding administrative business function of their businesses thereby facilitating the businesses can concentrate on their core competencies.

How Does Human Resources (HR) Outsourcing Helps?

Human resources outsourcing helps in boosting organizational performance with many strategic benefits like eliminating the redundant non-core HR functions, increasing cost competitiveness effectiveness and helps in maintaining strategic HR focus.

Thus, HR Outsourcing Can

- Help in structural reduction of the Human Resource Management (HRM) cost base, by identifying the non-value adding activities and eliminate the hidden HR operations costs.

- Help in identifying the inefficient Human Resources (HR) Administration processes and HR practices.
- Helps organization to focus on human resource performance.
- Help organizations to serve their employees better.

Human Resource Outsourcing Services

The role of human resource outsourcing services in an organization differs with the extent of outsourced functions. Some services go with the "all-or-nothing" approach, requiring that they handle all your HR functions or none at all. Others offer their services "a la carte," meaning one can pick and choose from the HR outsourcing services they offer.

HR Outsourcing Services and its Operational Models

Professional Employer Organization PEO

A Professional Employer Organization (PEO) assumes full legal responsibility of a company's Human Resources. The **PEO** and business owner work as associates, where **PEO** handles the human resource aspects and the owner handles core business.

Business Process Outsourcing BPO

Business Process Outsourcing refers to outsourcing in all fields for overall process improvements, not just outsourcing human resource functions. HR based BPO function ensures that organization is compatible with latest HR automation and technologies.

ASP

Application Service Providers (ASPs) offers HRIS support via latest HR software and web based HR solutions.

E-HR Services

E-HR services, outsourcing electronic HR services is a means to procure web aware online utilities for the organizational HR process improvement. The E-HR service providers offer value added web based applications to cater to the need of the employers.

HR Outsourcing Services Features

- **Payroll administration:** Produce checks, handle taxes and deal with sick time and vacation time.
- **Employee benefit administration:** Health, medical, life insurance plans, cafeteria plans, etc.
- **HR management:** Recruiting, hiring and firing. Also background interviews, exit interviews and wage reviews.
- **Risk management:** Workers' compensation, dispute resolution, safety inspection, office policies and handbooks.

THEME READING: TCS TO FOCUS ON HR OPERATIONS SOLUTIONS

IT services major, TCS, is scaling up its platform-based BPOs and one of its prime focus is human resources operation (HRO) solutions. "HRO solutions are gaining a lot of traction and we are in talks with a few clients. We have received letters of intent from these clients and are currently negotiating with them," said TCS CEO and executive director N Chandrasekaran.

(*Courtesy: July 18, 2008, The Economic Times*)

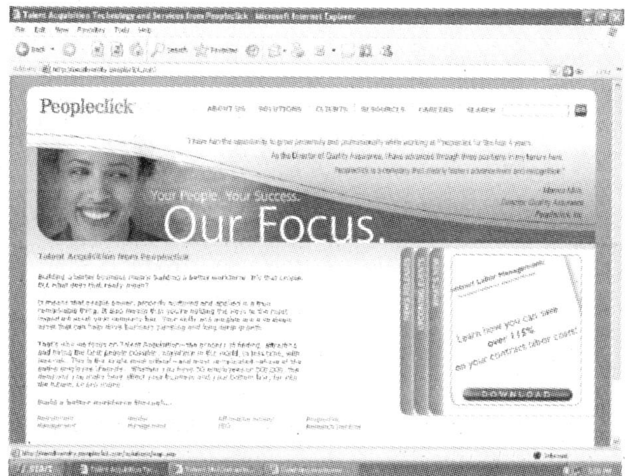

Fig. 6.12: An organization providing HRO services

Online HR Outsourcing Services

Online services tend to be limited in their offerings, but provide added options like Web access, which allows companies to view information (like benefits packages) and even make changes to such information online. Most HR Outsourcing companies will be able to provide employer and employees access to view their benefits plans, enroll in benefits, read policies and make changes to current data.

Benefits of Outsourcing HR Services

Human Resource Outsourcing (HRO) helps an organization to gain cost and time efficiencies and provides cutting edge over their human resource strategies and improve services to their employees. There is a comprehensive list of human resource outsourcing benefits. The benefits related to outsourcing human resource services include time and cost savings, control over hassle factors and perceived higher level of employer services.

Low Cost of Service

One of the most crucial factors that can't be ignored while making outsourcing HR decision is cost - both operating cost and cost avoidance. Any outsourcing HR company has to provide some level of savings. This cost is reflected in operating cost and cost avoidance, such as having to put in new technology and keeping it current.

Expected Higher Level of Service

There's a perceived higher level of service associated with HR outsourcing Companies. They specialize in providing efficient and cost effective services. With their highly skilled team of consultants; employers can expect a better career path for employees, and the ability to better retain them for a specified job.

Time Saving

Senior HR people are more interested in the business of their company than the business of human resource that is they are more concerned with well being as well as growth of the business in the long run. They would like to become more strategic, and the only way they can have the time to do so is to get rid of the time that's committed to some of the administrative functions by outsourcing them.

Controlling the Hassle Factors

There are loads of "hassle factors" like keeping track of all people, managing technology budgets, managing service level agreements etc. all these core competencies of business are really required, but these factors can easily be taken care by outsourcing HR company, to give employers ease from managing such complex functionalities.

Factors Involved in Using HRO for Rapid Organizational Transformation and Change

Resistance to change: As an organization in order to implement HRO it is strategically important to quickly overcome resistance from the organization itself in terms of its own policies and systems, internal environment and the mindset of the people. Speedy response enables executive management to run, not walk, in pursuit of corporate opportunities.

Organizational transformation: Secondly, transitioning rapidly from due diligence to acquisition to the overall organizational integration is critical. HR outsourcers are particularly good at this transition, since most of them only make money once they're up and running. And their domain-specific (e.g., HR) due-diligence teams are quite expert and can be a big help to an organization's internal team.

Business automation: Thirdly, the discipline of automated business processes (like institutionalizing a human resource management system), which meet current demand and adaptability to new HR operations, allows predictability in cost, quality and results through variable pricing and effective HR management markedly influences organizational growth and development.

Theme Reading: Crisis in Offshoring; Emerging Trends

Black book of Outsourcing's 2008 State of the Industry report has indicated that India's offshoring success story will need greater onshoring support to sustain it. Three Indian firms, Wipro (6), Satyam (7) and Genpact (8), figured in the top 10. TCS moved up to the rank 15 this year while HCL tumbled from 13 last year to 21. Conducted by the US-based consultancy firm Brown-wilson group, the report said that there is an indicative of the growing re-appreciation for the US-centric IT and ITES firms. HP emerged as the number one in the rankings, followed by Perot, CSC, Unisys and EDS. The report further indicates the rise of "reverse outsourcing", the phenomenon of Indian companies opening offices in USA and hiring logically. The reverse outsourcing development is too new for Indian companies and particularly how our industry giants will cope the new challenge would be worth watching.

(Courtesy: Deepshikha, M.,: "Offshoring slips on onshoring support lags", The Economic Times, 24th June, 2008, p. 5)

HRO Issues in Acquisitions

Post-merger integration challenges in any organization can be severe. Benefit plans of all types may need to be reviewed and revised. Employment policy standardization may involve evaluation of individual employment situations so as to avoid surprises and litigation. A company that has outsourced HR management functions can generally focus its attention on the key values of an HR department: alignment of HR strategies with corporate goals, design of plans for incentive compensation, retention, motivation, training, knowledge management and career path management. By having automated functions outsourced, the acquiring company can focus on speed and quality of workforce integration.

HRO Issues in Divestitures

Academicians, union leaders and management scholars have sometimes opined HRO contracts as a crutch to prepare for a divestiture of a distressed or "non-core/non-strategic" operation. In these situations, HRO avoids new investment in expensive HR software, hardware, real estate, supervisors, and costs of designing and running low-value, high-cost repetitive solutions. Often, Finance, HR, and IT departments jointly assess needs and capabilities and then outsource to avoid further cash drain. Quite naturally, HRO providers focus on customers in good financial condition. But customers should not hesitate to disclose the nature, scope and business reasons behind an outsourcing. Indeed, IT outsourcing providers deliver many IT- enabled services "on demand" or as a variable "utility." Like IT, HR administration can be a variable-cost "utility," providing financially-challenged customers with relief. In negotiating HRO deals, though, many organizations might find that certain vendors are better at this variable "utility" function than those of others. The scope of such deals needs to be tailored to achieve a balance between a customer's (an organization) volume commitments and a vendor's (Outsourced organization/consultant) need for volume-price adjustments.

HRO Issues in Turnarounds

Kodak used to be in consumer products, but price competition forced it to make radical shifts into industrial and medical markets. As a result, Kodak is now a leader in using outsourcing to renew its focus on the customer. Turnaround companies have been found to be in big trouble because they have continued to own their administrative processes, which piles on overwhelming regulatory compliance pressure and expense. By outsourcing HR administration, these corporations can focus on competing. For turnarounds, HRO is critical for accelerating organizational recovery. Management experts and industry captains therefore frequently advise using outsourcing as an essential tool for merger, acquisition, divestiture or turnaround situations.

QUESTION BANK

1. Define HRO. Why outsourcing of HR services has become important for organizations? Describe the salient features of HRO services.
2. How can HRO provide competitive edge to organizations?
3. What are the various HR outsourcing services and their various operational models available for client organizations?
4. What are the advantages and disadvantages of HRO? How can HRO contribute to employee retention?

Internet Exercises

- Study the following websites and share your findings on HRO with your friends:
  - http://www.getpeoplesmart.com/
  - http://www.xansa.com/services/hroutsourcing/
- Read the materials from the following hyperlinks and share your findings with your team: (http://www.financialexpress.com/news/Successful-HR-outsourcing-means-quality-service/171314/) and (www.financialexpress.com/news/**HR-outsourcing**-is-next-big-opportunity-experts/120325/)

Experiential Exercises

- "Outsourcing of HR activities would it be beneficial for talent management". Discuss the topic among your friends in the class.

ROLE OF HR IN LEARNING ORGANIZATIONS

Theme Reading: Sharing Knowledge – the Microsoft and GE Approaches

The Microsoft Approach

Microsoft as an organization has always emphasized that in today's highly competitive and dynamic business environment high individual knowledge is not enough for the survival and sustenance of any organization. An organization like Microsoft strongly believes that knowledge organizations like itself also requires a high corporate IQ profile to ensure long term sustenance. This IQ profile consists of business intelligence, market knowledge, and expertise of the company in terms of core competencies that are unique of its own. In order to achieve these Microsoft had always believed on the importance of constantly sharing information widely at all levels of the organization and enabling its employees "to build on each other's ideas". According to Bill Gates, organizations even need to go beyond this dimension for the creation of newer knowledge. This is why he commented "We read, ask questions, explore, go to lectures, compare notes and findings... consult experts, daydream, brainstorm, formulate and test hypotheses, build models and simulations, communicate what we're learning, and practice new skills".

The GE Approach

GE over the years had believed in the philosophy of inculcating a constant learning perspective in their organization. This learning could be achieved from past experience or from another GE business or even from a business rival.

At General Electric (GE) the outcome of this learning philosophy has reaped rich dividends for the organization. It has firstly ensured that the organization makes the most utilization of diversity in its business perspectives as well as that in its people. This had helped GE adopt a learning organization culture in any initiatives it had ventured over the years. According to Jack Welch, "What sets GE apart is a culture that uses diversity as a limitless source of learning opportunities, a storehouse of ideas whose breadth and richness is unmatched in world business. At the heart of this culture is an understanding that an organization's ability to learn, and translate that learning into action rapidly, is the ultimate competitive business advantage".

Learnings from GE and Microsoft

For instilling a learning culture organizations like those of GE and Microsoft have strongly emphasized on considering their human resources as their #1 assets and the source of developing new knowledge. Knowledge for GE or Microsoft has thereby become the corner stone for organizational development and emerged as the most productive wealth when dynamically shared by all organizational members. A learning organization according to knowledge workers and leaders of these organizations is "an organization that is continually expanding its capacity to create its mark for the future". It is continuously learning new ways of doing things and also (necessarily) involved in a continuous process of forgetting old ways of doing things. Organizations like GE, Motorola and Microsoft had emphasized on creating a learning environment in their organizations where people can draw upon resources to make sense out of things and construct meaningful solutions to problems. Thus it has become strategically important for today's organizations to constantly emphasize the importance of meaningful, authentic activities that would help their most valuable assets engage themselves into learning activities, constructing understandings and develop skills relevant to solve business problems on an ongoing basis.

Introduction to Learning Organizations

In organizational development (OD), **learning** is a characteristic of an *adaptive* organization, i.e., an organization that is able to sense changes in signals from its environment (both internal and external) and adapt accordingly. OD specialists endeavour to assist their clients to learn from experience and incorporate the learning as feedback into the planning process. The learning organization is an organization which facilitates the learning of all its members and continuously transforms itself. The 'learning organization' has its origins in companies like Shell. The learning organization is seen as a response to an increasingly unpredictable and dynamic business environment. Organizations are continuously changing either through mergers or some other means. Changes are significant and rapid in some cases. They are slow and not so significant in some other cases. In any case when the organizations are changing, they are trying to adapt themselves to the changing surroundings. In the process they are also learning. A learning organization is an organization that is continuously expanding its capacity to create its future.

Definitions of Learning Organizations

A learning organization alters the way a company thinks about learning and decision making (Solomon, 1994)[1]. It involves everyone within the organization, and provides a framework for "where people expand their capacity to create the results they truly desire, where new and expansive patterns of thinking are nurtured, where collective aspiration is set free, and where people continually are learning how to learn together" (Solomon, 1994)[1].

"The essence of organizational learning is the organization's ability to use the amazing mental capacity of all its members to create the kind of processes that will improve its own" (Nancy Dixon 1994)[2]

"A learning company is an organization that facilitates the learning of all its members and continually transforms itself". (M. Pedler, J. Burgoyne and Tom Boydell, 1991)[3]

"Organizations where people continually expand their capacity to create the results they truly desire, where new and expansive patterns of thinking are nurtured, where collective aspiration is set free, and where people are continually learning to learn together" (Tom Senge, et al, 1994)[4]

From the above definitions following are the points to be noted regarding learning organizations:

- Learning organizations are adaptive to their external environment
- They are continually involved so as to enhance their capability to change/adapt in response to changes in business or market environment
- Learning organizations attempt to develop collective as well as individual learning
- They utilize the results of learning to achieve better results and improve organizational as well as individual or team performances.

Disciplines of a Learning Organization

There are five disciplines of a learning organization. These are "Systems Thinking", "Personal Mastery", "Mental Models", "Shared Vision", and "Team Learning" (cited in Galagan, 1991)[5].

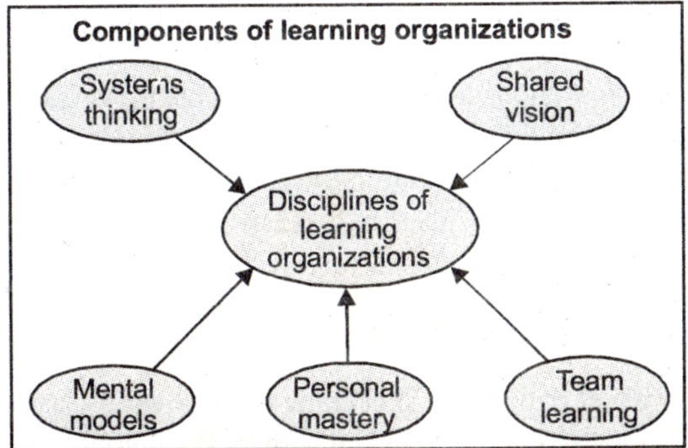

Fig. 6.13: Disciplines of a learning organization

The features of each of these disciplines are represented by the following table.

Disciplines of LO	Hallmarks
Systems thinking	• It involves looking at problems and goals as a part of a whole system where problem acts as the input, the learning process gives to the solution of the problem as the output. • It acts like a framework for seeing interrelationships rather than, things, for seeing patterns of change rather than static 'snap-shops'.
Personal mastery	• It is the discipline of continually clarifying and deepening our personal vision, of focusing our energies, of developing patience, and of seeing reality objectively. • Articulating the goals and objectives an individual wants to achieve also involves personal mastery.
Shared vision	• A shared vision is a mutual purpose among a group of people with common interests. • Shared vision binds people together around a common identity and a sense of destiny. • It builds a sense of commitment and facilitates open communication in the organization.
Mental models	• These are deeply ingrained assumptions, generalizations, or even pictures or images that influence people how they understand the world and enable them to take necessary actions. • They act as a tool for reflection and inquiry, to develop awareness of attitudes and perceptions and define the current reality of the organization.
Team learning	• It is facilitated through constant dialog and discussion within small groups/work teams. • Collective thinking is used to achieve a common objective or mutual learning. • Members of a team learn and grow together so as to develop intelligence and competence and leverage the knowledge of the whole together as one.

Exhibit: Jack Welch's Opinion on the Alignment of Mental Models

According to Jack Welch, the art of running a business is to assume that all important decision makers have to precisely access the same set of facts. If that happens, these decision makers would be able to reach roughly the same conclusion about how to deal with a business issue which is nothing but sharing the common "mental model". At the GE corporate executive council meetings he used to ensure that his key leaders exchanged their ideas on regular basis, which he considered was the foundation for organizational learning. By exchanging their ideas the leaders at GE were forming the same "Mental models" for developing innovative ideas for the business.

Exhibit: Team Learning at Boston Celtics

Boston Celtics (Celtics) is a basket ball team. This team was known for its remarkable performance in the World championship in between 1957 and 1969. The team was number one in 11 of 13 seasons. How this was possible let us go into the deep of it. The coach of the team was intensely focused on the bringing out the collective potential of his team by introducing "Team learning" as a key part of Celtics' every day practice. The coach along with his team members used to explore various ways to improve their game and tactics. Apart from this, ex-players used to give tips to the new players on how their competitor teams would be going to play for the day. The coach made sure that every player was on the team as long as he contributed to winning. Everybody's role in the team was clear.

(*Source: Scenarios: shooting the rapids, by Pierre Wack, Harvard Business Review, Nov/Dec 1985*)

Elements of a Learning Organization

Laura and Joel Connarton (2004)[6] have identified five key elements contributing to creating and maintaining a successful learning environment. These involve communication (Connarton, 2004)[6], rewarding the process, building a collabourative environment, formal company/job orientation, and capturing knowledge.

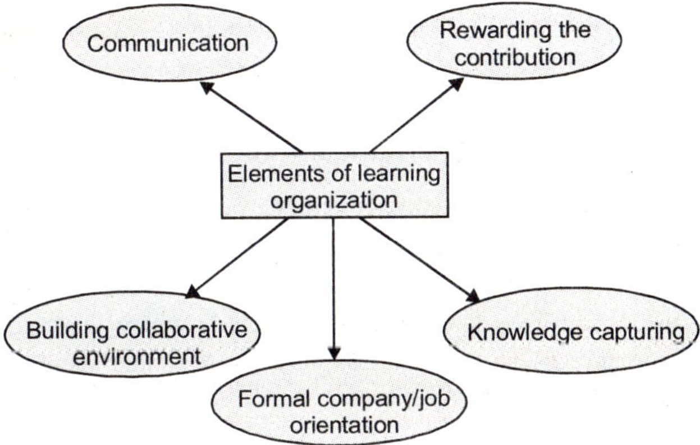

Fig. 6.14: Elements of a learning organization

Elements of LO	**Hallmarks**
Communication	• The role of communication is truly the central focus in creating and maintaining a learning organization. • Learning organizations typically have a free exchange and flow of information at all levels of the organization. • Systems are established to all individuals to network across organizational boundaries, broaden knowledge base and develop expertise.
Reward the process	• Processes that encourage cross-organizational interaction are rewarded. • Implementing programs that recognize and reward the acquisition of new skills, team-work as well as individual effort help to encourage creativity and enhances the level of employee motivation. • Celebration of the successes and accomplishments of the employees and teams also encourages continuous personal development which broadens the organization's "Knowledge IQ"

Building a collabourative environment	• Organizational support must flow from the top management downward and even at cross-sectional directions. • An environment of openness and trust encourages individuals to develop ideas, speak out, and to challenge actions. • Collabouration can be encouraged by having designated spaces for developing and exploiting information—such as conference rooms, bulletin boards, and groupwares to share and access knowledge.
Formal company/job orientation	• This involves a detailed presentation for new and existing employees and explains why the oragnization is in business, what the objectives of the company are, and how each department, or job, moves the company closer to its goals.
Capturing knowledge	• This requires systems that facilitate the retention of knowledge and learning that individuals hold within the organization. • This also involves developing a system whereby informations on learnings gained are recorded and retained for future use.

Why is it Important to Have Learning Organizations?

Companies are seeking to walk on the path of continuous improvement in their products and services, foster creativity and innovation through breakthrough strategies in order to stay into the highly competitive market scenario. This has resulted in a plethora of organizational development initiatives such as TQM (Total Quality Management) and BPR (Business Process Reengineering). This is where learning organizations have a competitive edge over other organizational models. Learning organizations can help organizations in the following ways:

- They help organizations to successfully cope with rapid and unexpected changes where existing 'programmed' responses are inadequate.
- They provide flexibility to cope with dynamically changing situations.
- They ensure that the organization's front-line staffs are more responsible so as to effectively respond with initiatives based on customer needs.
- Learning organizations facilitate in developing organizational capabilities for fast-paced innovation and inculcates a strong commitment to learn and love change.
- As the competitive business environment becomes more complex and challenging, the learning organizations provide a broader range of managerial beliefs, and a greater repertoire of managerial actions so as to facilitate fast paced growth.
- Learning organizations imbibe a strong people centric approach by linking the strategies of the organization with those with the people and creating an environment encouraging lifelong learning and knowledge sharing.

Exhibit: Learning and Development Perspectives in Dabur India

Dedicated to the
health and well being
of every household

Dabur's concern for its people can be understood by the following statement, "People are our most important asset. We add value through result driven training, and we encourage and reward excellence".

(*Courtesy: www.dabur.con/en/career/default.asp*)

The Learning and Rewarding Climate at Dabur

At Dabur, the above principle guides the entire organization in its relationship with the employees. The company believes that their people are the key facets of the organization and it is the contribution of the people that has enabled Dabur to achieve its current status. The company takes care of its employees and constantly encourages them into learning and development and also ensures that they recognize and reward employee contributions and good performances. The organization constantly emphasizes on special training and skill upgradation programs so as to keep its employees constantly abreast with the current business demands.

The Evidence

Dabur India was selected amongs the "25 Great places to work" in India (survey made by Business World) for the year 2005 and has secured the 10th rank in this august list.

Characteristics of Learning Organizations

The common features of a learning organization are as follows:

- **Learning culture and climate:** Learning organizations emphasize on creating an organizational climate that encourage and nurture continuous learning. There is a They strongly imbibe a commitment for innovation. In learning organizations, organizational culture and management style encourages experimentation, in order to learn from successes and failures.
- **Processes:** Learning organizations emphasize upon those organizational processes that encourage interaction across boundaries. These involve the organizational infrastructure, development and management processes, as opposed to business operational processes (the typical focus of many BPR initiatives).
- **Tools and techniques:** These are the methods that aid individual and group learning, such as creativity and various problem solving techniques used by the organization.
- **Skills and motivation:** These are indicated by the capability of the organization and their people to constantly involve and engage themselves to learn and adapt with the changing business environment.
- **Learning approaches to strategy:** This emphasizes on the importance of organizational policy and strategies and their implementation, evaluation and improvement which should be consciously structured as a learning process.

- **Participative policy making:** Participation and involvement should be the cornerstones of developing organizational policies and strategies. Opinion differences should be encouraged, disagreements should be used creatively, conflicts be managed positively in order to ensure effective business decisions.
- **Informating:** Learning organizations emphasize on having information systems that aim to constantly '**inform people**' as well as automate day to day operations.
- **Formative accounting and control:** In learning organizations, management systems should be accountable for effective accounting, budgeting and reporting in such a way that they could facilitate learning from the consequences of past or previous decisions taken by the organization.
- **Internal exchange:** In learning organizations all departments and internal units should view themselves and the employees as internal customers and suppliers, constantly being in dialogue with each other.
- **Reward flexibility:** Learning organizations should also emphasize on assumptions which underlie reward systems that are being made public with scope for further improvement and adjustment according to the needs of the business and market trends.
- **Enabling structures:** Learning organizations emphasize on giving space and headroom to meet the organization's present needs and respond to future business needs and challenges.
- **Boundary workers as environmental scanners:** Employees in learning organizations who are in constant touch with external contacts (for example, sales representatives and delivery agents) should function as environmental scanners. They should facilitate in terms of collecting negative and positive feedback and market knowledge so as to pass the same to other staffs in the organization.
- **Inter-company working:** Learning organizations should focus on sharing information so as to learn jointly with others outside the organization, such as key customers and suppliers.
- **Self-development for all:** Learning organizations ensure that resources and facilities are accessible to everyone in the organization so as to encourage learning and self-development at all levels in the organization.

THEME READING: THE LEARNING AND DEVELOPMENT CULTURE IN PANTALOONS

Pantaloon is not just an organization - it is an institution, a centre of learning and development. The company believes that knowledge is the only weapon at its disposal and the quest for the same is focused, systematic and unwavering. Pantaloon as an organization takes pride in challenging conventions and thinking out of the box, in travelling on the road less travelled. The company's corporate doctrine, 'Rewrite Rules, Retain Values' is derived from this spirit. The company believes that its most valuable assets are its "People". Young in spirit, adventurous in action, with an average age of 27 years, Pantaloon's skilled and qualified professionals work in an environment where change is the only constant.

Over the years, Pantaloon has accelerated growth through its ability to lead change. A number of its pioneering concepts have now emerged as industry standards. Today Pantaloon is one of the fastest growing retail companies in India. The way employees work at Pantaloons is distinctly "Pantaloon". The organization's courage to dream and to turn its dreams into reality – that change millions of Indian customer's lives, is the company's biggest advantage over its rivals. The same value proposition has been inculcated in Pantaloon's one of the biggest retail outlets "Big Bazaar". Pantaloon is an invitation to join a place where there are no boundaries to what an individual can achieve. It means never having to stop asking questions; it means never having to stop raising the bar. It is an opportunity to take risks, and it is this passion that makes the company's dreams a reality.

At Pantaloon, empowerment has been the buzzword that had motivated its employees over the years. Powered by the desire to create path-breaking practices and held together by values are the core mantras of people centric HR practices at Pantaloons. Out of the Box thinking has become a way of life at Pantaloon and living with the change, a habit. Leadership is a value that is followed by one and all at Pantaloon. Leadership is the quality that motivates people at Pantaloons to never stop learning, stretching to reach the next challenge, knowing that we will be rewarded along the way. Pantaloon provides enough challenges and opportunities for learning by involving people in handling multiple responsibilities, and then grooming them to play a larger role in the future. The "Work Culture" at pantaloons is a unique mix of preserving core Indian values and yet providing customers with a service, on par with international standards.

(Courtesy: http://www.pantaloon.com/career.asp, http://www.pantaloon.com/ourculture.asp)

Importance of Learning Culture in Learning Organizations

It is evident from the above write up on Pantaloons that a learning culture forms the cornerstone of any learning organization. This is achieved in the following way:

- **Future, External Orientation:** A learning culture constantly encourages organizations to develop an understanding of their business environment and help the senior management teams to have a vision of the future.
- **Free Exchange and Flow of Information:** A learning culture also ensures that systems are in place so as to ensure that expertises are available where they are needed. Learning cultures motivate individual employees to extensively form collabourations crossing organizational boundaries so as to develop their knowledge and expertise.
- **Commitment to Learning and Personal Development:** Learning cultures pervade at all levels in the organization. They inculcate support from top management and by involving people at all levels they engage a whole hearted commitment in the organization for learning on a regular basis.
- **Valuing People:** A learning culture stems out of the organization's commitment in valuing their people in terms of their ideas, creativity and "imaginative capabilities". An organization which successfully enriches and make the best utilization of these capabilities put themselves on the fast track of growth and development.
- **Climate of Openness and Trust:** Learning cultures motivate employees to develop creative ideas, to speak out, and challenge conventional actions and practices by inculcating a climate of openness and trust.
- **Learning from Experience:** A learning culture also lays considerable importance on learning from experience and past mistakes.

Key Management Processes Contributing to Learning Organizations

- **Strategic and Scenario Planning:** This involves strategic planning that enables the organization to look beyond the numbers, encourage challenging assumptions, and thinking 'outside of the box'. They even create opportunities for innovation by encouraging experimentation.
- **Competitor Analysis:** This involves an ongoing process of continuous monitoring and analysis of all key success factors and benchmarks in the external environment, including technology and strategic initiatives taken by business competitors.

- **Information and Knowledge Management:** These involve using techniques to identify, audit, value (cost/benefit), develop and exploit information as a resource and using the same for organizational change and development.
- **Capability Planning:** This involves profiling both qualitatively and quantitatively the competencies of the organization.
- **Team and Organization Development:** This involves the use of facilitators to help groups with work, job and organization design and team development - reinforcing values, developing vision, cohesiveness and a climate of stretching goals, sharing and support.
- **Performance Measurement:** Performance management initiatives should emphasize on applying and implementing appropriate measures and indicators of performance that could deliver continuous improvement in organizational performance. Tools like those of 'balanced scorecard' could be successfully instrumented to facilitate organizational development and learning.
- **Reward and Recognition Systems:** These involve processes and systems that recognize acquisition of new skills, team-work as well as individual contributions, celebrate successes and accomplishments, and encourage continuous personal development.

Barriers of Learning Organization

The following are some of the most common obstacles to becoming a learning organization:

- Operational/fire fighting preoccupation - not creating time to sit back and think strategically over the mistakes and problems
- Over emphasis on systems and process manuals (e.g. ISO 9000 documentation practices) and exclusion of other practical factors (like strategic decision-making).
- Reluctance to invest in training and development
- Impact of hidden personal agendas and role of power play and politics
- Too much emphasis on top-down driven management, tight supervision schedules and absence of effective empowerment.

Types of Organizational Learning

- **Incremental:** Incremental learning is characterized by simple, routine problem solving initiatives which demands little or no fundamental changes in the organization's thinking process or system.
- **Radical:** Radical learning can be described as breakthrough learning that directly challenges the prevailing mental models of an organization on which the entire organizational philosophy or system is being built.
- **Individual:** Individual learning involves the efforts and contributions put in by individual employees and members of an organization for their learning, self development and growth.
- **Team:** Team learning involves learning by collabourative and participative ways of sharing knowledge and learning together by contributing to generate creative and new ideas.
- **Organizational:** Organizational learning is a social process, involving interactions among all the above mentioned components so as to facilitate effective decision making.

Individual versus Organizational Learning

Learning by individuals in an organizational context is a well understood process. This is the traditional domain of human resources, including activities such as: training, increasing skills, work experience, and formal education. Given that the success of any organization is founded on the knowledge of the people who work for it, these activities will and, indeed, must continue. However, individual learning is not the only aspect of organizational learning.

A learning organization does not rely on passive or ad hoc process in the hope that organizational learning will take place through serendipity or as a by-product of normal work. A learning organization actively promotes, facilitates, and rewards collective learning that stems out in the form of a collective learning experience. Capturing individual learning for organizational development is in fact the first step to making it useful for creating a learning organization. There are many methods for capturing knowledge and experience, such as job experience, activity reports, lessons learned, interviews, and presentations. Capturing of knowledge also includes storage in repositories, databases, or libraries to ensure that it would be available whenever needed. An organization having a handful of such knowledge resources but without any effort to utilize them in their organization development has been described to be ineffective. Hence in the organizational learning process transferring knowledge forms an integral process of knowledge development.

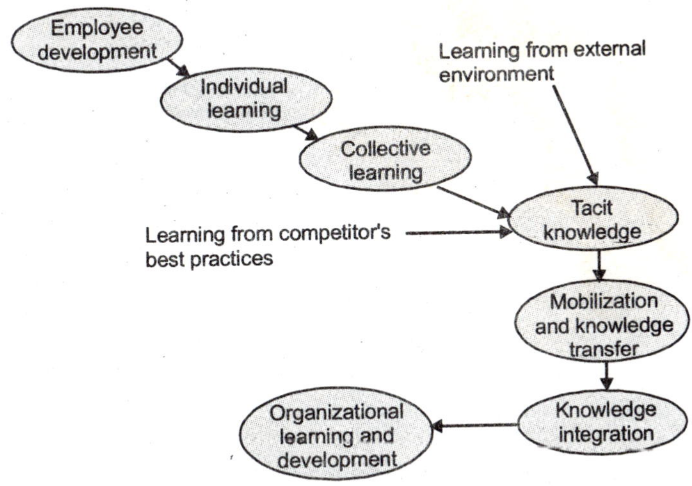

Fig. 6.15: Organizational learning and development process

Transferring knowledge requires that it be accessible to everyone when and where they need it. Modern organizations in the IT enabled era depend on sophisticated database management systems and Intranet networks to build such knowledge systems in their organizations. **Tacit knowledge** may be shared through communities of practice or consulting experts. It is also important that knowledge is presented in a way that employees at various levels of the organization can understand it and it must also suit their needs as and when required. Apart from this, **mobilizing knowledge** involves integrating and using relevant knowledge from many, often diverse, sources to solve a problem or address a business related issue. **Knowledge integration** requires interoperability standards among various repositories. Using knowledge may be through simple reuse of existing solutions that have worked previously. It may also come through adapting old solutions to new problems. Conversely, a learning organization learns from mistakes or recognizes when old solutions no longer apply. An organization must learn so that it can adapt to a changing business environment. Given the ever-accelerating rate of global-scale change, the more critical organizational learning and adaptation has become strategically important.

Levels of Organizational Learning

Organizational learning is a holistic process, involving interactions among many individuals leading to well-informed decision making. Thus organizations must emphasize on creating a culture that enables people to learn and adapt as a part of everyday working practices. As revealed by the above figure, the process of shifting from the individual to organizational learning involves a non-linear transformation that is much complex than what it appears to be in the given figure. For individual learning when somebody learns anything, it is available for his/her immediate use. On the other hand, in case of organizational learning organizations need to create, capture, transfer, and mobilize knowledge before it could be used for decision making. Although IT enabled technology supports this process, the success actually depends on how well the internal cultural environment is being built and change is managed in these organizations. There are four levels of organizational learning. These are as follows:

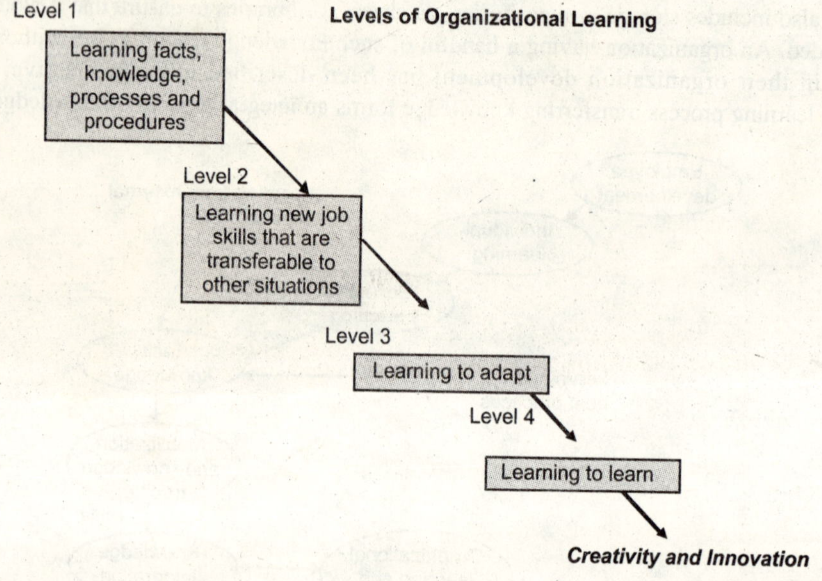

Fig. 6.16: Levels of organizational learning

The above model can be applied at not only for organizational learning, but also for catering to the **learning of individuals**, and that of **teams**. Organizations achieving learning to the Level 4 is said to master in terms of creativity and innovation.

Leveraging the Power of Knowledge in Learning Organizations

The above model has clearly established the importance of learning and knowledge building in terms of becoming learning organizations. This is achieved when organizations emphasize and consider:

- Learning as the key competency required for surviving competition in the knowledge economy.
- Learning as the catalyst and the intellectual resource to create a sustainable competitive advantage.
- Continuous learning as the cornerstone to obtain competitive advantage.

Guidelines for Becoming Learning Organizations

The following points can be placed as effective guidelines facilitating a learning organization. These are as follows, namely:

- **Starting at the top management level:** The strategic decisions makers should have consensus, high commitment be helpful to give an impetus towards the learning organization philosophy.
- **Start with a chronic problem:** Strategic decision makers should start the learning process by dissecting and investigating chronic problems that affect the organization's productivity.
- **Initiate a task force:** For taking any intervention for a learning organization, the management should initiate a task force with common responsibility, drive and vision.

- **Initiating organizational diagnosis:** OD experts and HR people need to ensure a holistic approach towards initiating organizational diagnosis with the involvement and participation of employees at all levels in the organization.
- **Link to an existing process or initiative:** Emphasis should be given to link the OD initiative to all the existing processes or initiatives in the organization.
- **Reviewing the existing systems and processes:** The organizations should also lay importance on conducting an audit so as to identify potent 'capability' gaps in their organizations.
- **Fostering a culture favouring creative idea building and moving for innovation and change.**

The HR Challenge: The challenge facing HR managers today is to make the effort needed to learn some of the new skill and techniques, and to put in processes that engage their workforce in programs of continuous capability development. Today's HR professionals have to ensure that organizational learning should be energizing, stimulating and fun for people. Retail giant Pantaloons is one such organization from our country which had successfully implemented such philosophies in their organization.

REFERENCES

1. Solomon, C. M. (1994): "HR facilitates the learning organization concept", Personnel Journal (73)11, p56, 9p, Retrieved February 12, 2005 from the University of Phoenix Library (EBSCO host Database) on the World Wide Web: http://ecampus.phoenix.edu.
2. Nancy Dixon (1994): "The Organizational Learning Cycle", McGraw-Hill Publications.
3. Mike Pedler, John Burgoyne and Tom Boydell, (1991): "The Learning Company: a Strategy for Sustainable Development", McGraw-Hill.
4. Peter M. Senge, C. Roberts, R.B. Ross, B.J. Smith, A. Kleiner, Nicholas Brierley (1994): "The Fifth Discipline Fieldbook: Strategies and Tools for Building a Learning Organization", Random House, Sydney.
5. Galaghan, P.A. (1991): "The learning organization made plain"; Training and Development, Retrieved February 12, 2005 from the University of Phoenix Library (EBSCO host Database) on the World Wide Web: http://ecampus.phoenix.edu
6. Connarton, L. and J. (2004): "Five elements of the learning organization"; Insights, Retrieved February 12, 2005 on the World Wide Web: http://www.elementsconsulting.com/insight/articles/learning_org/default.asp

QUESTION BANK

1. What do you mean by learning organizations? What are the five discipline of a learning organization?
2. What are the elements of a learning organization?
3. Why is it important to have learning organizations?
4. Describe the characteristic features of a learning organization.
5. How can organization develop a learning culture?
6. What are the barriers to a learning organization?
7. Classify various types of organizational learning.
8. What HR implications are important in the perspective of a learning organization?

Internet Exercises

Use internet resources and collect information regarding an organization which has successfully implemented learning organization philosophies for their business excellence.